MORNING

and

EVENING

MORNING

and

EVENING

A New Edition of the Classic Devotional Based on the Holy Bible, English Standard Version

Revised and updated by
Alistair Begg

CHARLES H. SPURGEON

CROSSWAY BOOKS

A DIVISION OF
GOOD NEWS PUBLISHERS
WHEATON, ILLINOIS

Library of Congress Cataloging-in-Publication Data
Spurgeon, C. H. (Charles Haddon), 1834-1892.
 [Morning and evening daily devotions]
 Morning and evening : a new edition of the classic devotional based on the Holy Bible, English Standard Version / C. H. Spurgeon ; edited by Alistair Begg.
  p. cm.
  ISBN 1-58134-466-X
 1. Devotional calendars—Baptists. 2. Bible—Meditations. I. Begg, Alistair, II. Title.
BV4811.S6669 2003
242'.2—dc21   2003015233

LB		13	12	11	10	09	08	07	06	
15	14	13	12	11	10	9	8	7	6	5	4

*"Morning by morning he awakens; he awakens my ear
to hear as those who are taught."*
ISAIAH 50:4

*"My soul will be satisfied as with fat and rich food, and
my mouth will praise you with joyful lips,
when I remember you upon my bed,
and meditate on you in the watches of the night."*
PSALM 63:5-6

INTRODUCTION

Spurgeon's daily devotional readings have stood the test of time and are unrivaled as an example of deep theological insight and warm pastoral concern. They are so classic that one hesitates to tamper with them.

In revising and updating the material, I have tried to make them more readable without spoiling the splendor of the language. Most of the changes are minor and will go largely undetected. On a few occasions, because of the difference between the King James Version and the English Standard Version, I was forced to take more liberty.

My goal throughout has been to fashion the material in such a way that it will be accessible to a far wider audience than before. Spurgeon's vocabulary is so vast that the reader may still find himself reaching for a dictionary, but this will surely be an added benefit!

Since I did not have the opportunity to ask Spurgeon's permission, when I meet him I will seek his forgiveness if in attempting to bring clarity I have clouded the issue. The reader must judge. My prayer is that another generation will emerge thankful to God for the work of Spurgeon, whose memory we revere and whose example of godly devotion we seek to follow.

ALISTAIR BEGG

January

❧ M O R N I N G ❧
THEY ATE OF THE FRUIT OF THE LAND OF CANAAN THAT YEAR.
— JOSHUA 5:12

Israel's weary wanderings were all over, and the promised rest was attained. No more moving tents, fiery serpents, fierce Amalekites, and howling wildernesses: They came to the land that flowed with milk and honey, and they ate the old corn of the land. Perhaps this year, beloved Christian reader, this may be your case or mine. Joyful is the prospect, and if faith be in active exercise, it will yield unalloyed delight. To be with Jesus in the rest, which remains for the people of God, is a cheering hope indeed, and to expect this glory so soon is a double bliss. Unbelief shudders at the Jordan that still rolls between us and the goodly land, but let us rest assured that we have already experienced more ills than death at its worst can cause us. Let us banish every fearful thought and rejoice with exceeding great joy in the prospect that this year we shall begin to be "forever with the Lord."

Some of the company will this year remain on earth, to do service for their Lord. If this should fall to our lot, there is no reason why the New Year's text should not still be true. "We who have believed enter that rest." The Holy Spirit is the earnest of our inheritance; He gives us glory begun below. In heaven believers are secure, and so are we preserved in Christ Jesus; there they triumph over their enemies, and we have victories too. Celestial spirits enjoy communion with their Lord, and this is not denied to us. They rest in His love, and we have perfect peace in Him; they sing His praise, and it is our privilege to bless Him too. We will this year gather celestial fruits on earthly ground, where faith and hope have made the desert like the garden of the Lord. Man ate angels' food of old, and why not now? O for grace to feed on Jesus, and so to eat of the fruit of the land of Canaan this year!

❧ E V E N I N G ❧
WE WILL EXULT AND REJOICE IN YOU. — SONG OF SOLOMON 1:4

We will be glad and rejoice in You. We will not open the gates of the year to the sorrowful notes of the organ, but to the sweet strains of the harp of joy and the high-sounding cymbals of gladness. "O come, let us sing to the LORD; let us make a joyful noise to the rock of our salvation."[1] We, the called and faithful and chosen, will drive away our griefs and set up our banners of confidence in the name of God. Let others lament over their troubles; we with joy will magnify the Lord. Eternal Spirit, our effectual Comforter, we who are the temples in which You dwell will never cease from adoring and blessing the name of Jesus. Jesus must have the crown of our heart's delight; we will not dishonor our Bridegroom by mourning in His presence. We are ordained to be the minstrels of the skies; let us rehearse our everlasting anthem before we sing it in the halls of the New Jerusalem. We will *exult and rejoice*: two words with one sense, double joy, blessedness upon blessedness. Need there be any limit to our rejoicing in the Lord even now? Do not men of grace find their Lord to be the sweetest of incense even now, and what better fragrance have they in heaven itself? We will be glad and rejoice *in You*. That last word is the meat in the dish, the kernel of the nut, the soul of the text. What heavens are laid up in Jesus! What rivers of infinite bliss have their source, aye, and every drop of their fullness in Him! Since, O sweet Lord Jesus, You are the present portion of Your people, favor us this year with such a sense of Your preciousness that from its first to its last day we may be glad and rejoice in You. Let January open with joy in the Lord, and December close with gladness in Jesus.

[1] Psalm 95:1

CONTINUE STEADFASTLY IN PRAYER. — COLOSSIANS 4:2

It is interesting to consider how large a portion of the Bible is occupied with the subject of prayer, either in furnishing examples, enforcing precepts, or pronouncing promises. We scarcely open the Bible before we read, "People began to call upon the name of the LORD;"[1] and just as we are about to close the volume, the "Amen" of an earnest supplication meets our ear. Instances are plentiful. Here we find a wrestling Jacob—there a Daniel who prayed three times a day—and a David who with all his heart called upon his God. On the mountain we see Elijah; in the dungeon Paul and Silas. We have multitudes of commands, and myriads of promises. What does this teach us, but the sacred importance and necessity of prayer? We may be certain that whatever God has made prominent in His Word, He intended to be conspicuous in our lives. If He has said much about prayer, it is because He knows we have much need of it. So deep are our necessities that until we are in heaven we must not cease to pray. Do you need nothing? Then I fear you do not know your poverty. Have you no mercy to ask of God? Then may the Lord's mercy show you your misery! A prayerless soul is a Christless soul. Prayer is the lisping of the believing infant, the shout of the fighting believer, the requiem of the dying saint falling asleep in Jesus. It is the breath, the watchword, the comfort, the strength, the honor of a Christian. If you are a child of God, you will seek your Father's face and live in your Father's love. Pray that this year you may be holy, humble, zealous, and patient; have closer communion with Christ, and enter more often into the banqueting-house of His love. Pray that you may be an example and a blessing to others, and that you may live more to the glory of your Master. The motto for this year must be, "Continue . . . in prayer."

❧ EVENING ❧
LET THE PEOPLES RENEW THEIR STRENGTH. — ISAIAH 41:1

All things on earth need to be renewed. No created thing continues by itself. "You renew the face of the ground,"[2] was the psalmist's utterance. Even the trees, which wear not themselves with care, nor shorten their lives with labor, must drink of the rain of heaven and draw from the hidden treasures of the soil. The cedars of Lebanon, which God has planted, only live because day by day they are full of sap freshly drawn from the earth. Neither can man's life be sustained without renewal from God. As it is necessary to repair the body by the frequent meal, so we must repair the soul by feeding upon the Book of God, or by listening to the preached Word, or by the soul-fattening table of the ordinances. How depressed are our graces when means are neglected! What poor starving souls they are who live without the diligent use of the Word of God and secret prayer! If our piety can live without God it is not of divine creating; it is but a dream; for if God had begotten it, it would wait upon Him as the flowers wait upon the dew. Without constant restoration we are not ready for the perpetual assaults of hell, or the stern afflictions of heaven, or even for the strife within. When the whirlwind shall be loosed, woe to the tree that has not sucked up fresh sap and grasped the rock with many inter-twisted roots. When tempests arise, woe to the mariners that have not strengthened their mast, nor cast their anchor, nor sought the haven. If we suffer the good to grow weaker, the evil will surely gather strength and struggle desperately for the mastery over us; and as a result a painful desolation and a lamentable disgrace may follow. Let us draw near to the footstool of divine mercy in humble entreaty, and we shall realize the fulfillment of the promise, "They who wait for the LORD shall renew their strength."[3]

[1] Genesis 4:26 [2] Psalm 104:30 [3] Isaiah 40:31

I WILL . . . GIVE YOU AS A COVENANT TO THE PEOPLE. — ISAIAH 49:8

Jesus Christ is Himself the sum and substance of the covenant, and as one of its gifts He is the property of every believer. Believer, can you estimate what you have received in Christ? "In him the whole fullness of deity dwells bodily."[1] Consider the word "God" and its infinity, and then meditate upon "perfect man" and all His beauty; for all that Christ, as God and man, ever had, or can have, is yours—out of pure free favor, given to you to be your entailed property forever. Our blessed Jesus, as God, is omniscient, omnipresent, omnipotent. Will it not console you to know that all these great and glorious attributes are altogether yours? Has He power? That power is yours to support and strengthen you, to overcome your enemies, and to preserve you even to the end. Has He love? Well, there is not a drop of love in His heart that is not yours; you may dive into the immense ocean of His love, and you may say of it all, "It is mine." Has He justice? It may seem a stern attribute, but even that is yours, for He will by His justice see to it that all that is promised to you in the covenant of grace shall be most certainly secured to you. And all that He has as perfect man is yours. As a perfect man the Father's delight was upon Him. He stood accepted by the Most High. O believer, God's acceptance of Christ is your acceptance; for the love that the Father set on a perfect Christ, He sets on you now. For all that Christ did is yours. That perfect righteousness which Jesus worked out, when through His stainless life He kept the law and made it honorable, is yours and is imputed to you. Christ is in the covenant.

My God, I am Thine—what a comfort divine!
What a blessing to know that the Savior is mine!
In the heavenly Lamb thrice happy I am,
And my heart it doth dance at the sound of His name.

∽ EVENING ∝

"THE VOICE OF ONE CRYING IN THE WILDERNESS:
'PREPARE THE WAY OF THE LORD,
MAKE HIS PATHS STRAIGHT.'" — LUKE 3:4

The voice crying in the wilderness demanded *a way for the Lord, a way prepared, and a way prepared in the wilderness.* I would be attentive to the Master's proclamation and give Him a road into my heart, cast up by gracious operations, through the desert of my nature. The four directions in the text[2] must have my serious attention.

Every valley must be exalted. Low and groveling thoughts of God must be given up; doubting and despairing must be removed; and self-seeking and carnal delights must be forsaken. Across these deep valleys a glorious causeway of grace must be raised.

Every mountain and hill shall be laid low. Proud creature-sufficiency, and boastful self-righteousness, must be leveled, to make a highway for the King of kings. Divine fellowship is never promised to haughty, high-minded sinners. The Lord has respect to the lowly and visits the contrite in heart, but the lofty are an abomination unto Him. My soul, beseech the Holy Spirit to set you right in this respect.

The crooked shall be made straight. The wavering heart must have a straight path of decision for God and holiness marked out for it. Double-minded men are strangers to the God of truth. My soul, take heed that in everything you are honest and true, as in the sight of the heart-searching God.

The rough places shall be made smooth. Stumbling-blocks of sin must be removed, and thorns and briers of rebellion must be uprooted. So great a visitor must not find miry ways and stony places when He comes to honor His favored ones with His company. Oh, that this evening the Lord may find in my heart a highway made ready by His grace, that He may make a triumphal progress through the utmost bounds of my soul, from the beginning of this year even to the end of it.

[1] Colossians 2:9   [2] Isaiah 40

GROW IN THE GRACE AND KNOWLEDGE OF OUR
LORD AND SAVIOR JESUS CHRIST. — 2 PETER 3:18

Grow in grace"—not in one grace only, but in all grace. Grow in that root-grace, *faith*. Believe the promises more firmly than you have done. Let faith increase in fullness, constancy, simplicity. Grow also in *love*. Ask that your love may become extended, more intense, more practical, influencing every thought, word, and deed. Grow likewise in *humility*. Seek to lie very low and know more of your own nothingness. As you grow *downward* in humility, seek also to grow *upward*—having nearer approaches to God in prayer and more intimate fellowship with Jesus. May God the Holy Spirit enable you to "*grow in . . . the knowledge of our Lord and Savior.*" He who grows not in the knowledge of Jesus, refuses to be blessed. To know Him is "life eternal," and to advance in the knowledge of Him is to increase in happiness. He who does not long to know more of Christ, knows nothing of Him yet. Whoever has sipped this wine will thirst for more, for although Christ does satisfy, yet it is such a satisfaction that the appetite is not choked, but whetted. If you know the love of Jesus as the hart pants for the water-brooks, so will you pant after deeper draughts of His love. If you do not desire to know Him better, then you love Him not, for love always cries, "Nearer, nearer." Absence from Christ is hell; but the presence of Jesus is heaven. Do not rest content without an increasing acquaintance with Jesus. Seek to know more of Him in His divine nature, in His human relationship, in His finished work, in His death, in His resurrection, in His present glorious intercession, and in His future royal advent. Live close to the Cross, and search the mystery of His wounds. An increase of love to Jesus and a more perfect apprehension of His love to us is one of the best tests of growth in grace.

❧ EVENING ✍
AND JOSEPH RECOGNIZED HIS BROTHERS,
BUT THEY DID NOT RECOGNIZE HIM. — GENESIS 42:8

This morning our desires went forth for growth in our acquaintance with the Lord Jesus; it may be well tonight to consider a kindred topic, namely, *our heavenly Joseph's knowledge of us*. This was most blessedly perfect long before we had the slightest knowledge of Him. "Your eyes saw my unformed substance; in your book were written, every one of them, the days that were formed for me, when as yet there were none of them."[1] Before we had a being in the world we had a being in His heart. When we were enemies to Him, He knew us, our misery, our madness, and our wickedness. When we wept bitterly in despairing repentance, and viewed Him only as a judge and a ruler, He viewed us as His brethren well beloved, and His heart yearned toward us. He never mistook His chosen but always beheld them as objects of His infinite affection. "The Lord knows those who are his"[2] is as true of the prodigals who are feeding pigs as of the children who sit at the table.

But, sadly *we did not know our royal Brother*, and out of this ignorance grew a host of sins. We withheld our hearts from Him and allowed Him no entrance to our love. We mistrusted Him and gave no credit to His words. We rebelled against Him and paid Him no loving homage. The Sun of Righteousness shone forth, and we could not see Him. Heaven came down to earth, and earth perceived it not. Let God be praised, those days are over with us; yet even now what we know of Jesus is small compared with what He knows of us. We have only begun to study Him, but He knows us altogether. It is a blessed circumstance that the ignorance is not on His side, for then it would be a hopeless case for us. He will not say to us, "I never knew you," but He will confess our names in the day of His appearing, and meanwhile will show Himself to us as He does not to the world.

[1] Psalm 139:16   [2] 2 Timothy 2:19

Light might well be good since it sprang from that fiat of goodness, "Let there be light." We who enjoy it should be more grateful for it than we are, and see more of God in it and by it. *Physical* light is said by Solomon to be sweet, but *gospel* light is infinitely more precious, for it reveals eternal things and ministers to our immortal natures. When the Holy Spirit gives us *spiritual* light and opens our eyes to behold the glory of God in the face of Jesus Christ, we behold sin in its true colors, and ourselves in our real position; we see the Most Holy God as He reveals Himself, the plan of mercy as He propounds it, and the world to come as the Word describes it. Spiritual light has many beams and prismatic colors, but whether they be knowledge, joy, holiness, or life, all are divinely good. If the light received be thus good, what must the *essential* light be, and how glorious must be the place where He reveals Himself. O Lord, since light is so good, give us more of it, and more of Yourself, the true light.

No sooner is there a good thing in the world than *a division is necessary*. Light and darkness have no communion; God has divided them—let us not confound them. Sons of light must not have fellowship with deeds, doctrines, or deceits of darkness. The children of the day must be sober, honest, and bold in their Lord's work, leaving the works of darkness to those who will dwell in it forever. Our churches should by discipline divide the light from the darkness, and we should by our distinct separation from the world do the same. In judgment, in action, in hearing, in teaching, in association, we must discern between the precious and the vile, and maintain the great distinction that the Lord made upon the world's first day. O Lord Jesus, be our light throughout the whole of this day, for Your light is the light of men.

Evening

This morning we noticed the goodness of the light, and the Lord's dividing it from the darkness. We now note the special eye that the Lord had for the light. "God saw the light"—He looked at it with complacency, gazed upon it with pleasure, saw that it "was good." If the Lord has given you light, dear reader, He looks on that light with peculiar interest; for not only is it dear to Him as His own handiwork, but it is like Himself, for "God is light." It is pleasant for the believer to know that God's eye tenderly observes that work of grace that He has begun. He never loses sight of the treasure that He has placed in our earthen vessels. Sometimes we cannot see the light, but God always sees the light, and that is much better than our seeing it. Better for the judge to see my innocence than for me to think I see it. It is very comfortable for me to know that I am one of God's people—but whether *I* know it or not, if the Lord knows it, I am still safe. This is the foundation, "The Lord knows those who are his."[1] You may be sighing and groaning because of inbred sin, and mourning over your darkness; yet the Lord sees "light" in your heart, for He has put it there, and all the cloudiness and gloom of your soul cannot conceal your light from His gracious eye. You may have sunk low in despondency, and even despair; but if your soul has any longing toward Christ, and if you are seeking to rest in His finished work, God sees the "light." He not only *sees* it, but He also *preserves* it in you. "I, the Lord, do keep it." This is a precious thought to those who, after anxious watching and guarding of themselves, feel their own powerlessness to do so. The light thus preserved by His grace, He will one day develop into the splendor of noonday, and the fullness of glory. The light within is the dawn of the eternal day.

[1] 2 Timothy 2:19

❧ MORNING ❧

CASTING ALL YOUR ANXIETIES ON HIM,
BECAUSE HE CARES FOR YOU. — 1 PETER 5:7

It is a happy way of soothing sorrow when we can feel, "He cares for me." Christian, do not dishonor religion by always wearing a brow of care; come, cast your burden upon your Lord. You are staggering beneath a weight that your Father would not feel. What seems to you a crushing burden would be to Him but as the small dust of the balance. Nothing is so sweet as to

> Lie passive in God's hands,
> And know no will but His.

O child of suffering, be patient; God has not passed you over in His providence. He who is the feeder of sparrows will also furnish you with what you need. Do not sit in despair; hope on, hope ever. Take up the arms of faith against a sea of trouble, and your opposition shall yet end your distresses. There is One who cares for you. His eye is fixed on you, His heart beats with pity for your woe, and His omnipotent hand shall bring you the needed help. The darkest cloud shall scatter itself in showers of mercy. The blackest gloom shall give place to the morning. He, if you are one of His family, will bind up your wounds and heal your broken heart. Do not doubt His grace because of your tribulation, but believe that He loves you as much in seasons of trouble as in times of happiness. What a serene and quiet life might you lead if you would leave providing to the God of providence! With a little oil in the cruse and a handful of meal in the barrel, Elijah outlived the famine, and you will do the same. If God cares for you, why do you need to care too? Can you trust Him for your soul and not for your body? He has never refused to bear your burdens; He has never fainted under their weight. Come, then, soul! Say good-bye to anxiety and leave all your concerns in the hand of a gracious God.

❧ EVENING ❧

NOW THE HAND OF THE LORD HAD BEEN UPON ME
THE EVENING BEFORE . . . — EZEKIEL 33:22

In the matter of *judgment* this may be the case, and if so, let me consider the reason for such a visitation and accept it as from His hand. I am not the only one who is chastened in the night season; let me cheerfully submit to the affliction and carefully endeavor to profit by it. But the hand of the Lord may also be felt in another manner, strengthening the soul and lifting the spirit upward toward eternal things. O that I may in this sense feel the Lord dealing with me! A sense of the divine presence and indwelling bears the soul toward heaven as upon the wings of eagles. At such times we are full to the brim with spiritual joy, and forget the cares and sorrows of earth; the invisible is near, and the visible loses its power over us. Servant-body waits at the foot of the hill, and the master-spirit worships upon the summit in the presence of the Lord. O that a hallowed season of divine communion may be granted to me this evening! The Lord knows that I need it very greatly. My graces languish, my corruptions rage, my faith is weak, my devotion is cold; all these are reasons why His healing hand should be laid upon me. His hand can cool the heat of my burning brow and calm the turmoil of my palpitating heart. That glorious right hand that molded the world can renew my mind; the unwearied hand that bears the earth's huge pillars can sustain my spirit; the loving hand that encloses all the saints can cherish me; and the mighty hand that breaks in pieces the enemy can subdue my sins. Why should I not feel that hand touching me this evening? Come, my soul, address God with the potent plea that Jesus' hands were pierced for your redemption, and you shall surely feel that same hand upon you that once touched Daniel and set him upon his knees that he might see visions of God.

FOR TO ME TO LIVE IS CHRIST. — PHILIPPIANS 1:21

The believer did not always live to Christ. He began to do so when God the Holy Spirit convinced him of sin, and when by grace he was brought to see the dying Savior making a propitiation for his guilt. From the moment of the new and heavenly birth the man begins to live to Christ. Jesus is to believers the one pearl of great price, for whom we are willing to part with all that we have. He has so completely won our heart that it beats alone for Him; to His glory we would live, and in defense of His Gospel we would die. He is the pattern of our life, and the model after which we would sculpture our character. Paul's words mean more than most men think; they imply that the *aim and end of his life* was Christ— nay, his life itself was Jesus. In the words of an ancient saint, he ate and drank and slept eternal life. Jesus was his very breath, the soul of his soul, the heart of his heart, the life of his life. Can you say, as a professing Christian, that you live up to this idea? Can you honestly say that for you to live is Christ? Your business—are you doing it *for Christ*? Is it not done for self-aggrandizement and for family advantage? Do you ask, "Is that a mean reason?" For the *Christian* it is. He professes to live for Christ; how can he live for another object without committing spiritual adultery? There are many who carry out this principle in some measure; but who is there that dares say that he has lived wholly for Christ as the apostle did? Yet this alone is the true life of a Christian—its source, its sustenance, its fashion, its end, all gathered up in one word—Christ. Lord, accept me; I present myself, praying to live only in You and to You. Let me be as the creature that stands between the plow and the altar, to work or to be sacrificed; and let my motto be, "Ready for either."

❧ EVENING ❧

MY SISTER, MY BRIDE. — SONG OF SOLOMON 4:12

Observe the sweet titles with which the heavenly Solomon with intense affection addresses His bride, the church. "*My sister*, one near to Me by ties of nature, partaker of the same sympathies. *My bride*, nearest and dearest, united to Me by the tenderest bands of love; My sweet companion, part of My own self. *My sister*, by My Incarnation, which makes Me bone of your bone and flesh of your flesh; *my bride*, by heavenly betrothal, in which I have married you to Myself in righteousness. *My sister*, whom I knew of old, and over whom I watched from her earliest infancy; *My bride*, taken from among the daughters, embraced by arms of love and joined to me forever." See how true it is that our royal Kinsman is not ashamed of us, for He dwells with manifest delight upon this twofold relationship. We have the word "my" twice in our version; as if Christ dwelt with rapture on His possession of His Church. His delights were with the sons of men because those sons of men were His own chosen ones. He, the Shepherd, sought the sheep because they were *His* sheep; He has gone about "to seek and to save that which was lost," because that which was lost was *His* long before it was lost to itself or lost to Him. The church is the exclusive portion of her Lord; none else may claim a partnership or pretend to share her love. Jesus, Your church delights to have it so! Let every believing soul drink solace out of these wells. Soul, Christ is near to you in ties of relationship. Christ is dear to you in bonds of marriage union, and you are dear to Him; behold, He grasps both of your hands with both His own, saying, "*My* sister, *my* bride." Consider how the Lord gets such a double hold of you that He neither can nor will ever let you go. Be not, O beloved, slow to return the hallowed flame of His love.

... GUILT FROM THE HOLY THINGS. — EXODUS 28:38

What a veil is lifted up by these words, and what a disclosure is made! It will be humbling and profitable for us to pause awhile and see this sad sight. The iniquities of our public worship, its hypocrisy, formality, lukewarmness, irreverence, wandering of heart, and forgetfulness of God—what a full measure have we there! Our work for the Lord, its emulation, selfishness, carelessness, slackness, unbelief—what a mass of defilement is there! Our private devotions, their laxity, coldness, neglect, sleepiness, and vanity—what a mountain of dead earth is there! If we looked more carefully, we should find this iniquity to be far greater than appears at first sight. Dr. Payson, writing to his brother, says, "My parish, as well as my heart, very much resembles the garden of the sluggard; and what is worse, I find that very many of my desires for the improvement of both, proceed either from pride or vanity or indolence. I look at the weeds, which overspread my garden, and breathe out an earnest wish that they were eradicated. But why? What prompts the wish? So that I may walk out and say to myself, 'In what fine order is my garden kept!' This is *pride*. Or, so that my neighbors may look over the wall and say, 'How finely your garden flourishes!' This is *vanity*. Or I may wish for the destruction of the weeds, because I am weary of pulling them up. This is indolence." So even our desires after holiness may be polluted by ill motives. Under the greenest sods worms hide themselves; we need not look long to discover them. How cheering is the thought that when the High Priest bore the iniquity of the holy things he wore upon his brow the words, "HOLINESS TO THE LORD," and even so while Jesus bears our sin, He presents before His Father's face not our unholiness, but His own holiness. O for grace to view our great High Priest by the eye of faith!

❧ EVENING ❧
FOR YOUR LOVE IS BETTER THAN WINE. — SONG OF SOLOMON 1:2

Nothing gives the believer so much joy as fellowship with Christ. He has enjoyment as others have in the common mercies of life—he can be glad both in God's gifts and God's works; but in all these separately, yes, and in all of them added together, he does not find such substantial delight as in the matchless person of his Lord Jesus. He has wine that no vineyard on earth ever yielded; he has bread that all the cornfields of Egypt could never bring forth. Where can such sweetness be found as we have tasted in communion with our Beloved? In our esteem, the joys of earth are little better than husks for pigs compared with Jesus, the heavenly manna. We would rather have one mouthful of Christ's love and a sip of his fellowship than a whole world full of carnal delights. What is the chaff to the wheat? What is the sparkling paste to the true diamond? What is a dream to the glorious reality? What is life's merriment compared to our Lord Jesus in His most despised estate? If you know anything of the inner life, you will confess that our highest, purest, and most enduring joys must be the fruit of the tree of life, which is in the midst of the Paradise of God. No spring yields such sweet water as that well of God, which was dug with the soldier's spear. All earthly bliss is of the earth earthy, but the comforts of Christ's presence are like Himself, heavenly. We can review our communion with Jesus and find in it no empty regrets; there are no dregs in this wine, no dead flies in this ointment. The joy of the Lord is solid and enduring. Vanity has not looked upon it, but discretion and prudence testify that it abides the test of years and is in time and in eternity worthy to be called "the only true delight." For nourishment, consolation, exhilaration, and refreshment, no wine can rival the love of Jesus. Let us drink to the full this evening.

I WILL BE THEIR GOD. — JEREMIAH 31:33

Christian, here is all you require. To make you happy you want something that shall satisfy you, and is not this enough? If you can pour this promise into your cup, will you not say, with David, "My cup overflows."[1] When this is fulfilled, "I am your God," are you not possessor of all things? Desire is insatiable as death, but He who fills all in all can fill it. The capacity of our wishes who can measure? But the immeasurable wealth of God can more than overflow it. I ask you if you are not complete when God is yours? Do you want anything but God? Is not His all-sufficiency enough to satisfy you if all else should fail? But you want more than quiet satisfaction; you desire *rapturous delight*. Come, soul, here is music fit for heaven in this your portion, for God is the Maker of heaven. Not all the music blown from sweet instruments or drawn from living strings can yield such melody as this sweet promise, "I will be their God." Here is a deep sea of bliss, a shoreless ocean of delight; come, bathe your spirit in it; swim an age, and you shall find no shore; dive throughout eternity, and you shall find no bottom. "I will be their God." If this does not make your eyes sparkle, and your heart beat fast with bliss, then assuredly your soul is not in a healthy state. But you want more than present delights—you crave something concerning which you may exercise *hope*; and what more can you hope for than the fulfillment of this great promise, "I will be their God"? This is the masterpiece of all the promises; its enjoyment makes a heaven below and will make a heaven above. Dwell in the light of your Lord, and let your soul be always ravished with His love. Get out the marrow and fatness that this portion yields you. Live up to your privileges, and rejoice with unspeakable joy.

❧ EVENING ☙
SERVE THE LORD WITH GLADNESS. — PSALM 100:2

Delight in divine service is a token of acceptance. Those who serve God with a sad countenance, because they do what is unpleasant to them, are not serving Him at all; they bring the *form* of loyalty, but the *life* is absent. Our God requires no slaves to grace His throne; He is the Lord of the empire of love, and would have His servants dressed in the uniform of joy. The angels of God serve Him with songs, not with groans; a murmur or a sigh would be a mutiny in their ranks. That obedience that is not voluntary is disobedience, for the Lord looks at the heart, and if He sees that we serve Him from force, and not because we love Him, He will reject our offering. Service coupled with cheerfulness is heart-service and therefore true. Take away joyful willingness from the Christian, and you have removed *the test of his sincerity*. If a man be driven to battle, he is no patriot; but he who marches into the fray with flashing eye and beaming face, singing, "It is sweet for one's country to die," proves himself to be sincere in his patriotism. Cheerfulness is *the support of our strength*; in the joy of the Lord are we strong. It acts as *the remover of difficulties*. It is to our service what oil is to the wheels of a railway carriage. Without oil the axle soon grows hot, and accidents occur; and if there be not a holy cheerfulness to oil our wheels, our spirits will be clogged with weariness. The man who is cheerful in his service of God proves that obedience is his element; he can sing,

> Make me to walk in your commands,
> It's a delightful road.

Reader, let us put this question—do *you* serve the Lord *with gladness*? Let us show to the people of the world, who think our religion to be slavery, that it is to us a delight and a joy! Let our gladness proclaim that we serve a good Master.

[1] Psalm 23:5

THERE IS LAID UP FOR ME THE CROWN OF RIGHTEOUSNESS.
— 2 TIMOTHY 4:8

Doubting one, you have often said, "I fear I shall never enter heaven." Fear not! All the people of God shall enter there. I love the quaint saying of a dying man who exclaimed, "I have no fear of going home; I have sent all ahead of me. God's finger is on the latch of my door, and I am ready for Him to enter." "But," said one, "are you not afraid lest you should miss your inheritance?" "Nay," said he, "nay; there is one crown in heaven which the angel Gabriel could not wear; it will fit no head but mine. There is one throne in heaven which Paul the apostle could not fill; it was made for me, and I shall have it." O Christian, what a joyous thought! Your portion is secure; "there remains a rest." "But cannot I forfeit it?" No, it is entailed. If I be a child of God I shall not lose it. It is mine as securely as if I were there. Come with me, believer, and let us sit upon the top of Nebo and view the goodly land, even Canaan. Do you see that little river of death glistening in the sunlight, and across it do you see the pinnacles of the eternal city? Do you mark the pleasant country and all its joyous inhabitants? Know, then, that if you could fly across you would see written upon one of its many mansions, "This remains for such a one, preserved for him only. He shall be caught up to dwell forever with God." Poor doubting one, see the fair inheritance; it is *yours*. If you believe in the Lord Jesus, if you have repented of sin, if you have been renewed in heart, you are one of the Lord's people, there is a place reserved for you, a crown laid up for you, a harp specially provided for you. No one else shall have your portion; it is reserved in heaven for you, and you shall have it before long, for there shall be no vacant thrones in glory when all the chosen are gathered in.

❧ EVENING ☙

IN MY FLESH I SHALL SEE GOD. — JOB 19:26

Consider the subject of Job's devout anticipation: "I shall see God." He does not say, "I shall see the saints"—though doubtless that will be untold happiness—but "I shall see God." It is not "I shall see the pearly gates, I shall behold the walls of jasper, I shall gaze upon the crowns of gold," but "I shall see God." This is the sum and substance of heaven; this is the joyful hope of all believers. It is their delight to see Him now in the ordinances by faith. They love to behold Him in communion and in prayer; but there in heaven they shall have an open and unclouded vision, and thus seeing "him as he is,"[1] shall be made completely like Him. *Likeness to God*—what more can we wish for? And *a sight of God*—what can we desire better? Some read the passage, "Yet I shall see God in my flesh" and find here an allusion to Christ as the Word made flesh, and that glorious beholding of Him that shall be the splendor of the latter days. Whether so or not, it is certain that Christ shall be the object of our eternal vision; nor shall we ever want any joy beyond that of seeing Him. Do not think that this will be a narrow sphere for the mind to dwell in. It is but one source of delight, but that source is infinite. All His attributes shall be subjects for contemplation, and as He is infinite under each aspect, there is no fear of exhaustion. His works, His gifts, His love to us, and His glory in all His purposes and in all His actions, these shall make a theme that will be ever new. The patriarch looked forward to this sight of God as *a personal* enjoyment. "Whom I shall see for myself, and my eyes shall behold, and not another."[2] Take realizing views of heaven's bliss; think what it will be *to you*. "*Your eyes* will behold the king in his beauty."[3] All earthly brightness fades and darkens as we gaze upon it, but here is a brightness that can never dim, a glory that can never fade—"*I shall see God.*"

[1] 1 John 3:2 [2] Job 19:27 [3] Isaiah 33:17

THESE HAVE NO ROOT. — LUKE 8:13

My soul, examine yourself this morning by the light of this text. You have received the Word with joy; your feelings have been stirred, and a lively impression has been made. But, remember, to receive the Word in the ear is one thing, and to receive Jesus into your very soul is quite another; superficial feeling is often joined to inward hardness of heart, and a lively impression of the Word is not always a lasting one. In the parable, the seed in one case fell upon ground having a rocky bottom, covered over with a thin layer of earth; when the seed began to take root, its downward growth was hindered by the hard stone, and therefore it spent its strength in pushing its green shoot aloft as high as it could. But having no inward moisture derived from root nourishment, it withered away. Is this my case? Have I been making a fair show in the flesh without having a corresponding inner life? Good growth takes place upward and downward at the same time. Am I rooted in sincere fidelity and love to Jesus? If my heart remains unsoftened and unfertilized by grace, the good seed may germinate for a season, but it must ultimately wither, for it cannot flourish on a rocky, unbroken, unsanctified heart. Let me dread a godliness as rapid in growth and as lacking in endurance as Jonah's vine; let me count the cost of being a follower of Jesus. Above all let me feel the energy of His Holy Spirit, and then I shall possess an abiding and enduring seed in my soul. If my mind remains as stubborn as it was by nature, the sun of trial will scorch, and my hard heart will help cast the heat the more terribly upon the ill-covered seed, and my religion will soon die, and my despair will be terrible. Therefore, O heavenly Sower, plow me first, and then cast the truth into me, and let me yield a bounteous harvest.

❤ E V E N I N G ❤
I HAVE PRAYED FOR YOU. — LUKE 22:32

How encouraging is the thought of the Redeemer's never-ceasing intercession for us. When we pray, He pleads for us; and when we are *not* praying, He is advocating our cause, and by His supplications shielding us from unseen dangers. Notice the word of comfort addressed to Peter—"Simon, Simon, behold, Satan demanded to have you, that he might sift you like wheat, but"[1]—what? "But go and pray for yourself"? That would be good advice, but it is not so written. Neither does He say, "But I will keep you watchful, and so you shall be preserved." That would be a great blessing. No, it is, "*But I have prayed for you* that your faith may not fail."[2] We little know what we owe to our Savior's prayers. When we reach the hilltops of heaven and look back upon all the way whereby the Lord our God has led us, how we shall praise Him who, before the eternal throne, undid the mischief that Satan was doing upon earth. How we shall thank Him because He never held His peace but day and night pointed to the wounds upon His hands and carried our names upon His breastplate! Even before Satan had begun to tempt, Jesus had forestalled him and entered a plea in heaven. Mercy outruns malice. Consider, He does not say, "Satan hath *desired* to have you." He checks Satan even in his very desire and nips it in the bud. He does not say, "But I have desired to pray for you." No, but "I *have* prayed for you—I have done it already; I have gone to court and entered a counterplea even before an accusation is made." O Jesus, what a comfort it is that You have pleaded our cause against our unseen enemies; You have unmasked their ambushes. Here is a matter for joy, gratitude, hope, and confidence.

[1] Luke 22:31 [2] Luke 22:32

YOU ARE CHRIST'S. — 1 CORINTHIANS 3:23

You *are* Christ's." You are His by donation, for the Father gave you to the Son; His by His purchase of blood, for He paid the price for your redemption; His by dedication, for you have consecrated yourself to Him; His by relation, for you are named by His name and made one of His brethren and joint-heirs. Labor practically to show the world that you are the servant, the friend, the bride of Jesus. When tempted to sin, reply, "I cannot do this great wickedness, for I am Christ's." Immortal principles forbid the friend of Christ to sin. When wealth is before you to be won by sin, say that you are Christ's, and touch it not. Are you exposed to difficulties and dangers? Stand fast in the evil day, remembering that you are Christ's. Are you placed where others are sitting down idly, doing nothing? Rise to the work with all your powers; and when the sweat stands upon your brow, and you are tempted to loiter, cry, "No, I cannot stop, for I am Christ's. If I were not purchased by blood, I might be like Issachar, crouching between two burdens; but I am Christ's and cannot loiter." When the siren song of pleasure would tempt you from the path of right, reply, "Your music cannot charm me; I am Christ's." When the cause of God invites you, give your goods and yourself away, for you are Christ's. Never contradict your profession. Be ever one of those whose manners are Christian, whose speech is like Jesus, whose conduct and conversation are so reminiscent of heaven that all who see you may know that you are the Savior's, recognizing in you His features of love and His countenance of holiness. "I am a Roman!" was of old a reason for integrity; far more, then, let your argument for holiness be, "I am Christ's!"

❧ EVENING ❧
I HAVE YET SOMETHING TO SAY ON GOD'S BEHALF. — JOB 36:2

We ought not to court publicity for our virtue or notoriety for our zeal; but at the same time it is a sin to be always seeking to hide what God has bestowed upon us for the good of others. A Christian is not to be a village in a valley, but "a city set on a hill";[1] he is not to be a candle under a bushel, but a candle in a candlestick, giving light to all. Retirement may be lovely in its season, and to hide one's self is doubtless modest, but the hiding of *Christ* in us can never be justified, and the keeping back of truth, which is precious to ourselves, is a sin against others and an offense against God. If you have a nervous temperament and a retiring disposition, take care that you do not indulge this trembling propensity, lest you should be useless to the church. Seek in the name of Him who was not ashamed of you to do some little violence to your feelings and tell others what Christ has told to you. If you cannot speak with trumpet tongue, use the still small voice. If the pulpit must not be your tribune, if the press may not carry on its wings your words, yet say with Peter and John, "I have no silver and gold, but what I do have I give to you."[2] By Sychar's well talk to the Samaritan woman, if you cannot preach a sermon on the mountain; utter the praises of Jesus in the house, if not in the temple; in the field, if not in the public square; in your own household, if you cannot in the great family of man. From the hidden springs within, let sweetly flowing streams of testimony flow forth, giving drink to every passerby. Hide not your talent; trade with it, and you shall bring in good interest to your Lord and Master. To speak for God will be refreshing to ourselves, cheering to saints, useful to sinners, and honoring to the Savior.

[1] Matthew 5:14   [2] Acts 3:6

   ❧   MORNING   ☙

JEHOSHAPHAT MADE SHIPS OF TARSHISH TO GO TO
OPHIR FOR GOLD, BUT THEY DID NOT GO,
FOR THE SHIPS WERE WRECKED AT EZION-GEBER. — 1 KINGS 22:48

Solomon's ships had returned in safety, but Jehoshaphat's vessels never reached the land of gold. Providence prospers one and frustrates the desires of another, in the same business and at the same spot; yet the Great Ruler is as good and wise at one time as another. May we have grace today, in the remembrance of this text, to bless the Lord for ships broken at Ezion-geber as well as for vessels filled with temporal blessings; let us not envy the more successful, nor murmur at our losses as though we were singularly and specially tried. Like Jehoshaphat, we may be precious in the Lord's sight, although our schemes end in disappointment.

The secret cause of Jehoshaphat's loss is well worthy of notice, for it is the root of very much of the suffering of the Lord's people; it was his alliance with a sinful family, his fellowship with sinners. In 2 Chronicles 20:37 we are told that the Lord sent a prophet to declare, "Because you have joined with Ahaziah, the LORD will destroy what you have made." This was a fatherly chastisement, which appears to have been considered blessed to him; for in the verse which succeeds our morning's text we find him refusing to allow his servants to sail in the same vessels with those of the wicked king. Would to God that Jehoshaphat's experience might be a warning to the rest of the Lord's people, to avoid being unequally yoked together with unbelievers! A life of misery is usually the lot of those who are united in marriage, or in any other way of their own choosing, with the men of the world. O for such love to Jesus that, like Him, we may be holy, harmless, undefiled, and separate from sinners; for if that is not the case with us, we may expect to hear it often said, "The Lord will destroy what you have made."

❧   EVENING   ☙

. . . MADE THE IRON FLOAT. — 2 KINGS 6:6

The axe head seemed hopelessly lost, and as it was borrowed, the honor of the prophetic band was likely to be imperiled, and so the name of their God to be compromised. Contrary to all expectation, the iron was made to mount from the depth of the stream and to swim; for things impossible with man are possible with God. I knew a man in Christ but a few years ago who was called to undertake a work far exceeding his strength. It appeared so difficult as to involve absurdity in the bare idea of attempting it. Yet he was called to it, and his faith rose with the occasion. God honored his faith, unlooked-for aid was sent, and the iron did swim. Another of the Lord's family was in dreadful financial straits. He would have been able to meet all claims and much more if he could have realized a certain portion of his estate, but he was overtaken with a sudden pressure. He sought for friends in vain, but faith led him to the unfailing Helper, and lo, the trouble was averted, his footsteps were enlarged, and the iron did swim. A third had a sorrowful case of depravity to deal with. He had taught, reproved, warned, invited, and interceded, but all in vain. Old Adam was too strong for young Melanchthon; the stubborn spirit would not relent. Then came an agony of prayer, and before long a blessed answer was sent from heaven. The hard heart was broken; the iron did swim.

Beloved reader, what is your desperate case? What heavy matter have you to deal with this evening? Bring it here. The God of the prophets lives, and lives to help His saints. He will not suffer you to lack any good thing. Believe in the Lord of hosts! Approach Him pleading the name of Jesus, and the iron shall swim; you too shall see the finger of God working marvels for His people. According to your faith be it unto you, and yet again the iron shall swim.

By the words "to save" we understand the whole of the great work of salvation, from the first holy desire onward to complete sanctification. The words are *multum in parvo* [much in little]: indeed, here is all mercy in a word. Christ is not only "mighty to save" those who repent, but He is able to make men repent. He will carry those to heaven who believe; but He is, moreover, mighty to give men new hearts and to work faith in them. He is mighty to make the man who hates holiness love it, and to constrain the despiser of His name to bend the knee before Him. And this is not all the meaning, for the divine power is equally seen in the after-work. The life of a believer is a series of miracles wrought by the Mighty God. The bush burns but is not consumed. He is mighty to keep His people holy after He has made them so, and to preserve them in His fear and love until He consummates their spiritual existence in heaven. Christ's power does not lie in making a believer and then leaving him to fend for himself; but He who begins the good work carries it on; He who imparts the first germ of life in the dead soul prolongs the divine existence and strengthens it until it breaks every bond of sin, and the soul leaps from earth, perfected in glory. Believer, here is encouragement. Are you praying for some beloved one? Oh, do not give up praying, for Christ is "mighty to save." You are powerless to reclaim the rebel, but your Lord is Almighty. Lay hold on that mighty arm and rouse it to put forth its strength. Does your own case trouble you? Fear not, for His strength is sufficient for you. Whether to begin with others or to carry on the work in you, Jesus is "mighty to save," the best proof of which lies in the fact that He has saved *you*. What a thousand mercies that you have not found Him mighty to destroy!

ᴄᴠ EVENING ᴊᴇ
BEGINNING TO SINK HE CRIED OUT, "LORD, SAVE ME." — MATTHEW 14:30

Sinking times are praying times with the Lord's servants. Peter neglected prayer at starting upon his venturous journey, but when he began to sink, his danger made him a suppliant, and his cry, though late, was not too late. In our hours of bodily pain and mental anguish, we find ourselves as naturally driven to prayer as the wreck is driven upon the shore by the waves. The fox runs to its hole for protection; the bird flies to the wood for shelter; and even so the tried believer hastens to the mercy-seat for safety. Heaven's great harbor of refuge is All-prayer; thousands of weather-beaten vessels have found a haven there, and the moment a storm comes on, it is wise for us to make for it with full sail.

Short prayers are long enough. There were but three words in the petition that Peter gasped out, but they were sufficient for his purpose. Not length but strength is desirable. A sense of need is a mighty teacher of brevity. If our prayers had less of the tail feathers of pride and more wing, they would be all the better. Verbiage is to devotion as chaff to the wheat. Precious things lie in small compass, and all that is real prayer in many a long address might have been uttered in a petition as short as that of Peter.

Our extremities are the Lord's opportunities. Immediately a keen sense of danger forces an anxious cry from us, the ear of Jesus hears, and with Him ear and heart go together, and the hand does not long linger. At the last moment we appeal to our Master, but His swift hand makes up for our delays by instant and effectual action. Are we nearly engulfed by the boisterous waters of affliction? Let us then lift up our souls unto our Savior, and we may rest assured that He will not suffer us to perish. When we can do nothing, Jesus can do everything; let us enlist His powerful aid upon our side, and all will be well.

❧ MORNING ❧

DO AS YOU HAVE SPOKEN. — 2 SAMUEL 7:25

God's promises were never meant to be thrown aside as wastepaper; He intended that they should be used. God's gold is not miser's money but is minted to be traded with. Nothing pleases our Lord better than to see His promises put in circulation; He loves to see His children bring them up to Him and say, "Lord, do as you have said." We glorify God when we plead His promises. Do you think that God will be any poorer for giving you the riches He has promised? Do you dream that He will be any less holy for giving holiness to you? Do you imagine He will be any less pure for washing you from your sins? He has said, "Come now, let us reason together, says the LORD: though your sins are like scarlet, they shall be as white as snow; though they are red like crimson, they shall become like wool."[1] Faith lays hold upon the promise of pardon, and it does not delay, saying, "This is a precious promise— I wonder if it be true?" but goes straight to the throne with it and pleads, "Lord, here is the promise. Do as you have said." Our Lord replies, "Be it unto you even as you will." When a Christian grasps a promise, if he does not take it to God, he dishonors Him; but when he hastens to the throne of grace and cries, "Lord, I have nothing to recommend me but this, You have said it," then his desire shall be granted. Our heavenly Banker delights to cash His own notes. Never let the promise rust. Draw the word of promise out of its sheath and use it with holy violence. Think not that God will be troubled by your importunately reminding Him of His promises. He loves to hear the loud outcries of needy souls. It is His delight to bestow favors. He is more ready to hear than you are to ask. The sun is not weary of shining, nor the fountain of flowing. It is God's nature to keep His promises; therefore go at once to the throne with, "Do as You have said."

❧ EVENING ❧

BUT I GIVE MYSELF TO PRAYER. — PSALM 109:4

Lying tongues were busy against the reputation of David, but he did not defend himself; he moved the case into a higher court and pleaded before the great King Himself. Prayer is the safest method of replying to words of hatred. The psalmist prayed in no coldhearted manner; he gave himself to the exercise—threw his whole soul and heart into it—straining every sinew and muscle, as Jacob did when wrestling with the angel. Thus, and thus only, shall any of us speed at the throne of grace. As a shadow has no power because there is no substance in it, even so that supplication in which a man's proper self is not thoroughly present in agonizing earnestness and vehement desire is utterly ineffectual, for it lacks that which would give it force. "Fervent prayer," says an old divine, "like a cannon planted at the gates of heaven, makes them fly open." The common fault with most of us is our readiness to yield to distractions. Our thoughts go roving here and there, and we make little progress toward our desired end. Like quicksilver our mind will not hold together but rolls off this way and that. How great an evil this is! It injures us, and what is worse, it insults our God. What should we think of a petitioner if, while having an audience with a prince, he should be playing with a feather or catching a fly?

Continuance and perseverance are intended in the expression of our text. David did not cry once and then relapse into silence; his holy clamor was continued till it brought down the blessing. Prayer must not be our intermittent work but our daily business, our habit and vocation. As artists give themselves to their models, and poets to their classical pursuits, so must we addict ourselves to prayer. We must be immersed in prayer as in our element, and so pray without ceasing. Lord, teach us so to pray, that we may be more and more efficacious in supplication.

[1] Isaiah 1:18

I AM THE ONE WHO HELPS YOU, DECLARES THE LORD. — ISAIAH 41:14

This morning let us hear the Lord Jesus speak to each one of us: "I will *help* you." "It is but a small thing for Me, your God, to *help* you. Consider what I have done already. What! Not help you? Why, I bought you with My blood. What! Not help you? I have died for you; and if I have done the greater, will I not do the less? *Help* you! It is the least thing I will ever do for you; I *have* done more, and will do more. Before the world began I chose you. I made the covenant for you. I laid aside My glory and became a man for you; I gave up My life for you; and if I did all this, I will surely help you now. In helping you, I am giving you what I have bought for you already. If you had need of a thousand times as much help, I would give it to you; you require little compared with what I am ready to give. It is much for you to need, but it is nothing for me to bestow. *Help* you? Fear not! If there were an ant at the door of your granary asking for help, it would not ruin you to give him a handful of your wheat; and you are nothing but a tiny insect at the door of My all-sufficiency. I will help you."

O my soul, is this not enough? Do you need more strength than the omnipotence of the united Trinity? Do you want more wisdom than exists in the Father, more love than displays itself in the Son, or more power than is manifest in the influences of the Spirit? Bring here your empty pitcher! Surely this well will fill it. Hurry, gather up your wants, and bring them here—your emptiness, your woes, your needs. Behold, this river of God is full for your supply; what else can you desire? Go forth, my soul, in this your might. The Eternal God is your helper!

Fear not, I am with you, oh, be not dismay'd!
I, I am your God, and will still give you aid.

❧ EVENING ❧

AN ANOINTED ONE SHALL BE CUT OFF AND
SHALL HAVE NOTHING. — DANIEL 9:26

Blessed be His name, there was no cause of death in Him. Neither original nor actual sin had defiled Him, and therefore death had no claim upon Him. No man could have taken His life from Him justly, for He had done no man wrong, and no man could even have taken Him by force unless He had been pleased to yield Himself to die. But lo, one sins, and another suffers. Justice was offended by us but found its satisfaction in Him. Rivers of tears, mountains of offerings, seas of the blood of bulls, and hills of frankincense could not have availed for the removal of sin; but Jesus was cut off for us, and the cause of wrath was cut off at once, for sin was put away forever. Herein is wisdom, whereby substitution, the sure and speedy way of atonement, was devised! Herein is condescension, which brought the Messiah, the Prince, to wear a crown of thorns and die upon the cross! Herein is love, which led the Redeemer to lay down His life for His enemies!

It is not enough, however, to admire the spectacle of the innocent bleeding for the guilty— we must make sure of our personal interest. The special object of the Messiah's death was the salvation of His Church. Do we have a part and a place among those for whom He gave His life as a ransom? Did the Lord Jesus stand as our representative? Are we healed by His stripes? It will be a terrible thing indeed if we should come short of a portion in His sacrifice; it were better for us than we had never been born. Solemn as the question is, it is a joyful circumstance that it is one that may be answered clearly and without mistake. To all who believe on Him the Lord Jesus is a present Savior, and upon them all the blood of reconciliation has been sprinkled. Let all who trust in the merit of Messiah's death be joyful at every remembrance of Him, and let their holy gratitude lead them to the fullest consecration to His cause.

THEN I LOOKED, AND BEHOLD, ON MOUNT ZION STOOD THE LAMB.
— REVELATION 14:1

The apostle John was privileged to look within the gates of heaven, and in describing what he saw, he begins by saying, "I looked, and, behold, . . . the Lamb." This teaches us that the chief object of contemplation in the heavenly state is "the Lamb of God, who takes away the sin of the world!"[1] Nothing else attracted the apostle's attention so much as the person of that Divine Being who has redeemed us by His blood. He is the theme of the songs of all glorified spirits and holy angels. Christian, here is joy for you; you have looked, and you have seen the Lamb. Through your tears your eyes have seen the Lamb of God taking away your sins. Rejoice then. In a little while, when your eyes shall have been wiped from tears, you will see the same Lamb exalted on His throne. It is the joy of your heart to hold daily fellowship with Jesus. You shall have the same joy to a higher degree in heaven; you shall enjoy the constant vision of His presence; you shall dwell with Him forever. "I looked, and, behold, . . . the Lamb." Why, that Lamb is heaven itself; for as good Rutherford says, "Heaven and Christ are the same thing." To be with Christ is to be in heaven, and to be in heaven is to be with Christ. That prisoner of the Lord very sweetly writes in one of his glowing letters, "O my Lord Jesus Christ, if I could be in heaven without you, it would be a hell; and if I could be in hell, and have you still, it would be a heaven to me, for you are all the heaven I want." It is true, is it not, Christian? Does not your soul say so?

Not all the harps above
Can make a heavenly place,
If God His residence remove,
Or but conceal His face.

All you need to make you blessed, supremely blessed, is to be with Christ.

❧ EVENING ❧

IT HAPPENED, LATE ONE AFTERNOON, WHEN DAVID AROSE
FROM HIS COUCH AND WAS WALKING ON THE ROOF
OF THE KING'S HOUSE . . . — 2 SAMUEL 11:2

At that hour David saw Bathsheba. We are never out of the reach of temptation. Both at home and away we are liable to meet with allurements to evil. The morning opens with peril, and the shades of evening find us still in jeopardy. They are well kept whom God keeps, but woe to those who go out into the world, or even dare to walk their own house unarmed. Those who think themselves secure are more exposed to danger than any others. The armor-bearer of Sin is Self-confidence.

David should have been engaged in fighting the Lord's battles, instead of which he rested in Jerusalem, giving himself up to luxurious repose, for he arose from his bed at eventide. Idleness and luxury are the devil's jackals and find him abundant prey. In stagnant waters noxious creatures swarm, and neglected soil soon yields a dense tangle of weeds and briars. Oh, for the constraining love of Jesus to keep us active and useful! When I see the King of Israel sluggishly leaving his couch at the close of the day and falling at once into temptation, let me take warning and set holy watchfulness to guard the door.

Is it possible that the king had mounted his housetop for retirement and devotion? If so, what a caution is given us to count no place, however secret, a sanctuary from sin! While our hearts are so like a tinderbox, and sparks so plentiful, we need to use all diligence in all places to prevent a blaze. Satan can climb housetops and enter closets, and even if we could shut out that foul fiend, our own corruptions are enough to work our ruin unless grace prevents it. Reader, beware of evening temptations. Be not secure. The sun is down, but sin is up. We need a watchman for the night as well as a guardian for the day. O blessed Spirit, keep us from all evil this night. Amen.

[1] John 1:29

THERE REMAINS A SABBATH REST FOR THE PEOPLE OF GOD. — HEBREWS 4:9

How different will be the state of the believer in heaven from what it is here! Here he is born to toil and suffer weariness, but in the land of the immortal, fatigue is never known. Anxious to serve his Master, he finds his strength unequal to his zeal; his constant cry is, "Help me to serve You, O my God." If he be thoroughly active, he will have much labor; not too much for his will, but more than enough for his power, so that he will cry out, "I am not wearied *of* the labor, but I am wearied *in it*." Ah, Christian, the hot day of weariness does not last forever. The sun is nearing the horizon; it shall rise again with a brighter day than you have ever seen upon a land where they serve God day and night, and yet rest from their labors. *Here* rest is but partial; *there* it is *perfect*. *Here* the Christian is always unsettled; he feels that he has not yet attained. *There* all are at rest; they have attained the summit of the mountain; they have ascended to the bosom of their God. Higher they cannot go. Ah, toil-worn laborer, only think of when you shall rest forever! Can you conceive it? It is a rest *eternal*; a rest that "remains." *Here* my best joys bear "mortal" on their brow. My fair flowers fade; my dainty cups are drained to dregs; my sweetest birds fall before Death's arrows; my most pleasant days are shadowed into nights; and the flood tides of my bliss subside into ebbs of sorrow. But *there* everything is immortal. The harp remains in tune, the crown unfading, the eye undimmed, the voice unfaltering, the heart unwavering; and the immortal being is wholly absorbed in infinite delight. Happy day when mortality shall be swallowed up of life, and the Eternal Sabbath shall begin!

❧ EVENING ❧

HE INTERPRETED TO THEM IN ALL THE SCRIPTURES THE
THINGS CONCERNING HIMSELF. — LUKE 24:27

The two disciples on the road to Emmaus had a most profitable journey. Their companion and teacher was *the best of tutors*, the interpreter one of a thousand, in whom are hid all the treasures of wisdom and knowledge. The Lord Jesus condescended to become a preacher of the Gospel, and He was not ashamed to exercise His calling before an audience of two persons. Neither does He now refuse to become the teacher of even one. Let us court the company of so excellent an Instructor, for till He is made unto us wisdom we shall never be wise unto salvation.

This unrivaled tutor used as His class-book *the best of books*. Although able to reveal fresh truth, He preferred to expound the old. He knew by His omniscience what was the most instructive way of teaching, and by turning at once to Moses and the prophets, He showed us that the surest road to wisdom is not speculation, reasoning, or reading human books, but meditation upon the Word of God. The readiest way to be spiritually rich in heavenly knowledge is to dig in this mine of diamonds, to gather pearls from this heavenly sea. When Jesus Himself sought to enrich others, He mined in the quarry of Holy Scripture.

The favored pair were led to consider *the best of subjects*, for Jesus spoke of Jesus and expounded the things concerning Himself. Here the diamond cut the diamond, and what could be more admirable? The Master of the House unlocked His own doors, conducted the guests to His table, and placed His own choice foods upon it. He who hid the treasure in the field Himself guided the searchers to it. Our Lord would naturally discourse upon the sweetest of topics, and He could find none sweeter than His own person and work. With an eye to these we should always search the Word. O for grace to study the Bible with Jesus as both our teacher and our lesson!

I SOUGHT HIM, BUT FOUND HIM NOT. — SONG OF SOLOMON 3:1

Tell me where you lost the company of Christ, and I will tell you the most likely place to find Him. Have you lost Christ in the closet by restraining prayer? Then it is there you must seek and find Him. Did you lose Christ by sin? You will find Christ in no other way but by the giving up of the sin, and seeking by the Holy Spirit to mortify the member in which the lust dwells. Did you lose Christ by neglecting the Scriptures? You must find Christ in the Scriptures. It is a true proverb, "Look for a thing where you dropped it—it is there." So look for Christ where you lost Him, for He has not gone away. But it is hard work to go back for Christ. Bunyan tells us that the pilgrim found the piece of the road back to the Arbor of Ease, where he lost his roll, the hardest he had ever traveled. Twenty miles onward is easier than to go one mile back for the lost evidence.

Take care, then, when you find your Master, to cling close to Him. But how is it you have lost Him? One would have thought you would never have parted with such a precious friend, whose presence is so sweet, whose words are so comforting, and whose company is so dear to you! How is it that you did not watch Him every moment for fear of losing sight of Him? Yet, since you have let Him go, what a mercy that you are seeking Him, even though you mournfully groan, "O that I knew where I might find Him!" Go on seeking, for it is dangerous to be without your Lord. Without Christ you are like a sheep without its shepherd, like a tree without water at its roots, like a withered leaf in the storm—not bound to the tree of life. With your whole heart seek Him, and He will be found by you. Only give yourself thoroughly up to the search, and truly you shall yet discover Him to your joy and gladness.

⁓   E V E N I N G   ⁓

THEN HE OPENED THEIR MINDS TO UNDERSTAND
THE SCRIPTURES. — LUKE 24:45

He whom we viewed last evening as opening Scripture, we here perceive opening the understanding. In the first work He has many fellow-laborers, but in the second He stands alone; many can bring the Scriptures to the mind, but the Lord alone can prepare the mind to receive the Scriptures. Our Lord Jesus differs from all other teachers. They reach the ear, but He instructs the heart; they deal with the outward letter, but He imparts an inward taste for the truth, by which we perceive its savor and spirit. The most unlearned of men become ripe scholars in the school of grace when the Lord Jesus by His Holy Spirit unfolds the mysteries of the kingdom to them and grants the divine anointing by which they are enabled to behold the invisible. Happy are we if we have had our understandings cleared and strengthened by the Master! How many men of profound learning are ignorant of eternal things! They know the killing letter of revelation, but its killing spirit they cannot discern; they have a veil upon their hearts that the eyes of carnal reason cannot penetrate. Such was our case a little time ago. We who now see were once utterly blind; truth was to us as beauty in the dark, a thing unnoticed and neglected. Had it not been for the love of Jesus we should have remained to this moment in utter ignorance, for without His gracious opening of our understanding, we could no more have attained to spiritual knowledge than an infant can climb the Pyramids or an ostrich fly up to the stars. Jesus' College is the only one in which God's truth can be really learned; other schools may teach us what is to be believed, but Christ's alone can show us how to believe it. Let us sit at the feet of Jesus and by earnest prayer call upon His blessed help, that our dull wits may grow brighter, and our feeble understandings may receive heavenly things.

    ❧ MORNING ❧

ABEL WAS A KEEPER OF SHEEP. — GENESIS 4:2

As a shepherd Abel *sanctified his work to the glory of God and offered a sacrifice of blood upon his altar, and the Lord had respect unto Abel and his offering.* This early type, a foreshadowing of our Lord, is exceedingly clear and distinct. Like the first streak of light that tinges the east at sunrise, it does not reveal everything, but it clearly manifests the great fact that the sun is coming. As we see Abel, a shepherd and yet a priest, offering a sacrifice of sweet fragrance unto God, we discern our Lord, who brings before His Father a sacrifice to which Jehovah ever has respect. Abel was hated by his brother—hated without a cause; and even so was the Savior. The natural and carnal man hated the accepted man in whom the Spirit of grace was found, and did not rest until his blood had been shed. Abel fell and sprinkled his altar and sacrifice with his own blood, and therein sets forth the Lord Jesus slain by the enmity of man while serving as a priest before the Lord. "The good shepherd lays down his life for the sheep."[1] Let us weep over Him as we view Him slain by the hatred of mankind, staining the horns of His altar with His own blood. *Abel's blood speaks.* "And the LORD said, 'What have you done? The voice of your brother's blood is crying to me from the ground.'"[2] The blood of Jesus has a mighty tongue, and the import of its prevailing cry is not vengeance but mercy. It is precious beyond all preciousness to stand at the altar of our Good Shepherd—to see Him bleeding there as the slaughtered priest, and then to hear His blood speaking peace to all His flock—peace in our conscience, peace between Jew and Gentile, peace between man and his offended Maker, peace all down the ages of eternity for blood-washed men. Abel is the first shepherd in order of time, but our hearts shall ever place Jesus first in order of excellence. Great Keeper of the sheep, we, the people of Your pasture, bless You with our whole hearts when we see You slain for us.

❧ EVENING ❧

TURN MY EYES FROM LOOKING AT WORTHLESS THINGS;
AND GIVE ME LIFE IN YOUR WAYS. — PSALM 119:37

There are various kinds of vanity. The cap and bells of the fool, the merriment of the world, the dance, and the cup of the dissolute—all these men know to be vanities; they wear upon their chest their proper name and title. Far more treacherous are those equally vain things—the cares of this world and the deceitfulness of riches. A man may follow vanity as truly in a portfolio as in a theater. If he is spending his life in amassing wealth, he passes his days in a vain show. Unless we follow Christ and make our God the great object of life, we only differ in appearance from the most frivolous. It is clear that there is much need of the prayer of our text: "Give me life in your ways." The psalmist confesses that he is dull, heavy, all but dead. Perhaps, dear reader, you feel the same. We are so sluggish that the best motives cannot quicken us, apart from the Lord Himself. What! Will not hell quicken me? Shall I think of sinners perishing, and yet not be awakened? Will not heaven quicken me? Can I think of the reward that awaits the righteous and yet be cold? Will not death quicken me? Can I think of dying and standing before my God, and yet be slothful in my Master's service? Will not Christ's love constrain me? Can I think of His dear wounds, can I sit at the foot of His cross, and not be stirred with fervency and zeal? It seems so! No mere consideration can quicken us to zeal, but God Himself must do it; hence the cry, "Give me life in *your* ways." The psalmist breathes out his whole soul in vehement pleadings; his body and his soul unite in prayer. "Turn my eyes," says the body. "Give me life," cries the soul. This is a fit prayer for every day. O Lord, hear it in my case this night.

[1] John 10:11 [2] Genesis 4:10

When Moses sang at the Red Sea, it was his joy to know that all Israel was safe. Not a drop of spray fell from that solid wall until the last of God's Israel had safely planted his foot on the other side of the flood. That done, immediately the floods dissolved into their proper place again, but not till then. Part of that song was, "You have led in your steadfast love the people whom you have redeemed."[1] In the last time, when the elect shall sing the song of Moses, the servant of God, and of the Lamb, it shall be the boast of Jesus, "Of all whom you have given me, I have lost none." In heaven there shall not be a vacant throne.

For all the chosen race
Shall meet around the throne,
Shall bless the conduct of His grace,
And make His glories known.

As many as God has chosen, as many as Christ has redeemed, as many as the Spirit has called, as many as believe in Jesus shall safely cross the dividing sea. We are not all safely landed yet:

Part of the host have crossed the flood,
And part are crossing now.

The vanguard of the army has already reached the shore. We are marching through the depths; we are at this day following hard after our Leader into the heart of the sea. Let us be of good cheer: The rearguard shall soon be where the vanguard already is; the last of the chosen ones shall soon have crossed the sea, and then shall be heard the song of triumph, when all are secure. But oh, if one were absent—oh, if one of His chosen family should be cast away, it would make an everlasting discord in the song of the redeemed and cut the strings of the harps of paradise, so that music could never be extorted from them.

&ea;   EVENING   &eb;
AND HE WAS VERY THIRSTY, AND HE CALLED UPON THE LORD AND SAID,
"YOU HAVE GRANTED THIS GREAT SALVATION BY THE HAND OF
YOUR SERVANT, AND SHALL I NOW DIE OF THIRST . . . ?" — JUDGES 15:18

Samson was thirsty and ready to die. The difficulty was totally different from any that the hero had met before. Merely to get thirst quenched is nothing like so great a matter as to be delivered from a thousand Philistines! But when the thirst was upon him, Samson felt that particular difficulty to be more weighty than the great past difficulty out of which he had so specially been delivered. It is very usual for God's people, when they have enjoyed a great deliverance, to find a little trouble too much for them. Samson slays a thousand Philistines and piles them up in heaps, and then faints for a little water! Jacob wrestles with God at Peniel and overcomes Omnipotence itself, and then goes "limping because of his hip!"[2] Strange that there must be a shrinking of the sinew whenever we win the day. As if the Lord must teach us our littleness, our nothingness, in order to keep us within bounds. Samson boasted right loudly when he said, "I have slain a thousand men." His boastful throat soon grew hoarse with thirst, and he betook himself to prayer. God has many ways of humbling His people. Dear child of God, if after great mercy you are laid very low, your case is not an unusual one. When David had mounted the throne of Israel, he said, "I am this day weak, though anointed king." You must expect to feel weakest when you are enjoying your greatest triumph. If God has wrought for you great deliverances in the past, your present difficulty is only like Samson's thirst, and the Lord will not let you faint, nor allow your enemy to triumph over you. The road of sorrow is the road to heaven, but there are wells of refreshing water all along the route. So, tested and tired pilgrim, cheer your heart with Samson's words, and rest assured that God will deliver you before long.

[1] Exodus 15:13 [2] Genesis 32:31

SON OF MAN, HOW DOES THE WOOD OF THE VINE SURPASS ANY WOOD,
THE VINE BRANCH THAT IS AMONG THE TREES
OF THE FOREST? — EZEKIEL 15:2

These words are for the humbling of God's people; they are called God's vine, but what are they by nature more than others? They, by God's goodness, have become fruitful, having been planted in a good soil; the Lord has trained them upon the walls of the sanctuary, and they bring forth fruit to His glory. But what are they without their God? What are they without the continual influence of the Spirit, begetting fruitfulness in them? O believer, learn to reject pride, seeing that you have no ground for it. Whatever you are, you have nothing to make you proud. The more you have, the more you are in debt to God; and you should not be proud of that which renders you a debtor. Consider your origin; look back to what you were. Consider what you would have been but for divine grace. Look upon yourself as you are now. Does not your conscience reproach you? Do not your thousand wanderings stand before you and tell you that you are unworthy to be called His son? And if He has made you anything, are you not taught thereby that it is grace that has made you to differ? Great believer, you would have been a great sinner if God had not made you to differ. O you who are valiant for truth, you would have been as valiant for error if grace had not laid hold upon you. Therefore, do not be proud, though you have a large influence—a wide domain of grace, for once you did not have a single thing to call your own except your sin and misery. Oh, strange infatuation that you, who has borrowed everything, should think of exalting yourself—a poor, dependent pensioner upon the bounty of your Savior, one who has a life that dies without fresh streams of life from Jesus, and yet is proud! Fie on you, O silly heart!

⤬ EVENING ⤬

"DOES JOB FEAR GOD FOR NO REASON?" — JOB 1:9

This was the wicked question of Satan concerning that upright man of old, but there are many in the present day concerning whom it might be asked with justice, for they love God after a fashion because He prospers them; but if things went ill with them, they would give up all their boasted faith in God. If they can clearly see that since the time of their supposed conversion the world has gone prosperously with them, then they will love God in their poor, carnal way; but if they endure adversity, they rebel against the Lord. Their love is the love of the table, not of the host; a love of the cupboard, not of the master of the house. As for the true Christian, he expects to have his reward in the next life and to endure hardness in this. The promise of the old covenant is adversity. Remember Christ's words—"Every branch of mine that does not bear fruit"—what?—"*he takes away, and every branch that does bear fruit he prunes, that it may bear more fruit.*"[1] If you bring forth fruit, you will have to endure affliction. "Alas," you say, "that is a terrible prospect." But this affliction works out such precious results, for the Christian who is the subject of it must learn to rejoice in tribulations because as his tribulations abound, so his consolations abound by Christ Jesus. Rest assured, if you are a child of God, you will be no stranger to the rod. Sooner or later every bar of gold must pass through the fire. Fear not, but rather rejoice that such fruitful times are in store for you, for in them you will be weaned from earth and made meet for heaven; you will be delivered from clinging to the present and made to long for those eternal things that are so soon to be revealed to you. When you feel that as regards the present you do serve God for nothing, you will then rejoice in the infinite reward of the future.

[1] John 15:2

I HAVE EXALTED ONE CHOSEN FROM THE PEOPLE. — PSALM 89:19

Why was Christ chosen out of the people? Speak, my heart, for heart-thoughts are best. Was it not that He might be able to be our brother, in the blest tie of kindred blood? Oh, what relationship there is between Christ and the believer! The believer can say, "I have a Brother in heaven. I may be poor, but I have a Brother who is rich and is a King, and will He allow me to be in want while He is on His throne? Oh, no! He loves me; He is my Brother." Believer, wear this blessed thought, like a necklace of diamonds, around the neck of your memory; put it, as a golden ring, on the finger of recollection, and use it as the King's own seal, stamping the petitions of your faith with confidence of success. He is a brother born for adversity—treat Him as such.

Christ was also chosen out of the people that He might know our wants and sympathize with us. "Who in every respect has been tempted as we are, yet without sin."[1] In all our sorrows we have His sympathy. Temptation, pain, disappointment, weakness, weariness, poverty—He knows them all, for He has felt all. Remember this, Christian, and let it comfort you. However difficult and painful your road, it is marked by the footsteps of your Savior; and even when you reach the dark valley of the shadow of death and the deep waters of the swelling Jordan, you will find His footprints there. Wherever we go, in every place, He has been our forerunner; each burden we have to carry has once been laid on the shoulders of Immanuel.

> His way was much rougher and darker than mine.
> Did Christ, my Lord, suffer, and shall I repine?

Take courage! Royal feet have left a blood-red track upon the road and consecrated the thorny path forever.

❧ EVENING ❧

WE WILL EXTOL YOUR LOVE MORE THAN WINE. — SONG OF SOLOMON 1:4

Jesus will not let His people forget His love. If all the love they have enjoyed should be forgotten, He will visit them with fresh love. "Do you forget my cross?" says He. "I will cause you to remember it; for at My table I will manifest Myself anew to you. Do you forget what I did for you in the council-chamber of eternity? I will remind you of it, for you shall need a counselor and shall find Me ready at your call." Mothers do not let their children forget them. If the boy has gone to Australia and does not write home, his mother writes, "Has John forgotten his mother?" Then there comes back a sweet epistle, which proves that the gentle reminder was not in vain. So is it with Jesus. He says to us, "Remember Me," and our response is, "We will remember Your love." *We will* remember Your love and its matchless history. It is as ancient as the glory that You had with the Father before the world was. We remember, O Jesus, Your eternal love when You became our Surety and chose us as Your bride. We remember the love that suggested the sacrifice of Yourself, the love that, until the fullness of time, mused over that sacrifice until what was written of You ("Lo, I come") was fulfilled. We remember Your love, O Jesus, as it was manifest to us in Your holy life, from the manger of Bethlehem to the Garden of Gethsemane. We track You from the cradle to the grave—for Your every word and deed was love—and we rejoice in Your love, which death did not exhaust—Your love that shone resplendent in Your resurrection. We remember that burning fire of love that will never let You hold Your peace until Your chosen ones be all safely housed, until Zion be glorified and Jerusalem settled on her everlasting foundations of light and love in heaven.

[1] Hebrews 4:15

    ❧ MORNING ❧

FOR HE WILL DELIVER YOU FROM THE SNARE
OF THE FOWLER. — PSALM 91:3

God delivers His people from the snare of the fowler in two senses. *From* and *out of.* First, He delivers them *from* the snare—He does not let them enter it; and secondly, if they should be caught in it, He delivers them *out of* it. The first promise is the most precious to some; the second is the best to others.

"He will deliver you *from* the snare." How? Trouble is often the means God uses to deliver us. God knows that our backsliding will soon end in our destruction, and He in mercy sends the rod. We say, "Lord, why is this?" not knowing that our trouble has been the means of delivering us from far greater evil. In this way many have been saved from ruin by their sorrows and their crosses. At other times God keeps His people *from* the snare of the fowler by giving them great spiritual strength, so that when they are tempted to do evil they say, "How then can I do this great wickedness and sin against God?"[1] But what a blessed thing it is that if the believer shall, in an evil hour, come into the net, yet God will bring him out of it! O backslider, be cast down, but do not despair. Wanderer though you have been, hear what your Redeemer says: "Return, O backsliding children; I will have mercy upon you." But you say you cannot return, for you are a captive. Then listen to the promise— "For he will deliver you from the snare of the fowler." You shall yet be brought out of all evil into which you have fallen, and though you shall never cease to repent of your ways, yet He who has loved you will not cast you away. He will receive you and give you joy and gladness, that the bones that He has broken may rejoice. No bird of paradise shall die in the fowler's net.

❧ EVENING ❧

BUT MARTHA WAS DISTRACTED WITH MUCH SERVING. — LUKE 10:40

Her fault was not that she *served*: The condition of a servant is commendable in the Christian. "I serve" should be the motto of all the princes of the royal family of heaven. Nor was it her fault that she had *"much* serving." We cannot do too much. Let us do all that we possibly can; let head and heart and hands be engaged in the Master's service. It was no fault of hers that she was busy preparing a feast for the Master. Happy Martha, to have an opportunity of entertaining so blessed a guest; and happy, too, to have the spirit to throw her whole soul so heartily into the engagement. Her fault was that she grew *"distracted* with much serving," so that she forgot *Him* and only remembered the service. She allowed service to override communion, and so presented one duty stained with the blood of another. We ought to be Martha and Mary in one: We should do much service and have much communion at the same time. For this we need great grace. It is easier to serve than to commune. Joshua never grew weary in fighting with the Amalekites; but Moses, on the top of the mountain in prayer, needed two helpers to sustain his hands. The more spiritual the exercise, the sooner we tire in it. The choicest fruits are the hardest to rear; the most heavenly graces are the most difficult to cultivate. Beloved, while we do not neglect external things, which are good enough in themselves, we ought also to see to it that we enjoy living, personal fellowship with Jesus. See to it that sitting at the Savior's feet is not neglected, even though it be under the specious pretext of doing Him service. The first thing for our soul's health, the first thing for His glory, and the first thing for our own usefulness is to keep ourselves in perpetual communion with the Lord Jesus and to see that the vital spirituality of our faith is maintained over and above everything else in the world.

[1] Genesis 39:9

JANUARY 25   ❧   MORNING   ❧

JANUARY 25   ❧   MORNING   ❧

I WILL RECOUNT THE STEADFAST LOVE OF THE LORD,
THE PRAISES OF THE LORD,
ACCORDING TO ALL THAT THE LORD HAS GRANTED US. — ISAIAH 63:7

And can you not do this? Are there no mercies that you have experienced? What! Though you are gloomy now, can you forget that blessed hour when Jesus met you and said, "Come unto me"? Can you not remember that rapturous moment when He snapped your fetters, dashed your chains to the earth, and said, "I came to break your bonds and set you free"? Or if the love of your conversion be forgotten, there must surely be some precious milestone along the road of life not quite grown over with moss, on which you can read a happy memorial of His mercy toward you. What! Did you never have a sickness like that which you are suffering now, and did He not restore you? Were you never poor before, and did He not supply your wants? Were you never in difficulties before, and did He not deliver you? Arise, go to the river of your experience and pull up a few bulrushes and fashion them into an ark, in which your infant-faith may float safely on the stream. Forget not what your God has done for you; turn over the book of your remembrance, and consider the days of old. Can you not remember the hill Mizar? Did the Lord never meet with you at Hermon? Have you never climbed the Delectable Mountains? Have you never been helped in time of need? I know you have. Go back, then, a little way to the choice mercies of yesterday, and though all may be dark now, light up the lamps of the past—they shall glitter through the darkness, and you shall trust in the Lord till the day break and the shadows flee away. "Remember your mercy, O LORD, and your steadfast love, for they have been from of old."[1]

❧   EVENING   ❧

DO WE THEN OVERTHROW THE LAW BY THIS FAITH?
BY NO MEANS!
ON THE CONTRARY, WE UPHOLD THE LAW. — ROMANS 3:31

When the believer is adopted into the Lord's family, his relationship to old Adam and the law ceases at once; but then he is under a new rule and a new covenant. Believer, you are God's child; it is your first duty to obey your heavenly Father. A servile spirit you have nothing to do with: You are not a slave but a child. And now, inasmuch as you are a beloved child, you are bound to obey your Father's faintest wish, the least intimation of His will. Does He bid you fulfill a sacred ordinance? It is at your peril that you neglect it, for you will be disobeying your Father. Does He command you to seek the image of Jesus? Is it not your joy to do so? Does Jesus tell you, "You therefore must be perfect, as your heavenly Father is perfect"?[2] Then not because the law commands, but because your Savior enjoins, you will labor to be perfect in holiness. Does He bid his saints to love one another? Do it, not because the law says, "Love your neighbor," but because Jesus says, "If you love me, you will keep my commandments."[3] And this is the commandment that He has given unto you, "that you love one another." Are you told to distribute to the poor? Do it, not because charity is a burden that you dare not shirk, but because Jesus teaches, "Give to him that asks of you." Does the Word say, "Love God with all your heart"? Look at the commandment and reply, "Ah, commandment, Christ has fulfilled you already. I have no need, therefore, to fulfill you for my salvation, but I rejoice to yield obedience to you because God is my Father now, and He has a claim upon me, which I would not dispute." May the Holy Ghost make your heart obedient to the constraining power of Christ's love, that your prayer may be, "I will run in the way of your commandments when you enlarge my heart!"[4] Grace is the mother and nurse of holiness, and not the apologist of sin.

[1] Psalm 25:6   [2] Matthew 5:48   [3] John 14:15   [4] Psalm 119:32

God's people are doubly His children. They are His offspring by creation, and they are His sons by adoption in Christ. Hence they are privileged to call Him, "Our Father in heaven." Father! Oh, what a precious word is that. Here is *authority*: "If I be a Father, where is My honor?" If you are sons, where is your obedience? Here is *affection* mingled with authority; an authority that does not provoke rebellion; an obedience demanded that is most cheerfully rendered—which would not be withheld even if it might. The obedience that God's children yield to Him must be *loving* obedience. Do not go about the service of God as slaves to their taskmaster's toil, but run in the way of His commands because it is your *Father's* way. Yield your bodies as instruments of righteousness, because righteousness is your Father's will, and *His* will should be the will of His child. *Father!* Here is a kingly attribute so sweetly veiled in love that the King's crown is forgotten in the King's face, and His scepter becomes, not a rod of iron, but a silver scepter of mercy—the scepter indeed seems to be forgotten in the tender hand of Him who wields it. *Father!* Here is honor and love. How great is a Father's love to his children! That which friendship cannot do, and mere benevolence will not attempt, a father's heart and hand must do for his sons. They are his offspring, and he must bless them; they are his children, and he must show himself strong in their defense. If an earthly father watches over his children with unceasing love and care, how much more does our heavenly Father? *Abba, Father!* He who can say this has uttered better music than cherubim or seraphim can reach. There is heaven in the depth of that word—Father! There is all I can ask, all my necessities can demand, all my wishes can desire. I have all in all to all eternity when I can say, "Father."

We must not cease to wonder at the great marvels of our God. It would be very difficult to draw a line between holy wonder and *real worship*; for when the soul is overwhelmed with the majesty of God's glory, though it may not express itself in song or even utter its voice with bowed head in humble prayer, yet it silently adores. Our incarnate God is to be worshiped as "the Wonderful." That God should consider His fallen creature, man, and instead of sweeping him away with the broom of destruction should Himself undertake to be man's Redeemer and to pay his ransom price is indeed marvelous! But to each believer redemption is most marvelous as he views it in relation to himself. It is a miracle of grace indeed that Jesus should forsake the thrones and royalties above to suffer ignominiously below *for you*. Let your soul lose itself in wonder, for wonder is in this way a very practical emotion. Holy wonder will lead you to *grateful worship* and *heartfelt thanksgiving*. It will cause within you *godly watchfulness*; you will be afraid to sin against such a love as this. Feeling the presence of the mighty God in the gift of His dear Son, you will put your shoes from off your feet, because the place whereon you stand is holy ground. You will be moved at the same time to *glorious hope*. If Jesus has done such marvelous things on your behalf, you will feel that heaven itself is not too great for your expectation. Who can be astonished at anything when he has once been astonished at the manger and the cross? What is there wonderful left after one has seen the Savior? Dear reader, it may be that from the quietness and solitariness of your life you are scarcely able to imitate the shepherds of Bethlehem, who told what they had seen and heard, but you can at least fill up the circle of the worshipers before the throne by wondering at what God has done.

AND FROM HIS FULLNESS WE HAVE ALL RECEIVED. — JOHN 1:16

These words tell us that there is a fullness in Christ. There is a fullness of essential Deity, for "in him the whole fullness of deity dwells bodily."[1] There is a fullness of perfect manhood, for in Him, bodily, that Godhead was revealed. There is a fullness of atoning efficacy in His blood, for "the blood of Jesus his Son cleanses us from all sin."[2] There is a fullness of justifying righteousness in His life, for "there is therefore now no condemnation for those who are in Christ Jesus."[3] There is a fullness of divine prevalence in His plea, for "He is able to save to the uttermost those who draw near to God through him, since he always lives to make intercession for them."[4] There is a fullness of victory in His death, for through death He destroyed him that had the power of death—that is, the devil. There is a fullness of efficacy in His resurrection from the dead, for by it "he has caused us to be born again to a living hope."[5] There is a fullness of triumph in His ascension, for "when he ascended on high he led a host of captives, and he gave gifts to men."[6] There is a fullness of blessings of every sort and shape; a fullness of grace to pardon, of grace to regenerate, of grace to sanctify, of grace to preserve, and of grace to perfect. There is a fullness at all times; a fullness of comfort in affliction, a fullness of guidance in prosperity. A fullness of every divine attribute—of wisdom, of power, of love; a fullness that it is impossible to survey, much less to explore. "For in him all the fullness of God was pleased to dwell."[7] Oh, what a fullness must this be of which *all* receive! Fullness, indeed, must there be when the stream is always flowing, and yet the well springs up as free, as rich, as full as ever. Come, believer, and get all your need supplied; ask largely, and you will receive largely, for this "fullness" is inexhaustible and is treasured up where all the needy may reach it, even in Jesus, Immanuel—God with us.

❧ EVENING ❧

BUT MARY TREASURED UP ALL THESE THINGS,
PONDERING THEM IN HER HEART. — LUKE 2:19

There was an exercise, on the part of this blessed woman, of three powers of her being: her *memory*—she kept all these things; her *affections*—she kept them in her heart; her *intellect*—she pondered them; so memory, affection, and understanding were all exercised about the things that she had heard. Beloved, remember what you have heard of your Lord Jesus and what He has done for you; make your heart the golden pot of manna to preserve the memorial of the heavenly bread whereon you have fed in days gone by. Let your memory treasure up everything about Christ that you have either felt or known or believed, and then let your fond affections hold *Him* fast forevermore. Love the person of your Lord! Bring forth the alabaster box of your heart, even though it be broken, and let all the precious ointment of your affection come streaming onto His pierced feet. Let your intellect be exercised concerning the Lord Jesus. Meditate upon what you read. Stop not at the surface; dive into the depths. Be not as the swallow, which touches the brook with her wing, but as the fish, which penetrates the lowest wave. Abide with your Lord: Let Him not be to you as a wayfaring man who tarries for a night, but constrain Him, saying, "Stay with us . . . the day is now far spent."[8] Hold Him, and do not let Him go. The word *ponder* means to weigh. Make ready the balances of judgment. Oh, but where are the scales that can weigh the Lord Christ? "He takes up the coastlands like fine dust"—who shall take *Him* up? He weighs "the mountains in scales"—in what scales shall we weigh *Him*?[9] If your understanding cannot comprehend, let your affections apprehend; and if your spirit cannot compass the Lord Jesus in the grasp of understanding, let it embrace Him in the arms of affection.

[1] Colossians 2:9   [2] 1 John 1:7   [3] Romans 8:1   [4] Hebrews 7:25   [5] 1 Peter 1:3   [6] Ephesians 4:8   [7] Colossians 1:19.
[8] Luke 24:29   [9] Isaiah 40:15, 12

. . . MATURE IN CHRIST. — COLOSSIANS 1:28

Do you not feel in your own soul that maturity is not in you? Does not every day teach you that? Every tear that trickles from your eye weeps "imperfection"; every harsh word that proceeds from your lip mutters "imperfection." You have too frequently had a view of your own heart to dream for a moment of any perfection *in yourself*. But amidst this sad consciousness of imperfection, here is comfort for you—you are perfect or "mature *in Christ.*" In God's sight you are complete in Him; *even now* you are "blessed in the Beloved."[1] But there is a second perfection, yet to be realized, that is just as sure. Is it not delightful to look forward to the time when every stain of sin shall be removed from the believer, and he shall be presented faultless before the throne, without spot or wrinkle or any such thing? The Church of Christ then will be so pure that not even the eye of Omniscience will see a spot or blemish in her; so holy and so glorious that Hart did not go beyond the truth when he said—

> With my Savior's garments on,
> Holy as the Holy One.

Then shall we know and taste and feel the happiness of this vast but short sentence, complete in Christ. Not till then shall we fully comprehend the heights and depths of the salvation of Jesus. Does not your heart leap for joy at the thought of it? Filthy as you are, you shall be clean. Oh, it is a marvelous salvation this! Christ takes a worm and transforms it into an angel; Christ takes a dirty and deformed thing and makes it clean and matchless in His glory, peerless in His beauty, and fit to be the companion of seraphs. O my soul, stand and admire this blessed truth of maturity in Christ.

∾ EVENING ∾
AND THE SHEPHERDS RETURNED, GLORIFYING AND
PRAISING GOD FOR ALL THEY HAD HEARD AND SEEN,
AS IT HAD BEEN TOLD THEM. — LUKE 2:20

What was the subject of their praise? They *praised God for what they had heard*—for the good tidings of great joy that a Savior was born unto them. Let us copy them; let us also raise a song of thanksgiving that we have heard of Jesus and His salvation. They also *praised God for what they had seen*. There is the sweetest music—what we have experienced, what we have felt within, what we have made our own. It is not enough to *hear* about Jesus: Mere hearing may tune the harp, but the fingers of living faith must create the music. If you have seen Jesus with the God-giving sight of faith, suffer no cobwebs to linger among the harp-strings, but loud with the praise of sovereign grace, awake your psaltery and harp. One point for which they praised God was *the agreement between what they had heard and what they had seen*. Observe the last sentence—"as it had been told them." Have you not found the Gospel to be in yourselves just what the Bible said it would be? Jesus said He would give you rest—have you not enjoyed the sweetest peace in Him? He said you would have joy and comfort and life through believing in Him—have you not received all these? Are not His ways ways of pleasantness, and His paths paths of peace? Surely you can say with the queen of Sheba, "The half was not told me."[2] I have found Christ more sweet than His servants ever said He was. I looked upon His likeness as they painted it, but it was a mere daub compared with Himself; for the King in His beauty outshines all imaginable loveliness. Surely what we have "*seen*" keeps pace with, no, far exceeds what we have "*heard*." Let us, then, glorify and praise God for a Savior so precious and so satisfying.

[1] Ephesians 1:6   [2] 1 Kings 10:7

... THE THINGS THAT ARE UNSEEN ... — 2 CORINTHIANS 4:18

In our Christian pilgrimage it is well, for the most part, to be looking forward. Forward lies the crown, and onward is the goal. Whether it be for hope, for joy, for consolation, or for the inspiring of our love, the future must, after all, be the grand object of the eye of faith. Looking into the future we see sin cast out, the body of sin and death destroyed, the soul made perfect and fit to be a partaker of the inheritance of the saints in light. Looking further yet, the believer's enlightened eye can see death's river passed, the gloomy stream forded, and the hills of light attained on which stands the celestial city. He sees himself enter within the pearly gates, hailed as more than conqueror, crowned by the hand of Christ, embraced in the arms of Jesus, glorified with Him, and made to sit together with Him on His throne, even as He has overcome and has sat down with the Father on His throne. The thought of this future may well relieve the darkness of the past and the gloom of the present. The joys of heaven will surely compensate for the sorrows of earth. Hush, hush, my doubts! Death is but a narrow stream, and you shall soon have forded it. Time, how short—eternity, how long! Death, how brief—immortality, how endless! The road is so, so short! I shall soon be there.

> When the world my heart is rending
> With its heaviest storm of care,
> My glad thoughts to heaven ascending,
> Find a refuge from despair.
> Faith's bright vision shall sustain me
> Till life's pilgrimage is past;
> Fears may vex and troubles pain me,
> I shall reach my home at last.

❧ EVENING ❧

THE DOVE CAME BACK TO HIM IN THE EVENING. — GENESIS 8:11

Blessed be the Lord for another day of mercy, even though I am now weary with its toils. Unto the preserver of men lift I my song of gratitude. The dove found no rest out of the ark and therefore returned to it; and my soul has learned yet more fully than ever, this day, that there is no satisfaction to be found in earthly things—God alone can give rest to my spirit. As to my business, my possessions, my family, my attainments, these are all well enough in their way, but they cannot fulfill the desires of my immortal nature. "Return, O my soul, to your rest; for the LORD has dealt bountifully with you."[1] It was at the still hour, when the gates of the day were closing, that with weary wing the dove came back to the master. O Lord, enable me this evening thus to return to Jesus. She could not endure to spend a night hovering over the restless waste, not can I bear to be even for another hour away from Jesus, the rest of my heart, the home of my spirit. She did not merely alight upon the roof of the ark—she "came back to him." Even so would my longing spirit look into the secret of the Lord, pierce to the interior of truth, enter into that which is within the veil, and reach to my Beloved in very deed. To Jesus must I come: Short of the nearest and dearest communion with Him my panting spirit cannot stay. Blessed Lord Jesus, be with me, reveal Yourself, and abide with me all night, so that when I awake I may be still with You. I note that the dove brought in her mouth an olive branch plucked off, the memorial of the past day and a prophecy of the future. Have I no pleasing record to bring home? No pledge and earnest of loving-kindness yet to come? Yes, my Lord, I present You my grateful acknowledgments for tender mercies that have been new every morning and fresh every evening; and now, I pray, put forth Your hand and take Your dove into Your bosom.

[1] Psalm 116:7

AND WHEN YOU HEAR THE SOUND OF MARCHING
IN THE TOPS OF THE BALSAM TREES,
THEN ROUSE YOURSELF. — 2 SAMUEL 5:24

The members of Christ's Church should be very prayerful, always seeking the unction of the Holy One to rest upon their hearts, that the kingdom of Christ may come, and that His "will be done, on earth as it is in heaven."[1] But there are times when God seems especially to favor Zion; such seasons ought to be to them like "the sound of marching in the tops of the balsam trees." We ought then to be doubly prayerful, doubly earnest, wrestling more at the throne than we have been used to do. Action should then be prompt and vigorous. The tide is flowing—now let us pull manfully for the shore. O for Pentecostal outpourings and Pentecostal labors. Christian, in yourself there are times "when you hear the sound of marching in the tops of the balsam trees." You have a peculiar power in prayer; the Spirit of God gives you joy and gladness; the Scripture is open to you; the promises are applied; you walk in the light of God's countenance; you have peculiar freedom and liberty in devotion, and more closeness of communion with Christ than before. Now, at such joyous periods when you hear the "sound of marching in the tops of the balsam trees," is the time to rouse yourself; now is the time to get rid of any evil habit, while God the Spirit helps your infirmities. Spread your sail; but remember what you sometimes sing—

I can only spread the sail;
But God must breathe the auspicious gale.

Only be sure you have the sail up. Do not miss the gale for want of preparation for it. Seek help from God, that you may be more earnest in duty when made more strong in faith, that you may be more constant in prayer when you have more liberty at the throne, that you may be more holy in your conversation while you live more closely with Christ.

❧ EVENING ❧

IN HIM WE HAVE OBTAINED AN INHERITANCE. — EPHESIANS 1:11

When Jesus gave Himself for us, He gave us all the rights and privileges that went with Himself; so now, although as eternal God He has essential rights to which no creature may venture to pretend, yet as Jesus, the Mediator, the federal Head of the covenant of grace, He has no heritage apart from us. All the glorious consequences of His obedience unto death are the joint riches of all who are in Him, and on whose behalf He accomplished the divine will. See, He enters into glory, but not for Himself alone, for it is written, "Jesus has gone as a forerunner *on our* behalf."[2] Does He stand in the presence of God? Christ appears "in the presence of God *on our* behalf."[3] Consider this, believer: You have no right to heaven in yourself; your right lies in Christ. If you are pardoned, it is through *His* blood; if you are justified, it is through *His* righteousness; if you are sanctified, it is because *He* is made of God unto you sanctification; if you shall be kept from falling, it will be because you are preserved in Christ Jesus; and if you are perfected at the last, it will be because you are complete in *Him.* Thus Jesus is magnified—for all is in Him and by Him; thus the inheritance is made certain to us—for it is obtained in Him; thus each blessing is the sweeter, and even heaven itself the brighter, because it is Jesus our Beloved in whom we have obtained all. Where is the man who shall estimate our divine portion? Weigh the riches of Christ in scales and His treasure in balances, and then think to count the treasures that belong to the saints. Reach the bottom of Christ's sea of joy, and then hope to understand the bliss that God has prepared for them that love Him. Overleap the boundaries of Christ's possessions, and then dream of a limit to the fair inheritance of the elect. "All are yours, and you are Christ's, and Christ is God's."[4]

[1] Matthew 6:10   [2] Hebrews 6:20   [3] Hebrews 9:24   [4] 1 Corinthians 3:22-23

It will always give a Christian the greatest calm, quiet, ease, and peace to think of the perfect righteousness of Christ. How often are the saints of God downcast and sad! I do not think they ought to be. I do not think they would be if they could always see their perfection in Christ. There are some who are always talking about corruption and the depravity of the heart and the innate evil of the soul. This is quite true, but why not go a little further and remember that we are perfect in Christ Jesus. It is no wonder that those who are dwelling upon their own corruption should wear such downcast looks; but surely if we call to mind "Christ Jesus, whom God made . . . our righteousness,"[1] we shall be of good cheer. What though distresses afflict me, though Satan assault me, though there may be many things to be experienced before I get to heaven, those are done for me in the covenant of divine grace; there is nothing wanting in my Lord—Christ has done it all. On the cross He said, "It is finished!" and if it be finished, then am I complete in Him and can rejoice with joy unspeakable and full of glory, "not having a righteousness of my own that comes from the law, but that which comes through faith in Christ, the righteousness from God that depends on faith."[2] You will not find on this side of heaven a holier people than those who receive into their hearts the doctrine of Christ's righteousness. When the believer says, "I live on Christ alone; I rest on Him solely for salvation; and I believe that, however unworthy, I am still saved in Jesus," then there rises up as a motive of gratitude this thought: "Shall I not live to Christ? Shall I not love Him and serve Him, seeing that I am saved by His merits?" "The love of Christ controls us,"[3] "that those who live might no longer live for themselves but for him who for their sake died and was raised."[4] If saved by imputed righteousness, we shall greatly value imparted righteousness.

❧ EVENING ☙
THEN AHIMAAZ RAN BY THE WAY OF THE PLAIN, AND OUTRAN THE CUSHITE. — 2 SAMUEL 18:23

Running is not everything. There is much in the way that we select: A swift foot over hill and down dale will not keep pace with a slower traveler upon level ground. How is it with my spiritual journey? Am I laboring up the hill of my own works and down into the ravines of my own humiliations and resolutions, or do I run by the plain way of "Believe and live"? How blessed is it to wait upon the Lord by faith! The soul runs without weariness and walks without fainting in the way of believing. Christ Jesus is the way of life, and He is a plain way, a pleasant way, a way suitable for the tottering feet and feeble knees of trembling sinners. Am I found in this way, or am I hunting after another track such as priestcraft or metaphysics may promise me? I read of the way of holiness, that the wayfaring man, though a fool, shall not err therein. Have I been delivered from proud reason and been brought as a little child to rest in Jesus' love and blood? If so, by God's grace I shall outrun the strongest runner who chooses any other path. This truth I may remember to my profit in my daily cares and needs. It will be my wisest course to go at once to my God, and not to wander in a roundabout manner to this friend and that. He knows my wants and can relieve them. To whom should I repair but to Himself by the direct appeal of prayer and the plain argument of the promise? "Straightforward makes the best runner." I will not parley with the servants but hasten to their master.

In reading this passage, it strikes me that if men vie with each other in common matters, and one outruns the other, I ought to be in solemn earnestness so to run that I may obtain. Lord, help me to gird up the loins of my mind, and may I press forward toward the mark for the prize of my high calling of God in Christ Jesus.

[1] 1 Corinthians 1:30   [2] Philippians 3:9   [3] 2 Corinthians 5:14   [4] 2 Corinthians 5:15

February

THEY SHALL SING OF THE WAYS OF THE LORD. — PSALM 138:5

The time when Christians begin to sing in the ways of the Lord is when they first lose their burden at the foot of the cross. Not even the songs of the angels seem so sweet as the first song of rapture that gushes from the inmost soul of the forgiven child of God. You know how John Bunyan describes it. He says when poor Pilgrim lost his burden at the cross, he gave three great leaps and went on his way singing,

> *Blest Cross! blest Sepulchre! blest rather be*
> *The Man that there was put to shame for me!*

Believer, do you recollect the day when *your* fetters fell off? Do you remember the place when Jesus met you and said, "I have loved you with an everlasting love. I have blotted out your transgressions like a cloud and your sins like mist; none of them shall be remembered against you." Oh, what a sweet season it is when Jesus takes away the pain of sin. When the Lord first pardoned my sin, I was so joyful that I could barely refrain from dancing. I thought on my road home from the house where I had been set at liberty that I must tell the stones in the street the story of my deliverance. So full was my soul of joy that I wanted to tell every snowflake that was falling from heaven of the wondrous love of Jesus, who had blotted out the sins of one of the chief of rebels. But it is not only at the commencement of the Christian life that believers have reason for song; as long as they live they discover cause to sing in the ways of the Lord, and their experience of His constant loving-kindness leads them to say, "I will bless the LORD at all times; his praise shall continually be in my mouth."[1] See to it, Christian, that you magnify the Lord *this day*.

> *Long as we tread this desert land,*
> *New mercies shall new songs demand.*

YOUR LOVE TO ME WAS EXTRAORDINARY. — 2 SAMUEL 1:26

Come, dear readers, let each one of us speak for himself of the wonderful love, not of Jonathan, but of Jesus. We will not relate what we have been told, but the things that we have tasted and handled—of the love of Christ. Your love to me, O Jesus, was wonderful when I was a stranger wandering far from You, fulfilling the desires of the flesh and of the mind. Your love restrained me from committing the sin that is unto death and withheld me from self-destruction. Your love held back the axe when Justice said, "Cut it down! Why does it clutter the ground?" Your love drew me into the wilderness, stripped me there, and made me feel the guilt of my sin and the burden of my iniquity. Your love spoke comfortably to me when I was deeply troubled—"Come to Me, and I will give you rest." Oh, how matchless Your love when, in a moment, You washed my sins away and made my polluted soul, which was crimson with the blood of my nativity and black with the grime of my transgressions, to be white as the driven snow and pure as the finest wool. How You commended Your love when You whispered in my ears, "I am yours, and you are Mine." Those were kind words when you declared, "The Father Himself loves you." And sweet were the moments when You commended to me the love of the Spirit. My soul shall never forget those chambers of fellowship where You unveiled Yourself to me. Moses had his cleft in the rock, where he saw the train, the back parts, of his God. We, too, have had our clefts in the rock, where we have seen the full splendors of the Godhead in the person of Christ. Did David remember the tracks of the wild goat, the land of Jordan and the Hermonites? We, too, can remember spots dear to our memory, equal to these in blessedness. Precious Lord Jesus, give us a fresh taste of Your wondrous love with which to begin the month. Amen.

[1] Psalm 34:1

❧ MORNING ❦
WITHOUT THE SHEDDING OF BLOOD THERE IS
NO FORGIVENESS OF SINS.—HEBREWS 9:22

This is the voice of unalterable truth. In none of the Jewish ceremonies were sins even typically removed without blood-shedding. In no case, by no means can sin be pardoned without atonement. It is clear, then, that there is no hope for me outside of Christ; for there is no other blood-shedding that is worth a thought as an atonement for sin. Am I, then, believing in Him? Is the blood of His atonement truly applied to my soul? All men are on the same level in terms of their need of Him. Even if we are moral, generous, amiable, or patriotic, the rule will not be altered to make an exception for us. Sin will yield to nothing less potent than the blood of Him whom God has set forth as a propitiation. What a blessing that there is the one way of pardon! Why should we seek another?

Persons of merely formal religion cannot understand how we can rejoice that all our sins are forgiven for Christ's sake. Their works and prayers and ceremonies give them very poor comfort; and their unease is no surprise, for they are neglecting the one great salvation and endeavoring to get remission without blood. My soul, sit down and recognize that a just God is bound to punish sin; then consider how that punishment all falls upon the Lord Jesus, and fall down in humble joy at the feet of Him whose blood has made atonement for you. It is useless when conscience is aroused to trust in feelings and evidences for comfort; this is a bad and sorry habit. The only cure for a guilty conscience is the sight of Jesus suffering on the cross. "The blood is the life," says the Levitical law, and let us rest assured that it is the life of faith and joy and every other holy grace.

> *Oh! how sweet to view the flowing*
> *Of my Savior's precious blood;*
> *With divine assurance knowing*
> *He has made my peace with God.*

❦ EVENING ❧
NOW THE RECORDS ARE ANCIENT.—1 CHRONICLES 4:22

But not so ancient as those precious things that are the delight of our souls. Let us for a moment recount them, repeating them as misers count their gold. *The sovereign choice* of the Father, by which He elected us unto eternal life, before creation, is a matter of vast antiquity, since no date can be conceived for it by the mind of man. We were chosen from before the foundations of the world. *Everlasting love* went with the choice, for it was not a bare act of divine will by which we were set apart, but the divine affections were concerned. The Father loved us in and from the beginning. Here is a theme for daily contemplation. *The eternal purpose* to redeem us from our foreseen ruin, to cleanse and sanctify us and at last to glorify us, was of infinite antiquity and runs side by side with immutable love and absolute sovereignty. *The covenant* is always described as being everlasting, and Jesus, the second party in it, is from eternity. He struck hands in sacred covenant long before the first stars began to shine, and it was in Him that the elect were ordained unto eternal life. In this way a most blessed covenant union was established between the Son of God and His elect people, which will remain as the foundation of their safety when time shall be no more. Is it not profitable to be conversant with these ancient things? Is it not shameful that they should be so readily neglected and even rejected by the majority of professing Christians? If they knew more of their own sin, would they not be more ready to adore distinguishing grace? Let us both admire and adore tonight, as we sing—

> *A monument of grace,*
> *A sinner saved by blood;*
> *The streams of love I trace*
> *Up to the Fountain, God;*
> *And in His sacred bosom see*
> *Eternal thoughts of Love to me.*

As God's creatures, we are all debtors to Him: to obey Him with all our body and soul and strength. Having broken His commandments, as we all have, we are debtors to His justice, and we owe to Him a vast amount that we are not able to pay. But of the *Christian* it can be said that he does not owe God's *justice* anything, for Christ has paid the debt His people owed; for this reason the believer is in debt to *love*. I am a debtor to God's grace and forgiving mercy; but I am no debtor to His justice, for He will never accuse me of a debt already paid. Christ said, "It is finished!" and by that He meant that whatever His people owed was wiped away forever from the book of remembrance. Christ has completely satisfied divine justice; the account is settled; the handwriting is nailed to the cross; the receipt is given, and we are no longer in debt to God's justice. But then it follows that since we are not debtors to our Lord in that sense, we become ten times more debtors to God than we should have been otherwise. Christian, pause and consider for a moment. What a debtor you are to divine *sovereignty*! How much you owe to His disinterested love, for He gave His own Son that He might die for you. Consider how much you owe to His forgiving *grace*, that even after ten thousand offenses He loves you as infinitely as ever. Consider what you owe to His *power*; how He has raised you from your death in sin; how He has preserved your spiritual life; how He has kept you from falling; and how, though a thousand enemies have surrounded your path, you have been able to hold on your way. Consider what you owe to His *immutability*. Though you have changed a thousand times, He has not changed once. You are as deep in debt as you can be to every attribute of God. To God you owe yourself and all you have: Offer yourself as a living sacrifice; it is but your reasonable service.

These words may be taken as expressions of the believer's desire for Christ's fellowship and his longing for present communion with Him. Where do You feed Your flock? In *Your house*? I will go, if I may find You there. In private *prayer*? Then I will pray without ceasing. In *the Word*? Then I will read it diligently. In *Your ordinances*? Then I will pursue them with all my heart. Tell me where this happens, for wherever You stand as the Shepherd, there will I lie down as a sheep; for no one but Yourself can supply my need. I cannot be satisfied to be apart from You. My soul hungers and thirsts for the refreshment of Your presence. "Where you make it lie down at noon." Whether at dawn or at noon, my only rest must be where You are and Your beloved flock. My soul's rest must be a grace-given rest and can only be found in You. Where is the shadow of that rock? Why should I not rest beneath it? "Why should I be as one that turns aside by the flocks of your companions?" (see v. 76). You have companions—why should I not be one? Satan tells me I am unworthy; but I always was unworthy, and yet You have long loved me; and therefore my unworthiness cannot be a barrier to having fellowship with You now. It is true I am weak in faith and prone to fall, but my very feebleness is the reason why I should always be where You feed Your flock, that I may be strengthened and preserved in safety beside the still waters. Why should I turn aside? There is no reason why I should, but there are a thousand reasons why I should not, for Jesus beckons me to come. If He withdrew Himself a little, it is but to make me value His presence more. Now that I am grieved and distressed at being away from Him, He will lead me again to that sheltered nook where the lambs of His fold are sheltered from the burning sun.

. . . EVEN AS THE LORD LOVES. — HOSEA 3:1

Believer, *look back* through all your experience, and think of the way in which the Lord your God has led you in the wilderness, and how He has fed and clothed you every day—how He has suffered your poor behavior—how He has put up with all your murmurings and all your longings after the flesh-pots of Egypt—how He has opened the rock to supply you and fed you with manna that came down from heaven. Think of how His grace has been sufficient for you in all your troubles—how His blood has been a pardon to you in all your sins—how His rod and His staff have comforted you. When you have then reflected upon the love of the Lord, let faith survey His love *in the future*, for remember that Christ's covenant and blood have something more in them than the *past*. He who has loved you and pardoned you will never cease to love and pardon. He is Alpha, and He shall be Omega also: He is first, and He shall be last. Therefore, remember when you pass through the valley of the shadow of death, you need fear no evil, for He is with you. When you stand in the cold floods of Jordan, you need not fear, for death cannot separate you from His love; and when you come into the mysteries of eternity you need not tremble, "For I am sure that neither death nor life, nor angels nor rulers, nor things present nor things to come, nor powers, nor height nor depth, nor anything else in all creation, will be able to separate us from the love of God in Christ Jesus our Lord."[1] Now, soul, is not your love refreshed? Does not this make you love Jesus? Does not a survey of the vastness of God's loving care stir your heart and compel you to delight yourself in the Lord your God? Surely as we meditate on the love of the Lord, our hearts burn within us, and we long to love Him more.

❧   EVENING   ❧

. . . A REFUGE FROM THE AVENGER OF BLOOD. — JOSHUA 20:3

It is said that in the land of Canaan, cities of refuge were so arranged that any man might reach one of them within half a day at the most. In the same way the word of our salvation is near to us; Jesus is a present Savior, and the way to Him is short. It is but a simple renunciation of our own merit and a laying hold of Jesus to be our all in all. With regard to the roads to the city of refuge, we are told that they were strictly preserved, every river was bridged, and every obstruction removed, so that the man who fled might find an easy passage to the city. Once a year the elders went along the roads to check on their condition, so that nothing might impede the flight of anyone and cause them, through delay, to be overtaken and slain. How graciously do the promises of the Gospel remove stumbling blocks from the way! Wherever there were junctions and turnings, there were signposts clearly stating, "To the city of refuge!" This is a picture of the road to Christ Jesus. It is no roundabout road of the law; it is no obeying this, that, and the other; it is a straight road: "Believe, and live." It is a road so hard that no self-righteous man can ever tread it, but so easy that every sinner who knows himself to be a sinner may by it find his way to heaven. As soon as the man seeking refuge reached the outskirts of the city, he was safe; it was not necessary for him to be beyond the walls—the suburbs themselves were sufficient protection. Learn from this that if you merely touch the hem of Christ's garment, you shall be made whole; if you can only lay hold upon him with "faith as a grain of mustard seed," you are safe.

> *A little genuine grace ensures*
> *The death of all our sins.*

So waste no time; do not dillydally, for the avenger of blood moves quickly; and it could be that he is at your heels even this evening.

---

[1] Romans 8:38-39

It is a sweet thought that Jesus Christ did not appear without His Father's permission, authority, consent, and assistance. He was sent by the Father, that He might be the Savior of men. We are too apt to forget that while there are distinctions as to the *persons* in the Trinity, there are no distinctions of *honor*. We are prone to ascribe the honor of our salvation, or at least the depths of its benevolence, more to Jesus Christ than to the Father. This is a very great mistake. Yes, Jesus came, but didn't His Father send Him? He spoke powerfully, but didn't His Father pour grace into His lips, that He might be an able minister of the new covenant? Whoever knows the Father and the Son and the Holy Spirit as they should know them never sets one before another in his love; he sees them together at Bethlehem, at Gethsemane, and on Calvary, all equally engaged in the work of salvation. O Christian, have you put your confidence in the Man Christ Jesus? Have you placed your trust solely on Him? And are you united with Him? Then believe that you are united with the God of heaven. Since to the Man Christ Jesus you are brother and live in close fellowship, you are in this way linked with God the Eternal, and "the Ancient of days" is your Father and your friend. Did you ever consider the depth of love in the heart of Jehovah, when God the Father equipped His Son for the great enterprise of mercy? If not, meditate today on this: *The Father* sent Him! Contemplate that subject. Think how Jesus works what *the Father* wills. In the wounds of the dying Savior view the love of the great I AM. Let every thought of Jesus be also connected with the Eternal, ever-blessed God, for "It was the will of the Lord to crush him; he has put him to grief."[1]

✎ EVENING ✎

This is a pointed way in which to begin a verse—"At that time Jesus declared." If you look at the context you will realize that no one had asked Him a question and that He was not in conversation with any human being. Yet it is written, "Jesus declared, I thank you, Father." When a man answers, he answers a person who has been speaking to him. Who, then, had been speaking to Christ? His Father. Yet there is no record of it; and this should teach us that Jesus had constant fellowship with His Father, and that God spoke into His heart so often, so continually, that it was not a circumstance peculiar enough to be recorded. It was the habit and life of Jesus to talk with God. Let us then learn the lesson that this simple statement concerning Him teaches us. May we also enjoy silent fellowship with the Father, so that often we answer Him, and although our friends don't know to whom we speak, we will be responding to that secret voice that they do not hear but that our own ear, opened by the Spirit of God, recognizes with joy. God has spoken to us; let us speak to God—either to affirm that God is true and faithful to His promise, or to confess the sin of which the Spirit of God has convinced us, or to acknowledge the mercy that God's providence has given, or to express agreement with the great truths that God the Holy Spirit has revealed to us. Intimate communion with the Father of our spirit is a great privilege! It is a secret hidden from the world, a joy with which even the nearest friend does not interfere. If we desire to hear the whispers of God's love, our ear must be purged and fit to listen to His voice. This very evening may our hearts be in such a condition, so that when God speaks to us, we, like Jesus, may be prepared at once to answer Him.

[1] Isaiah 53:10

PRAYING AT ALL TIMES. — EPHESIANS 6:18

What countless prayers we have offered from the first moment we learned to pray. Our first prayer was a prayer for ourselves; we asked that God would have mercy upon us and blot out our sin. He heard us. But when He had blotted out our sins like a cloud, then we had more prayers for ourselves. We have had to pray for sanctifying grace, for constraining and restraining grace; we have been led to crave for a fresh assurance of faith, for the comfortable application of the promise, for deliverance in the hour of temptation, for help in the line of duty, and for comfort in the day of trial. We have been compelled to go to God for our souls, as constant beggars asking for everything. Remember, child of God, you have never been able to get anything for your soul anywhere else. All the bread your soul has eaten has come down from heaven, and all the water it has drunk has flowed from the living rock—Christ Jesus the Lord. Your soul has never grown rich in itself; it has always been dependent upon the daily provision of God; and consequently your prayers have ascended to heaven for a vast range of spiritual mercies. Your wants were innumerable, and therefore the supplies have been infinitely great, and your prayers have been as varied as the mercies have been countless. So then have you not reason to say, "I love the Lord, because He has heard my voice and my pleas for mercy"? For as your prayers have been many, so also have God's answers been. He has heard you in the day of trouble, has strengthened you and helped you, even when you dishonored Him by trembling and doubting at His throne. Remember this, and let it fill your heart with gratitude to God, who has graciously heard your poor, weak prayers. "Bless the LORD, O my soul, and forget not all His benefits."[1]

❧ EVENING ❧
PRAY FOR ONE ANOTHER. — JAMES 5:16

Be encouraged to cheerfully offer intercessory prayer, by remembering that *such prayer is the sweetest God ever hears.* The prayer of Christ is of this character. In all the incense that our Great High Priest now puts into the golden censer, there is not a single grain for Himself. His intercession must be the most acceptable of all supplications—and the more our prayer like Christ's, the sweeter it will be. Thus while petitions for ourselves will be accepted, our pleadings for others, having in them more of the fruits of the Spirit—more love, more faith, more brotherly kindness—will be, through the precious merits of Jesus, the sweetest sacrifice that we can offer to God. Remember, again, that *intercessory prayer is exceedingly prevalent* [powerful]. What wonders it has accomplished! The Word of God teems with its marvelous deeds. Believer, you have a mighty engine in your hand; use it well, use it constantly, use it with faith, and you will surely be a blessing to others. When you have the King's ear, speak to Him for the suffering members of His body. When you are favored to draw very near to His throne, and the King says to you, "Ask, and it will be given to you," let your petitions be, not for yourself alone, but for the many who need His aid. If you have any grace at all and are not an intercessor, that grace must be as small as a grain of mustard seed. You have just enough grace to float your soul clear from the quicksand, but you have no depth of grace or else you would carry in your vessel a heavy cargo of the wants of others, and you would bring back from your Lord rich blessings for them that apart from you they might not have obtained.

> Oh, let my hands forget their skill,
> My tongue be silent, cold, and still,
> This bounding heart forget to beat,
> If I forget the mercy-seat!

[1] Psalm 103:2

ARISE AND GO. — MICAH 2:10

The hour is approaching when the message will come to us, as it comes to all, "Arise, and leave the home in which you lived, from the city in which you have done your business, from your family, from your friends. Arise, and take your final journey." And what do we know of the journey? And what do we know of the country to which we are going? We have read a little about it, and part has been revealed to us by the Spirit; but how little do we know of the realms of the future! We know that there is a black and stormy river called Death. God bids us cross it, promising to be with us. And after death, what comes? What wonder-world will open upon our astonished sight? What scene of glory will be unfolded to our view? No traveler has ever returned to tell. But we know enough of the heavenly land to make us welcome our summons there with joy and gladness. The journey of death may be dark, but we may face it fearlessly, knowing that God is with us as we walk through the gloomy valley, and therefore we need fear no evil. We shall be departing from all we have known and loved here, but we shall be going to our Father's house—to our Father's home, where Jesus is—to that royal "city that has foundations, whose designer and builder is God."[1] This will be our last relocation, to live forever with Him we love, in the midst of His people, in the presence of God. Christian, meditate much on heaven; it will help you to press on and to forget the difficulty of the journey. This vale of tears is but the pathway to the better country: This world of woe is but the stepping-stone to a world of bliss.

> Prepare us, Lord, by grace divine,
> For Thy bright courts on high;
> Then bid our spirits rise, and join
> The chorus of the sky.

❧ EVENING ❧

THEN THEY HEARD A LOUD VOICE FROM HEAVEN
SAYING TO THEM, "COME UP HERE." — REVELATION 11:12

Without considering these words in their prophetic connection, let us regard them as the invitation of our great Forerunner to His sanctified people. In due time there shall be heard "a loud voice from heaven" to every believer, saying, "Come up here." This should be to the saints *the subject of joyful anticipation*. Instead of dreading the time when we will leave this world to go to the Father, we should be longing for the hour of our emancipation. Our song should be—

> My heart is with Him on His throne,
> And ill can brook delay;
> Each moment listening for the voice,
> "Rise up and come away."

We are not called down to the grave but up to the skies. Our heaven-born spirits should long for their native air. Yet the heavenly summons should be *the object of patient waiting*. Our God knows best when to bid us, "Come up here." We must not wish to antedate the period of our departure. I know that strong love will make us cry,

> O Lord of Hosts, the waves divide,
> And land us all in heaven.

But patience must have her perfect work. God ordains with accurate wisdom the most fitting time for the redeemed to live below. Surely, if there could be regrets in heaven, the saints might mourn that they did not live longer here to do more good. Oh, for more sheaves for my Lord's harvest, more jewels for His crown! But how unless there be more work? True, there is the other side of it, that, living so briefly, our sins are the fewer; but oh, when we are fully serving God, and He is asking us to scatter precious seed and reap a hundredfold, we would even say it is well for us to stay where we are. Whether our Master shall say, "Go" or "Stay," let us be equally well pleased as long as He indulges us with His presence.

[1] Hebrews 11:10

YOU SHALL CALL HIS NAME JESUS. — MATTHEW 1:21

When a person is dear, everything connected with him becomes dear for his sake. Thus, so precious is the person of the Lord Jesus in the estimation of all true believers that everything about Him they consider to be inestimable beyond all price. "Your robes are all fragrant with myrrh and aloes and cassia," said David,[1] as if the very vestments of the Savior were so sweetened by His person that he could not but love them. It is certain that there is not a spot where His hallowed foot has trod, there is not a word that His blessed lips have uttered, nor a thought that His loving Word has revealed that is not precious to us beyond all price. And this is true of the *names* of Christ—they are all sweet in the believer's ear. Whether He is called the Husband of the church, her Bridegroom, her Friend; whether He is referred to as the Lamb slain from the foundation of the world—the King, the Prophet, or the Priest—every title of our Master—Shiloh, Emmanuel, Wonderful, the Mighty Counselor—every name is like the honeycomb dropping with honey, and luscious are the drops that distill from it. But if there is one name sweeter than another in the believer's ear, it is the name *Jesus.* Jesus! It is the name that moves the harps of heaven to melody. Jesus! The life of all our joys. If there is one name more charming, more precious than another, it is this name. It is the melody of our psalms. Many of our hymns begin with it, and scarcely any, that are good for anything, end without it. It is the sum total of all delights. It is the music with which the bells of heaven ring, a song in a word, an ocean for comprehension, a matchless oratorio in two syllables, a gathering up of the hallelujahs of eternity in five letters.

> *Jesus, I love Thy charming name,*
> *'Tis music to my ear.*

❧ EVENING ❧

HE WILL SAVE HIS PEOPLE FROM THEIR SINS. — MATTHEW 1:21

Many people, if they are asked what they understand by salvation, will reply, "Being saved from hell and taken to heaven." This is one result of salvation, but it is not one tenth of what is contained in that blessing. It is true our Lord Jesus Christ does redeem all His people from the wrath to come; He saves them from the fearful condemnation that their sins had brought upon them; but His triumph is far more complete than this. He saves His people "from their sins"—a complete deliverance from our worst foes. Where Christ works a saving work, He casts Satan from his throne and will not let him be master any longer. No man is a true Christian if sin reigns in his mortal body. Sin will be in us—it will never be utterly expelled till the spirit enters glory; but it will never have *dominion.* There will be a striving for dominion—a lusting against the new law and the new spirit that God has implanted—but sin will never get the upper hand so as to be absolute monarch of our nature. Christ will be Master of the heart, and sin must be mortified. The Lion of the tribe of Judah shall prevail, and the dragon shall be cast out. Professing Christian, is sin subdued in you? If your *life* is unholy, your *heart* is unchanged; and if your heart is unchanged, you are an unsaved person. If the Savior has not sanctified you, renewed you, given you a hatred of sin and a love of holiness, He has done nothing in you of a saving character. The grace that does not make a man better than others is a worthless counterfeit. Christ saves His people not in their sins but *from* them. ". . . for the holiness without which no one will see the Lord."[2] "Let everyone who names the name of the Lord depart from iniquity."[3] If not saved from sin, how shall we hope to be counted among His people? Lord, save me now from all evil, and enable me to honor my Savior.

[1] Psalm 45:8   [2] Hebrews 12:14   [3] 2 Timothy 2:19

AND WHEN DAVID INQUIRED OF THE LORD . . . — 2 SAMUEL 5:23

When David made this inquiry, he had just fought the Philistines and gained a classic victory. The Philistines came up in great numbers, but, by the help of God, David had easily put them to flight. Note, however, that when they came a second time, David did not go up to fight them without inquiring of the Lord. Once he had been victorious, and he might have said, as many have in other cases, "I shall be victorious again. I may rest quite sure that if I have conquered once I shall triumph yet again. Why should I delay by seeking God?" Not so David. He had gained one battle by the strength of the Lord; he would not venture upon another until he had ensured the same. He inquired, "Shall I go up against them?" He waited until God's sign was given. Learn from David to take no step without God. Christian, if you would know the path of duty, take God for your compass; if you would steer your ship through the dark billows, put the tiller into the hand of the Almighty. Many a rock might be escaped if we would let our Father take the helm; many a shoal or quicksand we might well avoid if we would leave it to His sovereign will to choose and to command. The Puritan said, "As sure as ever a Christian carves for himself, he'll cut his own fingers." This is a great truth. Another old divine said, "He that goes before the cloud of God's providence goes on a fool's errand," and so he does. We must mark God's providence leading us; and if providence delays, wait until providence comes. He who goes before providence will be very glad to retreat. "I will instruct you and teach you in the way you should go,"[1] is God's promise to His people. Let us, then, take all our perplexities to Him and say, "Lord, what will you have me do?" Do not leave your house this morning without inquiring of the Lord.

❧ EVENING ❧

LEAD US NOT INTO TEMPTATION;
BUT DELIVER US FROM EVIL. — LUKE 11:4 [KJV]

The things we are taught to seek or avoid in prayer, we should equally pursue or avoid in action. We should with sincerity avoid temptation, seeking to walk so guardedly in the path of obedience that we may never tempt the devil to tempt us. We are not to enter the jungle in search of the lion. We might pay dearly for such presumption. This lion may cross our path or leap upon us from the jungle, but we have nothing to do with hunting him. He that meets with him, even though he wins the day, will find it a tough struggle. Let the Christian pray that he may be spared the encounter. Our Savior, who had experience of what temptation meant, thus earnestly admonished His disciples, "Pray that you do not enter into temptation."

But let us do as we will, we shall be tempted; hence the prayer, "deliver us from evil." God had one Son without sin; but He has no son without temptation. The natural man is born to trouble as the sparks fly upward, and just as certain the Christian man is born to temptation. We must be always on our watch against Satan because, like a thief, he gives no intimation of his approach. Believers who have had experience of the ways of Satan know that there are certain seasons when he will most probably make an attack, just as at certain seasons bleak winds may be expected; thus the Christian is put on a double guard by fear of danger, and the danger is averted by preparing to meet it. Prevention is better than cure: It is better to be so well armed that the devil will not attack you than to endure the perils of the fight even though you come off a conqueror. Pray this evening first that you may not be tempted, and then if temptation be permitted, pray that you may be delivered from the evil one.

[1] Psalm 32:8

I KNOW HOW TO ABOUND. — PHILIPPIANS 4:12

There are many who know "how to be brought low" who have not learned "how to abound." When they are set upon the top of a pinnacle their heads grow dizzy, and they are ready to fall. The Christian disgraces his profession more often in prosperity than in adversity. It is a dangerous thing to be prosperous. The crucible of adversity is a less severe trial for the Christian than the place of prosperity. What leanness of soul and neglect of spiritual things have been brought on through the very mercies and bounties of God! Yet this is not a matter of necessity, for the apostle tells us that he knew how to abound. When he had much, he knew how to use it. Abundant grace enabled him to bear abundant prosperity. When he had a full sail he was loaded with much ballast, and so floated safely. It needs more than human skill to carry the brimming cup of earthly joy with a steady hand; yet Paul had learned that skill, for he declares, "In any and every circumstance, I have learned the secret of facing plenty and hunger." It is a divine lesson to know how to be full, for the Israelites were full once, but while the food was still in their mouths, the wrath of God came upon them. Many have asked for mercies, that they might satisfy their own hearts' lust. Fullness of bread has often made fullness of blood, and that has brought on emptiness of spirit. When we have plenty of God's providential mercies, it often happens that we have but little of God's grace, and little gratitude for the blessings we have received. We are full, and we forget God: Satisfied with earth, we are content to do without heaven. Rest assured, it is harder to know how to be full than it is to know how to be hungry—so desperate is the tendency of human nature to pride and forgetfulness of God. Take care that you ask in your prayers that God would teach you how to be full.

Let not the gifts Thy love bestows
Estrange our hearts from Thee.

❧   E V E N I N G   ❧

I HAVE BLOTTED OUT YOUR TRANSGRESSIONS LIKE A CLOUD AND
YOUR SINS LIKE MIST; RETURN TO ME,
FOR I HAVE REDEEMED YOU. — ISAIAH 44:22

Pay attention to THE INSTRUCTIVE PICTURE: Our sins are like a *cloud*. As clouds appear in many shapes and shades, so do our transgressions. As clouds obscure the light of the sun and darken the landscape below, so do our sins hide from us the light of Jehovah's face and cause us to sit in the shadow of death. They are earthborn things and arise from the miry places of our lives; and when they collect and their measure is full, they threaten us with storm and tempest. Sadly, unlike clouds, our sins yield us no genial showers but rather threaten to deluge us with a fiery flood of destruction. How can it be fair weather when the dark clouds of sin remain within our souls?

Let our happy gaze ponder THE NOTABLE ACT of divine mercy—"blotted out." God Himself appears upon the scene and in divine generosity, instead of manifesting His anger, reveals His grace. He at once and forever effectually removes the mischief, not by blowing away the cloud, but by blotting it out from existence once and for all. Against the justified man no sin remains; the great transaction of the cross has eternally removed his transgressions from him. On Calvary's summit the great deed, by which the sin of all the chosen was forever put away, was completely and effectually performed.

Practically let us obey THE GRACIOUS COMMAND: "Return to me." Why should pardoned sinners live at a distance from their God? If all of our sins have been forgiven, let no legal fear hold us back from the boldest access to our Lord. Let backslidings be bemoaned, but let us not persevere in them. Let us, in the power of the Holy Spirit, work strenuously to return to intimate communion with the Lord. O Lord, restore us now, tonight!

AND THEY RECOGNIZED THAT THEY HAD BEEN
WITH JESUS. — ACTS 4:13

A Christian should be a striking likeness of Jesus Christ. You have read lives of Christ, beautifully and eloquently written, but the best life of Christ is His living biography, written out in the words and actions of His people. If we were what we profess to be, and what we should be, we would be pictures of Christ; yes, such striking likenesses of Him that the world would not have to hold us to the mirror and say, "Well, it seems somewhat of a likeness"; they would, when they saw us, exclaim, "He has been with Jesus; he has been taught by Him; he is like Him; he has caught the very idea of the holy Man of Nazareth, and he works it out in his life and everyday actions." A Christian should be like Christ in his *boldness*. Never blush to own your Christianity; your profession will never disgrace you: Take care you never disgrace *that*. Be like Jesus, very valiant for your God. Imitate Him in your *loving* spirit; think kindly, speak kindly, and do kindly, that men may say of you, "He has been with Jesus." Imitate Jesus in His *holiness*. Was He zealous for His Master? So should you be, going about doing good. Do not waste time; it is too precious. Was He self-denying, never looking to His own interest? Be the same. Was He devout? Then be fervent in your prayers. Did He defer to His Father's will? So submit yourselves to Him. Was He patient? So learn to endure. And best of all, as the highest portraiture of Jesus, try to forgive your enemies, as He did; and let those sublime words of your Master, "Father, forgive them, for they know not what they do," always ring in your ears. Forgive, as you hope to be forgiven. Heap coals of fire on the head of your enemy by your kindness to him. Good for evil, remember, is Godlike. Be Godlike then; and in all ways and by all means so live that all may say of you, "He has been with Jesus."

ᴥ EVENING *ᴥ*
YOU HAVE ABANDONED THE LOVE YOU HAD AT FIRST.
— REVELATION 2:4

We will always remember that best and brightest of hours when we first saw the Lord, lost our burden, received the gift of grace, rejoiced in full salvation, and went on our way in peace. It was springtime in the soul; the winter was past; the mutterings of Sinai's thunders were hushed; the flashings of its lightnings were no more perceived; God was beheld as reconciled; the law threatened no vengeance, and justice demanded no punishment. Then the flowers appeared in our heart. Hope, love, peace, and patience sprang from the ground; the hyacinth of repentance, the snowdrop of pure holiness, the crocus of golden faith, the daffodil of early love—all decked the garden of the soul. The time of the singing of birds had arrived, and we rejoiced with thanksgiving; we magnified the holy name of our forgiving God, and our resolve was, "Lord, I am Yours, Yours alone. All I am, and all I have, I devote to You. You have bought me with Your blood—let me spend myself and be spent in Your service. In life and in death let me be consecrated to You." *How well have we kept this resolve*? Our first love burned with a holy flame of devotion to Jesus—is it the same *now*? Is it possible that Jesus may say to us, "I have something against you, because you have left your first love"? Sadly we have done little for our Master's glory. Our winter has lasted all too long. We are as cold as ice when we should feel a summer's glow and bloom with sacred flowers. We give God pennies when He deserves much more, deserves our heart's blood to be coined in the service of His church and of His truth. But shall we continue in this way? O Lord, after You have blessed us so richly, shall we be ungrateful and become indifferent to Your good cause and work? Quicken us that we may return to our first love and do our first works! Send us a joyful spring, O Sun of Righteousness.

   ❧ MORNING ❧

There is a perfect balance in this. God in His providence operates the scales; on one side He puts His people's trials, and on the other He puts their consolations. When the scale of trial is nearly empty, you will always find the scale of consolation in nearly the same condition; and when the scale of trials is full, you will find the scale of consolation just as heavy. When the dark clouds gather, the light is more brightly revealed to us. When night falls and the storm is brewing, the Heavenly Captain is always closest to His crew. It is a blessed thing that when we are most downcast, then we are most lifted up by the consolations of the Spirit. One reason is, *trials make more room for consolation*. Great hearts can only be made by great troubles. The spade of trouble digs the reservoir of comfort deeper and makes more room for consolation. God comes into our heart—He finds it full—He begins to break our comforts and to make it empty; then there is more room for grace. The humbler a man is, the more comfort he will always have, because he will be more fitted to receive it. Another reason why we are often happiest in our troubles is this—*then we have the closest dealings with God*. When the barn is full, man can live without God: When the purse is bursting with gold, we try to do without so much prayer. But when our shelter is removed, then we want our God; when the house is purged of idols, then we are compelled to honor the Lord. "Out of the depths I cry to you, O LORD!"[1] There is no cry so good as that which comes from the bottom of the mountains, no prayer half so hearty as that which comes up from the depths of the soul, through deep trials and afflictions. They bring us to God, and we are happier; for nearness to God is happiness. Come, troubled believer, do not fret over your heavy troubles, for they are the heralds of weighty mercies.

❧ EVENING ❧

God the Father revealed Himself to Old Testament believers before the coming of His Son and was known to Abraham, Isaac, and Jacob as God Almighty. Then Jesus came, and the ever-blessed Son in His own proper person was the delight of His people's eyes. At the time of the Redeemer's ascension, the Holy Spirit became the head of the present era, and His power was gloriously displayed in and after Pentecost. He remains at this hour the present Immanuel—God with us, dwelling in and with His people, quickening, guiding, and ruling in our lives. Is His presence recognized as it ought to be? We cannot control His working; He is sovereign in all His operations, but are we sufficiently anxious to obtain His help or sufficiently watchful lest we grieve Him and He withdraws His help? Without Him we can do nothing, but by His almighty energy the most extraordinary results can be produced: Everything depends upon His revealing or concealing His power. Do we always look up to Him for our inner life and our outward service with the respectful dependence that is appropriate? Do we not too often run before His call and act independently of His aid? Let us humble ourselves this evening for past neglect, and now entreat the heavenly dew to rest upon us, the sacred oil to anoint us, the celestial flame to burn within us. The Holy Spirit is not a temporary gift—He remains with the church. When we seek Him as we should, we will find Him. He is jealous, but He is full of pity; if He leaves in anger, He returns in mercy. Condescending and tender, He does not grow tired of us but constantly displays His grace.

Sin has been hammering my heart
Unto a hardness, void of love.
Let supplying grace to cross his art
Drop from above.

[1] Psalm 130:1

SEE WHAT KIND OF LOVE THE FATHER HAS GIVEN TO US,
THAT WE SHOULD BE CALLED CHILDREN OF GOD; AND SO WE ARE.
THE REASON WHY THE WORLD DOES NOT KNOW US IS THAT IT DID NOT
KNOW HIM. BELOVED, WE ARE GOD'S CHILDREN NOW. — 1 JOHN 3:1-2

See what kind of love the Father has given to us." Consider who we were and what we feel ourselves to be even now when corruption is at work within us, and you will wonder at our adoption. Yet we are called *God's children.* What a high relationship is that of a son, and what privileges it brings! What care and tenderness the son expects from his father, and what love the father feels toward the son! But all that, and more than that, we now have through Christ. As for the temporary drawback of suffering with the elder brother, this we accept as an honor: "The reason why the world does not know us is that it did not know him." We are content to be unknown with Him in His humiliation, for we are to be exalted with Him. "*Beloved, we are God's children now.*" That is easy to read, but it is not so easy to feel. How is it with your heart this morning? Are you in the lowest depths of sorrow? Does corruption rise within your spirit, and grace seem like a poor spark trampled underfoot? Does your faith almost fail you? Fear not, it is neither your graces nor feelings on which you are to live: you must live simply by faith in Christ. With all these things against us, now—in the very depths of our sorrow, wherever we may be—*now*, as much in the valley as on the mountain, "Beloved, we are God's children *now.*" "Ah, but," you say, "look at my condition! My graces are not bright; my righteousness does not shine with apparent glory." But read the next: "*What we will be has not yet appeared; but we know that when he appears we shall be like him.*" The Holy Spirit shall purify our minds, and divine power shall refine our bodies, and then we shall *see Him as He is.*

✦ E V E N I N G ✦

THERE IS THEREFORE NOW NO CONDEMNATION. — ROMANS 8:1

Come, my soul, think about this. Believing in Jesus, you are actually and effectually cleared from guilt; you are led out of prison. You are no longer in chains as a slave; you are delivered *now* from the bondage of the law; you are freed from sin and can walk around as a free man—the Savior's blood has procured your full acquittal. You now have a right to approach your Father's throne. No flames of vengeance are there to scare you now—no fiery sword; justice cannot strike the innocent. Your disabilities are removed. Once you were unable to see your Father's face; now you can. You could not speak with Him; but now you can approach Him with boldness. Once there was a fear of hell upon you; but now you have no fear of it, for how can there be punishment for the guiltless? He who believes is not condemned and cannot be punished. And more than all, the privileges you might have enjoyed, if you had never sinned, are yours now that you are justified. All the blessings that you would have had if you had kept the law are yours, because Christ has kept it for you. All the love and acceptance that perfect obedience could have obtained belong to you, because Christ was perfectly obedient on your behalf and has imputed all His merits to your account, that you might be exceedingly rich through Him who for your sake became exceedingly poor. How great the debt of love and gratitude you owe to your Savior!

> *A debtor to mercy alone,*
> *Of covenant mercy I sing;*
> *Nor fear with Your righteousness on,*
> *My person and offerings to bring:*
> *The terrors of law and of God,*
> *With me can have nothing to do;*
> *My Savior's obedience and blood*
> *Hide all my transgressions from view.*

AND FOR HIS ALLOWANCE, A REGULAR ALLOWANCE WAS
GIVEN HIM BY THE KING, ACCORDING TO HIS DAILY NEEDS,
AS LONG AS HE LIVED. — 2 KINGS 25:30

Jehoiachin was not sent away from the king's palace with provision to last him for months, but it was given to him as a daily supply. In this He provides us with a picture of the happy position of all the Lord's people. A daily portion is *all that a man really wants.* We do not need tomorrow's supplies; that day has not yet dawned, and its wants are as yet unborn. The experience that we may suffer in the month of June does not need to be quenched in February, for we do not feel it yet; if we have enough for each day as the days arrive, we shall never know want. Sufficient for the day is *all that we can enjoy.* We cannot eat or drink or wear more than the day's supply of food and clothing; the more we have, the more we have to store, and we worry about it being stolen. One cane helps a traveler, but a bundle of sticks is a heavy burden. Enough is not only as good as a feast, but it is all that the greediest glutton can truly enjoy. This is *all that we should expect*; a craving for more than this is ungrateful. When our Father does not give us more, we should be content with his daily allowance. Jehoiachin's case is ours; we have a sure portion, a portion *given to us by the king*, a *gracious* portion, and a *perpetual portion.* Here is surely ground for thankfulness.

Beloved Christian reader, in matters of grace *you need a daily supply.* You have no store of strength. Day by day you must seek help from above. It is a very happy assurance that *you are provided with a regular allowance.* In the Word, through the ministry, by meditation, in prayer, and waiting upon God you will receive renewed strength. In Jesus everything you need is provided for you. So *enjoy your continual allowance.* Never go hungry while the daily bread of grace is on the table of mercy.

❧ EVENING ❧

SHE HAD BEEN IMMEDIATELY HEALED. — LUKE 8:47

One of the most touching and instructive of the Savior's miracles is before us tonight. The woman was very ignorant. She imagined that virtue came out of Christ by a law of necessity, without His knowledge or direct will. Moreover, she was a stranger to the generosity of Jesus' character, or she would not have gone behind to steal the cure that He was so ready to provide. Misery should always place itself right in the face of mercy. Had she known the love of Jesus' heart, she would have said, "I need only to put myself where He can see me—His omniscience will teach Him my case, and His love will immediately work my cure." We admire her faith, but we marvel at her ignorance. After she had obtained the cure, she rejoiced with trembling: She was glad that the divine virtue had worked a marvel in her; but she feared in case Christ should retract the blessing and negate the grant of His grace. Little did she comprehend the fullness of His love! We do not have as clear a view of Him as we could wish; we do not know the heights and depths of His love. But we know of a certainty that He is too good to withdraw from a trembling soul the gift that it has been able to obtain. But here is the marvel of it: Although her knowledge was small, her faith, because it was real faith, saved her, and saved her at once. There was no tedious delay—faith's miracle was instantaneous. If we have faith as a grain of mustard seed, salvation is our present and eternal possession. If in the list of the Lord's children we are described as the feeblest of the family, yet, being heirs through faith, no power, human or devil, can eject us from salvation. If we dare not lean our heads upon His bosom with John, yet if we can venture in the crowd behind Him and touch the hem of his garment, we are made whole. Take courage, timid one! Your faith has saved you; go in peace. "Since we *have been* justified by faith, we *have* peace with God."[1]

[1] Romans 5:1

TO HIM BE THE GLORY BOTH NOW AND TO THE DAY OF ETERNITY.
— 2 PETER 3:18

Heaven will be full of the ceaseless praises of Jesus. Eternity! Your unnumbered years shall run their everlasting course, but forever and forever; "to him be the glory." Is He not a "priest forever after the order of Melchizedek"? "To him be the glory." Is He not king forever—King of kings and Lord of lords, the everlasting Father? "To him be the glory both now and to the day of eternity." His praises shall never end. That which was bought with blood deserves to last while immortality endures. The glory of the cross must never be eclipsed; the luster of the grave and of the resurrection must never be dimmed. O Jesus, You will be praised forever. So long as immortal spirits live—as long as the Father's throne endures—forever, forever, unto You shall be glory. Believer, you are anticipating the time when you will join the saints above in ascribing all glory to Jesus; but are you glorifying Him *now*? The apostle's words are, "To him be the glory both now and to the day of eternity." Will you not today make it your prayer? Lord, help me to glorify You. I am poor; help me to glorify You by contentment. I am sick; help me to give You honor by patience. I have talents; help me to extol You by spending them for You. I have time, Lord; help me to redeem it, that I may serve You. I have a heart to feel; Lord, let that heart feel no love but Yours, and glow with no flame but affection for You. I have a mind to think, Lord; help me to think *of* You and *for* You. You have put me in this world for something. Lord, show me what that is, and help me to work out my life-purpose. I cannot do much, but as the widow put in her two copper coins, which were all her living, so, Lord, I cast my time and eternity too into Your treasury. I am all Yours; take me, and enable me to glorify You *now*, in all that I say, in all that I do, and with all that I have.

❧ EVENING ❧

FROM IVORY PALACES STRINGED INSTRUMENTS MAKE YOU GLAD.
— PSALM 45:8

And who are those who enjoy the privilege of making the Savior glad? His church—His people. But is it possible? He makes *us* glad, but *how can we make Him glad*? By our love. We think it so cold, so faint; and so, indeed, we must sorrowfully confess it to be, but it is very sweet to Christ. Listen to such love expressed in Solomon's song: "How beautiful is your love, my sister, my bride! How much better is your love than wine!" See, loving heart, this is how He delights in you. When you rest in Him you do not only receive, but you also give Him joy; when you gaze with love upon His beauty, you not only obtain comfort but impart delight. Our *praise* also gives Him joy—not the song of the lips alone, but the melody of the heart's deep gratitude. Our *gifts* are also very pleasant to Him; He loves to see us lay our time, our talents, our substance upon the altar, not for the value of what we give, but for the sake of the motive from which the gift springs. To Him the lowly offerings of His saints are more acceptable than the thousands of gold and silver. *Holiness* is like frankincense and myrrh to Him. Forgive your enemy, and you make Christ glad; distribute of your substance to the poor, and He rejoices; be the means of saving souls, and you give Him to see of the travail of His soul; proclaim His Gospel, and you are a sweet savor unto Him; go among the ignorant and lift up the cross, and you have given Him honor. It is in your power even now to break the alabaster box and pour the precious oil of joy upon His head, like the woman in the Bible, whose testimony is still remembered wherever the Gospel is preached. Will you not join her in expressing your love and devotion for the Lord Jesus? And even in ivory palaces the songs of the saints will be heard.

   ❧ MORNING ❧

FOR I HAVE LEARNED IN WHATEVER SITUATION I AM
TO BE CONTENT. — PHILIPPIANS 4:11

These words show us that contentment is not a natural propensity of man. Weeds grow easily. Covetousness, discontent, and murmuring are as natural to man as thorns are to the soil. We do not need to sow thistles and brambles; they come up naturally enough, because they are indigenous to earth. And so we do not need to teach men to complain; they complain fast enough without any education. But the precious things of the earth must be cultivated. In order to have wheat, we must plow and sow; if we want flowers, there must be the garden, and all the gardener's care. Now, contentment is one of the flowers of heaven, and if we would have it, it must be cultivated; it will not grow in us by nature. It is the new nature alone that can produce it, and even then we must be specially careful and watchful that we maintain and cultivate the grace that God has sown in us. Paul says, "I have *learned . . .* to be content," as much as to say he did not know how at one time. It cost him some pains to discover that great truth. No doubt he sometimes thought he had learned, and then broke down. And when at last he had attained to it and could say, "I have learned in whatsoever situation I am to be content," he was an old, gray-headed man, upon the borders of the grave—a poor prisoner shut up in Nero's dungeon at Rome. We might well be willing to endure Paul's infirmities and share the cold dungeon with him, if we also might by some means attain to his good stature. Do not indulge the notion that you can be contented with *learning* or learn without discipline. It is not a power that may be exercised naturally but a science to be acquired gradually. We know this from experience. Christian, hush that murmur, even though it is natural, and continue as a diligent pupil in the College of Contentment.

❧ EVENING ❧

. . . YOUR GOOD SPIRIT. — NEHEMIAH 9:20

Common, too common, is the sin of forgetting the Holy Spirit. This is folly and ingratitude. He deserves better from us, for He is good, supremely good. As God, He is good essentially. He shares in the threefold ascription of "Holy, holy, holy" that ascends to the Triune God. He is unmixed purity, truth, and grace. He is *good benevolently*, tenderly bearing with our waywardness, striving with our rebellious wills, quickening us from our death in sin, and then training us for heaven as a loving father trains his children. How generous, forgiving, and tender is this patient Spirit of God. He is *good operatively*. All His works are good in the most eminent degree: He suggests good thoughts, prompts good actions, reveals good truths, applies good promises, assists in good attainments, and leads to good results. There is no spiritual good in all the world of which He is not the author and sustainer, and heaven itself will owe the perfect character of its redeemed inhabitants to His work. He is *good officially*: Whether as Comforter, Instructor, Guide, Sanctifier, Quickener, or Intercessor, He fulfills His office well, and each work is filled with the highest good to the church of God. Those who yield to His influences become good; those who obey His impulses do good; those who live under His power receive good. Let us then act toward Him according to the dictates of gratitude. Let us revere His person and adore Him as God over all, blessed forever; let us own His power and our need of Him by waiting upon Him in all our holy enterprises; let us hourly seek His help and never grieve Him; and let us speak His praise whenever occasion occurs. The church will never prosper until it more reverently believes in the Holy Spirit. He is so good and kind that it is sad indeed that He should be grieved by slights and negligences.

ISAAC SETTLED AT BEER-LAHAI-ROI. — GENESIS 25:11

Hagar had once found deliverance there, and Ishmael had drunk from the water so graciously revealed by the God who lives and sees the sons of men; but that was a merely casual visit, such as unbelievers pay to the Lord in times of need, when it suits them. They cry to Him in trouble but forsake Him in prosperity. Isaac *dwelt* there and made the well of the living and all-seeing God his constant source of supply. The usual tenor of a man's life, the *dwelling* of his soul, is the true test of his state. Perhaps the providential visitation experienced by Hagar struck Isaac's mind and led him to revere the place. Its mystical name endeared it to him; his frequent musings at its brim at evening made him familiar with the well. Meeting Rebecca there had made his spirit feel at home near the spot; but best of all, the fact that there he enjoyed fellowship with the living God had made him select that hallowed ground for his dwelling. Let us learn to live in the presence of the living God; let us ask the Holy Spirit that this day, and every other day, we may sense, "God, You see me." May the Lord be as a well to us, delightful, comforting, unfailing, springing up unto eternal life. The bottle of the creature cracks and dries up, but the well of the Creator never fails; happy is he who dwells at the well and as a result has abundant and constant supplies at hand. The Lord has been a sure helper to others: His name is Shaddai, God All-sufficient. Our hearts have often had most delightful communion with Him; through Him our soul has found her glorious Husband, the Lord Jesus; and in Him this day we live and move and have our being. Let us, then, dwell in closest fellowship with Him. Glorious Lord, constrain us, that we may never leave You but dwell by the well of the living God.

. . . ALTHOUGH THE LORD WAS THERE . . . — EZEKIEL 35:10

Edom's princes saw the whole country left desolate and counted upon its easy conquest; but there was one great difficulty in their way—quite unknown to them—"*The Lord was there*"; and in His presence lay the special security of the chosen land. Whatever may be the machinations and devices of the enemies of God's people, there is still the same effectual barrier to thwart their plan. The saints are God's heritage, and He is among them and will protect His own. This assurance grants us comfort in our troubles and spiritual conflicts! We are constantly opposed and yet perpetually preserved! How often Satan shoots his arrows against our *faith*, but our faith defies the power of hell's fiery darts; they are not only turned aside, but they are quenched upon its shield, for "the Lord was there." *Our good works* are the subjects of Satan's attacks. A believer never yet had a virtue or a grace that was not the target for hellish bullets: whether it was bright and sparkling hope, or warm and fervent love, or all-enduring patience, or zeal flaming like coals of fire, the old enemy of everything that is good has tried to destroy it. The only reason why anything virtuous or lovely survives in us is this: "the Lord was there."

If the Lord is with us through life, we do not need to fear death; for *when we come to die*, we will find that "the Lord is *there*." Where the billows are most tempestuous, and the water is most chill, we shall feel the bottom and know that it is good; our feet shall stand upon the Rock of Ages when time is passing away. Dear friend, from the beginning of a Christian's life to the end, the only reason he does not perish is because "*the Lord was there*." When the God of everlasting love shall change and leave His elect to perish, then may the church of God be destroyed; but not until then, because it is written, JEHOVAH SHAMMAH, "*The Lord was there*."

LET ME KNOW WHY YOU CONTEND AGAINST ME. — JOB 10:2

Perhaps, weary soul, the Lord is doing this to develop your graces. There are some of your graces that would never be *discovered* if it were not for your trials. Do you not know that your faith never looks as good in summer as it does in winter? Love is too often like a glowworm, showing but little light unless it is surrounded by darkness. Hope itself is like a star—not to be seen in the sunshine of prosperity, and only to be discovered in the night of adversity. Afflictions are often the black foils in which God sets the jewels of His children's graces, to make them shine brighter. It was only a little while ago that on your knees you were saying, "Lord, I fear I have no faith. Let me know that I have faith." Were you not really, though perhaps unconsciously, praying for trials? For how can you know that you have faith until your faith is exercised? Depend upon it—God often sends us trials so that our graces may be discovered and that we may be convinced of their existence. Besides, it is not merely discovery; *real growth* in grace is the result of sanctified trials. God often takes away our comforts and our privileges in order to make us better Christians. He trains His soldiers not in tents of ease and luxury, but by turning them out and subjecting them to forced marches and hard service. He makes them ford through streams, and swim through rivers, and climb mountains, and walk many long miles with heavy backpacks of sorrow. Well, Christian, may this not account for the troubles through which you are passing? Is the Lord bringing out your graces and making them grow? Is it for this reason He contends with you?

> *Trials make the promise sweet;*
> *Trials give new life to prayer;*
> *Trials bring me to His feet,*
> *Lay me low, and keep me there.*

⇛ EVENING ⇜

FATHER, I HAVE SINNED. — LUKE 15:18

It is quite certain that those whom Christ has washed in His precious blood need not make a confession of sin as culprits or criminals before God the Judge, because Christ has forever taken away all their sins in a legal sense, so that they no longer stand where they can be condemned, but are once for all accepted in the Beloved. But having become children, and offending as children, should they not every day go before their heavenly Father and confess their sin and acknowledge their iniquity in that character? Nature teaches that it is the duty of erring children to make a confession to their earthly father, and the grace of God in the heart teaches us that we, as Christians, owe the same duty to our heavenly Father. We daily offend and ought not to rest without daily pardon. Suppose that my trespasses against my Father are not at once taken to Him to be washed away by the cleansing power of the Lord Jesus—what will be the consequence? If I have not sought forgiveness and been washed from these offenses against my Father, I shall feel at a distance from Him; I shall doubt His love to me; I shall tremble before Him; I shall be afraid to pray to Him: I shall grow like the prodigal who, although still a child, was yet far away from his father. But if with a child's sorrow at offending so gracious and loving a Parent, I go to Him and tell Him everything, and do not rest until I realize that I am forgiven, then I shall feel a holy love to my Father and shall go through my Christian career not only as saved, but as one enjoying present peace in God through Jesus Christ my Lord. There is a wide distinction between confessing sin *as a culprit* and confessing sin *as a child*. The Father's bosom is the place for penitent confessions. We have been cleansed once for all, but our feet still need to be washed from the defilement of our daily walk as children of God.

    ❧ MORNING ❧

THUS SAYS THE LORD GOD:
THIS ALSO I WILL LET THE HOUSE OF ISRAEL ASK ME
TO DO FOR THEM. — EZEKIEL 36:37

Prayer is the forerunner of mercy. Turn to sacred history, and you will find that scarcely ever did a great mercy come to this world unheralded by supplication. You have found this true in your own personal experience. God has given you many an unsolicited favor, but still great prayer has always been the prelude of great mercy with you. When you first found peace through the blood of the cross, you had been praying much and earnestly interceding with God that He would remove your doubts and deliver you from your distresses. Your assurance was the result of prayer. When at any time you have had high and rapturous joys, you have been obliged to look upon them as answers to your prayers. When you have had great deliverances out of sore troubles and mighty help in great dangers, you have been able to say, "I sought the LORD, and He answered me and delivered me from all my fears."[1] Prayer is always the preface to blessing. It goes before the blessing *as the blessing's shadow*. When the sunlight of God's mercies rises upon our necessities, it casts the shadow of prayer far down upon the plain. Or, to use another illustration, when God piles up a hill of mercies, He Himself shines behind them, and He casts on our spirits the shadow of prayer, so that we may rest confident, if we are much in prayer, that our pleadings are the shadows of mercy. Prayer is thus connected with the blessing *to show us the value of it*. If we had the blessings without asking for them, we should think them common things; but prayer makes our mercies more precious than diamonds. The things we ask for are precious, but we do not realize their preciousness until we have sought them earnestly.

> *Prayer makes the darken'd cloud withdraw;*
> *Prayer climbs the ladder Jacob saw;*
> *Gives exercise to faith and love;*
> *Brings every blessing from above.*

❧ EVENING ❧

HE FIRST FOUND HIS OWN BROTHER SIMON. — JOHN 1:41

This case is an excellent pattern of all cases where spiritual life is vigorous. *As soon as a man has found Christ, he begins to find others*. I will not believe that you have tasted of the honey of the Gospel if you can eat it all yourself. True grace puts an end to all spiritual monopoly. Andrew *first* found his own brother Simon, and then others. *Relationship has a very strong demand upon our first individual efforts*. Andrew, you did well to begin with Simon. I doubt whether there are not some Christians giving away tracts at other people's houses who would do well to give away a tract at their own—whether there are not some engaged in works of usefulness abroad who are neglecting their special sphere of usefulness at home. You may or may not be called to evangelize the people in any particular locality, but certainly you are called to witness to your own servants, your own family and acquaintances. Let your faith begin at home. Many tradesmen export their best commodities—the Christian should not. He should have all his conversation everywhere be the best; but let him take care to display and share the sweetest fruit of spiritual life and testimony in his own family. When Andrew went to find his brother, he little imagined how eminent Simon would become. *Simon Peter was worth ten Andrews* so far as we can gather from sacred history, and yet Andrew was instrumental in bringing him to Jesus. You may be very deficient in talent yourself, and yet you may be the means of drawing to Christ one who shall become eminent in grace and service. Dear friend, you hardly know the possibilities that are in you. You may simply speak a word to a child, and in that child there may be slumbering a noble heart that shall stir the Christian church in years to come. Andrew has only two talents, but he finds Peter. Go out and do the same.

[1] Psalm 34:4

GOD, WHO COMFORTS THE DOWNCAST. — 2 CORINTHIANS 7:6

And who comforts like Him? Go to some poor, melancholy, distressed child of God; tell him sweet promises and whisper in his ear choice words of comfort; he is like the deaf adder that doesn't listen to the voice of the charmer, even though he charms wisely. He is drinking gall and wormwood, and no matter how you comfort him, you will only get a note or two of mournful resignation from him; you will bring forth no psalms of praise, no hallelujahs, no joyful sonnets. But let *God* come to His child, let Him lift up his countenance, and the mourner's eyes glisten with hope. Do you not hear him sing—

'Tis paradise, if you are here;
If you depart, 'tis hell.

You could not have cheered him: but the Lord has done it; He is the "God of all comfort."[1] There is no balm in Gilead, but there is balm in God. There is no physician among the creatures, but the Creator is Jehovah-rophi. It is marvelous how one sweet word of God will make whole songs for Christians. One word of God is like a piece of gold, and the Christian is the gold-beater and can hammer that promise out for weeks. So, then, poor Christian, you need not sit down in despair. Go to the Comforter, and ask Him to give you consolation. You are a poor, dry well. You have heard it said that when a pump is dry, you must pour water down it first of all, and then you will get water; and so, Christian, when you are dry, go to God, ask Him to shed abroad His joy in your heart, and then your joy shall be full. Do not go to earthly acquaintances, for you will find them to be Job's comforters; but go first and foremost to "God, who comforts the downcast," and you will soon say, "When the cares of my heart are many, Your consolations cheer my soul."

<hr/>

❧ EVENING ☙

THEN JESUS WAS LED UP BY THE SPIRIT INTO THE WILDERNESS
TO BE TEMPTED BY THE DEVIL. — MATTHEW 4:1

A holy character does not prevent temptation—Jesus was tempted. When Satan tempts us, his sparks fall upon tinder; but in Christ's case, it was like striking sparks on water; yet the enemy continued his evil work. Now, if the devil goes on striking when there is no result, how much more will he do it when he knows what inflammable stuff our hearts are made of. Though you become greatly sanctified by the Holy Spirit, expect that the great dog of hell will bark at you still. In the haunts of men we expect to be tempted, but even seclusion will not guard us from the same trial. Jesus Christ was led away from human society into the wilderness and was tempted by the devil. Solitude has its charms and its benefits and may be useful in checking the lust of the eye and the pride of life; but the devil will follow us into the most lovely retreats. Do not suppose that it is only the worldly-minded who have dreadful thoughts and blasphemous temptations, for even spiritually minded persons endure the same; and in the holiest position we may suffer the darkest temptation. The utmost consecration of spirit will not insure you against satanic temptation. Christ was consecrated through and through. It was His meat and drink to do the will of Him that sent Him— and yet He was tempted! Your hearts may glow with an angelic flame of love for Jesus, and yet the devil will try to bring you down to lukewarm uselessness. If you will tell me when God permits a Christian to lay aside his armor, I will tell you when Satan has left off temptation. Like the old knights in wartime, we must sleep with helmet and breastplate buckled on, for the arch-deceiver will seize our first unguarded moment to make us his prey. May the Lord keep us watchful in all seasons and grant us a final escape from the jaw of the lion and the paw of the bear.

[1] 2 Corinthians 1:3

... FOR HE HAS SAID ... — HEBREWS 13:5

If we can only grasp these words by faith, we have an all-conquering weapon in our hand. What doubt will not be slain by this two-edged sword? What fear is there that shall not fall smitten with a deadly wound before this arrow from the bow of God's covenant? Will not the distresses of life and the pangs of death, will not the internal corruptions and the external snares, will not the trials from above and the temptations from beneath all seem but light afflictions when we can hide ourselves beneath the bulwark of "he has said"? Yes; whether for delight in peace or for strength in our conflict, "he has said" must be our daily resort. And this may teach us the extreme value of searching the Scriptures. There may be a promise in the Word that would exactly fit your case, but you may not know of it, and therefore you miss its comfort. You are like prisoners in a dungeon, and there may be one key in the bunch that would unlock the door, and you might be free; but if you will not look for it, you may remain a prisoner still, though liberty is so near at hand. There may be a potent medicine in the great pharmacy of Scripture, and you may yet continue sick unless you will examine and search the Scriptures to discover what "he has said." Should you not, besides reading the Bible, store your memories richly with the promises of God? You can recollect the sayings of great men; you treasure up the verses of renowned poets. So should you not also be proficient in your knowledge of the Word of God, so that you may be able to quote it readily in solving a difficulty or overthrowing a doubt? Since "he has said" is the source of all wisdom and the fountain of all comfort, let it dwell in you richly, as "a spring of water welling up to eternal life."[1] In this way you will grow healthy, strong, and happy in the divine life.

✎ EVENING ✍
DO YOU UNDERSTAND WHAT YOU ARE READING? — ACTS 8:30

We would be more able teachers, and not so easily carried away by every wind of doctrine, if we sought to have a more intelligent understanding of the Word of God. As the Holy Spirit, the Author of the Scriptures, is the only one who can enlighten us rightly to understand them, we should constantly ask His help to lead us into truth. When the prophet Daniel was called upon to interpret Nebuchadnezzar's dream, what did he do? He set himself to earnest prayer that God would open up the vision. The apostle John, in his vision at Patmos, saw a book sealed with seven seals that none was found worthy to open or so much as to look upon. The book was afterward opened by the Lion of the tribe of Judah, who had prevailed to open it; but it is written first, "I wept much." The tears of John, which were his liquid prayers, were, so far as he was concerned, the sacred keys by which the folded book was opened. Therefore, if, for your own and others' profiting, you desire to be "filled with the knowledge of his will in all spiritual wisdom and understanding,"[2] remember that prayer is your best means of study. Like Daniel, you shall understand the dream and its interpretation when you have sought it from God; and like John you shall see the seven seals of precious truth unloosed after you have wept much. Stones are not broken except by a constant, diligent use of the hammer; and the stone-breaker must go down on his knees. Use the hammer of diligence, and let the knee of prayer be exercised, and there is not a stony doctrine in revelation that is useful for you to understand that will not fly into shivers under the exercise of prayer and faith. You may force your way through anything with the leverage of prayer. Thoughts and reasoning are like the steel wedges that give a hold upon truth; but prayer is the lever that pries open the iron chest of sacred mystery, that we may get the treasure hidden inside.

[1] John 4:14   [2] Colossians 1:9

HIS BOW REMAINED UNMOVED; HIS ARMS WERE MADE AGILE BY THE HANDS
OF THE MIGHTY ONE OF JACOB. — GENESIS 49:24

The strength that God gives to His Josephs is *real* strength; it is not a boasted valor, a fiction, a thing of which men talk but which ends in smoke; it is true—*divine strength.* Why does Joseph stand against temptation? Because God enables him. There is nothing that we can do without the power of God. All true strength comes from "the Mighty One of Jacob." Notice in what a *blessedly familiar way* God gives this strength to Joseph—"His arms were made agile by the hands of the Mighty One of Jacob." God is represented as putting His hands on Joseph's hands, placing His arms on Joseph's arms. Just as a father teaches his children, so the Lord teaches them that fear Him. He puts His arms upon them. Marvelous condescension! God Almighty, Eternal, Omnipotent, stoops from His throne and lays His hand upon the child's hand, stretching His arm upon the arm of Joseph, that he may be made strong! This strength was also covenant strength, for it is ascribed to "*the Mighty One of Jacob.*" Now, wherever you read of the God of Jacob in the Bible, you should remember the covenant with Jacob. Christians love to think of God's covenant. All the power, all the grace, all the blessings, all the mercies, all the comforts, all the things we have flow to us from the fountainhead, through the covenant. If there were no covenant, then we should fail indeed; for all grace proceeds from it, as light and heat from the sun. No angels ascend or descend except by the ladder that Jacob saw, at the top of which stood a covenant God. Christian, it may be that the archers have sorely grieved you and shot at you and wounded you, but still your bow remains unmoved. Be sure, then, to ascribe all the glory to Jacob's God.

❧ EVENING ❧

THE LORD IS SLOW TO ANGER AND GREAT IN POWER. — NAHUM 1:3

Jehovah "*is slow to anger.*" When mercy comes into the world, she drives winged horses; the axles of her chariot-wheels are red-hot with speed. But when wrath goes forth, it toils on with tardy footsteps, for God takes no pleasure in the sinner's death. God's rod of mercy is always in His hands outstretched; His sword of justice is in its scabbard, held down by that pierced hand of love that bled for the sins of men. "The LORD is slow to anger" because He is "*great in power.*" He is truly great in power who has power over himself. When God's power restrains Himself, then it is power indeed: The power that binds omnipotence is omnipotence surpassed. A man who has a strong mind can bear to be insulted and only resents the wrong when a sense of right demands his action. The weak mind is irritated at a little; the strong mind bears it like a rock that doesn't move though a thousand breakers dash upon it and cast their pitiful malice in spray upon its summit. God marks His enemies, and yet He bestirs not Himself but holds in His anger. If He were less divine than He is, He would long have since sent forth the whole of His thunders and emptied the cannons of heaven; He would have long ago blasted the earth with the wondrous fires of its lower regions, and man would have been utterly destroyed. But the greatness of His power brings us mercy. Dear reader, what is your condition this evening? Can you by humble faith look to Jesus and say, "My substitute, You are my rock, my trust"? Then, beloved, do not be afraid of God's power; for if by faith you have fled to Christ for refuge, the power of God need no more terrify you than the shield and sword of the warrior need terrify those whom he loves. Rather rejoice that He who is "great in power" is your Father and Friend.

No promise is for private application. Whatever God has said to one saint, He has said to all. When He opens a well for one, it is that all may drink. When He opens a granary-door to give out food, there may be one starving man who is the reason for it being opened, but all hungry saints may come and feed too. Whether He gave the word to Abraham or to Moses matters not, believer; He has given it to you as one of the covenanted seed. There is not a high blessing too lofty for you, nor a wide mercy too extensive for you. Lift up your eyes now to the north and to the south, to the east and to the west, for all this is yours. Climb to the mountaintop, and view the utmost limits of the divine promise, for the land is all your own. There is not a brook of living water of which you may not drink. If the land flows with milk and honey, eat the honey and drink the milk, for both are yours. Be bold to believe, for He has said, "I will never leave *you* nor forsake *you*." In this promise, God gives His people everything. "*I* will never leave you." Then no attribute of God can cease to be engaged for us. Is He mighty? He will show Himself strong on behalf of them that trust Him. Is He love? Then with loving-kindness will He have mercy upon us. Whatever attributes may compose the character of Deity, every one of them to its fullest extent shall be engaged on your side. To summarize, there is nothing you can want, there is nothing you can ask for, there is nothing you can need in time or in eternity, there is nothing living, nothing dying, there is nothing in this world, nothing in the next world, there is nothing now, nothing at the resurrection-morning, nothing in heaven that is not contained in this text—"I will never leave you nor forsake you."

You do not make your own cross, although unbelief is a master carpenter at cross-making; neither are you permitted to *choose* your own cross, although self-will wants to be lord and master. But your cross is prepared and appointed for you by divine love, and you must cheerfully accept it; you are to take up the cross as your chosen badge and burden, and not to stand complaining. This night Jesus bids you submit your shoulder to His easy yoke. Do not kick at it in petulance, or trample on it in pride, or fall under it in despair, or run away from it in fear, but take it up like a true follower of Jesus. Jesus was a cross-bearer; He leads the way in the path of sorrow. Surely you could not desire a better guide! And if He carried a cross, what nobler burden would you desire? The *Via Crucis* is the way of safety; fear not to tread its thorny paths.

Beloved, the cross is not made of feathers or lined with velvet; it is heavy and galling to disobedient shoulders; but it is not an iron cross, though your fears have painted it with iron colors; it is a wooden cross, and a man can carry it, for the Man of Sorrows tried the load. Take up your cross, and by the power of the Spirit of God you will soon be so in love with it that like Moses you would not exchange the reproach of Christ for all the treasures of Egypt. Remember that Jesus carried it; remember that it will soon be followed by the crown, and the thought of the coming weight of glory will greatly lighten the present heaviness of trouble. May the Lord help you bow your spirit in submission to the divine will before you fall asleep tonight, so that waking with tomorrow's sun, you may go forth to the day's cross with the holy and submissive spirit that is fitting for a follower of the Crucified.

I WILL SEND DOWN THE SHOWERS IN THEIR SEASON;
THEY SHALL BE SHOWERS OF BLESSING. — EZEKIEL 34:26

Here is *sovereign mercy*—"I will send down the showers in their season." Is it not sovereign, *divine mercy*? For who can say, "I will send down showers" except God? There is only one voice that can speak to the clouds and bid them send the rain. "Who sends down the rain upon the earth? Who scatters the showers upon the green herb? Do not I, the Lord?" So grace is the gift of God and is not to be created by man. It is also *needed grace*. What would the ground do without showers? You may break the clods, you may sow your seeds, but what can you do without the rain? Just as absolutely needful is the divine blessing; you work in vain until God the bestows the shower and sends salvation down. Then, it is *plenteous grace*. "I will send down the showers." It does not say, "I will send down drops," but "showers." So it is with grace. If God gives a blessing, He usually gives it in such a measure that there is not room enough to receive it. Plenteous grace! We need plenteous grace to keep us humble, to make us prayerful, to make us holy; plenteous grace to make us zealous, to preserve us through this life, and at last to land us in heaven. We cannot do without saturating showers of grace. Again, it is *seasonable grace*. "I will cause the shower to come down *in their season*." What is your season this morning? Is it the season of drought? Then that is the season for showers. Is it a season of great heaviness and black clouds? Then that is the season for showers. "As your days, so shall your strength be."[1] And here is a *varied* blessing. "I will give you *showers* of blessing." The word is in the plural. All kinds of blessings God will send. All God's blessings go together, like links in a golden chain. If He gives converting grace, He will also give comforting grace. He will send "showers of blessing." Look up today, O parched plant, and open your leaves and flowers for a heavenly watering.

❧ EVENING ❧

O LORD OF HOSTS, HOW LONG WILL YOU HAVE NO MERCY ON
JERUSALEM? . . . AND THE LORD ANSWERED GRACIOUS AND
COMFORTING WORDS TO THE ANGEL. — ZECHARIAH 1:12-13

What a sweet answer to an anxious inquiry! This night let us rejoice in it. O Zion, there are good things in store for you; your time of travail will soon be over; your children shall come forth; your captivity shall end. Bear patiently the rod for a season, and under the darkness still trust in God, for His love burns toward you. God loves the church with a love too deep for human imagination: He loves her with all His infinite heart. Therefore let her sons be of good courage; she cannot be far from prosperity to whom God speaks "gracious and comforting words." The prophet goes on to tell us: "I am exceedingly jealous for Jerusalem and for Zion." The Lord loves His church so much that He cannot bear that she should go astray to others; and when she has done so, He cannot endure that she should suffer too much or too heavily. He will not have his enemies afflict her: He is displeased with them because they increase her misery. When God seems most to leave His church, His heart is warm toward her. History shows that whenever God uses a rod to chasten His servants, He always breaks it afterwards, as if He loathed the rod that gave his children pain. "As a father shows compassion to his children, so the LORD shows compassion to those who fear him."[2] God has not forgotten us because He strikes—His blows are no evidences of absence of love. If this is true of His church *collectively*, it is also necessarily true of *each individual member*. You may fear that the Lord has passed you by, but it is not so: He who counts the stars and calls them by their names is in no danger of forgetting His own children. He knows your case as thoroughly as if you were the only creature He ever made or the only saint He ever loved. Approach Him and be at peace.

[1] Deuteronomy 33:25   [2] Psalm 103:13

... THE WRATH TO COME. — MATTHEW 3:7

It is pleasant to pass over a country after a storm has spent itself—to smell the freshness of the herbs after the rain has passed away, and to note the drops while they glisten like purest diamonds in the sunlight. That is the position of a Christian. He is going through a land where the storm has spent itself upon His Savior's head, and if there be a few drops of sorrow falling, they distill from clouds of mercy, and Jesus cheers him by the assurance that they are not for his destruction. But how terrible it is to witness the approach of a tempest—to note the forewarnings of the storm; to mark the birds of heaven as they droop their wings; to see the cattle as they lay their heads low in terror; to discern the face of the sky as it grows black, and to find the sun obscured, and the heavens angry and frowning! How terrible to await the dread advance of a hurricane, to wait in terrible apprehension till the wind rushes forth in fury, tearing up trees from their roots, forcing rocks from their pedestals, and hurling down all the dwelling-places of man! And yet, sinner, this is your present position. No hot drops have fallen as yet, but a shower of fire is coming. No terrible winds howl around you, but God's tempest is gathering its dread artillery. So far the water-floods are dammed up by mercy, but the floodgates will soon be opened: The thunderbolts of God are still in His storehouse, the tempest is coming, and how awful will that moment be when God, robed in vengeance, shall march forth in fury! Where, where, where, O sinner, will you hide your head, or where will you run to? May the hand of mercy lead you now to Christ! He is freely set before you in the Gospel: His pierced side is the place of shelter. You know your need of Him; believe in Him, cast yourself upon Him, and then the fury shall be past forever.

❧ EVENING ❧
BUT JONAH ROSE TO FLEE TO TARSHISH FROM THE PRESENCE OF THE LORD. HE WENT DOWN TO JOPPA. — JONAH 1:3

Instead of going to Nineveh to preach the Word, as God told him, Jonah disliked the work and went down to Joppa to escape from it. There are occasions when God's servants shrink from duty. But what is the consequence? What did Jonah lose by his conduct? *He lost the presence and comfortable enjoyment of God's love.* When we serve our Lord Jesus as believers should do, God is with us; and though we have the whole world against us, if we have God with us, what does it matter? But the moment we retreat and seek to establish our own agenda, we are at sea without a pilot. Then we will bitterly lament and groan out, "O my God, where have You gone? How could I have been so foolish as to shun Your service, and in this way lose all the bright shinings of Your face? This is a price too high. Let me return to my allegiance, that I may rejoice in Your presence." In the next place, *Jonah lost all peace of mind.* Sin soon destroys a believer's comfort. It is the poisonous tree whose leaves distill deadly drops that destroy the life of joy and peace. *Jonah lost everything upon which he might have drawn for comfort in any other case.* He could not plead the promise of divine protection, for he was not in God's ways; he could not say, "Lord, I meet with these difficulties in the discharge of my duty; therefore help me through them." He was reaping his own deeds; he was filled with his own ways. Christian, do not play the Jonah unless you wish to have all the waves and the billows rolling over your head. You will find in the long run that it is far harder to shun the work and will of God than to at once yield yourself to it. *Jonah lost his time,* for he had to go to Tarshish after all. It is hard to contend with God; let us yield ourselves to Him immediately.

SALVATION BELONGS TO THE LORD! — JONAH 2:9

Salvation is the work of God. It is He alone who quickens the soul "dead in . . . trespasses and sins,"[1] and He it is who maintains the soul in its spiritual life. He is both "Alpha and Omega." "Salvation belongs to the LORD!" If I am prayerful, God makes me prayerful; if I have graces, they are God's gifts to me; if I hold on in a consistent life, it is because He upholds me with His hand. I do nothing whatever toward my own preservation, except what God Himself first does in me. Whatever I have, all my goodness is of the Lord alone. Whenever I sin, that is my own doing; but when I act correctly, that is wholly and completely of God. If I have resisted a spiritual enemy, the Lord's strength nerved my arm. Do I live before men a consecrated life? It is not I, but Christ who lives in me. Am I sanctified? I did not cleanse myself: God's Holy Spirit sanctifies me. Am I separated from the world? I am separated by God's chastisements sanctified to my good. Do I grow in knowledge? The great Instructor teaches me. All my jewels were fashioned by heavenly art. I find in God all that I want; but I find in myself nothing but sin and misery. "He only is my rock and my salvation."[2] Do I feed on the Word? That Word would be no food for me unless the Lord made it food for my soul and helped me to feed upon it. Do I live on the bread that comes down from heaven? What is that bread but Jesus Christ Himself incarnate, whose body and whose blood I eat and drink? Am I continually receiving fresh supplies of strength? Where do I gather my might? My help comes from heaven's hills: Without Jesus I can do nothing. As a branch cannot bring forth fruit except it abide in the vine, no more can I, except I abide in Him. What Jonah learned in the ocean, let me learn this morning in my room: "Salvation belongs to the LORD."

❧ EVENING ❧
IF THE LEPROUS DISEASE HAS COVERED ALL HIS BODY,
HE SHALL PRONOUNCE HIM CLEAN OF THE DISEASE. — LEVITICUS 13:13

Although this regulation appears to be strange, yet there was wisdom in it, for the removal of the disease proved that the character was healthy. This evening it may be well for us to discover this principle to our profit. We, too, are in a sense lepers and may read the law of the leper as applicable to ourselves. When a man sees himself to be completely lost and ruined, covered with the defilement of sin, with no part free from pollution; when he disclaims all righteousness of his own and pleads guilty before the Lord, then he is clean through the blood of Jesus and the grace of God. Hidden, unfelt, unconfessed iniquity is the true leprosy of the soul; but when sin is seen and felt, it has received its deathblow, and the Lord looks with eyes of mercy upon the afflicted soul. Nothing is more deadly than self-righteousness or more hopeful than contrition. We must confess that we are "nothing else but sin," for no confession short of this will be the whole truth; and if the Holy Spirit is at work in us, convincing us of sin, there will be no difficulty about making such an acknowledgment—it will spring spontaneously from our lips. This text affords great comfort to truly awakened sinners: The very circumstance that so grievously discouraged them is here turned into a sign and symptom of a hopeful state! Digging out the foundation is the first thing in building—and a thorough sense of sin is one of the earliest works of grace in the heart. Spiritual lepers, aware of their condition, should take heart from the text and come as they are to Jesus.

> For let our debts be what they may, however great or small,
> As soon as we have naught to pay, our Lord forgives us all.
> 'Tis perfect poverty alone that sets the soul at large:
> While we can call one mite our own, we have no full discharge.

[1] Ephesians 2:1 [2] Psalm 62:2

YOU HAVE MADE THE LORD YOUR DWELLING PLACE—THE MOST HIGH,
WHO IS MY REFUGE. — PSALM 91:9

The Israelites in the wilderness were *continually exposed to change*. Whenever the pillar of cloud stopped, the tents were pitched; but the next day the morning sun arose, the trumpet sounded, the ark was in motion, and the fiery, cloudy pillar was leading the way through the narrow mountain passes, up the hillsides, or along the arid wastes of the wilderness. They scarcely had time to rest a little before they heard the sound of "Onward! this is not your rest; you must keep journeying onward toward Canaan!" They never stayed for long in one place. Even wells and palm trees could not detain them. They had an abiding home in their God; His cloudy pillar was their roof, and its flame by night their fireplace. They must go onward from place to place, continually changing, never having time to settle or to say, "Now we are secure; we will stay in this place." Moses says, "Though we are always changing, Lord, you have been our dwelling-place throughout all generations."[1] The Christian knows no change with regard to God. He may be rich today and poor tomorrow; he may be sick today and well tomorrow; he may be happy today and sad tomorrow—but there is no change regarding his relationship to God. If He loved me yesterday, He loves me today. My unmoving mansion of rest is my blessed Lord. Even when prospects are few and hopes are squashed and joy is waning, I have lost nothing of what I have in God. He is "my refuge" to which I continually return. I am a pilgrim in the world, but at home in my God. In the earth I wander, but in God I dwell in a quiet dwelling place.

☙ EVENING ❧

. . . WHOSE ORIGIN IS FROM OF OLD,
FROM ANCIENT DAYS. — MICAH 5:2

The Lord Jesus had purposes for His people *as their representative before the throne, long before they appeared upon the stage of time*. It was "from ancient days" that He signed the contract with His Father that He would pay blood for blood, suffering for suffering, agony for agony, and death for death on behalf of His people; it was "from ancient days" that He gave Himself up without a murmuring word. From the crown of His head to the sole of His foot He sweat great drops of blood; He was spat upon, pierced, mocked, torn, and crushed beneath the pains of death. All of this was "from ancient days." Let our souls pause in wonder at God's purposes from of old. Not only when you were born into the world did Christ love you, but His delights were with the sons of men before there were any sons of men! He often thought of them; from everlasting to everlasting He had set His affection upon them. Since He has been so long about your salvation, will not He accomplish it? Has He from everlasting been going forth to save me, and will He lose me now? It is inconceivable that having carried me in His hand, as His precious jewel, He would let me now slip from between His fingers. Did He choose me before the mountains were brought forth or the channels of the ocean were formed, and will He reject me now? Impossible! I am sure He would not have loved me for so long if He had not been a faithful Lover. If He could grow weary of me, He would have been tired of me long before now. If He had not loved me with a love as deep as hell and as strong as death, He would have turned from me long ago. What joy above all joys to know that I am His everlasting and inalienable inheritance, given to Him by His Father before the earth was formed! Everlasting love shall be the pillow on which I rest my head tonight.

[1] Psalm 90:1

❧ MORNING ❧

MY HOPE IS FROM HIM. — PSALM 62:5

It is the believer's privilege to use this language. If he is looking for anything from the world, it is a poor hope indeed. But if he looks to God for the supply of his needs, whether temporal or spiritual blessings, his hope will not be in vain. He may constantly draw from the bank of faith and get his need supplied out of the riches of God's loving-kindness. I know this: I would rather have God for my banker than all the Rothschilds. My Lord never fails to honor His promises; and when we bring them to His throne, He never sends them back unanswered. Therefore I will wait only at His door, for He always opens it with the hand of abundant grace. At this hour I will turn to Him afresh. But we have "hope" beyond this life. We will die soon; and still our "hope is from him." May we not expect that when we face illness He will send angels to carry us to His bosom? We believe that when the pulse is faint and the heart is weak, some angelic messenger shall stand and look with loving eyes upon us and whisper, "Come away!" As we approach the heavenly gate, we expect to hear the welcome invitation, "Come, you who are blessed by my Father, inherit the kingdom prepared for you from the foundation of the world."[1] We are expecting harps of gold and crowns of glory; we are hoping soon to be among the company of shining ones before the throne; we are looking forward and longing for the time when we shall be like our glorious Lord—for "We shall see him as he is."[2] Then if these are your hopes, O my soul, live for God; live with the desire and resolve to glorify Him from whose grace in your election, redemption, and calling you safely "hope" for the coming glory.

❧ EVENING ❧

THE JAR OF FLOUR WAS NOT SPENT, NEITHER DID
THE JUG OF OIL BECOME EMPTY, ACCORDING TO THE WORD
OF THE LORD THAT HE SPOKE BY ELIJAH. — 1 KINGS 17:16

Consider the faithfulness of divine love. It is clear that this woman had daily necessities. She had to feed her son and herself in a time of famine; and now, in addition, the prophet Elijah was also to be fed. But though the need was threefold, the supply was not spent, for it was *constant*. Each day she made withdrawals from the jar, but each day it remained the same. You, dear reader, have daily necessities, and because they come so frequently, you are apt to fear that the jar of flour will one day be empty, and the jug of oil will fail you. Rest assured that, according to the Word of God, this shall not be the case. Each day, though it bring its trouble, it shall also bring its help; and though you should live longer than Methuselah, and your needs should be as many as the sands of the seashore, yet God's grace and mercy will last through all your necessities, and you will never know a real lack. For three long years, in this widow's days, the heavens never saw a cloud, and the stars never wept a holy tear of dew upon the wicked earth: famine and desolation and death made the land a howling wilderness, but this woman was never hungry but always joyful in abundance. So it will be with you. You will see the sinner's hope perish, for he trusts in himself; you will see the proud Pharisee's confidence crumble, for he builds his hope upon the sand; you will even see your own plans blown apart, but you will discover that your daily needs are amply supplied. Better to have God for your guardian than the Bank of England for your possession. You might spend the wealth of the nations, but you can never exhaust the infinite mercies of God.

[1] Matthew 25:34 [2] 1 John 3:2

I HAVE LOVED YOU WITH AN EVERLASTING LOVE;
THEREFORE I HAVE CONTINUED MY FAITHFULNESS TO YOU. — JEREMIAH 31:3

The thunders of the law and the terrors of judgment are all used to bring us to Christ; but the final victory is the product of loving-kindness. The prodigal set out to his father's house from a sense of need; but his father saw him a great way off and ran to meet him, so that the last steps he took toward his father's house were with the kiss still warm upon his cheek and the welcome still music in his ears.

> Law and terrors do but harden
> All the while they work alone;
> But a sense of blood-bought pardon
> Will dissolve a heart of stone.

The Master came one night to the door and knocked with the iron hand of the law; the door shook and trembled upon its hinges. But the man piled every piece of furniture that he could find against the door, saying, "I will not admit the man." The Master turned away, but soon He returned, and with His own soft hand, using most that part where the nail had penetrated, He knocked again—softly and tenderly. This time the door did not shake, but, strange to say, it opened, and there upon his knees the once unwilling host was found rejoicing to receive his guest. "Come in, come in; you have knocked in such a tender way that my heart is turned to you. I could not think of your pierced hand leaving its blood-mark on my door and of your going away without my welcome. Your love has won my heart." And so it is in every case that loving-kindness wins the day. What Moses with the tablets of stone could never do, Christ does with His pierced hand. Such is the doctrine of effectual calling. Do I understand it experimentally? Can I say with the hymn-writer, "He drew me, and I followed on, glad to confess the voice divine"? If so, may He continue in His faithfulness to me until at last I shall sit down at the marriage supper of the Lamb.

❧ EVENING ❧

NOW WE HAVE RECEIVED . . . THE SPIRIT WHO IS FROM GOD,
THAT WE MIGHT UNDERSTAND THE THINGS
FREELY GIVEN US BY GOD. — 1 CORINTHIANS 2:12

Dear reader, have you received the Spirit who is from God? The necessity of the work of the Holy Spirit in the heart may be clearly seen from this fact, that *all which has been done by God the Father and by God the Son will be ineffectual to us unless the Spirit reveals these things to our souls.* What effect does the doctrine of election have upon any man until the Spirit of God enters into him? Election is a dead letter in my consciousness until the Spirit of God calls me out of darkness into marvelous light. *Then* through my calling, I see my election, and knowing myself to be called of God, I know myself to have been chosen in the eternal purpose. A covenant was made with the Lord Jesus Christ by His Father; but what good is that covenant to us until the Holy Spirit brings us its blessings and opens our hearts to receive them? These blessings in Christ Jesus are beyond our reach, but the Spirit of God takes them down and hands them to us, and so they actually become ours. Covenant blessings in themselves are like bread in heaven, far out of mortal reach, but the Spirit of God opens the windows of heaven and scatters the living bread around the camp of the redeemed. Christ's finished work is like wine stored in the wine-vat; through unbelief we can neither draw nor drink. The Holy Spirit dips our vessel into this precious wine, and then we drink; but without the Spirit we are as truly dead in sin as though the Father never had elected, and though the Son had never bought us with His blood. The Holy Spirit is absolutely necessary to our well-being. Let us walk lovingly toward Him and tremble at the thought of grieving Him.

March

❧ MORNING ❧

AWAKE, O NORTH WIND, AND COME, O SOUTH WIND!
BLOW UPON MY GARDEN, LET ITS SPICES FLOW. — SONG OF SOLOMON 4:16

Anything is better than the dead calm of indifference. Our souls may wisely desire the north wind of trouble if that is to become the means of our sanctification. So long as it cannot be said, "The Lord was not in the wind," we will not shrink from the most wintry blast that ever blew upon plants of grace. Did not the spouse in this verse humbly submit herself to the reproofs of her Beloved, only entreating Him to send forth His grace in some form, and making no stipulation as to the peculiar manner in which it should come? Did she not, like ourselves, become so utterly weary of deadness and unholy calm that she sighed for any visitation that would brace her to action? Yet she desires the warm south wind of comfort too, the smiles of divine love, the joy of the Redeemer's presence; these are often mightily effectual to arouse our sluggish life. She desires either one or the other, or both, so that she may but be able to delight her Beloved with the spices of her garden. She cannot endure to be unprofitable, nor can we. How cheering a thought that Jesus can find comfort in our poor feeble graces. Can it be? It seems far too good to be true. We may even court trial or death itself if by doing so we gladden Immanuel's heart. O that our heart were crushed to atoms if only by such bruising our Lord Jesus could be glorified. Graces unexercised are as sweet perfumes trapped in the bottle: The wisdom of God overrules diverse and opposite causes to produce the one desired result and makes both affliction and consolation produce the grateful aroma of faith, love, patience, hope, resignation, joy, and the other fair flowers of the garden. May we know by sweet experience what this means.

❧ EVENING ❧

BEHOLD, I AM LAYING IN ZION A STONE, A CORNERSTONE
CHOSEN AND PRECIOUS. — 1 PETER 2:6

As all the rivers run into the sea, so all delights center in the Lord Jesus. The glances of His eyes outshine the sun: the beauties of His face are fairer than the choicest flowers; no fragrance is like the breath of His mouth. Gems of the mine and pearls from the sea are worthless things when measured by His preciousness. Peter tells us that Jesus is precious, but he did not and could not tell us *how* precious, nor could any of us compute the value of God's unspeakable gift. Words cannot convey the preciousness of the Lord Jesus to His people, nor fully tell how essential He is to their satisfaction and happiness. Believer, have you not found in the occasion of plenty a sore famine if your Lord has been absent? The sun was shining, but Christ had hidden Himself, and all the world was dark to you; or it was night, and since the bright and morning star was gone, no other star could yield you so much as a ray of light. What a howling wilderness is this world without our Lord! If once He hides Himself from us, withered are the flowers of our garden; our pleasant fruits decay; the birds suspend their songs, and a tempest overturns our hopes. All earth's candles cannot make daylight if the Sun of Righteousness be eclipsed. He is the soul of our soul, the light of our light, the life of our life. Dear reader, what would you do in the world without Him when you wake up and look ahead to the day's battle? What would you do at night when you come home jaded and weary if there were no door of fellowship between you and Christ? Blessed be His name, He will not leave us to face the struggle without Him, for Jesus never forsakes His own. Yet, let the thought of what life would be without Him enhance His preciousness.

SAMUEL 13:20

MARCH 2

❧ MORNING ❧

BUT EVERY ONE OF THE ISRAELITES WENT DOWN
TO THE PHILISTINES TO SHARPEN HIS PLOWSHARE,
HIS MATTOCK, HIS AXE, OR HIS SICKLE. — 1 SAMUEL 13:20

We are engaged in a great war with the Philistines of evil. *Every weapon within our reach must be used*. Preaching, teaching, praying, giving—all must be brought into action, and talents that have been thought too mean for service must now be employed. These various tools may all be useful in slaying Philistines; rough tools may deal hard blows, and killing need not be elegantly done, so long as it is done effectually. Each moment of time, in season or out of season; each fragment of ability, educated or untutored; each opportunity, favorable or unfavorable, must be used, for our foes are many and our force but slender.

Most of our tools need sharpening; we need quickness of perception, tact, energy, promptness—in a word, complete adaptation—for the Lord's work. Practical common sense is a very scarce thing among the conductors of Christian enterprises. We might learn from our enemies if we would, and so *make the Philistines sharpen our weapons*. This morning let us note enough to sharpen our zeal during this day by the aid of the Holy Spirit. Witness the energy of some, how they travel over sea and land to make one proselyte—are they to monopolize all the earnestness? Consider what tortures some endure in the service of their idols! Are they alone to exhibit patience and self-sacrifice? Observe the prince of darkness, how persevering in his endeavors, how unabashed in his attempts, how daring in his plans, how thoughtful in his plots, how energetic in all! The devils are united as one man in their infamous rebellion, while we believers in Jesus are divided in our service of God and scarcely ever work with unanimity. O that from Satan's infernal industry we may learn to go about like good Samaritans, seeking whom we may bless!

❧ EVENING ❧

TO ME, THOUGH I AM THE VERY LEAST OF ALL THE SAINTS,
THIS GRACE WAS GIVEN, TO PREACH TO THE GENTILES
THE UNSEARCHABLE RICHES OF CHRIST. — EPHESIANS 3:8

The apostle Paul felt it a great privilege to be allowed to preach the Gospel. He did not look upon his calling as a drudgery, but he entered upon it with intense delight. Although Paul was thankful for his calling, his success in it greatly humbled him. The fuller a ship becomes, the deeper it sinks in the water. Idlers may indulge a fond conceit of their abilities, because they are untried; but the earnest worker soon learns his own weakness. If you seek humility, try hard work; if you would know your nothingness, attempt some great thing for Jesus. If you want to feel how utterly powerless you are apart from the living God, attempt especially the great work of proclaiming the unsearchable riches of Christ, and you will know, as you never knew before, what a weak, unworthy thing you are. Although the apostle thus knew and confessed his weakness, he was never perplexed as to the *subject* of his ministry. From his first sermon to his last, Paul preached Christ, and nothing but Christ. He lifted up the cross and extolled the Son of God who bled on it. Follow his example in all your personal efforts to spread the glad tidings of salvation, and let "Christ and him crucified" be your ever-recurring theme. The Christian should be like those lovely spring flowers that, when the sun is shining, open their golden cups, as if saying, "Fill us with your beams!" But when the sun is hidden behind a cloud, they close their cups and droop their heads. So should the Christian feel the sweet influence of Jesus. Jesus must be his sun, and He must be the flower that yields itself to the Sun of Righteousness. Oh, to speak of Christ alone—this is the subject that is both "seed to the sower and bread to the eater."[1] This is the live coal for the lip of the speaker, and the master-key to the heart of the hearer.

[1] Isaiah 55:10

I HAVE TRIED YOU IN THE FURNACE OF AFFLICTION. — ISAIAH 48:10

Comfort yourself, tried believer, with this thought: God says, "I have *chosen* thee in the furnace of affliction" [KJV]. Does not the Word come like a soft shower, assuaging the fury of the flame? Yea, is it not a protective shield, against which the heat has no power? Let affliction come—God has chosen me. Poverty, you may stride in at my door, but God is in the house already, and He has chosen me. Sickness, you may intrude, but I have balsam ready—God has chosen me. Whatever befalls me in this vale of tears, I know that He has "chosen" me. If, believer, you require still greater comfort, remember *that you have the Son of Man with you in the furnace.* In that silent chamber of yours, there sits by your side One whom you have not seen, but whom you love; and often when you do not know it, He comforts you in your affliction and softens the place of rest. You are in poverty; but in your lovely house the Lord of life and glory is a frequent visitor. He loves to come into these desolate places, that He may visit you. Your friend sticks closely to you. You cannot see Him, but you may feel the pressure of His hands. Do you not hear His voice? Even in the valley of the shadow of death He says, "Fear not, for I am with you; be not dismayed, for I am your God."[1] Remember that noble speech of Caesar: "Fear not, you carry Caesar and all his fortune." Fear not, Christian; Jesus is with you. In all your difficult trials, His presence is both your comfort and safety. He will never leave one whom He has chosen for His own. "Fear not, for I am with you" is His sure word of promise to His chosen ones in the "furnace of affliction." Will you not, then, take hold of Christ and say—

> *Through floods and flames, if Jesus lead,*
> *I'll follow where He goes.*

⚝ EVENING ⚞
HE SAW THE SPIRIT OF GOD DESCENDING LIKE A DOVE. — MATTHEW 3:16

As the Spirit of God descended upon the Lord Jesus, the head, so He also, in measure, descends upon the members of the mystical body. His descent is to us after the same fashion as that in which it fell upon our Lord. There is often a sudden *swiftness* about it; before we are even aware of it, we are impelled onward and heavenward beyond all expectation. Yet there is none of the hurry of earthly haste, for the wings of the dove are as soft as they are swift. *Quietness* seems essential to many spiritual operations; the Lord is in the still small voice, and like the dew, His grace is distilled in silence. The dove has always been the chosen type of *purity*, and the Holy Spirit is holiness itself. Where He comes, everything that is pure and lovely and of good report is made to abound, and sin and uncleanness depart. *Peace* reigns also where the Holy Dove comes with power; He bears the olive branch, which shows that the waters of divine wrath are assuaged. *Gentleness* is a sure result of the Sacred Dove's transforming power: Hearts touched by His benign influence are meek and lowly from that point and forever. *Harmlessness* follows as a matter of course; eagles and ravens may hunt their prey—the turtledove can endure wrong but cannot inflict it. We must be harmless as doves. The dove is an apt picture of *love*; the voice of the turtle is full of affection. And so the soul visited by the blessed Spirit abounds in love to God, in love to the brethren, and in love to sinners, and above all, in love to Jesus. The brooding of the Spirit of God upon the face of the deep first produced *order and life*, and in our hearts He causes and fosters new life and light. Blessed Spirit, as You did rest upon our dear Redeemer, even so rest upon us from this time forward and forever.

[1] Isaiah 41:10

MY GRACE IS SUFFICIENT FOR YOU. — 2 CORINTHIANS 12:9

If none of God's saints were poor and tried, we should not know half so well the consolations of divine grace. When we find the wanderer who has nowhere to lay his head who still can say, "I will trust in the Lord," or when we see the pauper starving on bread and water who still glories in Jesus, when we see the bereaved widow overwhelmed in affliction and yet having faith in Christ—oh, what honor it reflects on the Gospel. God's grace is illustrated and magnified in the poverty and trials of believers. Saints bear up under every discouragement, believing that all things work together for their good, and that out of apparent evils a real blessing shall ultimately spring—that their God will either work a deliverance for them speedily or most assuredly support them in the trouble, as long as He is pleased to keep them in it. This patience of the saints proves the power of divine grace. There is a lighthouse out at sea: It is a calm night—I cannot tell whether the edifice is firm. The tempest must rage about it, and then I shall know whether it will stand. So with the Spirit's work: If it were not on many occasions surrounded with tempestuous waters, we would not know that it was true and strong; if the winds did not blow upon it, we would not know how firm and secure it was. The masterworks of God are those men who stand in the midst of difficulties steadfast, unmovable—

> Calm mid the bewildering cry,
> Confident of victory.

The one who would glorify his God must be prepared to meet with many trials. No one can be illustrious before the Lord unless his conflicts are many. If, then, yours is a much-tried path, rejoice in it, because you will be better able to display the all-sufficient grace of God. As for His failing you, never dream of it—hate the thought. The God who has been sufficient until now should be trusted to the end.

✎ EVENING ✎

THEY FEAST ON THE ABUNDANCE OF YOUR HOUSE. — PSALM 36:8

Sheba's queen was amazed at the sumptuousness of Solomon's table. She lost all heart when she saw the provision of a single day; and she marveled equally at the company of servants who enjoyed the king's feast. But what is this in comparison to the abundance of the God of grace? Ten thousand thousand of His people are daily fed; hungry and thirsty, they bring large appetites with them to the banquet, but not one of them returns unsatisfied; there is enough for each, enough for all, enough forevermore. Although the company that eats at Jehovah's table is as countless as the stars of heaven, yet each one has his own portion. Think how much grace one saint requires, so much that nothing but the Infinite could supply him for one day; and yet the Lord spreads His table not for one, but for many saints; not for one day, but for many years; not for many years only, but for generation after generation. Consider the full feasting spoken of in the text; the guests at mercy's banquet are satisfied—more, abundantly satisfied, and not with ordinary fare, but with the peculiar abundance of God's own house; and such feasting is guaranteed by a faithful promise to all those children of men who put their trust under the shadow of Jehovah's wings. I once thought that if I could just get the leftovers at God's back door of grace I would be satisfied, like the woman who said, "The dogs eat the crumbs that fall from their masters' table." But no child of God is ever served with scraps and leftovers; like Mephibosheth, they all eat from the King's own table. In matters of grace, we all have Benjamin's portion—we all have ten times more than we could have expected; and though our necessities are great, yet are we often amazed at the marvelous fullness of grace that God gives us richly to enjoy.

LET US NOT SLEEP, AS OTHERS DO. — 1 THESSALONIANS 5:6

There are many ways of encouraging the Christian to stay awake. First, let me strongly advise Christians to talk to each other about the ways of the Lord. In Bunyan's *Pilgrim's Progress*, Christian and Hopeful, on their journey to the Celestial City, said to themselves, "To prevent drowsiness in this place, let us fall into good discourse." Christian inquired, "Brother, where shall we begin?" And Hopeful answered, "Where God began with us." Then Christian sang this song:

> When saints do sleepy grow, let them come hither,
> And hear how these two pilgrims talk together;
> Yea, let them learn of them, in any wise,
> Thus to keep open their drowsy slumb'ring eyes.
> Saints' fellowship, if it be managed well,
> Keeps them awake, and that in spite of hell.

Christians who isolate themselves and walk alone are very liable to grow drowsy. Keep Christian company, and you will be kept wakeful by it, and refreshed and encouraged to make quicker progress on the road to heaven. But as you enjoy fellowship with others in the ways of God, *take care that the theme of your conversation is the Lord Jesus.* Let the eye of faith be constantly looking to Him; let your heart be full of Him; let your lips speak of His worth. Friend, live near to the cross, and you will not sleep. *Work hard to impress yourself with a deep sense of the value of the place to which you are going.* If you remember that you are going to heaven, you will not sleep on the road. If you think that hell is behind you, and the devil pursuing you, you will not loiter. Would the innocent sleep with the enemy in pursuit and the city of refuge before him? Christian, will you sleep while the pearly gates are open—the songs of angels waiting for you to join them—a crown of gold ready for your brow? Ah, no! In holy fellowship continue to watch and pray, that you enter not into temptation.

❧ EVENING ❧

SAY TO MY SOUL, "I AM YOUR SALVATION!" — PSALM 35:3

What does this sweet prayer teach me? It shall be my evening's petition; but first let it grant me an instructive meditation. The text informs me first of all that *David had his doubts;* for why should he pray, "Say to my soul, 'I am your salvation'" if he were not sometimes exercised with doubts and fears? Let me, then, be encouraged that I am not the only saint who has to face such faltering faith. If David doubted, I need not conclude that I am not a Christian because I have doubts. The text reminds me that *David was not content while he had doubts and fears,* but he proceeded directly to the mercy-seat to pray for assurance, for he valued it as much as gold. I too must work to foster a continual sense of being accepted in the Beloved and must have no joy when His love is not shed abroad in my soul. When my Bridegroom is gone, my soul must long for Him. I learn also that *David knew where to obtain full assurance.* He went to his God in prayer, crying, "Say to my soul, 'I am your salvation.'" I need to be often alone with God if I am to enjoy a clear sense of Jesus' love. When my prayers cease, my eye of faith will grow dim. Much in prayer, much in heaven; slow in prayer, slow in progress. I notice that *David would not be satisfied unless his assurance had a divine source.* "Say to my soul . . ." Lord, speak to me! Nothing less than a divine testimony in the soul will ever content the true Christian. Moreover, David could not rest unless his assurance had *a vivid personality* about it. "Say to *my* soul, 'I am *your* salvation.'" Lord, if You said this to all the saints, it means little unless You should say it to me. Lord, I have sinned; I do not deserve Your smile; I scarcely dare to ask for it. But oh, say to *my* soul, even to *my* soul, "I am *your* salvation." Let me have a present, personal, infallible, indisputable sense that I am Yours and that You are mine.

❦ MORNING ❧

YOU MUST BE BORN AGAIN. — JOHN 3:7

Regeneration is a subject that lies at the very basis of salvation, and we should be very diligent to make sure that we really are "born again," for there are many who imagine they are, who are not. Be assured that to be *called* a Christian is not the same nature as *being* a Christian, and that being born in a Christian country and being recognized as professing the Christian religion is of no significance at all unless there be something more added to it. Being "born again" is a matter so *mysterious* that human words cannot describe it. "The wind blows where it wishes, and you hear its sound, but you do not know where it comes from or where it is goes. So it is with everyone who is born of the Spirit." Nevertheless, it is a change that is *known and felt*—known by works of holiness and felt by a gracious experience. This great work is *supernatural*. It is not an operation that a man performs for himself: A new principle is infused that works in the heart, renews the soul, and affects his whole life. It is not a change of my name, but a renewal of my nature, so that I am not the man I used to be, but a new man in Christ Jesus. To wash and dress a corpse is a far different thing from making it alive: Man can do the one—God alone can do the other. If you have, then, been "born again," your declaration will be, "O Lord Jesus, the everlasting Father, You are my spiritual Parent; if Your Spirit had not breathed into me the breath of a new, holy, and spiritual life, I would still be 'dead in trespasses and sins.' My heavenly life is wholly derived from You; to You I ascribe it. 'My life is hidden with Christ in God.' It is no longer I who live, but Christ who lives in me." May the Lord grant us assurance on this vital point, for to be unregenerate is to be unsaved, unpardoned, without God, and without hope.

❦ EVENING ❧

BEFORE DESTRUCTION A MAN'S HEART IS HAUGHTY. — PROVERBS 18:12

It is an old and common saying that "coming events cast their shadows before them." The wise man teaches us that a haughty heart is the precursor of evil. Pride is as clearly the sign of destruction as the change of mercury in the barometer is the sign of rain, and far more infallibly so than that. When men have ridden the high horse, destruction has always overtaken them. Let David's aching heart show that there is an eclipse of a man's glory when he dotes upon his own greatness (2 Samuel 24:10). Observe Nebuchadnezzar, the mighty builder of Babylon, creeping on the earth, devouring grass like a beast, his nails grown like the bird's claws, and his hair like eagle's feathers (Daniel 4:33). Pride made the boaster a beast, as once before it made an angel a devil. God hates high looks and never fails to bring them down. All the arrows of God are aimed at proud hearts. O Christian, is your heart haughty this evening? For pride can get into the Christian's heart as well as into the sinner's; it can delude him into dreaming that he is "rich, I have prospered, and I need nothing."[1] Are you glorying in your graces or your talents? Are you proud of yourself and your spiritual experiences? Be careful, reader—there is a destruction coming to you also. Your flaunting poppies of self-conceit will be pulled up by the roots, your mushrooming graces will wither in the burning heat, and your self-sufficiency will become as straw for the dunghill. If we forget to live at the foot of the cross in deepest lowliness of spirit, God will not forget to discipline us for our good. A destruction will come to you, O unduly exalted believer, the destruction of your joys and of your comforts, although there can be no destruction of your soul. Therefore, "Let the one who boasts, boast in the Lord."[2]

[1] Revelation 3:17 [2] 1 Corinthians 1:31

❧ MORNING ❧
HAVE FAITH IN GOD. — MARK 11:22

Faith gives feet to the soul, enabling it to march along the road of the commandments. Love can make the feet move more swiftly; but it is faith that carries the soul. Faith is the oil enabling the wheels of holy devotion and of practical holiness to move well; and without faith the wheels are taken from the chariot, and we drag ourselves along. With faith I can do all things; without faith I will be missing both the inclination and the power to do anything in the service of God. If you want to find the men who serve God best, you must look for men of faith. Little faith will save a man, but little faith cannot do great things for God. Poor Little-faith could not have fought "Apollyon"; it needed "Christian" to do that. Poor Little-faith could not have slain "Giant Despair"; it required "Great-heart's" arm to knock that monster down. Little faith will go to heaven most certainly, but it often has to hide itself in a nutshell, and it frequently loses all but its jewels. Little-faith says, "It is a rough road, beset with sharp thorns, and full of dangers; I am afraid to go;" but Great-faith remembers the promise, "Your bars shall be iron and bronze, and as your days, so shall your strength be";[1] and so she boldly ventures. Little-faith stands despondently, mingling her tears with the flood; but Great-faith sings, "When you pass through the waters, I will be with you; and through the rivers, they shall not overwhelm you,"[2] and she crosses the stream at once. Do you want to be comfortable and happy? To enjoy the journey do you desire cheerfulness rather than gloom? Then "have faith in God." If you love darkness and are satisfied to dwell in gloom and misery, then be content with little faith; but if you love the sunshine and would sing songs of rejoicing, covet earnestly this best gift, great faith.

❧ EVENING ❧
IT IS BETTER TO TAKE REFUGE IN THE LORD
THAN TO TRUST IN MAN. — PSALM 118:8

No doubt the reader has been tempted to rely upon the things that are seen instead of resting alone upon the invisible God. Christians often look to man for help and advice, and so spoil the noble simplicity of their reliance upon God. Does this evening's passage meet the eye of a child of God who is filled with anxiety? Then let us reason with you. You trust in Jesus, and only in Jesus, for your salvation; then why are you troubled? *"Because of my great care."* Is it not written, "Cast your burden upon the Lord"? "Do not be anxious about anything, but in everything by prayer and supplication with thanksgiving let your requests be made known to God."[3] Can you trust God for your physical needs? *"Ah! I wish I could."* If you cannot trust God with the physical, how dare you trust Him with the spiritual? Can you trust Him for your soul's redemption, and yet not rely upon Him for a few lesser mercies? Is God not enough for your need, or is His all-sufficiency too narrow for your wants? Do you need another to watch for you when you have Him who sees every secret thing? Is His heart faint? Is His arm weary? If so, seek another God; but if He is infinite, omnipotent, faithful, true, and all-wise, why do you run around seeking another confidence? Why do you scour the earth to find another foundation when this is strong enough to bear all the weight that you can ever build on it? Christian, do not mix your wine with water; do not tarnish the gold of faith with the dross of human confidence. Wait only upon God, and let your expectation be from Him. Do not covet Jonah's gourd but rest in Jonah's God. Let the sandy, shaky foundations be the choice of fools; but you, like one who sees the approaching storm, build for yourself an abiding place upon the Rock of Ages.

[1] Deuteronomy 33:25 [2] Isaiah 43:2 [3] Philippians 4:6

&* MORNING &*
THROUGH MANY TRIBULATIONS WE MUST ENTER
THE KINGDOM OF GOD. — ACTS 14:22

God's people have their trials. It was never God's plan, when He chose His people, that they should be untested. They were chosen in the furnace of affliction; they were never chosen for worldly peace and earthly joy. Freedom from sickness and the pains of mortality was never promised to them; but when their Lord drew up the charter of privileges, He included chastisements among the things to which they should inevitably be heirs. Trials are a part of our experience; they were predestinated for us in Christ's last legacy. As surely as the stars are fashioned by His hands, and their orbits fixed by Him, so surely are our trials allotted to us. He has ordained their season and their place, their intensity and the effect they shall have upon us. Good men must never expect to escape troubles; if they do, they will be disappointed, for none of their predecessors have been without them. Consider the patience of Job; remember Abraham, for he had his trials, and facing them with faith, he became the father of the faithful. Review the biographies of all the patriarchs, prophets, apostles, and martyrs, and you will find that each of those whom God made vessels of mercy were made to pass through the fire of affliction. God has ordained that the cross of trouble should be engraved on every vessel of mercy, as the royal insignia distinguishing the King's vessels of honor. But even though tribulation is the path of God's children, they have the comfort of knowing that their Master has walked it before them. They have His presence and sympathy to cheer them, His grace to support them, and His example to teach them how to endure; and when they reach "the kingdom," it will more than make amends for the "many tribulations" through which they passed to enter it.

&* EVENING &*
SHE CALLED HIS NAME BEN-ONI [SON OF SORROW];
BUT HIS FATHER CALLED HIM BENJAMIN
[SON OF MY RIGHT HAND]. — GENESIS 35:18

To every matter there is a bright as well as a dark side. Rachel was overwhelmed with the sorrow of her own travail and death; Jacob, while mourning the loss of his wife, could see the mercy of the child's birth. It is good for us if, while the flesh mourns over trials, our faith triumphs in divine faithfulness. Samson's lion yielded honey, and so will our adversities, if rightly considered. The stormy sea feeds multitudes with its fish; the wild wood blooms with beautiful flowers; the stormy wind sweeps away disease, and the biting frost loosens the soil. Dark clouds distill bright drops, and black earth grows lovely flowers. A vein of good is to be found in every mine of evil. Sad hearts have peculiar skill in discovering the most disadvantageous point of view from which to gaze upon a trial; if there were only one swamp in the world, they would soon be up to their necks in it, and if there were only one lion in the desert they would hear it roar. About us all there is a tinge of this wretched folly, and we are apt, at times, like Jacob, to cry, "All these things are against me." Faith's way of walking is to cast all care upon the Lord, and then to anticipate good results from the worst calamities. Like Gideon's men, she does not fret over the broken pitcher but rejoices that the lamp shines with even more brilliance. Out of the rough oyster-shell of difficulty she extracts the rare pearl of honor, and from the deep ocean-caves of distress she discovers the priceless coral of experience. When her flood of prosperity ebbs, she finds treasures hidden in the sands; and when her sun of delight goes down, she turns her telescope of hope to the starry promises of heaven. When death itself appears, faith points to the light of resurrection beyond the grave, thus making our dying Ben-oni to be our living Benjamin.

The superlative beauty of Jesus is all-attracting; it is not so much to be admired as to be loved. He is more than pleasant and fair—He is lovely. Surely the people of God can fully justify the use of this golden word, for He is the object of their warmest love, a love founded on the intrinsic excellence of His person, the complete perfection of His glory. Look, the disciples of Jesus know the sweetness of his voice and are able to say, "Do not His words cause our hearts to burn within us as He talks with us on the road?" You worshipers of Immanuel, look up to His head of much fine gold, and tell me, are not His thoughts precious unto you? Is not your adoration sweetened with affection as you humbly bow before that face that is as excellent as the cedars of Lebanon? Is there not a beauty in His every feature, and is not His whole person fragrant with such a savor of His goodness that we love Him? Is there one aspect of His being that is not attractive—one facet of His person that is not a blessing to our souls and a strong cord to bind our hearts? Our love is not as a seal set upon His heart of love alone; it is also fastened upon His arm of power, nor is there a single part of Him upon which it does not fix itself. We worship His whole person with the sweet fragrance of our fervent love. We would imitate His whole life and character. All other beings are incomplete; in Him there is all perfection. Even the best of His favored saints have had blots upon their garments and wrinkles upon their brows; He is nothing but loveliness. All earthly suns have their spots: This fair world has its wilderness; we cannot love the whole of the most lovely thing. But Christ Jesus is gold without alloy, light without darkness, glory without cloud. Yes, "he is *altogether* desirable."

❦ EVENING ❧

Communion with Christ is a certain cure for every ill. Whether it be the woodworm of sadness or the smothering impact of earthly treasure, close fellowship with the Lord Jesus will take bitterness from the one and excess from the other. Live near to Jesus, Christian, and it is a matter of secondary importance whether you live on the mountain of honor or in the valley of humiliation. Living near to Jesus, you are covered with the wings of God, and underneath you are the everlasting arms. Let nothing keep you from that hallowed communion that is the unique privilege of a life hidden in Christ. Do not be content with the occasional meeting, but always seek to retain His company, for only in His presence will you find either comfort or safety. Jesus should not be for us a friend who calls us now and then, but one with whom we are in constant touch. You have a difficult road before you: Make sure, pilgrim, that you do not go without your guide. You have to pass through the fiery furnace; do not enter unless, like Shadrach, Meshach, and Abednego, you have the Son of God to be your companion. You have to storm the walls of your corrupt heart: Do not attempt it until, like Joshua, you have seen the Captain of the Lord's host, with His sword drawn in His hand. When you meet with many temptations, do not rest upon the arm of flesh. In every case, in every condition, you will need Jesus, but most of all when the iron gates of death shall open to you. Keep close to the Captain of your salvation, lean upon His strength, ask Him to refresh you by His Spirit, and you will stand before Him at the end, without spot or blemish and at peace. Seeing you have lived with Him, and lived in Him here, you will abide with Him forever.

I SAID IN MY PROSPERITY, "I SHALL NEVER BE MOVED." — PSALM 30:6

Give a man wealth; let his ships bring home continually rich treasure; let the winds and waves appear to be his servants to carry his vessels across the bosom of the mighty deep; let his fields produce abundantly; let the weather be kind to his crops; let uninterrupted success attend him; let him stand among men as a successful merchant; let him enjoy continued health; allow him with braced nerve and brilliant eye to march through the world and live happily; give him the buoyant spirit; let him have a song perpetually on his lips; let his eye be ever sparkling with joy—and the inevitable consequence of such an easy life to any man, even though he may be the best Christian who ever breathed, will be *presumption*. Even David said, "I shall never be moved"; and we are not better than David, nor half so good. Brother, beware of the smooth places of the way; if you are treading them, or if the way be rough, thank God for it. If God should always rock us in the cradle of prosperity, if we were always enjoying good fortune, and there were no clouds in the sky, and no bitter drops in the wine of this life, we would become intoxicated with pleasure, and we would dream that we were standing—and stand we should, but it would be upon a pinnacle; like the man asleep upon the mast, each moment we would be in jeopardy.

We bless God, then, for our afflictions; we thank Him for our changes; we extol His name for losses of property; for we feel that if He had not chastened us in this way, we might have become too secure. Continued worldly prosperity is a fiery trial.

Afflictions, though they seem severe,
In mercy oft are sent.

❧ EVENING ☙

MAN . . . IS FEW OF DAYS AND FULL OF TROUBLE. — JOB 14:1

It may be of great service to us, before we fall asleep, to remember this mournful fact, for it may lead us to hold lightly to earthly things. There is nothing very pleasant in the recollection that we are not above the arrows of adversity, but it may humble us and prevent us from boasting like the psalmist that out mountain stands firm, that we shall never be moved. It may prevent us from making our roots too deep in this soil from which we are so soon to be transplanted into the heavenly garden. Let us keep in mind the frail tenure upon which we hold our *temporal mercies*. If we remember that all the trees of earth are marked for the woodman's axe, we will not be so ready to build our nests in them. We should love, but we should love with the love that expects death, and that reckons upon separations. Our *dear relations* are simply loaned to us, and the hour when we must return them to the lender's hand may be sooner than we think. This is also true of our *worldly goods*. Do not riches take to themselves wings and fly away? Our *health* is equally precarious. Frail flowers of the field, we must not reckon upon blooming forever. There is a time appointed for weakness and sickness, when we will have to glorify God by suffering and not by earnest activity. There is no single point in which we can hope to escape from the sharp arrows of affliction; out of our few days there is not one secure from sorrow. Man's life is a cask full of bitter wine; he who looks for joy in it would be better looking for honey in a salty ocean. Beloved reader, do not set your affections upon things of earth, but seek those things that are above, for *here* the moth devours, and the thief steals, but *there* all joys are perpetual and eternal. The path of trouble is the way home. Lord, make this thought a pillow for many a weary head!

... SIN ... SINFUL BEYOND MEASURE. — ROMANS 7:13

Beware of thinking lightly of sin. At the time of conversion, the conscience is so tender that we are afraid of the slightest sin. Young converts have a holy timidity, a godly fear of offending God. But sadly very soon the fine bloom upon these first ripe fruits is removed by the rough handling of the surrounding world: The sensitive plant of young piety turns into a willow in later life, too pliable, too easily yielding. It is sadly true that even a Christian may grow by degrees so callous that the sin that once startled him does not alarm him in the least. By degrees men get familiar with sin. The ear in which the cannon has been booming will not notice slight sounds. At first a little sin startles us; but soon we say, "Is it not a little one?" Then there comes another, larger, and then another, until by degrees we begin to regard sin as but a small matter; and this is followed by an unholy presumption: "We have not fallen into open sin. True, we tripped a little, but we stood upright for the most part. We may have uttered one unholy word, but as for most of our conversation, it has been consistent." So we toy with sin; we throw a cloak over it; we call it by dainty names. Christian, beware of thinking lightly of sin. Take heed in case you fall little by little. Sin a *little* thing? Is it not a poison? Who knows its deadliness? Sin a little thing? Do not the little foxes spoil the grapes? Doesn't the tiny coral insect build a rock that wrecks a navy? Do not little strokes fell lofty oaks? Will not continual drippings wear away stones? Sin a little thing? It put a crown of thorns on Jesus' head and pierced His heart! It made Him suffer anguish, bitterness, and woe. If you could weigh the least sin in the scales of eternity, you would run from it as from a serpent and abhor the slightest appearance of evil. Look upon all sin as that which crucified the Savior, and you will see it to be "sinful beyond measure."

❧ EVENING ☙
YOU SHALL BE CALLED SOUGHT OUT. — ISAIAH 62:12

The surpassing grace of God is seen very clearly in that we were not only sought, but sought *out*. Men *seek* for a thing that is lost upon the floor of the house, but in such a case there is only seeking, not seeking out. The loss is more perplexing and the search more persevering when a thing is sought *out*. We were mingled with the mire: We were as when some precious piece of gold falls into the sewer, and men gather out and carefully inspect a mass of abominable filth, and continue to stir and rake, and search among the heap until the treasure is found. Or, to use another figure, we were lost in a maze; we wandered here and there, and when mercy came after us with the Gospel, it did not find us at the first coming—it had to search for us and seek us out; for we as lost sheep were so desperately lost and had wandered into such a strange country that it did not seem possible that even the Good Shepherd could track our devious roamings. Glory be to unconquerable grace, we were *sought out*! No darkness could hide us, no filthiness could conceal us; we were found and brought home. Glory be to infinite love—God the Holy Spirit restored us!

If the lives of some of God's people could be written, they would fill us with holy astonishment. Strange and marvelous are the ways that God used in their case to find His own. Blessed be His name, He never relinquishes the search until the chosen are sought out effectually. They are not a people sought today and cast away tomorrow. Almightiness and wisdom combined will make no failures; they shall be called, "*Sought Out!*" That any should be sought out is matchless grace, but that *we* should be sought out is grace beyond degree! We can find no reason for it but God's own sovereign love and can only lift up our heart in wonder and praise the Lord that this night we wear the name of "*Sought Out*."

YOU SHALL LOVE YOUR NEIGHBOR. — MATTHEW 5:43

Love your neighbor." Perhaps he rolls in riches, and you are poor and living in your humble dwelling next-door to his mansion. Every day you see his estates, his fine clothes, and his extravagant parties. God has given him these gifts; covet not his wealth, and think no hard thoughts concerning him. Be content with what you have, if you cannot better it, but do not look upon your neighbor and wish that he was like you. Love him, and then you will not envy him.

Perhaps, on the other hand, you are rich, and the poor live nearby. Do not scorn to call them neighbors. Admit that you are bound to love them. The world calls them your inferiors. In what way are they inferior? They are far more your equals than your inferiors, for "He made from one man every nation of mankind to live on all the face of the earth."[1] Your clothes are better than theirs, but you are in no way better than them. They are men, and what are you more than that? Pay attention that you love your neighbor even though he be in rags or sunken in the depths of poverty.

But perhaps you say, "I cannot love my neighbors because no matter what I do for them they respond with ingratitude and contempt." All the more reason for the heroism of love. Would you be a featherbed warrior instead of bearing the rough fight of love? He who dares the most shall win the most; and if the path of love is rough, tread it boldly, still loving your neighbors through thick and thin. Heap coals of fire on their heads, and if they are hard to please, do not seek to please *them*, but to please *your Master*; and remember if *they* spurn your love, your Master has not spurned it, and your deed is as acceptable to Him as if it had been acceptable to them. Love your neighbor, for in so doing you are following the footsteps of Christ.

✎ EVENING ✎

TO WHOM DO YOU BELONG? — 1 SAMUEL 30:13

In the life of faith, neutrality is not an option. We are either ranked under the banner of the Lord Jesus, to serve and fight His battles, or we are slaves of the dark prince, Satan. "To whom do you belong?"

Reader, let me assist you in your response. *Have you been "born again"*? If you have, you belong to Christ; but without the new birth you cannot be His. *In whom do you trust?* For those who believe in Jesus are the sons of God. *Whose work are you doing?* You are sure to serve your master, for he whom you serve is thereby owned to be your lord. *What company do you keep?* If you belong to Jesus, you will keep company with those who wear the uniform of the cross. "Birds of a feather flock together." *What is your conversation?* Is it heavenly or is it earthly? *What have you learned from your Master?* For servants learn a great deal from the masters to whom they are apprenticed. If you have served your time with Jesus, it will be said of you, as it was of Peter and John, "they recognized that they had been with Jesus."[2]

We press the question, "To whom do you belong?" Answer honestly before you fall asleep for the night. If you are not Christ's, you are in a hard service—*run away from your cruel master*! Enter into the service of the Lord of Love, and you will enjoy a life of blessedness. If you *are* Christ's, let me advise you to do four things. You belong to Jesus—*obey Him*; let His word be your law; let His wish be your will. You belong to the Beloved; then *love Him*; let your heart embrace Him; let your whole soul be filled with Him. You belong to the Son of God; then *trust him*; rest on nothing or no one but on Him. You belong to the King of kings; then *be decided for Him*. Thus even without being marked with a sign everyone will know to whom you belong.

[1] Acts 17:26 [2] Acts 4:14

WHY ARE WE SITTING HERE UNTIL WE DIE? — 2 KINGS 7:3

Dear reader, this little book was mainly intended for the edification of believers, but if you are still unsaved, we are concerned for you, and we would like to say something that would be helpful to you. Open your Bible, and read this story of the lepers, and note their position, which was similar to yours. If you remain where you are, you must perish; if you go to Jesus you will live. "Nothing ventured, nothing gained" is the old proverb, and in your case the venture is not great. If you sit still in sullen despair, no one can pity you when your ruin comes; but if you were to die seeking mercy, if such a thing were possible, you would be the object of universal sympathy. None escape who refuse to look to Jesus; but you know that others are saved who believe in Him, for certain of your own friends and neighbors have received mercy. So why not you? Why not taste and see that the Lord is merciful? To perish is so awful that if you could only clutch at a straw, the instinct of self-preservation should lead you to stretch out your hand. We want to assure you, as from the Lord, that if you seek Him you will find Him. Jesus casts out none who come unto Him. You shall not perish if you trust Him; on the contrary, you shall find treasure far richer than what the poor lepers gathered in Syria's deserted camp. May the Holy Spirit embolden you to go at once, and you shall not believe in vain. Then when you are saved, share the good news with others. Do not hold back; tell your friends at church first, and join with them in fellowship; let the watchman of the city, the pastor, be informed of your discovery, and then proclaim the good news in every place. May the Lord God save you before the sun goes down this day.

❧ EVENING ❧

SO HE PUT OUT HIS HAND AND TOOK HER AND
BROUGHT HER INTO THE ARK WITH HIM. — GENESIS 8:9

Tired out by her wanderings, the dove finally returns to the ark as her only resting place. How heavily she flies—she will drop—she will never reach the ark! But she struggles on. Noah has been looking out for his dove all day long and is ready to receive her. She has just enough strength to reach the edge of the ark; she can hardly alight upon it and is ready to drop when Noah puts forth his hand and pulls her in unto him. Note that: "*brought her into the ark with him.*" She did not fly right in herself, because she was too fearful or too weary to do so. She flew as far as she could, and then he put out his hand and pulled her in with him. This act of mercy was shown to the wandering dove, and she was not scolded for her wanderings. Just as she was, she was pulled into the ark. So you, seeking sinner, with all your sin, will be received. "Only return"—those are God's two gracious words—"only return." What! Nothing else? No; "only return." She had no olive branch in her mouth this time, nothing at all but just herself and her wanderings; but it is "only return," and she does return, and Noah pulls her in. Wanderer, fly, fainting one; fly, dove, as you are. Though you imagine yourself to be as black as the raven with the filth of sin, come back to the Savior. Every moment you delay increases your misery; your attempts to plume yourself and make yourself fit for Jesus are all vanity. Come to Him just as you are. If you are running and hiding from God, then return as a backslider with all your backslidings about you. Return, return, return! Jesus is waiting for you! He will stretch forth His hand and pull you in—in to Himself, your heart's true home.

⤫ MORNING ⤫

It is a curious fact that there is such a thing as being proud of grace. A man says, "I have great faith—I shall not fall; poor little faith may, but I never shall." "I have fervent love," says another. "I can stand; there is no danger of my going astray." He who boasts of grace has little grace to boast of. Some who do this imagine that their graces can keep them, knowing not that the stream must flow constantly from the fountainhead or else the stream will soon be dry. If a continuous supply of oil does not come to the lamp, even though it may burn brightly today, it will smoke tomorrow, and noxious will be its scent. Pay attention that you do not glory in your graces, but let all your glorying and confidence be in Christ and His strength, for only in this way can you be kept from falling. Be much more diligent in prayer. Spend longer time in holy adoration. Read the Scriptures more earnestly and constantly. Watch your lives more carefully. Live nearer to God. Take the best examples for your pattern. Let your conversation be full of heaven. Let your hearts be perfumed with affection for men's souls. Live in such a way that men may recognize that you have been with Jesus and have learned of Him; and when that happy day shall come, when He whom you love shall say, "Come up higher," may it be your happiness to hear Him say, "You have fought the good fight, you have finished the race, and henceforth there is laid up for you the crown of righteousness that doesn't fade." Keep on, Christian, with care and caution! Go on, with holy fear and trembling! On, with faith and confidence in Jesus alone, and let your constant petition be, "Uphold me according to Your promise."[1] He alone is able "to keep you from stumbling and to present you blameless before the presence of his glory with great joy."[2]

⤫ EVENING ⤫

Fellow-pilgrim, do not say in your heart, "I will go here and there, and I will not sin," for you are never so out of danger of sinning as to boast of security. The road is very muddy; it will be hard to pick your path so as not to soil your garments. This is a dirty world, and you will need to stay alert if you are to keep your hands clean. There is a robber at every turn of the road to rob you of your jewels; there is a temptation in every mercy; there is a snare in every joy; and if you ever reach heaven, it will be a miracle of divine grace to be ascribed entirely to your Father's power. Be on your guard. When a man carries fireworks in his hand, he should be careful that he does not go near a candle; and you too must take care that you do not succumb to temptation. Even your everyday activities are sharp-edged tools; you must mind how you handle them. There is nothing in this world to foster a Christian's piety, but everything to destroy it. How concerned you should be to look up to God, that *He* may keep you! Your prayer should be, "Hold me up, and I shall be safe." Having prayed, you must also watch, guarding every thought, word, and action, with holy jealousy. Do not expose yourselves unnecessarily; but if called to exposure, if you are called to go where the darts are flying, never venture forth without your shield; for if once the devil finds you without your armor, he will rejoice that his hour of triumph is come and will soon make you fall down wounded by his arrows. Although you cannot be killed, you may be wounded. Be sober-minded; be watchful—danger may befall you at a time when everything seems to be secure. Therefore, pay attention, stay alert, watch and pray. No man ever fell into error through being too watchful. May the Holy Spirit guide us in all our ways, so they shall always please the Lord.

[1] Psalm 119:116 [2] Jude 24

❧ MORNING ❧
BE STRENGTHENED BY THE GRACE THAT IS IN
CHRIST JESUS. — 2 TIMOTHY 2:1

Christ has grace without measure in Himself, but He has not retained it for Himself. As the reservoir empties itself into the pipes, so Christ has emptied out His grace for His people. "From His fullness we have all received, grace upon grace."[1] He seems only to have all this in order to dispense to us. He stands like the fountain, always flowing, but only running in order to supply the empty pitchers and the thirsty lips that draw near to it. Like a tree, He bears sweet fruit, not to hang on branches, but to be gathered by those who need it. Grace, whether its work be to pardon, to cleanse, to preserve, to strengthen, to enlighten, to quicken, or to restore, is ever to be had from Him freely and without price; nor is there one form of the work of grace that He has not bestowed upon His people. As the blood of the body, though flowing from the heart, belongs equally to every member, so the influences of grace are the inheritance of every saint united to the Lamb; and herein there is a sweet communion between Christ and His church, inasmuch as they both receive the same grace. Christ is the head upon which the oil is first poured; but the same oil runs to the very skirts of the garments, so that the meanest saint has an unction of the same costly moisture as that which fell upon the head. This is true communion when the sap of grace flows from the stem to the branch, and when it is perceived that the stem itself is sustained by the very nourishment that feeds the branch. As we day by day receive grace from Jesus, and more constantly recognize it as coming from Him, we shall behold Him in communion with us and enjoy the joy of communion with Him. Let us make daily use of our riches and constantly come to Him as our own covenant Lord, taking from Him the supply of all we need with as much boldness as men take money from their own wallet.

❧ EVENING ❧
. . . HE DID WITH ALL HIS HEART, AND PROSPERED. — 2 CHRONICLES 31:21

This is no unusual occurrence; it is the general rule of the moral universe that the prosperous are those who do their work with all their hearts, while others are almost certain to fail when they go about their business halfheartedly. God does not give harvests to lazy men except harvests of thistles, nor is He pleased to send wealth to those who will not dig in the field to find its hidden treasure. It is universally confessed that if a man would prosper, he must be diligent in business. It is the same in the matter of faith as it is in other things. If you would prosper in your work for Jesus, let it be *heart* work, and let it be done with all your heart. Put as much force, energy, heartiness, and earnestness into faith as ever you do into business, for it deserves far more. The Holy Spirit helps our weaknesses, but He does not encourage our laziness; He loves active believers. Who are the most useful men in the Christian church? The men who do what they undertake for God *with all their hearts*. Who are the most successful Sunday school teachers? The most talented? No. The most zealous; those whose hearts are on fire—they are the ones who see their Lord riding forth prosperously in the majesty of His salvation. Wholeheartedness shows itself in *perseverance*; there may be failure at first, but the earnest worker will say, "It is the Lord's work, and it must be done; my Lord has called me to do it, and in His strength I will accomplish it." Christian, are you serving your Master with all your heart? Remember the earnestness of Jesus! Think what heart-work was His! He could say, "*Zeal for Your house has consumed me.*" When He sweat great drops of blood, it was no light burden He had to carry upon those blessed shoulders; and when He poured out His heart, it was no weak effort He was making for the salvation of His people. Was Jesus in earnest, and we are lukewarm?

[1] John 1:16

I AM A SOJOURNER WITH YOU. — PSALM 39:12

Yes, O Lord, *with* You, but not *to* You. All my natural alienation from You, Your grace has effectually removed; and now, in fellowship with Yourself, I walk through this sinful world as a pilgrim in a foreign country. You are a stranger in Your own world. Man forgets You, dishonors You, sets up new laws and alien customs, and knows You not. When Your dear Son came unto His own, His own received Him not. He was in the world, and the world was made by Him, and the world did not recognize Him. There was never a foreigner who stood out from the inhabitants of any country as much as your beloved Son among His mother's brethren. It is no marvel, then, if I who live the life of Jesus should be unknown and a stranger here below. Lord, I would not be a citizen where Jesus was an alien. His pierced hand has loosened the cords that once bound my soul to earth, and now I find myself a stranger in the land. My speech seems to these pagans among whom I dwell a strange tongue; my manners are singular, and my actions are outlandish. A prince would be more at home in the ghetto than I could ever be in the haunts of sinners. But here is the sweetness of my circumstance: I am a stranger *with You*. You are my fellow-sufferer, my fellow-pilgrim. Oh, what joy to wander in such blessed company! My heart burns within me on the journey when You speak to me, and though I am a traveler, I am far more blessed than those who sit on thrones, and far more at home than those who live in their comfortable homes.

> *To me remains nor place, nor time:*
> *My country is in every clime;*
> *I can be calm and free from care*
> *On any shore, since God is there.*
>
> *While place we seek, or place we shun,*
> *The soul finds happiness in none:*
> *But with a God to guide our way,*
> *'Tis equal joy to go or stay.*

❧ EVENING ❧

KEEP BACK YOUR SERVANT ALSO FROM PRESUMPTUOUS SINS. — PSALM 19:13

Such was the prayer of the *"man after God's own heart."* Did holy David need to pray like this? How needful, then, such a prayer must be for us babes in grace! It is as if he said, "Keep me back, or I shall rush headlong over the precipice of sin." Our evil nature, like an ill-tempered horse, is apt to run away. May the grace of God put the bridle upon it and hold it in, that it rush not into mischief. What would the best of us do if it were not for the checks that the Lord sets upon us both in providence and in grace! The psalmist's prayer is directed against the worst form of sin—that which is done with deliberation and willfulness. Even the holiest need to be "kept back" from the vilest transgressions. It is a solemn thing to find the apostle Paul warning saints against the most loathsome sins: "Put to death therefore what is earthly in you: sexual immorality, impurity, passion, evil desire, and covetousness, which is idolatry."[1] What! Do saints really need to be warned against such sins as these? Yes, they do. The whitest robes, unless their purity be preserved by divine grace, will be defiled by the blackest spots. Experienced Christian, do not boast in your experience; you will trip if you look away from Him who is able to keep you from falling. You whose love is fervent, whose faith is constant, whose hopes are bright, do not say, "We shall never sin," but rather cry, "Lead us not into temptation." There is enough kindling in the heart of the best of men to light a fire that shall burn to the lowest hell, unless God shall quench the sparks as they fall. Who would have dreamed that righteous Lot could be found drunk and committing immorality? Hazael said, "Is Your servant a dog, that he should do this thing?" and we are very apt to use the same self-righteous question. May infinite wisdom cure us of the madness of self-confidence.

[1] Colossians 3:5

REMEMBER THE POOR. — GALATIANS 2:10

Why does God allow so many of His children to be poor? He could make them all rich if He pleased; He could lay bags of gold at their doors; He could send them a large annual income; or He could scatter around their houses abundance of provisions, as once he made the quails lie in heaps around the camp of Israel and rained bread out of heaven to feed them. There is no necessity that they should be poor, except that He sees it to be best. "The cattle on a thousand hills"[1] are His—He could supply them; He could make the rich, the great, and the mighty bring all their power and riches to the feet of His children, for the hearts of all men are in His control. But He does not choose to do so. He allows them to experience need; He allows them to struggle in poverty and obscurity. Why is this? There are many reasons. One is, *to give us, who are favored with enough, an opportunity of showing our love to Jesus.* We show our love to Christ when we sing of Him and when we pray to Him; but if there were no needy people in the world, we should lose the sweet privilege of displaying our love by ministering by our gifts to His poorer brethren. He has ordained that in this way we should prove that our love stands not only in word, but in deed and in truth. If we truly love Christ, we will care for those who are loved by Him. Those who are dear to Him will be dear to us. Let us then look upon it not as a duty but as a privilege to relieve the poor of the Lord's flock, remembering the words of the Lord Jesus, "As you did it to one of the least of these my brothers, you did it to me."[2] Surely this assurance is sweet enough, and this motive strong enough to lead us to help others with a willing hand and a loving heart— recollecting that all we do for His people is graciously accepted by Christ as done to Himself.

❧ E V E N I N G ❧

BLESSED ARE THE PEACEMAKERS,
FOR THEY SHALL BE CALLED SONS OF GOD. — MATTHEW 5:9

This is the seventh of the beatitudes: and seven was the number of perfection among the Hebrews. It may be that the Savior placed the peacemaker seventh on the list because he most nearly approaches the perfect man in Christ Jesus. He who would have perfect blessedness, so far as it can be enjoyed on earth, must attain to this seventh benediction and become a peacemaker. There is a significance also in the position of the text. The verse that precedes it speaks of the blessedness of "the pure in heart, for they shall see God." It is important to understand that we are to be "first pure, then peaceable."[3] Our peaceableness is never to be a contract with sin or toleration of evil. We must set our faces like flint against everything that is contrary to God and His holiness: When purity in our souls is a settled matter, we can go on to peaceableness. In the same way, the verse that follows seems to have been put there on purpose. However peaceable we may be in this world, yet we shall be misrepresented and misunderstood; and we should not be surprised, for even the Prince of Peace, by His very peacefulness, brought fire upon the earth. He Himself, though He loved mankind and did no ill, was "despised and rejected by men; a man of sorrows, and acquainted with grief."[4] Just in case the peaceable in heart should be surprised when they meet with enemies, the following verse reads, "Blessed are those who are persecuted for righteousness' sake, for theirs is the kingdom of heaven." So, the peacemakers are not only pronounced to be blessed, but they are surrounded with blessings. Lord, give us grace to climb to this seventh beatitude! Purify our minds that we may be "first pure, then peaceable" and fortify our souls, that our peaceableness may not lead us into cowardice and despair when we are persecuted for Your sake.

[1] Psalm 50:10 [2] Matthew 25:40 [3] James 3:17 [4] Isaiah 53:3

❧ MORNING ❧

FOR IN CHRIST JESUS YOU ARE ALL SONS OF GOD,
THROUGH FAITH. — GALATIANS 3:26

The *fatherhood of God is common to all His children.* Ah, Little-faith, you have often said, "I wish that I had the courage of Great-heart, that I could wield his sword and be as valiant as he! But, alas, I stumble at every straw, and a shadow makes me afraid." Listen, Little-faith. Great-heart is God's child, and you are God's child too; and Great-heart is not one bit more God's child than you are. Peter and Paul, the highly-favored apostles, were of the family of the Most High; and so are you also. The weak Christian is as much a child of God as the strong one.

> *This cov'nant stands secure,*
> *Though earth's old pillars bow;*
> *The strong, the feeble, and the weak,*
> *Are one in Jesus now.*

All the names are in the same family register. One may have more grace than another, but God our heavenly Father has the same tender heart toward all. One may do more mighty works and may bring more glory to his Father, but he whose name is the least in the kingdom of heaven is as much the child of God as he who stands among the King's mighty men. Let this cheer and comfort us when we draw near to God and say, "Our Father."

Yet, while we are comforted by knowing this, let us not rest contented with weak faith but ask, like the apostles, to have it increased. However feeble our faith may be, if it is real faith in Christ, we shall reach heaven at last, but we shall not honor our Master much on our pilgrimage, neither shall we abound in joy and peace. If then you would live to Christ's glory and be happy in His service, seek to be filled with the spirit of adoption more and more completely, until perfect love shall cast out fear.

❧ EVENING ❧

AS THE FATHER HAS LOVED ME, SO HAVE I LOVED YOU. — JOHN 15:9

As the Father loves the Son, in the same manner Jesus loves His people. What is that divine method? He loved Him *without beginning,* and thus Jesus loves His members. "*I have loved you with an everlasting love.*"[1] You can trace the beginning of human affection; you can easily find the beginning of your love to Christ. But His love to us is a stream whose source is hidden in eternity. God the Father loves Jesus *without any change.* Christian, take this for your comfort, that there is no change in Jesus Christ's love to those who rest in Him. Yesterday you were on the mountain, and you said, "He loves me." Today you are in the valley of humiliation, but He loves you still the same. On the hills and among the peaks, you heard His voice, which spoke so sweetly of His love; and now on the sea, or even in the sea, when all His waves and billows go over you, His heart is still faithful to His ancient choice. The Father loves the Son *without any end,* and this is how the Son loves His people. Saint, you need not fear the prospect of death, for His love for you will never cease. Rest confident that even down to the grave Christ will go with you, and that up again from it He will be your guide to the celestial hills. Moreover, the Father loves the Son *without any measure,* and the same immeasurable love the Son bestows upon His chosen ones. The whole heart of Christ is dedicated to His people. He "loved us and gave himself for us." His is a love that passes knowledge. We have indeed an immutable Savior, a precious Savior, one who loves without measure, without change, without beginning, and without end, even as the Father loves Him! There is rich food here for those who know how to digest it. May the Holy Spirit lead us into its marrow and fatness!

[1] Jeremiah 31:3

... STRONG IN HIS FAITH. — ROMANS 4:20

Christian, take good care of your faith, for *faith is the only way in which you can obtain blessings.* If we want blessings from God, nothing can fetch them down but faith. Prayer cannot draw down answers from God's throne unless it is the earnest prayer of the man who believes. Faith is the angelic messenger between the soul and the Lord Jesus in glory. Let that angel be withdrawn, we can neither send up prayer, nor receive the answers. Faith is the telegraphic wire that links earth and heaven—on which God's messages of love fly so fast that before we call He answers, and while we are still speaking He hears us. But if that telegraphic wire of faith is snapped, how can we receive the promise? Am I in trouble? I can obtain help for trouble by faith. Am I beaten about by the enemy? My soul leans on God by faith. But take faith away—in vain I call to God. There is no road between my soul and heaven. In the deepest wintertime faith is a road on which the horses of prayer may travel—ay, and all the better for the biting frost; but blockade the road and how can we communicate with the Great King? Faith links me with divinity. Faith clothes me with the power of God. Faith engages on my side the omnipotence of Jehovah. Faith ensures every attribute of God in my defense. It helps me defy the hosts of hell. It makes me march in triumph over my enemies. But without faith how can I receive anything from the Lord? The one who wavers—who is like a wave of the sea—should not expect to receive anything from God! So, then, Christian, pay attention to your faith; for with it you can win all things, however poor you are, but without it you can obtain nothing. "If you can! All things are possible for one who believes."[1]

ℓ EVENING ℒ
AND SHE ATE UNTIL SHE WAS SATISFIED, AND
SHE HAD SOME LEFT OVER. — RUTH 2:14

Whenever we are privileged to eat the bread that Jesus gives, we are, like Ruth, satisfied with a full and sweet provision. When Jesus is the host, no guest goes empty from the table. Our *head* is satisfied with the precious truth that Christ reveals; our *heart* is content with Jesus as the altogether lovely object of affection; our *hope* is satisfied, for who do we have in heaven but Jesus? And our desire is fulfilled, for what more can we wish for than to "gain Christ and be found in him"?[2] Jesus fills our *conscience* until it is at perfect peace, our *judgment* with persuasion of the certainty of His teachings, our *memory* with recollections of what He has done, and our *imagination* with the prospects of what He is still to do. As Ruth was "satisfied," so is it with us. We have drunk deeply; we have thought that we could take in all of Christ; but when we have done our best, we have had to leave a vast remainder. We have sat at the table of the Lord's love and said, "Nothing but the infinite can ever satisfy me; I am such a great sinner that I must have infinite merit to wash my sin away." But we have had our sin removed and found that there was merit to spare; we have had our hunger relieved at the feast of sacred love and found that there was an abundance of spiritual food remaining. There are certain sweet things in the Word of God that we have not enjoyed yet, and that we are obliged to leave for a while; for we are like the disciples to whom Jesus said, "I still have many things to say to you, but you cannot bear them now."[3] Yes, there are graces to which we have not attained, places of fellowship nearer to Christ that we have not reached, and heights of communion that our feet have not climbed. At every banquet of love there are many baskets left over. Let us magnify the generosity of kindly Boaz.

[1] Mark 9:23   [2] Philippians 3:9   [3] John 16:12

❧ MORNING ❧

MY BELOVED. — SONG OF SOLOMON 2:8

This was a golden name that the ancient church in her most joyous moments ascribed to the Anointed of the Lord. When the time of the singing of birds was come, and the voice of the turtledove was heard in her land, the church's love-note was sweeter than either, as she sang, "*My beloved* is mine, and I am his; he grazes among the lilies." Ever in her song of songs she calls Him by that delightful name, "my beloved." Even in the long winter, when idolatry had withered the garden of the Lord, her prophets found space to lay aside the burden of the Lord for a little season and to say, "Let me sing for my beloved my love song concerning his vineyard." Though the saints had never seen His face, though as yet He was not made flesh, nor had dwelt among us, nor had man beheld His glory, yet He was the consolation of Israel, the hope and joy of all the chosen, the "beloved" of all those who were upright before the Most High. We, in the summer days of the church, are also able to speak of Christ as the best beloved of our soul and to feel that He is very precious, the "distinguished among ten thousand, and altogether desirable." Since the church loves Jesus and claims Him as her beloved, the apostle dares to defy the whole universe to separate her from the love of Christ and declares that neither tribulation, distress, persecution, famine, nakedness, danger, or the sword have been able to do it; nay, he joyously boasts, "In all these things we are more than conquerors through him who loved us."[1]

> *My sole possession is Thy love;*
> *In earth beneath, or heaven above,*
> *I have no other store;*
> *And though with fervent heart I pray,*
> *And plead with Thee day after day,*
> *I ask for nothing more.*

❧ EVENING ❧

HUSBANDS, LOVE YOUR WIVES, AS
CHRIST LOVED THE CHURCH. — EPHESIANS 5:25

What a golden example Christ gives to His disciples! Few masters could venture to say, "If you would practice my teaching, imitate my life." But as the life of Jesus is the exact transcript of perfect virtue, He can point to Himself as the paragon of holiness, as well as the teacher of it. The Christian should take nothing less than Christ for his model. Under no circumstances should we be content unless we reflect the grace that was in Him. As a husband, the Christian is to look upon the portrait of Christ Jesus, and he is to paint according to that copy. The true Christian is to be such a husband as Christ was to His church. The love of a husband is *special*. The Lord Jesus cherishes for the church a peculiar affection, which is set upon her above the rest of mankind: "I am praying for them. I am not praying for the world."[2] The elect church is the favorite of heaven, the treasure of Christ, the crown of His head, the bracelet of His arm, the breastplate of His heart, the very center and core of His love. A husband should love his wife with a *constant* love, for in this way Jesus loves His church. He does not vary in His affection. He may change in His display of affection, but the affection itself is still the same. A husband should love his wife with an *enduring* love, for nothing shall "separate us from the love of . . . Christ."[3] A true husband loves his wife with a *hearty* love, fervent and intense. It is not mere lip service. What more could Christ have done in proof of His love than He has done? Jesus has a *delighted love* toward His spouse: He prizes her affection and delights in her with sweet satisfaction. Believer, you wonder at Jesus' love; you admire it—*are you imitating it?* In your domestic relationships, is the rule and measure of your love *"even as Christ loved the church"*?

[1] Romans 8:37 [2] John 17:9 [3] Romans 8:39

YOU WILL BE SCATTERED, EACH TO HIS OWN HOME,
AND WILL LEAVE ME ALONE. — JOHN 16:32

Few had fellowship with the sorrows of Gethsemane. The majority of the disciples were not sufficiently advanced in grace to be admitted to behold the mysteries of the agony. Occupied with the Passover feast at their own houses, they represent the many who live upon the letter but are mere babes as to the spirit of the Gospel. To twelve, no, to only eleven the privilege was given to enter Gethsemane and see "this great sight." Out of the eleven, eight were left at a distance; they had fellowship, but not of that intimate sort to which men greatly beloved are admitted. Only three highly favored ones could approach the veil of our Lord's mysterious sorrow. Within that veil even they must not intrude; they remain a stone's throw apart. He must tread the winepress *alone*, and of the people there must be none with Him. Peter and the two sons of Zebedee represent the few eminent, experienced saints who may be written down as "Father"; those doing business on the great waters can in some degree measure the huge Atlantic waves of their Redeemer's passion. To some selected spirits it is given, for the good of others and to strengthen them for future, special, and tremendous conflict, to enter the inner circle and hear the pleadings of the suffering High Priest; they have fellowship with Him in his sufferings, becoming like Him in His death. Yet even these cannot penetrate the secret places of the Savior's woe. "Thine unknown sufferings" is the remarkable expression of the Greek liturgy: There was an inner chamber in our Master's grief, shut out from human knowledge and fellowship. There Jesus is *left alone.* Here Jesus was more than ever an "unspeakable gift!" Is not Watts right when he sings—

> *And all the unknown joys he gives,*
> *Were bought with agonies unknown.*

❧ EVENING ❧

CAN YOU BIND THE CHAINS OF THE PLEIADES OR
LOOSE THE CORDS OF ORION? — JOB 38:31

If we are inclined to boast of our abilities, the grandeur of nature will quickly show us how puny we are. We cannot move the least of all the twinkling stars or quench so much as one of the sunbeams of the morning. We speak of power, but the heavens laugh us to scorn. When the stars shine forth in spring-like joy, we cannot restrain their influences; and when Orion reigns above, and the year is bound in winter's chains, we cannot relax the icy grip. The seasons arrive by divine appointment, and it is impossible for men to change the cycle. Lord, what is man?

In the spiritual, as in the natural, world, man's power is limited on all hands. When the Holy Spirit sheds abroad His delights in the soul, none can disturb; all the cunning and malice of men are unable to prevent the genial, quickening power of the Comforter. When He deigns to visit a church and revive it, the most inveterate enemies cannot resist the good work; they may ridicule it, but they can no more restrain it than they can push back the spring when the Pleiades rule the hour. God wills it, and so it must be. On the other hand, if the Lord in sovereignty, or in justice, binds up a man so that his soul is in bondage, who can give him liberty? He alone can remove the winter of spiritual death from an individual or a people. He looses the bands of Orion, and none but He. What a blessing it is that He can do it. O that He would perform the wonder tonight. Lord, end my winter, and let my spring begin. I cannot with all my longings raise my soul out of her death and dullness, but all things are possible with You. I need heavenly influences, the clear shinings of Your love, the beams of Your grace, the light of Your countenance—these are as summer suns to me. I suffer greatly from sin and temptation; these are my terrible wintry signs. Lord, work wonders in me, and for me. Amen.

❧ **MORNING** ☙

AND GOING A LITTLE FARTHER HE FELL
ON HIS FACE AND PRAYED. — MATTHEW 26:39

There are several instructive features in our Savior's prayer in His hour of trial. It was *lonely prayer*. He withdrew even from His three favored disciples. Believer, be diligent in solitary prayer, especially in times of trial. Family prayer, social prayer, prayer in the church will not be sufficient; these are very precious, but the fragrance of heaven will be sweetest in your private devotions, where no ear hears but God's.

It was *humble prayer*. Luke says He knelt, but another evangelist says He "fell on His face." Where, then, must be *your* place, you humble servant of the great Master? What dust and ashes should cover *your* head! Humility gives us a good foothold in prayer. There is no hope of prevailing with God unless we abase ourselves, that He may exalt us in due time.

It was *filial prayer*. "Abba, Father." You will find it a stronghold in the day of trial to plead your adoption. You have no rights as a subject—you have forfeited them by your treason; but nothing can forfeit a child's right to a father's protection. Do not be afraid to say, "My Father, hear my cry."

Observe that it was *persevering prayer*. He prayed three times. Do not stop until you prevail. Be like the importunate widow, whose continual coming earned what her first supplication could not win. Continue in prayer with a thankful heart.

Lastly, *it was the prayer of resignation*. "Nevertheless, not as I will, but as you will." Let it be as God wills, and God will determine for the best. Be content to leave your prayer in His hands, who knows when to give, and how to give, and what to give, and what to withhold. So pleading, earnestly, importunately, yet with humility and resignation, you will surely prevail.

❧ **EVENING** ☙

FATHER, I DESIRE THAT THEY ALSO,
WHOM YOU HAVE GIVEN ME,
MAY BE WITH ME WHERE I AM. — JOHN 17:24

O death! Why do you touch the tree beneath whose spreading branches weariness finds rest? Why do you snatch away the excellent of the earth, in whom is all our delight? If you must use your axe, use it upon the trees that yield no fruit; then you may be thanked. But why will you chop down the best trees? Hold your axe, and spare the righteous. But no, it must not be; death strikes the best of our friends; the most generous, the most prayerful, the most holy, the most devoted must die. And why? It is through Jesus' prevailing prayer—"Father, I desire that they also, whom you have given me, may be with me where I am." It is *that* which bears them on eagle's wings to heaven. Every time a believer moves from this earth to paradise, it is an answer to Christ's prayer. A good old divine remarks, "Many times Jesus and His people pull against one another in prayer. You bend your knee in prayer and say 'Father, I desire that Your saints be with me where *I* am'; Christ says, 'Father, I desire that they also, whom you have given me, may be with me where I am.'" In this way the disciple is at cross-purposes with his Lord. The soul cannot be in both places: The beloved one cannot be with Christ and with you too. Now, which of the two who plead shall win the day? If you had your choice, if the King should step from His throne and say, "Here are two supplicants praying in opposition to one another," which shall be answered? Oh, I am sure, though it were agony, you would jump to your feet and say, "Jesus, not my will, but Yours be done." You would give up your prayer for your loved one's life, if you could realize the thoughts that Christ is praying in the opposite direction—"Father, I desire that they also, whom you have given me, may be with me where I am." Lord, You shall have them. By faith we let them go.

HIS SWEAT BECAME LIKE GREAT DROPS OF BLOOD
FALLING DOWN TO THE GROUND. — LUKE 22:44

The mental pressure arising from our Lord's struggle with temptation so forced his frame to an unnatural excitement that his pores sent forth, as it were, great drops of blood, which fell down to the ground. This proves *how tremendous must have been the weight of sin*, that it was able to crush the Savior to this extent! This demonstrates *the mighty power of His love*. It is a very helpful observation that the sap, which exudes from the tree without it being cut, is always the best. This precious camphor tree yielded sweet spices when it was wounded by the whips and pierced by the nails on the cross; but consider how it produces its best spice when there is no whip, no nail, no wound. This presents the *voluntariness of Christ's sufferings*, since without a lance the blood flowed freely. No need to put on the leech or apply the knife; it flows spontaneously. No need for the rulers to cry, "Spring up, O well"; of itself it flows in crimson torrents. When men suffer great pain of mind, the blood apparently rushes to the heart. The cheeks are pale; a fainting fit comes on; the blood has gone inward as if to nourish the inner man while passing through its trial. But look at Christ in His agony; he is so utterly oblivious of self that instead of His agony driving His blood to the heart to nourish Himself, it drives it outward falling to the ground. The agony of Christ, inasmuch as it pours Him out upon the ground, pictures the fullness of the offering that He made for men.

Can we fathom how intense the wrestling must have been through which he passed, and will we not hear its voice *to us*? "In your struggle against sin you have not yet resisted to the point of shedding your blood."[1] Behold the great Apostle and High Priest of our profession, and sweat even to blood rather than yield to the great tempter of your souls.

I TELL YOU, IF THESE WERE SILENT, THE VERY STONES
WOULD CRY OUT. — LUKE 19:40

But could the stones cry out? Assuredly they could if He who opens the mouth of the dumb should bid them lift up their voice. Certainly if they were to speak, they would have much to declare in praise of Him who created them by the word of His power; they could extol the wisdom and power of their *Maker* who called them into being. Shall *we* not speak well of Him who made us new and out of stones raised up children unto Abraham? The old rocks could tell of chaos and order and the handiwork of God in successive stages of creation's drama; are *we* not also able to talk of God's decrees, of God's great work in ancient times, in all that He did for His church in the days of old? If the stones were to speak, they could tell of their *breaker*, how he took them from the quarry and made them fit for the temple. And aren't we also able to tell of our glorious Breaker, who broke our hearts with the hammer of His Word, that He might build us into His temple? If the stones should cry out, they would magnify their *builder*, who polished them and fashioned them into a beautiful palace; and shall not we talk of our Architect and Builder, who has put us in our place in the temple of the living God? If the stones could cry out, they might have a long, long story to tell by way of memorial, for many a time a great stone has been rolled as a memorial before the Lord; and we too can testify, stones of help and pillars of remembrance. The broken stones of the law cry out against us, but Christ Himself, who has rolled away the stone from the door of the tomb, speaks for us. Stones might well cry out, but we will not let them: We will silence their noise as we break into sacred song and bless the majesty of the Most High; we will spend all our days glorifying Him whom Jacob calls the Shepherd and Stone of Israel.

[1] Hebrews 12:4

HE WAS HEARD BECAUSE OF HIS REVERENCE. — HEBREWS 5:7

How amazing is this reverence in light of the infernal suggestion *that He was utterly forsaken.* There may be sterner trials than this, but surely it is *one* of the worst to be utterly forsaken. "See," said Satan, "you have a friend nowhere! Your Father has closed the door of His compassion against you. Not an angel in His courts will stretch out his hand to help you. All heaven is alienated from You; You are left alone. The companions from whom You have taken sweet counsel, what are they worth? Son of Mary, see there Your brother James, see there Your loved disciple John, and Your bold apostle Peter, how the cowards sleep when You are in Your sufferings! Look! You have no friend left in heaven or earth. All hell is against You. I have stirred up my infernal den. I have sent my letters throughout all regions summoning every prince of darkness to set upon You this night, and we will spare no arrows—we will use all our infernal might to overwhelm You; and what will You do, You solitary one?" In the face of his cruel trial an angel appears to strengthen Him. "He was heard because of His reverence." He was no more alone, but heaven was with Him. Perhaps this is the reason why He came three times to His disciples.

> *Backwards and forwards thrice He ran,*
> *As if He sought some help from man.*

He would see for Himself whether it were really true that all men had forsaken Him. He found them all asleep; but perhaps He gained some faint comfort from the thought that they were sleeping not from treachery, but from sorrow; the spirit indeed was willing, but the flesh was weak. In that dark valley He was heard because of His reverence. Jesus was heard in His deepest trial; my soul, you shall be heard also.

☜ EVENING ☞

IN THAT SAME HOUR HE REJOICED IN THE HOLY SPIRIT. — LUKE 10:21

The Savior was "a man of sorrows,"[1] but every thoughtful mind has discovered the fact that down deep in His innermost soul He carried an inexhaustible treasury of refined and heavenly joy. Of all the human race, there was never a man who had a deeper, purer, or more abiding peace than our Lord Jesus Christ. "He was anointed with the oil of gladness beyond your companions."[2] His vast benevolence must, from the very nature of things, have afforded Him the deepest possible delight, for benevolence is joy. There were a few remarkable seasons when this joy manifested itself. "In that same hour Jesus rejoiced in the Holy Spirit, and said, I thank you, Father, Lord of heaven and earth. . . ."[3] Christ had His songs, even in the darkness; even though His face was marred, and His countenance had lost the luster of earthly happiness, yet sometimes it was illumined with a matchless splendor of unparalleled satisfaction as He thought upon the recompense of the reward and in the midst of the congregation sang His praise unto God. In this, the Lord Jesus is a blessed picture of His church on earth. At this hour the church expects to walk in sympathy with her Lord along a thorny road; through much tribulation she is making her way to the crown. To bear the cross is her office, and to be scorned and counted an alien by her mother's children is her lot; and yet the church has a deep well of joy, of which none can drink but her own children. There are stores of wine and oil and corn hidden in the midst of our Jerusalem, upon which the saints of God are continuously sustained and nurtured. And sometimes, as in our Savior's case, we have our seasons of intense delight, for "There is a river whose streams make glad the city of God."[4] Even though we are exiles, we rejoice in our King; yes, in Him we exceedingly rejoice, while in His name we set up our banners.

[1] Isaiah 53:3   [2] Psalm 45:7   [3] Luke 10:21   [4] Psalm 46:4

The kisses of an enemy are deceitful. Let me be on my guard when the world puts on a loving face, for it will, if possible, betray me as it did my Master, with a kiss. Whenever a man is about to stab religion, he usually professes very great reverence for it. Let me beware of sleek-faced hypocrisy, which is assistant to heresy and infidelity. Knowing how easily the unrighteous are deceived, let me be wise as a serpent to detect and avoid the designs of the enemy. The young man, devoid of understanding, was led astray by the kiss of the strange woman: May my soul be so graciously instructed today that the seductive tones of the world may have no effect upon me. Holy Spirit, let me not, a poor frail son of man, be betrayed with a kiss!

But what if I should be guilty of the same dreadful sin as Judas, that son of perdition? I have been baptized into the name of the Lord Jesus; I am a member of His visible church; I sit at the Communion table: All these are so many kisses of my lips. Am I sincere in them? If not, I am a base traitor. Do I live in the world as carelessly as others do, and yet make a profession of being a follower of Jesus? Then I am exposing my faith to ridicule and leading men to speak evil of the very name Christian. Surely if I act inconsistently, I am a Judas, and it were better for me if I had never been born. Dare I hope that I am innocent in this matter? Then, O Lord, keep me so. O Lord, make me sincere and true. Preserve me from every false way. Never let me betray my Savior. I do love You, Lord Jesus, and though I often grieve You, I still desire to remain faithful even unto death. O God, forbid that I should be a high-sounding professor and then fall at last into the lake of fire because I betrayed my Master with a kiss.

❧ EVENING ❧
THE SON OF MAN. — JOHN 3:13

How constantly our Master used the title, "the Son of man!" If He had chosen, He might always have spoken of Himself as the Son of God, the Everlasting Father, the Wonderful Counselor, the Prince of Peace; but behold the lowliness of Jesus! He prefers to call Himself the Son of man. Let us learn a lesson of humility from our Savior; let us never court great titles nor proud degrees. There is here, however, a far sweeter thought. Jesus loved manhood so much that He delighted to honor it; and since it is a high honor, and indeed the greatest dignity of manhood, that Jesus is the Son of man, He is willing to display this name, that He may as it were hang royal stars upon the breast of manhood and display the love of God to Abraham's seed. *Son of man*—whenever He said this, He shed a halo around the head of Adam's children. Yet there is perhaps a more precious thought still. Jesus Christ called Himself the Son of man to express His oneness and sympathy with His people. In this way He reminds us that He is the one whom we may approach without fear. As a man, we may take to Him all our griefs and troubles, for He knows them by experience. In that He Himself has suffered as "the Son of Man," He is able to rescue and comfort us. We bless You, Lord Jesus, for using such a title to remind us and assure us that You are a brother. This is for us a token of Your grace, Your humility, Your love.

Oh see how Jesus trusts Himself
Unto our childish love,
As though by His free ways with us
Our earnestness to prove!

His sacred name a common word
On earth He loves to hear;
There is no majesty in Him
Which love may not come near.

❧ MORNING ❧

JESUS ANSWERED . . . "SO, IF YOU SEEK ME,
LET THESE MEN GO." — JOHN 18:8

Mark, my soul, the care that Jesus displayed even in His hour of trial toward his precious sheep! The ruling passion is strong in death. He resigns Himself to the enemy, but He interposes a word of power to set His disciples free. As to Himself, like a sheep before her shearers He is dumb and opens not His Mouth, but for His disciples' sake He speaks with almighty energy. Herein is love—constant, self-forgetting, faithful love. But is there not far more here than is immediately apparent? Do we not have the very soul and spirit of the atonement in these words? The Good Shepherd lays down His life for the sheep and pleads that they must therefore go free. The Surety is bound, and justice demands that those for whom He stands as substitute should go free. In the middle of Egypt's bondage, the voice rang out with power, "*Let these men go.*" Out of slavery of sin and Satan the redeemed must come. In every cell of the dungeons of Despair, the sound is echoed, "*Let these men go,*" and out come Despondency and Fearful. Satan hears the well-known voice and lifts his foot from the neck of the fallen; and Death hears it, and the grave opens her gates to let the dead arise. These men go the way of progress, holiness, triumph, glory, and none shall dare to keep them from it. No lion shall hinder their progress, and no fierce opponent shall prevent them. The Lord Jesus has drawn the cruel hunters upon Himself, making the most timid of His followers to discover perfect peace in His unbounded love. The thundercloud has burst over the cross of Calvary, and the pilgrims of Zion shall never be smitten by the bolts of vengeance. Come, my heart, rejoice in the immunity that your Redeemer has secured for you, and bless His name all day and every day.

❧ EVENING ❧

. . . WHEN HE COMES IN THE GLORY OF HIS FATHER
WITH THE HOLY ANGELS. — MARK 8:38

If we have been partakers with Jesus in His shame, we shall also share with Him the luster that surrounds Him when He appears again in glory. Are you in communion with Christ Jesus? Does a vital union bind you to Him? Then you are today with Him in His shame; you have taken up His cross and have gone with Him outside the camp bearing His reproach; you will doubtless be with Him when the cross is exchanged for the crown. But examine yourself this evening; for if you are not with Him in regeneration, you will not be with Him when He comes in His glory. If you run from the dark side of fellowship, you will not understand its bright, happy chapter when the King comes *with all His holy angels.* What! *Are angels with Him?* And yet He did not take up angels—He took up the seed of Abraham. Are the holy angels *with Him?* Come, my soul; if you are indeed His own beloved, you cannot be far from Him. If His friends and His neighbors are called together to see His glory, shall you be distant? Though it be a day of judgment, yet you cannot be far from that heart that, having admitted angels into intimacy, has admitted you into union with Himself. Has He not said to you, O my soul, "I will betroth you to me in righteousness and in justice, in steadfast love and in mercy"? Has He not declared us to be in union with Him? If the angels, who are but friends and neighbors, shall be with Him, it is abundantly certain that His own beloved in whom is all His delight shall be near to Him and sit at His right hand. Here is a morning star of hope for you, of such exceeding brilliance that it may well light up your darkest and most desolate experience.

THEN ALL THE DISCIPLES LEFT HIM AND FLED. — MATTHEW 26:56

He never deserted them, but they in cowardly fear of their lives fled from Him at the very outset of His sufferings. This is but one instructive instance of the frailty of all believers if left to themselves; they are but sheep at best, and they flee when the wolf appears. They had all been warned of the danger and had promised to die rather than leave their Master; and yet they were seized with sudden panic and took to their heels. It may be that I, at the opening of this day, have braced myself to bear a trial for the Lord's sake, and I imagine myself able for the challenge; but let me be careful in case with the same evil heart of unbelief I should depart from my Lord as the apostles did. It is one thing to promise, and quite another to perform. It would have been to their eternal honor to have stood manfully at Jesus' side; they fled from honor. May I be kept from imitating them! Where else could they have been so safe as near their Master, who could presently call for twelve legions of angels? They fled from their true safety. O God, let me not play the fool also. Divine grace can make the coward brave. The smoking flax can flame forth like fire on the altar when the Lord wills it. These very apostles who were timid as hares grew to be bold as lions after the Spirit had descended upon them, and even so the Holy Spirit can make my wretched spirit brave to confess my Lord and witness for His truth.

What anguish must have filled the Savior as He saw His friends so faithless! This was one bitter ingredient in His cup; but that cup is drained dry; let me not put another drop in it. If I forsake my Lord, I shall crucify Him afresh and put Him to an open shame. Keep me, O blessed Spirit, from such a shameful end.

❧ EVENING ❧

SHE SAID, "YES, LORD, YET EVEN THE DOGS
EAT THE CRUMBS THAT FALL
FROM THEIR MASTERS' TABLE." — MATTHEW 15:27

This woman gained comfort in her misery by thinking *great thoughts of Christ*. The Master had talked about the children's bread. "Now," she argued, "since You are the Master of the table of grace, I know that You are a generous housekeeper, and there is sure to be plenty of bread on Your table. There will be such an abundance for the children that there will be crumbs to throw on the floor for the dogs, and the children will fare none the worse because the dogs are fed." She thought Him one who kept so fine a table that all that she needed would only be a crumb in comparison; yet remember, what she wanted was to have the devil cast out of her daughter. It was a very great thing to her, but she had such a high esteem of Christ that she said, "It is nothing to Him; it is but a crumb for Christ to give." This is the royal road to comfort. Great thoughts of your sin alone will drive you to despair; but great thoughts of Christ will guide you into the haven of peace. "My sins are many, but oh, it is nothing to Jesus to take them all away. The weight of my guilt presses me down as a giant's foot would crush a worm, but it is no more than a grain of dust to Him, because He has already borne its curse in His own body on the tree. It will be only a small thing for Him to give me full remission, although it will be an infinite blessing for me to receive it." The woman opens her needy soul very wide, expecting great things of Jesus, and He fills it with His love. Dear reader, do the same. *She won the victory by believing in Him.* Her case is an instance of prevailing faith; and if we would conquer like her, we must imitate her tactics.

... THE LOVE OF CHRIST THAT SURPASSES KNOWLEDGE. — EPHESIANS 3:19

The love of Christ in its sweetness, its fullness, its greatness, its faithfulness passes all human comprehension. Where can we find the words to describe His matchless, His unparalleled love toward the children of men? It is so vast and boundless that, as the swallow simply skims the water without diving into its depths, so all descriptive words merely touch the surface, while immeasurable depths lie below. Well might the poet say,

O love, thou fathomless abyss!

For this love of Christ is indeed measureless and fathomless; no one can fully comprehend it. Before we can have any right idea of the love of Jesus, we must understand His previous glory in its height of majesty, and His incarnation upon the earth in all its depths of shame. But who can tell us the majesty of Christ? When He was enthroned in the highest heavens He was very God of very God. By Him the heavens were made, and all its inhabitants. His own almighty arm upheld the spheres; the praises of cherubim and seraphim perpetually surrounded Him; the full chorus of the hallelujahs of the universe flowed without ceasing to the foot of his throne. He reigned supreme above all His creatures, God over all, blessed forever. Who can tell His height of glory then? And who, on the other hand, can tell how low He descended? To be a man was something; to be a man of sorrows was far more. To bleed and die and suffer—these were much for Him who was the Son of God; but to suffer such unparalleled agony—to endure a death of shame and desertion by His Father—this is a depth of condescending love that the most inspired mind must utterly fail to fathom. Herein is love! And truly it is love that "surpasses knowledge." O let this love fill our hearts with adoring gratitude and lead us to practical demonstrations of its power.

❧ EVENING ❧
AS A PLEASING AROMA I WILL ACCEPT YOU. — EZEKIEL 20:41

The merits of our great Redeemer are as a pleasing aroma to the Most High. Whether we speak of the active or passive righteousness of Christ, there is an equal fragrance. There was a pleasing aroma in His active life by which He honored the law of God and made every precept to glitter like a precious jewel in the pure setting of His own person. Such, too, was His passive obedience, when He endured with unmurmuring submission hunger and thirst, cold and nakedness, and at the end sweat as it were great drops of blood in Gethsemane. He gave His back to the smiters and His cheeks to them that plucked out the hair and was fastened to the cruel wood, that He might suffer the wrath of God in our behalf. These two things are sweet before the Most High; and for the sake of His doing and His dying, His substitutionary sufferings and His vicarious obedience, the Lord our God accepts us. What a preciousness there must be in Him to overcome our lack of preciousness! What a pleasing aroma to put away our nasty odor! What a cleansing power in His blood to take away sin such as ours! And what glory in His righteousness to make such unacceptable creatures to be accepted in the Beloved! Consider, believer, how sure and unchanging is our acceptance, since it is *in Him*! Take care that you never doubt your acceptance in Jesus. You cannot be accepted without Christ; but when you have received His merit, you cannot be unaccepted. Despite all your doubts and fears and sins, Jehovah's gracious eye never looks upon you in anger; though He sees sin in you, in yourself, yet when He looks at you through Christ, He sees no sin. You are always accepted in Christ, are always blessed and dear to the Father's heart. Therefore lift up a song, and as you see the smoking incense of the Savior's merit coming up this evening before the sapphire throne, let the incense of your praise go up also.

❧ MORNING ☙

ALTHOUGH HE WAS A SON, HE LEARNED OBEDIENCE
THROUGH WHAT HE SUFFERED. — HEBREWS 5:8

We are told that the Captain of our salvation was made perfect through suffering; therefore we who are sinful and who are far from being perfect must not wonder if we are called to pass through suffering too. Shall the head be crowned with thorns while the other parts of the body enjoy only comfort and ease? Must Christ pass through seas of His own blood to win the crown while we walk to heaven dry-shod in silver slippers? No; our Master's experience teaches us that suffering is necessary, and the true-born child of God must not, would not, escape it if he could. But there is one very comforting thought in the fact of Christ's "being made perfect" through suffering—it is that He can have complete sympathy with us. He is not a high priest who is "unable to sympathize with our weaknesses."[1] In this sympathy of Christ we find a sustaining power. One of the early martyrs said, "I can bear it all, for Jesus suffered, and He suffers in me now; He sympathizes with me, and this makes me strong." Believer, grasp this thought in every agonizing experience. Let the thought of Jesus strengthen you as you follow in His steps. Find a sweet support in His sympathy; and remember that to suffer is an honorable thing—to suffer for Christ is glory. The apostles rejoiced that they were counted worthy to do this. Just so far as the Lord shall give us grace to suffer *for* Christ, to suffer *with* Christ, just so far does He honor us. The jewels of a Christian are his afflictions. The regalia of the kings whom God has anointed are their troubles, their sorrows, and their griefs. Let us not, therefore, shun being honored. Let us not turn aside from being exalted. Griefs exalt us, and troubles lift us up. "If we endure, we will also reign with him."[2]

❧ EVENING ☙

I CALLED HIM, BUT HE GAVE NO ANSWER. — SONG OF SOLOMON 5:6

Prayer sometimes lingers, like a petitioner at the gate, until the King comes with the blessings that she seeks. The Lord, when He has given great faith, has been known to test it by long delays. He has allowed His servants' voices to echo in their ears as if the heavens were brass. They have knocked at the golden gate, but it has remained immovable, as though it were rusted upon its hinges. Like Jeremiah, they have cried, "You have wrapped yourself with a cloud so that no prayer can pass through."[3] In this manner true saints have continued to wait patiently without a reply, not because their prayers were not strong, nor because they were unaccepted, but because it so pleased Him who is a Sovereign and who gives according to His own pleasure. If it pleases Him to test our patience, shall He not do as He wishes with His children? Beggars must not be choosers either as to time, place, or form. But we must be careful not to take delays in prayer for denials. God's postdated checks will be punctually honored; we must not allow Satan to shake our confidence in the God of truth by pointing to our unanswered prayers. Unanswered petitions are not unheard. God keeps a file for our prayers—they are not blown away by the wind; they are treasured in the King's archives. This is a registry in the court of heaven in which every prayer is recorded. Struggling believer, your Lord has as it were a tear-bottle in which the costly drops of your sacred grief are put away, and a book in which your holy groanings are numbered. By-and-by your case shall prevail. Can you not be content to wait a little? Will the Lord's time not be better than yours? By-and-by He will comfortably appear, to your soul's joy, and will cause you to put away the sackcloth and ashes of long waiting and put on the scarlet and fine linen of full fruition.

[1] Hebrews 4:15 [2] 2 Timothy 2:12 [3] Lamentations 3:44

HE POURED OUT HIS SOUL TO DEATH AND WAS NUMBERED
WITH THE TRANSGRESSORS. — ISAIAH 53:12

Why did Jesus cause Himself to be enrolled among sinners? This wonderful condescension was justified by many powerful reasons. *By doing so He could better become their advocate.* In some trials there is an identification of the counselor with the client, nor can they be looked upon in the eye of the law as separate from each other. Now, when the sinner is brought to the bench, Jesus appears there Himself. *He* stands to answer the accusation. He points to His side, His hands, His feet, and challenges Justice to bring anything against the sinners whom He represents. He pleads His blood, and pleads so triumphantly, being numbered with them and having a part with them, that the Judge proclaims, "Let them go, deliver them from the pit, for He has provided a ransom." Our Lord Jesus was numbered with the transgressors in order that they might *feel their hearts drawn toward Him.* Who can be afraid of one whose name appears on the same list with us? Surely we may come boldly to Him and confess our guilt. He who is numbered with us cannot condemn us. Was He not entered in the transgressor's list *that we might be written in the red roll of the saints?* He was holy and written among the holy; we were guilty and numbered among the guilty. He transfers His name from that list to this dark indictment, and our names are taken from the indictment and written in the roll of acceptance, for there is a complete transfer made between Jesus and His people. All our condition of misery and sin Jesus has taken; and all that Jesus has comes to us. His righteousness, His blood, and everything that He has He gives us as our dowry. Rejoice, believer, in your union to Him who was numbered among the transgressors; and prove that you are truly saved by being clearly identified with those who are new creatures in Him.

❧ EVENING ❧

LET US TEST AND EXAMINE OUR WAYS, AND
RETURN TO THE LORD! — LAMENTATIONS 3:40

The wife who fondly loves her absent husband longs for his return; a long protracted separation from him is a semi-death to her spirit. And so it is with souls who love the Savior much; they need to see His face; they cannot bear that He should be away, thus depriving them of communion with Him. A reproaching glance, an uplifted finger will be grievous to loving children who fear to offend their tender father and are only happy in his smile. Beloved, it was so once this way with you. A text of Scripture, a threatening, a touch of the rod of affliction, and you went to your Father's feet, crying, "Let me know why you contend against me." Is that still the case? Or are you content to follow Jesus from a distance? Can you contemplate broken communion with Christ without being alarmed? Can you bear to have your Beloved walking contrary to you, because you walk contrary to Him? Have your sins separated between you and your God, and is your heart at rest? Let me affectionately warn you, for it is a grievous thing when we can live contentedly without the present enjoyment of the Savior's face. *Let us work to feel what an evil thing this is*—little love to our own dying Savior, little joy in His company, little time with the Beloved! Hold a true Lent in your souls, while you sorrow over your hardness of heart. Do not stop at sorrow! Remember where you first received salvation. *Go at once to the cross.* There, and there only, can you get your spirit quickened. No matter how hard, how insensible, how dead we may have become, let us go again in all the rags and poverty and defilement of our natural condition. Let us clasp that cross, let us look into those languid eyes, let us bathe in that fountain filled with blood—this will bring back to us our first love; this will restore the simplicity of our faith and the tenderness of our heart.

WITH HIS STRIPES WE ARE HEALED. — ISAIAH 53:5

Pilate delivered our Lord to be scourged. The Roman scourge was a most dreadful instrument of torture. It was made of the sinews of oxen, and sharp bones were intertwined among the sinews, so that every time the lash came down, these pieces of bone inflicted fearful laceration and tore off the flesh from the bone. The Savior was, no doubt, bound to the column, and thus beaten. He had been beaten before; but this from the Roman soldiers was probably the most severe of His flagellations. My soul, stand here and weep over His poor, stricken body.

Believer in Jesus, can you gaze upon Him without tears as He stands before you, the mirror of agonizing love? He is at once fair as the lily for innocence and red as the rose with the crimson of His own blood. As we feel the sure and blessed healing that His stripes have wrought in us, does not our heart melt at once with love and grief? If ever we have loved our Lord Jesus, surely we must feel that affection glowing now within our hearts.

> *See how the patient Jesus stands,*
> *Insulted in His lowest case!*
> *Sinners have bound the Almighty's hands,*
> *And spit in their Creator's face.*

> *With thorns His temples gor'd and gash'd*
> *Send streams of blood from every part;*
> *His back's with knotted scourges lash'd.*
> *But sharper scourges tear His heart.*

We may long to go to our bedrooms and weep; but since our business calls us away, we will first ask the Lord Jesus to print the image of His bleeding self upon the tablets of our hearts all the day, and at nightfall we will return to commune with Him and sorrow that our sin should have cost Him so dearly.

❧ EVENING ❧
THEN RIZPAH THE DAUGHTER OF AIAH TOOK SACKCLOTH AND SPREAD IT FOR HERSELF ON THE ROCK, FROM THE BEGINNING OF HARVEST UNTIL RAIN FELL UPON THEM FROM THE HEAVENS. AND SHE DID NOT ALLOW THE BIRDS OF THE AIR TO COME UPON THEM BY DAY, OR THE BEASTS OF THE FIELD BY NIGHT. — 2 SAMUEL 21:10

If the love of a woman to her slain sons could make her prolong her mournful vigil for so long a period, shall we grow tired of considering the sufferings of our blessed Lord? She drove away the birds of prey, and shall not we chase from our meditations those worldly and sinful thoughts that defile both our minds and the sacred themes upon which we are occupied? Be gone, you birds of evil wing! Leave the sacrifice alone! She bore the heat of summer, the night dews and the rains, unsheltered and alone. Sleep was chased from her weeping eyes: her heart was too full for slumber. Consider how she loved her children! Shall Rizpah endure while we quit at the first little inconvenience or trial? Are we such cowards that we cannot bear to suffer with our Lord? She chased away even the wild beasts with unusual courage, and will we not be ready to encounter every foe for Jesus' sake? Her children were slain by other hands than hers, and yet she wept and watched. What ought we to do who have by our sins crucified our Lord? Our obligations are boundless; our love should be fervent and our repentance thorough. To watch with Jesus should be our business, to protect His honor our occupation, to abide by His cross our solace. Those ghastly corpses might well have frightened Rizpah, especially by night, but in our Lord, at whose cross we are sitting, there is nothing revolting but everything attractive. Never was living beauty so enchanting as a dying Savior. Jesus, we will watch with You still, and may You graciously unveil Yourself to us; then shall we not sit beneath sackcloth but in a royal pavilion.

April

❱❲ MORNING ❱❲

LET HIM KISS ME WITH THE KISSES OF HIS MOUTH.
— SONG OF SOLOMON 1:2

For several days we have been dwelling upon the Savior's passion, and for some little time to come we shall linger there. In beginning a new month, let us seek the Lord with the desire that glowed in the heart of this woman. See how she leaps at once to *Him*. There are no introductions; she does not even mention His name. She is in the heart of her theme at once, for she speaks of *Him* who was the only Him in the world to her. How bold is her love! it was true condescension that allowed the sinful woman to anoint Jesus' feet with spices—it was rich love that allowed the gentle Mary to sit at His feet and learn of Him; but in this picture we see strong, fervent love, aspiring to higher tokens of affection and closer signs of fellowship. Esther trembled in the presence of Ahasuerus, but the woman in joyful liberty of perfect love knows no fear. If we have received the same free spirit, we may also ask the same. By "kisses" we suppose to be intended those varied manifestations of affection by which the believer is made to enjoy the love of Jesus. The kiss of *reconciliation* we enjoyed at our conversion, and it was sweet as honey dropping from the comb. The kiss of *acceptance* is still warm on our brow, as we know that He has accepted us through rich grace. The kiss of daily, present *communion* is that which we long to be repeated day after day, till it is changed into the kiss of *reception*, which removes the soul from earth, and the kiss of *consummation* that fills it with the joy of heaven. Faith is our walk, but intimate fellowship is our rest. Faith is the road, but communion with Jesus is the well from which the pilgrim drinks. O lover of our souls, do not be distant. Let the lips of Your blessing meet the lips of our asking; let the lips of Your fullness touch the lips of our need, and immediately our joy will be full.

❱❲ EVENING ❱❲

IT IS THE TIME TO SEEK THE LORD. — HOSEA 10:12

The month of April is said to derive its name from the Latin verb *aperio*, which means *to open*, because all the buds and blossoms are now opening, and we have arrived at the gates of the flowery season. Reader, if you are not yet saved, may your heart, in keeping with the universal awakening of nature, be opened to receive the Lord. Every blossoming flower warns you that *it is time to seek the Lord*; do not be out of tune with nature, but let your heart bud and bloom with holy desires. If you tell me that the warm blood of youth leaps in your veins, then I entreat you, give your vigor to the Lord. It was my unspeakable happiness to be called in early youth, and I am thankful to the Lord every day for that. Salvation is priceless, let it come when it may, but oh, an early salvation has a double value in it. Young men and women, since you may die before you reach your prime, *"It is the time to seek the Lord."* You who feel the first signs of decay, quicken your pace: That chest pain, that biopsy report, are warnings that you must not trifle with; with you it is definitely time to seek the Lord. Did I observe a little gray, a little thinning in your hair? Years are flying by, and death is drawing nearer by the day; let each return of spring arouse you to set your house in order. Dear reader, if you are now advanced in years, let me entreat and implore you to delay no longer. There is a day of grace for you now—be thankful for that—but it is a limited season and grows shorter every time the clock ticks. Here in the silence of your room, on this first night of another month, I speak to you as best I can by paper and ink, and from my inmost soul, as God's servant, I lay before you this warning, *"It is the time to seek the Lord."* Do not make light of this; it may be your last call from destruction, the final syllable from the lip of grace.

❧ MORNING ❧

BUT HE GAVE HIM NO ANSWER, NOT EVEN TO A SINGLE CHARGE.
— MATTHEW 27:14

Jesus had never been slow of speech when He could bless the sons of men, but He would not say a single word for Himself. "No man ever spoke like this man," and no man was ever silent like Him. Was this singular silence *the index of His perfect self-sacrifice*? Did it show that He would not utter a word to prevent His crucifixion, which He had dedicated as an offering for us? Had He so entirely surrendered Himself that He would not interfere on His own behalf, even in the smallest details, but be crowned and killed an unstruggling, uncomplaining victim? Was this silence *a type of the defenselessness of sin*? Nothing can be said to excuse human guilt; and, therefore, He who bore its whole weight stood speechless before His judge. Patient silence is *the best reply to a world of cruel opposition*. Calm endurance answers some questions infinitely more conclusively than the loftiest eloquence. The best apologists for Christianity in the early days were its martyrs. The anvil breaks a host of hammers by quietly bearing their blows. Did not the silent Lamb of God furnish us with *a grand example of wisdom*? Where every word was occasion for new blasphemy, it was the line of duty to provide no fuel for the flame of sin. The ambiguous and the false, the unworthy and mean will soon enough confound themselves, and therefore the true can afford to be quiet and find silence to be its wisdom. Evidently our Lord, by His silence, furnished *a remarkable fulfillment of prophecy*. A long defense of Himself would have been contrary to Isaiah's prediction: "Like a lamb that is led to the slaughter, and like a sheep that before its shearers is silent, so he opened not his mouth."[1] By His silence He declared Himself to be the true Lamb of God. As such we worship Him this morning. Be with us, Jesus, and in the silence of our heart let us hear the voice of Your love.

❧ EVENING ❧

HE SHALL SEE HIS OFFSPRING; HE SHALL PROLONG HIS DAYS; THE WILL OF
THE LORD SHALL PROSPER IN HIS HAND. — ISAIAH 53:10

Ask God to fulfill this promise quickly, all you who love the Lord. It is easy work to pray when our desires are fixed and established on God's own promise. How can He who gave the word refuse to keep it? Immutable truth cannot demean itself by a lie, and eternal faithfulness cannot degrade itself by neglect. God must bless His Son—His covenant binds Him to it. The Spirit prompts us to ask for Jesus what God the Father decrees to give Him. Whenever you are praying for the kingdom of Christ, let your eyes behold the dawning of the blessed day that draws near, when the Crucified will receive His coronation in the place where men rejected Him. Take courage, you who prayerfully work for Christ with only scant success—it will not always be this way; better times are ahead. Your eyes cannot see the wonderful future: borrow the telescope of faith; wipe the misty breath of your doubts from the viewfinder; look through it and behold the coming glory. Reader, let us ask, *do you* make this your constant prayer? Remember that the same Christ who tells us to say, "Give us each day our daily bread," first gave us this petition, "Hallowed be your name; your kingdom come; your will be done in earth as it is in heaven." Do not let your prayers be all about your own sins, your own desires, your own imperfections, your own trials, but let them climb the starry ladder and get up to Christ Himself, and then as you draw near to the blood-sprinkled mercy-seat, offer this prayer continually: "Lord, extend the kingdom of Your dear Son." When you fervently present such a petition, it will elevate the spirit of all your devotions. Make sure that you prove the sincerity of your prayer by working to promote the Lord's glory.

[1] Isaiah 53:7

SO THEY TOOK JESUS, AND HE WENT OUT. — JOHN 19:16-17

He had spent the night in agony, and in the early morning He was hurried from the hall of Caiaphas to Pilate, from Pilate to Herod, and from Herod back again to Pilate. Consequently his strength was almost gone, but He was granted neither food nor rest. They were eager for His blood and therefore led Him out to die, burdened with the cross. At this sad procession the women wept, and my soul weeps in turn.

What do we learn here as we see our blessed Lord led forth? Do we not perceive the truth, which was foreshadowed in *the scapegoat*? Remember how the high priest brought the scapegoat and put both his hands upon its head, confessing the sins of the people, so that those sins might be transferred from the people and laid upon the goat. Then the goat was led away into the wilderness, and it carried away the sins of the people, so that if they looked for them they could not be found. Now we see Jesus brought before the priests and rulers, who pronounce Him guilty. God Himself imputes our sins *to Him*: "the Lord has laid on him the iniquity of us all";[1] "He made him to be sin."[2] And as the substitute for our guilt, bearing our sin upon His shoulders, represented by the cross, we see the great Scapegoat led away by the appointed officers of justice. Beloved, can you feel assured that He carried *your* sin? As you look at the cross upon His shoulders, does it represent *your* sin? There is one way by which you can tell whether He carried your sin or not. Have you laid your hand upon His head, confessed your sin, and trusted in Him? Then your sin no longer lies on you; it has all been transferred by blessed imputation to Christ, and He bears it on His shoulder as a load heavier than the cross.

Do not allow this picture to disappear until you have rejoiced in your own deliverance and bowed in adoring wonder before the Redeemer upon whom your iniquities were laid.

❧ E V E N I N G ❧

ALL WE LIKE SHEEP HAVE GONE ASTRAY; WE HAVE TURNED EVERY ONE
TO HIS OWN WAY; AND THE LORD HAS LAID ON HIM
THE INIQUITY OF US ALL. — ISAIAH 53:6

Here a confession of sin is shared by all the elect people of God. They have all fallen, and therefore, in one voice, from the first who entered heaven to the last who shall arrive they all say, "All we like sheep have gone astray." This confession is not only unanimous, it is also *special* and particular: "We have turned every one to his own way." All are sinful, but each individual faces his or her own peculiar sinfulness, which is not found in someone else. It is the mark of genuine repentance that while it naturally associates itself with other penitents, it also takes up a position of loneliness. "We have turned every one to his own way" is a confession that each individual had sinned against light peculiar to himself or sinned with an aggravation that he could not perceive in others. This confession is *unreserved*; there is not a word to detract from its force, nor a syllable by way of excuse. This confession bids farewell to every plea of self-justification. It is the declaration of those who are consciously guilty—guilty with aggravations, guilty without excuse: they stand with their weapons of rebellion broken in pieces and cry, "All we like sheep have gone astray; we have turned every one to his own way." Yet we hear no mournful wailings attending this confession of sin; for the next sentence makes it almost a song. "The LORD has laid on him the iniquity of us all." It is the most grievous sentence of the three, but it overflows with comfort. How strange that where misery was concentrated, mercy reigned; where sorrow reached her climax, weary souls find rest. The Savior bruised is the healing of bruised hearts. Consider how the humble confession gives way to assured confidence by simply gazing at Christ on the cross!

[1] Isaiah 53:6   [2] 2 Corinthians 5:21

FOR OUR SAKE HE MADE HIM TO BE SIN WHO KNEW NO SIN,
SO THAT IN HIM WE MIGHT BECOME THE
RIGHTEOUSNESS OF GOD. — 2 CORINTHIANS 5:21

Mourning Christian, why are you weeping? Are you mourning over your own sins and failings? Look to your perfect Lord, and remember, you are complete in Him. You are in God's sight as perfect as if you had never sinned; more than that, the Lord our Righteousness has clothed you with a royal robe of righteousness, which is wholly undeserved—you have the righteousness of God. You who are mourning by reason of inbred sin and depravity, remember, none of your sins can condemn you. You have learned to hate sin; but you have also learned how that sin is not yours—it was laid upon Christ's head. Your standing is not in yourself—it is in Christ. Your acceptance is not in yourself, but in your Lord; you are just as accepted by God today, with all your sinfulness, as you will be when you stand before His throne, free from all corruption. So I urge you, take hold of this precious thought—*perfection in Christ*! For you are "complete in him."[1] With your Savior's garment on, you are as holy as the Holy One. "Who is to condemn? Christ Jesus is the one who died— more than that, who was raised—who is at the right hand of God, who indeed is interceding for us."[2] Christian, let your heart rejoice, for you are "accepted in the beloved"[3]—what do you have to fear? Keep a smile on your face! Live near your Master; live in the suburbs of the Heavenly City; for soon, when your time has come, you will rise up to where Jesus sits and reign at His right hand; and all because the Lord Jesus was made "to be sin who knew no sin, so that in him we might become the righteousness of God."

❧ EVENING ❧

COME, LET US GO UP TO THE MOUNTAIN OF THE LORD. — ISAIAH 2:3

It is exceedingly beneficial to our souls to rise above this present evil world to something nobler and better. The cares of this world and the deceitfulness of riches are apt to choke everything good within us, and we grow fretful, desponding, perhaps proud and carnal. It is good for us to cut down these thorns and briers, because heavenly seed sown among them is not likely to yield a harvest. Where will we find a better scythe with which to cut them down than communion with God and the things of the kingdom? There are places in the world where the lowlands are a breeding ground for sickness. Doctors will often suggest that their patients head for the mountains where they can breathe the clear, fresh air. Heeding such advice, the valley dwellers leave their homes among the marshes and the fever mists to inhale the bracing elements upon the hills. It is to such an exploit of climbing that I invite you this evening. May the Spirit of God assist us to leave the mists of fear and the fevers of anxiety and all the ills that gather in this valley of earth, and to ascend the mountains of anticipated joy and blessedness. May God the Holy Spirit cut the cords that keep us here below and enable us to climb! We are too often like chained eagles fastened to the perch, and even worse, unlike the eagle, we begin to love our chain and might even, if it came to the test, be loath to have it snapped. May God now grant us grace, if we cannot escape from the chain as to our flesh, yet to do so as to our spirits; and leaving the body, like a servant, at the foot of the hill, may our soul, like Abraham, reach the top of the mountain, so that we can enjoy communion with the Most High.

[1] Colossians 2:10, KJV   [2] Romans 8:34   [3] Ephesians 1:6

... LAID ON HIM THE CROSS, TO CARRY IT BEHIND JESUS.
— LUKE 23:26

We see in Simon's carrying the cross a picture of the work of the church throughout all generations; she is the cross-bearer after Jesus. Notice, Christian, that Jesus does not suffer so as to prevent your suffering. He bears a cross, not that you may escape it, but that you may endure it. Christ exempts you from sin, but not from sorrow. Remember that, and expect to suffer. But let us comfort ourselves with this thought, that in our case, as in Simon's, *it is not our cross* but Christ's cross that we carry. When you are persecuted for your piety, when your faith is the occasion of cruel jokes, then remember it is not *your* cross, it is Christ's cross; and what a privilege it is to carry the cross of our Lord Jesus!

You carry the cross after Him. You have blessed company; your path is marked with the footprints of your Lord. The mark of His blood-red shoulder is upon that heavy burden. It is *His* cross, and He goes before you as a shepherd goes before his sheep. Take up your cross daily, and follow Him.

Do not forget, also, that *you bear this cross in partnership*. It is the opinion of some that Simon only carried one end of the cross, and not the whole of it. That is very possible. Christ may have carried the heavier part, against the transverse beam, and Simon may have borne the lighter end. Certainly that is the case with you; you only carry the light end of the cross—Christ bore the heavier end.

And remember, *though Simon had to bear the cross for only a short while, it gave him lasting honor*. Even so, the cross we carry is only for a little while at most, and then we shall receive the crown, the glory. Surely we should love the cross and, instead of shrinking from it, *count it very dear*, for it works out for us an eternal weight of glory beyond all comparison.

❧ EVENING ☙
HUMILITY COMES BEFORE HONOR. — PROVERBS 15:33

Humiliation of soul always *brings a positive blessing with it*. If we empty our hearts of self, God will fill them with His love. If we desire close communion with Christ, we should remember the word of the Lord: "This is the one to whom I will look: he who is humble and contrite in spirit and trembles at my word."[1] Stoop if you want to climb to heaven. Is it not said of Jesus, "He who descended is the one who also ascended"?[2] So must you. You must grow downwards, that you may grow upwards; for the sweetest fellowship with heaven will be enjoyed by humble souls and by them alone. God will deny no blessing to a thoroughly humbled spirit. "Blessed are the poor in spirit, for theirs is the kingdom of heaven,"[3] with all its riches and treasures. All of God's resources will be made available to the soul that is humble enough to be able to receive them without growing proud because of it. God blesses each of us up to the level and extent of what it is safe for Him to do. If you do not get a blessing, it is because it is not safe for you to have one. If our heavenly Father were to let your unhumbled spirit win a victory in His holy war, you would snatch the crown for yourself, and in the next battle you would fall a victim. He keeps you low for your own safety! When a man is sincerely humble and never tries to take the credit or the praise, there is scarcely any limit to what God will do for him. Humility makes us ready to be blessed by the God of all grace and equips us to deal efficiently with our fellows. True humility is a flower that will adorn any garden. This is a sauce that will season every dish of life and improve it in every case. Whether in prayer or praise, whether in work or suffering, the genuine salt of humility cannot be used in excess.

[1] Isaiah 66:2   [2] Ephesians 4:10   [3] Matthew 5:3

Jesus, bearing His cross, went to suffer outside the gate. The Christian's reason for leaving the camp of the world's sin and religion is not because he loves to be isolated, but because *Jesus did so*; and the disciple must follow his Master. Christ was "not of the world." His life and His testimony were a constant protest against conformity with the world. Although He displayed overflowing affection for men, He was still separate from sinners. In the same way Christ's people must "go to him." They must take their position "outside the camp," as witness-bearers for the truth. They must be prepared to walk the straight and narrow path. They must have bold, unflinching, lion-like hearts, loving Christ first, and His truth next, and Christ and His truth more than all the world. Jesus desires His people to "go . . . outside the camp" *for their own sanctification.* You cannot grow in grace to any high degree while you are conformed to the world. The life of separation may be a path of sorrow, but it is the highway of safety; and though the separated life may be painful and make every day a battle, yet it is a happy life after all. No joy can excel that of the soldier of Christ: Jesus reveals Himself so graciously and gives such sweet refreshment that the warrior feels more calm and peace in his daily strife than others in their hours of rest. The highway of holiness is the highway of communion. It is in this way we shall hope *to win the crown* if we are enabled by divine grace faithfully to follow Christ "outside the camp." The crown of glory will follow the cross of separation. A moment's shame will be well rewarded by eternal honor; a little while of witness-bearing will seem nothing when we are forever with the Lord.

∼ EVENING ∼

Our Lord Jesus, by His death, did not purchase a right to just a part of us, but to all of us. He pondered in His passion our complete sanctification—spirit, soul, and body, that in every area He Himself might reign supreme without a rival. It is the business of the newborn nature that God has given to the regenerate to assert the rights of the Lord Jesus Christ. My soul, insofar as you are a child of God, you must conquer all the rest of yourself that remains unblessed; you must subdue all your powers and passions, and you must never be satisfied until He who is King by purchase also becomes King by gracious coronation and reigns in you supreme. Seeing, then, that sin has no right to any part of us, we are involved in good and lawful warfare when we seek, in the name of God, to drive it out. Since my body is a member of Christ, shall I tolerate subjection to the prince of darkness? My soul, Christ has suffered for your sins and redeemed you with His most precious blood; do not allow your memory to store up evil thoughts or your passions to be the occasion of sin. Do not allow your judgment to be perverted by error or your will to be led in chains of iniquity. No, my soul, you are Christ's, and sin has no right to you.

Be courageous concerning this, O Christian! Be not dispirited, as though your spiritual enemies could never be destroyed. You are able to overcome them—but not in your own strength—the weakest of them would be too much for you; but you can and shall overcome them through the blood of the Lamb. If you wonder how to dispossess them since they are greater and mightier than you, go to the strong for strength, wait humbly upon God, and the mighty God of Jacob will surely come to your rescue, and you will sing of victory through His grace.

An instructive writer has made a mournful list of the honors that the blinded people of Israel awarded to their long-expected King. (1) They gave Him *a procession of honor*, in which Roman legionaries, Jewish priests, and men and women took part, He Himself bearing His cross. This is the triumph that the world awards to Him who comes to overthrow man's greatest enemy. Derisive shouts are His only acclamations, and cruel taunts His only songs of praise. (2) They presented Him with *the wine of honor*. Instead of a golden cup of generous wine, they offered Him the criminal's anesthetic potion, which He refused in order that he might, in all its unmitigated horror, taste death; and afterwards when He cried, "I thirst," they gave Him vinegar mixed with gall, thrust to His mouth upon a sponge. What wretched, detestable inhospitality to the King's Son. (3) He was provided with *a guard of honor*, who showed their esteem of Him by gambling over His clothes, which they had seized as their treasure. The bodyguard of Jesus was a quaternion of brutal gamblers. (4) *A throne of honor* was found for Him upon the bloody tree. The cross was, in fact, the full expression of the world's feeling toward Him. "There," they seemed to say, "you Son of God, this is the manner in which God Himself should be treated, could we reach Him." (5) *The title of honor* was nominally "King of the Jews," but this was distinctly repudiated. They really called Him "King of thieves" by preferring Barabbas and by placing Jesus in the place of highest shame between two thieves. In this way His glory was turned into shame by the sons of men, but it shall nevertheless still gladden the eyes of saints and angels, world without end.

In this *solemn confession*, it is helpful to observe that David plainly names his sin. He does not call it manslaughter or speak of it as an imprudence by which an unfortunate accident occurred to a worthy man, but he calls it by its true name, "bloodguiltiness." He did not actually kill the husband of Bathsheba; but still it was planned in David's heart that Uriah should die, and David was before the Lord responsible for his murder. Learn in confession to be honest with God. Do not give fair names to foul sins; call them what you will, they will smell no sweeter. What God sees them to be, that you should work to feel them to be; and with an honest, open heart acknowledge their real character. Observe that David was evidently oppressed with the heinousness of his sin. It is easy to use words, but it is difficult to feel their meaning. The fifty-first Psalm is the photograph of a contrite spirit. Let us seek to display the same brokenness of heart; because no matter how excellent our words may be, if our heart is not conscious of the hell-deservingness of sin, we cannot expect to find forgiveness.

Our text has in it *an earnest prayer*—it is addressed to the God of *salvation*. It is His prerogative to forgive; it is His very name and office to save those who seek His face. Better still, the text calls Him the God of *my* salvation. We bless His name, in that while we are still going to Him through Jesus' blood, we may rejoice in the God of *our* salvation.

The psalmist ends with *a commendable vow*: If God will deliver him he will sing—actually, he will "*sing aloud*." Who can mute their praise in light of such a mercy as this! But note the subject of the song—"*your righteousness*." We must sing of the finished work of a precious Savior; and the one who knows this forgiving love the best will sing the loudest of us all.

FOR IF THEY DO THESE THINGS WHEN THE WOOD IS GREEN, WHAT WILL HAPPEN WHEN IT IS DRY? — LUKE 23:31

Among other interpretations of this suggestive question, the following is full of teaching: "If the innocent substitute for sinners suffers in this way, what will be done when the sinner himself—the dry tree—falls into the hands of an angry God?" When God saw Jesus in the sinner's place, He did not spare Him; and when He finds the unregenerate without Christ, He will not spare them. O sinner, Jesus was led away by His enemies; and you will be dragged away by fiends to the place appointed for you. Jesus was deserted by God; and if He, who was only imputedly a sinner, was deserted, how much more will you be? *"Eloi, eloi, lama sabachthani?"* What an awful shriek! But what will be your cry when you shall say, "O God! O God! Why have You forsaken me?" and the answer shall come back, "Because you have ignored all My counsel and would have none of My reproof, I also will laugh at your calamity; I will mock when terror strikes you." If God did not spare His own Son, how much less will He spare you! What whips of stinging pain will be yours when your conscience smites you with all its terrors. You rich, you merry, you most self-righteous sinners—who would stand in your place when God says, "Awake, O sword, against the man that rejected Me; smite him, and let him feel the sting forever"? Jesus was spat upon. Sinner, what shame will be yours! We cannot sum up in one word all the mass of sorrows that met upon the head of Jesus who died for us; therefore it is impossible for us to tell you what streams, what oceans of grief must roll over *your* spirit if you die as you are now. You may die in this state; you may die now. By the agonies of Christ, by His wounds and by His blood, do not bring upon yourselves the wrath to come! Trust in the Son of God, and you shall never die.

❧ EVENING ☙

I WILL FEAR NO EVIL, FOR YOU ARE WITH ME. — PSALM 23:4

Consider how the Holy Spirit can make the Christian independent of outward circumstances. What a bright light may shine within us when it is really dark outside! How firm, how happy, how calm, how peaceful we may be when the world shakes, and the foundations of the earth are removed! Even death itself, with all its terrible influences, has no power to suspend the music of a Christian's heart, but instead makes that music sweeter, clearer, more heavenly, until the last kind act that death can do is allow the earthly song to melt into the heavenly chorus, the temporal joy into the eternal bliss! Let us have confidence, then, in the blessed Spirit's power to comfort us. Dear reader, are you facing poverty? Do not fear—the Holy Spirit can give you, in your need, a greater plenty than the rich have in their abundance. You never know what joys may be stored up for you in the cottage around which grace will plant the roses of contentment. Are you conscious of your physical frailty? Do you anticipate sleepless nights and painful days? Do not be sad! Your bed may become a throne to you. You cannot tell how every pain that shoots through your body may be a refining fire to consume your dross—a beam of glory to light up the secret parts of your soul. Is your eyesight failing? Jesus will be your light. Is your hearing deteriorating? Jesus' name will be your soul's best music, and His person your dear delight. Socrates used to say, "Philosophers can be happy without music," and Christians can be happier than philosophers when all outward causes of rejoicing are removed. In You, my God, my heart shall triumph, no matter my circumstances! By Your power, O blessed Spirit, my heart shall rejoice even though all things should fail me here below.

❧ MORNING ☙
AND THERE FOLLOWED HIM A GREAT MULTITUDE OF THE PEOPLE
AND OF WOMEN WHO WERE MOURNING
AND LAMENTING FOR HIM. — LUKE 23:27

Among the rabble that hounded the Redeemer to His doom, there were some gracious souls whose bitter anguish found an outlet in wailing and lamentations—suitable music to accompany that woeful march. When I can, in imagination, see the Savior bearing His cross to Calvary, my soul joins the godly women and weeps with them; for, indeed, there is true cause for grief—cause lying deeper than those mourning women recognized. They bewailed innocence maltreated, goodness persecuted, love bleeding, meekness about to die; but my heart has a deeper and more bitter cause to mourn. My sins were the scourges that lacerated those blessed shoulders and crowned with thorns those bleeding brows: my sins cried, "Crucify Him! crucify Him!" and laid the cross upon His gracious shoulders. His being led forth to die is sorrow enough for one eternity: but my having been His murderer is more, infinitely more, grief than one poor fountain of tears can express. The reason for those women's love and tears is plain to read, but they could not have had greater reasons for love and grief than my heart has. The widow of Nain saw her son restored—but I myself have been raised to newness of life. Peter's mother-in-law was cured of the fever—but I of the greater plague of sin. Out of Magdalene seven devils were cast—but a whole legion out of me. Mary and Martha were favored with visits—but He dwells with me. His mother bore His body—but He is formed in me, the hope of glory. Since I am not behind the holy women in debt, let me not be behind them in gratitude or sorrow.

> *Love and grief my heart dividing,*
> *With my tears His feet I'll lave—*
> *Constant still in heart abiding,*
> *Weep for Him who died to save.*

❧ EVENING ☙
YOUR GENTLENESS MADE ME GREAT. — PSALM 18:35

These words are capable of being translated, "Your *goodness* made me great." David gratefully ascribed all his greatness not to his own goodness, but to the goodness of God. "Your *providence*" is another reading; and providence is nothing more than goodness in action. Goodness is the bud of which providence is the flower, or goodness is the seed of which providence is the harvest. Some render it, "Your *help*," which is just another word for providence, providence being the firm ally of the saints, aiding them in the service of their Lord. Or again, "Your *humility* made me great." "Your *condescension*" may perhaps serve as a comprehensive reading, combining all these ideas, including *humility*. God's making Himself little is the cause of our being made great. We are so little that if God should display His greatness without condescension, we would be trampled under His feet; but God, who must stoop to view the skies and bow to see what angels do, turns His eye yet lower and looks to the lowly and contrite and makes them great. There are still other translations. For example, the Septuagint reads, "Your *discipline*"—Your fatherly correction—"made me great," while another paraphrase reads, "Your *word* increased me." Still the idea is the same. David ascribes all his own greatness to the condescending goodness of his Father in heaven. May this attitude be echoed in our hearts this evening while we cast our crowns at Jesus' feet and cry, "Your gentleness made me great." How marvelous is our experience of God's gentleness! How gentle His corrections! How gentle His patience! How gentle His teachings! How gentle His invitations! Meditate upon this theme, believer. Let gratitude be awakened; let humility be deepened; let love be quickened before you fall asleep tonight.

The hill of comfort is the hill that is called The Skull or Calvary; the house of consolation is built with the wood of the cross; the temple of heavenly blessing is based upon the riven rock—riven by the spear that pierced His side. No scene in sacred history ever gladdens the soul like Calvary's tragedy.

> *Is it not strange, the darkest hour*
> *That ever dawned on sinful earth,*
> *Should touch the heart with softer power,*
> *For comfort, than an angel's mirth?*
> *That to the Cross the mourner's eye should turn,*
> *Sooner than where the stars of Bethlehem burn?*

Light springs from the midday-midnight of Golgotha, and every herb of the field blooms sweetly beneath the shadow of the once accursed tree. In that place of thirst, grace has dug a fountain that runs continually with water pure as crystal, each drop capable of alleviating the woes of mankind. You who have had your seasons of conflict will confess that it was not at Olivet that you ever found comfort, not on the hill of Sinai, nor on Tabor; but Gethsemane and Golgotha have been a means of comfort to you. The bitter herbs of Gethsemane have often taken away the pains in your life; and the groans of Calvary yield rare and rich comfort. We never would have known Christ's love in all its heights and depths if He had not died; nor could we guess the Father's deep affection if He had not given His Son to die. The common mercies we enjoy all sing of love, just as the seashell, when we put it to our ears, whispers the sounds of the deep sea from which it came; but if we desire to hear the ocean itself, we must not look at everyday blessings, but at the transactions of the crucifixion. If you want to know love, then go afresh to Calvary and see the Man of Sorrows die.

Storms and darkness, combined with imminent risk of shipwreck, had brought the crew of the vessel into a sorry predicament; only one man among them remained perfectly calm, and by his word the rest were reassured. Paul was the only man who had enough heart to say, "I urge you to take heart." There were veteran Roman soldiers on board, and brave sailors, but their poor Jewish prisoner had more spirit than all of them. He had a secret Friend who kept his courage up. The Lord Jesus sent a heavenly messenger to whisper words of comfort in Paul's ear, and as a result his face shone, and he spoke like a man at ease.

If we fear the Lord, we may look for His timely intervention when our case is at its worst. Angels are not kept from us by storms or hindered by darkness. Seraphs do not think it is beneath them to visit the poorest of the heavenly family. If angels' visits are few and far between at ordinary times, they will be frequent in our nights of tempest and storm. Friends may leave us when we are under pressure, but our awareness of the members of the angelic world will be far more apparent. Strengthened by loving words brought to us from the throne via Jacob's ladder, we will be able to do daring feats. Dear reader, are you facing an hour of distress? Then ask for particular help. Jesus is the angel of the covenant, and if you earnestly seek His presence, it will not be denied. The encouragement which that presence brings will be remembered by those who, like Paul, have had the angel of God standing by them in a night of storm, when anchors slipped and shipwreck threatened.

> *O angel of my God, be near,*
> *Amid the darkness hush my fear;*
> *Loud roars the wild tempestuous sea,*
> *Thy presence, Lord, shall comfort me.*

I AM POURED OUT LIKE WATER, AND ALL MY BONES ARE OUT OF JOINT.
— PSALM 22:14

Did earth or heaven ever witness a sadder spectacle than this? In soul and body, our Lord felt Himself to be weak as water poured upon the ground. The placing of the cross in its socket had shaken Him with great violence, had strained all the ligaments, pained every nerve, and more or less dislocated all His bones. Burdened by His own weight, the impressive sufferer felt the strain increasing every moment of those six long hours. His sense of faintness and general weakness were overpowering, and He felt Himself to be nothing but a mass of misery and swooning sickness. When Daniel saw the great vision, he describes his sensations in this way: "No strength was left in me. My radiant appearance was fearfully changed, and I retained no strength."[1] How much more devastating must it have been for Jesus when He saw the dreadful vision of the wrath of God and felt it in His own soul! Sensations that our Lord endured, we could not have faced, and unconsciousness would have had to come to our rescue. In His case He was wounded and *felt* the sword; He drained the cup and *tasted* every drop.

> O King of Grief! (a title strange, but true,
> To Thee of all kings only due)
> O King of Wounds! how shall I grieve for Thee,
> Who in all grief savest me!

As we kneel before our ascended Savior's throne, let us carefully remember the way by which He prepared it as a throne of grace for us; let us in spirit drink of His cup, that we may be strengthened for our hour of heaviness whenever it may come. In His natural body every member suffered, and so must it be in the spiritual; just as out of all His griefs and woes His body emerged uninjured to glory and power, similarly His mystical body will come through the furnace with not so much as the smell of smoke upon it.

❧ EVENING ❧

CONSIDER MY AFFLICTION AND MY TROUBLE, AND
FORGIVE ALL MY SINS. — PSALM 25:18

It is good for us when prayers about our sorrows are linked with pleas concerning our sins— when, being under God's hand, we do not focus exclusively on our pain, but remember our sins against God. It is also good to take both sorrow and sin to the same place. It was to God that David carried his sorrow: It was to God that David confessed his sin. Notice, then, *we must take our sorrows to God*. Even your little sorrows you may cast upon God, for He counts the hairs of your head; and your great sorrows you may commit to Him, for He holds the ocean in the hollow of His hand. Go to Him, whatever your present trouble may be, and you will find Him able and willing to relieve you. *But we must take our sins to God too*. We must carry them to the cross, that the blood may fall upon them, to purge away their guilt and to destroy their defiling power.

The special lesson of the text is this:—*we are to go to the Lord with sorrows and with sins in the right spirit*. Note that all David asks concerning his sorrow is, "*Consider* my affliction and my trouble"; but the next petition is vastly more explicit, definite, decided, plain— "*Forgive* all my sins." Many sufferers would have reversed it: "Remove my affliction and my pain, and consider my sins." But David does not; he cries, "Lord, when it comes to my affliction and my pain, I will not dictate to Your wisdom. Lord, look at them—I will leave them to You. I would like to have my pain removed, but do as You will. But as for my sins, Lord, I know what needs to happen—I must have them forgiven; I cannot endure to live under their curse for a moment." A Christian counts sorrow lighter in the scale than sin; he can bear to have troubles continue, but he cannot bear the burden of his transgressions.

[1] Daniel 10:8

MY HEART IS LIKE WAX; IT IS MELTED WITHIN MY BREAST.
— PSALM 22:14

O ur blessed Lord experienced a terrible sinking and melting of soul. "A man's spirit will endure sickness, but a crushed spirit who can bear?"[1] Deep spiritual depression is the most devastating of all trials; nothing compares to it. No wonder the suffering Savior cries to His God, "Do not be far off," for more than at any other time a man needs his God when his heart is melted within him because of heaviness. Believer, come to the cross this morning, and humbly worship the King of glory as one who has been brought far lower, in mental distress and inward anguish, than anyone among us; and consider Him a faithful High Priest who is able to sympathize with our weakness. Especially let those of us whose sadness springs directly from the withdrawal of a present sense of our Father's love enter into near and intimate communion with Jesus. Let us not give in to despair; our Master has already walked this dark road. Our souls may sometimes long and faint, and thirst even to the point of anguish, to see the light of the Lord's face; at such times let us calm ourselves by focusing on the sympathy of our great High Priest. Our drops of sorrow may be forgotten in the ocean of His griefs; how high ought our love to rise! O strong and deep love of Jesus, come in like a flood, cover all my powers, drown all my sins, wash away all my cares, lift up my earthbound soul, and bring me up to my Lord's feet. Let me lie, a poor broken shell, washed up by His love, having no virtue or value; but knowing that if He will bend His ear to me, He will hear within my heart faint echoes of the vast waves of His own love that have brought me to where I am happy to stay, even at His feet forever.

❧ EVENING ❨

. . . THE KING'S GARDEN . . . — NEHEMIAH 3:15

M ention of the king's garden by Nehemiah brings to mind the *paradise* that the King of kings prepared for Adam. Sin has utterly ruined that delightful dwelling and has driven out the children of men to till the ground, which yields thorns and thistles to them. My soul, remember the Fall, for it was *your* fall. Weep much because the Lord of love was so shamefully ill treated by the head of the human race, of which you are a member, as undeserving as any. Behold how dragons and demons dwell on this fair earth, which was once a garden of delights.

Look now at another King's garden, which the King waters with His bloody sweat— *Gethsemane*, whose bitter herbs are far sweeter to renewed souls than the luscious fruits of Eden. In Gethsemane the mischief of the serpent in the first garden was undone: There the curse was lifted from earth and borne by the woman's promised seed. My soul, learn to ponder Christ's agony and passion; visit the garden of the olive-press, and view your great Redeemer rescuing you from your lost condition. This is the garden of gardens; indeed, here the soul may see the guilt of sin and the power of love, two sights that surpass all others.

Is there no other King's garden? Yes, *my heart*, or should be. How do the flowers flourish? Do any choice fruits appear? Does the King walk there and rest in the arbor of my spirit? Let me ensure that the plants are trimmed and watered, and the mischievous foxes hunted out. Come, Lord, and let the heavenly wind blow at Your coming, that the spices of Your garden may cast their fragrance everywhere. I must not forget the King's garden of *the church*. O Lord, send prosperity to it. Rebuild her walls, nourish her plants, ripen her fruits, and from the huge wilderness reclaim the wasteland and make of it a King's garden.

[1]Proverbs 18:14

MY BELOVED IS TO ME A SACHET OF MYRRH. — SONG OF SOLOMON 1:13

Myrrh may well be chosen to typify Jesus because of *its preciousness, its perfume,* its *pleasantness, its healing, preserving, disinfecting qualities, and its connection with sacrifice.* But why is He compared to "a *sachet* of myrrh"? First, because it speaks of plenty. He is not a drop of it—He is a basketful. He is not a sprig or flower of it, but a whole bundle. There is enough in Christ for all my needs; do not let me be slow to avail myself of Him. Our well-beloved is compared to a "sachet," again, for *variety,* for there is in Christ not only the one thing needful, but "in him the whole fullness of deity dwells bodily";[1] everything needful is in Him. Consider the numerous aspects of Christ, and you will see a marvelous variety—Prophet, Priest, King, Husband, Friend, Shepherd. Consider Him in His life, death, resurrection, ascension, second coming; view Him in His virtue, gentleness, courage, self-denial, love, faithfulness, truth, righteousness—everywhere He is a sachet of preciousness. He is a "sachet of myrrh" for *preservation*—not loose myrrh tied up, but myrrh to be stored in a container. We must value Him as our best treasure; we must prize His words and His ordinances; and we must keep our thoughts of Him and our knowledge of Him as under lock and key, in case the devil should steal anything from us. Furthermore, Jesus is a "sachet of myrrh" *for specialty.* The emblem suggests the idea of distinguishing, discriminating grace. From before the foundation of the world, He was set apart for His people; and He gives His perfume only to those who understand how to enter into communion with Him, to have close dealings with Him—blessed people whom the Lord has admitted into His secrets, and for whom He sets Himself apart. Choice and happy are those who can say, "My beloved is to me a sachet of myrrh."

🙠　EVENING　🙢
HE SHALL LAY HIS HAND ON THE HEAD OF THE BURNT OFFERING, AND IT
SHALL BE ACCEPTED FOR HIM TO MAKE ATONEMENT FOR HIM.
— LEVITICUS 1:4

Our Lord's being "made . . . sin"[2] for us is pictured here by the very significant transfer of sin to the bullock, which was done by the elders of the people. The laying of the hand was not a mere touch of contact, for in some other places of Scripture the original word has the meaning of leaning heavily, as in the expression, "Your wrath lies heavy upon me" (Psalm 88:7). Surely this is the very essence and nature of faith, which not only brings us into contact with the great Substitute, but also teaches us to lean upon Him with all the burden of our guilt. Jehovah made all the offenses of His covenant people rest upon the Substitute, and each one of the chosen is brought personally to confirm this solemn covenant act, when by grace he is enabled by faith to lay his hand upon the head of the Lamb that was slain before the foundation of the world. Believer, do you remember that wonderful day when you first realized pardon through Jesus the sin-bearer? Can you make a glad confession and join with the writer in saying, "My soul recalls the day of deliverance with delight. Burdened with guilt and full of fears, I saw my Savior as my Substitute, and I laid my hand upon Him—timidly at first, but courage grew and confidence was confirmed until I leaned my soul entirely upon Him. And now it is my unceasing joy to know that my sins are no longer imputed to me but are laid on Him. Like the debts of the wounded traveler, Jesus, like the good Samaritan, has said of all my future sinfulness, 'Set that to My account.'" Blessed discovery! Eternal solace of a grateful heart!

My numerous sins transferr'd to Him,
Shall never more be found,
Lost in His blood's atoning stream,
Where every crime is drown'd!

[1] Colossians 2:9　[2] 2 Corinthians 5:21

ALL WHO SEE ME MOCK ME; THEY MAKE MOUTHS AT ME;
THEY WAG THEIR HEADS. — PSALM 22:7

Mockery was a large factor in our Lord's suffering. Judas mocked Him in the garden; the chief priests and scribes laughed Him to scorn; Herod set Him at nothing; the servants and the soldiers jeered at Him and brutally insulted Him; Pilate and his guards ridiculed His royalty; and on the tree all sorts of horrible jibes and hideous taunts were hurled at Him. Ridicule is always hard to bear, but when we are in intense pain it is so heartless, so cruel, that it cuts us to the quick. Consider the Savior crucified, racked with anguish far beyond anything we can imagine, and then picture that motley multitude, all wagging their heads or making mouths in bitter contempt of the poor suffering victim! Surely there must have been something more in the Crucified One than they could see, or else such a great and mingled crowd would not have unanimously "honored" Him with such contempt. Was it not evil confessing, in the very moment of its greatest apparent triumph, that after all it could do no more than mock at that victorious goodness that was then reigning on the cross? O Jesus, "despised and rejected by men,"[1] how could You die for men who treated You so badly? Here is amazing love, love divine, love beyond degree. We despised You in our pre-converted days, and even since our new birth we have given the world a place in our hearts, and yet You bled to heal our wounds and died to give us life. O that we could set You on a glorious high throne in all men's hearts! We would ring out Your praises over land and sea until men would universally adore you just as they once unanimously rejected You.

> Your creatures wrong Thee, O sovereign Good!
> You are not loved, because not understood:
> This grieves me most, that vain pursuits beguile
> Ungrateful men, regardless of Thy smile.

❧ EVENING ❧

TELL THE RIGHTEOUS THAT IT SHALL BE WELL WITH THEM. — ISAIAH 3:10

It *is well with the righteous ALWAYS.* If it had said, "Tell the righteous that it is well with them in their prosperity," we would be thankful for so great a blessing, for prosperity is an hour of peril. It is a gift from heaven to be safe from its snares. If it had read, "It is well with them when under persecution," we would be thankful for such a comforting assurance, for persecution is hard to bear; but when no time is mentioned, all time is included. God's shalls must always be understood in their largest sense. From the beginning of the year to the end of the year, from the first gathering of evening shadows until a new day dawns, in all conditions and under all circumstances, it will be well with the righteous. It is so well with him that we could not imagine it to be better, for he is *well fed*—he feeds upon the flesh and blood of Jesus; he is *well clothed*—he wears the imputed righteousness of Christ; he is *well housed*—he dwells in God; he is *well married*—his soul is knit in bonds of marriage to Christ; he is *well provided for*—for the Lord is his Shepherd; he is *well endowed*—for heaven is his inheritance. It is well with the righteous—*well upon divine authority*; the mouth of God speaks the comforting assurance. O beloved, if God declares that all is well, ten thousand devils may declare it to be ill, but we may laugh them all to scorn. Blessed be God for a faith that enables us to believe God when the creatures contradict Him. It is, says the Word, at all times well with you, righteous one; then, beloved, if you cannot see it, let God's Word assure you; believe it on divine authority with more confidence than if your eyes and your feelings told it to you. Those God blesses are blessed indeed, and what His lip declares is truth most sure and steadfast.

[1] Isaiah 53:3

MY GOD, MY GOD, WHY HAVE YOU FORSAKEN ME? — PSALM 22:1

Here we view the Savior in the depth of His sorrows. No other place displays the griefs of Christ like this, and no other moment at Calvary is so full of agony as when His cry rends the air—"My God, my God, why have you forsaken me?" At this moment physical weakness was united with acute mental torture from the shame and ignominy through which He had to pass; His grief culminated in suffering the spiritual agony beyond all telling that resulted from the departure of His Father's presence. This was the black midnight of His horror—when He descended the abyss of suffering. No man can enter into the full meaning of these words. Some of us think at times that *we* could cry, "My God, my God, why have you forsaken me?" There are seasons when the brightness of our Father's smile is eclipsed by clouds and darkness; but let us remember that God never really does forsake us. It is only a seeming forsaking with us, but in Christ's case it was a real forsaking. We grieve at a little withdrawal of our Father's love; but the real turning away of God's face from His Son—who can calculate how deep the agony that caused Him?

In our case, our cry is often dictated by unbelief: In His case, it was the utterance of a dreadful fact, for God had really turned away from Him for a season. Poor, distressed soul who once lived in the sunshine of God's face but now in darkness, remember that He has not really forsaken you. God in the clouds is as much our God as when He shines forth in all the beauty of His grace; but since even the *thought* that He has forsaken us gives us agony, what must the suffering of the Savior have been when He exclaimed, "My God, my God, why have you forsaken me?"

✎ EVENING ✎

BE THEIR SHEPHERD AND CARRY THEM FOREVER. — PSALM 28:9

God's people need to be carried. They are very heavy by nature. They have no wings, or if they have, they are like the dove of old that lay among the pots; and they need divine grace to make them rise up on wings covered with silver and with feathers of yellow gold. By nature sparks fly upward, but the sinful souls of men fall downward. O Lord, "carry them forever"! David himself said, "To you, O LORD, I lift up my soul,"[1] and here he feels the necessity that other men's souls should be lifted up as well as his own. When you ask for this blessing, do not forget to seek it for others also. There are three ways in which God's people require to be carried or lifted up. *They require to be lifted up in character.* Lift them up, Lord; do not allow Your people to be like the rest of the world! The world lies in the wicked one; lift them out of it! The world's people are looking for silver and gold, seeking their own pleasures and the gratification of their lusts; but, Lord, carry Your people up beyond all this; keep them from being "muck-rakers," as John Bunyan calls the man who was always scraping for gold! Set their hearts upon their risen Lord and the heavenly heritage! Moreover, *believers need to be carried in conflict.* In the battle, if they seem to fall, Lord, be pleased to give them the victory. If the foot of the enemy is upon their necks for a moment, help them to grasp the sword of the Spirit and eventually to win the battle. Lord, lift up Your children's spirits in the day of conflict; do not let them sit in the dust, mourning forever. Do not allow the adversary to disturb their peace and make them fret; but if they have been, like Hannah, persecuted, let them sing of the mercy of a delivering God.

We may also ask our Lord to *carry them at the last!* Lift them up by taking them home; carry their bodies from the tomb, and raise their souls to Your eternal kingdom in glory.

[1] Psalm 25:1

... THE PRECIOUS BLOOD OF CHRIST. — 1 PETER 1:19

Standing at the foot of the cross, we see hands and feet and side all distilling crimson streams of "precious blood." It is "precious" because of its *redeeming* and *atoning efficacy*. By it the sins of Christ's people are atoned for; they are redeemed from under the law; they are reconciled to God, made one with Him. Christ's blood is also "precious" in its *cleansing power*; it cleanses from all sin. "Though your sins are like scarlet, they shall be as white as snow."[1] Through Jesus' blood there is not a spot left upon any believer; no wrinkle nor any such thing remains. O precious blood that makes us clean, removing the stains of our iniquity and permitting us to stand accepted in the Beloved despite the many ways in which we have rebelled against our God. The blood of Christ is also "precious" in its *preserving power*. We are safe from the destroying angel under the sprinkled blood. Remember, it is *God's seeing* the blood that is the true reason for our being spared. Here is comfort for us when the eye of faith is dim, for God's eye is still the same. The blood of Christ is "precious" also in its *sanctifying influence*. The same blood that justifies by taking away sin also quickens the new nature and leads it onward to subdue sin and to obey the commands of God. There is no greater motive for holiness than that which streams from the veins of Jesus. And "precious," unspeakably precious, is this blood because it has an *overcoming power*. It is written, "And they have conquered him by the blood of the Lamb."[2] How could they do otherwise? He who fights with the precious blood of Jesus fights with a weapon that cannot know defeat. The blood of Jesus! Sin dies at its presence; death ceases to be death: Heaven's gates are opened. The blood of Jesus! We shall march on, conquering and to conquer, so long as we can trust its power!

❧ EVENING ❧
SO HIS HANDS WERE STEADY UNTIL THE GOING DOWN OF THE SUN.
— EXODUS 17:12

The prayer of Moses was so mighty that everything depended upon it. The petitions of Moses disconcerted the enemy more than the fighting of Joshua. Yet both were needed. In the soul's conflict, force and fervor, decision and devotion, valor and vehemence must join their forces, and all will be well. You must wrestle with your sin, but the major part of the wrestling must be done alone in private with God. Prayer like Moses' holds up the token of the covenant before the Lord. The rod was the emblem of God's working with Moses, the symbol of God's government in Israel. Learn, praying saint, to hold up the promise and the oath of God before Him. The Lord cannot deny His own declarations. Hold up the rod of promise, and have what you seek.

Moses grew tired, and then his friends assisted him. Whenever your prayer loses vigor, let faith support one hand, and let holy hope lift up the other, and prayer seating itself upon the stone of Israel, the rock of our salvation, will persevere and prevail. Beware of growing faint in your devotion. If Moses felt it, who can escape? It is far easier to fight with sin in public than to pray against it in private. It has been observed that while Joshua never grew weary in the fighting, Moses did grow weary in the praying; the more spiritual an exercise, the more difficult it is for flesh and blood to maintain it. Let us cry, then, for special strength, and may the Spirit of God, who helps our weaknesses as He helped Moses, enable us like him to continue with our steady hands "*until the going down of the sun,*" until the evening of life is over, until we shall come to the rising of a better sun in the land where prayer is swallowed up in praise.

[1] Isaiah 1:18   [2] Revelation 12:11

YOU HAVE COME . . . TO THE SPRINKLED BLOOD THAT SPEAKS A BETTER
WORD THAN THE BLOOD OF ABEL. — HEBREWS 12:22, 24

Reader, have *you* come to "the sprinkled blood"? The question is not whether you have come to a knowledge of doctrine or an observance of ceremonies or to a certain form of experience, but *have you come to the blood of Jesus?* The blood of Jesus is the life of all vital godliness. If you have truly come to Jesus, we know how you came—the Holy Spirit kindly brought you there. You came to the sprinkled blood with no merits of your own. Guilty, lost, and helpless, you came to take that blood, and that blood alone, as your everlasting hope. You came to the cross of Christ with a trembling and an aching heart; and what a precious sound it was to you to hear the voice of the blood of Jesus! The dropping of His blood is as the music of heaven to the penitents of earth. We are full of sin, but the Savior bids us lift our eyes to Him; and as we gaze upon His streaming wounds, each drop of blood, as it falls, cries, "It is finished; I have made an end of sin; I have brought in everlasting righteousness." Sweet language of the precious blood of Jesus! If you have come to that blood once, you will come to it constantly. Your life will be "looking to Jesus." Your whole conduct will be epitomized in this—"to whom coming." Not to whom I *have* come, but to whom I am *always coming.* If you have ever come to the sprinkled blood, you will feel your need of coming to it every day. He who does not desire to wash in it *every day* has never washed in it at all. Believers constantly feel it to be their joy and privilege that there is still a fountain opened. Past experiences are doubtful food for Christians; a present coming to Christ alone can give us joy and comfort. This morning let us sprinkle our doorpost fresh with blood, and then feast upon the Lamb, assured that the destroying angel must pass us by.

❧ EVENING ☙

WE WISH TO SEE JESUS. — JOHN 12:21

The constant cry of the world is, "Who will show us any good?" They seek satisfaction in earthly comforts, enjoyments, and riches. But the quickened sinner knows of only one good. "I wish I knew where I might find *Him*!" When he is truly awakened to feel his guilt, if you could lay a fortune before him he would say, "Take it away: I want to find *Him.*" It is a blessed thing for a man when he has brought his desires into focus, so that they all center in one object. When he has fifty different desires, his heart resembles a stagnant pool spreading out into a marsh, breeding disease; but when all his desires are channeled in one direction, his heart becomes like a river of pure water, running swiftly to fertilize the fields. Happy is he who has one desire, if that one desire is set on Christ, though it may not yet have been realized. When a soul desires Jesus, it is a sure indication of divine work within. Such a man will never be content with mere externals. He will say, "I want Christ; I *must* have Him—mere ordinances are of no use to me. I want *Himself*; do not offer me these; you offer me the empty pitcher, while I am dying of thirst; give me water or I die. Jesus is my soul's desire. I wish to see Jesus!"

Is this your condition, my reader, at this moment? Have you only one desire, and is that for Christ? Then you are not far from the kingdom of heaven. Have you only one wish in your heart, and that is that you may be washed from all your sins in Jesus' blood? Can you really say, "I would give all I have to be a Christian. I would give up everything I have and hope for, in order to know that I have an interest in Christ"? Then, despite all your fears, be encouraged—the Lord loves you, and you will come out into daylight soon and rejoice in the liberty with which Christ makes you free.

SHE TIED THE SCARLET CORD IN THE WINDOW. — JOSHUA 2:21

Rahab depended for her preservation upon the promise of the spies, whom she regarded as the representatives of the God of Israel. Her faith was simple and firm, but it was very obedient. To tie the scarlet cord in the window was a very trivial act in itself, but she dared not run the risk of omitting it. Come, my soul, is there not here a lesson for you? Have you been attentive to all your Lord's will, even though some of His commands should seem nonessential? Have you observed in His own way the two ordinances of believers' baptism and the Lord's Supper? To neglect these is to display the unloving disobedience in your heart. From now on be blameless in everything, even the tying of a thread, if that is what's commanded.

This act of Rahab provides an even more solemn lesson. Have I implicitly trusted in the precious blood of Jesus? Have I tied the scarlet cord, with an intricate knot in my window, so that my trust can never be removed? Or can I look out toward the Dead Sea of my sins or the Jerusalem of my hopes without seeing the blood and seeing all things in connection with its blessed power? The passer-by can see a cord of such a conspicuous color if it hangs from the window: It will be good for me if my life makes the efficacy of the atonement conspicuous to all onlookers. What is there to be ashamed of? Let men or devils gaze if they want, the blood is my boast and my song. My soul, there is One who will see that scarlet cord, even when because your faith is weak you cannot see it yourself; Jehovah, the Avenger, will see it and pass over you. Jericho's walls fell flat: Rahab's house was on the wall, and yet it stood undisturbed. My nature is built into the wall of humanity, and yet when destruction smites the race, I will be secure. My soul, tie the scarlet cord in the window again, and rest in peace.

✋ EVENING ✍

BUT YOU SAID, I WILL SURELY DO YOU GOOD. — GENESIS 32:12

When Jacob was on the other side of the brook Jabbok, and Esau was coming with armed men, Jacob earnestly sought God's protection, and the ground of his appeal was this: "But you said, I will surely do you good." What force is in that plea! He was holding God to His word—"You said." The attribute of God's faithfulness is a splendid horn of the altar to lay hold upon; but the promise, which contains the attribute and something more, is mightier still—"You said, I will surely do you good." Would *He* say it and then not do it? "Let God be true though everyone were a liar."[1] Will *He* not be true? Will *He* not keep His word? Will not every word that comes out of His lips stand fast and be fulfilled? Solomon, at the opening of the temple, used this same mighty plea. He pleaded with God to remember the word that He had spoken to his father David and to bless that place. When a man gives a promissory note, his honor is engaged; he signs his name, and he must honor it when the due time comes or else he loses credit. It shall never be said that God dishonors His bills. The credit of the Most High was never impeached, and never shall be. He is punctual to the second: He is never before His time, but He is never behind it. Search God's Word through, and compare it with the experience of God's people, and you will find the two tally from beginning to end. Many an ancient patriarch has said with Joshua, "Not one word has failed of all the good things that the LORD your God promised concerning you. All have come to pass."[2] If you have a divine promise, you need not plead it with an "if"; you may urge it with certainty. The Lord meant to fulfill the promise or He would not have given it. God does not give His words merely to keep us quiet and to keep us hopeful for a while with the intention of putting us off in the end; but when He speaks, it is because He means to do as He has said.

[1] Romans 3:4   [2] Joshua 23:14

AND BEHOLD, THE CURTAIN OF THE TEMPLE WAS TORN IN TWO,
FROM TOP TO BOTTOM. — MATTHEW 27:51

No small miracle was performed in the tearing of so strong and thick a curtain; but it was not intended merely as a display of power—many lessons were contained in it. *The old law of ordinances* was put away and, like a worn-out garment, torn and set aside. When Jesus died, the sacrifices were all finished, because they were fulfilled in Him; and therefore the place of sacrifice, the temple, was marked with a clear sign of this change. With the curtain torn, *all the hidden things of the old dispensation became apparent*: The mercy-seat could now be seen, and the glory of God gleaming above it. By the death of our Lord Jesus we have a clear revelation of God, for He was "not like Moses, who would put a veil over his face."[1] Life and immortality are now brought to light, and things that have been hidden since the foundation of the world are displayed in Him. *The annual ceremony of atonement was also abolished.* The atoning blood that once every year was sprinkled inside the curtain was now offered once for all by the great High Priest, and therefore the place of the symbolical rite was finished. No blood of bullocks or of lambs is needed now, for Jesus has entered inside the curtain with his own blood. Therefore *access to God is now permitted* and is the privilege of every believer in Christ Jesus. It is not just a small opening through which we may peer at the mercy-seat, but the tear reaches from the top to the bottom. We may come with boldness to the throne of heavenly grace. Is it wrong to suggest that the opening of the Holy of Holies in this marvelous manner by our Lord's expiring cry was signifying *the opening of the gates of paradise* to all the saints by virtue of the Passion? Our bleeding Lord has the key of heaven; He opens and no man shuts; let us enter in with Him to the heavenly places and sit with Him there until our common enemies shall be made His footstool.

✺   EVENING   ✺

THE WORDS OF THE AMEN. — REVELATION 3:14

The word *Amen* solemnly confirms what went before, and Jesus is the great Confirmer; immutable forever is "the Amen" in all *His promises. Sinner,* I would comfort you with this reflection. Jesus Christ said, "Come to me, all who labor and are heavy laden, and I will give you rest."[2] If you come to Him, He will say "Amen" in your soul; His promise shall be true *to you.* He said in the days of His flesh, "A bruised reed he will not break."[3] Poor, broken, bruised heart, if you come to Him, He will say "Amen" to you, and it will be true in your soul as in hundreds of cases in years gone by. *Christian,* isn't this very comforting to you also, that there is not a word that has come from the Savior's lips that He has ever retracted? The words of Jesus will stand when heaven and earth pass away. If you get ahold of but half a promise, you will find it true. Watch out for those who ignore the promises and so miss much of the comfort of God's Word.

Jesus is Yes and Amen in all *His offices.* He was a Priest to pardon and cleanse once; He is Amen as Priest still. He was a King to rule and reign for His people and to defend them with His mighty arm; He is an Amen King, the same still. He was a Prophet of old, to foretell good things to come; His words remain trustworthy and true—He is an Amen Prophet. He is Amen as to the merit of His blood; He is Amen as to His righteousness. That sacred robe will remain most fair and glorious when nature shall decay. He is Amen in every single title that He bears; your Husband, never seeking a divorce; your Friend, sticking closer than a brother; your Shepherd, with you in death's dark vale; your Help and your Deliverer; your Refuge and your Strong Tower; the Vessel of your strength, your confidence, your joy, your all in all, and your Yes and Amen in everything.

[1] 2 Corinthians 3:13   [2] Matthew 11:28   [3] Matthew 12:20

... THAT THROUGH DEATH HE MIGHT DESTROY THE ONE WHO HAS THE
POWER OF DEATH. — HEBREWS 2:14

Child of God, death has lost its sting, because the devil's power over it is destroyed. Stop fearing death! Ask God the Holy Spirit to grant you an intimate knowledge and a firm belief in your Redeemer's death, so that you may be strengthened for that journey. Living near the cross of Calvary, you may learn to think of death with pleasure and welcome it when it comes with intense delight. It is blessed to die in the Lord: It is a covenant blessing to sleep in Jesus. Death is no longer banishment; it is a return from exile, a going home to the many mansions where the loved ones are already living. The distance between glorified spirits in heaven and militant saints on earth seems great; but it is not. We are not far from home—a moment will bring us there. The sail is spread; the soul is launched upon the deep. How long will its voyage be? How many weary winds must beat upon the sail before it shall be berthed in the port of peace? How long shall that soul be buffeted on the waves before it comes to that sea that knows no storm? Listen to the answer: "away from the body and at home with the Lord."[1] The ship has just departed, but it is already at its destination. It simply spread its sail, and it was there. Like that ship of old upon the Lake of Galilee, a storm had tossed it, but Jesus said, "Peace, be still," and *immediately* it came to land. Do not think that a long period intervenes between the instant of death and the eternity of glory. When the eyes close on earth, they open in heaven. The chariots of fire are not an instant on the road. So child of God, what is there for you to fear in death, seeing that through the death of your Lord Jesus its curse and sting are destroyed? And now it is like a Jacob's ladder with its base in a dark grave, but with its top reaching to everlasting glory.

❧ EVENING ☙

FIGHT THE LORD'S BATTLES. — 1 SAMUEL 18:17

The Christian is involved in a continual war, with Jesus Christ as the Captain of their salvation. He has said, "Behold, I am with you always, to the end of the age."[2] Listen to the battle cries! Now let the people of God stand firm in their ranks, and let no man's heart fail him. We may feel in these days that we are losing the battle and unless the Lord Jesus shall lift His sword we do not know what may become of the church of God in our time; but let us be courageous and bold. Seldom has there been a time like this as biblical Christianity trembles on the brink of capitulation to pluralism and empty religious routine. We are in great need of a bold voice and a strong hand to preach and publish the Gospel for which martyrs bled and confessors died. The Savior is, by His Spirit, still on earth; let this encourage us. He is always ever in the middle of the fight, and therefore the outcome of the battle is not in doubt. And as the conflict rages, what a deep satisfaction it is to know that the Lord Jesus, in His office as our great Intercessor, is prevalently pleading for His people! Turn your anxious gaze from the battle below, where, enshrouded in smoke, the faithful fight in garments rolled in blood. And lift your eyes above where the Savior lives and pleads, for while He intercedes, the cause of God is safe. Let us fight as if it all depended upon us, but let us look up and know that it all depends upon Him.

On the basis of our Savior's atoning sacrifice and in the strength of the Holy Spirit's power, we charge you who love Jesus to fight bravely in this holy war, for truth and righteousness, for the kingdom and the crown. Onward! The battle is not yours but God's, and you will yet hear Him say, "Well done, brave warrior, well done!"

[1] 2 Corinthians 5:8   [2] Matthew 28:20

The essence of Job's comfort lies in the little word "my"—"my Redeemer"—and in the fact that the Redeemer lives. Oh, to get hold of a living Christ. We must get a share in Him before we can enjoy Him. What is gold to me while it is still in the mine? It is gold in my possession that will satisfy my necessities by purchasing the things I need. So a Redeemer who does not redeem *me*, an avenger who will never stand up for my blood, what benefit is there in that? Do not rest content until by faith you can say, "Yes, I cast myself upon my living Lord; and He is mine." You may hold Him with a feeble hand and half think it presumption to say, "He lives as *my* Redeemer." But remember, if you have faith even as a grain of mustard seed, that little faith *entitles* you to say it. But there is also another word here, which expresses Job's strong confidence: "*I know.*" To say, "I hope so, I trust so" is comfortable, and there are thousands in the fold of Jesus who hardly ever get much further. But to reach the essence of consolation you must say, "I know." Ifs, buts, and maybes are sure destroyers of peace and comfort. Doubts are dreary things in times of sorrow. Like wasps they sting the soul! If I have any suspicion that Christ is not mine, then there is vinegar mingled with the gall of death. But if I know that Jesus lives for me, then darkness is not dark: Even the night is light about me. Surely if Job, in those ages before the coming of Christ, could say, "I know," *we* should not speak less positively. God forbid that our positiveness should be presumption. Let us make sure that our evidences are right, in case we build upon an ungrounded hope; and then let us not be satisfied with the mere foundation, for it is from the upstairs rooms that we get the panoramic views. A living Redeemer, truly mine, is unspeakable joy.

❧ EVENING ❧
. . . WHO IS AT THE RIGHT HAND OF GOD. — ROMANS 8:34

He who was once despised and rejected by men now occupies the honorable position of a beloved and honored Son. The right hand of God is *the place of majesty and favor.* Our Lord Jesus is His people's representative. When He died for them, they had rest; when He rose again for them, they had liberty; when He sat down at His Father's right hand, they had favor and honor and dignity. The raising and elevation of Christ is the elevation, the acceptance, and the glorifying of all His people, for He is their head and representative. This sitting at the right hand of God, then, is to be viewed as the reception of the Representative and therefore the acceptance of *our* souls. Believer, this is why you are free from condemnation. "Who is he that condemneth?" [KJV]. Who will condemn those men who are in Jesus at the right hand of God?

The right hand is *the place of power.* Christ at the right hand of God has all the power in heaven and on earth. Who will fight against the people who have such power vested in their Captain? My soul, what can destroy you if Omnipotence is your helper? If the protection of the Almighty covers you, what sword can harm you? Be sure of this: If Jesus is your all-prevailing King and has trampled your enemies beneath His feet, if sin, death, and hell are all defeated by Him, and you are represented in Him, there exists no possibility of your being destroyed.

> *Jesu's tremendous name*
> *Puts all our foes to flight:*
> *Jesus, the meek, the angry Lamb,*
> *A Lion is in fight.*
>
> *By all hell's host withstood;*
> *We all hell's host o'erthrow;*
> *And conquering them, through Jesu's blood*
> *We still to conquer go.*

GOD EXALTED HIM. — ACTS 5:31

Jesus, our Lord, who once was crucified, dead, and buried, now sits upon the throne of glory. The highest place that heaven affords is His by undisputed right. It is vital and helpful to remember that the exaltation of Christ in heaven is a *representative exaltation.* He is exalted at the Father's right hand, and though as Jehovah He had eminent glories, in which finite creatures cannot share, yet as the Mediator, the honors that Jesus wears in heaven are the heritage of all the saints. It is delightful to think of how close Christ's union is with His people. We are actually one with Him; we are members of His body; and His exaltation is our exaltation. He will allow us to sit upon His throne, even as He has overcome and is seated with His Father on His throne. He has a crown, and He gives us crowns too. He has a throne, but He is not content with having a throne to Himself; on His right hand there must be His queen, dressed in fine gold. He cannot be glorified without His bride. Look up, believer, to Jesus now. Let the eye of your faith see Him with many crowns upon His head; and remember that one day you will be like Him, when you will see Him as He is. You shall not be as great as He is, you will not be as divine; but you will, in some measure, share the same honors and enjoy the same happiness and the same dignity that He possesses. Be content to live unknown for a little while and to walk your weary way through the fields of poverty or up the hills of affliction; for soon enough you will reign with Christ, for He has "made [us] a kingdom and priests to our God," and we shall reign forever and ever.[1] What a wonderful thought for the children of God! We have Christ for our glorious representative in heaven's courts right now, and soon He will come and receive us to Himself, to be with Him there, to see His glory and to share His joy.

❧ EVENING ☙

YOU WILL NOT FEAR THE TERROR OF THE NIGHT. — PSALM 91:5

What is this "terror"? It may be the cry of fire or the noise of thieves or intrigued appearances or the shriek of sudden sickness or death. We live in the world of death and sorrow; we may anticipate facing ills and difficulties during the night as well as in the glare of the noonday sun. This should not alarm us, for whatever the terror may be, the promise is that the believer shall not be afraid. Why should he be? Let us put this more closely— why should *we?* God our Father is here, and will be with us all through the lonely hours. He is an almighty Watcher, a sleepless Guardian, a faithful Friend. Nothing can happen without His direction, for even hell itself is under His control. Darkness is not dark to Him. He has promised to be a wall of fire around His people—and who can break through such a barrier? Unbelievers may well be afraid, for they have an angry God above them, a guilty conscience within them, and a yawning hell beneath them. But we who rest in Jesus are saved from all these by His rich mercy. If we give way to foolish fear, we will dishonor our testimony and lead others to doubt the reality of godliness. We ought to be afraid of being afraid, in case we should grieve the Holy Spirit by foolish distrust. Down, then, you dismal forebodings and groundless apprehensions—God has not forgotten to be gracious, nor held back His tender mercies. It may be night in the soul, but there need be no terror, for the God of love does not change. Children of light may walk in darkness, but they are not therefore cast away. No, they are now enabled to prove their adoption by trusting in their heavenly Father in a way that hypocrites cannot do.

> Though the night be dark and dreary,
> Darkness cannot hide from Thee;
> You are He, who, never weary,
> Watchest where Your people be.

[1] Revelation 5:10

NO, IN ALL THESE THINGS WE ARE MORE THAN CONQUERORS
THROUGH HIM WHO LOVED US. — ROMANS 8:37

We go to Christ for forgiveness, and then too often look to the law for power to fight our sins. Paul issues this rebuke: "O foolish Galatians! Who has bewitched you? . . . Let me ask you only this: Did you receive the Spirit by works of the law or by hearing with faith? Are you so foolish? Having begun by the Spirit, are you now being perfected by the flesh?"[1] Take your sins to Christ's cross, for the flesh can only be crucified there: We are crucified *with Him*. The only weapon to fight sin with is the spear that pierced the side of Jesus. To give an illustration—if you want to overcome an angry temper, how do you go about it? It is very possible that you have never tried the right way of going to Jesus with it. How did I get salvation? I came to Jesus just as I was, and I trusted Him to save me. I must kill my angry temper in the same way. It is the only way in which I can ever kill it. I must go to the cross with it and say to Jesus, "Lord, I trust You to deliver me from it." This is the only way to give it a deathblow. Are you covetous? Do you feel the world entangle you? You may struggle against this evil as long as you please, but if it is your besetting sin, you will never be delivered from it in any other way than by the blood of Jesus. Take it to Christ. Tell Him, "Lord, I have trusted You, and Your name is Jesus, for You save Your people from their sins. Lord, this is one of my sins; save me from it!" Ordinances are nothing without Christ as a means of mortification. Your prayers, and your repentances, and your tears—the whole of them put together—are worth nothing apart from Him. Only Jesus can do helpless sinners good, and helpless saints too. You must be conquerors through Him who has loved you if you will be a conqueror at all. Our laurels must grow among His olives in Gethsemane.

∾ EVENING ∾

AND BETWEEN THE THRONE AND THE FOUR LIVING CREATURES AND
AMONG THE ELDERS I SAW A LAMB STANDING,
AS THOUGH IT HAD BEEN SLAIN. — REVELATION 5:6

Why should our exalted Lord appear in glory with His wounds? The wounds of Jesus are His glories, His jewels, His sacred ornaments. To the eye of the believer, Jesus is altogether lovely. We see Him as the lily of matchless purity, and as the rose crimsoned with His own blood. We behold the beauty of Christ in all His earthly pilgrimage, but there never was such matchless beauty as when He hung upon the cross. There we saw all His beauties in perfection, all His attributes developed, all His love drawn out, all His character expressed. Beloved, the wounds of Jesus are far fairer in our eyes than all the splendor and pomp of kings. The thorny crown is more than an imperial diadem. It is true that He no longer bears the scepter of reed, but there was even in that ignominy a glory that never flashed from a scepter of gold. Jesus wears the appearance of a slain Lamb as His royal dress in which He wooed our souls and redeemed them by His complete atonement. And these are not only the ornaments of Christ: They are the *trophies* of His love and of His victory. He has divided the spoil with the strong. He has redeemed for Himself a great multitude that no one can count, and these scars are the memorials of the fight. If Christ loves to retain the thought of His sufferings for His people, then *how precious should his wounds be to us*!

> *Behold how every wound of His*
> *A precious balm distils,*
> *Which heals the scars that sin had made,*
> *And cures all mortal ills.*

> *Those wounds are mouths that preach His grace,*
> *The ensigns of His love;*
> *The seals of our expected bliss*
> *In paradise above.*

[1] Galatians 3:1-3

BECAUSE OF ALL THIS WE MAKE A FIRM COVENANT. — NEHEMIAH 9:38

There are many occasions in our experience when we may very rightly, and with benefit, renew our covenant with God. After *recovery from sickness* when, like Hezekiah, we have had a new lease of years added to our life, we may do so appropriately. After any *deliverance from trouble*, when our joys spring forth anew, let us again visit the foot of the cross and renew our consecration. Especially let us do this after any *sin that has grieved the Holy Spirit* or brought dishonor upon the cause of God; let us then look to that blood that can make us whiter than snow and again offer ourselves to the Lord. We should not only let *our troubles* confirm our dedication to God, but *our prosperity* should do the same. If we ever meet with occasions that deserve to be called "crowning mercies," then surely, if He has crowned us, we ought also to crown our God; let us bring out again all the jewels of the divine regalia that have been stored in the jewel-closet of our heart, and let our God sit upon the throne of our love, arrayed in royal apparel. If we could learn to profit by our prosperity, we would not need to face so much adversity. If we would gather from a kiss all the good it might confer upon us, we would not have to bear the imprint of punishment so often. Have we recently received some blessing that we hadn't expected? Has the Lord opened our way? Can we sing of mercies multiplied? Then this is the day to put our hand upon the horns of the altar and say, "Bind me here, my God; bind me here with cords, even forever." Just as we need the fulfillment of new promises from God, let us offer renewed prayers that our old vows may not be dishonored. This morning let us make with Him a firm covenant because of the sacrifice of Jesus that we have been considering with gratitude for the last month.

❧ EVENING ❧

THE FLOWERS APPEAR ON THE EARTH, THE TIME OF SINGING HAS COME,
AND THE VOICE OF THE TURTLEDOVE IS HEARD IN OUR LAND.
— SONG OF SOLOMON 2:12

The season of spring is welcome in its freshness. The long and dreary winter helps us to appreciate spring's genial warmth, and its promise of summer enhances its present delights. After periods of spiritual depression, it is delightful to see again the light of the Sun of Righteousness. Our slumbering graces rise from their lethargy, like the crocus and the daffodil from their beds of earth; and our heart is made glad with delicious notes of gratitude, far more tuneful than the warbling of birds. The comforting assurance of peace, which is infinitely more delightful than the turtledove's cooing, is heard within the soul. This is the time for the soul to seek communion with her Beloved; now she must rise from her natural sordidness and come away from her old associations. If we do not hoist the sail when the breeze is favorable, we make a grave mistake: Times of refreshing should never be allowed to pass us by. When Jesus Himself visits us in tenderness and entreats us to arise, can we be so ungrateful as to refuse His request? He has risen so that He may draw us after Him. He, by His Holy Spirit, has revived us so that we may in newness of life ascend to the heavenlies and enjoy fellowship with Him. We bid farewell to the coldness and indifference of a spiritual winter when the Lord creates a spring within. Then our sap flows with vigor, and our branches blossom with high resolve. O Lord, if it is not springtime in my chilly heart, I pray You make it so, for I am tired of living at a distance from You. When will You bring this long and dreary winter to an end? Come, Holy Spirit, and renew my soul! Quicken me, restore me, and have mercy on me! This very night I earnestly implore you, Lord, to take pity upon Your servant and send me a happy revival of spiritual life!

❧ MORNING ❧

I hear the voice of my Beloved! He speaks to *me*! Fair weather is smiling upon the face of the earth, and He does not want me to be spiritually asleep while nature is all around me awaking from her winter's rest. He bids me "Arise," as well He might, for I have been lying long enough among the weeds of worldliness. He is risen, and I am risen in Him; so why should I still cleave to the dust? From lower loves, desires, pursuits, and aspirations, I want to rise to Him. He calls me by the sweet title "my love" and counts me "beautiful"; this is a good argument for my rising. If He has exalted me and thinks me fair, how can I linger in the tents of wickedness and make my friends in the wrong company? He bids me "Come away"; further and further from everything selfish, groveling, worldly, sinful, He calls me; yes, from the outwardly religious world that doesn't know Him and has no sympathy with the mystery of godliness. "Come away" has no harsh sound to my ear, and what is there to hold me in this wilderness of vanity and sin? My Lord, I want desperately to come away, but I am held among the thorns and cannot escape from them as I wish. I would, if it were possible, close my eyes and ears and heart to sin. You call me to Yourself by saying, "Come away," and this is indeed a melodious call. To come to You is to come home from exile, to reach the shore out of the raging storm, to finally rest after hard labor, to reach the goal of my desires and the summit of my wishes. But, Lord, how can a stone rise; how can a lump of clay come away from the horrible pit? Please raise me; draw me by Your grace. Send Your Holy Spirit to kindle sacred flames of love in my heart, and I will continue to rise until one day I will leave life and time behind me and come away indeed.

❧ EVENING ❧

What is your desire this evening? Is it focused on heavenly things? Do you long to enjoy the high doctrine of eternal love? Do you desire liberty in very close communion with God? Do you aspire to know the heights and depths and lengths and breadths of His love? Then you must draw near to Jesus; you must get a clear sight of Him in His preciousness and completeness: you must view Him in His work—in His role as prophet, friend, and king—and in His person. He who understands Christ, receives an anointing from the Holy One, by which He knows all things. Christ is the great master-key of all the chambers of God: There is no treasure-house of God that will not open and yield up all its wealth to the soul that lives near to Jesus. Are you saying, "I wish that He would live in my heart and make it His dwelling-place forever"? Open the door, beloved, and He will come into your soul. He has been knocking continually in order that you and He may break bread together. *He eats with you* because you provide the house or the heart, and *you with Him* because He brings the meal. He could not eat with you if it were not in your heart, you finding the house; nor could you eat with Him, for you would have an empty table if He did not bring the food with Him. Fling wide, then, the portals of your soul. He will come with that love that you long to feel; He will come with that joy into which you cannot work your poor depressed spirit; He will bring the peace that now you do not have; He will come with His flagons of wine and sweet apples of love and will cheer you until you have no other sickness but that of overpowering, divine love. Only open the door to Him, drive out His enemies, give Him the keys of your heart, and He will live there forever. What wondrous love that brings such a guest to dwell in such a heart!

DO THIS IN REMEMBRANCE OF ME. — 1 CORINTHIANS 11:24

It appears that Christians may forget Christ! There would be no need for this loving exhortation if there were not a fearful possibility that our memories might prove treacherous. Nor is this an empty notion: It is, sadly too well confirmed in our experience, not as a possibility, but as a lamentable fact. It appears almost impossible that those who have been redeemed by the blood of the dying Lamb and loved with an everlasting love by the eternal Son of God could forget that gracious Savior; but if startling to the ear, sadly it is too apparent to the eye to allow us to deny the crime. Forget Him who never forgot us! Forget Him who poured His blood out for our sins! Forget Him who loved us even to death! Can it be possible? Yes, it is not only possible, but conscience confesses that it is too sadly a fault with all of us that we treat Him as a stranger, like an overnight guest. Instead of Him being a permanent resident in our memories, we treat Him as a visitor. The cross where one would expect that memory would linger and disinterest would be an unknown intruder is desecrated by the feet of forgetfulness. Doesn't your conscience say that this is true? Don't you find yourselves forgetful of Jesus? Some other love steals away your heart, and you are unmindful of Him upon whom your affection ought to be set. Some earthly business engrosses your attention when you ought to be fixed steadily upon the cross. It is the incessant turmoil of the world, the constant attraction of earthly things, that takes the soul away from Christ. While memory works to preserve a poisonous weed, it allows the rose of Sharon to wither. Let us charge ourselves to tie a heavenly forget-me-not around our hearts for Jesus our Beloved, and whatever else we let slip, let us hold tight to Him.

❧ EVENING ❧

BLESSED IS THE ONE WHO STAYS AWAKE. — REVELATION 16:15

I die every day,"[1] said the apostle. This was the life of the early Christians; they went everywhere with their lives in their hands. We are not at this time being called to pass through the same fearful persecutions: if we were, the Lord would give us grace to bear the test. But the tests of Christian life, at the present moment, though outwardly not so terrible, are still more likely to overcome us than even those of the fiery age. We have to bear the sneer of the world—that is small; its flatteries, its soft words, its oily speeches, its fawning, its hypocrisy are far worse. Our danger is that we might grow rich and become proud; we might give ourselves up to the fashions of this present evil world and lose our faith. Or if wealth does not test us, worldly care is quite as mischievous. If we cannot be torn in pieces by the roaring lion, we may be hugged to death by the bear. The devil cares very little which it is, as long as he destroys our love for Christ and our confidence in Him. I am afraid that the Christian church is far more likely to lose her integrity in these soft and easy days than in those rougher times. We must stay awake now, for we are crossing enchanted ground and are most likely to fall asleep to our own ruin, unless our faith in Jesus is a reality and our love for Jesus an ardent flame. Many in these days of easy-believism are likely to prove to be tares, and not wheat; hypocrites with attractive masks on their faces, but not the true-born children of the living God. Christian, do not think that these are times in which you can dispense with watchfulness or with holy ardor; you need these things more than ever, and may God the eternal Spirit display His omnipotence in you, that you may be able to say, in all these softer things as well as in the rougher, "We are more than conquerors through him who loved us."[2]

[1] 1 Corinthians 15:31   [2] Romans 8:37

GOD, OUR GOD, SHALL BLESS US. — PSALM 67:6

It is strange how little use we make of the spiritual blessings that God gives us, but it is even stranger that we make such little use of God Himself. Though He is "our God," we scarcely give ourselves to Him, and we ask so little of Him. How seldom do we seek counsel at the hands of the Lord! How often do we go about our business without seeking His guidance! In our troubles how we constantly struggle to bear our burdens ourselves instead of casting them upon the Lord, that He may sustain us! This is not because we may not, for the Lord seems to say, "I am yours, soul; come and make use of Me as you will. You may freely come to My store, and the more you come, the more welcome you will be." It is our own fault if we do not enjoy the riches of our God. Since you have such a friend, and He invites you, draw from Him daily. Never be wanting while you have a God to go to; never fear or faint while you have God to help you; go to your treasure and take whatever you need—there is all that you can ever want. Learn the divine skill of making God all things to you. He can supply you with everything; or better still, He can be everything to you. Let me urge you, then, to make use of your God. Make use of Him *in prayer*. Go to Him often, because He is *your* God. Will you fail to use such a great privilege? Run to Him; tell Him all your needs. Use Him constantly *by faith* at all times. If some dark providence has cast a shadow on you, use God as a sun; if some strong enemy has attacked you, find in Jehovah a shield, for He is a sun and shield to His people. If you have lost your way in the mazes of life, use Him as a guide, for He will direct you. Whatever you are, and wherever you are, remember, God is just *what* you want and just *where* you want, and that He can do everything you want.

&ea; EVENING &es;
THE LORD IS KING FOREVER AND EVER. — PSALM 10:16

Jesus Christ is not a tyrant claiming *divine right*, but He is really and truly the Lord's anointed! "For in him all the fullness of God was pleased to dwell."[1] God has given to Him all power and all authority. As the Son of man, He is now head over all things in His church, and He reigns over heaven and earth and hell with the keys of life and death at His belt. Certain princes have been glad to call themselves kings by the *popular will*, and certainly our Lord Jesus Christ is such in His church. If it could be put to the vote whether He should be King in the church, every believing heart would crown Him. We ought to crown Him more gloriously than we do! We would regard no expense too great if we could glorify Christ. Suffering would be pleasure, and loss would be gain, if through that we could surround His brow with brighter crowns and make Him more glorious in the eyes of men and angels. Yes, He shall reign. Long live the King! All hail to You, King Jesus! Go on, you virgin souls who love your Lord. Bow at His feet; cover His path with the lilies of your love and the roses of your gratitude: "Bring forth the royal diadem, and crown Him Lord of all." Our Lord Jesus is King in Zion by *right of conquest*: He has taken the hearts of His people by storm and has defeated their enemies who held them in cruel bondage. In the Red Sea of His own blood, our Redeemer has drowned the Pharaoh of our sins: Shall He not be Lord and King? He has delivered us from sin's dominion and from the heavy curse of the law: Shall not the Liberator be crowned? We are His portion, whom He has taken out of the hand of the enemy with His sword and with His bow: Who will snatch His conquest from His hand? All hail, King Jesus! We gladly own Your gentle sway! Rule in our hearts forever, You lovely Prince of Peace.

[1] Colossians 1:19

❧ MORNING ☙

REMEMBER YOUR WORD TO YOUR SERVANT,
IN WHICH YOU HAVE MADE ME HOPE. — PSALM 119:49

Whatever your particular need may be, you will find some promise in the Bible related to it. Are you faint and feeble because your way is rough and you are weary? Here is the promise—"He gives power to the faint."[1] When you read such a promise, take it back to the great Promiser and ask Him to fulfill His own word. Are you seeking for Christ and thirsting for closer communion with Him? This promise shines like a star upon you— "Blessed are those who hunger and thirst for righteousness, for they shall be satisfied."[2] Take that promise to the throne continually; do not plead anything else, but go to God over and over again with this—"Lord, You have said it; do as You have said." Are you distressed because of sin and burdened with the heavy load of your iniquities? Listen to these words—"I, I am he who blots out your transgressions for my own sake, and I will not remember your sins."[3] You have no merit of your own to plead why He should pardon you, but plead His written promises and He will perform them. Are you afraid that you might not be able to hold on to the end and that after having thought yourself a child of God you should prove a castaway? If that is your condition, take this word of grace to the throne and plead it: "The mountains may depart and the hills be removed, but my steadfast love shall not depart from you."[4] If you have lost the sweet sense of the Savior's presence and are seeking Him with a sorrowful heart, remember the promises: "Return to me . . . and I will return to you."[5] "For a brief moment I deserted you, but with great compassion I will gather you."[6] Feast your faith upon God's own Word, and whatever your fears or wants, take them to the Bank of Faith with your Father's note, which reads, "Remember your word to your servant, in which you have made me hope."[7]

❧ EVENING ☙

ALL THE HOUSE OF ISRAEL HAVE A HARD FOREHEAD AND
A STUBBORN HEART. — EZEKIEL 3:7

Are there no exceptions? No, not one. Even God's chosen are described in this way. If the best are so bad, then what must the worst be like? Come, my heart, consider to what extent you share in this universal accusation; as you think, prepare to be ashamed of those things of which you are guilty. The first charge is *impudence*, or hardness of forehead, an absence of holy shame, an unholy boldness in evil. Before my conversion, I could sin and feel no regret, hear of my guilt and remain unhumbled, and even confess my iniquity without any accompanying humiliation. When a sinner goes to God's house and pretends to pray to Him and praise Him, he displays a brazen-facedness of the worst kind! Sadly, since the day of my new birth I have doubted my Lord to His face, murmured unblushingly in His presence, worshiped Him in a slovenly manner, and sinned without bewailing myself on account of it. If my forehead were not like a diamond, harder than flint, I would display more holy fear and a far deeper contrition of spirit. Woe is me, for I am one of the impudent house of Israel. The second charge is *hard-heartedness*, and I dare not attempt to plead innocent here. Once I had nothing but a heart of stone, and although through grace I now have a new and fleshy heart, much of my former stubbornness remains. I am not affected by the death of Jesus as I ought to be; neither am I moved as I should be by the lostness of my fellowmen, the wickedness of the times, the chastisement of my heavenly Father, and my own failures. O that my heart would melt at the recital of my Savior's sufferings and death. Would to God I were rid of this dreadful burden within me, this hateful body of death. Blessed be the name of the Lord, the disease is not incurable; the Savior's precious blood is the universal remedy, and it will effectually soften me, even me, until my heart melts as wax before the fire.

[1] Isaiah 40:29 [2] Matthew 5:6 [3] Isaiah 43:25 [4] Isaiah 54:10 [5] Zechariah 1:3 [6] Isaiah 54:7 [7] Psalm 119:49

YOU ARE MY REFUGE IN THE DAY OF DISASTER. — JEREMIAH 17:17

The path of the Christian is not always bright with sunshine; he has his seasons of darkness and of storm. It is true that God's Word says, "Her ways are ways of pleasantness, and all her paths are peace";[1] and it is a great truth that faith is calculated to give a man happiness below as well as bliss above. But life confirms that if the experience of the righteous is "like the light of dawn, which shines brighter and brighter until full day,"[2] sometimes that light is eclipsed. At certain periods clouds cover the believer's sun, and he walks in darkness and sees no light. There are many who have rejoiced in the presence of God for a season; they have basked in the sunshine in the early stages of their Christian life; they have walked along the "green pastures" by the side of the "still waters." But suddenly they find that the glorious sky is clouded; instead of the promised land they have to endure the wilderness; in place of sweet waters, they find troubled streams, bitter to their taste, and they say, "Surely, if I were a child of God, this would not happen." Do not say that if you are walking in darkness. The best of God's saints must drink the bitter potion; the dearest of His children must bear the cross. No Christian has enjoyed perpetual prosperity; no believer can always keep his heart in constant tune. Perhaps the Lord gave you in the beginning a smooth and unclouded path because you were weak and timid. He moderated the wind on account of your weakness, but now that you are stronger in the spiritual life, you must enter upon the riper and rougher experience of God's full-grown children. We need winds and tempests to exercise our faith, to tear off the rotten branches of self-reliance, and to root us more firmly in Christ. The day of evil reveals to us the value of our glorious hope.

&. EVENING ƒ

THE LORD TAKES PLEASURE IN HIS PEOPLE. — PSALM 149:4

How comprehensive is the love of Jesus! There is no part of His people's interests that He does not consider, and there is nothing that concerns their welfare that is not important to Him. He doesn't merely think of you, believer, as an immortal being, but as a mortal being too. Do not deny it or doubt it: "Even the hairs of your head are all numbered."[3] "The steps of a man are established by the LORD, when he delights in his way."[4] It would be sad for us if this covering of love did not tackle all our concerns, for what mischief might be done to us in that part of our lives that did not come under our gracious Lord's protection! Believer, rest assured that the heart of Jesus cares about your smallest concerns. The breadth of His tender love is such that you may turn to Him in every case; for in all your afflictions He is afflicted, and just like a father cares for his children, so He cares for you. The smallest interests of all His saints are all borne upon the heart of the Son of God. And what a heart He has, which does not merely understand the nature of His people but also comprehends their diverse and innumerable concerns. Do you think, Christian, that you can measure the love of Christ? Consider what His love has brought you—justification, adoption, sanctification, eternal life! The riches of His goodness are unsearchable; you will never be able to convey them or even conceive them. Oh, the breadth of the love of Christ! Shall such a love as this have only half our hearts? Shall it have a cold love in return? Shall Jesus' marvelous loving-kindness and tender care be met with only faint response and delayed acknowledgment? My soul, tune your harp to a glad song of thanksgiving! Go to your rest rejoicing, for you are not a desolate wanderer but a beloved child, watched over, cared for, supplied, and defended by your Lord.

[1] Proverbs 3:17 [2] Proverbs 4:18 [3] Matthew 10:30 [4] Psalm 37:23

AND ALL THE PEOPLE OF ISRAEL GRUMBLED. — NUMBERS 14:2

There are grumblers among Christians now, just as there were in the camp of Israel of old. There are those who, when punished, cry out against the affliction. They ask, "Why am I afflicted? What have I done to be chastened in this manner?" A word with you, grumbler! Why should you grumble against the dealings of your heavenly Father? Can He treat you more severely than you deserve? Consider what a rebel you once were, but He has pardoned you! Surely, if He in His wisdom considers it necessary to chasten you, you should not complain. After all, are you punished as severely as your sins deserve? Consider the corruption that is in your heart, and then will you wonder that so much of the rod is necessary to root it out? Weigh yourself, and discern how much dross is mingled with your gold; and do you think the fire is too hot to purge away the amount of dross you have? Doesn't your proud rebellious spirit prove that your heart is not thoroughly sanctified? Aren't those grumbling words contrary to the holy, submissive nature of God's children? Isn't the correction necessary? But if you *will* grumble against the chastening, pay attention, for it will go hard with grumblers. God always chastises His children twice if they do not respond properly the first time. But know this—"He does not willingly afflict or grieve the children of men."[1] All His corrections are sent in love, to purify you and to draw you nearer to Himself. Surely it must help you to bear the chastening with submission if you are able to recognize your *Father's* hand. "For the Lord disciplines the one he loves, and chastises every son whom he receives."[2] ". . . nor grumble the way some of them did and were destroyed by the Destroyer."[3]

❧ EVENING ☙
HOW PRECIOUS TO ME ARE YOUR THOUGHTS, O GOD!
— PSALM 139:17

Divine omniscience provides no comfort to the ungodly mind, but to the child of God it overflows with consolation. God is always thinking about us, never turns His mind from us, always has us before His eyes; and this is precisely how we would want it, because it would be dreadful to exist for a moment outside the observation of our heavenly Father. His thoughts are always tender, loving, wise, prudent, far-reaching, and they bring countless benefits to us: It is consequently a supreme delight to remember them. The Lord always thought about His people: hence their election and the covenant of grace by which their salvation is secured. He will always think upon them: hence their final perseverance by which they shall be brought safely to their final rest. In all our wanderings the watchful glance of the Eternal Watcher is constantly fixed upon us—we never roam beyond the Shepherd's eye. In our sorrows He observes us incessantly, and not a painful emotion escapes Him; in our toils He notices all our weariness, and He writes all the struggles of His faithful ones in His book. These thoughts of the Lord encompass us in all our paths and penetrate the innermost region of our being. Not a nerve or tissue, valve or vessel of our bodily frame is uncared for; all the details of our little world are thought upon by the great God.

Dear reader, is this precious to you? Then hold to it. Do not be led astray by those philosophical fools who preach an impersonal God and talk of self-existent, self-governing matter. The Lord lives and thinks upon us; this is a far too precious truth for us to be easily robbed of it. To be noticed by a nobleman is valued so highly that he who has it counts his fortune made; but how much greater is it to be thought of by the King of kings! If the Lord thinks upon us, all is well, and we may rejoice evermore.

[1] Lamentations 3:33 [2] Hebrews 12:6 [3] 1 Corinthians 10:10

May

His cheeks are like beds of spices, mounds of sweet-smelling herbs. — Song of Solomon 5:13

Here we are in the month when flowers come! March winds and April showers have done their work, and the earth is all dressed with beauty. Come, my soul, put on your springtime clothes and gather garlands of heavenly thoughts. You know where to go, for the "beds of spices" are well known, and you have so often smelled the perfume of "sweet-smelling herbs" that you will go at once to Him who is altogether lovely and find all loveliness and all joy in Him. His cheek, which once was so rudely smitten with a rod, often covered with tears of sympathy and defiled by man—that cheek smiles with mercy and is a fragrant aroma to my heart. You did not hide Your face from shame and spitting, O Lord Jesus, and therefore I will find my dearest delight in praising You. Your face was furrowed by the plow of grief, and blood flowed freely from Your thorn-crowned brow; such marks of unbounded love fill my soul far more than words can tell. If I may not see the whole of His face, I would behold His cheeks, for the least glimpse of Him is exceedingly refreshing to my spiritual sense and yields a variety of delights. In Jesus I find not only fragrance but a bed of spices; not one herb, but all kinds of sweet herbs. He is to me parsley, sage, rosemary, and thyme. When He is with me, it is May all year round, and my soul goes forth to wash its happy face in the morning-dew of His grace and to solace herself with the singing of the birds of His promises. Precious Lord Jesus, let me in very deed know the blessedness that dwells in abiding, unbroken fellowship with You. I am a poor, worthless one whose cheek You have deigned to kiss! O let me kiss You in return with the kisses of my lips.

❧ Evening ❧

I am a rose of Sharon. — Song of Solomon 2:1

Whatever beauty there may be in the material world, Jesus Christ possesses all of that in the spiritual world to the nth degree. Among flowers the rose is regarded as the sweetest, but Jesus is infinitely more beautiful in the garden of the soul than a rose in the gardens of earth. He takes the first place as the fairest among ten thousand. He is the sun, and all others are the stars; the heavens and the day are dark in comparison with Him, *for the King in His beauty transcends all.* "I am a rose of *Sharon.*" This was the best and rarest of roses. Jesus simply is not "a rose"; He is "a rose of Sharon," just as He calls His righteousness "gold," and then adds, "the gold of Ophir"[1]—the best of the best. He is positively lovely, and superlatively the loveliest. *There is variety in His beauty.* The rose is delightful to the eye, and its scent is pleasant and refreshing; so each of the senses of the soul, whether it be the taste or feeling, the hearing, the sight, or the spiritual smell, finds appropriate gratification in Jesus. *Even the recollection of His love is sweet.* Take a rose of Sharon, pull it leaf from leaf, and place the leaves in the jar of memory, and you will find each leaf retains its fragrance, filling the house with perfume. Christ *satisfies the highest taste* of the most educated spirit to the full. The greatest amateur in perfumes is quite satisfied with a rose: And when the soul has arrived at her highest pitch of true taste, she will still be content with Christ; indeed, she shall be more able to appreciate Him. Heaven itself possesses nothing that excels a rose of Sharon. What emblem can fully set forth His beauty? Human speech and earthborn things fail to tell of Him. Earth's choicest beauties combine to provide ultimately a feeble picture of His glory. Blessed rose, bloom in my heart forever!

[1] 1 Chronicles 29:4

MORNING

I DO NOT ASK THAT YOU TAKE THEM OUT OF THE WORLD, BUT THAT YOU KEEP THEM FROM THE EVIL ONE. — JOHN 17:15

In God's own time every believer will experience the sweet and blessed occasion of going home to be with Jesus. In a few more years the Lord's soldiers, who are presently fighting "the good fight of the faith,"[1] will have finished the battle and will have entered into the joy of their Lord. But although Christ prays that His people may eventually be with Him where He is, He does not ask that they may be taken at once away from this world to heaven. He wishes them to stay here. Yet how often is the weary pilgrim heard to pray, "Oh, that I had wings like a dove! I would fly away and be at rest."[2] But Christ does not pray like that; He leaves us in His Father's hands until, like shocks of fully ripe corn, we shall each be gathered into our Master's garner. Jesus does not plead for our instant removal by death, because our earthly journey is needful for others even when daunting for us. He asks that we may be kept from evil, but He never asks for us to be admitted to the inheritance in glory until it is time. Christians often want to die when they have any trouble. Ask them why, and they tell you, "Because we would rather be with the Lord." I wonder whether it is not so much that they long to be with the Lord as it is because they want to be free of their troubles; otherwise they would feel the same desire to die at other times when not under the pressure of trial. They want to go home not so much for the Savior's company as to be at rest. Now it is quite right to desire to depart if we can do it in the same spirit that Paul did—because to be with Christ is far better; but the wish to escape from trouble is a selfish one. Rather let your longing be to glorify God by your life down here as long as He pleases, even though you live in the midst of toil and conflict and suffering. Leave Him to say when it is enough.

EVENING

THESE ALL DIED IN FAITH. — HEBREWS 11:13

Consider the epitaph of all those blessed saints who fell asleep before the coming of our Lord! The issue is not how they died—whether of old age or by violent means—but that whatever their diverse experiences, they are united in Him: "These all died in faith." In faith they lived—it was their comfort, their guide, their motive, and their support; and in the same spiritual grace they died, ending their life-song in the sweet melody that had followed them through life. They did not die trusting in the flesh or their own attainments; they never wavered from their first way of acceptance with God but held to the way of faith to the end. Faith is as precious to die by as to live by.

Dying in faith has distinct reference to *the past*. They believed the promises that had gone before and were assured that their sins were blotted out through the mercy of God. Dying in faith has to do with *the present*. These saints were confident of their acceptance with God; they enjoyed the benefits of His love and rested in His faithfulness. Dying in faith looks into *the future*. They fell asleep, affirming that the Messiah would surely come and that when He in the last days appeared upon the earth, they would rise from their graves to behold Him. To them the pains of death were but the birth-pangs of a better state. Take courage, my soul, as you read this epitaph. Your journey, through grace, is one of faith, not sight, and this has always been the pathway of the brightest and the best. Faith was the orbit in which these stars of the first magnitude shone in their day; and happy are you to be in their company. Look again tonight to Jesus, the founder and perfecter of your faith, and thank Him for giving you like precious faith with souls now in glory.

[1] 1 Timothy 6:12 [2] Psalm 55:6

IN THE WORLD YOU WILL HAVE TRIBULATION. — JOHN 16:33

Are you asking why this should be, believer? Look upward to your heavenly Father, and behold Him pure and holy. Do you know that you are one day to be like Him? Will you easily be conformed to His image? Will you not require much refining in the furnace of affliction to purify you? Will it be an easy thing to get rid of your corruptions and make you perfect even as your Father in heaven is perfect? Next, Christian, turn your eye *downward*. Do you know what foes you have beneath your feet? You were once a servant of Satan, and no king will willingly lose his subjects. Do you think that Satan will leave you alone? No, he will always be at you, for he "prowls around like a roaring lion, seeking someone to devour."[1] Expect trouble, then, Christian, when you look beneath you. Then look *around you*. Where are you? You are in enemy country, a stranger and an alien. The world is not your friend. If it is, then you are not God's friend, for whoever is the friend of the world is the enemy of God. Be certain that you will find enemies everywhere. When you sleep, remember that you are resting on the battlefield; when you travel, suspect an ambush in every hedge. As mosquitoes are said to bite strangers more than natives, so the trials of earth will be sharpest to you. Lastly, look *within you*, into your own heart, and observe what is there. *Sin* and *self* are still within. If you had no devil to tempt you, no enemies to fight you, and no world to ensnare you, you would still find in yourself enough evil to be a sore trial to you, for "the heart is deceitful above all things, and desperately sick."[2] Expect trouble then, but do not despair on account of it, for God is with you to help and to strengthen you. He has said, "call upon me in the day of trouble; I will deliver you, and you shall glorify me."[3]

❧ EVENING ☙

A VERY PRESENT HELP. — PSALM 46:1

Covenant blessings are not meant only to be observed but to be appropriated. Even our Lord Jesus is given to us for our present use. Believer, you do not make use of Christ as you ought to do. When you are in trouble, why do you not tell Him all your grief? Does He not have a sympathizing heart, and can He not comfort and relieve you? No, you are going to all your friends, except your best Friend, and telling your story everywhere, except into the heart of your Lord. Are you burdened with this day's sins? Here is a fountain filled with blood: Use it, saint, use it. Has a sense of guilt returned upon you? The pardoning grace of Jesus may be proved again and again. Come to Him at once for cleansing. Do you deplore your weakness? He is your strength: Why not lean upon Him? Do you feel naked? Come here, soul; put on the robe of Jesus' righteousness. Do not stand looking at it, but wear it. Strip off your own righteousness, and your own fears too: Put on the fair white linen, for it was meant to *wear*. Do you feel yourself sick? Call upon the Beloved Physician, and He will give the medicine that will revive you. You are poor, but remember you have a kinsman, who is incredibly wealthy. What! Will you not go to Him and ask Him to give you from His abundance when He has promised that you will be joint heir with Him and has credited all that He is and all that He has to your account? There is nothing Christ dislikes more than for His people to make a show of coming to Him and yet not to use Him. He loves to be employed by us. The more burdens we put on His shoulders, the more precious He will be to us.

> *Let us be simple with Him, then,*
> *Not backward, stiff, or cold,*
> *As though our Bethlehem could be*
> *What Sinai was of old.*

[1] 1 Peter 5:8   [2] Jeremiah 17:9   [3] Psalm 50:15

    ❧   M ORNING   ☙

O ne great besetting sin of ancient Israel was idolatry, and the church is vexed with a tendency to the same folly. The ancient gods of man's invention have mostly disappeared,
but the shrines of pride are not forsaken, and the golden calf still stands. Self makes an
empty display, and the flesh sets up its altars wherever it can find space for them. Favorite
children are often the cause of much sin in believers; the Lord is grieved when He sees us
doting upon them beyond measure; they will live to be as great a curse to us as Absalom
was to David, or they will be taken from us to leave our homes desolate. If Christians desire
to grow thorns with which to stuff their sleepless pillows, let them dote on their children.

It is accurate to say that "such are not gods," for the objects of our foolish love are
very doubtful blessings, the solace that they yield us now is dangerous, and the help that they
can give us in the hour of trouble is small indeed. Why, then, are we so bewitched with
vanities? We pity the poor heathen who worships a god of stone, and yet we worship a
god of gold. Where is the vast superiority between a god of flesh and one of wood? The principle, the sin, the folly is the same in either case; the only difference is that our crime is
more aggravated because we have more light, and sin in the face of it. The heathen bows
to a false deity, but the true God he has never known; we commit two evils, inasmuch as
we forsake the living God and turn to idols. May the Lord purge us all from this grievous
iniquity!

> The dearest idol I have known,
> Whate'er that idol be;
> Help me to tear it from Thy throne,
> And worship only Thee.

❧   E VENING   ☙

P eter earnestly exhorted the scattered saints to love each other "earnestly from a pure
heart" (verse 22), and he did so not on the basis of the law or human nature or philosophy, but from that high and divine nature that God has implanted in His people. In the
same way that a sensible tutor of princes might seek to foster in them a kingly spirit and
dignified behavior, finding arguments in their position and pedigree, so, looking upon God's
people as heirs of glory, princes of royal blood, descendants of the King of kings, earth's truest
and oldest aristocracy, Peter said to them in essence, "See that you love one another because
of your noble birth, being born of imperishable seed, because of your pedigree, being
descended from God, the Creator of all things, and because of your immortal destiny, for you
shall never pass away, though the glory of the flesh shall fade and even its existence shall
cease." We would do well if, in the spirit of humility, we recognized the true dignity of our
regenerated nature and lived up to it. What is a Christian? If you compare him with a king,
he adds priestly sanctity to royal dignity. The king's royalty often lies only in his crown, but
with a Christian it is infused into his inmost nature. He is as much above his fellows through
his new birth as a man is above the beast that perishes. Surely he shall conduct himself in
all his dealings as one who is different from the crowd, chosen out of the world, distinguished
by sovereign grace, part of God's "peculiar people."[1] Such trophies of God's grace cannot
grovel in the dust like some, nor live in the fashion of the world's citizens. Let the dignity of
your nature and the brightness of your prospects, O believers in Christ, constrain you to hold
fast to holiness and to avoid the very appearance of evil.

[1] Titus 2:14, KJV

I WILL BE THEIR GOD, AND THEY SHALL BE MY PEOPLE.

— 2 CORINTHIANS 6:16

What a sweet title: "my people"! What a cheering revelation: "their God"! What a wealth of meaning is couched in those two words, "my people!" Here is *speciality*. The whole world is God's; the heaven, even the heaven of heavens, is the Lord's, and He reigns among the children of men. But of those whom He has chosen, whom He has purchased to Himself, He says what He says not of others—"my people." In this word there is the idea of *proprietorship*. In a special manner "the LORD's portion is his people, Jacob his allotted heritage."[1] All the nations upon earth are His; the whole world is in His power. But His people, His chosen, are more especially His possession, for He has done more for them than for others. He has bought them with His blood; He has brought them to Himself; He has set His great heart upon them; He has loved them with an everlasting love, a love that many waters cannot quench and that the revolutions of time will never in the least degree diminish. Dear friends, can you by faith see yourselves in that number? Can you look up to heaven and say, "My Lord and my God: mine by that sweet *relationship* that entitles me to call You Father; mine by that hallowed *fellowship* that I rejoice to enjoy with You when You are pleased to show Yourself to me as You do not to the world"? Can you read the Bible and find there the guarantee of your salvation? Can you read your title written in precious blood? Can you, by humble faith, lay hold of Jesus' garments and say, "My Christ"? If you can, then God says of you, and of others like you, "My people;" for if God be your God and Christ your Christ, the Lord has a special interest in you; you are the object of His choice, accepted in His beloved Son.

✎ EVENING ✐

WHOEVER GIVES THOUGHT TO THE WORD WILL DISCOVER GOOD, AND
BLESSED IS HE WHO TRUSTS IN THE LORD. — PROVERBS 16:20

Wisdom is man's true strength; and under its guidance he is best able to find and fulfill his reason for living. Wisely handling the matter of life gives to man the richest enjoyment and presents the noblest occupation for his powers; and in this way he finds good in the fullest sense. Without wisdom, man is like a wild donkey running here and there, wasting strength that might have been profitably employed. Wisdom is the compass by which man is to steer across the trackless waste of life; without it he is a derelict vessel, the victim of winds and waves. A man must be prudent in such a world as this or he will find no good, but will be betrayed into unnumbered ills. The pilgrim will sorely wound his feet among the briers of the wood of life if he does not pick his steps with the utmost caution. He who is in a wilderness infested with thieves must handle matters wisely if he would journey safely. If, trained by the Great Teacher, we will follow where He leads, we will find good even in the darkness, and celestial fruits to be tasted, and songs of paradise to be sung amid the groves of earth. But where shall this wisdom be found? Many have dreamed of it without possessing it. Where will we learn it? Let us listen to the voice of the Lord, for He has declared the secret. He has revealed to the sons of men where true wisdom lies, and we have it in the text, "blessed is he who trusts in the LORD." *The true way to handle a matter wisely is to trust in the Lord.* This is the sure clue to the most intricate labyrinths of life; follow it and find eternal bliss. He who trusts in the Lord has a diploma for wisdom granted by inspiration: Happy is he now, and happier he shall be above. Lord, in this sweet evening walk with me in the garden, and teach me the wisdom of faith.

[1] Deuteronomy 32:9

WE ABIDE IN HIM. — 1 JOHN 4:13

Do you want a house for your soul? You may ask, "How much does it cost?" Something less than proud human nature would like to pay. It is without money and without price. But you would like to pay a respectable rent! You would love to do something to win Christ? Then you cannot have the house, for it is without price. Will you take my Master's house on a lease for all eternity, with nothing to pay for it, nothing but the rent of loving and serving Him forever? Will you take Jesus and dwell in Him? This house is furnished with all you want; it is filled with riches more than you can spend as long as you live. In this house you can have intimate communion with Christ and feast on His love; the tables are well-stocked with food for you to live on forever; in it, when weary, you can find rest with Jesus; and from it you have a view of heaven itself. Will you have the house? If you are homeless, you will say, "I should like to have the house; but may I have it?" Yes; the key is, "Come to Jesus." "But," you say, "I am too shabby for such a house." Never mind; there are garments inside. If you feel guilty and condemned, come; and though the house is too good for you, Christ will make you good enough for the house soon enough. He will wash you and cleanse you, and you will yet be able to sing, "We dwell in Him." Believer, your happiness will be multiplied in having such a dwelling-place! What a privilege for you to live in such a secure dwelling—a place of safety. And dwelling in Him, you have not only a perfect and secure house, but an *everlasting* one. When this world shall have melted like a dream, our house shall live and stand more imperishable than marble, more solid than granite, self-existent as God, for it is God Himself—"We abide in him."

❧ EVENING ☙

ALL THE DAYS OF MY SERVICE I WOULD WAIT. — JOB 14:14

A short stay on earth will make heaven more heavenly. Nothing makes rest so enjoyable as work; nothing renders security so pleasant as exposure to danger. The bitter cups of earth will give a relish to the new wine that sparkles in the golden bowls of heaven. Our battered armor and scarred countenances will render more glorious our victory above, when we are welcomed to the seats of those who have overcome the world. We would not have *full fellowship with Christ* if we did not sojourn for a while below, for He was baptized with a baptism of suffering among men, and we must be baptized with the same if we would share His kingdom. Fellowship with Christ is so honorable that the sorest sorrow is a light price by which to procure it. Another reason for our lingering here is *for the good of others.* We would not wish to enter heaven till our work is done, and it may be that we still have a part to play shining as light in the dark wilderness of sin. Our prolonged stay here is doubtless *for God's glory.* A tested saint, like a well-cut diamond, glitters much in the King's crown. Nothing reflects so much honor on a workman as a protracted and severe trial of his work and his triumphant endurance of the ordeal without giving in or giving up. We are God's workmanship, and He will be glorified by our afflictions. It is for the honor of Jesus that we endure the trial of our faith with sacred joy. Let each man surrender his own longings to the glory of Jesus and declare: "If my lying in the dust would elevate my Lord by so much as an inch, let me still lie among the pots of earth. If to live on earth forever would make my Lord more glorious, it should be my heaven to be shut out of heaven." Our time is fixed and settled by eternal decree. Let us not be anxious about it, but wait with patience until the gates of pearl shall open.

MANY FOLLOWED HIM, AND HE HEALED THEM ALL.
— MATTHEW 12:15

What a variety of sickness must have been presented to the gaze of Jesus! Yet we do not read that He was disgusted but patiently waited on every case. What a combination of evils must have met at His feet! What sickening ulcers and putrefying sores! Yet He was ready for every new shape of the monster of evil and was victor over it in every form. Wherever the arrow landed, He quenched its fiery power. Fevers, lameness, sadness, or the cold of dropsy; the lethargy of madness, leprosy, and blindness—all knew the power of His word and fled at His command. In every aspect of the battle He was triumphant over evil and received the homage of delivered captives. He came, He saw, He conquered everywhere. It is still the case today. Whatever my own condition may be, the beloved Physician can heal me; and whatever may be the state of others whom I may remember at this moment in prayer, I may have hope in Jesus that He will be able to heal them of their sins. My child, my friend, my dearest one—I can have hope for each, for all, when I remember the healing power of my Lord; and on my own account, however severe my struggle with sins and infirmities, I can still rejoice and be confident. He who on earth walked the hospitals still dispenses His grace and works wonders among the sons of men: Let me go to Him immediately and earnestly.

Let me praise Him this morning as I remember how He worked His spiritual cures, which brings Him the most renown. It was by taking upon Himself our sicknesses. "With his stripes we are healed."[1] The church on earth is full of souls healed by our beloved Physician; and the inhabitants of heaven confess that "he healed them all." Come, then, my soul, declare far and wide the virtue of His grace, and "it shall make a name for the LORD, an everlasting sign that shall not be cut off."[2]

❧ EVENING ❧

JESUS SAID TO HIM, "GET UP, TAKE UP YOUR BED, AND WALK."
— JOHN 5:8

Like many others, this impotent man had been waiting for a wonder to be performed and a sign to be given. He grew tired watching the pool, but no angel came, or at least not for him; still considering it to be his only chance, he kept waiting, not knowing that there was One near him whose word could heal him in a moment. Many are in the same condition. They are waiting for some singular emotion, remarkable impression, or celestial vision; but they wait and watch in vain. Even supposing that, in a few cases, remarkable signs are seen, yet these are rare, and no man has a right to look for them in his own case—especially not the man who feels his inability to take advantage of the moving of the water even if it came. It is sad to think of how many tens of thousands are waiting on the use of means and ordinances and vows and resolutions and have been waiting for so long and completely in vain. Meanwhile these poor souls forget that Jesus is near, and He bids them look to Him and be saved. He could heal them at once, but they prefer to wait for an angel and a wonder. To trust Him is the sure way to every blessing, and He is worthy of the most implicit confidence; but unbelief makes them prefer to wait for the water to stir than to embrace the warm welcome of His love. May the Lord turn His eye upon the multitudes who are in that position tonight; may He forgive their lack of faith in His divine power and call them by His sweet constraining voice to rise from the bed of despair and in the energy of faith take up their bed and walk. O Lord, hear our prayer for such as these in the sunset hour, and before a new dawn may they look and live.

Thankful reader, is there anything in this portion for you?

[1] Isaiah 53:5   [2] Isaiah 55:12

THE MAN WHO HAD BEEN HEALED DID NOT KNOW WHO IT WAS.
— JOHN 5:13

Years pass quickly for the happy and the healthy; but thirty-eight years of disease must have seemed like forever in the life of the poor impotent man. When Jesus, therefore, healed him by a word while he lay at the pool of Bethesda, the man was delightfully *aware of a change*. Even so the sinner who has for weeks and months been paralyzed with despair and has wearily sighed for salvation is very conscious of the change when the Lord Jesus speaks the word of power and gives joy and peace in believing. The evil removed is too great to be removed without our discerning it; the life imparted is too remarkable to be possessed and remain inoperative; and the change is too marvelous not to be perceived. Yet the poor man was *ignorant of the author* of his cure; he did not know this person, or the part that he played, or the plan that had brought Him among men. Hearts that feel the power of His blood may still be ignorant of His ways. We must not be too quick to condemn men for lack of knowledge; but where we can see the faith that saves the soul, we must believe that salvation has been bestowed. The Holy Spirit makes men penitents long before He makes them ministers; and he who believes what he knows shall soon know more clearly what he believes. Ignorance is, however, an evil; for this poor man was much *tantalized by the Pharisees* and was quite unable to cope with them. It is good to be able to answer our critics; but we cannot do so if we do not know the Lord Jesus clearly and with understanding. The cure of his ignorance, however, soon followed the cure of his infirmity, for he was *visited by the Lord* in the temple; and after that gracious discourse, he was soon declaring to all "that it was Jesus who had healed him." Lord, if You have saved me, show me Yourself, that I may declare You to the sons of men.

❧ EVENING ❧

AGREE WITH GOD, AND BE AT PEACE. — JOB 22:21

In order to properly "agree with God, and be at peace," we must know Him as He has revealed Himself, not only in *the unity of His essence and subsistence*, but also in *the plurality of His persons*. God said, "Let us make man in our image"[1]—man must not be content until he knows something of the "us" from whom his being was derived. Endeavor to know the Father. Approach Him in deep repentance, and confess that you are not worthy to be called His son; receive the kiss of His love; let the ring that is the token of His eternal faithfulness be on your finger; sit at His table and let your heart rejoice in His grace. Then press forward and seek to know much of *the Son of God* who although He is the brightness of His Father's glory humbled Himself and became man for our sakes. Know Him in the singular complexity of His nature: eternal God, and yet suffering, finite man; follow Him as He walks the waters with the tread of deity, and as He sits down at the well tired in the weariness of humanity. Do not be satisfied unless you know much of Jesus Christ as your Friend, your Brother, your Husband, your all. Do not forget *the Holy Spirit*. Endeavor to obtain a clear view of His nature and character, His attributes, and His works. Behold the Spirit of the Lord, who first of all moved upon chaos and brought forth order, who now visits the chaos of your soul and creates the order of holiness. Behold Him as the Lord and giver of spiritual life, the Illuminator, the Instructor, the Comforter, and the Sanctifier. Behold Him as He descends upon the head of Jesus, and then as He rests upon *you*. Such an intelligent, scriptural, and experiential belief in the Trinity is yours if you truly know God; and such knowledge *brings peace indeed*.

[1] Genesis 1:26

... WHO HAS BLESSED US IN CHRIST WITH EVERY SPIRITUAL BLESSING.
— EPHESIANS 1:3

Christ bestows all the goodness of the past, the present, and the future upon His people. In the mysterious ages of the past the Lord Jesus was His Father's first elect, and in His *election* He gave us an interest, for we were chosen in Him from before the foundation of the world. He had from all eternity the prerogatives of *Sonship*, as His Father's only-begotten and well-beloved Son; and He has, in the riches of His grace, by adoption and regeneration, elevated us to sonship also, so that to us He has given "the right to become children of God."[1] The *eternal covenant*, which He has confirmed by an oath, is ours, for our strong consolation and security. In the *everlasting settlements of predestinating wisdom* and omnipotent decree, the eye of the Lord Jesus was fixed upon us; and we may rest assured that in the whole roll of destiny there is not a line that militates against the interests of His redeemed. The *great betrothal* of the Prince of Glory is ours, for it is to us that He is engaged, as the wedding feast shall soon declare to an assembled universe. The *marvelous incarnation* of the God of heaven, with all the amazing condescension and humiliation that attended it, is ours. The bloody sweat, the scourge, the cross are ours forever. Whatever blissful consequences flow from *perfect obedience, finished atonement, resurrection, ascension, or intercession*, all are ours by His own gift. Upon His breastplate He is now bearing our names; and in His authoritative pleadings at the throne He remembers us and pleads our case. His *dominion* over principalities and powers, and His absolute majesty in heaven, He employs for the benefit of them who trust in Him. His high estate is as much at our service as was His obedience unto death. He who gave Himself for us in the depths of woe and death does not withdraw His help now that He is enthroned in the highest heavens.

❧ EVENING ❧

COME, MY BELOVED, LET US GO OUT INTO THE FIELDS . . . LET US . . . SEE
WHETHER THE VINES HAVE BUDDED. — SONG OF SOLOMON 7:11-12

The bride was about to engage in hard work and desired her beloved's company in it. She does not say, "I will go," but "let us go." In like fashion, it is a blessing to work when Jesus is at our side! It is the business of God's people to be trimmers of God's vines. Like our first parents, we are put into the garden of the Lord for usefulness; let us then go out into the fields. When God's people are thinking properly, they desire to enjoy communion with Christ. Some may imagine that they cannot serve Christ actively and still have fellowship with Him; they are mistaken. There is no doubt that we may easily neglect our inward life in outward exercises and be forced to say, "They made me keeper of the vineyards, but my own vineyard have I not kept!"[2] There is no reason why this should be the case except for our own foolishness and neglect. It is certain that a professing Christian may do nothing and end up just as lifeless in spiritual things as those who are most busy. Mary was not praised for sitting still, but for her *sitting at Jesus' feet*. Even so, Christians are not to be praised for neglecting duties under the pretense of having secret fellowship with Jesus: It is not sitting, but sitting at Jesus' feet that is commendable. Do not think that activity is in itself an evil: It is a great blessing and a means of grace to us. Paul called it a grace given to him to be allowed to preach; and every form of Christian service may become a personal blessing to those engaged in it. Those who have most fellowship with Christ are not recluses or hermits, who have time on their hands, but tireless workers who are toiling for Jesus and who, in their endeavor, have Him side by side with them, so that they are workers together with God. Let us remember then, in anything we have to do for Jesus, we *can* do it and *should* do it in close communion with Him.

[1] John 1:12   [2] Song of Solomon 1:6

BUT IN FACT CHRIST HAS BEEN RAISED FROM THE DEAD.
— 1 CORINTHIANS 15:20

The whole system of Christianity rests upon the fact that "Christ has been raised from the dead;" for "If Christ has not been raised, then our preaching is in vain and your faith is in vain" (verse 13). The *divinity* of Christ finds its surest proof in His resurrection, since He was "declared to be the Son of God in power according to the Spirit of holiness by his resurrection from the dead."[1] It would not be unreasonable to doubt His Deity if He had not risen. Furthermore, Christ's *sovereignty* depends upon His resurrection: "For to this end Christ died and lived again, that he might be Lord both of the dead and of the living."[2] Again, our *justification*, that choice blessing of the covenant, is linked with Christ's triumphant victory over death and the grave, for He "was delivered up for our trespasses and raised for our justification."*[3] More than this, our very *regeneration* is connected with His resurrection, for we are "born again to a living hope through the resurrection of Jesus Christ from the dead."[4] And most certainly our *ultimate resurrection* rests here, for "If the Spirit of him who raised Jesus from the dead dwells in you, he who raised Christ Jesus from the dead will also give life to your mortal bodies through his Spirit who dwells in you."[5] If Christ is not risen, then we will not rise; but if He is risen, then those who are asleep in Christ have not perished but in their flesh shall surely see God. In this way the silver thread of resurrection runs through all the believer's blessings, from his regeneration onward to his eternal glory, and ties them all together. How important for believers is this glorious fact, and how they rejoice that beyond a doubt it is established, that "in fact Christ has been raised from the dead."

> The promise is fulfill'd,
> Redemption's work is done,
> Justice with mercy's reconciled,
> For God has raised His Son.

❧ EVENING ❧

. . . THE ONLY SON FROM THE FATHER, FULL OF GRACE AND TRUTH.
— JOHN 1:14

Believer, *you* can bear your testimony that Christ is *the only Son from the Father*, as well as the firstborn from the dead. You can say, "He is divine to me, even if He is regarded as simply human by the world. He has done for me what only God could do. He has subdued my stubborn will, melted a rebellious heart, opened gates of brass, and snapped bars of iron. He has turned my mourning into laughter and my desolation into joy; He has led my captivity captive and made my heart rejoice with joy unspeakable and full of glory. Let others think of Him as they will—to me He must be the only Son from the Father: Blessed be His name. And He is *full of grace*. If He had not been, I would never have been saved. He drew me when I struggled to escape from His grace; and when at last I came trembling like a condemned culprit to His mercy-seat He said, 'Take heart, My son; your sins are forgiven.' And He is *full of truth*. His promises have been true; not one has failed. I testify that no servant ever had such a master as He; no brother ever had such a relative as He has been to me; no spouse ever had such a husband as Christ has been to my soul; no sinner ever had a better Savior, no mourner a better comforter than Christ has been to my spirit. He is all I need! In life He is my life, and in death He will be the death of death; in poverty Christ is my riches; in sickness He is my great physician; in darkness He is my star, and in brightness He is my sun; He is the manna of the camp in the wilderness, and it is He who makes the feast in the promised land. Jesus is to me all grace and no wrath, all truth and no falsehood: And of truth and grace He is *full*, infinitely full. My soul, tonight bless with all your might 'the only Son.'"

[1] Romans 1:4   [2] Romans 14:9   [3] Romans 4:25   [4] 1 Peter 1:3   [5] Romans 8:11

I AM WITH YOU ALWAYS. — MATTHEW 28:20

It is good that there is One who is always the same and who is always with us. It is good that there is one stable rock amidst the billows of the sea of life. Let us not set our soul's affections upon rusting, moth-eaten, decaying treasures but set our hearts upon Him who remains faithful forever. Let us not build our house upon the moving quicksands of a deceitful world but base our hopes upon this rock that, amid descending rain and roaring floods, shall stand immovably secure. My soul, I charge you, lay up your treasure in the only secure cabinet; store your jewels where you can never lose them. Put your all in Christ; set all your affections on His person, all your hope in His merit, all your trust in His efficacious blood, all your joy in His presence, and then you may laugh at loss and defy destruction. Remember that all the flowers in the world's garden fade by turns, and the day comes when nothing will be left but the black, cold earth and death will soon put out your candle. How sweet to have the sunlight when the candle is gone! The dark flood must soon roll between you and all you have; so join your heart to Him who will never leave you; trust Him who will go with you through the surging current of death's stream and who will bring you safely to the celestial shore and have you sit with Him in heavenly places forever. In the sorrows of affliction, tell your secrets to the Friend who sticks closer than a brother. Trust all your concerns to Him who can never be taken from you, who will never leave you, and who will never let you leave Him, even "Jesus Christ [who] is the same yesterday and today and forever."[1] "I am with you always" is enough for my soul to live upon no matter who forsakes me.

✑ EVENING ✐

ONLY BE STRONG AND VERY COURAGEOUS. — JOSHUA 1:7

The tender love of God for His servants makes Him concerned for how they feel inside. He wants them to be courageous. Some people think it is okay for a believer to be vexed with doubts and fears, but God does not think so. From this text it is clear that our Master does not want us entangled with fears. He desires for us to live without fretfulness, doubt, and cowardice. Our Master does not think as lightly of our unbelief as we do. When we are despondent, we are subject to a grievous ailment that is not to be trifled with but instead taken at once to the beloved Physician. Our Lord does not like to see our faces sad. It was a law of Ahasuerus that no one should come into the king's court dressed in mourning: This is not the law of the King of kings, for we may come to Him in mourning. But He still would have us put off the spirit of heaviness and put on the garment of praise, for there are so many reasons to rejoice. The Christian ought to be of a courageous spirit, in order that the Lord may be glorified when trials are bravely endured. The fearful and fainthearted *dishonor their God.* Besides, *what a bad example it is.* This disease of doubtfulness and discouragement is an epidemic that spreads quickly among the Lord's flock. One downcast believer makes twenty souls sad. Moreover, unless your courage is kept up, *Satan will be too much for you.* Let your spirit be joyful in God your Savior; the joy of the Lord shall be your strength, and no fiend of hell shall make headway against you. But cowardice lets the banner fall. Moreover, *work is easy* for the cheerful spirit; and *success waits upon cheerfulness.* The workers, rejoicing in their God, believing with all their heart, have success guaranteed. To sow in hope will be to reap in joy; therefore, dear reader, "be strong and very courageous."

[1] Hebrews 13:8

I WILL LOVE HIM AND MANIFEST MYSELF TO HIM. — JOHN 14:21

The Lord Jesus gives special revelations of Himself to His people. Even if Scripture did not declare this, many of the children of God could testify to the truth of it from their own experience. They have had manifestations of their Lord and Savior, Jesus Christ, in a peculiar manner, such as no mere reading or hearing could afford. In the biographies of eminent saints, you will find many instances recorded in which Jesus has been pleased in a very special manner to speak to their souls and to unfold the wonders of His person; in this way their souls have been steeped in happiness, and they have thought themselves to be in heaven. Although they were not there, they were close to the threshold of it—for when Jesus manifests Himself to His people, it is heaven on earth; it is paradise in embryo; it is bliss begun. Special manifestations of Christ exercise a holy influence on the believer's heart. One effect will be *humility*. If a man says, "I have had such-and-such spiritual communications, I am a great man," he has never had any communion with Jesus at all; for "the LORD regards the lowly, but the haughty he knows from afar."[1] He does not need to come near the haughty to know them and will never give them any visits of love. Another effect will be *happiness*; for in God's presence there are pleasures forevermore. *Holiness* will be sure to follow. A man who has no holiness has never had this manifestation. Some men profess a great deal; but we must not believe anyone unless we see that his actions agree with what he says. "Do not be deceived: God is not mocked."[2] He will not bestow His favors upon the wicked, for He will neither cast away a perfect man, nor will He respect an evildoer. Thus there will be three effects of nearness to Jesus—humility, happiness, and holiness. May God give them to you, Christian!

❧ **EVENING** ❧

DO NOT BE AFRAID TO GO DOWN TO EGYPT, FOR THERE I WILL MAKE YOU INTO A GREAT NATION. I MYSELF WILL GO DOWN WITH YOU TO EGYPT, AND I WILL ALSO BRING YOU UP AGAIN. — GENESIS 46:3-4

Jacob must have shuddered at the thought of leaving the land of his fathers to live among heathen strangers. It was *a new scene, and likely to be a trying one*: Who shall venture among citizens of a foreign power without some anxiety? Yet the way was *evidently appointed* for him, and therefore he resolved to go. This is frequently the experience of believers; they are called to face perils and temptations. At such times *let them imitate Jacob's example* by offering sacrifices of prayer to God and seeking His direction. Let them not take a step until they have waited upon the Lord for His blessing: Then *they will have Jacob's companion* to be their friend and helper. How blessed to feel assured that the Lord is with us in all our ways and condescends to enter into our humiliations and banishments! Even at such times we may bask in the sunshine of our Father's love. We need not hesitate to go where He promises His presence; even the darkest valley grows bright with the radiance of this assurance. Marching onward with faith in their God, believers *shall have Jacob's promise.* They will be brought up again, whether it be from the troubles of life or the chambers of death. Jacob's offspring came out of Egypt in due time, and so shall all the faithful pass unscathed through the tribulations of life and the terror of death. Let us exercise Jacob's confidence. *"Do not be afraid"* is the Lord's command and His divine encouragement to those who at His bidding are launching upon new seas; God's presence and preservation forbid so much as one unbelieving fear. Without our God we would be afraid to move; but when He bids us to, it would be dangerous to linger. Reader, go forward, and do not be afraid.

[1] Psalm 138:6   [2] Galatians 6:7

WEEPING MAY TARRY FOR THE NIGHT, BUT JOY COMES WITH THE MORNING.
— PSALM 30:5

Christian, if you are in a night of trial, think of tomorrow; cheer up your heart with the thought of the coming of your Lord. Be patient, for "Lo! He comes with clouds descending."

Be patient! The farmer waits until He reaps His harvest. Be patient; for you know who has said, "Behold, I am coming soon, bringing my recompense with Me, to repay everyone for what he has done." If you are presently in wretched circumstances, remember:

A few more days of marching into battle,
Then you will receive the crown.

Your head may be bowed with thorny troubles now, but it shall wear a starry crown before long. Your heart may be filled with care—it shall be filled with the praise of heaven soon. Your clothes may be soiled with dust now; soon they shall be gloriously white. Wait a little longer. How trivial our troubles and trials will seem when we look back upon them! Looking at them here in the prospect, they seem immense; but when we get to heaven we shall view everything from a new perspective.

Our trials will then seem light and momentary afflictions. Let us go on boldly; even if the night be ever so dark, the morning comes, which is more than they can say who are shut up in the darkness of hell. Do you know what it is then to live on the future—to live on expectation—to anticipate heaven? You are happy, believer, to have such a sure and comforting hope. It may be all dark now, but it will soon be light; it may be all trial now, but it will soon be all happiness. What does it matter if "weeping may tarry for the night" when "joy comes with the morning"?

❧ EVENING ❧

THE LORD IS MY PORTION. — PSALM 119:57

Look at your possessions, believer, and compare your portion with the circumstances of your friends. Some of them have their portion in the field; they are rich, and their harvests yield them a golden increase; but what are harvests compared with your God, who is the God of harvests? What are bursting granaries compared with Him who feeds you with the bread of heaven? Some have their portion in the city; their wealth is abundant and flows to them in constant streams until they become a very reservoir of gold; but what is gold compared with your God? You could not live on it; your spiritual life could not be sustained by it. Could it grant peace to a troubled conscience? Apply it to a sad heart, and see if it could prevent a single groan or minimize one grief. But you have God, and in Him you have more than gold or riches could ever buy. Some have their portion in something most men love—applause and fame; but ask yourself, is not your God more to you than that? Do you think that human accolades or thunderous applause could prepare you to face death or encourage you in the prospect of judgment? No! There are sorrows in life that wealth cannot alleviate; and there is the deep need of a dying hour, for which no riches can provide. But when you have *God* for your portion, you have more than everything else put together. In Him every need is met, whether in life or in death. With God for your portion you are rich indeed, for He will supply your need, comfort your heart, relieve your grief, guide your steps, walk with you in the dark valley, and then take you home to enjoy Him as your portion forever. "I have enough," said Esau; this is the best thing a worldly man can say, but Jacob replied in essence, "I have everything," which is a note too high for carnal minds.

FELLOW HEIRS WITH CHRIST. — ROMANS 8:17

The boundless realms of His Father's universe belong by right to Christ. As "heir of all things,"[1] He is the sole proprietor of the vast creation of God, and He has admitted us to claim it all as ours, by making us His fellow heirs. The golden streets of paradise, the pearly gates, the river of life, the transcendent bliss, and the unutterable glory are all, by our blessed Lord, made ours for an everlasting possession. All that He has, He shares with His people. The royal crown He has placed upon the head of His Church, granting her a kingdom, and calling her sons a royal priesthood, a generation of priests and kings. He uncrowned Himself that we might have a coronation of glory; He would not sit upon His own throne until He had procured a place upon it for all who overcome by His blood. Crown the head, and the whole body shares the honor. Here then is the reward of every Christian conqueror! Christ's throne, crown, scepter, palace, treasure, robes, heritage are yours. He deems His happiness completed by His people sharing it. "The glory that you have given me I have given to them."[2] "These things I have spoken to you, that my joy may be in you, and that your joy may be full."[3] The smiles of His Father are all the sweeter to Him because His people share them. The honors of His kingdom are more pleasing because His people appear with Him in glory. More valuable to Him are His conquests since they have taught His people to overcome. He delights in His throne because on it there is a place for them. He rejoices in His royal robes since they cover His people. He delights all the more in His joy because He calls them to enter into it.

❧ EVENING ☙

HE WILL GATHER THE LAMBS IN HIS ARMS;
HE WILL CARRY THEM IN HIS BOSOM. — ISAIAH 40:11

Who is He of whom such gracious words are spoken? He is *the Good Shepherd*. Why does He carry the lambs in His bosom? Because *He has a tender heart, and any weakness at once melts His heart.* The sighs, the ignorance, the feebleness of the little ones of His flock draw forth His compassion. *It is His office,* as a faithful High Priest, to consider the weak. Besides, *He purchased them with blood; they are His property*: He must and will care for those who cost Him so dearly. Then He is *responsible for each lamb*, bound by covenant love not to lose one. Moreover, *they are all a part of His glory and reward.*

But how may we understand the expression, "he will *carry* them"? Sometimes He carries them by *not permitting them to endure much trial.* Providence deals tenderly with them. Often they are carried by being filled with *an unusual degree of love*, so that they bear up and stand fast. Though their knowledge may not be deep, they have great sweetness in what they do know. Frequently He carries them by giving them *a very simple faith*, which takes the promise just as it stands and in childlike trust runs with every trouble straight to Jesus. The simplicity of their faith gives them an unusual degree of confidence, which carries them above the world.

He carries the lambs "*in his bosom.*" Here is *boundless affection.* Would He put them in His bosom if He did not love them much? Here is *tender nearness*: They are so near that they could not possibly be nearer. Here is *a holy relationship*: There are precious love-passages between Christ and His weak ones. Here is *perfect safety*: In His bosom who can hurt them? They must hurt the Shepherd first. Here is *perfect rest and sweetest comfort.* Surely we are not sufficiently aware of the infinite tenderness of Jesus!

[1] Hebrews 1:2   [2] John 17:22   [3] John 15:11

EVERYONE WHO BELIEVES IS FREED FROM EVERYTHING [JUSTIFIED, KJV].
— ACTS 13:38

The believer in Christ receives a present justification. Faith does not produce this fruit later on, but *now*. So far as justification is the result of faith, it is given to the soul in the moment when it closes with Christ and accepts Him as its all in all. Are those who stand before the throne of God justified now? So are we as certainly and as clearly justified as those who have entered into the portals of heaven. The thief upon the cross was justified the moment that he turned the eye of faith to Jesus; and Paul, at the end of his life, after years of service, was not more justified than the thief who had no service at all. We are *today* accepted in the Beloved, *today* absolved from sin, *today* acquitted at the bar of God's judgment. What a soul-stirring thought! There are some benefits that we will not be able to enjoy until we enter heaven; but this is our immediate possession. This is not like the corn of the land, which we can never eat until we cross the Jordan; but this is part of the manna in the wilderness, a portion of our daily nutriment with which God supplies us in all our comings and goings. We are *now*—even *now*—pardoned; even *now* are our sins put away; even *now* we stand in the sight of God accepted, as though we had never been guilty. "There is therefore *now* no condemnation for those who are in Christ Jesus."[1] There is not a sin in the Book of God, even now, against one of His people. Who dares to lay anything to their charge? There is neither speck, nor spot, nor wrinkle, nor anything remaining upon any one believer in this matter of being justified in the sight of the Judge of all the earth. Let our present privileges awaken us to present duty, and now, while life lasts, let us spend and be spent for our sweet Lord Jesus.

❧ EVENING ❧
. . . MADE PERFECT. — HEBREWS 12:23

Remember that there are two kinds of perfection that the Christian needs—the perfection of justification in the person of Jesus, and the perfection of sanctification accomplished in him by the Holy Spirit. At present, corruption still remains even in the hearts of the regenerate—experience soon teaches us this. Within us there still are lusts and evil imaginations. But I rejoice to know that the day is coming when God shall finish the work that He has begun; and He will present my soul not only perfect in Christ, but perfect through the Spirit, without spot or blemish or any such thing. Can it be true that this poor sinful heart of mine is to become holy even as God is holy? Can it be that this spirit, which often cries, "Wretched man that I am! Who will deliver me from this body of death?"[2] shall get rid of sin and death—that I will have no evil sounds to vex my ears, and no unholy thoughts to disturb my peace? May this happy hour come quickly! When I cross the Jordan, the work of sanctification will be finished; but not until that moment shall I ever claim perfection in myself. Then my spirit will have its last baptism in the Holy Spirit's fire. I think I long to die to receive that last and final purification that will usher me into heaven. An angel will not be any purer than I shall be, for I shall be able to say, in a double sense, "I am clean," through Jesus' blood and through the Spirit's work. We should extol the power of the Holy Spirit who makes us fit to stand before our Father in heaven! Yet we must not allow the hope of perfection there to make us content with imperfection now. If it does this, our hope cannot be genuine; for a good hope is a purifying thing, even now. Grace must be at work in us *now* or it will not be perfected in us *then*. Let us pray to "be filled with the Spirit,"[3] that we may *increasingly* bring forth the fruits of righteousness.

[1] Romans 8:1   [2] Romans 7:24   [3] Ephesians 5:18

GOD, WHO RICHLY PROVIDES US WITH EVERYTHING TO ENJOY.
— 1 TIMOTHY 6:17

Our Lord Jesus is always giving and does not for a single moment withdraw His hand. As long as there is a vessel of grace not yet full to the brim, the oil shall not be withheld. He is an ever-shining sun; He is manna in unfailing supply; He is a rock in the desert, sending constant streams of life from His pierced side; the rain of His grace is always falling; the river of His bounty is ever-flowing, and the wellspring of His love is a constant tide. As the King can never die, so His grace can never fail. Every day we pluck His fruit, and every day His branches bend down to our hand with a fresh supply of mercy. There are seven feast-days in His weeks, and as many banquets in His years. Who has ever returned from His door unblessed? Who has ever risen from His table unsatisfied? His mercies are new every morning and fresh every evening. Who can calculate the number of His benefits or value the extent of His provision? Every passing day we are the beneficiaries of a myriad of mercies. The wings of our hours are covered with the silver of His kindness and with the yellow gold of His affection. The river of time bears from the mountains of eternity the golden sands of His favor. The countless stars serve as the standard bearers of incalculable blessings. Who can measure the benefits that He bestows on His servant or recount the extent of His mercies toward His own? How shall my soul extol Him who loads us with daily benefits, and who crowns us with loving-kindness? O that my praise could be as endless as His provision. O miserable tongue, how can you be silent? Wake up, I pray, lest I call you no more my glory, but my shame. "Awake, O harp and lyre! I will awake the dawn."[1]

AND HE SAID, "THUS SAYS THE LORD, 'I WILL MAKE THIS DRY STREAMBED
FULL OF POOLS.' FOR THUS SAYS THE LORD, 'YOU SHALL NOT SEE
WIND OR RAIN, BUT THAT STREAMBED SHALL BE FILLED WITH WATER,
SO THAT YOU SHALL DRINK, YOU, YOUR LIVESTOCK,
AND YOUR ANIMALS.'" — 2 KINGS 3:16-17

The armies of the three kings were famishing and in need of water. God was about to send it, and in these words the prophet announced the coming blessing. Here was a case of *human helplessness*: Not a drop of water could all the valiant men procure from the skies or find in the wells of earth. In similar fashion the people of the Lord are often at their wits' end—seeing their helplessness, and then learning where their help is to be found. Notice that people were to *prepare in faith to receive the divine blessing*. They were to dig the trenches in which the water would be held. The church must learn by her efforts and prayers to make herself ready to be blessed; she must make the pools, and the Lord will fill them. This must be done in faith, in the full assurance that the blessing is about to descend. They were soon to discover a unique provision of the water they required. The shower did not pour from the clouds, as in Elijah's case; but in a silent and mysterious manner the pools were filled. The Lord has His own sovereign modes of action: He is not tied to process and time as we are but does as He pleases among the sons of men. Our part is to humbly receive from Him, and not to dictate to Him. We must also notice *the remarkable abundance of the supply*—there was enough for the needs of all. And so it is in the gospel blessing. All the needs of the congregation and of the entire church will be met by divine power in answer to prayer; and above all this, victory shall be quickly given to the armies of the Lord.

What am I doing for Jesus? What trenches am I digging? O Lord, make me ready to receive the blessing that You are so willing to bestow.

[1] Psalm 57:8

WHOEVER SAYS HE ABIDES IN HIM OUGHT TO WALK IN THE SAME WAY
IN WHICH HE WALKED. — 1 JOHN 2:6

Why should Christians imitate Christ? They should do it *for their own sakes*. If they desire to be spiritually healthy—if they want to escape the sickness of sin and enjoy the vigor of growing grace, Jesus must be their model. For their own happiness' sake, if they would drink deeply of His love, if they would enjoy holy and happy communion with Jesus, if they would be lifted up above the cares and troubles of this world, let them walk even as He walked. There is nothing that is able to assist you in walking directly toward heaven like wearing the image of Jesus on your heart to rule all its emotions. It is when, by the power of the Holy Spirit, you are enabled to walk with Jesus in His very footsteps that you are most happy and most known to be the sons of God. Peter at a distance is both unsafe and uneasy. Next, for *religion's sake* strive to be like Jesus. Poor religion, you have been fiercely attacked by cruel foes, but you have not been wounded half as much by your enemies as you have by your friends. Who made those wounds in the fair hand of godliness? The professing Christian who used the dagger of hypocrisy. The man who with disguises enters the fold, being nothing but a wolf in sheep's clothing, worries the flock more than the lion outside. There is no weapon half so deadly as a Judas-kiss. Inconsistent professing Christians injure the Gospel more than the sneering critic or the heretic. But especially for *Christ's own sake*, imitate His example. Christian, do you love your Savior? Is His name precious to you? Is His cause dear to you? Would you see the kingdoms of the world become His? Is it your desire that He should be glorified? Are you longing that souls should be won to Him? If so, *imitate* Jesus; be "a letter of Christ . . . known and read by all."[1]

❧   EVENING   ❧

YOU ARE MY SERVANT, I HAVE CHOSEN YOU. — ISAIAH 41:9

If we have received the grace of God in our hearts, its practical effect has been to make us God's *servants*. We may be unfaithful servants, we certainly are unprofitable ones, but yet, blessed be His name, we are His servants, wearing His uniform, eating at His table, and obeying His commands. We were once the servants of sin, but He who made us free has now taken us into His family and taught us obedience to His will. We do not serve our Master perfectly, but we would if we could. As we hear God's voice saying unto us, "You are My servant," we can answer with David, "I am your servant. . . . You have loosed my bonds."[2] But the Lord calls us not only His *servants*, but His *chosen* ones—"I have chosen you." We have not chosen Him first, but He has chosen us. If we are now God's servants, it wasn't always so; the change must be ascribed to sovereign grace. The eye of sovereignty singled us out, and the voice of unchanging grace declared, "I have loved you with an everlasting love."[3] Long before time began or space was created, God had written upon His heart the names of His elect people, had predestinated them to be conformed unto the image of His Son, and ordained them heirs of all the fullness of His love, His grace, and His glory. What comfort is here! Having loved us for so long, will the Lord then reject us? He knew how stiff-necked we would be, He understood that our hearts were evil, and yet He made the choice. Our Savior is no fickle lover. He dos not feel enchanted for a while with some gleams of beauty from His church's eye and then afterwards reject her because of her unfaithfulness. No, He married her in old eternity; and He hates divorce! The eternal choice is a bond upon *our* gratitude and upon *His* faithfulness, which neither can disown.

[1] 2 Corinthians 2:2-3 [2] Psalm 116:16 [3] Jeremiah 31:3

IN HIM THE WHOLE FULLNESS OF DEITY DWELLS BODILY, AND
YOU HAVE BEEN FILLED IN HIM. — COLOSSIANS 2:9-10

All the attributes of Christ, as God and man, are at our disposal. All the fullness of the Godhead, whatever that marvelous term may encompass, is ours to make us complete. He cannot endow us with the attributes of Deity; but He has done all that can be done, for He has made even His divine power and Godhead subservient to our salvation. His omnipotence, omniscience, omnipresence, immutability and infallibility are all combined for our defense. Stand up, believer, and witness the Lord Jesus hitching the whole of His divine Godhead to the chariot of salvation! How vast His grace, how firm His faithfulness, how unswerving His immutability, how infinite His power, how limitless His knowledge! The Lord Jesus made all these pillars of the temple of salvation; and all, without any lessening of their infinity, are covenanted to us as our perpetual inheritance. The fathomless love of the Savior's heart is ours in every drop; every sinew in the arm of strength, every jewel in the crown of majesty, the immensity of divine knowledge, and the sternness of divine justice—all are ours and shall be employed for us. The whole of Christ, in His adorable character as the Son of God, is by Himself made ours to most richly enjoy. His wisdom is our direction, His knowledge our instruction, His power our protection, His justice our guarantee, His love our comfort, His mercy our solace, and His immutability our trust. He holds nothing back but opens the recesses of the Mount of God and bids us dig in its mines for the hidden treasures. "All, all, all are yours," He says, "sated with favor, and full of the blessing of the Lord." How wonderful to see Jesus in this way, and to call upon Him with the certain confidence that in seeking the intervention of His love or power, we are simply asking for what He has already faithfully promised.

❦ EVENING ❧
. . . LATER . . . — HEBREWS 12:11

How happy are tested Christians, *later*. There is no deeper calm than that which follows the storm. Who has not rejoiced in clear shinings after rain? Victorious banquets are for well-accomplished soldiers. After killing the lion we eat the honey; after climbing the Hill Difficulty,[1] we sit down in the arbor to rest; after traversing the Valley of Humiliation, after fighting with Apollyon, the shining one appears, with the healing branch from the tree of life. Our sorrows, like the passing hulls of the ships upon the sea, leave a silver line of holy light behind them "later." It is peace, sweet, deep peace, that follows the horrible turmoil that once reigned in our tormented, guilty souls. Consider, then, the happy condition of a Christian! He has his best things last, and therefore in this world he receives his worst things first. But even his worst things are "later" good things, hard plowings yielding joyful harvests. Even now he grows rich by his losses, he rises by his falls, he lives by dying, and he becomes full by being emptied; if, then, his grievous afflictions yield him so much peaceable fruit in this life, what will be the full vintage of joy "later" in heaven? If his dark nights are as bright as the world's days, what shall his days be? If even his starlight is more splendid than the sun, what must his sunlight be? If he can sing in a dungeon, how sweetly will he sing in heaven! If he can praise the Lord in the fires, how will he extol Him before the eternal throne! If evil be good to him *now*, what will the overflowing goodness of God be to him *then*? Oh, blessed "later"! Who would not be a Christian? Who would not bear the present cross for the crown that comes afterwards? But here is work for patience, for the rest is not for today, nor the triumph for the present, but "later." Wait, my soul, and let patience have her perfect work.

[1] *Pilgrim's Progress*

I HAVE SEEN SLAVES ON HORSES, AND PRINCES WALKING ON
THE GROUND LIKE SLAVES. — ECCLESIASTES 10:7

Upstarts frequently steal the highest places, while the truly great struggle in obscurity. This is a riddle in providence whose solution will one day gladden the hearts of the upright; but it is so common a fact that none of us should complain if we face the experience. When our Lord was on earth, although He is the Prince of the kings of the earth, yet He walked the footpath of weariness and service as the Servant of servants. It should then be no surprise if His followers, who are princes in His line, should also be looked down upon as inferior and contemptible persons. The world is upside-down, and therefore the first are last and the last first. Consider how the servile sons of Satan lord it in the earth! What a high horse they ride! How they exalt themselves. David wanders on the mountains, while Saul reigns in state; Elijah is complaining in the cave, while Jezebel is boasting in the palace. Yet who would wish to take the places of the proud rebels? And who, on the other hand, might not envy the despised saints? When the wheel turns, those who are lowest rise, and the highest sink. Patience, then, believer, eternity will right the wrongs of time.

Let us not fall into the error of letting our passions and sinful appetites ride in triumph, while our nobler powers walk in the dust. Grace must reign as a prince and make the members of our bodies instruments of righteousness. The Holy Spirit loves order, and He therefore sets our powers and faculties in proper rank and place, giving the highest room to those spiritual faculties that link us with the great King; let us not disturb the divine arrangement but ask for grace to keep our body under control and bring it into subjection. We were not made new to allow our passions to rule over us, but in order that, as kings, we may reign in Christ Jesus over the triple kingdom of spirit, soul, and body, to the glory of God the Father.

❧   EVENING   ❧

AND HE ASKED THAT HE MIGHT DIE. — 1 KINGS 19:4

It was a remarkable thing that the man who was never to die, for whom God had ordained an infinitely better lot, the man who would be carried to heaven in a chariot of fire and be translated and not see death, should thus pray, "Take away my life, for I am no better than my fathers." We have here a memorable proof that God does not always answer prayer in kind, though He always does in effect. He gave Elijah something better than what he asked for, and thus really heard and answered him. It was strange that the lion-hearted Elijah should be so depressed by Jezebel's threat as to ask to die, and yet it was so kind on the part of our heavenly Father not to take His desponding servant at his word. There is a limit to the doctrine of the prayer of faith. We are not to expect that God will give us everything we choose to ask for. We know that we sometimes ask and do not receive because we ask wrongly. If we ask for that which is not promised—if we run counter to the spirit that the Lord would have us cultivate—if we ask contrary to His will or to the decrees of His providence—if we ask merely for selfish gratification and without a concern for His glory, we must not expect that we will receive. But when we ask in faith, without doubting, if we do not receive the precise thing for which we asked, we shall receive an equivalent, and more than an equivalent, for it. As one remarks, "If the Lord does not pay in silver, He will in gold; and if He does not pay in gold, He will in diamonds." If He does not give you precisely what you ask for, He will give you that which is tantamount to it, and that which you will be happy to receive in its place. So, dear reader, be much in prayer, and make this evening a time of earnest intercession, but be careful what you ask for!

WONDROUSLY SHOW YOUR STEADFAST LOVE. — PSALM 17:7

When we give our hearts with our offerings, we do well, but we must often admit to failure in this respect. Not so our Master and our Lord. His favors are always performed with the love of His heart. He does not send us the cold meat and the broken pieces from the table of His luxury, but He dips our portion in His own dish and seasons our provisions with the spices of His fragrant affections. When He puts the golden coins of His grace into our palms, He accompanies the gift with such a warm pressure of our hand that the manner of His giving is as precious as the gift itself. When He comes into our houses on His errands of love, He does not act as some austere visitors do in a poor man's cottage, but He sits by our side, not despising our poverty, nor blaming our weakness. Beloved, with what smiles does He speak! What golden sentences drop from His gracious lips! What embraces of affection does He bestow upon us! If He had only given us pennies, the way He gave would have made them as gold! But as it is, the expensive gifts are set in the golden basket of His pleasant demeanor. It is impossible to doubt the sincerity of His love, for there is a bleeding heart stamped upon the face of all His coins. He gives generally and without holding back. He gives no hint that we are burdensome to Him, no cold looks for His poor dependents; instead He rejoices in His mercy and presses us to His bosom while He is pouring out His life for us. There is a fragrance in His ointment that nothing but His heart could produce; there is a sweetness in His honeycomb that could not be unless the very essence of His soul's affection had been mingled with it. Oh, the rare communion that such singular devotion provides! May we continually taste and know the blessedness of it!

❧ Evening ☙

I LED THEM WITH CORDS OF KINDNESS, WITH THE BANDS OF LOVE.
— HOSEA 11:4

Our heavenly Father often leads us with the cords of love; but how slow we are to run toward Him! How reluctantly we respond to His gentle impulses! *He leads us to exercise a more simple faith in Him*; but we have not yet learned to trust like Abraham. We do not leave our worldly cares with God, but, like Martha, we burden ourselves with much serving. Our meager faith brings leanness to our souls; we do not open our mouths wide, though God has promised to fill them. Does He not this evening lead us to trust Him? Can we not hear Him say, "Come, My child, and trust Me. The curtain is opened; enter into My presence, and come boldly to the throne of My grace. I am worthy of your complete confidence; cast your cares on Me. Shake yourself from the dust of your cares, and put on the garments of joy." But, sadly though called with tones of love to the blessed exercise of this comforting grace, we will not come. At another time *He leads us to closer communion with Himself*. We have been sitting on the doorstep of God's house, and He invites us into the banqueting hall to eat with Him, but we decline the honor. There are secret rooms not yet opened to us, which Jesus invites us to enter, but we hold back. Shame on our cold hearts! We are but poor lovers of our sweet Lord Jesus, not fit to be His servants, much less to be His brides, and yet He has exalted us to be bone of His bone and flesh of His flesh, married to Him by a glorious marriage-covenant. Herein is love! But it is a love that *takes no denial*. If we do not obey the gentle leadings of His love, He will send affliction to drive us into closer intimacy with Himself. He is determined to bring us close to Him. What foolish children we are to refuse those bands of love, and in doing so to bring upon ourselves painful discipline, which He exercises for our good!

... IF INDEED YOU HAVE TASTED THAT THE LORD IS GOOD.
— 1 PETER 2:3

If." Then this is not a matter to be taken for granted concerning every one of the human race. "If"—then there is a possibility and a probability that some may not have tasted that the Lord is gracious. "If"—then this is not a general but a special mercy; and it is necessary to ask whether we know the grace of God by inward experience. There is no spiritual favor that may not be a matter for heart-searching.

But while this should be a matter of earnest and prayerful inquiry, no one ought to be content while there is any such thing as an "if" about his having tasted that the Lord is good. A jealous and holy distrust of self may give rise to the question even in the believer's heart, but the *continuance* of such a doubt would be an evil indeed. We must not rest without a desperate struggle to clasp the Savior in the arms of faith and say, "I know whom I have believed, and I am convinced that he is able to guard until that Day what has been entrusted to me."[1] Do not rest, believer, until you have a full assurance of your interest in Jesus. Let nothing satisfy you until, by the infallible witness of the Holy Spirit bearing witness with your spirit, you are identified as a child of God. Do trifle with this. Do not be satisfied with "perhaps" or "if" or "maybe." Build on eternal truths; really build upon them. Let your anchor be cast into that which is within the veil, and see to it that your soul is linked to the anchor by a cable that will not break. Get beyond these dreary "ifs"; stay no longer in the wilderness of doubts and fears; cross the Jordan of distrust, and enter the promised land of peace, where the land ceases not to flow with milk and honey.

❧ EVENING ☙

THERE IS GRAIN FOR SALE IN EGYPT. — GENESIS 42:2

Famine pinched all the nations, and it seemed inevitable that Jacob and his family should suffer great want; but the God of providence, who never forgets the objects of electing love, had stored a granary for His people by giving the Egyptians warning of the scarcity and leading them to treasure up the grain from the years of plenty. Little did Jacob expect deliverance from Egypt, but there was grain in store for him. Believer, though all things are apparently against you, rest assured that God has made a reservation on your behalf; in the roll of your griefs there is a saving clause. Somehow He will deliver you, and somewhere He will provide for you. Your rescue may come from a very unexpected source, but help will definitely come in your extremity, and you will magnify the name of the Lord. If men do not feed you, ravens will; and if the earth does not yield wheat, heaven will drop manna. Therefore be of good courage, and rest quietly in the Lord. God can make the sun rise in the west if He pleases and can make the source of distress a channel of delight. The grain in Egypt was all in the hands of the beloved Joseph; he opened or closed the granaries at will. And so the riches of providence are all in the absolute power of our Lord Jesus, who will dispense them generously to His people. Joseph was abundantly ready to help his own family; and Jesus is unceasing in His faithful care for His brethren. Our responsibility is to go after the help that is provided for us: We must not sit still in despondency, but stir ourselves. Prayer will bring us quickly into the presence of our royal Brother. Once before His throne we have only to ask and receive. His stores are not exhausted; there is still grain: His heart is not hard; He will give the grain to us. Lord, forgive our unbelief, and this evening constrain us to draw largely from Your fullness and receive grace for grace.

[1] 2 Timothy 1:12

HE LED THEM BY A STRAIGHT WAY. — PSALM 107:7

Changing circumstances often causes the anxious believer to ask, "Why is this happening to me?" I looked for light, but darkness came; for peace, but faced trouble. I said in my heart, my mountain stands firm, I shall never be moved. Lord, You hide Your face, and I am troubled. Only yesterday I could read my title clearly; but today my evidences are blurred, and my hopes are clouded. Yesterday I could climb the mountain and view the landscape and rejoice with confidence in my future inheritance; today my spirit has no hopes, but many fears; no joys, but great distress. Is this part of God's plan for me? Can this be the way in which God would bring me to heaven? Yes, it is even so. The eclipse of your faith, the darkness of your mind, the fainting of your hope—all these things are just parts of God's method of making you ready for the great inheritance, which you will soon enjoy. These trials are for the testing and strengthening of your faith—they are waves that wash you further upon the rock—they are winds that steer your ship more quickly toward the desired haven. What David wrote then will be true of you: "he brought them to their desired haven" (verse 30). By honor and dishonor, by evil report and by good report, by plenty and by poverty, by joy and by distress, by persecution and by peace—by all these things your spiritual life is maintained, and by each of these you are helped on your way. Do not think, believer, that your sorrows are out of God's plan; they are necessary parts of it. "Through many tribulations we must enter the kingdom."[1] Learn, then, to "count it all joy . . . when you meet trials of various kinds."[2]

> O let my trembling soul be still,
> And trust Thy wise, Thy holy will!
> I cannot, Lord, Thy purpose see,
> Yet all is well since ruled by Thee.

❧ EVENING ❧

BEHOLD, YOU ARE BEAUTIFUL, MY BELOVED. — SONG OF SOLOMON 1:16

From every angle our Well-beloved is most fair. Our various experiences are meant by our heavenly Father to provide new vantage points from which we may view the loveliness of Jesus. How friendly are our trials when they allow us a clearer view of Jesus than ordinary life could afford us! We have seen Him from the mountain peaks, and He has shone upon us as the sun in His strength; but we have seen Him also from the lions' dens, and even there He has lost none of His loveliness. In the experience of suffering and pain, from the borders of the grave, we have turned our eyes to our soul's spouse, and He has never been other than "beautiful." Many of His saints looked upon Him from the gloom of dungeons and from the martyr's flames; yet they never uttered an ill word of Him, but died extolling His surpassing charms. To keep our gaze on the Lord Jesus is noble and pleasant employment. Is it not unspeakably delightful to view the Savior in all His works and to perceive Him matchless in each? To shift the kaleidoscope, as it were, and to find fresh combinations of matchless grace? In the manger and in eternity, on the cross and on His throne, in the garden and in His kingdom, among thieves or in the midst of cherubim, He is everywhere glorious in His beauty. Examine carefully every little act of His life and every trait of His character, and He is as lovely in the minute as in the majestic. Judge Him as you will, you cannot censure; weigh Him as you please, and He will not be found wanting. Eternity shall not discover the shadow of a spot in our Beloved, but rather as ages revolve, His hidden glories will shine with even more inconceivable splendor, and His unutterable loveliness will continually ravish all celestial minds.

[1] Acts 14:22   [2] James 1:2

THE LORD WILL FULFILL HIS PURPOSE FOR ME. — PSALM 138:8

It is clear that the confidence that the psalmist expresses is a *divine confidence*. He did not say, "*I* have enough grace to perfect that which concerns me—my faith is so steady that it will not falter—my love is so warm that it will never grow cold—my resolution is so firm that nothing can move it." No, his dependence was on the Lord alone. If we display a confidence that is not grounded on the Rock of ages, our confidence is worse than a dream; it will fall upon us and cover us with its ruins, to our sorrow and confusion. The psalmist was wise; he rested on nothing less than the *Lord's* work. It is the Lord who has begun the good work within us; it is He who has carried it on; and if He does not finish it, it never will be completed. If there is one stitch in the celestial garment of our righteousness that we must insert ourselves, then we are lost; but this is our confidence—what the Lord begins, He completes. He *has* done it all, *must* do it all, and *will* do it all. Our confidence must not be in what we have done, nor in what we have resolved to do, but entirely in what *the Lord* will do. Unbelief insinuates: "You will never be able to stand. Look at the evil of your heart—you can never conquer sin; remember the sinful pleasures and temptations of the world that beset you—you will be certainly allured by them and led astray." True, we would certainly perish if left to our own strength. If by ourselves we navigate the most frail vessels of our lives over so rough a sea, we might well give up the voyage in despair; but thanks be to God, He will complete that which concerns us and bring us to the desired haven. We can never be too confident when we confide in Him alone, and never too eager to have such a trust.

❧ EVENING ❧

YOU HAVE NOT BOUGHT ME SWEET CANE WITH MONEY.
— ISAIAH 43:24

Worshipers at the temple were keen to bring presents of sweet perfumes to be burned upon the altar of God. But Israel, in the time of her backsliding, became ungenerous and made fewer offerings to her Lord. This was an evidence of coldness of heart toward God and His house. Reader, does this never happen with you? Is it not possible that the complaint of this text may occasionally, if not frequently, be brought against you? Those who are poor in pocket, if rich in faith, will be accepted even though their gifts are small; but, poor reader, do you give in fair proportion to the Lord, or is the widow's mite kept back from the sacred treasury? The rich believer should be thankful for the wealth entrusted to him but should not forget his large responsibility, for where much is given, much will be required. But, rich reader, are you mindful of your obligations, and is your giving to the Lord proportionate to the benefit you enjoy? Jesus gave His blood for us; what shall we give to Him? We are His, and He has purchased us for Himself—can we act as if we were our own? O for more consecration! O for more love! Blessed Jesus, how good it is of You to accept our sweet cane bought with money! Nothing is too costly as a tribute to Your unrivaled love, and yet You receive with favor the smallest sincere token of affection! You receive our poor forget-me-nots and love-tokens as though they were intrinsically precious, though indeed they are but as the bunch of wild flowers that the child brings to his mother. Let us never grow stingy toward You, and from this hour may we never hear You complain of us again for withholding the gifts of our love. We will give You the firstfruits of our increase and pay You tithes of all, and then we will confess, "of your own have we given you."[1]

[1] 1 Chronicles 29:14

BLESSED BE GOD, BECAUSE HE HAS NOT REJECTED MY PRAYER.
— PSALM 66:20

In looking back upon the character of our prayers, if we do it honestly, we shall be filled with wonder that God has ever answered them. There may be some who think their prayers worthy of acceptance—as the Pharisee did; but the true Christian, who sees things clearly, must surely weep over his prayers, and if he could retrace his steps he would desire to pray more earnestly. Remember, Christian, how *cold* your prayers have been. When in your closet you should have wrestled as Jacob did; but instead your petitions have been faint and few—far removed from that humble, believing, persevering faith that cries, "I will not let you go unless you bless me." Yet, how wonderful to know that God has heard these cold prayers of yours, and not only heard, but answered them. Reflect also how *infrequent* have been your prayers unless you have been in trouble, and then you have gone often to the mercy-seat: But when deliverance has come, what happened to your constant supplication? Yet, even though you have stopped praying as you once did, God has not stopped blessing. When you have neglected the mercy-seat, God has not deserted it, but the bright light of His glory has remained visible between the wings of the cherubim. How marvelous that the Lord should pay attention to our intermittent spasms of prayerfulness that ebb and flow with our needs. What a God He is to hear the prayers of those who come to Him when they have pressing concerns but neglect Him when they have received a mercy; who approach Him when they are forced to come but who almost forget to address Him when benefits are plentiful and sorrows are few. Let His gracious kindness in hearing such prayers touch our hearts, so that from now on we may be found "praying at all times in the Spirit, with all prayer and supplication."[1]

❧ EVENING ☙

ONLY LET YOUR MANNER OF LIFE BE WORTHY OF THE GOSPEL OF CHRIST.
— PHILIPPIANS 1:27

The apostle's concern is not simply with our talk and conversation with one another, but with the whole course of our life and behavior in the world. The Greek word translated "manner of life" signifies the actions and the privileges of citizenship: And in this way we are commanded to let our actions, as citizens of the New Jerusalem, be worthy of the Gospel of Christ. What "manner of life" is this? In the first place, *the Gospel is very simple.* So Christians should be simple and plain in their habits. There should be about our manner, our speech, our dress, our whole behavior that simplicity that is the very soul of beauty. The Gospel is *preeminently true.* It is gold without dross; and the Christian's life will be lusterless and valueless without the jewel of truth. The Gospel is a very *fearless Gospel*; it boldly proclaims the truth, whether men like it or not. We must be equally faithful and unflinching. But the Gospel is also *very gentle.* We see this in Jesus: "a bruised reed he will not break."[2] Some professing Christians are sharper than a thorn-hedge; such men are not like Jesus. Let us seek to win others by the gentleness of our words and deeds. The Gospel is *very loving.* It is the message of the God of love to a lost and fallen race. Christ's command to His disciples was, "Love one another." We need more real, hearty union with and love for all the saints, more tender compassion toward the souls of the worst and vilest of men! We must not forget that the Gospel of Christ is *holy.* It never excuses sin: It pardons it, but only through an atonement. If our life is to resemble the Gospel, we must shun not merely the grosser vices, but everything that would hinder our perfect conformity to Christ. For His sake, for our own sakes, and for the sake of others, we must strive day by day to let our manner of life be more in accordance with His Gospel.

[1] Ephesians 6:18   [2] Matthew 12:20

DO NOT FORSAKE ME, O LORD! — PSALM 38:21

We frequently pray that God would not forsake us in the hour of trial and temptation, but we are prone to forget that we need to pray like this at *all times*. There is no moment of our life, however holy, in which we can do without His constant upholding. Whether in light or in darkness, in communion or in temptation, we need always to pray, "Do not forsake me, O LORD!" "Hold me up, that I may be safe."[1] A little child, while learning to walk, always needs the nurse's aid. The ship left by the pilot drifts immediately off course. We cannot do without continued aid from above; let it then be your prayer today, "Do not forsake me. Father, do not forsake Your child, lest he fall by the hand of the enemy. Shepherd, do not forsake Your lamb, lest he wander from the safety of the fold. Farmer, do not forsake Your crops, lest they wither and die. 'Do not forsake me, O LORD,' now or at any moment of my life. Do not forsake me in my joys, lest they absorb my heart. Do not forsake me in my sorrows, lest I murmur against You. Do not forsake me in the day of my repentance, lest I lose the hope of pardon and fall into despair; and do not forsake me in the day of my strongest faith, lest faith degenerate into presumption. Do not forsake me, for without You I am weak, but with You I am strong. Do not forsake me, for my path is dangerous and full of snares, and I cannot do without Your guidance. As the hen does not forsake her brood, so You, O Lord protect me, and permit me to find my refuge in You. 'Be not far from me, for trouble is near, and there is none to help.'[2] 'Cast me not off; forsake me not, O God of my salvation!'"[3]

> *Forever in our cleansed breast,*
> *May Thy Eternal Spirit rest;*
> *And make our secret soul to be*
> *A temple clean and pure for Thee.*

❧ EVENING ❧
AND THEY ROSE THAT SAME HOUR AND RETURNED TO JERUSALEM. . . .
THEN THEY TOLD WHAT HAD HAPPENED ON THE ROAD, AND
HOW HE WAS KNOWN TO THEM. — LUKE 24:33, 35

When the two disciples had reached Emmaus and were refreshing themselves at the evening meal, the mysterious stranger who had so enchanted them on the road took bread and broke it, made Himself known to them, and then vanished out of their sight. They had constrained Him to stay with them because the day was far spent; but now, although it was much later, their love was a lamp to their feet, indeed wings also. They forgot the darkness, their weariness was all gone, and immediately they headed back the seven miles to tell the wonderful news of a risen Lord who had appeared to them on the road. They reached the Christians in Jerusalem and were received by a burst of joyful news before they could tell their own tale. These early Christians were all on fire to speak of Christ's resurrection and to proclaim what they knew of the Lord; they happily shared their experiences. This evening let their example impress us deeply. We also must bear our witness concerning Jesus. John's account of the sepulcher needed to be supplemented by Peter; and Mary could speak of something further still; the combined accounts provide us with a complete testimony from which nothing necessary is missing. Each of us has peculiar gifts and personal experiences; but the one object God has in view is the maturing of the whole Body of Christ. We must, therefore, bring our spiritual possessions and lay them at the apostles' feet, that we may share all of what God has given to us. Withhold no part of the precious truth, but speak what you know and declare what you have seen. Do not allow the toil or darkness or possible unbelief of your friends to dissuade you. Let us rise and march to the place of duty, and there declare what great things God has shown to our soul.

[1] Psalm 119:117   [2] Psalm 22:11   [3] Psalm 27:9

CAST YOUR BURDEN ON THE LORD, AND HE WILL SUSTAIN YOU.
— PSALM 55:22

Care, even when addressed to legitimate matters, if it is carried to excess, has in it the nature of sin. Again and again Jesus exhorted His followers to avoid anxious care. The apostles reiterated the call; and it is one that cannot be neglected without involving transgression: For the very essence of anxious care is imagining that we are wiser than God and putting ourselves in His place as if we could do for Him what He has undertaken to do for us. We attempt to think of things that we imagine Him forgetting; we work to take upon ourselves a heavy burden, as if He were unable or unwilling to take it for us. Now this disobedience to His plain precept, this unbelief in His Word, this presumption that intrudes upon His province, is all sinful. But more than this, anxious care often leads to acts of sin. If we cannot calmly leave our affairs in God's hand but attempt to carry our own burden, we will be tempted to use wrong means to help ourselves. This sin leads to a forsaking of God as our counselor and resorting instead to human wisdom. This is going to the broken well instead of to the fountain, a sin of which Israel was guilty in the past. Anxiety makes us doubt God's loving-kindness, and so our love to Him grows cold; we feel mistrust, and in this we grieve the Spirit of God, so that our prayers are hindered, our consistent example spoiled, and our life one of self-seeking. Such lack of confidence in God leads us to wander far from Him; but if through simple faith in His promise we cast each burden as it comes upon Him and are "not . . . anxious about anything"[1] because He undertakes to care for us, it will keep us close to Him and strengthen us against temptation. "You keep him in perfect peace whose mind is stayed on you, because he trusts in you."[2]

⚘ EVENING ⚘

CONTINUE IN THE FAITH. — ACTS 14:22

Perseverance is the badge of true saints. The Christian life is not only a *beginning* in the ways of God, but also means *continuing* in those ways as long as life lasts. It is with a Christian as it was with the great Napoleon: He said, "Conquest has made me what I am, and conquest must maintain me." So under God, dear believer in the Lord, conquest has made you what you are, and conquest must sustain you. Your motto must be, "Aim higher." The only true conqueror who shall be crowned in the end is he who continues until war's trumpet is blown no more. Perseverance is, therefore, the target of all our spiritual enemies. The *world* does not object to your being a Christian for a time, if she can tempt you to quit your pilgrimage and settle down to trade with her in Vanity Fair. The *flesh* will seek to ensnare you and to prevent your pressing on to glory. "Being a pilgrim is weary work and makes me wonder: Am I always to be mortified? Am I never to be indulged? Can I not have at least a holiday from this constant warfare?" *Satan* will make many a fierce attack on your perseverance; it will be the target for all his arrows. He will strive to hinder you *in service*: He will insinuate that you are doing no good and that you need to rest. He will endeavor to make you weary of *suffering*; he will whisper, "Curse God, and die." Or he will attack your *steadfastness*: "What is the good of being so zealous? Be quiet like the rest; sleep as others do, and let your lamp go out like the foolish virgins." Or he will assail your *doctrinal sentiments*: "Why do you hold to these doctrinal creeds? Sensible men are getting more liberal; they are removing the old landmarks: Fall in with the times." So, Christian, wear your shield close to your armor and cry earnestly to God, that by His Spirit you may endure to the end.

[1] Philippians 4:6 [2] Isaiah 26:1

SO MEPHIBOSHETH LIVED IN JERUSALEM,
FOR HE ATE ALWAYS AT THE KING'S TABLE.
NOW HE WAS LAME IN BOTH HIS FEET. — 2 SAMUEL 9:13

Mephibosheth was not an attractive guest at the royal table; yet he had an open invitation because King David could see in his face the features of the beloved Jonathan. Like Mephibosheth, we may exclaim to the King of Glory, "What is Your servant, that You should show regard for a dead dog such as I?" But still the Lord invites us to share intimately with Him, because He sees in our countenances the remembrance of His dearly-beloved Jesus. It is on account of Jesus that the Lord's people are dear to God. Such is the love that the Father bears to His only begotten that for His sake He raises His lowly brothers and sisters from poverty and exile to enjoy the king's court, noble rank, and royal provision. Their *deformity shall not rob them of their privileges.* Lameness is no bar to sonship; the disabled is as much the heir as if he could run like a gazelle. Our ability to enter may be impaired but not our right of entry. A king's table is a noble hiding-place for lame legs, and at the gospel feast we learn to rejoice in infirmities because the power of Christ rests upon us. Yet serious *disability may spoil the journey of the best-loved saints.* Here is one feasted by David, and yet so lame in both his feet that he could not go up with the king when he fled from the city and was therefore maligned and injured by his servant. Saints whose faith is weak and whose knowledge is limited are great losers; they are exposed to many enemies and cannot follow the king wherever he goes. *This disease is frequently the result of a fall.* Bad nursing in their spiritual infancy often causes converts to fall into a despondency from which they never recover, and sin in other cases brings broken bones. Lord, help the lame to leap like the hart, and satisfy all Your people with the bread of Your table!

⇛ EVENING ⇚

WHAT IS YOUR SERVANT, THAT YOU SHOULD SHOW REGARD FOR
A DEAD DOG SUCH AS I? — 2 SAMUEL 9:8

If Mephibosheth was humbled by David's kindness, what shall we be in the presence of our gracious Lord? The more grace we have, the less we shall think of ourselves, for grace, like light, reveals our impurity. Eminent saints have scarcely known what to compare themselves to, their sense of unworthiness has been so clear and keen. "I am," says the godly Rutherford, "a dry and withered branch, a piece of dead carcass, dry bones, and not able to step over a straw." In another place he writes, "Apart from their open outbursts, I am too much like Judas and Cain." The meanest objects in nature appear to the humbled mind to have a preference above itself, because they have never contracted sin: A dog may be greedy, fierce, or filthy, but it has no conscience to violate, no Holy Spirit to resist. A dog may be appear to be worthless, and yet by a little kindness it is soon won to love its master and is faithful to death; but we forget the goodness of the Lord and do not follow His call. The term *dead dog* is the most expressive of all terms of contempt, but it is not too strong to express the self-abhorrence of well-taught believers. They do not display false modesty; they mean what they say; they have weighed themselves in the balances of the sanctuary and discovered the vanity of their nature. At best we are but clay, animated dust; but viewed as sinners, we are monsters indeed. Let it be published in heaven as a miracle that the Lord Jesus should set His heart's love upon people like us. Dust and ashes though we be, we must and will magnify the exceeding greatness of His grace. Could His heart not find rest in heaven? Does He need to come to these tents for a spouse and choose a bride from the children of men? Let the heavens and earth break forth into song and give all the glory to our sweet Lord Jesus.

WHOM HE JUSTIFIED HE ALSO GLORIFIED. — ROMANS 8:30

Here is a precious truth for you, believer. You may be poor or suffering or unknown, but for your encouragement take a moment to review your calling and the consequences that flow from it, and especially the blessed result spoken of here. As surely as you are God's child today, so surely will all your trials soon come to an end, and you shall be rich to an extent that is hard to imagine. Wait awhile, and your weary head will wear the crown of glory, and the worker's hand shall grasp the palm-branch of victory. Do not bemoan your troubles, but rather rejoice that before long you will be where no longer "shall there be mourning nor crying nor pain anymore."[1] The chariots of fire are at your door, and it will take only a moment to transport you to the glorified. The everlasting song is almost on your lip. The portals of heaven stand open for you. Do not think that you can fail to enter into your rest. If He has called you, nothing can divide you from His love. Distress cannot sever the bond; the fire of persecution cannot burn the link; the hammer of hell cannot break the chain. You are secure; that voice which called you at first shall call you yet again from earth to heaven, from death's dark gloom to immortality's unuttered splendors. Rest assured, the heart of Him who has justified you beats with infinite love toward you. You will soon be with the glorified, where your portion is; you are only waiting here to be made ready for the inheritance, and with that done, the wings of angels shall carry you far away, to the mount of peace and joy and blessedness, where

> Far from a world of grief and sin,
> With God eternally shut in,

you shall rest forever and ever.

❧ EVENING ❧

THIS I CALL TO MIND, AND THEREFORE I HAVE HOPE.
— LAMENTATIONS 3:21

Memory is frequently the slave of despondency. Despairing minds remember every dark prediction in the past and expand upon every gloomy feature in the present; in this way memory, clothed in sackcloth, presents to the mind a cup of bitter-tasting herbs. There is, however, no necessity for this. Wisdom can readily transform memory into an angel of comfort. That same recollection that on the one hand brings so many gloomy omens may be trained instead to provide a wealth of hopeful signs. She need not wear a crown of iron; she may encircle her brow with a tiara of gold, all spangled with stars. Such was Jeremiah's experience: in the previous verse memory had brought him to deep humiliation of soul: "My soul continually remembers it and is bowed down within me"; but now this same memory restored him to life and comfort. "But this I call to mind, and therefore I have hope." Like a two-edged sword, his memory first killed his pride with one edge and then slew his despair with the other. As a general principle, if we would exercise our memories more wisely, we might, in our very darkest distress, strike a match that would instantaneously kindle the lamp of comfort. There is no need for God to create a new thing upon the earth in order to restore believers' joy; if they would prayerfully rake the ashes of the past, they would find light for the present; and if they would turn to the book of truth and the throne of grace, their candle would soon shine as before. Let us then remember the loving-kindness of the Lord and rehearse His deeds of grace. Let us open the volume of recollection, which is so richly illuminated with memories of His mercy, and we will soon be happy. Thus memory may be, as Coleridge calls it, "the bosom-spring of joy," and when the Divine Comforter bends it to His service, it is then the greatest earthly comfort we can know.

[1] Revelation 21:4

YOU HAVE LOVED RIGHTEOUSNESS AND HATED WICKEDNESS.
— PSALM 45:7

Be angry and do not sin."[1] There can hardly be goodness in a man if he is not angered by sin; he who loves truth must hate every false way. How our Lord Jesus hated it when the temptation came! Three times it assailed Him in different forms, but He responded with, "Be gone, Satan." He hated it in others, no less fervently by showing His hatred often more in tears of pity than in words of rebuke; yet what language could be more stern, more Elijah-like, than such words as, "Woe to you, scribes and Pharisees, hypocrites! For you devour widows' houses, and for a pretense you make long prayers." He hated wickedness so much that He bled to wound it to the heart; He died that it might die; He was buried that He might bury it in His tomb; and He rose that He might forever trample it beneath His feet. Christ is in the Gospel, and that Gospel is opposed to wickedness in every shape. Wickedness arrays itself in fine clothes and imitates the language of holiness; but the precepts of Jesus, like His famous scourge of small cords, chase it out of the temple and will not tolerate it in the church. So, too, in the heart where Jesus reigns, what a war is waged between Christ and Satan! And when our Redeemer shall come to be our Judge, those thundering words, "Depart from me, you cursed" that are, indeed, but a prolongation of His life-teaching concerning sin shall manifest His abhorrence of iniquity. As warm as His love is to sinners, so hot is His hatred of sin; as perfect as is His righteousness, so complete shall be the destruction of every form of wickedness. Glorious champion of right, and destroyer of wrong, for this cause God has anointed You with the oil of gladness above Your fellows.

EVENING

CURSED BEFORE THE LORD BE THE MAN WHO RISES UP AND
REBUILDS THIS CITY, JERICHO. — JOSHUA 6:26

If the man who rebuilt Jericho was cursed, how much more does the man who works to restore false religion among us deserve the same. In our fathers' days the gigantic walls of false religion fell by the power of their faith, the perseverance of their efforts, and the blast of their gospel trumpets; and now there are some who would like to rebuild those false systems upon their old foundations. Lord, we pray, be pleased to thwart these unrighteous endeavors, and pull down every stone that they build. It should be a serious business with us to be thoroughly purged of every error that tends to foster the spirit of falsehood, and when we have made a clean sweep at home we should seek in every way to oppose its all too rapid spread abroad in the church and in the world. This we may accomplish only in secret by fervent prayer and in public by faithful witness. We must warn with judicious boldness those who are inclined toward the errors of false religion; we must instruct the young in gospel truth and tell them of the dark doings of falsehood in earlier times. We must assist in spreading the light more thoroughly through the land, for false teachers, like owls, hate daylight. Are we doing all we can for Jesus and the Gospel? If not, our negligence plays into the hands of the heretics. What are we doing to spread the Bible, which is the antidote to falsehood? Are we sending out good, sound gospel writings? Luther once said, "The devil hates goose quills," and, no doubt, he has good reason; the writer's pen blessed by the Holy Spirit has damaged his evil kingdom greatly. If the thousands who read this short word tonight will do all they can to hinder the rebuilding of this accursed Jericho, the Lord's glory shall spread quickly among the sons of men. Reader, what can you do? What will you do?

[1] Ephesians 4:26

CATCH THE FOXES FOR US, THE LITTLE FOXES THAT SPOIL THE VINEYARDS.
— SONG OF SOLOMON 2:15

A little thorn can cause much suffering. A small cloud may hide the sun. Tiny foxes spoil the vineyards; and little sins do mischief to the tender heart. These small sins burrow in the soul and fill it with what is hateful to Christ, and thus our comfortable fellowship and communion with Him is spoiled. A great sin cannot destroy a Christian, but a little sin can make him miserable. Jesus will not walk with His people unless they drive out every known sin. He says, "If you keep my commandments, you will abide in my love, just as I have kept my Father's commandments and abide in his love."[1] Some Christians rarely enjoy their Savior's presence. How is this? Surely it must be an affliction for a tender child to be separated from his father. Are you a child of God, and yet satisfied to live without seeing your Father's face? What! You are the spouse of Christ, and yet content to be absent from His company! Surely, you have fallen into a sad state, for the pure spouse of Christ mourns like a dove without her mate when he has left her. Here is the question: What has driven Christ from you? He hides His face behind the wall of your sins. That wall may be made up of little pebbles as easily as of great stones. The sea is made of drops; the rocks are made of grains: And the sea that divides you from Christ may be filled with the drops of your little sins; and the rock that almost wrecked the vessel of your life may have been made by the daily working of the coral insects of your little sins. If you would live with Christ and walk with Christ and see Christ and have fellowship with Christ, pay attention to "the little foxes that spoil the vineyard, for our vineyards are in blossom." Jesus invites you to go *with Him* against them. He will surely, like Samson, take the foxes at once and easily. Go with Him to the hunting.

❧ EVENING ☙

. . . SO THAT WE WOULD NO LONGER BE ENSLAVED TO SIN.
— ROMANS 6:6

Christian, why would you play with sin? *Has it not cost you enough already?* Burnt child, will you play with the fire? What! When you have already been between the jaws of the lion, will you step a second time into his den? Have you not had enough of the old serpent? Did he not poison all your veins once, and will you play at the cobra's den and put your hand in the dragon's lair a second time? Do not be not so mad, so foolish! Did sin ever yield you real pleasure? Did you find solid satisfaction in it? If so, go back to your old drudgery, and wear the chain again, if it delights you. But inasmuch as sin never gave you what it promised to bestow but deluded you with lies, do not be snared by the old fowler: Be free, and let the memory of your enslavement prevent you from entering the net again! *It is contrary to the designs of eternal love*, which are all focused on your purity and holiness; therefore do not run counter to the purposes of your Lord. Another thought should restrain you from sin. *Christians can never sin cheaply*; they pay a heavy price for iniquity. Transgression destroys peace of mind, obscures fellowship with Jesus, hinders prayer, brings darkness over the soul; therefore do not be the serf and slave of sin. There is still a higher argument: Each time you serve sin you are "crucifying once again the Son of God . . . and holding him up to contempt."[2] Can you bear that thought? If you have fallen into any special sin during this day, it may be that my Master has sent this admonition this evening to bring you back before you have wandered very far. Turn to Jesus afresh. He has not forgotten His love for you; His grace is still the same. With weeping and repentance, come to His footstool, and you shall be reunited in His love; you will be set upon a rock again, and your goings shall be established.

[1] John 15:10 [2] Hebrews 6:6

AND THE KING CROSSED THE BROOK KIDRON. — 2 SAMUEL 15:23

David passed that gloomy brook when fleeing with his sorry company from his traitorous son. The man after God's own heart was not exempt from trouble; in fact, his life was full of it. He was both the Lord's Anointed and the Lord's Afflicted. Why then should we expect to escape? At sorrow's gates the noblest of our race have waited with ashes on their heads. Why then should we complain as though some strange thing had happened unto us?

The King of kings Himself was not favored with a more cheerful or royal road. He passed over the filthy ditch of Kidron, through which the filth of Jerusalem flowed. God had one Son without sin, but not a single child without the rod. It is a great joy to believe that Jesus has been tempted in all points just as we are. What is our Kidron this morning? Is it a faithless friend, a sad bereavement, a slanderous reproach, a dark foreboding? The King has passed over all these. Is it bodily pain, poverty, persecution, or contempt? Over each of these Kidrons the King has gone before us. "In all their affliction he was afflicted."[1] The idea that trials are an unusual experience should be banished at once and forever, for He who is the Head of all saints knows by experience the grief that we consider so peculiar. All the citizens of Zion must be free of the Honorable Company of Mourners, of which the Prince Immanuel is Head and Captain.

Although David was abased, yet he returned in triumph to his city, and David's Lord rose victorious from the grave; so let us then be of good courage, for we also shall win the day. We will joyfully draw water out of the wells of salvation, even though we are presently faced with the harmful streams of sin and sorrow. Courage, soldiers of the Cross, the King himself triumphed after going over Kidron, and so will you.

↪ EVENING ↫

. . . WHO HEALS ALL YOUR DISEASES. — PSALM 103:3

Humbling as is the statement, yet the fact is certain that we are all more or less suffering under the disease of sin. What a comfort to know that we have a great Physician who is both able and willing to heal us! Let us think of Him for a moment tonight. His cures are very *speedy*—there is life for a look at Him; His cures are *radical*—He strikes at the center of the disease; and so His cures are sure and certain. He never fails, and *the disease never returns*. There is no relapse where Christ heals, no fear that His patients should be merely patched up for a season. He makes new men of them: He also gives them a new heart and puts a right spirit within them. He is well skilled in *all* diseases. Physicians generally have some *specialty*. Although they may know a little about almost all our pains and ills, there is usually one disease that they have studied more than others; but Jesus Christ is thoroughly acquainted with the whole of human nature. He is as much at home with one sinner as with another, and He never yet met an unusual case that was difficult for Him. He has had extraordinary complications of strange diseases to deal with, but He has known exactly with one glance of His eye how to treat the patient. He is the only universal doctor; and the medicine He gives is the only true panacea, healing in every instance. Whatever our spiritual malady may be, we should apply at once to this Divine Physician. There is no brokenness of heart that Jesus cannot bind up. "The blood of Jesus his Son cleanses us from all sin."[2] We have only to think of the myriads who have been delivered from all sorts of diseases through the power and virtue of His touch, and we will joyfully put ourselves in His hands. We trust Him, and sin dies; we love Him, and grace lives; we wait for Him, and grace is strengthened; we see Him as he is, and grace is perfected forever.

[1] Isaiah 63:9   [2] 1 John 1:7

June

AND THERE WAS EVENING AND THERE WAS MORNING, THE FIRST DAY.
— GENESIS 1:5

Was it so even in the beginning? Did light and darkness divide the realm of time in the first day? Then it should be no surprise if I have also changes in my circumstances from the sunshine of prosperity to the midnight of adversity. It will not always be the sunshine of noonday, even in my soul; I must expect at times to mourn the absence of my former joys and seek my Beloved in the night. I am not alone in this, for all the Lord's loved ones have had to sing the mingled song of judgment and mercy, of trial and deliverance, of mourning and delight. It is one of the arrangements of divine providence that day and night will not cease either in the spiritual or natural creation until we reach the land of which it is written, "there will be no night there."[1] What our heavenly Father ordains is wise and good.

What, then, my soul, is it best for you to do? Learn first to *be content* with this divine order and be willing, with Job, to receive evil from the hand of the Lord as well as good. Then work at *beginning and ending your days with joy*. Praise the Lord for the sun of joy when it rises and for the gloom of evening as it falls. There is beauty in both sunrise and sunset; sing of it, and glorify the Lord. Like the nightingale, sound your notes at all hours. *Believe that the night is as useful as the day*. The dews of grace fall heavily in the night of sorrow. The stars of promise shine forth gloriously against the darkness of grief. *Continue your service* under all circumstances. If in the day your watchword is *work*, at night exchange it for *watch*. Every hour has its duty; so continue in your calling as the Lord's servant until He shall suddenly appear in His glory. My soul, your evening of old age and death is drawing near; do not dread it, for it is part of the day, and the Lord has said in essence, "I will cover him all the day long."

❧ E V E N I N G ❧

FOR THE LORD . . . MAKES HER WILDERNESS LIKE EDEN.
— ISAIAH 51:3

In my mind's eye I see a howling wilderness, a great and terrible desert, like the Sahara. I perceive nothing in it to relieve the eye; all around I am wearied with a vision of hot and arid sand, on which are ten thousand bleaching skeletons of wretched men who have expired in anguish, having lost their way in the pitiless waste. What an appalling sight! How horrible! A sea of sand without boundary and without an oasis, a cheerless graveyard for a forlorn race. But look and wonder! All of a sudden, springing from the scorching sand I see a well-known plant; and as it grows it buds, the bud expands—it is a rose, and at its side a lily bows its modest head—and, miracle of miracles, as the fragrance of those flowers is diffused, the wilderness is transformed into a fruitful field, and all around it blossoms abundantly like the glory of Lebanon, the excellency of Carmel and Sharon. Do not call it Sahara; call it Paradise. Do not refer to it any longer as the valley of death, for where the skeletons lay bleaching in the sun, a resurrection is proclaimed, and up spring the dead, a mighty army, full of life immortal. Jesus is that well-known plant, and His presence makes everything new. The wonder is no less in each individual's salvation. I can see you, dear reader, cast out, an infant, unclothed, unwashed, defiled with your own blood, and left to be food for beasts of prey. But look, a jewel has been thrown into your bosom by a divine hand, and for its sake you have been pitied and guarded by divine providence; you are washed and cleansed from your defilement; you are adopted into heaven's family; the fair seal of love is upon your forehead, and the ring of faithfulness is on your hand—you are now a prince to God, though once an orphan and a castaway. Cherish then the matchless power and grace that changes deserts into gardens and makes the barren heart sing for joy.

[1] Revelation 21:25

    ❧ MORNING ❧

FOR THE DESIRES OF THE FLESH ARE AGAINST THE SPIRIT, AND THE DESIRES OF THE SPIRIT ARE AGAINST THE FLESH. — GALATIANS 5:17

In every believer's heart there is a constant struggle between the old nature and the new. The old nature is very active and loses no opportunity of employing all the weapons in its deadly arsenal against newborn grace; while on the other hand, the new nature is always on the lookout to resist and destroy its enemy. Grace within us will employ prayer and faith and hope and love to cast out the evil; it takes to itself "the whole armor of God"[1] and wrestles vigorously. These two opposing natures will never stop struggling as long as we are in this world. Bunyan's Christian fought Apollyon in a battle lasting three hours, but the battle of Christian with himself lasted all the way from the entry Gate to the River Jordan. The enemy is so securely entrenched within us that he can never be driven out while we are in this body: But although we are closely followed, and often in fierce conflict, we have an Almighty helper, Jesus, the Captain of our salvation, who is always with us and who assures us that we shall eventually be more than conquerors through Him. With such assistance the newborn nature is more than a match for its enemies. Are you fighting with the adversary today? Are Satan, the world, and the flesh all against you? Do not be discouraged nor dismayed. Fight on! For God Himself is with you. *Jehovah Nissi* is your banner, and *Jehovah Rophi* is the healer of your wounds. Do not fear, you will overcome, for who can defeat Omnipotence? Fight on, "looking to Jesus";[2] and although the conflict is long and tough, the victory will be sweet, and the promised reward will be glorious.

> *From strength to strength go on;*
> *Wrestle, and fight, and pray,*
> *Tread all the powers of darkness down,*
> *And win the well-fought day.*

❧ EVENING ❧

TEACHER. — MATTHEW 19:16

If the young man in the Gospel used this title in speaking to our Lord, it is only right that we should address Him in this way. He is indeed my Teacher in that He rules and teaches me. I am glad to run His errands and to sit at His feet. I am both His servant and His disciple and count it my highest honor to serve Him in this way. He is a good teacher. If He should ask me why I call Him "*good*," I could answer easily. It is true that "no one is good except God alone,"[3] but then He is God, and all the goodness of Deity shines in Him. In my experience I have found Him to be good, indeed so good that all the good I have has come to me through Him. He was good to me when I was dead in sin, for He raised me by His Spirit's power; He has been good to me in all my needs, trials, struggles, and sorrows. There could never be a better Teacher, for His service is freedom, His rule is love: I wish I were one thousandth part as good a servant. When He teaches me, He is unspeakably good, His doctrine is divine, His manner is gracious, His spirit is gentleness itself. There is no error in His instruction: Pure is the golden truth that He presents, and all His teachings lead to goodness, sanctifying as well as edifying the disciple. Angels know that He is good and delight to worship at His footstool. The ancient saints proved Him to be a good Teacher, and each of them rejoiced to sing, "I am Your servant, O Lord!" My own humble testimony must certainly be to the same effect. I will declare this before my friends and neighbors, for possibly they may be led by my testimony to seek my Lord Jesus as their Teacher. O I long that they might do so! They would never regret the decision. If they would submit to His easy yoke, they would find themselves in such royal service that they would never want to leave. The school of grace rejoices to have such a Teacher!

[1] Ephesians 6:11   [2] Hebrews 12:2   [3] Mark 10:18.

THESE WERE THE POTTERS [WHO] LIVED THERE IN THE KING'S SERVICE.
— 1 CHRONICLES 4:23

Potters were among the ranks of manual workers, but the king needed potters, and therefore they were elevated to royal service, although the material upon which they worked was nothing but clay. In the same way we also may be engaged in the most menial part of the Lord's work, but it is a great privilege to do anything for the King; and therefore we will play our part, hoping that, although we live among the pots, we will soar in the service of our Master. These people *dwelt among plants and hedges* and had rough, rustic hedging and ditching work to do. They may have wanted to live in the city, amid its life, society, and refinement, but they kept their assigned places because they were doing the king's work. There is no ideal place for us to serve God except the place He sets us down. We are not to run from it on a whim or sudden notion, but we should serve the Lord in it by being a blessing to those among whom we live. These potters and gardeners had *royal company*, for they lived with the king, and although among hedges and plants, they lived with the king *there*. No lawful place or gracious occupation, however menial, can keep us from communion with our Lord. In hovels, run-down neighborhoods, and jails, we may keep company *with the King*. In all works of faith we can count upon Jesus' fellowship. It is when we are in His work that we may reckon on His smile. You unknown workers who are serving the Lord amid the dirt and wretchedness of the lowest of the low, be of good cheer, for jewels have often been found among rubbish, earthen pots have been filled with heavenly treasure, and ugly weeds have been transformed into precious flowers. Dwell with the King and do His work, and when He writes His chronicles, your name shall be recorded.

❧ EVENING ☙

HE HUMBLED HIMSELF. — PHILIPPIANS 2:8

Jesus is the great teacher of lowliness of heart. Every day we need to learn from Him. Witness the Master taking a towel and washing His disciples' feet! Follower of Christ, will you not humble yourself? Consider Him the Servant of servants, and surely you cannot be proud! This sentence sums up His life: "He humbled Himself." Isn't it true to say that on earth he was always stripping off first one robe of honor and then another until, naked, He was fastened to the cross and emptied Himself, pouring out His lifeblood, giving it up for all of us, until they laid Him penniless in a borrowed grave? Our dear Redeemer was brought low! How then can we be proud? Stand at the foot of the cross and count the purple drops by which you have been cleansed; see the crown of thorns; mark His scourged shoulders; see hands and feet given up to the rough iron, and His whole self to mockery and scorn; see the bitterness and the pains of inward grief, showing themselves in His outward frame; hear the beleaguered cry, "My God, my God, why have You forsaken me?" And if you do not lie prostrate on the ground before that cross, you have never seen it: If you are not humbled in the presence of Jesus, you do not know Him. You were so lost that nothing could save you but the sacrifice of God's only Son. Think of that, and as Jesus stooped for you, bow yourself in lowliness at His feet. A sense of Christ's amazing love for us has a greater tendency to humble us than even an awareness of our own guilt. May the Lord bring our thoughts to Calvary; then our position will no longer be that of the pompous man of pride, but we will take the humble place of one who loves much because he has been forgiven much. Pride cannot live beneath the cross. Let us sit there and learn our lesson, and then rise and carry it into practice.

❧ MORNING ❧
THE GOODNESS AND LOVING KINDNESS OF GOD OUR SAVIOR.
— TITUS 3:4

How sweet it is to see Jesus fellowshiping with His own beloved people! There can be nothing more delightful than when the Holy Spirit leads us into this fertile field of delight. Let the mind for a moment consider the history of the Redeemer's love, and a thousand evidences of His kindness will come to mind. The purpose of them all has been to draw us to Christ and to weave the mind of Christ into the thoughts and emotions of the renewed soul. When we meditate upon this amazing love and see the Head of the church endowing her with all His wealth and power, our souls may well faint for joy. Who is able to endure such a weight of love? Even a partial sense of it, which the Holy Spirit sometimes grants us, is more than the soul can contain; how transforming a complete view of it must be! When the soul shall learn to discern all the Savior's gifts and is granted the wisdom to fathom them and the time to meditate upon them, such as heaven will afford us, we will then commune with Jesus in a more intimate manner than at present. But who can imagine the sweetness of such fellowship? It must be one of the things that have not entered into the heart of man, but that God has prepared for them that love Him. If we could burst open the door of our Joseph's granaries and see the plenty that He has stored up for us, we would be overwhelmed with His love. By faith we see, as in a mirror dimly, the reflected image of His unbounded treasures, but when we actually see the heavenly things themselves, with our own eyes, how deep will be the stream of fellowship in which our soul shall bathe! Until then our loudest songs shall be reserved for our loving benefactor, Jesus Christ our Lord, whose love to us is wonderful, surpassing the love of a man for a woman.

❧ EVENING ❧
. . . TAKEN UP IN GLORY. — 1 TIMOTHY 3:16

We have seen the Lord Jesus in the days of His flesh, humiliated and scorned: "He was despised and rejected by men; a man of sorrows, and acquainted with grief."[1] He whose brightness is as the morning wore the sackcloth of sorrow as His daily dress: Shame was His belt, and reproach was His cloak. Yet now that He has triumphed over all the powers of darkness upon the bloody tree, our faith sees Him returning, robed in the splendor of victory. How glorious He must have been in the eyes of seraphs, when a cloud received Him out of sight and He ascended to heaven! Now He wears the glory that He had with God before creation, and yet another glory above all—that which He has earned in the fight against sin, death, and hell. As victor He wears the illustrious crown. Listen to the swelling song! It is a new and sweeter song: "Worthy is the Lamb who was slain, for by Your blood You ransomed people for God!" He wears the glory of an Intercessor who can never fail, of a Prince who can never be defeated, of a Conqueror who has defeated every foe, of a Lord who has the allegiance of every subject. Jesus wears all the glory that heaven can bestow upon Him, all that ten thousand times ten thousand angels can minister to Him. You cannot with the utmost stretch of imagination conceive of His exceeding greatness; yet there will be a further revelation of it when He shall descend from heaven in great power, with all the holy angels—"Then he will sit on his glorious throne."[2] The splendor of that glory seen will ravish the hearts of His people. This isn't the end, for eternity will sound His praise. "Your throne, O God, is forever and ever!"[3] Reader, if you would rejoice in Christ's glory *then*, He must be glorious in your sight *now*. So, is He?

[1] Isaiah 53:3 [2] Matthew 25:31 [3] Psalm 45:6

AND THE LORD SHUT HIM IN. — GENESIS 7:16

Noah was shut in away from all the world by the hand of divine love. The door of God's electing purpose separates us from the world, which lies in the wicked one. We are not of the world even as our Lord Jesus was not of the world. Into the sin, the folly, the pursuits of the crowd we cannot enter; we cannot play in the streets of Vanity Fair with the children of darkness, for our heavenly Father has shut us in. Noah was shut in *with his God.* "Come into the ark," was the Lord's invitation, by which He clearly showed that He Himself intended to dwell in the ark with Noah and his family. In this manner all the chosen live in God and God in them. Happy people to be enclosed in the same circle that contains God in the Trinity of His persons—Father, Son, and Spirit. Let us never be inattentive to that gracious call, "Come, my people, enter your chambers, and shut your doors behind you; hide yourselves for a little while until the fury has passed by." Noah was so shut in that *no evil could reach him.* Floods simply lifted toward heaven, and winds helped him on his way. Outside the ark all was ruin, but inside all was rest and peace. Without Christ we perish, but in Christ Jesus there is perfect safety. Noah was so shut in that *he could not even desire to come out,* and those who are in Christ Jesus are in Him forever. They are there forever because eternal faithfulness has shut them in, and infernal malice cannot drag them out. God closes, and no man opens; and when in the last days as Master of the house He shall rise and close the door, it will be futile for mere professors to knock and cry, "Lord, Lord open for us," for that same door which closes in the wise virgins will shut out the foolish forever. Lord, close me in by Your grace.

❧ EVENING ☙
ANYONE WHO DOES NOT LOVE DOES NOT KNOW GOD. — 1 JOHN 4:8

The distinguishing mark of a Christian is his confidence in Christ's love for him and in the offering of his love to Christ. First, faith sets her seal upon the man by enabling the soul to say with the apostle, "Christ loved me and gave himself for me."[1] Then love gives the countersign and stamps upon the heart gratitude and love to Jesus in return. "We love because he first loved us."[2] In those grand old ages, which are the heroic period of the Christian religion, this double mark was clearly seen in all believers in Jesus; they were men who knew the love of Christ and rested upon it as a man leans upon a staff whose trustiness he has proved. The love that they felt toward the Lord was not a quiet emotion that they hid within themselves in the secret place of their souls and that they only spoke about in private or when they met on the first day of the week and sang hymns in honor of Christ Jesus the crucified; it was a passion with them of such a vehement and all-consuming energy that it was visible in all their actions, evident in their conversation, and seen in their eyes, even in their casual glances. Love for Jesus was a flame that fed upon the core and heart of their being and therefore by its own force burned its way into their demeanor and shone there. Zeal for the glory of King Jesus was the seal and mark of all genuine Christians. Because of their dependence upon Christ's love they *dared* much, and because of their love for Christ they *did* much, and it is the same now. The children of God are ruled in their inmost powers by love. The love of Christ constrains them; they rejoice that divine love is set upon them, they feel it shed abroad in their hearts by the Holy Spirit, who is given to them, and then by force of gratitude they love the Savior with a pure and fervent heart. My reader, do *you* love Him? Before you sleep, give an honest answer to this weighty question!

[1] Galatians 2:20   [2] 1 John 4:19

BEHOLD, I AM OF SMALL ACCOUNT. — JOB 40:4

Here is a cheering word for you, poor lost sinner! You think you shouldn't come to God because *you* are of small account. Now, there is not a saint alive on earth who has not felt this way. If Job and Isaiah and Paul were all obliged to say, "I am of small account," then, sinner, will you be ashamed to join in the same confession? If divine grace does not eradicate all sin from the believer, how do you hope to do it yourself? And if God loves His people while they are of small account, do you think your condition will prevent Him from loving you? Believe on Jesus, you outcast of the world's society! Jesus calls *you*, and just as you are.

> *Not the righteous, not the righteous;*
> *Sinners, Jesus came to call.*

Declare, even now, "You have died for sinners. I am a sinner, Lord Jesus; sprinkle Your blood on me." If you will confess your sin, you will find pardon. If now, with all your heart, you will say, "I am unclean, wash me," you will be washed now. If the Holy Spirit enables you to cry from your heart

> *Just as I am, without one plea*
> *But that Thy blood was shed for me,*
> *And that Thou bid me come to Thee,*
> *O Lamb of God, I come, I come!*

you will rise from reading this morning's portion with all your sins pardoned; and though you woke this morning with every sin that man has ever committed on your head, you will rest tonight accepted in the Beloved. Although you were once degraded with the rags of sin, you will be adorned with a robe of righteousness and appear as white as the angels are. For "now," mark it, "*Now* is the favorable time."[1] If you "trust him who justifies the ungodly,"[2] you are saved. May the Holy Spirit give you saving faith in Him who receives those who are of small account.

☙ EVENING ❧

ARE THEY ISRAELITES? SO AM I. — 2 CORINTHIANS 11:22

We have here *a personal claim*, and one that *needs proof*. The apostle knew that *his* claim was indisputable, but there are many people who have no right to the title yet still claim to belong to the Israel of God. If we are confidently declaring, "I am also an Israelite," let us only say it after we have searched our hearts as in the presence of God. But if we can give proof that we are following Jesus, if we can say from the heart, "I trust Him wholly, trust Him only, trust Him simply, trust Him now, and trust Him ever," then the position that the saints of God hold also belongs to us. All their enjoyments are our possessions; we may be the very least in Israel, "least of all saints," but since the mercies of God belong to the saints *as saints*, and not as advanced saints or well-taught saints, we may put in our plea and say, "Are they Israelites? So am I. The promises are mine, grace is mine, and glory will be mine." The claim, rightfully made, is one that will yield untold comfort. When God's people are rejoicing that they are His, what a happiness to be able to say, "So am I!" When they speak of being pardoned and justified and accepted in the Beloved, how joyful to respond, "Through the grace of God, so am I." But this claim not only has its enjoyments and privileges, but also its conditions and duties. We must share with God's people in cloud as well as in sunshine. When we hear them spoken of with contempt and ridicule for being Christians, we must come boldly forward and say, "So am I." When we see them working for Christ, giving their time, their talent, their whole heart to Jesus, we must be able to say, "So do I." Let us then prove our gratitude by our devotion and live as those who, having claimed a privilege, are willing to take the responsibility connected with it.

[1] 2 Corinthians 6:2   [2] Romans 4:5

❧ MORNING ❧

You have good reason to "hate evil," for just consider what harm it has already caused you. What a world of mischief sin has brought into your heart! Sin blinded you so that you could not see the beauty of the Savior; it made you deaf so that you could not hear the Redeemer's tender invitations. Sin turned your feet into the way of death and poured poison into the very fountain of your being; it tainted your heart and made it "deceitful above all things, and desperately sick."[1] What a creature you were when evil had done its utmost with you, before divine grace intervened! You were an heir of wrath just like others; you ran with the crowd to do evil. We were all like this, but Paul reminds us, "but you were washed, you were sanctified, you were justified in the name of the Lord Jesus Christ and by the Spirit of our God."[2] We have good reason, indeed, for hating evil when we look back and trace its deadly workings. We were in such a sorry state that our souls would have been lost if omnipotent love had not intervened to redeem us. Even now it is an active enemy, always looking for ways to harm us and to drag us to perdition. Therefore "hate evil," Christian, unless you desire trouble. If you want to cover your path with thorns and plant nettles in your pillow, then fail to "hate evil"; but if you would live a happy life and die a peaceful death, then walk in all the ways of holiness, hating evil right to the end. If you truly love your Savior and want to honor Him, then "hate evil." We know of no cure for the love of evil in a Christian like daily communion with the Lord Jesus. Be often with Him, and it is impossible for you to be at peace with sin.

> Order my footsteps by Thy Word,
> And make my heart sincere;
> Let sin have no dominion, Lord,
> But keep my conscience clear.

❧ EVENING ❧

If you want to see souls converted, if you want to hear the cry that "the kingdom of the world has become the kingdom of our Lord,"[3] if you want to place crowns upon the head of the Savior and see His throne lifted high, then be filled with zeal. For under God, the way the world will be converted is by the zeal of the church. Every element of grace will do its work, but zeal will be first; prudence, knowledge, patience, and courage will follow in their places, but zeal must lead the charge. It is not the extent of your knowledge, though that is useful, it is not the extent of your talent, though that is not to be despised, it is your zeal that will do great exploits. This zeal is the fruit of the Holy Spirit: It draws its vital force from *the continued operations* of the Holy Spirit in the soul. If our inner life dwindles, if our heart beats slowly before God, we will not know zeal; but if everything inside is strong and vigorous, then we cannot but feel a loving urgency to see Christ's kingdom come, and His will done on earth, even as it is in heaven. A deep *sense of gratitude* will nourish Christian zeal. When we reflect on the miry pit from which we were lifted, we find plenty of reason for spending ourselves for God. And zeal is also stimulated by *the thought of the eternal future*. It looks with tearful eyes down to the flames of hell, and it cannot sleep: It looks up with anxious gaze to the glories of heaven, and it cannot stay still. It feels that time is short compared with the work to be done, and therefore it devotes all that it has to the cause of its Lord. And it is continually strengthened by *remembering Christ's example*. He was clothed with zeal as with a cloak. How swift the chariot-wheels of duty went with Him! He never loitered on the way. Let us prove that we are His disciples by displaying the same spirit of zeal.

[1] Jeremiah 17:9 [2] 1 Corinthians 6:11 [3] Revelation 11:15

FOR MANY FELL, BECAUSE THE WAR WAS OF GOD. — 1 CHRONICLES 5:22

Warrior, as you fight under the banner of the Lord Jesus, observe this verse with holy joy, for as it was in the days of old, so is it now: If the war is of God, the victory is sure. The armies of God could barely muster forty-five thousand fighting men, and yet in their war with the enemy, they captured "a hundred thousand men," "for they cried to God in the battle, and he granted their urgent plea because they trusted in him." The Lord saves not by many, nor by few; it is ours to go in Jehovah's name even if we are only a handful of men, for the Lord of Hosts is with us as our Captain. They did not neglect their weapons, but neither did they place their trust in them; we must use all fitting means, but our confidence must rest in the Lord alone, for He is the sword and the shield of His people. The great reason for their extraordinary success lay in the fact that "the war was of God." Beloved, in fighting with sin in us and around us, with error doctrinal or practical, with spiritual wickedness in high places or low places, with devils and the devil's allies, you are waging Jehovah's war, and unless He himself can be defeated, you do not need to fear defeat. Do not tremble before superior numbers; do not shrink from difficulties or impossibilities; do not flinch at wounds or death; strike with the two-edged sword of the Spirit, and the dead shall lie in heaps. The battle is the Lord's, and He will deliver His enemies into our hands. With steadfast foot, strong hand, dauntless heart, and flaming zeal, rush to the conflict, and the hosts of evil will fly like chaff before the gale.

Stand up! stand up for Jesus!
The strife will not be long;
This day the noise of battle,
The next the victor's song:
To him that overcometh,
A crown of life shall be;
He with the King of glory
Shall reign eternally.

❧ EVENING ❧

NOW YOU SHALL SEE WHETHER MY WORD WILL COME TRUE
FOR YOU OR NOT. — NUMBERS 11:23

God had made a positive promise to Moses that for the space of a whole month He would feed the vast company in the wilderness with meat. Moses is then overtaken by a fit of unbelief, looks to the outward means, and is at a loss to know how the promise can be fulfilled. He looked to the creature instead of the Creator. But does the Creator expect the creature to fulfill His promise for Him? No; He who makes the promise always fulfills it by His own unaided omnipotence. If He speaks, it is done—done by Himself. His promises do not depend for their fulfillment upon the cooperation of the puny strength of man. We can immediately see the mistake that Moses made. And yet how routinely we do the same! God has promised to supply our needs, and we look to the creature to do what God has promised to do; and then, because we perceive the creature to be weak and feeble, we indulge in unbelief. Why do we look in that direction at all? Will you look to the North Pole to gather fruits ripened in the sun? You would be acting no more foolishly in doing this than when you look to the weak for strength, and to the creature to do the Creator's work. Let us, then, put the question on the right footing. The ground of faith is not the sufficiency of the visible means for the performance of the promise, but the all-sufficiency of the invisible God, who will definitely do what He has said. If after clearly seeing that the onus lies with the Lord and not with the creature we dare to indulge in mistrust, the question of God comes home forcefully to us: "Is the LORD's hand shortened?" May it also be that in His mercy the question will be accompanied by this blessed declaration: "Now you shall see whether my word will come true for you or not."

    MORNING

Some Christians are sadly prone to look on the *dark* side of everything, and to dwell more upon what they have gone through than upon what God has done for them. Ask for their impression of the Christian life, and they will describe their continual conflicts, their deep afflictions, their sad adversities, and the sinfulness of their hearts, but with scarcely any reference to the mercy and help that God has provided them. But a Christian whose soul is in a *healthy* state will come forward joyously and say, "I will not speak about myself, but to the honor of my God. He has brought me up out of a horrible pit and out of the miry clay and set my feet upon a rock and established my goings; and He has put a new song in my mouth, even praise to our God. The Lord has done great things for me—I am glad." This summary of experience is the very best that any child of God can present. It is true that we endure trials, but it is just as true that we are delivered out of them. It is true that we have our corruptions, and sadly we acknowledge this, but it is just as true that we have an all-sufficient Savior who overcomes these corruptions and delivers us from their dominion. In looking back, it would be wrong to deny that we have been in the Slough of Despond and have crept along the Valley of Humiliation, but it would be equally wicked to forget that we have been *through* them safely and profitably; we have not remained in them, thanks to our Almighty Helper and Leader, who has "brought us out to a place of abundance."[1] The deeper our troubles, the louder our thanks to God, who has led us through them all and preserved us until today. Our griefs cannot spoil the melody of our praise; we consider them to be the "bass line" of our life's song, "The LORD has done great things for us; we are glad."

EVENING

The Greek word translated *search* signifies a strict, close, diligent, curious search, the kind men make when they are seeking gold, or hunters when they are in pursuit of game. We must not be content with giving a superficial glance to one or two chapters, but with the candle of the Spirit we must deliberately seek out the meaning of the Word. Holy Scripture *requires searching*—much of it can only be learned by careful study. There is milk for babies, but also meat for strong men. The rabbis wisely say that a mountain of matter hangs upon every word, indeed, upon every title of Scripture. Tertullian declared, "I adore the fullness of the Scriptures." The person who merely skims the Book of God will not profit from it; we must dig and mine until we obtain the treasure. The door of the Word only opens to the key of diligence. The Scriptures *demand to be searched.* They are the writings of God, bearing the divine stamp and imprimatur—who shall dare to treat them casually? To despise them is to despise the God who wrote them. God forbid that any of us should allow our Bibles to become witnesses against us in the great day of account. The Word of God *will repay searching.* God does not ask us to sift through a mountain of chaff with only here and there a grain of wheat in it, but the Bible is sifted corn—we have only to open the granary door and find it. Scripture grows upon the student. It is full of surprises. Under the teaching of the Holy Spirit, to the searching eye, it glows with splendor of revelation, like a vast temple paved with gold and roofed with rubies, emeralds, and all manner of gems. There is no merchandise like the merchandise of scriptural truth. Finally, *the Scriptures reveal Jesus*: "They that bear witness about me." No more powerful motive can be urged upon Bible readers than this: He who finds Jesus finds life, heaven, and all things. Happy are they who, in searching the Bible, discover their Savior.

[1] Psalm 66:12

   ❧ **MORNING** ❧

WE LIVE TO THE LORD. — ROMANS 14:8

If God had willed it, each of us might have entered heaven at the moment of conversion. It was not absolutely necessary for our preparation for immortality that we should linger here. It is possible for a man to be taken to heaven and to be found fit to partake in the inheritance of the saints in light, even though he has only just believed in Jesus. It is true that our sanctification is a long and continued process, and we shall not be perfected until we lay aside our bodies and enter within the veil; but nevertheless, if the Lord had wanted to, He could have changed us from imperfection to perfection and have taken us to heaven at once. Why then are we here? Would God keep His children out of paradise a single moment longer than was necessary? Why is the army of the living God still on the battlefield when one charge might give them the victory? Why are His children still wandering here and there through a maze when a single word from His lips would bring them into the center of their hopes in heaven? The answer is—they are here that they may *"live to the Lord"* and may bring others to know His love. We remain on earth as sowers to scatter good seed, as plowmen to break up the fallow ground, as heralds publishing salvation. We are here as "the salt of the earth,"[1] to be a blessing to the world. We are here to glorify Christ in our daily life. We are here as workers for Him, and as workers together with Him. Let us see that our life fulfills this purpose. Let us live zealous, useful, holy lives, to "the praise of his glorious grace."[2] Meanwhile we long to be with Him and daily sing—

> *My heart is with Him on His throne,*
> *And ill can brook delay;*
> *Each moment listening for the voice,*
> *"Rise up, and come away."*

❧ **EVENING** ❧

IT IS THEY THAT BEAR WITNESS ABOUT ME. — JOHN 5:39

Jesus Christ is the Alpha and Omega of the Bible. He is the constant theme of its sacred pages; from beginning to end they bear witness to Him. At the creation we immediately recognize Him as one of the sacred Trinity; we catch a glimpse of Him in the promise of the woman's seed; we see Him pictured in the ark of Noah; we walk with Abraham as He sees Messiah's day; we live in the tents of Isaac and Jacob, feeding upon the gracious promise; and in the numerous types of the law, we find the Redeemer abundantly foreshadowed. Prophets and kings, priests and preachers all look one way—they all stand as the cherubs did over the ark, desiring to look within and to read the mystery of God's great propitiation. Even more obvious in the New Testament we discover that Jesus is the one pervading subject. It is not that He is mentioned every so often or that we can find Him in the shadows; no, the whole substance of the New Testament is Jesus crucified, and even its closing sentence sparkles with the Redeemer's name. We should always read Scripture in this light; we should consider the Word to be like a mirror into which Christ looks down from heaven; and then we, looking into it, see His face reflected—darkly, it is true, but still in such a way as to be a blessed preparation for one day seeing Him face to face. The New Testament contains Jesus Christ's letters to us, which are perfumed by His love. These pages are like the garments of our King, and they all bear His fragrance. Scripture is the royal chariot in which Jesus rides, and it is paved with love for the daughters of Jerusalem. The Scriptures are like the swaddling clothes of the holy child Jesus; unroll them, and there you find your Savior. The essence of the Word of God is Christ.

[1] Matthew 5:13 [2] Ephesians 1:6

WE LOVE BECAUSE HE FIRST LOVED US. — 1 JOHN 4:19

There is no light in the planet but that which proceeds from the sun; and there is no true love for Jesus in the heart but that which comes from the Lord Jesus Himself. From this overflowing fountain of the infinite love of God, all our love to God must spring. This truth is foundational, that we love Him for no other reason than because He first loved us. Our love for Him is *the result* of His love for us. When studying the works of God, anyone may respond with cold admiration, but the warmth of love can only be kindled in the heart by God's Spirit. What a wonder that any of us, knowing what we're like, should ever have been brought to love Jesus at all! How marvelous that when we had rebelled against Him, He should, by a display of such amazing love, seek to draw us back. We would never have had a grain of love toward God unless it had been sown in us by the sweet seed of His love for us. Love, then, has for its parent the love of God shed abroad in the heart: But after it is divinely born, it must *be divinely nourished*. It is not like a plant, which will flourish naturally in human soil—it must be watered from above. Love for Jesus is a flower of a delicate nature, and if it received no nourishment but that which could be drawn from the rock of our hearts, it would soon wither. As love comes from heaven, so it must feed on heavenly bread. It cannot exist in the wilderness unless it be fed by manna from on high. Love must feed on love. The very soul and life of our love for God is His love for us.

I love Thee, Lord, but with no love of mine,
For I have none to give;
I love Thee, Lord; but all the love is Thine,
For by Thy love I live.
I am as nothing, and rejoice to be
Emptied, and lost, and swallowed up in Thee.

❦ EVENING ❧

THERE HE BROKE THE FLASHING ARROWS, THE SHIELD, THE SWORD, AND THE WEAPONS OF WAR. — PSALM 76:3

Our Redeemer's glorious cry of "It is finished" was the death-knell of all the adversaries of His people, the breaking of "the weapons of war." Behold the hero of Golgotha using His cross as an anvil, and His wounds as a hammer, dashing to pieces bundle after bundle of our sins, those poisoned "flashing arrows," trampling on every indictment and destroying every accusation. What glorious blows the mighty Breaker gives with a hammer far more powerful than the fabled weapon of Thor! How the diabolical darts break in pieces, and the infernal swords are broken like old clay pots! Consider how He draws from its sheath of hellish workmanship the dreadful sword of satanic power! He snaps it across His knee as a man breaks dry sticks and throws it into the fire. Beloved, no sin of a believer can now be an arrow bringing death, no condemnation can now be a sword to kill him, for the punishment of our sin was borne by Christ, and a full atonement was made for all our iniquities by our blessed Substitute and Surety. Who now accuses? Who now condemns? Christ has died, yes, has risen again. Jesus has removed the weapons of hell, has quenched every fiery dart, and has broken the head off every arrow of wrath; the ground is covered with the splinters and relics of the weapons of hell's warfare, which are only visible to us to remind us of our former danger and of our great deliverance. Sin no longer has dominion over us. Jesus has made an end of it and put it away forever. Our enemy's destructions have come to a perpetual end. Declare all the wonderful works of the Lord, all you who make mention of His name; do not be silent, neither by day, nor when the sun goes down. Bless the Lord, O my soul.

YOU HAVE BEEN WEIGHED IN THE BALANCES AND FOUND WANTING.
— DANIEL 5:27

It is good to regularly weigh ourselves in the scale of God's Word. You will find it a holy exercise to read some Psalm of David and, as you meditate upon each verse, to ask yourself, "Can I say this? Have I felt as David felt? Has my heart ever been broken on account of sin, as his was when he penned his penitential psalms? Has my soul been full of true confidence in the hour of difficulty as his was when he sang of God's mercies in the cave of Adullam or in the holds of Engedi? Do I take the cup of salvation and call upon the name of the Lord?" Then turn to the life of Christ, and as you read, ask yourself how far you are conformed to His likeness. Endeavor to discover whether you have the meekness, the humility, the lovely spirit that He constantly urged and displayed. Then take the epistles, and see whether you can go with the apostle in what he said of his experience. Have you ever cried out as he did, "Wretched man that I am! Who will deliver me from this body of death"?[1] Have you ever felt his self-abasement? Have you seemed to yourself the chief of sinners, and less than the least of all the saints? Have you known anything of his devotion? Could you join with him and say, "For to me to live is Christ, and to die is gain"?[2] If in this way we read God's Word as a test of our spiritual condition, we will often have good reason to pause and say, "Lord, I feel I have never yet been here. O bring me here! Give me the true penitence about which I am reading. Give me real faith; give me warmer zeal; inflame me with more fervent love; grant me the grace of meekness; make me more like Jesus. Do not allow me to be 'found wanting' when weighed in the balances of the Bible, in case I be found wanting in the scales of judgment." "Judge not, that you be not judged."[3]

❧ EVENING ❧

. . . WHO SAVED US AND CALLED US TO A HOLY CALLING.
— 2 TIMOTHY 1:9

The apostle uses the perfect tense and says, "who *saved* us." Believers in Christ Jesus *are* saved. They are not looked upon as people who are in a hopeful state and may ultimately be saved, but they *are* already saved. Salvation is not a blessing to be enjoyed upon our dying bed and to be sung of in a future state above, but a matter to be obtained, received, promised, and enjoyed now. The Christian is perfectly saved *in God's purpose*; God has ordained him to salvation, and that purpose is complete. He is saved also as to the *price that has been paid for him*: "It is finished" was the cry of the Savior before He died. The believer is also perfectly saved *in His covenant Head*, for as he fell in Adam, so he lives in Christ. This complete salvation is accompanied by *a holy calling*. Those whom the Savior saved upon the cross are in due time effectually called by the power of God the Holy Spirit to holiness: They leave their sins; they endeavor to be like Christ; they choose holiness, not out of any compulsion, but from the power of a new nature, which leads them to rejoice in holiness just as naturally as when previously they delighted in sin. God neither chose them nor called them because they were holy, but He called them that they might be holy, and holiness is the beauty produced by His workmanship in them. The excellencies that we see in a believer are as much the work of God as the Atonement itself. In this way the fullness of the grace of God is beautifully displayed. Salvation must be of grace, because the Lord is the author of it: And what motive but grace could move Him to save the guilty? Salvation must be of grace because the Lord works in such a manner that our righteousness is forever excluded. Such is the believer's privilege—*a present salvation*; such is the evidence that he is called to it—*a holy life*.

[1] Romans 7:24   [2] Philippians 1:21   [3] Matthew 7:1

LET THE ONE WHO DESIRES TAKE THE WATER OF LIFE WITHOUT PRICE.
— REVELATION 22:17

The invitation is to "take . . . without price." Jesus wants no payment or preparation. He seeks no recommendation from our virtuous emotions. If you have no good feelings, but if you are willing, you are invited; therefore come! If you have no belief and no repentance, come to Him, and He will give them to you. Come just as you are, and take without money and without price. He gives Himself to the needy. In nineteenth-century Britain the drinking fountains at the corners of the streets were valuable institutions; it would have been a strange and foolish sight to see someone standing at the fountain declaring, "I cannot drink because I do not have any money." However poor an individual may be, there is the fountain, and just as he is, he may drink of it without cost. Thirsty passengers, as they go by, whether they are dressed poorly or expensively, do not look for any authorization to drink; the existence of the fountain is sufficient warrant for taking its water freely. The generosity of some good friends has put in place the refreshing supply, and we take it and ask no questions. Perhaps the only people who go thirsty through the street where there is a drinking fountain are the fine ladies and gentlemen who are in their carriages. They are very thirsty but cannot think of being so vulgar as to get out to drink. It would demean them, they think, to drink at a common drinking fountain: so they ride by with parched lips. How many there are who are rich in their own good works and cannot therefore come to Christ! "I will not be saved," they say, "in the same way as the prostitute or the blasphemer." What! Go to heaven in the same way as a chimney sweep? Is there no pathway to glory but the path that led the dying thief there? I will not be saved that way. Such proud boasters must remain without the living water; but "Let the one who desires *take the water of life without price.*"

REMOVE FAR FROM ME FALSEHOOD AND LYING. — PROVERBS 30:8

DO NOT FORSAKE ME, O LORD! — PSALM 38:21

Here we have two great lessons—what to deprecate and what to supplicate. The happiest state of a Christian is the holiest state. Just as there is the most heat nearest to the sun, so there is the most happiness closest to Christ. No Christian enjoys comfort when his eyes are fixed on falsehood—he finds no satisfaction unless his soul is quickened in the ways of God. The world may find happiness elsewhere, but he cannot. I do not blame ungodly men for rushing to their pleasures. Why should I? Let them have their fill. That is all they have to enjoy. A converted wife who despaired of her husband was always very kind to him, for she said, "I fear that this is the only world in which he will be happy, and therefore I have made up my mind to make him as happy as I can in it." Christians must seek their delights in a higher sphere than the tasteless trifles or sinful enjoyments of the world. Empty pursuits are dangerous to renewed souls. We have heard of a philosopher who, while he looked *up* to the stars, fell into a pit; but how deeply do they fall who look *down*. Their fall is fatal. No Christian is safe when his soul is lazy, and his God is far from him. Every Christian is always safe as to the great matter of his standing in Christ, but he is not safe as regards his experience in holiness and communion with Jesus in this life. Satan does not often attack a Christian who is living near to God. It is when the Christian departs from God, becomes spiritually starved, and tries to feed on lies that the devil discovers his moment of advantage. He may sometimes stand foot to foot with the child of God who is active in his Master's service, but the battle is generally brief. He who slips as he goes down into the Valley of Humiliation will find that with every false step he invites the devil's attack. O for grace to walk humbly with our God!

❧ MORNING ❦

DELIGHT YOURSELF IN THE LORD. — PSALM 37:4

The teaching of these words must seem very surprising to those who are strangers to vital godliness, but to the sincere believer it is only the reminder of a recognized truth. The life of the believer is described as a *delight* in God, and we are reminded of the great fact that genuine faith overflows with happiness and joy. Ungodly persons and mere professors never look upon religion as a joyful thing; to them it is service, duty, or necessity, but never pleasure or delight. If they attend to religion at all, it is either because of what they might get or because they are afraid of the consequences of neglect. The thought of *delight* in religious exercise is so strange to most men that no two words in their language stand further apart than *holiness* and *delight*. But believers who know Christ understand that delight and faith are so wonderfully united that the gates of hell cannot manage to separate them. Those who love God with all their hearts find that His ways are ways of pleasantness, and all His paths are peace. The saints discover in Christ such joy, such overflowing delight, such blessedness that far from serving Him from custom, they would follow Him even though the whole world rejected Him. We do not fear God because of any compulsion; our faith is no shackle, our profession is no bondage, we are not dragged to holiness, nor driven to duty. No, our piety is our pleasure, our hope is our happiness, our duty is our delight.

Delight and true faith are as interwoven as root and flower, as indivisible as truth and certainty; they are, in fact, two precious stones glittering side by side in a setting of gold.

> 'Tis when we taste Thy love,
> Our joys divinely grow,
> Unspeakable like those above,
> And heaven begins below.

❧ EVENING ❦

TO US, O LORD, BELONGS OPEN SHAME . . . BECAUSE WE HAVE
SINNED AGAINST YOU. — DANIEL 9:8

A deep sense and clear view of sin, its dreadfulness, and the punishment that it deserves should make us lie low before the throne. We have sinned as Christians. It is sad that it should be so. We have been favored, and yet we have been ungrateful; privileged beyond most, but we have not brought forth fruit in proportion. Who is there, although he may have been engaged in the Christian warfare for years, who will not blush when he looks back upon the past? As for our days before we were born again, may they be forgiven and forgotten; but since then, though we have not sinned as before, yet we have sinned against light and against love—light that has really penetrated our minds, and love in which we have rejoiced. The sin of a pardoned soul is an atrocity! An unpardoned sinner sins cheaply compared with the sin of one of God's elect, who has had communion with Christ and leaned upon Him for his comfort. Look at David! Many will talk of his sin, but I ask you to look at his repentance and hear his broken bones as each one of them moans out its mournful confession! Consider his tears as they fall upon the ground, and the deep sighs with which he accompanies the softened music of his harp! We have strayed: Let us, therefore, seek the spirit of penitence. Look again at Peter! We often speak of how he denied Christ. Remember, it is written, "He wept bitterly." Do *we* have no denials of our Lord to be lamented with tears? These sins of ours, before and after conversion, would consign us to the place of inextinguishable fire if it were not for God's sovereign mercy, which snatched us like sticks from the fire. My soul, bow down under a sense of your natural sinfulness, and worship your God. Admire the grace that saves you—the mercy that spares you—the love that pardons you!

AND SARAH SAID, GOD HAS MADE LAUGHTER FOR ME;
EVERYONE WHO HEARS WILL LAUGH OVER ME. — GENESIS 21:6

It was far above the power of nature, and even contrary to its laws, that the aged Sarah should be honored with a son; and even so it is beyond all ordinary rules that I, a poor, helpless, undone sinner, should find grace to carry in my soul the indwelling Spirit of the Lord Jesus. I, who once despaired, as well I might, for my nature was as dry and withered and barren and accursed as a howling wilderness, even I have been made to bring forth fruit unto holiness. Well may my mouth be filled with joyous laughter, because of the singular, surprising grace that I have received from the Lord, for I have found Jesus, the promised seed, and He is mine forever. Today I will sing psalms of triumph to the Lord who has remembered my low estate, for "my heart exults in the LORD; my strength is exalted in the LORD. My mouth derides my enemies, because I rejoice in your salvation."[1]

My desire is that all those who hear of my great deliverance from hell and my most blessed visitation from heaven will laugh for joy with me. I want to surprise my family with my abundant peace; I want to delight my friends with my ever-increasing happiness; I want to edify the church with my grateful confessions, and even impress the world with the cheerfulness of my daily conversation. Bunyan tells us that Mercy laughed in her sleep, and no wonder when she dreamed of Jesus; my joy should not be less than hers while Christ is the theme of my daily thoughts. The Lord Jesus is a deep sea of joy: My soul shall dive in and shall be swallowed up in the delights of His company. Sarah looked on Isaac and laughed without restraint, and all her friends laughed with her. And you, my soul, look on Jesus, and invite heaven and earth to unite in your unspeakable joy.

❦   EVENING   ❧

. . . WHO OPENS AND NO ONE WILL SHUT. — REVELATION 3:7

Jesus is the keeper of the gates of paradise, and before every believing soul He sets an open door, which no man or devil will be able to close. What joy it will be to find that faith in Him is the golden key to the everlasting doors. My soul, do you carry this key close to you, or are you trusting in some dishonest locksmith who will fail you in the end? Pay attention to a parable of the preacher, and remember it. The great King has made a banquet, and He has proclaimed to all the world that no one will enter except those who bring with them the fairest flower that blooms. The spirits of men advance to the gate by thousands, and each one brings the flower that he esteems the queen of the garden; but in crowds they are driven from the royal presence and do not enter into the festive halls. Some are carrying the poisonous plant of superstition, others the flaunting poppies of empty religion, and some the hemlock of self-righteousness; but these are not precious to the King, and so those carrying them are shut out of the pearly gates. My soul, have you gathered the rose of Sharon? Do you wear the lily of the valley on your lapel constantly? If so, when you arrive at the gates of heaven you will know its value, for you only have to show this choicest of flowers, and the Porter will open and without a moment's delay, for to that rose the Porter always opens. You will find your way with the rose of Sharon in your hand up to the throne of God Himself, for heaven itself possesses nothing that excels its radiant beauty, and of all the flowers that bloom in paradise, none of them can rival the lily of the valley. My soul, get Calvary's blood-red rose into your hand by faith, by love wear it, by communion preserve it, by daily watchfulness make it your all in all, and you will be blessed beyond all bliss, happy beyond a dream. Jesus, be mine forever, my God, my heaven, my all.

[1] 1 Samuel 2:1

❧ MORNING ☙

I GIVE THEM ETERNAL LIFE, AND
THEY WILL NEVER PERISH. — JOHN 10:28

The Christian should never think or speak lightly of unbelief. For when a child of God mistrusts His love, His truth, His faithfulness, it is greatly displeasing to Him. How can we ever grieve Him by doubting His upholding grace? Christian, it is contrary to every promise of God's precious Word that you would ever be forgotten or left to perish. If it could be so, how could He be true who has said, "Can a woman forget her nursing child, that she should have no compassion on the son of her womb? Even these may forget, yet I will not forget you."[1] What would be the value of the promise—"'The mountains may depart and the hills be removed, but my steadfast love shall not depart from you, and my covenant of peace shall not be removed,' says the LORD, who has compassion on you"?[2] What truth would there be in Christ's words—"I give them eternal life, and they will never perish, and no one will snatch them out of my hand. My Father, who has given them to me, is greater than all, and no one is able to snatch them out of the Father's hand"?[3] What value would there be in the doctrines of grace? They would be all disproved if one child of God should perish. What value could be placed in the veracity of God, His honor, His power, His grace, His covenant, His oath, if any of those for whom Christ died, and who have put their trust in Him, should nevertheless be cast away? Banish then those unbelieving fears, which so dishonor God. Arise, shake yourself from the dust, and put on your beautiful clothes. Remember, it is sinful to doubt His Word in which He has promised you that you will never perish. Let the eternal life within you express itself in confident rejoicing.

The gospel bears my spirit up:
A faithful and unchanging God
Lays the foundation for my hope,
In oaths, and promises, and blood.

❧ EVENING ☙

THE LORD IS MY LIGHT AND MY SALVATION; WHOM SHALL I FEAR?
THE LORD IS THE STRONGHOLD OF MY LIFE;
OF WHOM SHALL I BE AFRAID? — PSALM 27:1

The LORD is my light and my salvation." Here is personal interest: *"my light," "my salvation"*; the soul is assured of it, and therefore declares it boldly. Into the soul at the new birth divine light is poured as the forerunner of salvation; where there is not enough light to reveal our own darkness and to make us long for the Lord Jesus, there is no evidence of salvation. After conversion our God is our joy, comfort, guide, teacher, and in every sense our light: He is light within us, light around us, light reflected from us, and light to be revealed to us. Note, it does not just say that the Lord gives light, but that He is light; nor that He gives salvation, but that He is salvation; so, then, whoever by faith has laid hold upon God has all the covenant blessings in their possession. Once this fact is assured, the deduction from it is put in the form of a question, *"Whom shall I fear?"* A question that is its own answer. The powers of darkness are not to be feared, for the Lord, our light, destroys them; and we need not dread the damnation of hell, for the Lord is our salvation. This is a very different challenge from that of boastful Goliath, for it rests not upon the conceited vigor of human strength, but upon the real power of the omnipotent I AM. *"The LORD is the stronghold of my life."* Here is a third glowing quality showing that the writer's hope was fastened with a threefold cord that could not be broken. It is no surprise that we accumulate terms of praise where the Lord lavishes deeds of grace. Our life derives all its strength from God; and if He deigns to make us strong, we cannot be weakened by all the cunning movements of our adversary. *"Whom shall I fear?"* The bold question looks into the future as well as the present. "If God is for us, who can be against us,"[4] either now or in time to come?

[1] Isaiah 49:15 [2] Isaiah 54:10 [3] John 10:28-29 [4] Romans 8:31

This prayer is remarkable for its brevity, but it may be offered *humbly, regularly*, and *profitably*. David was saddened that the numbers of the faithful were so small, and therefore he lifted up his heart in supplication: When the creature failed, he flew to the Creator. He evidently felt his own weakness, or he would not have cried for help; but at the same time he obviously intended to give himself for the cause of truth, for the cry "save" is inapplicable where we do not exert ourselves. Note the *directness, clearness of perception*, and *distinctness of utterance* in this petition of few words, distinguishing it from the long, rambling outpourings of certain professors. The psalmist runs straight toward his God with a well-considered prayer; he knows what he is seeking and where to seek it. Lord, teach us to pray in the same direct manner.

The occasions when prayer is needed are constant. In providential afflictions how necessary prayer is for tested believers who find all other helpers failing them. Students in *doctrinal difficulties* will find help by lifting up this cry of "Save, O LORD" to the Holy Spirit, the great Teacher. Spiritual warriors in *inward conflicts* may send to the throne of grace for reinforcements, and this will be a model for their request. Those who are engaged in *heavenly toil* may in this way obtain grace in time of need. Seeking sinners, in *doubts and alarms*, may offer up the same simple supplication; in fact, in all these cases, times, and places this will serve the turn of needy souls. "Save, O LORD" will suit us in living and dying, suffering or working, rejoicing or sorrowing. In Him our help is found; let us not be slow to cry to Him.

The answer to the prayer is certain, if it is sincerely offered through Jesus. The Lord's character assures us that He will not leave His people; His relationship as Father and Husband guarantee us His help. God's gift of Jesus is a pledge of every good thing; and His sure promise stands, "Fear not, I will help you."

This well was famous in the wilderness because it was *the subject of a promise*: "That is the well of which the LORD said to Moses, 'Gather the people together, so that I may give them water.'" The people needed water, and it was promised by their gracious God. We need fresh supplies of heavenly grace, and in the covenant the Lord has pledged Himself to give us all we require. The well also became *the cause of a song*. Before the water gushed out, cheerful faith prompted the people to sing; and as they saw the crystal fountain bubbling up, the music grew more joyful. In similar fashion, we who believe the promise of God should rejoice in the prospect of divine revivals in our souls, and as we experience them our holy joy should overflow. Are we thirsting? Then let us not grumble but sing. Spiritual thirst is bitter to bear, but we need not bear it—the promise indicates a well; so let us be of good heart, and look for it. Moreover, the well was *the center of prayer*. "Spring up, O well." What God has promised to give, we must seek after, or we show that we have neither desire nor faith. This evening let us ask that the Scripture we have read, and our devotional exercises, may not be an empty formality but a channel of grace to our souls. May God the Holy Spirit work in us with all His mighty power, filling us with all the fullness of God. Lastly, the well was *the object of effort*. "The nobles of the people delved, with the scepter and with their staffs." The Lord wants us to be active in obtaining grace. Our implements are ill suited for digging in the sand, but we must use them to the best of our ability. Prayer must not be neglected; the gathering of God's people must not be forsaken; ordinances must not be set aside. The Lord will give us His peace most generously, but not on the path of laziness. Let us, then, stir ourselves to seek Him in whom we find all our fresh and flowing springs.

❧ MORNING ❧

YOUR REDEEMER. — ISAIAH 54:5

Jesus, the Redeemer, is altogether ours and ours forever. All the *offices* of Christ are held on our behalf. He is King for us, priest for us, and prophet for us. Whenever we read a new title of the Redeemer, let us appropriate Him as ours under that name as much as under any other. The shepherd's staff, the father's rod, the captain's sword, the priest's miter, the prince's scepter, the prophet's mantle—all are ours. Jesus has no dignity that He will not employ for our exaltation, and no prerogative that He will not exercise for our defense. His fullness of *Godhead* is our unfailing, inexhaustible treasure-house.

His *manhood* also, which he took upon Him for us, is ours in all its perfection. To us our gracious Lord communicates the spotless virtue of a stainless character; to us He gives the meritorious efficacy of a devoted life; on us He bestows the reward procured by obedient submission and unceasing service. He makes the perfect garment of His life our covering beauty, the glittering virtues of His character our ornaments and jewels, and the superhuman meekness of His death our boast and glory. He bequeaths us His manger, from which we learn how God came down to man, and His cross to teach us how man may go up to God. All His thoughts, emotions, actions, utterances, miracles, and intercessions were for us. He walked the path of sorrow on our behalf and has left to us as His heavenly legacy the full results of all the labors of His life. He is now as much ours as He will be; and He does not shrink to acknowledge Himself "*our* Lord Jesus Christ," though He is the blessed and only Potentate, the King of kings and Lord of lords. Christ everywhere and in every way is our Christ, forever and ever most richly to enjoy. O my soul, by the power of the Holy Spirit, call Him this morning "your Redeemer."

❧ EVENING ❧

I CAME TO MY GARDEN, MY SISTER, MY BRIDE. — SONG OF SOLOMON 5:1

The heart of the believer is Christ's garden. He bought it with His precious blood, and He enters it and claims it as His own. A garden *implies separation*. It is not the open field; it is not a wilderness; it is walled around or hedged in. If only we could see the wall of separation between the church and the world made broader and stronger. It is sad to hear Christians saying, "Well, there is no harm in this; there is no harm in that," and by this approach getting as near to the world as possible. Grace is at a low ebb in the soul that is always inquiring about how far it may go in worldly conformity. A garden is *a place of beauty*; it far surpasses the wild uncultivated lands. The genuine Christian must seek to be more excellent in his life than the best moralist, because Christ's garden ought to produce the best flowers in all the world. Even the best is poor compared with what Christ deserves; let us not disappoint Him with withering and feeble plants. The rarest, richest, choicest lilies and roses ought to bloom in the place that Jesus calls His own. The garden is *a place of growth*. The believer must not remain undeveloped, just mere buds and blossoms. We should grow in grace and in the knowledge of our Lord and Savior Jesus Christ. Growth should be rapid where Jesus is the gardener and the Holy Spirit the dew from heaven. A garden is *a place of retirement*. So the Lord Jesus Christ would have us reserve our souls as a place in which He can show Himself, in a way that He does not to the world. As Christians we should be far keener to keep our hearts closely shut up for Christ! We often worry and trouble ourselves, like Martha, with much serving, and like her we do not have the room for Christ that Mary had, and we do not sit at His feet as we ought. May the Lord grant the sweet showers of His grace to water His garden today.

❧ MORNING ❧

The blessings of today would be rich if all of us were filled with the Holy Spirit. It would be impossible to overestimate the consequences of this sacred filling of the soul. Life, comfort, light, purity, power, peace, and many other precious blessings are inseparable from the Spirit's gracious presence. As sacred *oil*, He anoints the head of the believer, setting him apart to the priesthood of saints and giving him grace to execute his office properly. As the only truly purifying *water* He cleanses us from the power of sin and sets us apart to holiness, enabling us to desire and then to do what pleases the Lord. As the *light*, He revealed Himself to us in our darkness, and now He reveals the Lord Jesus to us and in us and guides us in the way of righteousness. Enlightened by His pure celestial ray, we are no longer in darkness but light in the Lord. *As fire*, He purges us from dross and sets our consecrated nature ablaze. He is the sacrificial flame by which we are enabled to offer our whole souls as a living sacrifice unto God. As heavenly *dew*, He removes our barrenness and fertilizes our lives. How we long for Him to come upon us from above at this early hour! Such morning dew would be a sweet beginning to the day. As the *dove*, with wings of peaceful love He broods over His Church and over the souls of believers, and as a Comforter He dispels the cares and doubts that spoil the peace of His beloved. He descends upon the chosen as He did upon Christ at His baptism and bears witness to their sonship by working in them a filial spirit by which they cry, "Abba, Father." As the *wind*, He brings the breath of life to men; blowing where He wills, He performs the quickening operations by which the spiritual creation is animated and sustained. Would to God that we might feel His presence this day and every day.

❧ EVENING ❧
MY BELOVED IS MINE, AND I AM HIS; HE GRAZES AMONG THE LILIES.
UNTIL THE DAY BREATHES AND THE SHADOWS FLEE, TURN,
MY BELOVED, BE LIKE A GAZELLE OR A YOUNG STAG
ON CLEFT MOUNTAINS. — SONG OF SOLOMON 2:16-17

Surely if there is a happy verse in the Bible it is this—"My beloved is mine, and I am his." It is so peaceful, so full of assurance, so overflowing with happiness and contentment, that it might well have been written by the same hand that penned the Twenty-third Psalm. Yet though the prospect is very bright and lovely—as fair a scene as earth can display—it is not an entirely sunlit landscape. There is a cloud in the sky, which casts a shadow over the scene. Listen: "Until the day breathes and the shadows flee."

There is a word, too, about the "cleft mountains," or "the mountains of division," and to our love, anything like division is bitterness. Beloved, this may be your present state of mind. You do not doubt your salvation, you know that Christ is yours, but you are not feasting with Him. You understand your vital interest in Him, so that you do not have a shadow of a doubt about being His and of His being yours, but still His left hand is not under your head, nor does His right hand embrace you. A shade of sadness is cast over your heart, perhaps by affliction, certainly by the temporary absence of your Lord, so that even while exclaiming, "I am his," you are forced to take to your knees and to pray, "Until the day breathes, and the shadows flee, turn, my beloved."

"Where is He?" asks the soul. And the answer comes, "He grazes among the lilies." If we would find Christ, we must get into communion with His people, we must come to the ordinances with His saints. Oh, for an evening glimpse of Him! Oh, to eat with Him tonight!

FOR BEHOLD, I WILL COMMAND, AND SHAKE THE HOUSE OF ISRAEL
AMONG ALL THE NATIONS AS ONE SHAKES WITH A SIEVE,
BUT NO PEBBLE SHALL FALL TO THE EARTH. — AMOS 9:9

Every sifting comes by *divine command and permission*. Satan must ask permission before he can lay a finger upon Job. In actual fact, in some sense our siftings are *directly the work of heaven*, for in the text God says that He will "shake the house of Israel." Satan, like a slave, may hold the sieve, hoping for the worst; but the overruling hand of the Master is accomplishing His purpose by the very process that the enemy hopes will be destructive. Precious children of God, even though you are shaken, be comforted by the blessed fact that the Lord directs the whole process for His own glory and for your eternal profit.

The Lord Jesus will graciously and yet firmly *divide that which is precious from that which is of little account*. All are not Israel that are of Israel; the grain on the barn floor is not clean and pure, and so the shaking process must be performed. In the sieve, husks and chaff fly before the wind, and only solid substance will remain.

Observe the *complete safety of the Lord's wheat*; even a pebble has a promise of preservation. God Himself sifts, and therefore it is stern and terrible work; He sifts them in all places, "among all the nations"; He sifts them in the most effective manner, "as one shakes with a sieve"; and yet in all this, not the smallest, lightest, or most shriveled grain is permitted to fall to the ground. Every individual believer is precious in the sight of the Lord. A shepherd would not lose one sheep, nor a jeweler one diamond, nor a mother one child, nor a man one limb of his body; nor will the Lord lose one of His redeemed people. However little we may be, if we are the Lord's, we may rejoice that we are preserved in Christ Jesus.

❧ EVENING ❧

AND IMMEDIATELY THEY LEFT THEIR NETS AND FOLLOWED HIM.
— MARK 1:18

When they heard the call of Jesus, Simon and Andrew obeyed at once without hesitation. If we did likewise and punctually with resolute zeal put into practice what we hear immediately, then our attendance at the means of grace and our reading of good books could not fail to enrich us spiritually. He will not lose his loaf who has taken care to eat it immediately; neither can he be deprived of the benefit of the doctrine who has already acted upon it. Most readers and hearers become moved to decide to take action; but sadly, the proposal is a blossom that has not flowered, and as a result no fruit comes from it; they wait, they waver, and then they forget, until, like the ponds on frosty nights, when the sun shines by day, they are only thawed in time to be frozen again. That fatal *tomorrow* is blood-red with the murder of good resolutions; it is the slaughterhouse of the innocents. We are very concerned that our little book of "Evening Readings" should not be fruitless, and therefore we pray that readers may not be readers only, but doers of the Word. *The practice of truth is the fruit of profitable reading.* Should the reader be impressed with any duty while perusing these pages, let him be quick to fulfill it before the holy glow has departed from his soul, and let him leave his nets and all that he has rather than be found rebellious to the Master's call. Do not give place to the devil by delay! Act while opportunity and desire are working in happy partnership. Do not be caught in your own nets, but break the meshes of worldliness, and go where glory calls you. Happy is the writer who will meet with readers resolved to carry out his teachings: His harvest will be a hundredfold, and his Master will have great honor. We can only pray that this might be our reward from these brief meditations and hurried hints. Grant it, O Lord, to Your servant!

YOU ARE THE MOST HANDSOME OF THE SONS OF MEN. — PSALM 45:2

The entire person of Christ is like one diamond, and His life in every dimension leaves one lasting impression. He is altogether complete, not only in His various parts, but as a gracious all-glorious whole. His character is not a mass of bright colors mixed confusedly, nor a heap of precious stones laid carelessly on top of each other; He is a picture of beauty and a breastplate of glory. In Him, all the things of good repute are in their proper places and assist in adorning each other. Not one feature in His glorious person attracts attention at the expense of others; but He is perfectly and altogether lovely.

Oh, Jesus, Your power, Your grace, Your justice, Your tenderness, Your truth, Your majesty, and Your immutability combine to make a man, or rather a God-man, whom neither heaven nor earth has ever seen elsewhere. Your infancy, Your eternity, Your sufferings, Your triumphs, Your death, and Your immortality are all woven into one gorgeous tapestry, without seams or tears. You are music without discord; You are all things, and yet not diverse. As all the colors blend into one resplendent rainbow, so all the glories of heaven and earth meet in You and unite so perfectly that there is no one like You in all things; indeed, if all the virtues of the most excellent were bound in one bundle, they could not rival You, mirror of all perfection. You have been anointed with the holy oil, which Your God has reserved for You alone; and as for Your fragrance, it is the holy perfume that cannot be matched even with the chemist's skill; each spice is fragrant, but the compound is divine.

Oh, sacred symmetry! oh, rare connection
Of many perfects, to make one perfection!
Oh, heavenly music, where all parts do meet
In one sweet strain, to make one perfect sweet!

❧ EVENING ❧

BUT GOD'S FIRM FOUNDATION STANDS. — 2 TIMOTHY 2:19

The foundation upon which our faith rests is this, that "in Christ God was reconciling the world to himself, not counting their trespasses against them."[1] The great fact on which genuine faith relies is that "the Word became flesh and dwelt among us,"[2] and that "Christ also suffered once for sins, the righteous for the unrighteous, that he might bring us to God";[3] "He himself bore our sins in his body on the tree";[4] "Upon him was the chastisement that brought us peace, and with his stripes we are healed."[5] In one word, the great pillar of the Christian's hope is *substitution*. The vicarious sacrifice of Christ for the guilty, Christ being made sin for us that we might be made the righteousness of God in Him, Christ offering up a true and proper expiatory and substitutionary sacrifice in the room, place, and stead of as many as the Father gave Him, who are known to God by name and are recognized in their own hearts by their trusting in Jesus—this is the cardinal fact of the Gospel. If this foundation were removed, what could we do? But it stands firm as the throne of God. We know it; we rest on it; we rejoice in it; and our delight is to hold it, to meditate upon it, and to proclaim it, while we desire to be stirred and moved by gratitude for it in every part of our life and conversation. In these days a direct attack is made upon the doctrine of the Atonement. Men cannot bear substitution. They gnash their teeth at the thought of the Lamb of God bearing the sin of man. But we, who know by experience the preciousness of this truth, will proclaim it confidently and unceasingly and in defiance of them. We will neither dilute it nor change it, nor distort it in any shape or fashion. It shall still be Christ, a *positive substitute*, bearing human guilt and suffering in the place of men. We cannot, dare not give it up, for it is our life, and despite every controversy we affirm that "God's firm foundation stands."

[1] 2 Corinthians 5:19   [2] John 1:14   [3] 1 Peter 3:18   [4] 1 Peter 2:24   [5] Isaiah 53:5

&ea; MORNING &es;

IT IS HE WHO SHALL BUILD THE TEMPLE OF THE LORD AND
SHALL BEAR ROYAL HONOR. — ZECHARIAH 6:13

Christ Himself is the builder of His spiritual temple, and He has built it on the mountains of His unchangeable affection, His omnipotent grace, and His infallible truthfulness. But as it was in Solomon's temple, so in this: The materials need to be prepared. There are the cedars of Lebanon, but they are not framed for the building; they are not cut down and shaped and made into those planks of cedar whose fragrant beauty will make glad the courts of the Lord's house in paradise. There are also the rough stones still in the quarry, which must be hewn out and squared. All this is Christ's own work. Each individual believer is being prepared and polished and made ready for his place in the temple; but Christ's own hand performs the preparation-work. Afflictions cannot sanctify, except when they are used by Him to fulfill His purpose. Our prayers and efforts cannot make us ready for heaven, apart from the hand of Jesus, who fashions our hearts correctly.

As in the building of Solomon's temple, where "neither hammer nor axe nor any tool of iron was heard"[1] because it all arrived perfectly ready for the exact spot it was to occupy, so is it with the temple that Jesus builds; the preparation is all done on earth. When we reach heaven, there will be no sanctifying us there, no squaring us with affliction, no maturing us with suffering. No, we must be made ready here—and all that Christ will do He will do now; and when He has done it, we will be ferried by a loving hand across the stream of death and brought to the heavenly Jerusalem, to live as eternal pillars in the temple of our Lord.

> Beneath His eye and care,
> The edifice shall rise,
> Majestic, strong, and fair,
> And shine above the skies.

&ea; EVENING &es;

. . . IN ORDER THAT THE THINGS THAT CANNOT BE SHAKEN MAY REMAIN.
— HEBREWS 12:27

We have many things in our possession at the present moment that can be shaken, and it is not good for a Christian to rely upon them, for there is nothing stable beneath these rolling skies; change is written upon all things. Yet we have certain "things that *cannot* be shaken," and I invite you this evening to think of them—that if the things that can be shaken should all be taken away, you may derive real comfort from the things that cannot be shaken and that will remain. Whatever your losses have been, or may be, you enjoy present salvation. You are standing at the foot of Christ's cross, trusting alone in the merit of His precious blood, and no rise or fall of the markets can interfere with your salvation in Him; no breaking of banks, no failures and bankruptcies can touch that. Then you are *a child of God* this evening. God is your Father. No change of circumstances can ever rob you of that. Even if by loss you are brought to poverty and stripped bare, you can still say, "He is still my Father. In my Father's house are many rooms; therefore I will not be troubled." You have another permanent blessing, namely, *the love of Jesus Christ.* He who is God and man loves you with all the strength of His affectionate nature—nothing can affect that. The fig tree may not blossom, and the flocks may dwindle and wander from the field, but it does not matter to the man who can sing, "My Beloved is mine, and I am His." Our best portion and richest heritage we cannot lose. Whatever troubles come, let us play the man; let us show that we are not like little children cast down by what happens to us in this poor fleeting state of time. Our country is Immanuel's land, our hope is fixed in heaven, and therefore, calm as the summer's ocean, we will see the wreck of everything earthborn and yet rejoice in the God of our salvation.

[1] 1 Kings 6:7

EPHRAIM IS A CAKE NOT TURNED. — HOSEA 7:8

A cake not turned is *uncooked on one side*; and so Ephraim was, in many respects, untouched by divine grace: Though there was partial obedience, there was too much rebellion left. My soul, I charge you to see whether this is true of you. Are you thorough in the things of God? Has grace gone to the very center of your being so that its divine operation is felt in all your powers, your actions, your words, and your thoughts? To be sanctified, spirit, soul, and body, should be your aim and prayer; and although sanctification might not be complete in you, still it must be at work in you. There must not be the appearance of holiness in one place and reigning sin in another; otherwise you will also be a cake not turned.

A cake not turned is *soon burnt on the side nearest the fire*, and although no man can have too much religion, there are some who seem burnt black with bigoted zeal for that part of truth that they overemphasize; others are charred to a cinder with a self-congratulatory pharisaic performance of those religious activities that suit their mood. The assumed appearance of superior sanctity frequently accompanies a total absence of all vital godliness, and the saint in public is a devil in private. He deals in flour by day and in soot by night. The cake that is burned on one side is dough on the other.

This is true of me, Lord Jesus; turn me! Turn my unsanctified nature to the fire of Your love, and let it feel the sacred glow, and let my burnt side cool a little while I learn my own weakness and lack of heat when I am removed from Your heavenly flame. Let me not be a double-minded man, but one who is entirely under the powerful influence of reigning grace. I know only too well that if I am left like a cake unturned, and am not on both sides the subject of Your grace, I will be consumed forever in everlasting burnings.

❧ EVENING ☙
WE WAIT EAGERLY FOR ADOPTION AS SONS. — ROMANS 8:23

Even in this world saints are God's children, but the only way that people will discover this is by certain moral characteristics. The adoption is not displayed; the children are not yet openly declared. Among the Romans a man might adopt a child and keep it private for a long time; but there was a second adoption in public; when the child was brought before the constituted authorities, its old clothes were removed, and the father who took it to be his child gave it clothing suitable to its new status in life. "Beloved, we are God's children now, and what we will be has not yet appeared."[1] We are not yet clothed in the apparel of heaven's royal family; we are wearing in this flesh and blood just what we wore as the children of Adam. But we know that "when *he* appears" who is "the firstborn among many brothers,"[2] we will be like Him, for we will see Him as He is. Can't you imagine that a child taken from the lowest ranks of society and adopted by a Roman senator would say to himself, "I long for the day when I shall be publicly adopted. Then I shall discard these poor clothes and be dressed in clothes that depict my senatorial rank"? Glad for what he has already received, he still groans until he gets the fullness of what has been promised to him. So it is with us today. We are waiting until we put on our proper clothes and are declared as the children of God for all to see. We are young nobles and have not yet worn our crowns. We are young brides, and the marriage day has not arrived, but our fiancée's love for us leads us to long and sigh for the bridal morning. Our very happiness makes us long for more; our joy, like a swollen stream, longs to spring up like a fountain, leaping to the skies, heaving and groaning within our spirit for lack of space and room by which to reveal itself to men.

[1] 1 John 3:2 [2] Romans 8:29

❧ MORNING ❧

A WOMAN IN THE CROWD RAISED HER VOICE AND SAID TO HIM,
"BLESSED IS THE WOMB THAT BORE YOU, AND THE BREASTS AT WHICH YOU
NURSED!" BUT HE SAID, "BLESSED RATHER ARE THOSE WHO HEAR
THE WORD OF GOD AND KEEP IT!" — LUKE 11:27-28

It is fondly imagined by some that it must have been a very special privilege to be the mother of our Lord, because they suppose that she had the benefit of looking into His very heart in a way in which we cannot hope to do. There may be an appearance of plausibility in this notion, but not much. We do not know that Mary knew more than others; what she did know she did well to store in her heart; but she does not appear from anything we read in the Gospels to have been a better-instructed believer than any of Christ's other disciples. All that she knew we also may discover. Are you surprised by this? Here is a text to prove it: "The friendship of the LORD is for those who fear him, and he makes known to them his covenant."[1] Remember the Master's words—"No longer do I call you servants, for the servant does not know what his master is doing; but I have called you friends, for all that I have heard from my Father I have made known to you."[2] The Divine Revealer of secrets tells us His heart, and He keeps nothing back that is needful for us. His own assurance is, "If it were not so, would I have told you . . . ?"[3] Does He not today reveal Himself to us in a way that He does not to the world? And since this is so we will not ignorantly cry, "Blessed is the womb that bore you," but we will intelligently bless God that, having heard the Word and kept it, we first of all have as real a communion with the Savior as His mother had, and in the second place as true an acquaintance with the secrets of His heart as she can be supposed to have obtained. Happy soul to enjoy this privilege!

❧ EVENING ❧

SHADRACH, MESHACH, AND ABEDNEGO ANSWERED AND SAID . . .
"BE IT KNOWN TO YOU, O KING,
THAT WE WILL NOT SERVE YOUR GODS." — DANIEL 3:16, 18

The narrative of the manly courage and marvelous deliverance of these three holy children, or rather champions, is well calculated to engender in the minds of believers firmness and steadfastness in upholding the truth in the teeth of tyranny and in the very jaws of death. Here is a wonderful example especially for young Christians, teaching them that when it comes to faith in action they must never sacrifice their consciences. Lose everything rather than lose your integrity, and when everything is gone, still hold fast a clear conscience as the rarest jewel that can adorn the bosom of a mortal. Do not be guided by expediency but by divine authority. Follow the right at every hazard. When you see no obvious advantage, then walk by faith and not by sight. Honor God by trusting Him when it comes to matters of loss for the sake of principle. See whether He will be your debtor! See if He does not even in this life prove His word that "there is great gain in godliness with contentment,"[4] and that for those who "seek first the kingdom of God and his righteousness . . . all these things will be added to you."[5] Should it happen that in the providence of God you are a loser for conscience's sake, you will find that if the Lord does not pay you back in the silver of earthly prosperity, He will discharge His promise in the gold of spiritual joy. Remember that a man's life does not consist in the abundance of what he possesses. To wear an honest spirit, to have a heart void of offense, to have the favor and smile of God is greater riches than all the gold and diamonds in the world. "Better is a dinner of herbs where love is than a fattened ox and hatred with it."[6] An ounce of contentment is worth a ton of gold.

[1] Psalm 25:14 [2] John 15:15 [3] John 14:2 [4] 1 Timothy 6:6 [5] Matthew 6:33 [6] Proverbs 15:17

GET YOU UP TO A HIGH MOUNTAIN. — ISAIAH 40:9

Our knowledge of Christ is somewhat like climbing one of the mountains in Wales. When you are at the base you see only a little: the mountain itself appears to be only half as high as it really is. Confined in a little valley, you discover scarcely anything but the rippling brooks as they descend into the stream at the foot of the mountain. Climb the first rising knoll, and the valley lengthens and widens beneath your feet. Go higher, and you see the country for four or five miles around, and you are delighted with the widening prospect. Higher still, and the scene enlarges; until at last, when you are on the summit and look east, west, north, and south, you see almost all of England lying before you. There is a forest in some distant county, perhaps two hundred miles away, and here the sea, and there a shining river and the smoking chimneys of a manufacturing town, or the masts of the ships in a busy port. All these things please and delight you, and you say, "I could not have imagined that so much could be seen at this elevation." Now, the Christian life is of the same order. When we first believe in Christ, we see only a little of Him. The higher we climb, the more we discover of His beauty. But who has ever gained the summit? Who has known all the heights and depths of the love of Christ that passes knowledge? When Paul had grown old and was sitting gray-haired and shivering in a dungeon in Rome, he was able to say with greater emphasis than we can, "I know whom I have believed,"[1] for each experience had been like the climbing of a hill, each trial had been like ascending another summit, and his death seemed like gaining the top of the mountain, from which he could see the whole panorama of the faithfulness and love of Him to whom he had committed his soul. Get up, dear friend, into a high mountain.

∽ EVENING ∝

BUT THE DOVE FOUND NO PLACE TO SET HER FOOT. — GENESIS 8:9

Reader, can you find rest apart from the ark, Christ Jesus? Then consider that your religion may be in vain. Are you satisfied with anything short of a conscious knowledge of your union and interest in Christ? Then woe to you. If you profess to be a Christian while finding full satisfaction in worldly pleasures and pursuits, your profession is probably false. If your soul can stretch herself at rest and find the bed long enough and the blanket broad enough to cover it in the chambers of sin, then you are a hypocrite and far away from any proper thoughts of Christ or awareness of His preciousness. But if, on the other hand, you feel that if you could indulge in sin without punishment, that would be a punishment itself, and that if you could have the whole world and live in it forever, it would be quite enough misery not to be separated from it, for your God—your God—is what your soul longs for, then be of good courage, you are a child of God. With all your sins and imperfections, take this for your comfort: If your soul has no rest in sin, you are not as the sinner is! If you are still crying after and craving after something better, Christ has not forgotten you, for you have not quite forgotten Him. The believer cannot do without his Lord; words are inadequate to express his thoughts of Him. We cannot live on the sands of the wilderness—we want the manna that drops from heaven; the pitchers of self-confidence cannot produce for us a drop of moisture, but we drink of the rock that follows us, and that rock is Christ. When you feed on Him, your soul can sing, "He who satisfies me with good so that my youth is renewed like the eagle's";[2] but if you don't have Him, your wine cellar and well-stocked pantry can give you no sort of satisfaction: Learn to lament over them in the words of wisdom, "Vanity of vanities, all is vanity!"

[1] 2 Timothy 1:12   [2] See Psalm 103:5

W hat must be the apostate professor's doom when his naked soul appears before God? How will he bear to hear that voice telling him that he is banished forever from His presence and that he will not be the recipient of mercy? "Depart from Me, you cursed; you have rejected knowledge, and I reject you." What will be this wretch's shame at the last great day when, before the assembled crowds, the apostate shall be unmasked? See the profane, and sinners who never professed faith, lifting themselves up from their beds of fire to point at him. "There he is," says one; "will he preach the gospel in hell?" "There he is," says another; "he rebuked me for cursing and was a hypocrite himself!" "Aha!" says another; "here comes a psalm-singing Methodist—one who was always at his meeting; he is the man who boasted of his being sure of everlasting life, and here he is!" No greater eagerness will ever be seen among satanic tormentors than in that day when devils drag the hypocrite's soul down to perdition. Bunyan pictures this with massive but awful grandeur of poetry when he speaks of the back way to hell. Seven devils bound the wretch with nine cords and dragged him from the road to heaven, in which he had professed to walk, and thrust him through the back door into hell. Watch out for that back way to hell, professors! "Examine yourselves, to see whether you are in the faith."[1] Pay attention to your condition, and see whether you are in Christ or not. It is the easiest thing in the world to give high marks when grading your own paper. Be honest and fair. Be gracious to all, but be rigorous with yourself. Remember, if you are not building on the rock, your house will collapse. May the Lord give you sincerity, constancy, and firmness; and in no day, however evil, may you be led to turn aside.

ex.   E V E N I N G   *ex.*

B anish forever any thought of indulging the flesh if you want to live in the power of your risen Lord. It is incongruous for a man who is alive in Christ to dwell in the corruption of sin. "Why do you seek the living among the dead?" said the angel to the women. Should the living dwell in the tombs? Should divine life be imprisoned in the burial ground of fleshly lust? How can we partake of the cup of the Lord and yet drink the cup of the devil? Surely, believer, from blatant lusts and sins you are delivered, but have you also escaped from those that are more secret and delusive? Have you left behind the lust of pride? Have you escaped from laziness? Have you given up trusting in earthly things? Are you seeking each day to live above worldliness, the pride of life, and the ensnaring grip of greed? Remember, it is in order that you might know such victory that you have been enriched with the treasures of God. If you are really the chosen of God, and beloved by Him, do not allow all this lavish treasure of grace to be wasted on you. Pursue holiness; it is the Christian's crown and glory. An unholy church is useless to the world and of no esteem among men. It is an abomination, hell's laughter, heaven's abhorrence. The worst evils that have ever come upon the world have been brought upon her by an unholy church. O Christian, the vows of God are upon you. You are God's servant: Act as such. You are God's king: Reign over your lusts. You are God's chosen: Do not associate with Satan. Heaven is your portion: Live like a heavenly spirit, and in this way you will prove that you have true faith in Jesus, for there cannot be faith in the heart unless there is holiness in the life.

Lord, I desire to live as one
Who bears a blood-bought name,
As one who fears but grieving Thee,
And knows no other shame.

[1] 2 Corinthians 13:5

ONLY YOU MUST NOT GO VERY FAR AWAY. — EXODUS 8:28

This is a crafty word from the lip of the arch-tyrant Pharaoh. If the poor enslaved Israelites must leave Egypt, then he bargains with them that it shall not be very far away—not too far for them to escape the terror of his arms and the observation of his spies. After the same fashion, the world hates the nonconformity of nonconformity or the dissidence of dissent; it would rather we were more charitable and not deal with things too severely. Death to the world and burial with Christ are experiences that worldly minds treat with ridicule, and as a result baptism, which pictures them, is almost universally neglected and even condemned. Worldly wisdom recommends the path of compromise and talks of "moderation." According to this carnal policy, purity is admitted to be very desirable, but we are warned against being too precise; truth is of course to be followed, but error is not to be severely denounced. "Yes," says the world, "be spiritually minded by all means, but do not deny yourself a little friendship with the world, the odd journey to Vanity Fair. What's the good of denouncing this empty lifestyle when it is so fashionable and everybody does it?" Multitudes of professors succumb to this cunning advice, to their own eternal ruin. If we are going to really follow the Lord, we must be prepared to walk the narrow path and join Moses who refused to enjoy the pleasures of sin for a season. We must leave behind the world's maxims— its pleasure, and its religion too—and go far away to the place where the Lord calls His sanctified ones. When the town is on fire, our house cannot be too far from the flames. When disease is rampant, it is hard to escape it. The further from a poisonous snake the better, and the further from worldly conformity the better. To all true believers let the trumpet-call be sounded: "Therefore go out from their midst, and be separate from them."[1]

❧ EVENING ❧

EACH ONE SHOULD REMAIN IN THE CONDITION IN WHICH HE WAS CALLED.
— 1 CORINTHIANS 7:20

Some people have the foolish notion that the only way in which they can live for God is by becoming pastors, missionaries, or Bible teachers. How many would be excluded from any opportunity of spiritual usefulness if this were the case. Beloved, it is not office— it is sincerity; it is not position—it is grace that will enable us to serve and glorify God. God is definitely glorified at the workbench, where the godly worker fulfills his task singing of the Savior's love. In this humble setting God is glorified far more than in many a lofty pulpit where official religion performs its scanty duties. The name of Jesus is glorified by the taxicab driver as he blesses God and speaks to his passengers of the living hope. He will be more useful than the popular preacher who goes about peddling the Gospel for profit. God is glorified when we serve Him in our proper vocations. Take care, dear reader, that you do not neglect the path of duty by leaving your occupation, and take care you do not dishonor your profession while in it. Think little of yourselves, but do not think too little of your callings. Every lawful trade may be sanctified by the Gospel to noblest ends. Turn to the Bible, and you will find the most menial forms of labor connected either with most daring deeds of faith or with persons whose lives have been illustrations of holiness. Therefore do not be discontented with your calling. Whatever God has made your position or your work, remain in that, unless you are quite sure that He calls you to something else. Let your first concern be to glorify God to the best of your ability where you are. Fill your present sphere to His praise, and if He needs you in another, He will show it you. This evening lay aside anxious ambition, and embrace peaceful content.

[1] 2 Corinthians 6:17

❧ MORNING ❧
LOOKING TO JESUS. — HEBREWS 12:2

It is always the Holy Spirit's work to turn our eyes away from self to Jesus. But Satan's work is just the opposite; he is constantly trying to make us look at ourselves instead of Christ. He insinuates, "Your sins are too great for pardon; you have no faith; you do not repent enough; you will never be able to continue to the end; you do not have the joy of His children; you have such a wavering hold on Jesus." All these are thoughts about self, and we will never find comfort or assurance by looking within. But the Holy Spirit turns our eyes entirely away from self: He tells us that we are nothing, but that Christ is everything. Remember, therefore, it is not *your hold* of Christ that saves you—it is Christ; it is not *your joy* in Christ that saves you—it is Christ; it is not even faith in Christ, although that is the instrument—it is Christ's blood and merits. Therefore, do not look so much to your hand with which you are grasping Christ as to Christ; do not look to your hope but to Jesus, the source of your hope; do not look to your faith, but to Jesus, the founder and perfecter of your faith. We will never find happiness by looking at our prayers, our deeds, or our feelings; it is what *Jesus* is, not what we are, that gives rest to the soul. If we are to overcome Satan and have peace with God, it must be by "looking to Jesus." Keep your eye simply on Him; let His death, His sufferings, His merits, His glories, His intercession be fresh upon your mind. When you waken in the morning look to Him; when you lie down at night look to Him. Do not let your hopes or fears come between you and Jesus; follow hard after Him, and He will never fail you.

> My hope is built on nothing less
> Than Jesus' blood and righteousness:
> I dare not trust the sweetest frame,
> But wholly lean on Jesus' name.

❧ EVENING ❧

BUT AARON'S STAFF SWALLOWED UP THEIR STAFFS. — EXODUS 7:12

This incident is an instructive illustration of the certain victory of God's handiwork over all opposition. Whenever a divine principle is set in the heart, even though the devil may create a counterfeit and produce swarms of opponents, we may be sure that God is in the work, and it will swallow up all its foes. If God's grace takes possession of a man, the world's magicians may throw down all their staffs, and every staff may be as cunning and poisonous as a serpent; but Aaron's staff will swallow up their staffs. The sweet attractions of the cross will woo and win the man's heart, so that although he had lived only for this deceitful earth, he will now have an eye for heaven, and his mind will be set on the things that are above. When grace has won the day, the unbeliever begins to seek the world to come. The same fact is to be observed in the life of the believer. A company of enemies assailed our faith—our old sins; the devil threw them down before us, and they turned to serpents. What numbers of them! But the cross of Jesus destroys them all. Faith in Christ makes short work of all our sins. Then the devil has launched another host of serpents in the form of worldly trials, temptations, unbelief; but faith in Jesus is more than a match for them and overcomes them all. The same absorbing principle shines in the faithful service of God! With an enthusiastic love for Jesus, difficulties are surmounted; sacrifices become pleasures; sufferings are honors. But if faith is a consuming passion in the heart, then it follows that there are many people who profess it but do not have it; for what they have will not bear this test. Examine yourself, my reader, on this point. Aaron's staff *proved* its heaven-given power. Is your faith doing so? If Christ is anything, He must be everything. Do not rest until love and faith in Jesus are the master passions of your soul!

✨ M O R N I N G ✨

EVEN SO, THROUGH JESUS, GOD WILL BRING WITH HIM THOSE WHO
HAVE FALLEN ASLEEP. — 1 THESSALONIANS 4:14

Let us not imagine that *the soul* sleeps in insensibility. "Today you will be with me in paradise" is the whisper of Christ to every dying saint. They sleep in Jesus, but their souls are before the throne of God, praising Him day and night in His temple, singing hallelujahs to Him who washed them from their sins in His blood. The body sleeps in its lonely bed of earth, beneath the coverlet of grass. But what is this sleep? The idea connected with sleep is "*rest*," and that is the thought that the Spirit of God would convey to us. Sleep makes each night a sabbath for the day. Sleep shuts tight the door of the soul and bids all intruders wait for a while, that the life within may enter its summer garden of ease. The toil-worn believer quietly sleeps, as does the weary child when it slumbers on its mother's breast. Happy are they who die in the Lord; they rest from their labors, and their works follow them. Their quiet repose will never be broken until God shall rouse them to give them their full reward. Guarded by angelic watchers, curtained by eternal mysteries, they sleep on, the inheritors of glory, until the fullness of time shall bring the fullness of redemption. What an awaking will be theirs! They were laid in their last resting place, weary and worn, but they will not rise in that condition. They went to their rest with furrowed brow and wasted features, but they wake up in beauty and glory. The shriveled seed, so devoid of form and beauty, rises from the dust a glorious flower. The winter of the grave gives way to the spring of redemption and the summer of glory. Blessed is death, since through the divine power it removes our working clothes and dresses us with the wedding garment of incorruption. Blessed are those who sleep in Jesus.

✨ E V E N I N G ✨

AND SO IN THE MATTER OF THE ENVOYS OF THE PRINCES OF BABYLON,
WHO HAD BEEN SENT TO HIM TO INQUIRE ABOUT THE SIGN THAT HAD
BEEN DONE IN THE LAND, GOD LEFT HIM TO HIMSELF,
IN ORDER TO TEST HIM AND TO KNOW ALL THAT WAS IN HIS HEART.
— 2 CHRONICLES 32:31

Hezekiah was growing so inwardly great and priding himself so much upon the favor of God that self-righteousness crept in, and because he trusted in himself, the grace of God was for a time, in its more active operations, withdrawn. If the grace of God were to leave the best Christian, there is enough sin in his heart to make him the worst of transgressors. If left to yourselves, you who are warmest for Christ would cool down like Laodicea into sickening lukewarmness: You who are sound in the faith would be white with the leprosy of false doctrine; you who now walk before the Lord in excellency and integrity would reel to and fro and stagger with a drunkenness of evil passion. Like the moon, we borrow our light; bright as we are when grace shines on us, we are darkness itself when the Sun of Righteousness withdraws Himself. *Therefore, let us cry to God to never leave us.* "Take not Your Holy Spirit from me! Do not withdraw from us Your indwelling grace! Have You not said, 'I, the LORD, am its keeper; every moment I water it. Lest anyone punish it, I keep it night and day'?[1] Lord, keep us everywhere. Keep us when we're in the valley so that we do not grumble against Your humbling hand; keep us when we're on the mountain, so we do not lose our balance by being lifted up; keep us in youth, when our passions are strong; keep us in old age, when becoming conceited in our wisdom, we may therefore prove greater fools than those who are young and silly; keep us when we come to die, in case at the very end we should deny You! Keep us living, keep us dying, keep us working, keep us suffering, keep us fighting, keep us resting, keep us everywhere, for everywhere we need You, O our God!"

[1] Isaiah 27:3

❧ MORNING ❧

Behold the superlative generosity of the Lord Jesus, for He has given us His all. Although a tithe of His possessions would have made a universe of angels, rich beyond all thought, yet He was not content until He had given us all that He had. It would have been surprising grace if He had allowed us to eat the crumbs of His abundance beneath the table of His mercy; but He will do nothing by half measures. He makes us sit with Him and share the feast. If He had given us some small donation from His royal treasure, we would have had cause to love Him eternally; but in fact He wants His bride to be as rich as Himself, and He will not have a glory or a grace in which she will not share. He has not been content with less than making us joint-heirs with Himself, so that we might have equal possessions. He has emptied all His riches into the members of the church and has shared everything with His redeemed. There is not one room in His house the key of which He will keep from His people. He gives them complete freedom to take all that He has to enjoy as their own; He loves to see them enjoy His treasure and take as much as they can possibly carry. The limitless fullness of His all-sufficiency is as free to the believer as the air he breathes. Christ has put the cup of His love and grace to the believer's lip and invites him to drink of it forever; if he could empty it, he is welcome to do so, but as he cannot exhaust it, he is invited to drink abundantly, for it is all his own. What truer proof of fellowship can heaven or earth provide?

When I stand before the throne
Dressed in beauty not my own;
When I see Thee as Thou art,
Love Thee with unsinning heart;
Then, Lord, shall I fully know—
Not till then—how much I owe.

❧ EVENING ❧

At the very time when the Chaldeans surrounded Jerusalem, and when the sword, famine, and pestilence had desolated the land, Jeremiah was commanded by God to purchase a field and have the deed of transfer legally sealed and witnessed. This was a strange purchase for a rational man to make. Caution could not justify it, for it was buying with hardly a probability that the purchaser would ever enjoy the possession. But it was enough for Jeremiah that his God had instructed him, for he knew with certainty that God will be justified of all His children. He reasoned thus: "Lord God, You can make this plot of ground useful to me; You can rid this land of these oppressors; You can make me sit under my vine and my fig-tree in the heritage that I have bought; for You made the heavens and the earth, and there is nothing too hard for You." There was a majesty in the early saints, who dared to do at God's command things that human reason would condemn. Whether it be a Noah who is to build a ship on dry land, an Abraham who is to offer up his only son, a Moses who is to despise the treasures of Egypt, or a Joshua who is to besiege Jericho for seven days, using no weapons but the blasts of trumpets, they all act upon God's command, contrary to the dictates of human reason; and the Lord gives them a rich reward as the result of their obedient faith. Would to God we had in contemporary Christianity a more potent infusion of this heroic faith in God. If we would venture more upon the naked promise of God, we would enter a world of wonders to which as yet we are strangers. May Jeremiah's place of confidence become ours—nothing is too hard for the God that created the heavens and the earth.

July

IT SHALL CONTINUE IN SUMMER AS IN WINTER. — ZECHARIAH 14:8

The streams of living water that flow from Jerusalem are not dried up by the parching heats of sultry midsummer any more than they are frozen by the cold winds of blustering winter. Rejoice, O my soul, that you are spared to testify of the faithfulness of the Lord. The seasons change, and you change, but your Lord abides evermore the same, and the streams of His love are as deep, as broad, and as full as ever. The heats of business cares and scorching trials make me need the cooling influences of the river of His grace; I may go at once and drink to the full from the inexhaustible fountain, for in summer and in winter it pours forth its flood. The upper springs are never scanty, and blessed be the name of the Lord, the lower springs cannot fail either. Elijah found Cherith dried up, but Jehovah was still the same God of providence. Job said his brethren were like deceitful brooks, but he found his God an overflowing river of consolation. The Nile is the great confidence of Egypt, but its floods are variable; our Lord is evermore the same. By turning the course of the Euphrates, Cyrus took the city of Babylon; but no power, human or infernal, can divert the current of divine grace. The tracks of ancient rivers have been found all dry and desolate, but the streams that take their rise on the mountains of divine sovereignty and infinite love shall ever be full to the brim. Generations melt away, but the course of grace is unaltered. The river of God may sing with greater truth than the brook in the poem—

> Men may come, and men may go,
> But I go on forever.

How happy you are, my soul, to be led beside such still waters! Never wander to other streams, lest you hear the Lord's rebuke, "What do you gain by going to Egypt to drink the waters of the Nile?"[1]

❧ EVENING ❧

. . . THE SOUND OF THE LORD GOD WALKING IN THE GARDEN
IN THE COOL OF THE DAY. — GENESIS 3:8

My soul, now that the cool of the day has come, retire awhile and hearken to the voice of God. He is always ready to speak with you when you are prepared to hear. If there is any slowness to commune, it is not on His part, but altogether on yours, for He stands at the door and knocks, and if His people will but open, He rejoices to enter. But in what state is my heart, which is my Lord's garden? May I venture to hope that it is well trimmed and watered and is bringing forth fruit fit for Him? If not, He will have much to reprove, but still I pray Him to come to me, for nothing can so certainly bring my heart into a right condition as the presence of the Sun of Righteousness, who brings healing in His wings. Come, therefore, O Lord, my God, my soul invites You earnestly and waits for You eagerly. Come to me, O Jesus, my well-beloved, and plant fresh flowers in my garden, such as I see blooming in such perfection in Your matchless character! Come, O my Father, who is the Gardener, and deal with me in Your tenderness and prudence! Come, O Holy Spirit, and saturate my whole nature, as the herbs are now moistened with the evening dews. O that God would speak to me. Speak, Lord, for Your servant hears! O that He would walk with me; I am ready to give up my whole heart and mind to Him, and every other thought is hushed. I am only asking what He delights to give. I am sure that He will condescend to have fellowship with me, for He has given me His Holy Spirit to abide with me forever. Sweet is the cool twilight, when every star seems like the eye of heaven and the cool wind is as the breath of celestial love. My Father, my elder Brother, my sweet Comforter, speak now in loving-kindness, for You have opened my ear and I am not rebellious.

[1] Jeremiah 2:18

OUR HEART IS GLAD IN HIM. — PSALM 33:21

Blessed is the fact that Christians can rejoice even in the deepest distress; although trouble may surround them, they still sing; and like many birds, they sing best in their cages. The waves may roll over them, but their souls soon rise to the surface and see the light of God's countenance; they have a buoyancy about them that keeps their head always above the water and helps them to sing amid the tempest, "God is with me still." To whom shall the glory be given? Oh, to Jesus—it is all by Jesus. Trouble does not necessarily bring consolation with it to the believer, but the presence of the Son of God with him in the fiery furnace fills his heart with joy. He is sick and suffering, but Jesus visits him and makes his bed for him. He is dying, and the cold, chilly waters of Jordan are gathering about him up to the neck, but Jesus puts His arms around him and cries, "Fear not, beloved; to die is to be blessed; the waters of death have their fountainhead in heaven; they are not bitter—they are sweet as honey, for they flow from the throne of God." As the departing saint wades through the stream, and the billows gather around him, and heart and flesh fail him, the same voice sounds in his ears: "Fear not, for I am with you; be not dismayed, for I am your God."[1] As he nears the borders of the infinite unknown and is almost frightened to enter the realm of shades, Jesus says, "Fear not, little flock, for it is your Father's good pleasure to give you the kingdom."[2] Thus strengthened and consoled, the believer is not afraid to die; no, he is even willing to depart, for since he has seen Jesus as the morning star, he longs to gaze upon Him as the sun in his strength. Truly, the presence of Jesus is all the heaven we desire. He is at once

The glory of our brightest days;
The comfort of our nights.

❧ EVENING ❧

TO YOU, O LORD, I CALL; MY ROCK, BE NOT DEAF TO ME, LEST,
IF YOU BE SILENT TO ME, I BECOME LIKE THOSE WHO GO
DOWN TO THE PIT. — PSALM 28:1

A cry is the natural expression of sorrow, and a suitable utterance when all other modes of appeal fail us; but the cry must be alone directed to the Lord, for to cry to man is to waste our entreaties upon the air. When we consider the readiness of the Lord to hear and His ability to aid, we shall see good reason for directing all our appeals at once to the God of our salvation. It will be in vain to call to the rocks in the day of judgment, but our Rock attends to our cries.

"*Be not deaf to me.*" Mere formalists may be content without answers to their prayers, but genuine suppliants cannot; they are not satisfied with the results of prayer itself in calming the mind and subduing the will—they must go further and obtain actual replies from heaven or they cannot rest; and those replies they long to receive at once—they dread even a little of God's silence. God's voice is often so terrible that it shakes the wilderness; but His silence is equally full of awe to an eager suppliant. When God seems to close His ear, we must not therefore close our mouths but rather cry with more earnestness; for when our note grows shrill with eagerness and grief, He will not long deny us a hearing. What a dreadful case we would be in if the Lord should become forever deaf to our prayers. "*Lest, if you be silent to me, I become like those who go down to the pit.*" Deprived of the God who answers prayer, we would be in a more pitiable plight than the dead in the grave and would soon sink to the same level as the lost in hell. We *must* have answers to prayer: Ours is an urgent case of dire necessity; surely the Lord will speak peace to our agitated minds, for He never can find it in His heart to permit His own elect to perish.

[1] Isaiah 41:10 [2] Luke 12:32

THE UGLY, THIN COWS ATE UP THE SEVEN ATTRACTIVE, PLUMP COWS.
— GENESIS 41:4

Pharaoh's dream has too often been my waking experience. My days of laziness have ruinously destroyed all that I had achieved in times of zealous endeavor; my seasons of coldness have frozen all the genial glow of my periods of fervency and enthusiasm; and my fits of worldliness have thrown me back from my advances in the divine life. I had need to beware of lean prayers, lean praises, lean duties, and lean experiences, for these will eat up the fat of my comfort and peace. If I neglect prayer for never so short a time, I lose all the spirituality to which I had attained; if I draw no fresh supplies from heaven, the old corn in my granary is soon consumed by the famine that rages in my soul. When the caterpillars of indifference, the worms of worldliness, and the snares of self-indulgence lay my heart completely desolate and make my soul languish, all my former fruitfulness and growth in grace avails me nothing whatever. How anxious should I be to have no lean-fleshed days, no ill-favored hours! If every day I journeyed toward the goal of my desires I would soon reach it, but backsliding leaves me still far from the prize of my high calling and robs me of the advances that I had so strenuously made. The only way in which all my days can be like the fat cows is to feed them in the right meadow, to spend them with the Lord, in His service, in His company, in His fear, and in His way. Why should not every year be richer than the past, in love and usefulness and joy? I am nearer the celestial hills; I have had more experience of my Lord and should be more like Him. O Lord, keep far from me the curse of leanness of soul; let me not have to bemoan such leanness, but may I be well-fed and nourished in Your house, that I may praise Your name.

❧ EVENING ❧

IF WE ENDURE, WE WILL ALSO REIGN WITH HIM. — 2 TIMOTHY 2:12

We *must not imagine that we are suffering for Christ and with Christ if we are not in Christ.* Beloved friend, are you trusting in Jesus only? If not, whatever you may have to mourn over on earth, you are not suffering with Christ and have no hope of reigning with Him in heaven. Neither are we to conclude that all a Christian's sufferings are sufferings with Christ, for *it is essential that he be called by God to suffer.* If we are rash and imprudent and run into positions for which neither providence nor grace has fitted us, we ought to question whether we are not rather sinning than communing with Jesus. If we let passion take the place of judgment, and self-will reign instead of scriptural authority, we shall fight the Lord's battles with the devil's weapons, and if we cut our own fingers we must not be surprised. Again, *in troubles that come upon us as the result of sin, we must not dream that we are suffering with Christ.* When Miriam spoke evil of Moses, and the leprosy polluted her, she was not suffering for God. Moreover, suffering that God accepts *must have God's glory as its end.* If I suffer that I may earn a name or win applause, I shall get no other reward than that of the Pharisee. It is required also *that love for Jesus and love for His people should always be the mainspring of all our patience. We must manifest the Spirit of Christ* in meekness, gentleness, and forgiveness. Let us search and see if we truly *suffer with Jesus.* And if we do suffer in this way, what is our "slight momentary affliction"[1] compared with *reigning with Him?* Oh, it is so blessed to be in the furnace with Christ, and such an honor to stand in the jail with Him, that if there were no future reward, we might count ourselves happy in present honor; but when the recompense is so eternal, so infinitely more than we had any right to expect, shall we not take up the cross with enthusiasm and go on our way rejoicing?

[1] 2 Corinthians 4:16

SANCTIFY THEM IN THE TRUTH. — JOHN 17:17

Sanctification begins in regeneration. The Spirit of God implants in man that new living principle by which he becomes "a new creation"[1] in Christ Jesus. This work, which begins in the new birth, is carried on in two ways—mortification, whereby the lusts of the flesh are subdued and kept under, and vivification, by which the life that God has put within us is made to be a well of water springing up unto everlasting life. This is carried on every day in what is called *perseverance*, by which the Christian is preserved and continued in a gracious state and is made to abound in good works unto the praise and glory of God; and it culminates or comes to perfection in glory, when the soul, being thoroughly purged, is caught up to dwell with holy beings at the right hand of the Majesty on high. But while the Spirit of God is thus the author of sanctification, yet there is a visible agency employed that must not be forgotten. "Sanctify them," said Jesus, "in the *truth*; your word is truth." The passages of Scripture that prove that the instrument of our sanctification is the Word of God are numerous. The Spirit of God brings to our minds the precepts and doctrines of truth and applies them with power. These are heard in the ear, and being received in the heart, they work in us to will and to do God's good pleasure. The truth is the sanctifier, and if we do not hear or read the truth, we shall not grow in sanctification. We only progress in sound living as we progress in sound understanding. "Your word is a lamp to my feet and a light to my path."[2] Do not say of any error, "It is a mere matter of opinion." No man indulges an error of judgment without sooner or later tolerating an error in practice. Hold fast the truth, for by doing so you shall be sanctified by the Spirit of God.

❧ EVENING ☙

HE WHO HAS CLEAN HANDS AND A PURE HEART,
WHO DOES NOT LIFT UP HIS SOUL TO WHAT IS FALSE AND
DOES NOT SWEAR DECEITFULLY. — PSALM 24:4

Outward practical holiness is a very precious mark of grace. It is to be feared that many professors have perverted the doctrine of justification by faith in such a way as to treat good works with contempt; if so, they will receive everlasting contempt at the last great day. If our hands are not clean, let us wash them in Jesus' precious blood, and so let us lift up pure hands unto God. But "*clean hands*" will not suffice unless they are connected with "*a pure heart*." True religion is heart-work. We may wash the outside of the cup and the plate as long as we please, but if the inward parts be filthy, we are filthy altogether in the sight of God, for our hearts are more truly ourselves than our hands are. The very life of our being lies in the inner nature, and hence the imperative need of purity within. The pure in heart shall see God; all others are but blind bats.

The man who is born for heaven "*does not lift up his soul to what is false.*" All men have their joys by which their souls are lifted up. The worldling lifts up his soul in carnal delights, which are mere empty vanities; but the saint loves more substantial things; like Jehoshaphat, he is lifted up in the ways of the Lord. He who is content with husks will be reckoned with the swine. Does the world satisfy you? Then you have your reward and portion in this life; make much of it, for you will know no other joy.

"*Does not swear deceitfully.*" The saints are men of honor still. The Christian man's word is his only oath; but that is as good as twenty oaths of other men. False speaking will shut any man out of heaven, for a liar shall not enter into God's house, whatever may be his professions or doings. Reader, does the text before us condemn you, or do you hope to ascend into the hill of the Lord?

[1] 2 Corinthians 5:17   [2] Psalm 119:105

CALLED TO BE SAINTS. — ROMANS 1:7

We are very apt to regard the apostolic saints as if they were "saints" in a more special manner than the other children of God. All are "saints" whom God has called by His grace and sanctified by His Spirit; but we are apt to look upon the *apostles* as extraordinary beings, scarcely subject to the same weaknesses and temptations as ourselves. Yet in doing so we forget this truth, that the nearer a man lives to God, the more intensely has he to mourn over his own evil heart; and the more his Master honors him in His service, the more the evil of the flesh vexes and teases him day by day. The fact is, if we had seen the apostle Paul, we would have thought him remarkably like the rest of the chosen family: And if we had talked with him, we would have said, "We find that his experience and ours are much the same. He is more faithful, more holy, and more deeply taught than we are, but he has the self-same trials to endure. Actually, in some respects he is more sorely tried than ourselves." Do not, then, look upon the ancient saints as being exempt either from infirmities or sins; and do not regard them with that mystic reverence that will almost make us idolaters. Their holiness is attainable even by us. We are "called to be saints" by that same voice that con-strained them to their high vocation. It is a Christian's duty to force his way into the inner cir-cle of saintship; and if these saints were superior to us in their attainments, as they certainly were, let us follow them; let us emulate their passion and holiness. We have the same light that they had, the same grace is accessible to us, and why should we rest satisfied until we have equaled them in heavenly character? They lived *with* Jesus, they lived *for* Jesus, there-fore they grew *like* Jesus. Let us live by the same Spirit as they did, "looking to Jesus,"[1] and our saintship will soon be apparent.

❧ EVENING ❧

TRUST IN THE LORD FOREVER, FOR THE LORD GOD IS
AN EVERLASTING ROCK. — ISAIAH 26:4

Seeing that we have such a God to trust, let us rest upon Him with all our weight; let us resolutely drive out all unbelief and endeavor to get rid of doubts and fears, which spoil our comfort, since there is no excuse for fear when God is the foundation of our trust. A loving parent would be sorely grieved if his child could not trust him; and how ungenerous, how unkind is our conduct when we put so little confidence in our heavenly Father, who has never failed us and who never will. It would be good if doubting was banished from the household of God; but it is to be feared that old Unbelief is as nimble today as when the psalmist asked, "Will the Lord spurn forever, and never again be favorable?"[2] David had not tested the mighty sword of the giant Goliath for long, and yet he said, "There is none like that."[3] He had tried it once in the hour of his youthful victory, and it had proved itself to be of the right metal, and therefore he praised it ever afterwards. Even so should we speak well of our God; there is none like unto Him in the heaven above or the earth beneath. "To whom will you liken me and make me equal, and compare me, that we may be alike?"[4] There is no rock like the rock of Jacob, our enemies themselves being judges. So far from tolerating doubts to live in our hearts, we will take the whole detestable crew, as Elijah did the prophets of Baal, and slay them over the brook; and for a stream to kill them at, we will select the sacred torrent that flows from our Savior's wounded side. We have been in many trials, but we have never yet been placed where we could not find in our God all that we needed. Let us then be encouraged to trust in the Lord forever, assured that His ever-lasting strength will be, as it has been, our deliverance and comfort.

[1] Hebrews 12:2   [2] Psalm 77:7   [3] 1 Samuel 21:9   [4] Isaiah 46:5

WHOEVER LISTENS TO ME WILL DWELL SECURE AND WILL BE AT EASE,
WITHOUT DREAD OF DISASTER. — PROVERBS 1:33

Divine love is clearly observable when it shines in the face of judgments. Fair is that single star that smiles through the gaps in the thunderclouds; bright is the oasis that blooms in the wilderness of sand; so fair and so bright is love in the midst of wrath. When the Israelites provoked the Most High by their continued idolatry, He punished them by withholding both dew and rain, so that their land was visited by a sore famine; but while He did this, He took care that His own chosen ones should be secure. If all other brooks are dry, yet shall there be one reserved for Elijah; and when that fails, God shall still preserve for him a place of sustenance. Not only so, the Lord also had a remnant according to the election of grace, who were hidden by fifties in a cave; and though the whole land was subject to famine, yet these fifties in the cave were fed, and fed from Ahab's table too by His faithful, God-fearing steward, Obadiah.[1] Let us from this draw the inference that come what may, God's people are safe. Let convulsions shake the solid earth, let the skies themselves be torn apart, yet amid the wreck of worlds the believer shall be as secure as in the calmest hour of rest. If God cannot save His people *under* heaven, He will save them *in* heaven. If the world becomes too hot to hold them, then heaven shall be the place of their reception and their safety. Be confident then, when you hear of wars and rumors of wars. Let no agitation distress you; don't be unsettled by fear of evil. Whatever happens on the earth, the believer is sheltered beneath the broad wings of Jehovah and shall be secure. Take your stand upon His promise; rest in His faithfulness, and boldly face the darkest future, for there is nothing in it harmful for you. Your sole concern should be to display to the world the blessedness of taking heed to the voice of wisdom.

❧ EVENING ❧

HOW MANY ARE MY INIQUITIES AND MY SINS? — JOB 13:23

Have you ever really weighed and considered how great the sin of God's people is? Think how heinous is your own transgression, and you will find that not only does a sin here and there tower up like an alp, but that your iniquities are heaped upon each other, as in the old fable of the giants who piled Pelian upon Ossa,[2] mountain upon mountain. What an aggregate of sin there is in the life of one of the most sanctified of God's children! Attempt to multiply this, the sin of one only, by the multitude of the redeemed, "a great multitude that no one could number,"[3] and you will have some conception of the great mass of the guilt of the people for whom Jesus shed His blood. But we arrive at a more adequate idea of the magnitude of sin by the greatness of the remedy provided. It is the blood of Jesus Christ, God's only and well-beloved Son. God's Son! Angels cast their crowns before Him! All the choral symphonies of heaven surround His glorious throne. "God over all, blessed forever. Amen."[4] And yet He takes upon Himself the form of a servant and is scourged and pierced, bruised and torn, and at last slain; nothing but the blood of the incarnate Son of God could make atonement for our offenses. No human mind can adequately estimate the infinite value of the divine sacrifice, for although the sin of God's people is great, the atonement that takes it away is immeasurably greater. Therefore, even when sin rolls in like a flood, and the remembrance of the past is bitter, the believer can still stand before the blazing throne of the great and holy God and cry, "Who is to condemn? Christ Jesus is the one who died— more than that, who was raised."[5] While the recollection of the believer's sin fills him with shame and sorrow, its very darkness serves to show the brightness of mercy; guilt is the dark night in which the fair star of divine love shines with serene splendor.

[1] 1 Kings 18:1-16 [2] The giant sons of Iphimedia who tried to reach Olympus by piling Mt. Pelian on Mt. Ossa (*The Odyssey*). [3] Revelation 7:9 [4] Romans 9:5 [5] Romans 8:34

BROTHERS, PRAY FOR US. — 1 THESSALONIANS 5:25

This one morning in the year we reserved to remind each reader of the importance of praying for ministers, and we earnestly implore every Christian household to heed this request first uttered by Paul and now repeated by us. Brothers, our work is solemnly momentous, involving good or ill to thousands; we deal with souls for God on eternal business, and our word is either a savor of life unto life or of death unto death. A very heavy responsibility rests upon us, and it will be no small mercy if at the last we be found clear of the blood of all men. As officers in Christ's army, we are the special target of the hostility of men and devils; they watch for our faltering and work to trip us at the heels. Our sacred calling involves us in temptations from which you are exempt; above all it too often draws us away from our personal enjoyment of truth into a ministerial and official consideration of it. We meet with many difficult cases, and our wits are at a quandary; we observe very sad backslidings, and our hearts are wounded; we see millions perishing, and our spirits sink. We wish to encourage you by our preaching; we desire to be a blessing to your children; we long to be useful both to saints and sinners. Therefore, dear friends, intercede for us with our God. We are miserable men if we miss the help of your prayers, but happy are we if we live in your supplications. You do not look to us but to our Master for spiritual blessings, and yet how many times has He given those blessings through His ministers; ask then, again and again, that we may be the earthen vessels into which the Lord may put the treasure of the Gospel. We, the whole company of missionaries, ministers, and students, do in the name of Jesus beseech you: *"Brothers, pray for us."*

❧ EVENING ❧

WHEN I PASSED BY YOU . . . I SAID TO YOU . . . "LIVE!" — EZEKIEL 16:6

Believer, consider gratefully this mandate of mercy. Note that this decree of God is *majestic.* In our text we find a sinner with nothing in him but sin, expecting nothing but wrath; but the eternal Lord passes by in His glory. He looks, He pauses, and He pronounces the solitary but royal word, "Live." Only God can speak in this way, dispensing life with a single syllable! Again, this decree is *manifold.* When He says "Live," it includes many things. Here is judicial life. The sinner is ready to be condemned, but the Mighty One says, "Live," and he rises pardoned and absolved. It is spiritual life. We did not know Jesus—our eyes could not see Christ, our ears could not hear His voice—but Jehovah said "Live," and we who were dead in trespasses and sins were quickened. Moreover, it includes glory-life, which is the perfection of spiritual life. "I said to you . . . 'Live,'" and that word rolls on through all the years of time till death comes; and even in the shadows of death, the Lord's voice is still heard—"Live!" In the morning of the resurrection it is that self-same voice that is echoed by the archangel, "Live," and as holy spirits rise to heaven to be blessed forever in the glory of their God, it is in the power of this same word, "Live." Note again, that it is an *irresistible* decree. Saul of Tarsus is on the road to Damascus to arrest the saints of the living God. A voice is heard from heaven, and a light is seen above the brightness of the sun, and Saul is crying out, "Who are you, Lord?"[1] This decree is of *free grace.* When sinners are saved, it is only and solely because God *will* do it to magnify His free, unpurchased, unsought grace. Christians, see your position—debtors to grace; show your gratitude by earnest, Christlike lives; and as God has called you to live, see to it that you do so in sincerity.

[1] Acts 9:5

❧ MORNING ☙

TELL ME WHERE YOUR GREAT STRENGTH LIES. — JUDGES 16:6

Where does the secret strength of faith lie? It lies in the food it feeds on; for faith studies what the promise is—an emanation of divine grace, an overflowing of the great heart of God. And faith says, "My God could not have given this promise except from love and grace; therefore it is quite certain His Word will be fulfilled." Then faith thinks, "*Who gave this promise?*" It considers not so much its greatness as, "Who is the author of it?" She remembers that it is God, who cannot lie—God omnipotent, God immutable—and therefore concludes that the promise must be fulfilled; and onward she proceeds in this firm conviction. She remembers *why the promise was given*—namely, for God's glory—and she feels perfectly sure that God's glory is safe, that He will never stain His own insignia, nor spoil the sparkle of His own crown; and therefore the promise must and will stand. Then faith also considers the amazing *work of Christ* as being a clear proof of the Father's intention to fulfill His word. "He who did not spare his own Son but gave him up for us all, how will he not also with him graciously give us all things?"[1] Moreover, faith looks back upon *the past*, for her battles have strengthened her, and her victories have given her courage. She remembers that God has never failed her, that He never once failed any of His children. She recalls times of great peril when deliverance came, hours of awful need when as her day her strength was found, and she cries, "No, I never will be led to think that He can change and leave His servant now. Thus far the Lord has helped me, and He will help me still." Thus faith views each promise in its connection with the promise-giver and, because she does so, can with assurance say, "Surely goodness and mercy shall follow me all the days of my life!"[2]

❧ EVENING ☙

LEAD ME IN YOUR TRUTH AND TEACH ME, FOR YOU ARE THE GOD OF MY SALVATION; FOR YOU I WAIT ALL THE DAY LONG. — PSALM 25:5

When the believer has begun with trembling feet to walk in the way of the Lord, he still asks to be led onward like a little child upheld by its parent's helping hand, and he yearns to receive further instruction in the alphabet of truth. Experimental teaching is the burden of this prayer. David knew much, but he felt his ignorance and desired to be still in the Lord's school: four times over in two verses he applies for a scholarship in the college of grace. It would be better for many professors if instead of following their own devices and cutting out new paths of thought for themselves, they would inquire for the good old ways of God's own truth and beseech the Holy Ghost to give them sanctified understandings and teachable spirits. "*For you are the God of my salvation.*" Jehovah is the Author and Perfecter of salvation to His people. Reader, is He the God of *your* salvation? Do you find in the Father's election, in the Son's atonement, and in the Spirit's quickening all the grounds of your eternal hopes? If so, you may use this as an argument for obtaining further blessings; if the Lord has ordained to save you, surely He will not refuse to instruct you in His ways. It is a happy thing when we can address the Lord with the confidence that David displays here; it gives us great power in prayer and comfort in trial. "*For you I wait all the day long.*" Patience is the fair handmaid and daughter of faith; we cheerfully wait when we are certain that we shall not wait in vain. It is our duty and our privilege to wait upon the Lord in service, in worship, in expectancy, in trust all the days of our life. Our faith will be tried faith, and if it is of the true kind, it will bear continued trial without yielding. We shall not grow weary of waiting upon God if we remember how long and how graciously He once waited for us.

[1] Romans 8:32 [2] Psalm 23:6

FORGET NOT ALL HIS BENEFITS. — PSALM 103:2

It is a delightful and profitable occupation to mark the hand of God in the lives of ancient saints and to observe His goodness in delivering them, His mercy in pardoning them, and His faithfulness in keeping His covenant with them. But would it not be even more interesting and profitable for us to observe the hand of God in our own lives? Should we not look upon our own history as being at least as full of God, as full of His goodness and of His truth, as much a proof of His faithfulness and veracity as the lives of any of the saints who have gone before? We do our Lord an injustice when we suppose that He performed all His mighty acts and showed Himself strong for those in the early time but does not perform wonders or lay bare His arm for the saints who are now upon the earth. Let us review our own lives. Surely in these we may discover some happy incidents, refreshing to ourselves and glorifying to our God. Have you had no *deliverances*? Have you passed through no rivers, supported by the divine presence? Have you walked through no fires unharmed? Have you had no *manifestations*? Have you had no choice *favors*? The God who gave Solomon the desire of his heart, has He never listened to you and answered your requests? That God of lavish bounty of whom David sang, "who satisfies you with good,"[1] has He never filled *you* up to overflowing? Have you never been made to lie down in green pastures? Have you never been led by the still waters? Surely the goodness of God has been the same to us as to the saints of old. Let us, then, weave His mercies into a song. Let us take the pure gold of thankfulness and the jewels of praise and make them into another crown for the head of Jesus. Let our souls produce music as sweet and as exhilarating as came from David's harp while we praise the Lord whose mercy endures forever.

❧ EVENING ❧
AND GOD SEPARATED THE LIGHT FROM THE DARKNESS. — GENESIS 1:4

A believer has two principles at work within him. In his natural estate he was subject to one principle only, which was darkness; now light has entered, and the two principles disagree. Consider the apostle Paul's words in the seventh chapter of Romans: "I find it to be a law that when I want to do right, evil lies close at hand. For I delight in the law of God, in my inner being, but I see in my members another law waging war against the law of my mind and making me captive to the law of sin that dwells in my members."[2] How is this state of things occasioned? "God separated the light from the darkness." Darkness, by itself, is quiet and undisturbed, but when the Lord sends in light, there is a conflict, for the one is in opposition to the other, a conflict that will never end until the believer is altogether light in the Lord. If there is a division *inside* the individual Christian, there is certain to be *a division outside*. As soon as the Lord gives light to any man, he proceeds to separate himself from the darkness around; he withdraws from a merely worldly religion of outward ceremony, for nothing short of the Gospel of Christ will now satisfy him, and he removes himself from worldly society and frivolous amusements and seeks the company of the saints, for "We know that we have passed out of death into life, because we love the brothers."[3] The light gathers to itself, and the darkness to itself. What God has separated, let us never try to unite; but as Christ went outside the camp, bearing His reproach, let us come out from the ungodly and be a special people. He was holy, harmless, undefiled, separate from sinners; and as He was, so we are to be nonconformists to the world, dissenting from all sin, and distinguished from the rest of mankind by our likeness to our Master.

[1] Psalm 103:5 [2] Romans 7:21-23 [3] 1 John 3:14

❧ MORNING ❧

What is meant by our being citizens in heaven? It means that we are *under heaven's government.* Christ, the King of Heaven, reigns in our hearts; our daily prayer is, "Your will be done, on earth as it is in heaven."[1] The proclamations issued from the throne of glory are freely received by us: The decrees of the Great King we cheerfully obey. Then as citizens of the New Jerusalem, *we share heaven's honors.* The glory that belongs to beatified saints belongs to us, for we are already sons of God, already princes of the blood imperial; already we wear the spotless robe of Jesus' righteousness; already we have angels for our servants, saints for our companions, Christ for our Brother, God for our Father, and a crown of immortality for our reward. We share the honors of citizenship, for we have come to the general assembly and the Church of the firstborn, whose names are written in heaven. As citizens, we have *common rights to all the property of heaven.* Ours are its gates of pearl and walls of chrysolite, ours the azure light of the city that needs no candle nor light of the sun, ours the river of the water of life and the twelve kinds of fruit that grow on the trees planted on its banks; there is nothing in heaven that does not belong to us. "The present or the future"[2]—all is ours. Also as citizens of heaven we *enjoy its delights.* Do they rejoice in heaven over sinners that repent—prodigals who have returned? So do we. Do they chant the glories of triumphant grace? We do the same. Do they cast their crowns at Jesus' feet? Such honors we have we cast there too. Are they charmed with His smile? It is just as sweet to us who live below. Do they look forward, waiting for His second advent? We also look and long for His appearing. If, then, we are *citizens of heaven,* let our walk and actions be consistent with our high dignity.

❧ EVENING ❧

The evening was "darkness," and the morning was "light," and yet *the two together are called by the name that is given to the light alone!* This is somewhat remarkable, but it has an exact analogy in spiritual experience. In every believer there is darkness and light, and yet he is not to be named a sinner because there is sin in him, but he is to be named a saint because he possesses some degree of holiness. This will be a most comforting thought to those who are mourning their infirmities and who ask, "Can I be a child of God while there is so much darkness in me?" Yes; like the "day," you do not take your name from the evening, but from the morning; and you are spoken of in the Word of God as if you were even now perfectly holy, as you will be soon. You are called the child of light, even though there is darkness in you still. You are named after what is the predominating quality in the sight of God, which will one day be the only principal remaining. Notice that *the evening comes first.* Naturally we are darkness first in order of time, and the gloom is often first in our mournful apprehension, driving us to cry out in deep humiliation, "God, be merciful to me, a sinner."[3] The place of the morning is second; it dawns when grace overcomes nature. It is a blessed maxim of John Bunyan, "That which is last, lasts forever." That which is first yields in due season to the last; but nothing comes after the last. So though you are naturally darkness, once you become light in the Lord, there is no evening to follow; "your sun shall no more go down."[4] The first day in this life is an evening and a morning; but the second day, when we shall be with God forever, shall be a day with no evening, but one, sacred, high, eternal noon.

[1] Matthew 6:10 [2] 1 Corinthians 3:22 [3] Luke 18:13 [4] Isaiah 60:20

JULY 11   ❧ MORNING ❧

AFTER YOU HAVE SUFFERED A LITTLE WHILE, THE GOD OF ALL
GRACE . . . WILL HIMSELF RESTORE, CONFIRM, STRENGTHEN,
AND ESTABLISH YOU. — 1 PETER 5:10

You have seen the arch of heaven as it spans the plain: Glorious are its colors, and rare its hues. It is beautiful, but, sadly, it passes away, and the rainbow is no more. The fair colors give way to the fleecy clouds, and the sky is no longer brilliant with the tints of heaven. It is not *established*. How can it be? A glorious show made up of transitory sunbeams and passing raindrops—how can it remain? The graces of the Christian character must not resemble the rainbow in its transitory beauty but, on the contrary, must be established, settled, abiding. Seek, O believer, that every good thing you have may be an abiding thing. May your character not be a writing upon the sand, but an inscription upon the rock! May your faith be no "baseless fabric of a vision," but may it be built of material able to endure that awful fire that shall consume the wood, hay, and stubble of the hypocrite. May you be rooted and grounded in love. May your convictions be deep, your love real, your desires sincere. May your whole life be so settled and established that all the blasts of hell and all the storms of earth will never be able to remove you. But notice how this blessing of being established in the faith is gained. The apostle's words point us to *suffering* as the means employed— "*After you have suffered a little while.*" It is of no use to hope that we shall be well rooted if no rough winds pass over us. Those old gnarlings on the root of the oak tree and those strange twistings of the branches all tell of the many storms that have swept over it, and they are also indicators of the depth into which the roots have forced their way. So the Christian is made strong and firmly rooted by all the trials and storms of life. Do not shrink then from the tempestuous winds of trial, but take comfort, believing that by their rough discipline God is fulfilling this benediction to you.

❧ EVENING ❧

TELL YOUR CHILDREN OF IT, AND LET YOUR CHILDREN TELL
THEIR CHILDREN, AND THEIR CHILDREN TO
ANOTHER GENERATION. — JOEL 1:3

In this simple way, by God's grace, a living testimony for truth is always to be kept alive in the land: The beloved of the Lord are to hand down their witness for the Gospel and the covenant to their heirs, and these again to their next descendants. This is our *first* duty; we are to begin at the family hearth: He is a bad preacher who does not commence his ministry at home. The heathen are to be sought by all means, and the highways and hedges are to be searched, but home has a prior claim, and woe to those who reverse the order of the Lord's arrangements. To teach our children is a *personal* duty; we cannot delegate it to Sunday school teachers or other friendly helpers. These can assist us but cannot deliver us from the sacred obligation; substitutes and sponsors are wicked devices in this case: Mothers and fathers must, like Abraham, command their households in the fear of God and talk with their offspring concerning the wondrous works of the Most High. Parental teaching is a *natural* duty. Who is better fitted to look after the child's well-being than those who are the authors of his actual being? To neglect the instruction of our children is worse than brutish. Family religion is *necessary* for the nation, for the family itself, and for the church of God. By a thousand plots empty religion is secretly advancing in our land, and one of the most effectual means for resisting its inroads is routinely neglected—namely, the instruction of our children in the faith. It is time for parents to awaken to a sense of the importance of this matter. It is a pleasant duty to talk of Jesus to our sons and daughters, and the more so because it has often proved to be an *accepted* work, for God has saved the children through the parents' prayers and admonitions. May every house into which this volume shall come honor the Lord and receive His smile.

    ❧   MORNING   ❧

BELOVED IN GOD THE FATHER. . . . SANCTIFIED IN CHRIST JESUS. . . .
IN THE SANCTIFICATION OF THE SPIRIT.
— JUDE 1; 1 CORINTHIANS 1:2; 1 PETER 1:2

Consider the union of the three Divine Persons in all their gracious acts. How unwisely do those believers talk who make preferences in the Persons of the Trinity, who think of Jesus as if He were the embodiment of everything lovely and gracious, while the Father they regard as severely just but destitute of kindness. Equally wrong are those who magnify the decree of the Father and the atonement of the Son so as to depreciate the work of the Spirit. In works of grace none of the Persons of the Trinity act separately from the rest. They are as united in their works as in Their essence. In Their love toward the chosen They are one, and in the actions that flow from that great central source They are still undivided. Notice this especially in the matter of sanctification. While it is right to speak of sanctification as the work of the Spirit, yet we must make sure that we do not view it as if the Father and the Son were not involved. It is correct to speak of sanctification as the work of the Father, of the Son, and of the Spirit. Still God says, "Let *us* make man in our image, after our likeness,"[1] and so we are "*his* workmanship, created in Christ Jesus for good works, which God prepared beforehand, that we should walk in them."[2] See the value that God sets upon real holiness, since the three Persons in the Trinity are represented as co-working to produce a Church without "spot or wrinkle or any such thing."[3] And you, believer, as the follower of Christ, must also set a high value on holiness—upon purity of life and godliness of conversation. Value the blood of Christ as the foundation of your hope, and never speak disparagingly of the work of the Spirit. This day let us live in such a way as to manifest the work of the Triune God in us.

❧   EVENING   ❧

HIS HEAVENLY KINGDOM. — 2 TIMOTHY 4:18

The city of the great King is a place of *active service*. Ransomed spirits serve Him day and night in His temple. They never cease to fulfill the good pleasure of their King. They always rest, so far as ease and freedom from care is concerned, and never rest, in the sense of indolence or inactivity. Jerusalem the golden is the place of *communion* with all the people of God. We shall sit with Abraham, Isaac, and Jacob in eternal fellowship. We shall hold high converse with the noble host of the elect, all reigning with Him who by His love and His powerful arm has brought them safely home. We shall not sing solos, but in chorus shall we praise our King. Heaven is a place of *victory realized*. Whenever, Christian, you have achieved a victory over your lusts—whenever after hard struggling, you have laid a temptation dead at your feet—you have in that hour a foretaste of the joy that awaits you when the Lord shall soon tread Satan under your feet, and you shall find yourself more than a conqueror through Him who has loved you. Paradise is a place of *security*. When you enjoy the full assurance of faith, you have the pledge of that glorious security that shall be yours when you are a perfect citizen of the heavenly Jerusalem. O my sweet home, Jerusalem, happy harbor of my soul! Thanks, even now, to Him whose love has taught me to long for you; but louder thanks in eternity, when I shall possess you.

My soul has tasted of the grapes,
And now it longs to go
Where my dear Lord His vineyard keeps
And all the clusters grow.

Upon the true and living vine,
My famish'd soul would feast,
And banquet on the fruit divine,
An everlasting guest.

[1] Genesis 1:26   [2] Ephesians 2:10   [3] Ephesians 5:27

Anger is not always or necessarily sinful, but it has such a tendency to run wild that whenever it displays itself, we should be quick to question its character, with this inquiry, "Do you do well to be angry?" It may be that we can answer, "Yes." Very frequently anger is the madman's firebrand, but sometimes it is Elijah's fire from heaven. We do well when we are angry with sin, because of the wrong that it commits against our good and gracious God; or with ourselves because we remain so foolish after so much divine instruction; or with others when the sole cause of anger is the evil that they do. He who is not angry at transgression becomes a partaker in it. Sin is a loathsome and hateful thing, and no renewed heart can patiently endure it. God himself is angry with the wicked every day, and it is written in His Word, "O you who love the LORD, hate evil."[1] Far more frequently it is to be feared that our anger is not commendable or even justifiable, and then we must answer, "No." Why should we be fretful with children, passionate with servants, and wrathful with companions? Is such anger honorable to our Christian profession or glorifying to God? Is it not the old evil heart seeking to gain dominion, and should we not resist it with all the might of our newborn nature? Many professors give way to temper as though it were useless to attempt resistance; but let the believer remember that he must be a conqueror in every point, or else he cannot be crowned. If we cannot control our tempers, what has grace done for us? Someone told Mr. Jay that grace was often grafted on a crab-stump. "Yes," he said, "but the fruit will not be crabs." We must not make natural infirmity an excuse for sin, but we must fly to the cross and pray the Lord to crucify our tempers, and renew us in gentleness and meekness after His own image.

❨ EVENING ❩

It is impossible for any human speech to express the full meaning of this delightful phrase, "*God is for me.*" He was for us before the worlds were made. He was for us or He would not have given His well-beloved Son; He was for us when He smote the Only-begotten and laid the full weight of His wrath upon Him—He was for *us*, though He was against *Him*. He was "for us" when we were ruined in the Fall—He loved us notwithstanding all. He was for us when we were rebels against Him and with a high hand were bidding Him defiance. He was for us or He would not have brought us humbly to seek His face. He has been for us in many struggles; we have been summoned to encounter hosts of dangers; we have been assailed by temptations from without and within—how could we have remained unharmed to this hour if He had not been for us? He is for us with all the infinity of His being, with all the omnipotence of His love, with all the infallibility of His wisdom. Arrayed in all His divine attributes, He is for us—eternally and immutably for us; for us when the heavens shall be rolled up like a worn-out robe; for us throughout eternity. And because He is for us, the voice of prayer will always ensure His help. "*Then my enemies will turn back in the day when I call.*" This is no uncertain hope, but a well-grounded assurance—"*this I know.*" I will direct my prayer unto You and will look up for the answer, assured that it will come and that my enemies shall be defeated, for "God is for me." O believer, how happy you are with the King of kings on your side! How safe with such a Protector! How sure your cause pleaded by such an Advocate! If God be for you, who can be against you?

[1] Psalm 97:10

IF YOU WIELD YOUR TOOL ON IT YOU PROFANE IT. — EXODUS 20:25

God's altar was to be built of unhewn stones, that no trace of human skill or labor might be seen upon it. Human wisdom delights to trim and arrange the doctrines of the cross into a system more artificial and more congenial to the depraved tastes of fallen nature; instead, however, of improving the Gospel carnal wisdom pollutes it, until it becomes another gospel and not the truth of God at all. All alterations and amendments of the Lord's own Word are defilements and pollutions. The proud heart of man is very anxious to have a hand in the justification of the soul before God; preparations for Christ are dreamed of, humblings and repentings are trusted in, good works are put forth, natural ability is much vaunted, and by all means the attempt is made to lift up human tools upon the divine altar. It would be best if sinners would remember that so far from perfecting the Savior's work, their carnal confidences only pollute and dishonor it. The Lord alone must be exalted in the work of atonement, and not a single mark of man's chisel or hammer will be endured. There is an inherent blasphemy in seeking to add to what Christ Jesus in His dying moments declared to be finished or to improve that in which the Lord Jehovah finds perfect satisfaction. Trembling sinner, away with your tools, and fall upon your knees in humble supplication; accept the Lord Jesus to be the altar of your atonement, and rest in Him alone.

Many professors may take warning from this morning's text as to the doctrines that they believe. There is among Christians far too much inclination to square and reconcile the truths of revelation. This is a form of irreverence and unbelief; let us strive against it and receive truth as we find it, rejoicing that the doctrines of the Word are unhewn stones, and so are all the more fit to build an altar for the Lord.

✧ EVENING ✧

TOWARD THE DAWN . . . MARY MAGDALENE . . . WENT TO SEE THE TOMB.
— MATTHEW 28:1

Let us learn from Mary Magdalene how to obtain fellowship with the Lord Jesus. Notice how she sought. She sought the Savior *very early* in the morning. If you can wait for Christ and be patient in the hope of having fellowship with Him at some distant season, you will never have fellowship at all; for the heart that is fitted for communion is a hungering and a thirsting heart. She sought Him also with *very great boldness*. Other disciples fled from the tomb, for they trembled and were amazed; but Mary, it is said, "stood"[1] at the tomb. If you would have Christ with you, seek Him boldly. Let nothing hold you back. Defy the world. Press on where others flee. She sought Christ *faithfully*—she stood *at the tomb*. Some find it hard to stand by a living Savior, but she stood by a dead one. Let us seek Christ after this mode, cleaving to the very least thing that has to do with Him, remaining faithful though all others should forsake Him. Note further, she sought Jesus *earnestly*—she stood "weeping." Those teardrops were as spells that led the Savior captive and made Him come forth and show Himself to her. If you desire Jesus' presence, weep after it! If you cannot be happy unless He come and say to you, "You are My beloved," you will soon hear His voice. Lastly, she sought the Savior *only*. What did she care about angels? She turned herself back from them; her search was only for her Lord. If Christ is your one and only love, if your heart has cast out all rivals, you will soon enjoy the comfort of His presence. Mary Magdalene sought thus *because she loved much*. Let us arouse ourselves to the same intensity of affection; let our heart, like Mary's, be full of Christ, and our love, like hers, will be satisfied with nothing short of Himself. O Lord, reveal Yourself to us this evening!

[1] John 20:11

FIRE SHALL BE KEPT BURNING ON THE ALTAR CONTINUALLY;
IT SHALL NOT GO OUT. — LEVITICUS 6:13

Keep the altar of *private prayer* burning. This is the very life of all piety. The sanctuary and family altars borrow their fires here; therefore let this burn well. Secret devotion is the very essence, evidence, and barometer of vital and experimental [experiential] religion.

Burn here the fat of your sacrifices. Let your closet seasons be, if possible, regular, frequent, and undisturbed. Effectual prayer avails much. Have you nothing to pray for? Let us suggest the church, the ministry, your own soul, your children, your relations, your neighbors, your country, and the cause of God and truth throughout the world. Let us examine ourselves on this important matter. Do we engage with lukewarmness in private devotion? Is the fire of devotion burning dimly in our hearts? Do the chariot wheels drag heavily? If so, let us be alarmed at this sign of decay. Let us go with weeping, and ask for the Spirit of grace and of supplications. Let us set apart special seasons for extraordinary prayer. For if this fire should be smothered beneath the ashes of a worldly conformity, it will dim the fire on the family altar and lessen our influence both in the church and in the world.

The text will also apply to *the altar of the heart*. This is a golden altar indeed. God loves to see the hearts of His people glowing toward Himself. Let us give to God our hearts, all blazing with love, and seek His grace, that the fire may never be quenched, for it will not burn if the Lord does not keep it burning. Many foes will attempt to extinguish it; but if the unseen hand behind the wall pours on the sacred oil, it will blaze higher and higher. Let us use texts of Scripture as fuel for our heart's fire; they are live coals. Let us attend to sermons, but above all, let us be much alone with Jesus.

❧ EVENING ☙

HE APPEARED FIRST TO MARY MAGDALENE. — MARK 16:9

Jesus "appeared first to Mary Magdalene," probably not only on account of her great love and persevering seeking, but because, as the context intimates, she had been *a special trophy of Christ's delivering power*. Learn from this that the greatness of our sin before conversion should not make us imagine that we may not be specially favored with the very highest grade of fellowship. She was one who had left all to become *a constant attendant on the Savior*. He was her first, her chief, object. Many who were on Christ's side did not take up Christ's cross; *she* did. *She spent her substance in relieving His wants*. If we would see much of Christ, let us *serve* Him. Tell me who they are who sit most often under the banner of His love and drink the deepest from the cup of communion, and I am sure they will be those who give most, who serve best, and who abide closest to the bleeding heart of their dear Lord. But notice *how* Christ revealed Himself to this sorrowing one—by a *word*: "Mary."[1] It needed but one word *in His voice*, and at once she knew Him. *Her heart expressed allegiance by another word*, but her heart was too full to say more. That one word would naturally be the most fitting for the occasion. It implies obedience. She said, "*Master*" [KJV]. There is no state of mind in which this confession of allegiance will be too cold. When your spirit glows most with the heavenly fire, then you will say, "I am your servant. . . . You have loosed my bonds."[2] If you can say, "Master," if you feel that His will is your will, then you stand in a happy, holy place. He must have said, "Mary," or else you could not have said, "Rabboni," "Master." See, then, from all this how Christ honors those who honor Him, how love draws our Beloved, how it needs but one word of His to turn our weeping to rejoicing, how His presence makes the heart's sunshine.

[1] John 20:16   [2] Psalm 116:16

❧ MORNING ❧

Work hard to maintain a sense of your entire dependence upon the Lord's good will and pleasure for the continuance of your richest enjoyments. Never try to live on the old manna, nor seek to find help in Egypt. All must come from Jesus or you are undone forever. Old anointings will not suffice to impart unction to your spirit; your head must have fresh oil poured upon it from the golden horn of the sanctuary, or it will cease from its glory. Today you may be upon the summit of the mount of God, but He who has put you there must keep you there or you will sink far more speedily than you imagine. Your mountain only stands firm when He settles it in its place; if He hides His face, you will soon be troubled. If the Savior should see fit, there is not a window through which you see the light of heaven that He could not darken in an instant. Joshua bade the sun stand still, but Jesus can shroud it in total darkness. He can withdraw the joy of your heart, the light of your eyes, and the strength of your life; in His hand your comforts lie, and at His will they can depart from you. Our Lord is determined that we shall feel and recognize this hourly dependence, for He only permits us to pray for "daily bread," and only promises that our strength will be equal to our days. Is it not best for us that it should be so, that we may often repair to His throne and constantly be reminded of His love? Oh, how rich the grace that supplies us so continually and does not refrain itself because of our ingratitude! The golden shower never ceases; the cloud of blessing tarries evermore above our dwelling. O Lord Jesus, we would bow at Your feet, conscious of our utter inability to do anything without You, and in every favor that we are privileged to receive, we would adore Your blessed name and acknowledge Your unexhausted love.

❧ EVENING ❧

A selfish man in trouble is exceedingly hard to comfort, because the springs of his comfort are entirely within himself, and when he is sad all his springs are dry. But a large-hearted man full of Christian generosity has other springs from which to supply himself with comfort beside those that lie within. He can go to his God first of all and there find abundant help; and he can discover arguments for consolation in things relating to the world at large, to his country, and, above all, to the Church. David in this Psalm was exceedingly sorrowful; he wrote, "I am like an owl of the waste places; I lie awake; I am like a lonely sparrow on the housetop."[1] The only way in which he could comfort himself was in the reflection that God would arise and have mercy upon Zion. Though *he* was sad, yet Zion should prosper; however low his own estate, yet Zion would arise. Christian man, learn to comfort yourself in God's gracious dealing toward the Church. That which is so dear to your Master, should it not also be supremely precious to you? Although your path be dark, can you not cheer your heart with the triumphs of His cross and the spread of His truth? Our own personal troubles are forgotten while we look not only upon what God *has* done and is doing for Zion, but on the glorious things He *will yet do* for His Church. Try this approach, O believer, whenever you are sad of heart and in heaviness of spirit: Forget yourself and your little concerns, and seek the welfare and prosperity of Zion. When you kneel in prayer to God, limit not your petition to the narrow circle of your own life, tried though it be, but send out your longing prayers for the church's prosperity. "Pray for the peace of Jerusalem,"[2] and your own soul shall be refreshed.

[1] Psalm 102:6-7 [2] Psalm 122:6

FOR WE KNOW, BROTHERS LOVED BY GOD, THAT HE HAS CHOSEN YOU.
— 1 THESSALONIANS 1:4

Many persons want to know their election before they look to Christ, but that is not possible; it is only to be discovered by "looking to Jesus."[1] If you desire to ascertain your own election, after the following manner shall you assure your heart before God. Do you feel yourself to be a lost, guilty sinner? Go straight to the cross of Christ, and tell Jesus so, and tell Him that you have read in the Bible, "Whoever comes to me I will never cast out."[2] Tell Him that He has said, "The saying is trustworthy and deserving of full acceptance, that Christ Jesus came into the world to save sinners."[3] Look to Jesus and believe on Him, and you shall make proof of your election directly, for as surely as you believe, you are elect. If you will give yourself wholly up to Christ and trust Him, then you are one of God's chosen ones; but if you stop and say, "I want to know first whether I am elect," you do not know what you are asking. Go to Jesus, just as you are, in all your guilt. Leave all curious inquiry about election alone. Go straight to Christ, and hide in His wounds, and you shall know your election. The assurance of the Holy Spirit shall be given to you, so that you shall be able to say, "I know whom I have believed, and I am convinced that he is able to guard until that Day what has been entrusted to me."[4] Christ was at the everlasting council— He can tell you whether you were chosen or not; but you cannot find it out in any other way. Go and put your trust in Him, and His answer will be, "I have loved you with an everlasting love; therefore I have continued my faithfulness to you."[5] There will be no doubt about His having chosen *you* when you have chosen *Him*.

> *Sons we are through God's election,*
> *Who in Jesus Christ believe.*

❧ EVENING ☙

LET NOT ONE OF THEM ESCAPE. — 1 KINGS 18:40

When the prophet Elijah had received the answer to his prayer, and the fire from heaven had consumed the sacrifice in the presence of all the people, he called upon the assembled Israelites to take the priests of Baal and sternly cried, "Let not one of them escape." He took them all down to the brook Kishon and slew them there. So must it be with our sins—they are all doomed; not one must be preserved. Our darling sin must die. Do not spare it because it cries. Strike though it be as dear as a beloved son. Strike, for God struck at sin when it was laid upon His own Son. With stern unflinching purpose you must condemn to death that sin that was once the idol of your heart. Do you ask how you are to accomplish this? Jesus will be your power. You have grace to overcome sin, given you in the covenant of grace; you have strength to win the victory in the crusade against inward lusts because Christ Jesus has promised to be with you even unto the end. If you would triumph over darkness, set yourself in the presence of the Sun of Righteousness. There is no place so well adapted for the discovery of sin and recovery from its power and guilt as the immediate presence of God. Job never knew how to get rid of sin half as well as he did when his eye of faith rested upon God, and then he abhorred himself and repented in dust and ashes. The fine gold of the Christian is often becoming dim. We need the sacred fire to consume the dross. Let us fly to our God. He is a consuming fire; He will not consume our spirit, but our sins. Let the goodness of God excite us to a sacred jealousy and to a holy revenge against those iniquities that are hateful in His sight. Go forth to battle in His strength and utterly destroy the accursed crew: "Let not one of them escape."

[1] Hebrews 12:2   [2] John 6:37   [3] 1 Timothy 1:15   [4] 2 Timothy 1:12   [5] Jeremiah 31:3

❧ MORNING ❧

The camp of Dan brought up the rear when the armies of Israel were on the march. The Danites occupied *the hindmost place*, but their position wasn't important, since they were as truly part of the company as were the foremost tribes. They followed the same fiery cloudy pillar, ate of the same manna, drank of the same spiritual rock, and journeyed to the same inheritance. Come, my heart, cheer up, even though last and least; it is your privilege to be in the army and to fare as they fare who lead the expedition. Someone must be at the rear in honor and esteem, someone must do menial work for Jesus, and why shouldn't it be me? In a poor village among an ignorant peasantry or in a back street among degraded sinners, I will work on and take my assigned place at the rear.

The Danites occupied *a very useful place*. Stragglers have to be picked up on the march, and lost property has to be gathered from the field. Fiery spirits may dash forward over untrodden paths to learn fresh truth and win more souls to Jesus; but some of a more conservative spirit may be well engaged in reminding the church of her ancient faith and restoring her fainting sons. Every position has its duties, and the slowly moving children of God will find their peculiar state one in which they may be eminently a blessing to the whole company.

The rear guard is *a place of danger*. There are foes behind us as well as before us. Attacks may come from any quarter. We read that Amalek fell upon Israel and slew some who were at the rear. The experienced Christian will find much work for his weapons in aiding those poor doubting, desponding, wavering souls who are slowest in faith, knowledge, and joy. These must not be left unaided, and therefore let it be the business of well-taught saints to bear their standards among the rear guard. My soul, watch tenderly to help the stragglers today.

❧ EVENING ❧

Locusts always keep their rank, and although their number is legion, they do not crowd upon each other, so as to throw their columns into confusion. This remarkable fact in natural history shows how thoroughly the Lord has infused the spirit of order into His universe, since the smallest animate creatures are as much controlled by it as are the rolling spheres or the angelic throng. It would be wise for believers to be ruled by the same influence in all their spiritual life. *In their Christian graces* no one virtue should usurp the sphere of another or feed off the rest for its own support. Affection must not smother honesty, courage must not elbow weakness out of the field, modesty must not jostle energy, and patience must not slaughter resolution. So also with *our duties*. One must not interfere with another; public usefulness must not injure private piety; church work must not push family worship into a corner. It is wrong to offer God one duty stained with the blood of another. Each thing is beautiful in its season, but not otherwise. The same rule applies to *our personal position*. We must take care to know our place, take it, and keep to it. We must minister as the Spirit has given us ability, and not intrude upon our fellow servant's domain. Our Lord Jesus taught us not to covet the high places, but to be willing to be the least among our brothers and sisters. Let us say no to an envious, ambitious spirit; let us feel the force of the Master's command and do as He bids us, keeping in step with the rest of the company. Tonight let us see whether we are keeping the unity of the Spirit in the bonds of peace, and let our prayer be that in all the churches of the Lord Jesus peace and order may prevail.

God's great design in all His works is the manifestation of His own glory. Any aim less than this would be unworthy of Himself. But how shall the glory of God be manifested to such fallen creatures as we are? Man's eye is not single in its focus; he always has a side glance toward his own honor, has too high an estimate of his own powers, and so is not qualified to behold the glory of the Lord. It is clear, then, that self must stand out of the way, that there may be room for God to be exalted. And this is the reason why He often brings His people into straits and difficulties, that, being made conscious of their own folly and weakness, they may be fitted to behold the majesty of God when He comes to work their deliverance. He whose life is one even and smooth path will see but little of the glory of the Lord, for he has few occasions of self-emptying and hence but little fitness for being filled with the revelation of God. They who navigate little streams and shallow creeks know but little of the God of tempests; but they who are "doing business on the great waters"[1] see "his wondrous works in the deep."[2] Among the huge waves of bereavement, poverty, temptation, and reproach, we learn the power of Jehovah, because we feel the littleness of man. Thank God, then, if you have been led by a rough road: It is this that has given you your experience of God's greatness and loving-kindness. Your troubles have enriched you with a wealth of knowledge to be gained by no other means: Your trials have been the crevice of the rock in which Jehovah has set you, as He did His servant Moses, that you might behold His glory as it passed by. Praise God that you have not been left to the darkness and ignorance that continued prosperity might have involved, but that in the great fight of affliction you have been qualified for the outshinings of His glory in His wonderful dealings with you.

⚙ EVENING ⚙
A BRUISED REED HE WILL NOT BREAK, AND
A SMOLDERING WICK HE WILL NOT QUENCH. — MATTHEW 12:20

What is weaker than the bruised reed or the smoldering wick? *A reed* that grows in the marshland—let a wild duck land on it, and it snaps; let but the foot of man brush against it, and it is bruised and broken; every wind that flits across the river moves it to and fro. You can conceive of nothing more frail or brittle or whose existence is more in jeopardy than a bruised reed. Then look at the smoldering wick—what is it? It has a spark within it, it is true, but it is almost smothered; an infant's breath might blow it out; nothing has a more precarious existence than its flame. *Weak things* are here described; yet Jesus says of them, "The smoldering wick I will not quench; the bruised reed I will not break." Some of God's children are made strong to do mighty works for Him; God has His Samsons here and there who can pull up Gaza's gates and carry them to the top of the hill. He has a few mighties who are lionlike men, but the majority of His people are a timid, trembling race. They are like starlings, frightened at every passerby, a little fearful flock. If temptation comes, they are taken like birds in a snare; if trial threatens, they are ready to faint. Their frail craft is tossed up and down by every wave; they drift along like a seabird on the crest of the billows—weak things, without strength, without wisdom, without foresight. Yet, weak as they are, and *because* they are so weak, they have this promise made especially to them. Herein is grace and graciousness! Herein is love and loving-kindness! How it opens to us the compassion of Jesus—so gentle, tender, considerate! We need never shrink back from *His* touch. We need never fear a harsh word from *Him*; though He might well chide us for our weakness, He rebukes not. Bruised reeds shall have no blows from Him, and the smoldering wick no damping frowns.

[1] Psalm 107:23   [2] Psalm 107:24

THE GUARANTEE OF OUR INHERITANCE. — EPHESIANS 1:14

Oh, what enlightenment, what joys, what consolation, what delight of heart is experienced by that man who has learned to feed on Jesus, and on Jesus alone. Yet the realization that we have of Christ's preciousness is, in this life, imperfect at best. As an old writer says, "'Tis but a taste!" We have tasted "that the LORD is good,"[1] but we do not yet know *how* good and gracious He is, although what we know of His sweetness makes us long for more. We have enjoyed the firstfruits of the Spirit, and they have set us hungering and thirsting for the fullness of the heavenly vintage. We groan within ourselves, waiting for the adoption. *Here* we are like Israel in the wilderness, who had but one cluster from the vine; *there* we shall be in the vineyard. Here we see the manna falling small, like coriander seed; but there shall we eat the bread of heaven and the old corn of the kingdom. We are but beginners now in spiritual education, for although we have learned the first letters of the alphabet, we cannot read words yet, much less can we put sentences together. But as one says, "He that has been in heaven but five minutes knows more than the general assembly of divines on earth." We have many unfulfilled desires at present, but soon every wish shall be satisfied, and all our powers shall find the sweetest employment in that eternal world of joy. O Christian, anticipate heaven for a few years. Within a very little time you will be rid of all your trials and your troubles. Your eyes now suffused with tears shall weep no longer. You will gaze in ineffable rapture upon the splendor of Him who sits upon the throne. Better still, you shall sit upon His throne. The triumph of His glory shall be shared by you; His crown, His joy, His paradise—these will be yours, and you will be co-heir with Him who is the heir of all things.

❧ EVENING ❧

AND NOW WHAT DO YOU GAIN BY GOING TO EGYPT
TO DRINK THE WATERS OF THE NILE? — JEREMIAH 2:18

By different miracles, by various mercies, by strange deliverances Jehovah had proved Himself to be worthy of Israel's trust. Yet they broke down the hedges with which God had enclosed them as a sacred garden; they forsook their own true and living God and followed after false gods. Constantly the Lord reproved them for this infatuation, and our text displays God's remonstrating with them, "And now what do you gain by going to Egypt to drink the waters of the Nile?" "Why are you wandering and leaving your own cool stream? Why do you forsake Jerusalem and turn aside to the wasteland? Why are you so strangely set on mischief that you cannot be content with what is good and healthy, but instead chase after what is evil and deceitful?" Is there not here a word of exposition and warning to the Christian? O true believer, called by grace and washed in the precious blood of Jesus, you have tasted a better drink than the muddy river of this world's pleasure. You have fellowship with Christ; you have obtained the joy of seeing Jesus and resting in His loving embrace. Do the trifles, the songs, the honors, the merriment of this earth content you after that? Have you eaten the bread of angels, and can you live on scraps? Good Rutherford once said, "I have tasted of Christ's own manna, and it has put my mouth out of taste for the brown bread of this world's joys." I think it should be so with you. If you are wandering after the waters of Egypt, O return quickly to the one living fountain: The waters of the Nile may be sweet to the Egyptians, but they will prove only bitterness to you. What have you to do with them? *Jesus asks you this question this evening*—what will you answer Him?

[1] Psalm 34:8

SHE WAGS HER HEAD BEHIND YOU—THE DAUGHTER OF JERUSALEM.
— ISAIAH 37:22

Reassured by the Word of the Lord, the poor trembling citizens of Zion grew bold and shook their heads at Sennacherib's boastful threats. Strong faith enables the servants of God to look with calm contempt upon their most haughty foes. *We know that our enemies are attempting impossibilities.* They seek to destroy eternal life, which cannot die while Jesus lives—to overthrow the citadel, against which the gates of hell shall not prevail. They kick against the goads to their own wounding and defiantly charge against God to their own hurt.

We know their weakness. What are they but men? And what is man but a worm? They roar and swell like waves of the sea, foaming out their own shame. When the Lord arises, they shall fly as chaff before the wind and be consumed as crackling thorns. Their utter powerlessness to do damage to the cause of God and His truth may make the weakest soldiers in Zion's ranks laugh them to scorn.

Above all, *we know that the Most High is with us,* and when He clothes Himself in armor, where are His enemies? If He comes forth from His place, the fragments of the earth will not long contend with their Maker. His rod of iron shall dash them in pieces like a potter's vessel, and their very remembrance shall perish from the earth. Away, then, all fears—the kingdom is safe in the King's hands. Let us shout for joy, for the Lord reigns, and His foes shall be as straw for compost.

> As true as God's own word is true;
> Nor earth, nor hell, with all their crew,
> Against us shall prevail.
> A jest, and byword, are they grown;
> God is with us, we are his own,
> Our victory cannot fail.

❧ E V E N I N G ✍

WHY DO I GO MOURNING? — PSALM 42:9

Can you answer this, believer? Can you find any reason why you are so often mourning instead of rejoicing? Why yield to gloomy anticipations? Who told you that the night would never end in day? Who told you that the sea of circumstances would ebb out till there should be nothing left but long stretches of the mud of horrible poverty? Who told you that the winter of your discontent would proceed from frost to frost, from snow and ice and hail to deeper snow and yet more heavy tempest of despair? Don't you know that day follows night, that flood comes after ebb, that spring and summer succeed winter? Be full of hope! Hope forever! For God does not fail you. Do you not know that God loves you in the midst of all this? Mountains, when in darkness hidden, are as real as in day, and God's love is as true to you now as it was in your brightest moments. No father chastens always. The Lord hates the rod as much as you do; He only cares to use it for that reason that would make you willing to receive it—namely, it brings about your lasting good. You will yet climb Jacob's ladder with the angels and behold Him who sits at the top of it—your covenant God. You will yet, amidst the splendors of eternity, forget the trials of time or only remember them to bless the God who led you through them and works your lasting good by them. Come, sing in the midst of tribulation. Rejoice even while passing through the furnace. Make the wilderness blossom like the rose! Cause the desert to ring with your exulting joys, for these light afflictions will soon be over, and then, forever with the Lord, your bliss shall never wane.

> Faint not nor fear, His arms are near,
> He changeth not, and thou art dear;
> Only believe and you shalt see,
> That Christ is all in all to thee.

Christ Jesus is joined unto His people in marriage-union. In love He espoused His Church as a chaste virgin, long before she fell under the yoke of bondage. Full of burning affection He toiled, like Jacob for Rachel, until the whole of her purchase-money had been paid; and now, having sought her by His Spirit and brought her to know and love Him, He awaits the glorious hour when their mutual bliss shall be consummated at the marriage-supper of the Lamb. The glorious Bridegroom has not yet presented His betrothed, perfected and complete, before the Majesty of heaven; she has not yet actually entered upon the enjoyment of her dignities as His wife and queen. She is as still a wanderer in a world of woe, a dweller in the tents of Kedar;[1] but she is even now the bride, the spouse of Jesus, dear to His heart, precious in His sight, written on His hands, and united with His person. On earth He exercises toward her all the affectionate offices of Husband. He makes rich provision for her wants, pays all her debts, allows her to assume His name and to share in all His wealth. Nor will He ever act otherwise to her. The word *divorce* He will never mention, for He hates it. Death inevitably severs the conjugal tie between the most loving mortals, but it cannot divide the links of this immortal marriage. In heaven they marry not but are as the angels of God; yet there is this one marvelous exception to the rule, for in Heaven Christ and His Church shall celebrate their joyous nuptials. This affinity, as it is more lasting, so is it more near than earthly marriage. The love of husband, no matter how pure and fervent, is but a faint picture of the flame that burns in the heart of Jesus. Passing all human union is that mystical cleaving unto the Church, for which Christ left His Father and became one flesh with her.

If there be one place where our Lord Jesus most fully becomes the joy and comfort of His people, it is where He plunged deepest into the depths of woe. Come, gracious souls, and behold the Man in the garden of Gethsemane; behold His heart so brimming with love that He cannot hold it in—so full of sorrow that it must find expression. Behold the bloody sweat as it distills from every pore of His body and falls upon the ground. Behold the Man as they drive the nails into His hands and feet. Look up, repenting sinners, and see the sorrowful image of your suffering Lord. Consider Him as the ruby drops stand on the thorn-crown and adorn with priceless gems the diadem of the King of Misery. Behold the Man when all His bones are out of joint, and He is poured out like water and brought into the dust of death; God has forsaken Him, and hell surrounds Him. Look and see, was there ever sorrow like His sorrow that is done unto Him? All passersby pause and look upon this spectacle of grief, a wonder to men and angels, an unparalleled phenomenon. Behold the Emperor of Woe who had no equal or rival in His agonies! Gaze upon Him, you mourners, for if there is no consolation in a crucified Christ there is no joy in earth or heaven. If in the ransom price of His blood there is no hope, there is no joy in the harps of heaven, and the right hand of God shall know no pleasures forevermore. We need only sit more continually at the cross to be less troubled with our doubts and woes. We need only see *His* sorrows, and *our* sorrows we shall be ashamed to mention; we need only gaze into His wounds and heal our own. If we would live properly, it must be by the contemplation of His death; if we would rise to dignity, it must be by considering His humiliation and His sorrow.

[1] Psalm 120:5

YOU WERE LIKE ONE OF THEM. — OBADIAH 11

Brotherly kindness was due from Edom to Israel in the time of need, but instead of showing kindness, the men of Esau joined with Israel's enemies. Special stress in the sentence before us is laid upon the word *you*, as when Caesar cried to Brutus, "and *you*, Brutus." A bad action may be all the worse because of the person who has committed it. When *we* sin, who are the chosen favorites of heaven, we sin with an emphasis; ours is a crying offense because we are so peculiarly indulged. If an angel should lay his hand upon us when we are doing evil, he need not use any other rebuke than the question, "What, *you*? What are *you* doing here?" Having been gloriously forgiven, delivered, instructed, enriched, blessed, do we dare give ourselves to evil? God forbid!

A few minutes of confession may be beneficial to you, gentle reader, this morning. Have you never been like the wicked? At an evening party certain men laughed at uncleanness, and the joke was not altogether offensive to your ear—*even you were as one of them.* When hard things were spoken concerning the ways of God, you were bashfully silent; and so, to onlookers, *you were as one of them.* When worldlings were bartering in the market and driving hard bargains, were you not as one of them? When they were pursuing vanity without restraint, were you not as greedy for gain as they were? Could any difference be discerned between you and them? *Is there any difference?* Here we come to close quarters. Be honest with your own soul, and make sure that you are a new creature in Christ Jesus; but when this is sure, walk carefully in case anyone should again be able to say, "You also are one of them."[1] You would not desire to share their eternal doom. Why then be like them here? Do not enter into their secret, in case you enter into their ruin. Side with the afflicted people of God, and not with the world.

❦ EVENING ❧

THE BLOOD OF JESUS HIS SON CLEANSES US FROM ALL SIN. — 1 JOHN 1:7

Cleanses," says the text—not "*shall* cleanse." There are multitudes who think that as a dying hope they may look forward to pardon. Oh, how infinitely better to have cleansing now than to depend on the bare possibility of forgiveness when I come to die. Some imagine that a sense of pardon is an attainment only obtainable after many years of Christian experience. But forgiveness of sin is a *present* reality—a privilege for this day, a joy for this very hour. The moment a sinner trusts Jesus he is fully forgiven. The text, being written in the present tense, also indicates *continuance*; it was "cleanses" yesterday, it is "cleanses" today, it will be "cleanses" tomorrow. This is the way it will always be with you, Christian, until you cross the river; every hour you may come to this fountain, for it cleanses still. Notice, likewise, the *completeness* of the cleansing: "The blood of Jesus his Son cleanses us from *all* sin"—not only from sin, but "from all sin." Reader, I cannot convey the exceeding sweetness of this word, but I pray that God the Holy Ghost will give you a taste of it. Manifold are our sins against God. Whether the bill be little or great, the same receipt can discharge one as the other. The blood of Jesus Christ is as blessed and divine a payment for the transgressions of blaspheming Peter as for the shortcomings of loving John. Our iniquity is gone, all gone at once, and all gone forever. Blessed completeness! What a sweet theme to dwell upon as one gives himself to sleep.

> *Sins against a holy God;*
> *Sins against His righteous laws;*
> *Sins against His love, His blood;*
> *Sins against His name and cause;*
> *Sins immense as is the sea—*
> *From them all He cleanseth me.*

[1] Luke 22:58

STAND FIRM, AND SEE THE SALVATION OF THE LORD. — EXODUS 14:13

These words contain God's command to the believer when he is reduced to great straits and brought into extraordinary difficulties. He cannot retreat; he cannot go forward; he is shut up on the right hand and on the left; what is he now to do? The Master's word to him is, "Stand firm." It will be well for him if at such times he listens only to his Master's word, for other and evil advisers come with their suggestions. *Despair* whispers, "Lie down and die; give it all up." But God would have us put on a cheerful courage and even in our worst times rejoice in His love and faithfulness. *Cowardice* says, "Retreat; go back to the worldling's way of action; you cannot play the Christian's part—it is too difficult. Relinquish your principles." But however much Satan may urge this course upon you, you cannot follow it if you are a child of God. His divine decree has bid you go from strength to strength, and so you shall, and neither death nor hell shall turn you from your course. Even if you are called to stand firm for a while, this is in order to renew your strength for some greater advance in due time. *Precipitancy* cries, "Do something. Stir yourself; to stand still and wait is sheer idleness." We *must* be doing something at once—we must do it, so we think—instead of looking to the Lord, who will not only do something but will do everything. *Presumption* boasts, "If the sea is before you, march into it and expect a miracle." But faith listens neither to presumption, nor to despair, nor to cowardice, nor to precipitancy, but it hears God say, "Stand firm," and immovable as a rock it stands. "*Stand firm*"—keep the posture of an upright man, ready for action, expecting further orders, cheerfully and patiently awaiting the directing voice; and it will not be long before God shall say to you, as distinctly as Moses said it to the people of Israel, "Go forward."

❦ EVENING ❧

HIS CAMP IS EXCEEDINGLY GREAT. — JOEL 2:11

Consider, my soul, the mightiness of the Lord who is your glory and defense. He is a man of war; Jehovah is His name. All *the forces of heaven* are at His command; legions wait at His door; cherubim and seraphim, watchers and holy ones, principalities and powers are all attentive to His will. If our eyes were not blinded by the dust of sin, we should see horses of fire and chariots of fire round about the Lord's servants. *The powers of nature* are all subject to the absolute control of the Creator: Stormy wind and tempest, lightning and rain, snow and hail, and the soft dews and cheering sunshine come and go at His decree. The bands of Orion He looses, and He binds the sweet influences of the Pleiades.[1] Earth, sea, and air and the places under the earth are the barracks for Jehovah's great armies; space is His camping ground, light is His banner, and flame is His sword. When He goes forth to war, famine ravages the land, pestilence smites the nations, hurricane sweeps the sea, tornado shakes the mountains, and earthquake makes the solid world to tremble. As for *animate creatures*, they all own His dominion, and from the great fish that swallowed the prophet down to "all manner of flies," which plagued the field of Zoan,[2] all are His servants, and even the caterpillars and the worms are squadrons of His great army, for His camp is very great. My soul, see to it that you are at peace with this mighty King. Be sure to enlist under His banner, for to war against Him is madness, and to serve Him is glory. Jesus, Immanuel, God with us, is ready to receive recruits for the army of the Lord: If I am not already enlisted, let me go to Him before I sleep and beg to be accepted through His merits; and if I be already, as I hope I am, a soldier of the cross, let me be of good courage, for the enemy is powerless compared with my Lord, whose camp is very great.

[1] Job 38:31 [2] Psalm 78:43-45

HE LEFT HIS GARMENT IN HER HAND AND FLED AND
GOT OUT OF THE HOUSE. — GENESIS 39:12

In contending with certain sins there remains no mode of victory but by flight. The ancient naturalists wrote much of basilisks, whose eyes fascinated their victims and rendered them easy victims; so the mere gaze of wickedness puts us in solemn danger. He who would be safe from acts of evil must hurry away from occasions of it. A covenant must be made with our eyes not even to look upon the cause of temptation, for such sins only need a spark to begin with and a blaze follows in an instant. Who would carelessly enter the leper's prison and sleep amid its horrible corruption? Only he who desires to be leprous himself. If the sailor knew how to avoid a storm, he would do anything rather than run the risk of weathering it. Cautious navigators have no desire to see how near the quicksand they can sail or how often they may touch a rock without springing a leak; their aim is to keep as nearly as possible in the midst of a safe channel.

Today I may be exposed to great peril; let me have the serpent's wisdom to keep out of it and avoid it. The wings of a dove may be of more use to me today than the jaws of a lion. It is true I may be an apparent loser by declining evil company, but I had better leave my cloak than lose my character; it is not needful that I should be rich, but it is imperative for me to be pure. No ties of friendship, no chains of beauty, no flashings of talent, no shafts of ridicule must turn me from the wise resolve to flee from sin. I am to resist the devil, and he will flee from me; but the lusts of the flesh *I* must flee, or they will surely overcome me. O God of holiness, preserve us like Joseph, that we may not be seduced by the subtle, vile suggestions of the temptress. May the horrible trinity of the world, the flesh, and the devil never overcome us!

∾   EVENING   ∾

. . . IN THEIR DISTRESS EARNESTLY SEEK ME. — HOSEA 5:15

Losses and adversities are frequently the means that the Great Shepherd uses to bring home His wandering sheep; like fierce dogs they worry the wanderers back to the fold. Well-fed lions defy our attempts to tame them; they must be brought down from their great strength, and their stomachs must be lowered, and then they will submit to the tamer's hand. How often have we seen the Christian rendered obedient to the Lord's will by the absence of bread and the presence of difficulty. When rich and increased in goods, many professors carry their heads much too loftily and speak exceeding boastfully. Like David, they flatter themselves: "My mountain stands firm; I shall never be moved."[1] When the Christian grows wealthy, is in good repute, or has good health and a happy family, he too often admits Mr. Carnal-Security[2] to feast at his table, and then if he is a true child of God there is a rod preparing for him. Wait awhile, and perhaps you will see his substance melt away as a dream. There goes a portion of his estate—how soon the acres change hands. That debt, that dishonored bill—how fast his losses roll in—where will they end? It is a blessed sign of divine life if, when these embarrassments occur one after another, he begins to be distressed about his backslidings and turns afresh to God. Blessed are the waves that wash the mariner upon the rock of salvation! Losses in business are often sanctified to our soul's enriching. If the chosen soul will not come to the Lord full-handed, it shall come empty. If God, in His grace, finds no other means of making us honor Him among men, He will cast us into the deep; if we fail to honor Him on the pinnacle of riches, He will bring us into the valley of poverty. Yet do not faint, heir of sorrow, when you are rebuked in this fashion; rather, recognize the loving hand that chastens and say, "I will arise and go to my Father."[3]

[1] See Psalm 30:6-7 [2] *The Holy War* (John Bunyan) [3] Luke 15:18

MAKE EVERY EFFORT TO SUPPLEMENT YOUR FAITH WITH VIRTUE,
AND VIRTUE WITH KNOWLEDGE, [ETC.] — 2 PETER 1:5-6

If you would enjoy the eminent grace of the full assurance of faith, under the blessed Spirit's influence and assistance, do what the Scripture tells you: "*Make every effort.*" Take care that your *faith* is the right kind—that it is not a mere belief of doctrine, but a simple faith, depending on Christ and on Christ alone. Pay careful attention to your *courage.* Plead with God that He would give you the face of a lion, that you may, with a consciousness of right, go on boldly. Study the Scriptures diligently and get *knowledge*; for a knowledge of doctrine will help a great deal to confirm faith. Try to understand God's Word; let it dwell in your heart richly.

When you have done this, add to your "knowledge . . . *self-control.*" Pay attention to your body and soul. Be controlled in speech, life, heart, and thought. Add to this, by God's Holy Spirit, *patience*; ask Him to give you that patience that endures affliction, which, when it is tried, will come forth as gold. Array yourself with patience, so that you do not murmur or be depressed in your afflictions. When that grace is won, look to *godliness.* Godliness is something more than religion. Make God's glory your object in life; live in His sight; dwell close to Him; seek fellowship with Him; then you will have "godliness"; and to that add *brotherly love.* Have a love for all the saints: And add to that a *charity* that opens its arms to all men and loves their souls. When you are adorned with these jewels, and just in proportion as you practice these heavenly virtues, you will come to know by clearest evidence "your calling and election." "Make every effort," if you would get assurance, for lukewarmness and doubting very naturally go hand in hand.

❦ EVENING ❧

. . . TO MAKE THEM SIT WITH PRINCES. — PSALM 113:8

Our spiritual privileges are of the highest order. "With princes" *is the place of select society.* "Indeed our fellowship is with the Father and with his Son Jesus Christ."[1] There is no more select society than this! "But you are a chosen race, a royal priesthood, a holy nation."[2] ". . . to the assembly of the firstborn who are enrolled in heaven."[3] The saints *have direct and immediate access*: Princes are admitted to royalty when common people must stand afar off. The child of God has free access to the inner courts of heaven. "For through him we both have access in one Spirit to the Father."[4] "Let us then with confidence draw near," says the apostle, "*to the throne* of grace."[5] Among princes there is *abundant wealth*, but what is the abundance of princes compared with the riches of believers? For "all are yours, and you are Christ's, and Christ is God's."[6] "He who did not spare his own Son but gave him up for us all, how will he not also with him graciously give us all things?"[7] Princes have *peculiar power.* A prince of heaven's empire has great influence: He wields a scepter in his own domain; he sits upon Jesus' throne, for "You have made them a kingdom and priests to our God, and they shall reign on the earth."[8] We reign over the united kingdom of time and eternity. Princes, again, have *special honor.* We may look down upon all earthborn dignity from the eminence upon which grace has placed us. For what is human grandeur to this: "[He] raised us up with him and seated us with him in the heavenly places in Christ Jesus"?[9] We share the honor of Christ, and compared with this, earthly splendors are not worth a thought. Communion with Jesus is a richer gem than ever glittered in a royal crown. Union with the Lord is an emblem of beauty outshining all the blaze of imperial pomp.

[1] 1 John 1:3   [2] 1 Peter 2:9   [3] Hebrews 12:23   [4] Ephesians 2:18   [5] Hebrews 4:16   [6] 1 Corinthians 3:22-23
[7] Romans 8:32   [8] Revelation 5:10   [9] Ephesians 2:6

... PRECIOUS AND VERY GREAT PROMISES. — 2 PETER 1:4

If you would know experimentally [experientially] the preciousness of the promises and enjoy them in your own heart, *meditate much upon them.* There are promises that are like grapes in the winepress; if you will tread them, the juice will flow. Thinking over the hallowed words will often be the prelude to their fulfillment. While you are musing upon them, the benefit that you are seeking will insensibly come to you. Many a Christian who has thirsted for the promise has found the favor that it ensured gently distilling into his soul even while he has been considering the divine record; and he has rejoiced that he was ever led to lay the promise near his heart.

But besides *meditating* upon the promises, *seek in your soul to receive them as being the very words of God.* Say to your soul: "If I were dealing with a man's promise, I would carefully consider the ability and the character of the man who had covenanted with me. So with the promise of God, my eye must not be so much fixed upon the greatness of the mercy—that may stagger me—as upon the greatness of the promiser—that will cheer me. My soul, it is God, even your God, God who cannot lie, who speaks to you. This word of His that you are now considering is as true as His own existence. He is an unchangeable God. He has not altered the thing that has gone out of His mouth, nor called back one single soothing sentence. Nor does He lack any power; it is the God who made the heavens and the earth who has spoken. Nor can He fail in wisdom as to the time when He will bestow the favors, for He knows when it is best to give and when better to withhold. Therefore, seeing that it is the word of a God so true, so immutable, so powerful, so wise, I will and must believe the promise." If in this way we meditate upon the promises and consider the Promiser, we shall experience their sweetness and obtain their fulfillment.

❧ EVENING ❧

WHO SHALL BRING ANY CHARGE AGAINST GOD'S ELECT?
— ROMANS 8:33

Most blessed challenge! How unanswerable it is! Every sin of the elect was laid upon the great Champion of our salvation, and by the atonement carried away. There is no sin in God's book against His people: He sees no sin in Jacob, neither iniquity in Israel; they are justified in Christ forever. When the guilt of sin was taken away, the punishment of sin was removed. For the Christian there is no stroke from God's angry hand—no, not so much as a single frown of punitive justice. The believer may be chastised by his Father, but God the Judge has nothing to say to the Christian except "I have absolved you: you are acquitted." For the Christian there is no penal death in this world, much less any second death. He is completely freed from all the punishment as well as the guilt of sin, and the power of sin is removed too. It may stand in our way and agitate us with perpetual warfare; but sin is a conquered foe to every soul in union with Jesus. There is no sin that a Christian cannot overcome if he will only rely upon his God to do it. They who wear the white robe in heaven overcame through the blood of the Lamb, and we may do the same. No lust is too mighty, no besetting sin too strongly entrenched; we can overcome through the power of Christ. Do believe it, Christian—your sin is a condemned thing. It may kick and struggle, but it is doomed to die. God has written condemnation across its brow. Christ has crucified it, nailing it to His cross. Go now and mortify it, and may the Lord help you to live to His praise, for sin with all its guilt, shame, and fear is gone.

> *Here's pardon for transgressions past,*
> *It matters not how black their cast;*
> *And, O my soul, with wonder view,*
> *For sins to come here's pardon too.*

I WAS BRUTISH AND IGNORANT; I WAS LIKE A BEAST TOWARD YOU.
— PSALM 73:22

Remember, this is the confession of the man of God; and in telling us his inner life, he writes, "I was brutish and ignorant." The word *"brutish"* conveys the extent of his wayward folly. In an earlier verse of the Psalm, the psalmist writes, "I was envious of *the arrogant* when I saw the prosperity of the wicked," which shows that his ignorant reaction was sinful. He puts himself down as being "brutish," and in doing so conveys the intensity of his feelings. His attitude and reaction was sinful. He could not excuse it but deserved to be condemned because of its perverseness and willful ignorance. He had been envious of the immediate prosperity of the ungodly, forgetting the ultimate, dreadful end that they faced. Are we any better than him that we should call ourselves wise? Do we profess that we have attained perfection or have been so disciplined that our stubbornness has been removed? This would be pride indeed! If the psalmist was foolish, how foolish are *we* when we fail to see ourselves! Look back, believer: Think of when you doubted God when He was so faithful to you; think of your foolish outcry of "Not so, my Father" when He crossed His hands in affliction to give you the greater blessing; think of the many times when you have read His providences in the dark, misinterpreted His dealings, and groaned, "All these things are against me" when they are in fact working together for your good! Think how often you have chosen sin because of its pleasure, when indeed that pleasure was a root of bitterness to you! Surely if we know our own heart we must plead guilty to the indictment of a sinful folly; and conscious of this "brutishness," we must learn to say with the psalmist, *"You guide me with Your counsel."*

❧ EVENING ❧

HE WENT ABOUT DOING GOOD. — ACTS 10:38

Few words, but yet an exquisite miniature of the Lord Jesus Christ. There are not many touches, but they are the strokes of a master's pencil. Of the Savior and only of the Savior is this true in the fullest, broadest, and most unqualified sense. "He went about doing good." From this description it is evident that He did good *personally*. The evangelists constantly tell us that He touched the leper with His own finger, that He anointed the eyes of the blind, and that in cases where He was asked to speak the word only at a distance, He did not usually comply but went Himself to the sickbed and there personally worked the cure. A lesson to us, if we would do good, to do it ourselves. Give gifts with your own hand; a kind look or word will enhance the value of the gift. Speak to a friend about his soul; your loving appeal will have more influence than a whole library of tracts. Our Lord's mode of doing good sets forth His *constant activity*! He did not only the good that came close to hand, but He "went about" on His errands of mercy. Throughout the whole land of Judea there was scarcely a village or a hamlet that was not gladdened by the sight of Him. How this reproves the creeping, loitering manner in which many professors serve the Lord. Let us gird up the loins of our mind and not grow weary in doing good. Does the text not imply that Jesus Christ *went out of His way to do good*? "He went *about* doing good." He was never deterred by danger or difficulty. He sought out the objects of His gracious intentions. So must we. If old plans will not answer, we must try new ones, for fresh experiments sometimes achieve more than regular methods. Christ's *perseverance*, and the *unity* of His purpose, are also hinted at, and the practical application of the subject may be summed up in the words, "Christ . . . leaving you an example, so that you might follow in his steps."[1]

[1] 1 Peter 2:21

NEVERTHELESS, I AM CONTINUALLY WITH YOU. — PSALM 73:23

"N*evertheless*"—as if, notwithstanding all the foolishness and ignorance that David had just been confessing to God, not one atom was it less true and certain that David was saved and accepted, and that the blessing of being constantly in God's presence was undoubtedly his. Fully conscious of his own lost estate and of the deceitfulness and vileness of his nature, yet, by a glorious outburst of faith, he sings, "Nevertheless, I am continually with you." Believer, you are forced to enter into Asaph's confession and acknowledgment; endeavor in like spirit to say "nevertheless, since I belong to Christ I am continually with God!" By this is meant continually upon His *mind*—He is always thinking of me for my good. Continually before His *eye*—the eye of the Lord never sleeps but is perpetually watching over my welfare. Continually in His *hand*, so that none shall be able to pluck me away. Continually on His *heart*, worn there as a memorial, even as the high priest bore the names of the twelve tribes upon his heart forever. You always think of me, O God. The tender mercies of Your love continually yearn toward me. You are always making providence work for my good. You have set me as a signet upon Your arm; Your love is strong as death, and many waters cannot quench it; neither can the floods drown it. Surprising grace! You see me in Christ, and though in myself disapproved, You behold me as wearing Christ's garments and washed in His blood, and so I stand accepted in Your presence. I am therefore continually in Your favor—"continually with you." Here is comfort for the tried and afflicted soul; vexed with the tempest within, look at the calm without. "*Nevertheless*"—O say it in your heart, and take the peace it gives. "Nevertheless, I am continually with you."

❧ EVENING ❧

ALL THAT THE FATHER GIVES ME WILL COME TO ME. — JOHN 6:37

This declaration involves *the doctrine of election*: There are some whom the Father gave to Christ. It involves *the doctrine of effectual calling*: These who are given must and shall come; however stoutly they may set themselves against it, yet they shall be brought out of darkness into God's marvelous light. It teaches us *the indispensable necessity of faith*, for even those who are given to Christ are not saved except they come to Jesus. Even *they* must come, for there is no other way to heaven but by the door, Christ Jesus. All that the Father gives to our Redeemer *must come to Him*; therefore none can come to heaven except they come to Christ.

Oh, the power and majesty that rest in the words *"will come."* He does not say they have power to come, nor that they may come if they will, but they *"will come."* The Lord Jesus by His messengers, His Word, and His Spirit sweetly and graciously compels men to come in, that they may eat of His marriage supper; and this He does not by any violation of the free agency of man, but by the power of His grace. I may exercise power over another man's will, and yet that other man's will may be perfectly free, because the constraint is exercised in a manner accordant with the laws of the human mind. Jehovah Jesus knows how by irresistible arguments addressed to the understanding, by mighty reasons appealing to the affections, and by the mysterious influence of His Holy Spirit operating upon all the powers and passions of the soul so to subdue the whole man, whereas he was once rebellious, that he yields cheerfully to His government, subdued by sovereign love. But how shall those be known whom God has chosen? By this result: that they do willingly and joyfully accept Christ and come to Him with simple and unfeigned faith, resting upon Him as all their salvation and all their desire. Reader, have you come to Jesus in this way?

AND PETER REMEMBERED. . . . AND HE BROKE DOWN AND WEPT.
— MARK 14:72

It has been thought by some that as long as Peter lived, the fountain of his tears began to flow whenever he remembered that he had denied his Lord. It is not unlikely that it was so (for his sin was very great, and grace in him had afterwards a perfect work). This same experience is common to all the redeemed family according to the degree in which the Spirit of God has removed the natural heart of stone. We, like Peter, remember *our boastful promise*: "Though they all fall away because of you, I will never fall away."[1] We eat our own words with the bitter herbs of repentance. When we think of what we vowed we would be and of what we have been, we may weep whole showers of grief. He remembered *denying his Lord*—the place in which he did it, the little cause that led him into such heinous sin, the oaths and blasphemies with which he sought to confirm his falsehood, and the dreadful hardness of heart that drove him to do so again and yet again. Can we, when we are reminded of our sins and their exceeding sinfulness, remain stolid and stubborn? Will we not make our house a place of sacrifice and cry to the Lord for renewed assurances of pardoning love? May we never take a dry-eyed look at sin, in case we discover our tongue parched in the flames of hell. Peter also remembered *his Master's look of love*. The Lord followed up the rooster's warning voice with an admonitory look of sorrow, pity, and love. That glance was never out of Peter's mind so long as he lived. It was far more effectual than ten thousand sermons would have been without the Spirit. The penitent apostle would be sure to weep when he remembered the *Savior's full forgiveness*, which restored him to his former place. To think that we have offended so kind and good a Lord is more than sufficient reason for being constant weepers. Lord, smite our rocky hearts, and make the waters flow.

❧ EVENING ❧

WHOEVER COMES TO ME I WILL NEVER CAST OUT. — JOHN 6:37

There is *no expiration date* on this promise. It does not merely say, "I will not cast out a sinner at his first coming," but "I will never cast him out." The original reads, "I will not, not cast out," or "I will never, never cast out." The text means that Christ will not at *first* reject a believer, and that as He will not do it at first, so He will not to the last.

But suppose the believer sins after coming? "If anyone does sin, we have an advocate with the Father, Jesus Christ the righteous."[2] But suppose that believers backslide? "I will heal their apostasy; I will love them freely, for my anger has turned from them."[3] But believers may fall under temptation! "God is faithful, and he will not let you be tempted beyond your ability, but with the temptation he will also provide the way of escape, that you may be able to endure it."[4] But the believer may fall into sin as David did! Yes, but He will "Purge me with hyssop, and I shall be clean; wash me, and I shall be whiter than snow."[5]

Once in Christ, in Christ forever,
Nothing from His love can sever.

Jesus said, "I give them eternal life, and they will never perish, and no one will snatch them out of my hand."[6] What do you say to this, O trembling, feeble mind? This is a precious mercy. Coming to Christ, you do not come to One who will treat you well for a little while and then send you about your business, but He will receive you and make you His bride, and you shall be His forever! Live no longer in the spirit of bondage to fear, but in the spirit of adoption, which cries, "Abba, Father!" Oh, the grace of these words: "I will never cast out."

[1]Matthew 26:33 [2]1 John 2:1 [3]Hosea 14:4 [4]1 Corinthians 10:13 [5]Psalm 51:7 [6]John 10:28

I IN THEM. — JOHN 17:23

If this is the union between our souls and the person of our Lord, how deep and broad is the channel of our communion! This is no narrow channel through which a threadlike stream may wind its way; it is a river of amazing depth and breadth, along whose glorious length a ponderous volume of living water may roll its floods. Consider how He has set before us an open door; let us not be slow to enter. This city of communion has many pearly gates, every gate is made of one pearl, and each gate is thrown open wide so that we may enter, assured of welcome. If there were but one small loophole through which to talk with Jesus, it would be a high privilege to thrust a word of fellowship through the narrow door; how much we are blessed in having so large an entrance! If the Lord Jesus were far away from us, with many a stormy sea between, we would long to send a messenger to Him to carry Him our love and bring us tidings from His Father's house; but consider His kindness—He has built His house next-door to ours. More than that, He lives with us and makes His home in our poor humble hearts, so He may have continual fellowship with us. O how foolish must we be if we do not live in constant communion with Him. When the road is long and dangerous and difficult, it is no surprise that friends seldom meet each other; but when they live together, shall Jonathan forget his David? A wife may, when her husband is on a journey, spend many days without conversing with him, but she could never endure to be separated from him if she knew him to be in one of the rooms of her own house. Why, believer, do you not sit at His banquet of wine? Seek your Lord, for He is near; embrace Him, for He is your Brother. Hold Him fast, for He is your Husband; and press Him to your heart, for He is your kith and kin.

↭ EVENING ↭

NOW THESE, THE SINGERS . . . WERE ON DUTY DAY AND NIGHT.
— 1 CHRONICLES 9:33

It was so well organized in the temple that the sacred refrain never ceased, for the singers constantly praised the Lord, whose mercy endures forever. As mercy did not cease to rule either by day or by night, so neither did music hush its holy sound. My heart, there is a lesson sweetly taught to you in the ceaseless song of Zion's temple. You are a constant debtor; therefore see to it that your gratitude, like charity, never fails. God's praise is constant in heaven, which is to be your final dwelling-place; so learn to practice the eternal hallelujah. Around the earth as the sun scatters its light, its beams awaken grateful believers to tune their morning hymn, so that by the priesthood of the saints perpetual praise is kept up at all hours; they surround our globe in a mantle of thanksgiving and girdle it with a golden belt of song.

The Lord always deserves to be praised for what He is in Himself, for His works of creation and providence, for His goodness toward His creatures, and especially for the transcendent act of redemption and all the marvelous blessings that flow from it. It is always beneficial to praise the Lord; such praise cheers the day and brightens the night; it lightens toil and softens sorrow; and over earthly gladness it sheds a sanctifying radiance that makes it less liable to blind us with its glare. Do we not have something to sing about at this moment? Can we not weave a song out of our present joys or our past deliverances or our future hopes? Earth yields her summer fruits: The hay is baled, the golden grain invites the scythe, and the sun tarries to shine upon a fruitful earth and shorten the interval of shade, that we may extend the hours of devoted worship. By the love of Jesus, let us be stirred up to close the day with a psalm of sanctified gladness.

August

LET ME GO TO THE FIELD AND GLEAN AMONG THE EARS OF GRAIN.
— RUTH 2:2

Downcast and troubled Christian, come and glean today in the broad field of promise. Here is an abundance of precious promises, which meet your needs exactly. Take this one: "A bruised reed he will not break, and a faintly burning wick he will not quench."[1] Is that not helpful to you? A reed, helpless, insignificant, and weak, a bruised reed, out of which no music can come, weaker than weakness itself—yet He will not break you, but on the contrary, will restore and strengthen you. You are like the smoking wick: No light, no warmth, can come from you, but He will not extinguish you; He will blow with His sweet breath of mercy until He fans you into a flame. Would you glean another ear? "Come to me, all who labor and are heavy laden, and I will give you rest."[2] What gentle words! Your heart is tender, and the Master knows it, and therefore He speaks so softly to you. Will you not obey Him and come to Him even now? Take another ear of corn: "Fear not, you worm Jacob, you men of Israel! I am the one who helps you, declares the LORD; your Redeemer is the Holy One of Israel."[3] How can you fear with such a wonderful assurance as this? You may gather ten thousand golden ears such as this: "I have blotted out your transgressions like a cloud and your sins like mist."[4] Or this: "Though your sins are like scarlet, they shall be as white as snow; though they are red like crimson, they shall become like wool."[5] Or this: "The Spirit and the Bride say, Come. And let the one who is thirsty come; let the one who desires take the water of life without price."[6] Our Master's field is very rich, as you can see. Plenty of promises lie before you, believer! Gather them up, make them your own, for Jesus wants you to have them. Do not be afraid; only believe! Grasp these sweet promises, thresh them out by meditation, and feed on them with joy.

✎ EVENING ✎

YOU CROWN THE YEAR WITH YOUR BOUNTY. — PSALM 65:11

All the year round, every hour of every day, God is richly blessing us; when we are asleep and when we awaken, His mercy waits upon us. The sun may leave us a legacy of darkness, but God never ceases to shine upon His children with beams of love. Like a river, His loving-kindness is always flowing, with a fullness as inexhaustible as His own nature. Like the atmosphere that constantly surrounds the earth and is always ready to support the life of man, the kindness of God surrounds all His creatures; in it, as in their element, they live and move and have their being. Just as the sun on summer days gladdens us with warmer and brighter rays than at other times, and as rivers in certain seasons are swollen by the rain, and as the air itself is sometimes filled with fresher breezes than at other times, so is it with the mercy of God; it has its golden hours, its overflowing days, when the Lord magnifies His grace before the children of men. *The joyful days of harvest* are a special season of abundant favor. It is the glory of autumn that the ripe gifts of providence are then generously bestowed; it is the mellow season when we enjoy all that we had hoped for. The joy of harvest is great. The reapers are happy to fill their arms with the abundance of heaven. The psalmist tells us that the harvest is the crowning of the year. Surely these crowning mercies merit a crowning thanksgiving! Let us render it by the *inward emotions of gratitude.* Let our hearts be warmed; let our spirits remember, meditate, and think upon this goodness of the Lord. Then let us *praise Him with our lips* and honor and magnify His name who is the source of all this goodness. Let us glorify God by *offering our gifts* to His cause. A practical proof of our gratitude is a special thank-offering to the Lord of the harvest.

[1]Isaiah 42:3 [2]Matthew 11:28 [3]Isaiah 41:14 [4]Isaiah 44:22 [5]Isaiah 1:18 [6]Revelation 22:17

WHO WORKS ALL THINGS ACCORDING TO THE COUNSEL OF HIS WILL.
— EPHESIANS 1:11

Our belief in God's wisdom supposes and necessitates that He has a settled purpose and plan in the work of salvation. What would *creation* have been without His design? Is there a fish in the sea or a bird in the air that was formed by chance? No; in every bone, joint, and muscle, sinew, gland, and blood-vessel, you see the presence of a God working everything according to the design of infinite wisdom. And will God be present in creation, ruling over all, but not in *grace*? Shall the new creation have the fickle genius of free will to preside over it when divine counsel rules the old creation? Look at *providence*! We know that not even a sparrow falls to the ground without our Father. Even the hairs of your head are all numbered. God weighs the mountains of our grief in scales, and the hills of our tribulation in balances. And shall there be a God in providence and not in grace? Shall the shell be ordained by wisdom and the kernel left to blind chance? No; He knows the end from the beginning. He sees in its appointed place not merely the cornerstone that He has laid in fair colors, in the blood of His dear Son, but He sees each of the chosen stones taken out of the quarry of nature, placed in their ordained position, and polished by His grace. He sees the whole from corner to cornice, from base to roof, from foundation to pinnacle. In His mind he has a clear knowledge of every stone that will be put in its prepared space, and how vast the structure will be when the capstone is set in place with shouts of "Grace! Grace!" In the end it will be clearly seen that in every child of God, Jehovah did as He planned with His own; and in every part of the work of grace He accomplished His purpose and glorified His own name.

❧ EVENING ❧

SO SHE GLEANED IN THE FIELD UNTIL EVENING. — RUTH 2:17

Let me learn from Ruth, the gleaner. As she went out to gather the ears of corn, so must I set out for the fields of prayer, meditation, the ordinances, and hearing the Word to gather spiritual food. *The gleaner gathers her portion ear by ear*; her gains are little by little: So I must be content to search for single truths, if they come just one at a time. Every ear helps to make a bundle, and every gospel lesson assists in making us wise for salvation. *The gleaner keeps her eyes open*: If she stumbled dreamlike among the stubble, she would have no load to carry home rejoicingly at evening. I must be careful in religious exercises in case they become unprofitable to me; I fear I have lost quite a bit already. I need to estimate my opportunities properly and glean with greater diligence. *The gleaner stoops for all she finds*, and I must do the same. Proud minds criticize and object, but humble minds glean and receive benefit. A lowly heart is the key to profitably hearing the Gospel. The soul-saving Word is not received except with meekness. A stiff back makes for a bad gleaner. Pride is a vile robber and must not be tolerated for a moment. *What the gleaner gathers, she keeps*: If she dropped one ear to find another, the result of her day's work would be but meager; she is as careful to retain as to obtain, and so at last she makes great gains. How often do I forget all that I hear; the second truth pushes the first out of my head, and so my reading and hearing end in much ado about nothing! Do I understand the importance of storing up the truth? Hunger helps to make the gleaner wise; if she has no corn in her hand, there will be no bread on her table; she works under a sense of necessity, and consequently she moves swiftly and her grasp is firm. My need is even greater, Lord; help me to feel it, that it may urge me onward to glean in fields that yield to diligence a plenteous reward.

❧ MORNING ☙

Quietly contemplate the Lamb as the light of heaven. Light in Scripture is the emblem of *joy*. The joy of the saints in heaven is comprised in this: *Jesus* chose us, loved us, bought us, cleansed us, robed us, kept us, glorified us: We are here entirely through the Lord Jesus. Each one of these thoughts shall be as sweet as a cluster of grapes. Light is also the cause of *beauty*. Nothing of beauty is left when the light is gone. Without light no radiance flashes from the sapphire, no peaceful ray proceeds from the pearl; and so all the beauty of the saints above comes from Jesus. As planets, they reflect the light of the Sun of Righteousness; they live as beams proceeding from the central orb. If He withdrew, they must die; if His glory were veiled, their glory must expire. Light is also the emblem of *knowledge*. In heaven our knowledge will be perfect, but the Lord Jesus Himself will be the fountain of it. Dark providences we've never understood will then be clearly seen, and all that puzzles us now will become plain to us in the light of the Lamb. Oh, what discoveries there will be, and what glorifying of the God of love! Light also means *manifestation*. Light manifests. In this world it does not yet appear what we shall be. God's people are a hidden people, but when Christ receives His people into heaven, He will touch them with the wand of His own love and change them into the image of His manifested glory. They were poor and wretched, but what a transformation! They were stained with sin, but one touch of His finger, and they are as bright as the sun and as clear as crystal. What a display! All this proceeds from the exalted Lamb. Whatever there may be of transcendent splendor, Jesus will be the center and soul of it all. Plan on being present to see Him in His own light, the King of kings and Lord of lords!

❧ EVENING ☙

Jesus is passing through the crowd heading for the house of Jairus, so that he might raise the ruler's dead daughter. He is so extravagant in His goodness that He works another miracle on His way there. It is enough for most of us, if we have one purpose, to go immediately and accomplish it, without impulsively expending our energies on the way. Rushing to the rescue of a drowning friend, we cannot afford to use up our strength upon someone else in similar danger. It is enough for a tree to yield one sort of fruit and for a man to fulfill his own peculiar calling. But the Lord Jesus is not limited in His power or restricted in His mission. He is so prolific in grace that, like the sun that shines as it rolls onward in its orbit, His path is radiant with loving-kindness. He is a swift arrow of love that not only reaches its ordained target but perfumes the air through which it flies. Virtue is always going out of Jesus, just as sweet fragrance exudes from flowers; and it will always be emanating from Him, like water from a sparkling fountain. What delightful encouragement this truth affords us! If our Lord is so ready to heal the sick and bless the needy, then, my soul, do not be slow to put yourself in His path so that He may smile on you. Do not be lazy in asking, since He is so generous in giving. Pay careful attention to His Word now and at all times, so that Jesus may speak through it to your heart. Pitch your tent wherever He is so that you can obtain His blessing. When He is present to heal, may He not heal you? Be certain that He is present even now, for He always comes to hearts that need Him. And do you not need Him? *He* knows the extent of your need; so turn your gaze, look upon your distress, and call upon Him while He is near.

❧ MORNING ❧

THE PEOPLE WHO KNOW THEIR GOD SHALL STAND FIRM.
— DANIEL 11:32

Every believer understands that to know God is the highest and best form of knowledge; and this spiritual knowledge is a source of strength to the Christian. It strengthens his *faith*. Believers are constantly referred to in the Bible as people who are enlightened and taught by the Lord; they are said to "have been anointed by the Holy One,"[1] and it is the Spirit's peculiar office to lead them into all truth, so that they might grow in their faith. Knowledge strengthens *love* as well as faith. Knowledge opens the door, and then through that door we see our Savior. Or to put it another way, knowledge paints the portrait of Jesus, and when we see that portrait, then we love Him. We cannot love a Christ whom we do not know at least in some degree. If we know only a little of the excellencies of Jesus, what He has done for us and what He is doing now, we cannot love Him much; but the more we know Him, the more we will love Him. Knowledge also strengthens *hope*. How can we hope for something if we do not know of its existence? Hope may be the telescope, but until we receive instruction, our ignorance blocks our view, and we can see nothing. Knowledge removes the blockage, and when we look through the bright optic glass we discover the glory to be revealed and anticipate it with joyful confidence. Knowledge supplies us with reason for *patience*. How will we have patience unless we know something of the sympathy of Christ and understand the good that comes out of the correction that our heavenly Father sends us? There is not a single Christian who, under God, will not be fostered and brought to perfection by holy knowledge. It is then very important that we should grow not only in grace, but in the knowledge of our Lord and Savior Jesus Christ.

❧ EVENING ❧

I STRUCK YOU AND ALL THE PRODUCTS OF YOUR TOIL WITH BLIGHT
AND WITH MILDEW AND WITH HAIL. — HAGGAI 2:17

How destructive is the hail to the standing crops, beating out the precious grain upon the ground! How grateful we should be when the corn is spared so terrible a ruin! Let us offer to the Lord thanksgiving. Even more to be dreaded are those mysterious destroyers—fungus, rust, and mildew. They turn the ear into a mass of soot or render it putrid or dry up the grain, and all in a manner so beyond all human control that the farmer is compelled to cry, "This is the finger of God." Innumerable minute fungi cause the mischief, and if it weren't for the goodness of God, the rider on the black horse would soon scatter famine over the land. Infinite mercy spares the food of men, but in view of the active agents that are ready to destroy the harvest, wisdom teaches us to pray, "Give us this day our daily bread." The curse is everywhere, and we are in constant need of the blessing. When blight and mildew come, they are chastisements from heaven, and men must learn to deal with them accordingly.

Spiritually, mildew is not an uncommon evil. When our work is most promising, this blight appears. We hoped for many conversions, and instead we find a general apathy, an abounding worldliness, or a cruel hardness of heart! There may be no blatant sin in those for whom we are working, but there is a deficiency of sincerity and decision that is sadly disappointing. We learn from this to depend upon the Lord and the necessity of prayer so that no blight will fall upon our work. Spiritual pride or laziness will soon bring upon us the dreadful evil, and only the Lord of the harvest can remove it. Mildew may even attack our own hearts and shrivel our prayers and dampen our zeal. May it please the great Gardener to avert so serious a calamity. Shine, blessed Sun of Righteousness, and drive the diseases away.

[1] 1 John 2:20

WE KNOW THAT FOR THOSE WHO LOVE GOD ALL THINGS WORK TOGETHER FOR GOOD. — ROMANS 8:28

Upon some points a believer is absolutely sure. He knows, for instance, that God sits in the center of the vessel when it rocks most. He believes that an invisible hand is always on the world's tiller, and that wherever providence may drift, God is steering it. That reassuring knowledge prepares him for everything. He looks over the raging waters and sees the spirit of Jesus walking on the water, and he hears a voice saying, "It is I—do not be afraid." He knows too that God is always wise, and knowing this, he is confident that there can be no accidents, no mistakes and that nothing can occur that ought not to happen. He can say, "If I should lose everything, it is better that I should lose it than keep it if it is God's will: The worst disaster is the wisest and the kindest thing that I could face if God ordains it." "We know that for those who love God all things work together for good." The Christian does not merely hold this as a theory, but *he knows it* as a matter of fact. So far everything *has* worked for good; the poisonous drugs mixed in proper proportions have effected the cure; the sharp cuts of the scalpel have cleaned out the disease and facilitated the healing. Every event as yet has worked out the most divinely blessed results; and so, believing that God rules all, that He governs wisely, that He brings good out of evil, the believer's heart is assured, and he is learning to meet each trial calmly when it comes. In the spirit of true resignation the believer can pray, "Send me what You will, my God, as long as it comes from You; there never was a poor portion that came from Your table to any of Your children."

Do not say, my soul, "Where will God find one to relieve my care?"
Remember that Omnipotence has servants everywhere.
His method is sublime and His heart profoundly kind,
God is never too early and never behind!

☙ EVENING ❧

SHALL YOUR BROTHERS GO TO THE WAR WHILE YOU SIT HERE? — NUMBERS 32:6

Family brings its obligations. The people of Reuben and the people of Gad would have been unbrotherly if they had claimed the land that had been conquered and had left the rest of the people to fight for their portions alone. We have received great benefits as a result of the efforts and sufferings of the saints in years gone by, and if we do not make some return to the Church of Christ by giving her our best energies, we are unworthy to be enrolled in her ranks. Others are bravely combating the errors of the age or excavating the dying from amid the ruins of the Fall, and if we fold our hands in idleness we put ourselves in danger. The Master of the vineyard inquires, "Why do you stand here all day doing nothing?" What is the lazy man's excuse? Serving Jesus becomes the duty of all because it is cheerfully and generously rendered by some. The toils of devoted missionaries and fervent ministers shame us if we continue to sit in laziness. It is the residents of "easy street" who are tempted to run from trials: They would like to escape the cross but still wear the crown; to them the question for this evening's meditation is very relevant. If the most precious are tested in the fire, are we to escape the crucible? If the diamond must be cut and fashioned on the wheel, are we to be made perfect without suffering? Who has commanded the wind to stop blowing because our ship is on the ocean? Why should we be treated better than our Lord? The firstborn endured suffering, so why not His younger brothers? It is a cowardly pride that would choose a soft pillow and a silk couch for a soldier of the cross. Far wiser is the one who first resigns himself to God's will and then as he grows in grace learns to delight in it. So he picks berries on the path of duty, gathers lilies at the foot of the cross, and like Samson discovers honey in the lion.

WATCHMAN, WHAT TIME OF THE NIGHT? — ISAIAH 21:11

What enemies are around? Errors abound, and new ones appear every hour: Against what heresy am I to be on my guard? Sins creep from their lurking places when the darkness reigns; I need to climb the watchtower and give myself to prayer. Our heavenly Protector anticipated all the attacks that are about to be made upon us, and when the evil designed for us is still in the desire of Satan, He prays for us that our faith will not fail when we are sifted as wheat. Continue then, gracious Watchman, to warn us of our foes, and for Zion's sake do not remain silent.

"Watchman, what time of the night?" *What weather is coming for the Church?* Are the clouds rolling in, or is it all clear and fair overhead? We must care for the Church of God with sincere and thoughtful love; and now that empty religion and irreligion both threaten, let us observe the signs of the times and prepare for conflict.

"Watchman, what time of the night?" *What stars are visible?* What precious promises are relevant to our circumstances? You sound the alarm and also give us the consolation. Christ, like the North Star, is always fixed in His place, and all the stars are secure in the right hand of their Lord.

But, watchman, *when comes the morning?* The Bridegroom delays. Are there no signs of His appearing as the Sun of Righteousness? Hasn't the morning star arisen as the pledge of day? When will the day dawn and the shadows flee away? O Jesus, if You don't come in person to Your waiting Church today, still come in Spirit to my sighing heart, and make it sing for joy.

> *Now all the earth is bright and glad*
> *With the fresh morn;*
> *But all my heart is cold, and dark and sad:*
> *Sun of the soul, let me behold Thy dawn!*
> *Come, Jesus, Lord,*
> *O quickly come, according to Thy word.*

❧ EVENING ☙

MAY THE WHOLE EARTH BE FILLED WITH HIS GLORY! AMEN AND AMEN!
— PSALM 72:19

This is a large petition. To intercede for a whole city needs a stretch of faith, and there are times when praying for one man is more than we can handle. But how far-reaching was the psalmist's dying intercession! How comprehensive! How sublime! "May the whole earth be filled with his glory." Not a single country is exempt even if it is crushed by the foot of superstition; this does not exclude a single nation however uncivilized. For the terrorist as well as for the civilized, for all places and races this prayer is uttered: It encompasses the whole circle of the world and omits no one. We must be up and doing for our Master, or we cannot honestly offer such a prayer. The petition is not asked with a sincere heart unless we endeavor, with God's help, to extend the kingdom of our Master. Are there not some who *neglect* both to pray and to work? Reader, is it *your* prayer? Turn your eyes to Calvary. Look at the Lord of Life nailed to a cross, with a crown of thorns upon His brow, with bleeding head and hands and feet. What! Can you look upon this miracle of miracles, the death of the Son of God, without feeling within your heart a marvelous adoration that language never can express? And when you feel the blood applied to your conscience and know that He has blotted out your sins, *you are not a man* unless you jump from your knees to cry, "May the whole earth be filled with his glory! Amen, and Amen!" Can you bow before the Crucified in humble adoration and not wish to see your Monarch Master of the world? You only pretend to love your Prince if you do not desire to see Him the universal ruler. Your piety is worthless unless it leads you to wish that the same mercy that has been shown to you may bless the whole world. Lord, it is harvesttime; put in Your sickle and reap.

RIGHTLY DO THEY LOVE YOU. — SONG OF SOLOMON 1:4

Believers love Jesus with a deeper affection then they dare to give to any other being. They would sooner lose father and mother than part with Christ. They hold all earthly comforts with a loose hand, but they carry Him locked tight in their hearts. They voluntarily deny themselves for His sake, but they are not to be driven to *deny* Him. It is a feeble love that the fire of persecution can dry up; the true believer's love is a deeper stream than this. Men have tried to divide the faithful from their Master, but their attempts have been fruitless in every age. Neither crowns of honor, nor frowns of anger have been able to untie this loving knot. This is not just a routine attachment that the world's power may eventually dissolve. Neither man nor devil have found a key that opens this lock. Never has the craft of Satan been more at fault than when he has exercised it in seeking to break this union of two divinely welded hearts. It is written, and nothing can blot out the sentence, "*Rightly do they love you.*" The intensity of the love of the upright, however, is not so much to be judged by how it appears as by what the upright long for. It is our daily lament that we cannot love enough. If only our hearts were capable of holding more and reaching further. Like Samuel Rutherford, we sigh and cry, "Oh, for as much love as would go round about the earth, and over heaven—yes, the heaven of heavens, and ten thousand worlds—that I might expand it all upon this fairest Lord Jesus." Unfortunately, our longest reach is only a span of love, and our affection is like a drop in a bucket compared with what He deserves. Measure our love by our intentions, and it is strong indeed; we trust that the Lord judges it in this way. If only we could give all the love in all hearts in one great offering, a gathering together of all loves to Him who is altogether lovely!

EVENING
SATAN HINDERED US. — 1 THESSALONIANS 2:18

Since the first hour in which goodness came into conflict with evil, it has never ceased to be true in spiritual experience that Satan hinders us. From all points of the compass, all along the line of battle, in the advance party or in the rear, at the dawn of day and in the midnight hour, Satan hinders us. If we work in the field, he seeks to break our implements; if we build a wall, he tries to cast down the stones; if we are serving God in suffering or in conflict—everywhere Satan hinders us. He hinders us when we are first coming to Jesus Christ. We had fierce conflicts with Satan when we first looked to the cross and lived. Now that we are saved, he tries to prevent our growth in Christian character. You may be congratulating yourself: "So far I have walked consistently; no one can challenge my integrity." Beware of boasting, for your virtue will soon be tested; Satan will direct his engines against the very virtue for which you are most famous. If you have to this point been a firm believer, your faith will soon be attacked; if you have been meek like Moses, expect to be tempted to speak unadvisedly with your lips. The birds will peck at your ripest fruit, and the wild boar will dash his tusks at your choicest vines. Satan is sure to hinder us when we are faithful in prayer. He hinders our persistence and weakens our faith in order that, if possible, we may miss the blessing. Satan is equally vigilant in obstructing Christian effort. There was never a revival of religion without a revival of his opposition. As soon as Ezra and Nehemiah began to work, Sanballat and Tobiah were stirred up to hinder them. What then? We are not alarmed because Satan hinders us, for it is a proof that we are on the Lord's side and are doing the Lord's work, and in His strength we will win the victory and triumph over our adversary.

❧ MORNING ❧

THEY WEAVE THE SPIDER'S WEB. — ISAIAH 59:5

Observe the spider's web and find in it a most suggestive picture of the hypocrite's religion. *It is meant to catch his prey*: The spider fattens himself on flies, and the Pharisee has his reward. Foolish people are easily trapped by the loud professions of pretenders, and even the more discerning cannot always escape. Philip baptized Simon Magus, whose deceitful declaration of faith was so quickly exposed by the stern rebuke of Peter. Routine and reputation, praise and promotion, along with other flies, are the small game that hypocrites take in their nets. A spider's web is *a marvel of skill*: Look at it and admire the tricks of this cunning hunter. The deceiver's religion is equally seductive. How does he make so barefaced a lie appear to be a truth? How can he make his tinsel look so much like gold? A spider's web *emerges all from the creature itself*. The bee gathers her wax from flowers; the spider doesn't, but still she spins her material to great length. In the same way hypocrites find their trust and hope within themselves; their anchor was forged on their own anvil, and their rope twisted by their own hands. They rest upon their own foundation and carve out the pillars from their own house, scorning the thought of being debtors to the sovereign grace of God. But a spider's web is *very frail*. It is curiously constructed, but not enduringly manufactured. It is no match for the servant's broom or the traveler's staff. The hypocrite does not need a battery of cannons to blow his hope to pieces; a mere puff of wind will do it. Hypocritical cobwebs will soon come down when the broom of destruction begins its purifying work. Which reminds us of one more thought—namely, that such cobwebs *are not to be tolerated in the Lord's house*: He will see to it that the webs and those who spin them will be utterly destroyed. My soul, make sure to rest on something better than a spider's web. Take the Lord Jesus as your eternal hiding-place.

❧ EVENING ❧

ALL THINGS ARE POSSIBLE FOR ONE WHO BELIEVES.
— MARK 9:23

Many professed Christians are always doubting and fearing, and they forlornly think that this is the inevitable state of believers. This is a mistake, for "all things are possible for one who believes"; and it is possible for us to arrive at a place where a doubt or a fear shall be like a migrant bird flitting across the soul but never lingering there. When you read of the high and sweet communions enjoyed by favored saints, you sigh and murmur in the chamber of your heart, "Sadly, these are not for me." But, climber, if you exercise your faith, you will before long stand on the sunny pinnacle of the temple, for "all things are possible for one who believes." You hear of exploits that holy men have done for Jesus—what they have enjoyed of Him, how much they have been like Him, how they have been able to endure great persecutions for His sake—and you say, "But as for me, I am useless. I can never reach these heights." But there is nothing that one saint was that you may not be. There is no elevation of grace, no attainment of spirituality, no clearness of assurance, no place of duty, that is not open to you if you have but the power to believe. Lay aside your sackcloth and ashes, and rise to the dignity of your true position; you are impoverished not because you have to be but because you want to be. It is not right that you, a child of the King, should grovel in the dust. Rise! The golden throne of assurance is waiting for you! The crown of communion with Jesus is ready to adorn your brow. Wrap yourself in scarlet and fine linen, and eat lavishly every day; for if you believe, you can eat the royal portion, your land will flow with milk and honey, and your soul shall be satisfied in God. Gather golden sheaves of grace, for they await you in the fields of faith. "All things are possible for one who believes."

THE CITY HAS NO NEED OF SUN OR MOON TO SHINE ON IT.
— REVELATION 21:23

Further on, in the better world, the residents are not dependent upon creature comforts. They do not need new clothes; their white robes never wear out, nor do they become soiled or tattered. They don't need medicine to heal diseases, for no one will ever say, "I am sick." They do not need sleep to restore their strength—they do not rest by day or night as they praise God in His temple. They do not need social relationships to grant comfort, and whatever happiness they may derive from association with their fellows is not essential to their bliss, for the presence of Jesus is enough for their largest desires. They do not need teachers there; they doubtless commune with one another concerning the things of God, but they do not need to be instructed; they will all be taught of the Lord. We receive donations at the King's gate, but they feast at the table itself. Here we lean upon the friendly arm, but there they lean upon the Beloved and upon Him alone. Here we need the help of our companions, but there they find all they need in Christ Jesus. Here we look to the food that perishes and to the clothing that decays before the moth, but there they find everything in God. We use the bucket to fetch water from the well, but there they drink from the fountainhead and put their lips down to the living water. Now the angels bring us blessings, but then we will not need messengers from heaven. They do not need angels there to bring their love-notes from God because they see *Him* face to face. What a blessed time it will be when having moved beyond every secondary cause we rest upon the bare arm of God! What a glorious hour when God, and not His creatures—the Lord, and not His works—will be our daily joy! Our souls will then have attained the perfection of bliss.

⚬ EVENING ⚬

HE APPEARED FIRST TO MARY MAGDALENE, FROM WHOM HE HAD
CAST OUT SEVEN DEMONS. — MARK 16:9

Mary of Magdala was *the victim of a fearful evil.* She was possessed not just by one demon, but by seven. These dreadful inmates caused much pain and pollution to the poor frame in which they had found a lodging. Hers was a hopeless, horrible case. She could not help herself, and no human power could set her free. But Jesus passed that way, and without being asked and probably while being resisted by the poor demoniac, He uttered the word of power, and Mary of Magdala became *a trophy of the healing power of Jesus.* All seven demons left her, left her never to return, forcibly ejected by the Lord of all. What a blessed deliverance! What a happy change! From delirium to delight, from despair to peace, from hell to heaven! Immediately she became *a constant follower of Jesus,* listening to His every word, following His winding steps, sharing His busy life; and in all this she became *His generous helper,* first among that band of healed and grateful women who ministered to Him out of their means. When Jesus was lifted up in crucifixion, Mary remained *the sharer of His shame:* We find her first watching from a distance and then drawing near to the foot of the cross. She could not die on the cross with Jesus, but she stood as near it as she could, and when His blessed body was taken down, she watched to see how and where it was laid. She was *the faithful and watchful believer,* last at the sepulcher where Jesus slept, first at the grave where He arose. Her loyalty and love made her *a favored beholder of her beloved Master,* who deigned to call her by her name and to make her *His messenger of good news* to the trembling disciples and Peter. Grace found her useless and made her useful, cast out her demons and gave her to behold angels, delivered her from Satan and united her forever to the Lord Jesus. May we also be such miracles of grace!

CHRIST WHO IS YOUR LIFE. — COLOSSIANS 3:4

Paul's marvelously rich expression indicates that Christ is the *source* of our life. You has He quickened who "were dead in . . . trespasses and sins."[1] The same voice that brought Lazarus out of the tomb raised us to newness of life. He is now the *substance* of our spiritual life. It is by His life that we live; He is in us, the hope of glory, the spring of our actions, the central thought that moves every other thought. *Christ is the sustenance of our life.* What can the Christian feed upon but Christ, the living bread? "This is the bread that comes down from heaven, so that one may eat of it and not die."[2] Remember, weary pilgrims in this wilderness of sin, that you will never get a morsel to satisfy your spiritual hunger unless you find it in Him! *Christ is the solace of our life.* All our true joys come from Him; and in times of trouble, His presence is our consolation. There is nothing worth living for but Him; and His loving-kindness is better than life! *Christ is the object of our life.* As the ship speeds toward the port, so hurries the believer toward the haven of his Savior's heart. As the arrow flies to its target, so the Christian flies toward the perfecting of his fellowship with Christ Jesus. As the soldier fights for his captain and is crowned in his captain's victory, so the believer contends for Christ and gets his triumph out of the triumphs of his Master. "For [him] to live is Christ."[3] *Christ is the exemplar of our life.* Where the same life is found inside, there will, there must be, to a great extent, the same developments outside; and if we live in close fellowship with the Lord Jesus we shall grow like Him. We will set Him before us as our divine example, and we will seek to follow in His footsteps, until He shall become *the crown of our life in glory.* How safe, how honored, how happy is the Christian since Christ is his life!

❧   E V E N I N G   ☙

THE SON OF MAN HAS AUTHORITY ON EARTH TO FORGIVE SINS.
— MATTHEW 9:6

Consider here the Great Physician's mighty power: the power to forgive sin! While He lived here below, before the ransom had been paid, before the blood had been literally sprinkled on the mercy-seat, He had power to forgive sin. Has He no power to do it now that He has died? What power must dwell in Him who to the utmost penny has faithfully discharged the debts of His people! He has unlimited power now that He has finished transgression and made an end of sin. If you doubt it, see Him rising from the dead! Behold Him in ascending splendor, raised to the right hand of God! Hear Him pleading before the eternal Father, pointing to His wounds, declaring the merit of His sacred passion! What power to forgive is here! He ascended on high, and He gave gifts to men. He is exalted on high to give repentance and forgiveness of sins. The most crimson sins are removed by the crimson of His blood. At this moment, dear reader, whatever your sinfulness, Christ has power to pardon, power to pardon *you*, and millions just like you. A word will speak it. He has nothing more to do to win your pardon; all the atoning work is done. He can, in answer to your tears, forgive your sins today and make you know it. He can breathe into your soul at this very moment a peace with God that passes all understanding, which shall spring from perfect remission of your many iniquities. Do you believe that? I trust you believe it. May you even now experience the power of Jesus to forgive sin! Waste no time in applying to the Physician of souls; hasten to Him with words like these:

> *Jesus! Master! hear my cry;*
> *Save me, heal me with a word;*
> *Fainting at Thy feet I lie,*
> *Thou my whisper'd plea has heard.*

[1] Ephesians 2:1   [2] John 6:50   [3] Philippians 1:21

OH, THAT I WERE AS IN THE MONTHS OF OLD. — JOB 29:2

Many Christians are able to view the past with pleasure but regard the present with dissatisfaction. They look back upon the days that they have spent in communing with the Lord as being the sweetest and the best they have ever known; but as to the present, it is as if they were smothered by a heavy blanket of gloom and dreariness. Once they lived near Jesus, but now they feel that they have wandered from Him, and they say, "Oh, that I were as in the months of old." They complain that they have lost their evidences, or that they no longer have peace of mind, or that they have no enjoyment in the means of grace, or that their conscience is hardened, or that they are no longer as zealous for God's glory as they once were. The causes of this mournful state of things are many. It may arise through a comparative *neglect of prayer*, for a neglected closet is the beginning of all spiritual decline. Or it may be the result of *idolatry*. The heart has been occupied with something else, more than with God; the affections have been set on the things of earth instead of the things of heaven. A jealous God will not be content with a divided heart; He must be loved first and best. He will withdraw the sunshine of His presence from a cold, wandering heart. Or the cause may be found in *self-confidence* and *self-righteousness*. Pride is busy in the heart, and self is exalted instead of lying low at the foot of the cross. Christian, if you are not now as you "were . . . in the months of old," do not be content to simply *wish* for a return of your former happiness, but go at once to seek your Master and tell Him your sad state. Ask His grace and strength to enable you to walk more closely with Him; humble yourself before Him, and He will lift you up and allow you once more to enjoy the light of His countenance. Do not sit down to sigh and lament; while the beloved Physician lives there is hope; there is a certainty of recovery even for the worst cases.

❧ EVENING ☙

ETERNAL COMFORT. — 2 THESSALONIANS 2:16

Comfort." There is music in the word: Like David's harp, it charms away the evil spirit of melancholy. It was a distinguished honor to Barnabas to be called "the son of encouragement";[1] it is one of the illustrious names of a greater than Barnabas, for the Lord Jesus is the comfort of Israel. "*Eternal* comfort"! This is the best of all, for the everlasting nature of comfort is its crown and glory. What is this "eternal comfort"? It includes a sense of pardoned sin. A Christian man has received in his heart the witness of the Spirit that his iniquities are put away like a cloud, and his transgressions like a thick cloud. If sin is pardoned, is that not an eternal comfort? Next, the Lord gives His people an abiding sense of being accepted in Christ. The Christian knows that God looks upon him as standing in union with Jesus. Union with the risen Lord is a comfort of the most abiding order; it is, in fact, everlasting. Let sickness prostrate us—haven't we seen hundreds of believers as happy in the weakness of disease as they would have been in the enjoyment of blooming health? If death's arrows pierce us to the heart, our comfort does not die, for we have often heard the songs of saints as they rejoiced because the living love of God was shed abroad in their hearts in dying moments. Yes, a sense of acceptance in the Beloved is an eternal comfort. Moreover, the Christian is convinced of his security. God has promised to save those who trust in Christ: The Christian does trust in Christ, and he believes that God will be as good as His word and will save him. He feels that he is safe by virtue of his being bound up with the person and work of Jesus. Herein is comfort such as can be found nowhere else and in no one else!

[1] Acts 4:36

❧ MORNING ❧

There are no real causes for anxiety as long as this blessed sentence is true. *On earth* the Lord's power controls the rage of the wicked as readily as the rage of the sea; His love refreshes the poor with mercy as easily as the earth with showers. Majesty gleams in flashes of lightning amid the tempest's horrors, and the glory of the Lord is seen in its grandeur in the fall of empires and the crash of thrones. In all our conflicts and tribulations, we may behold the hand of the divine King.

> God is God; He sees and hears
> All our troubles, all our tears.
> Soul, forget not, in your pains,
> God o'er all forever reigns.

In hell, evil spirits acknowledge, with misery, His undoubted supremacy. When permitted to roam about, it is with a chain at their heel; the bit is in the mouth of the beast, and the hook in the jaws of the monster. Death's darts are under the Lord's jurisdiction, and the grave's prisons have divine power as their jailer. The terrible vengeance of the Judge of all the earth causes fiends to cower and tremble.

> Fear not death, nor Satan's thrusts,
> God defends who in Him trusts;
> Soul, remember, in your pains,
> God o'er all forever reigns.

In heaven there are none who doubt the sovereignty of the King Eternal, but all fall on their faces to do Him homage. Angels are His courtiers, the redeemed His favorites, and all delight to serve Him day and night. May we soon reach the city of the great King!

> For this life's long night of sadness
> He will give us peace and gladness.
> Soul, remember, in your pains,
> God o'er all forever reigns.

❧ EVENING ❧
THE BOW IS SEEN IN THE CLOUDS. — GENESIS 9:14

The rainbow, the symbol of the covenant with Noah, foreshadows our Lord Jesus, who is the Lord's witness to the people. When may we *expect to see the token of the covenant?* The rainbow is only to be seen painted upon a *cloud.* When the sinner's conscience is dark with clouds, when he remembers his past sin and mourns and laments before God, Jesus Christ is revealed to him as the covenant Rainbow, displaying all the glorious hues of the divine character and declaring peace. To the believer, when his trials and temptations surround him, it is sweet to behold the person of our Lord Jesus Christ—to see Him bleeding, living, rising, and pleading for us. God's rainbow is hung over the cloud of our sins, our sorrows, and our woes, to prophesy deliverance. By itself a *cloud* does not give a rainbow; there must be *the crystal drops* to reflect the light of the sun. So, our sorrows must not only threaten, but they must really fall upon us. There would have been no Christ for us if the vengeance of God had been merely a threatening cloud: Punishment must fall in terrible drops upon Him. Until there is a *real* anguish in the sinner's conscience, there is no Christ for him; until the chastisement that he feels becomes grievous, he cannot see Jesus. But there must also be a sun; for clouds and drops of rain do not make rainbows unless the sun shines. Beloved, our God, who is as the sun to us, always shines, but we do not always see Him—clouds hide His face; but no matter what drops may be falling or what clouds may be threatening, if *He* shines there will be a rainbow at once. It is said that when we see the rainbow, the shower is over. It is certain that when Christ comes, our troubles withdraw; when we look on Jesus, our sins vanish, and our doubts and fears subside. When Jesus walks upon the waters of the sea, how profound the calm!

THE CEDARS OF LEBANON THAT HE PLANTED. — PSALM 104:16

Lebanon's cedars are emblematic of the Christian, in that *they owe their planting entirely to the Lord*. This is quite true of every child of God. He is not man-planted, nor self-planted, but God-planted. The mysterious hand of the divine Spirit dropped the living seed into a heart that He had Himself prepared for its reception. Every true heir of heaven knows that it is God who planted him. Moreover, the cedars of Lebanon *do not depend upon man for their watering*; they stand on the lofty rock, unmoistened by human irrigation; and yet our heavenly Father supplies them. So it is with the Christian who has learned to live by faith. He is independent of man, even in temporal things; for his continued maintenance he looks to the Lord his God, and to Him alone. The dew of heaven is his portion, and the God of heaven is his fountain. Again, the cedars of Lebanon *are not protected by any mortal power*. They owe nothing to man for their preservation from stormy wind and tempest. They are God's trees, kept and preserved by Him, and by Him alone. It is precisely the same with the Christian. He is not a hothouse plant, sheltered from temptation; he stands in the most exposed position; he has no shelter, no protection, except this, that the broad wings of the eternal God always cover the cedars that He Himself has planted. Like cedars, believers are *full of sap*, having enough vitality to stay green, even amid the winter's snows. Lastly, the flourishing and majestic condition of the cedar *is to the praise of God only*. The Lord, even the Lord alone, has been everything to the cedars, and therefore David very sweetly puts it in one of the psalms, "Praise the Lord! Fruit trees and all cedars."[1] In the believer there is nothing that can magnify man; he is planted, nourished, and protected by the Lord's own hand, and therefore to Him let all the glory be ascribed.

❧ EVENING ☙

I WILL REMEMBER MY COVENANT. — GENESIS 9:15

Note the form of this promise. God does not say, "And when you shall look upon the bow, and *you* shall remember My covenant, *then* I will not destroy the earth," but it is gloriously put, not upon *our* memory, which is fickle and frail, but upon *God's* memory, which is infinite and immutable. "When . . . the bow is seen in the clouds, I will remember my covenant." It is not my remembering God—it is God's remembering *me* that is the ground of my safety; it is not my laying hold of His covenant, but His covenant's laying hold on me. Glory be to God! The ramparts of salvation are secured by divine power, and even the minor towers, which we could imagine being left to man, are guarded by almighty strength. Even the *remembrance* of the covenant is not left to our memories, for *we* might forget; but our Lord cannot forget the names of those whom He has graven on the palms of His hands. It is with us as it was with Israel in Egypt; the blood was upon the lintel and the two sideposts, but the Lord did not say, "When *you* see the blood I will pass over you," but "When *I* see the blood I will pass over you." My looking to Jesus brings me joy and peace, but it is God's looking to Jesus that secures my salvation and that of all His elect, since it is impossible for our God to look at Christ, our bleeding Surety, and then to be angry with us for sins already punished in Him. It is not left with *us* even to be saved by remembering the covenant. There is not a single thread of human effort in this fabric. It is not *of* man, neither *by* man, but of the Lord alone. We *should* remember the covenant, and we *shall* do it, through divine grace; but the hinge of our safety does not hang there—it is God's remembering *us*, not our remembering *Him*; and hence the covenant is *an everlasting covenant*.

[1] Psalm 148:9

YOU, O LORD, HAVE MADE ME GLAD BY YOUR WORK. — PSALM 92:4

Do you believe that your sins are forgiven and that Christ has made a full atonement for them? Then what a joyful Christian *you ought to be*! How you should live above the common trials and troubles of the world! Since sin is forgiven, can it matter what happens to you now? Luther said, "Smite, Lord, smite, for my sin is forgiven; if You have forgiven me, smite as hard as You will." And in a similar spirit you may say, "Send sickness, poverty, losses, crosses, persecution, what You will. *You have forgiven me*, and my soul is glad." Christian, if you are thus saved, while you are glad, *be grateful and loving*. Cling to that cross that took your sin away; serve Him who served you. "I appeal to you therefore, brothers, by the mercies of God, to present your bodies as a living sacrifice, holy and acceptable to God, which is your spiritual worship."[1] Do not let your zeal evaporate in some little exuberant song. Show your love in meaningful ways. Love the brethren of Him who loved you. If there is a Mephibosheth anywhere who is disabled, help him for Jonathan's sake. If there is a poor tried believer, weep with him, and bear his cross for the sake of Him who wept for you and carried your sins. Since you are forgiven freely for Christ's sake, go and tell others the joyful news of pardoning mercy. Do not be contented with this unspeakable blessing for yourself alone, but publish widely the story of the cross. Holy gladness and holy boldness will make you a good preacher, and all the world will be a pulpit for you to preach in. Cheerful holiness is the most forcible of sermons, but the Lord must give it to you. Seek it this morning before you go into the world. When it is the Lord's work in which we rejoice, we need not be afraid of being too glad.

❧ EVENING ❧

I KNOW THEIR SUFFERINGS. — EXODUS 3:7

The child is cheered as he sings, "This my father knows"; and shall we not be comforted as we discern that our dear and tender Friend knows all about us?

1. *He is the Physician*, and if He knows everything, there is no need for the patient to know. Calm down, you silly, fluttering heart, prying, peeping, and suspecting! What you don't know now, you will know later; and meanwhile Jesus, the beloved Physician, knows your soul in adversities. Why does the patient need to analyze all the medicine or estimate all the symptoms? This is the Physician's work, not mine; it is my business to trust, and His to prescribe. If He shall write His prescription in a fashion that I cannot read, I will not be uneasy on that account, but will rely upon His unfailing skill to make everything clear in the result, no matter how mysterious the process.

2. *He is the Master*, and *His* knowledge is to serve us instead of our own; we are to obey, not to judge: "The servant does not know what his master is doing."[2] Shall the architect explain his plans to every bricklayer on the job? If he knows his own intent, is it not enough? The pot upon the wheel cannot guess to what pattern it will be conformed, but if the potter understands his art, the ignorance of the clay is irrelevant. My Lord must not be cross-questioned any more by one so ignorant as I am.

3. *He is the Head*. All understanding centers there. What judgment has the arm? What comprehension has the foot? All the power to know lies in the head. Why should the member have a brain of its own when the head fulfills for it every intellectual office? Here, then, the believer must rest his comfort in sickness—not that he himself can see the end, but that Jesus knows all. Sweet Lord, be forever eye and soul and head for us, and let us be content to know only what You choose to reveal.

[1] Romans 12:1   [2] John 15:15

AUGUST 15   MORNING

ISAAC WENT OUT TO MEDITATE IN THE FIELD TOWARD EVENING.
— GENESIS 24:63

Isaac's evening occupation was very admirable. If those who spend so many hours in idle company, light reading, and useless pastimes could learn wisdom, they would find more profitable society and more interesting engagements in meditation than in the vanities that now hold such appeal for them. We would all know more, live closer to God, and grow in grace if we were alone more often. Meditation chews the cud and extracts the real nutriment from the mental food gathered elsewhere. When Jesus is the theme, meditation is sweet indeed. Isaac found Rebecca while engaged in private musings; many others have found their best beloved there.

Isaac's choice of place was very admirable. The field provides a study full of texts for thought. From the cedar to the hyssop, from the soaring eagle down to the chirping grasshopper, from the blue expanse of heaven to a drop of dew, all these things are full of teaching, and when the eye is divinely opened, that teaching flashes upon the mind far more vividly than from books. Our little rooms are neither so healthy, so suggestive, so agreeable, or so inspiring as the fields. Let us count nothing common or unclean but feel that all created things point to their Maker, and the field will at once be holy ground.

The season was very admirable. The season of sunset as it draws a veil over the day is a fitting time for the soul's repose when earthborn cares yield to the joys of heavenly communion. The glory of the setting sun excites our wonder, and the solemnity of approaching night awakens our awe. If the business of this day will permit it, it will be well, dear reader, if you can spare an hour to walk in the field at evening; but if not, the Lord is in the town too and will meet with you in your chamber or in the crowded street. Let your heart go out to meet Him.

EVENING

AND I WILL GIVE YOU A NEW HEART . . . A HEART OF FLESH.
— EZEKIEL 36:26

A "heart of flesh" is known by its *tenderness concerning sin.* To have indulged a foul imagination or to have allowed a wild desire to linger even for a moment is quite enough to make a heart of flesh grieve before the Lord. The heart of stone calls a great iniquity nothing, but not so the heart of flesh.

> *If to the right or left I stray,*
> *That moment, Lord, reprove;*
> *And let me weep my life away,*
> *For having grieved Thy love.*

The heart of flesh is *tender to God's will.* Unlike a strong heart that refuses to bow before God's dictates, when the heart of flesh is given, the will quivers like an aspen leaf in every breath of heaven and bows like a willow in every breeze of God's Spirit. The natural will is cold, hard iron, which refuses to be hammered into form, but the renewed will, like molten metal, is quickly molded by the hand of grace. In the fleshy heart there is *a tenderness of the affections.* The hard heart does not love the Redeemer, but the renewed heart burns with affection toward Him. The hard heart is selfish and coldly demands, "Why should I weep for sin? Why should I love the Lord?" But the heart of flesh says, "Lord, You know that I love You; help me to love You more!" There are many privileges of this renewed heart. It is here the Spirit dwells; it is here that Jesus lives. It is fitted to receive every spiritual blessing, and every blessing comes to it. It is prepared to yield every heavenly fruit to the honor and praise of God, and therefore the Lord delights in it. A tender heart is the best defense against sin and the best preparation for heaven. A renewed heart stands on its watchtower looking for the coming of the Lord Jesus. Do you have this heart of flesh?

ASCRIBE TO THE LORD THE GLORY DUE HIS NAME. — PSALM 29:2

God's glory is the result of His nature and acts. He is glorious in His character, for there is such a store of everything that is holy and good and lovely in God that He must be glorious. The actions that flow from His character are also glorious; but while He intends that they should display to His creatures His goodness and mercy and justice, He is equally concerned that the glory associated with them should be given only to Himself. Not that there is anything in ourselves in which we may glory; for who makes us different from another? And what do we have that we did not receive from the God of all grace? Then how careful we ought to be to *walk humbly before the Lord*! The moment we glorify ourselves, since there is room for one glory only in the universe, we set ourselves up as rivals to the Most High. Shall an insect that's been around for only an hour glorify itself against the sun that warmed it into life? Shall the clay pot exalt itself above the man who fashioned it upon the wheel? Shall the dust of the desert strive with the whirlwind? Or the drops of the ocean struggle with the storm? Give to the Lord, all you righteous, give to the Lord glory and strength; give to Him the honor that is due His name. It is, perhaps, one of the hardest struggles of the Christian life to learn this sentence—"Not to us, O LORD, not unto us, but to your name give glory."[1] It is a lesson that God is always teaching us, and teaching us sometimes by the most painful discipline. Let a Christian begin to boast, "I can do all things," without adding "through Christ who strengthens me," and before long he will have to groan, "I can do nothing" and bemoan himself in the dust. When we do anything for the Lord, and He is pleased to accept our doings, let us lay our crown at His feet and exclaim, "Not I, but the grace of God that is with me."[2]

～ EVENING ～
. . . OURSELVES, WHO HAVE THE FIRSTFRUITS OF THE SPIRIT.
— ROMANS 8:23

Present possession is declared. At this present moment we have the firstfruits of the Spirit. We have repentance, that gem of the first water; faith, that priceless pearl; hope, the heavenly emerald; and love, the glorious ruby. We are already made new creatures in Christ Jesus by the effectual working of God the Holy Spirit. This is called the firstfruit because *it comes first*. As the wave-sheaf was the first of the harvest, so the spiritual life, and all the graces that adorn that life, are the first operations of the Spirit of God in our souls. *The firstfruits were the pledge of the harvest.* As soon as the Israelite had plucked the first handful of ripe ears, he looked forward with glad anticipation to the time when the wagon would creak beneath the sheaves. So, brethren, when God gives us things that are pure, lovely, and of good report, as the work of the Holy Spirit, these are to us the indications of the coming glory. *The firstfruits were always holy to the Lord*, and our new nature, with all its powers, is a consecrated thing. The new life is not ours that we should ascribe its excellence to our own merit; it is Christ's image and creation and is ordained for His glory. But *the firstfruits were not the harvest*, and the works of the Spirit in us at this moment are not the consummation—the perfection is still to come. We must not boast that we have attained, and so reckon the first sheaf to be all the produce of the year: We must hunger and thirst for righteousness and long for the day of full redemption. Dear reader, this evening open your mouth wide, and God will fill it. Let the blessing in present possession excite in you a sacred greed for more grace. Groan within yourself for higher degrees of consecration, and your Lord will grant them to you, for He is able to do far more abundantly than all that we ask or think.

[1] Psalm 115:1 [2] 1 Corinthians 15:10

Meditate a little on this steadfast love of the Lord. It is *tender love*. With gentle, loving touch, He heals the brokenhearted and binds up their wounds. He is as gracious in the manner of His steadfast love as in the matter of it. It is *great steadfast love*. There is nothing little in God; His steadfast love is like Himself—it is infinite. You cannot measure it. His mercy is so great that it forgives great sins to great sinners after great lengths of time and then gives great favors and great privileges and raises us up to great enjoyments in the great heaven of the great God. It is *undeserved steadfast love*, as indeed all true mercy must be, for deserved mercy is only a misnomer for justice. There was no right on the sinner's part to the kind consideration of the Most High; had the rebel been doomed at once to eternal fire he would have richly merited the doom, and if delivered from wrath, sovereign love alone has found a cause, for there was none in the sinner himself. It is *rich steadfast love*. Some things are great but have little efficacy in them, but this steadfast love is a tonic to your drooping spirits, a golden ointment to your bleeding wounds, a heavenly bandage to your broken bones, a royal chariot for your weary feet, a bosom of love for your trembling heart. It is *manifold steadfast love*. As Bunyan says, "All the flowers in God's garden are double." There is no single steadfast love. You may think you have only one steadfast love, but you will find it to be a whole cluster of mercies. It is *abounding steadfast love*. Millions have received it, but far from its being exhausted, it is as fresh, as full, and as free as ever. *It is unfailing steadfast love*. It will never leave you. If mercy is your friend, mercy will be with you in temptation to keep you from yielding, with you in trouble to prevent you from sinking, with you in living to be the light and life of your countenance, and with you in dying to be the joy of your soul when earthly comfort is ebbing fast.

❧ EVENING ❧

THIS ILLNESS DOES NOT LEAD TO DEATH. — JOHN 11:4

From our Lord's words we learn that there is a limit to illness. Here is a "lead to" within which its ultimate end is restrained and beyond which it cannot go. Lazarus might pass through death, but death was not to be the conclusion of his illness. In all illness the Lord says to the waves of pain, "You may go so far, but no further." His fixed purpose is not the destruction but the instruction of His people. Wisdom hangs up the thermometer at the furnace mouth and regulates the heat.

1. *The limit is encouragingly comprehensive.* The God of providence has limited the time, manner, intensity, repetition, and effects of all our sicknesses; each throb is decreed, each sleepless hour predestined, each relapse ordained, each depression of spirit foreknown, and each sanctifying result eternally purposed. Nothing great or small escapes the ordaining hand of Him who numbers the hairs of our head.

2. *This limit is wisely adjusted* to our strength, to the purpose designed, and to the grace apportioned. Affliction is not haphazard—the weight of every stroke of the rod is accurately measured. He who made no mistakes in balancing the clouds and stretching out the heavens commits no errors in measuring out the ingredients that compose the medicine of souls. We cannot suffer too much nor be relieved too late.

3. *The limit is tenderly appointed.* The knife of the heavenly Surgeon never cuts deeper than is absolutely necessary. "He does not willingly afflict or grieve the children of men."[1] A mother's heart cries, "Spare my child"; but no mother is more compassionate than our gracious God. When we consider how hardmouthed we are, it is a wonder that we are not driven with a sharper bit. The thought is full of comfort that He who has established the boundary lines of our lives has also determined the boundaries of our tribulation.

[1] Lamentations 3:33

FOREIGNERS HAVE COME INTO THE HOLY PLACES OF THE LORD'S HOUSE.
— JEREMIAH 51:51

In this account the faces of the Lord's people were covered with shame, for it was a terrible thing for men to intrude upon the Holy Place that was reserved exclusively for the priests. Everywhere around us we see similar cause for sorrow. How many ungodly men are now studying with a view to entering the ministry! What a crying sin is that solemn lie by which our whole population is nominally part of a National Church! How fearful it is that ordinances should be pressed upon the unconverted, and that among the more enlightened churches of our land there should be such laxity of discipline. If the thousands who will read this portion will take this matter before the Lord Jesus today, He will interfere and avert the evil that otherwise will come upon His Church. To adulterate the church is to pollute a well, to pour water upon fire, to sow a fertile field with stones. May we all have grace to maintain in our own proper way the purity of the Church as being an assembly of believers and not a nation, an unsaved community of unconverted men.

Our zeal must, however, begin at home. Let us examine *ourselves* as to our right to eat at the Lord's Table. Let us see to it that we are wearing our wedding garment, lest we ourselves should be regarded as foreigners in the Lord's holy place. Many are called, but few are chosen; the way is narrow, and the gate is strait. O for grace to come to Jesus aright, with the faith of God's elect. He who smote Uzzah for touching the ark is very jealous of His two ordinances. As a true believer I may approach them freely; as a foreigner I must not touch them in case I die. Heart-searching is the duty of all who are baptized or come to the Lord's Table. "Search me, O God, and know my heart! Try me and know my thoughts!"[1]

Evening

AND THEY OFFERED HIM WINE MIXED WITH MYRRH,
BUT HE DID NOT TAKE IT. — MARK 15:23

A golden truth is couched in the fact that the Savior pushed the myrrhed wine-cup from His lips. On the heights of heaven the Son of God stood of old, and as He looked down upon our globe He measured the long descent to the utmost depths of human misery. He considered the sum total of all the agonies that expiation would require and didn't shrink. He solemnly determined that to offer a sufficient atoning sacrifice He must go the whole way, from the highest to the lowest, from the throne of highest glory to the cross of deepest woe. This myrrhed cup, with its anesthetic influence, would have prevented Him from experiencing the utter limit of misery, and therefore He refused it. He would not stop short of all He had undertaken to suffer for His people. How many of us have cried for comfort in our grief to keep us from injury! Reader, did you never pray to be relieved of hard service or suffering with a petulant and willful eagerness? In a moment providence has taken from you the desire of your eyes. Say, Christian, if you were told, "If you want, your loved one will live, but God will be dishonored," could you have put away the temptation and said, "Your will be done"? It is good to be able to say, "My Lord, if for other reasons I do not need to suffer, yet if I can honor You more by suffering, and if the loss of my earthly goods will bring You glory, then let it be. I refuse the comfort if it stands in the way of Your honor." Let us learn to walk in the footsteps of our Lord, cheerfully enduring trial for His sake, promptly and willingly putting away the thought of self and comfort when it would interfere with our completing the work that He has given us to do. Great grace is needed, but great grace is provided.

[1] Psalm 139:23

❧ MORNING ✍

HE SHALL STAND AND SHEPHERD HIS FLOCK
IN THE STRENGTH OF THE LORD. — MICAH 5:4

Christ's reign in His Church is that of a *shepherd-king*. He has supremacy, but it is the superiority of a wise and tender shepherd over his needy and loving flock. He commands and receives obedience, but it is the willing obedience of the well-cared-for sheep, rendered joyfully to their beloved Shepherd, whose voice they know so well. He rules by the force of love and the energy of goodness.

His reign is *practical in its character*. It is said, "He shall *stand and shepherd*." The great Head of the church is actively engaged in providing for His people. He does not sit down upon the throne in empty state or hold a scepter without wielding it in government. No; He stands and shepherds. The expression "shepherd" in the original is like an analogous one in the Greek that means to do everything expected of a shepherd: to guide, to watch, to preserve, to restore, to tend, as well as to feed.

His reign is *continual in its duration*. It is said, "*He shall stand* and shepherd"; not "He shall feed now and then and leave His position"; not "He shall one day grant a revival and then next day leave His Church to barrenness." His eyes never slumber, and His hands never rest; His heart never ceases to beat with love, and His shoulders are never weary of carrying His people's burdens.

His reign is *effectually powerful in its action*; "He shall . . . shepherd his flock in the strength of the LORD." Wherever Christ is, there is God; and whatever Christ does is the act of the Most High. It is a joyful truth to consider that He who stands today representing the interests of His people is very God of very God, to whom every knee shall bow. We are happy to belong to such a shepherd, whose humanity communes with us and whose divinity protects us. Let us worship and bow down before Him as the people of His pasture.

❧ EVENING ✍

YOU TAKE ME OUT OF THE NET THEY HAVE HIDDEN FOR ME,
FOR YOU ARE MY REFUGE. — PSALM 31:4

Our spiritual foes belong to the serpent's brood and seek to ensnare us by subtlety. This prayer presupposes the possibility of the believer being caught like a bird. The catcher does his work so skillfully that simple souls are soon surrounded by the net. The request is that even out of Satan's snares the captive may be delivered; this is a proper petition, and one that can be granted: eternal love can rescue the saint from between the jaws of the lion and out of the depths of hell. It may need a sharp pull to save a soul from the net of temptations and a mighty pull to extricate a man from the snares of malicious cunning, but the Lord is equal to every emergency, and the most skillfully placed nets of the hunter will never be able to hold His chosen ones. There will be grief for those who are so clever at net laying; those who tempt others shall be destroyed themselves.

"*For you are my refuge*." What a wonderful encouragement is found in these few words! How joyfully may we encounter toils, and how cheerfully may we endure sufferings when we can lay hold upon the strength of the Lord. Divine power will thwart all the endeavors of our enemies, confound their politics, and frustrate their foolish tricks. Happy is the man who has such matchless might engaged upon his side. Our own strength would serve us poorly when trapped in the nets of our cunning enemy, but the Lord's refuge is always available; we have only to ask, and we will find it near at hand. If by faith we are depending solely on the strength of the mighty God of Israel, then our dependence may become the occasion of our prayer.

Lord, evermore Thy face we seek:
Tempted we are, and poor, and weak;
Keep us with lowly hearts, and meek.
Let us not fall. Let us not fall.

THE SWEET PSALMIST OF ISRAEL. — 2 SAMUEL 23:1

Among all the saints whose lives are recorded in Holy Scripture, David possesses an experience of the most striking, varied, and instructive character. In his history we meet with trials and temptations that are not found, as a whole, in other saints of ancient times, and as a result he provides us with a shadowy picture of our Lord. David knew the trials of all ranks and conditions of men. Kings have their troubles, and David wore a crown. The peasant has his cares, and David handled a shepherd's crook. The wanderer has many hardships, and David hid in the caves of Engedi. The captain has his difficulties, and David found the sons of Zeruiah too hard for him. The psalmist also faced trials from his friends; his counselor Ahithophel forsook him: "[He] who ate my bread, has lifted his heel against me."[1] His worst foes came from his own household: His children were his greatest affliction. The temptations of poverty and wealth, of honor and reproach, of health and weakness all tried their power upon him. He had temptations from without to disturb his peace and from within to mar his joy. David no sooner escaped from one trial than he fell into another, no sooner emerged from one season of despondency and alarm than he was again brought into the lowest depths and all God's waves and billows rolled over him. This is probably the reason that David's psalms are so universally the delight of experienced Christians. Whatever our frame of mind, whether ecstasy or depression, David has exactly described our emotions. He was an able master of the human heart because he had been tutored in the best of all schools—the school of heartfelt, personal experience. As we are instructed in the same school, as we grow mature in grace and in years, we increasingly appreciate David's psalms and find them to be "green pastures."[2] My soul, let David's experience cheer and counsel you today.

☙ EVENING ❧

AND THEY RESTORED JERUSALEM AS FAR AS THE BROAD WALL. — NEHEMIAH 3:8

Well-fortified cities have broad walls, and so did Jerusalem in her glory days. The New Jerusalem must, similarly, be surrounded and preserved by a broad wall of nonconformity to the world and *separation* from its patterns and ideas. There is a tendency today to break down this holy barrier and make the distinction between the Church and the world merely nominal. Believers are no longer fixed on godliness, questionable literature is widely read, frivolous pastimes are eagerly indulged, and a general laxity threatens to deprive the Lord's special people of those sacred distinctives that separate them from sinners. It will be a bad day for the Church and the world when the proposed amalgamation is complete, and the sons of God and the daughters of men shall be united, and another deluge of wrath is ushered in. Beloved reader, make it your aim in heart, in word, in dress, in action to maintain the broad wall, remembering that the friendship of this world is enmity against God.

The Broad Wall provided a pleasant place of *relaxation* for the inhabitants of Jerusalem, from which they enjoyed sweeping views of the surrounding country. This reminds us of the Lord's exceeding broad commandments, which provide a pathway to freedom and communion with Jesus. From here we look upon the scenes of earth and gaze toward the glories of heaven. Separated from the world, and denying ourselves all ungodliness and fleshly lusts, we are not in prison, nor restricted within narrow boundaries; no, we walk in freedom, because we keep His commands. Come, reader; this evening walk with God in His statutes. As friend met friend upon the city wall, so meet your God on the path of holy prayer and meditation. You have every right to stand upon the walls of salvation, for you have been given the key to the King's city—you are a citizen of the metropolis of the universe.

[1] Psalm 41:9   [2] Psalm 23:2

WHOEVER BRINGS BLESSING WILL BE ENRICHED, AND
ONE WHO WATERS WILL HIMSELF BE WATERED. — PROVERBS 11:25

We are taught here the great lesson that to get, we must give; to accumulate, we must scatter; to make ourselves happy, we must make others happy; and in order to become spiritually vigorous, we must seek the spiritual good of others. In watering others, we are ourselves watered. How? Our efforts to be useful *bring out our powers for usefulness*. We have latent talents and unused gifts that become apparent by exercise. Our strength for work is even hidden from ourselves until we take our stand and fight the Lord's battles or climb the mountains of difficulty. We do not know what tender sympathies we possess until we try to dry the widow's tears and soothe the orphan's grief. We often find in attempting to teach others that we *gain instruction for ourselves*. What gracious lessons some of us have learned in visiting the sick! We went to teach the Scriptures, and we came away blushing that our knowledge of them was so poor. In our conversation with humble saints, we are taught the way of God more perfectly for ourselves and get a deeper insight into divine truth. So watering others *makes us humble*. We discover how much grace there is where we had not looked for it, and how much the humble saint may outstrip us in knowledge. Our own *comfort is also increased* by working for others. We endeavor to cheer them, and the consolation gladdens our own heart. Consider the two men in the snow—one massaged the other's limbs to keep him from dying, and in doing so kept his own blood circulating and saved his own life. Remember the poor widow who supplied the prophet's needs from her own meager resources, and from that day she never experienced need again. Give, and it will be given to you—good measure, pressed down, shaken together and running over.

❧   EVENING   ❧

I DID NOT SAY TO THE OFFSPRING OF JACOB, "SEEK ME IN VAIN."
— ISAIAH 45:19

We can gain a great deal of comfort by considering what God has *not* said. What He has said is full of comfort and delight; but what He has *not* said is scarcely less rich in consolation. It was what God *had not said* that preserved the kingdom of Israel in the days of Jeroboam the son of Joash, for "the LORD had not said that he would blot out the name of Israel from under heaven" (2 Kings 14:27). In our text we have an assurance that God *will* answer prayer because He "did *not* say to the offspring of Jacob, 'Seek me in vain.'" Those of you who are prone to self-condemnation should remember that, let your doubts and fears say what they will, if *God* has not cut you off from mercy, there is no need for despair: Even the voice of conscience carries little weight if it is not seconded by the voice of God. We should tremble at what God *has* said! But do not allow your rambling thoughts to overwhelm you with despondency and sinful despair. Many timid persons have been vexed by the suspicion that there may be something in God's decree that shuts *them* out from hope, but we have here a complete rebuttal of that troublesome fear, for no true seeker can be decreed to wrath. "I did not speak in secret, in a land of darkness; I did not say [even in the secret of my unsearchable decree] . . . , 'Seek me in vain.'" God has clearly revealed that He *will* hear the prayer of those who call upon Him, and that declaration cannot be contradicted. He has spoken so firmly, so truthfully, so righteously that there can be no room for doubt. He does not reveal His mind in unintelligible words, but He speaks plainly and positively. "Everyone who asks receives."[1] Doubter, believe this sure truth—that prayer must and will be heard, and that never, even in the secrets of eternity, has the Lord said to any living soul, "Seek me in vain."

[1] Matthew 7:8

❧ MORNING ☙

I ADJURE YOU, O DAUGHTERS OF JERUSALEM,
IF YOU FIND MY BELOVED, THAT YOU TELL HIM I AM SICK
WITH LOVE. — SONG OF SOLOMON 5:8

Such is the language of the believer panting after present fellowship with Jesus—*he is sick for his Lord*. Gracious souls are never perfectly at ease except when they are in close communion with Christ; for when they are away from Him, they lose their peace. The nearer to Him, the nearer to the perfect calm of heaven; the nearer to Him, the fuller the heart is, not only of peace, but of life and vigor and joy, for these all depend on constant fellowship with Jesus. What the sun is to the day, what the moon is to the night, what the dew is to the flower, such is Jesus Christ to us. What bread is to the hungry, clothing to the naked, the shadow of a great rock to the traveler in a sun-scorched land, such is Jesus Christ to us. And therefore if we are not consciously one with Him, we should not be surprised if our spirit cries in the words of the Song, "I adjure you, O daughters of Jerusalem, if you find my beloved, that you tell him I am sick with love." *This earnest longing after Jesus has a blessing attending it*: "Blessed are those who hunger and thirst for righteousness";[1] and therefore, supremely blessed are those who thirst for the Righteous One. Blessed is that hunger, since it comes from God: If I do not experience the blessedness of being filled, I will come again in my emptiness and eagerness until I am filled with Christ. If I do not yet feed on Jesus, I will continue to hunger and thirst after Him. There is a hallowedness about that hunger, since it sparkles among the beatitudes of our Lord. But the blessing *involves a promise*. These hungry ones "*shall be satisfied*" with what they desire. If in this way Christ causes us to long after Him, He will certainly satisfy those longings; and when He does come to us, as come He will, *how sweet it will be!*

❧ EVENING ☙

THE UNSEARCHABLE RICHES OF CHRIST. — EPHESIANS 3:8

My Master has riches beyond the calculation of arithmetic, the measurement of reason, the dream of imagination, or the eloquence of words. They are *unsearchable*! You may look and study and ponder, but Jesus is a greater Savior than you think Him to be even when your thoughts are at their best. My Lord is more ready to pardon than you are to sin, more able to forgive than you are to transgress. My Master is more willing to supply your needs than you are to confess them. Do not tolerate small thoughts of the Lord Jesus. When you put the crown on His head, you will only crown Him with silver when He deserves gold. *My Master has riches of happiness to bestow upon you now*. He can make you to lie down in green pastures and lead you beside still waters. There is no music like His music that He, the Shepherd, plays for His sheep as they lie down at His feet. There is no love like His; neither earth nor heaven can match it. To know Christ and to be found in Him is real life and true joy. My Master does not treat His servants meanly; He gives to them the way a king gives to a king. He gives them two heavens—a heaven below in serving Him here, and a heaven above in delighting in Him forever. *His unsearchable riches will be known best in eternity*. On the way to heaven He will give you all you need. He will defend you and provide for you en route, but it will be at the end of your journey when you will hear the songs of triumph, the shouts of salvation, and you will have a face-to-face view of the glorious and beloved One. "The unsearchable riches of Christ"! This is the tune for the minstrels of earth and the song for the musicians of heaven. Lord, teach us more and more of Jesus, and we will declare the good news to others.

[1] Matthew 5:6

I WILL REJOICE IN JERUSALEM AND BE GLAD IN MY PEOPLE;
NO MORE SHALL BE HEARD IN IT THE SOUND OF WEEPING AND
THE CRY OF DISTRESS. — ISAIAH 65:19

In heaven the glorified do not weep, for *all outward causes of grief are gone*. There are no broken friendships, nor unfulfilled longings in heaven. Poverty, famine, danger, persecution, and slander are unknown there. There will be no pain to distress us, no anxious thoughts of death or bereavement to sadden. Those there do not weep, for *they are perfectly sanctified*. No evil heart of unbelief prompts them to depart from the living God; they are faultless before His throne and fully conformed to His image. Well might they stop mourning since they have stopped sinning. They do not weep, because *all fear of change is past*. They know that they are eternally secure. Sin is shut out, and they are shut in. They are safe in a city that will never be taken; they bask in a sun that shall never set; they drink of a river that will never run dry; they pluck fruit from a tree that will never wither. Countless cycles may revolve, but eternity will not be exhausted; and while eternity endures, their immortality and blessedness shall endure with it. They are forever with the Lord. They do not weep because *every desire is fulfilled*. They cannot wish for anything that they do not have. Eye and ear, heart and hand, judgment, imagination, hope, desire and will—all the faculties are completely satisfied; and although our present ideas of what God has prepared for those who love him are imperfect, still we know by the revelation of the Spirit that the saints above are supremely blessed. The joy of Christ, which is an infinite fullness of delight, is in them. They bathe themselves in the bottomless, shoreless sea of infinite blessing. That same joyful rest awaits us. It may not be too long before the weeping willow is exchanged for the palm-branch of victory, and sorrow's tears will be transformed into the pearls of everlasting bliss. "Therefore encourage one other with these words."[1]

EVENING

. . . SO THAT CHRIST MAY DWELL IN YOUR HEARTS THROUGH FAITH.
— EPHESIANS 3:17

It is desirable beyond measure that we, as believers, should keep the person of Jesus constantly before us, to stir up our love for Him and to grow in our knowledge of Him. I would to God that my readers were all entered as diligent scholars in Jesus' college, students of *Corpus Christi*, or the body of Christ, resolved to get a good degree in the learning of the cross. But to have Jesus ever near, the heart must be full of Him, welling up with His love and even running over; so the apostle prays "that Christ may *dwell in your hearts.*" Look at how close he wants Jesus to be! You cannot get a subject closer to you than to have it in your heart. "*That Christ may dwell*"; not that He may call upon you sometimes, as a casual visitor may stay overnight, but that He may *dwell*; that Jesus may become the Lord and permanent resident of your inmost being, never to leave again.

Observe the words—that He may dwell *in your heart*, the best room in the house! Not in your thoughts alone, but in your affections; not merely in the mind's meditations, but in the heart's emotions. We should long to love Christ in an enduring way—not a love that flames up and then dies out into the darkness of a few embers, but a constant flame, fed by sacred fuel, like the fire upon the altar that never went out. This cannot be accomplished except by faith. Faith must be strong or love will not be fervent; the root of the flower must be healthy or we cannot expect the blossom to be glorious. Faith is the plant's root, and love is the plant's blossom. Now, reader, Jesus cannot be in your heart's love unless you have a firm hold of Him by your heart's faith; and, therefore, pray that you may always trust Christ in order that you may always love Him. If love is cold, be sure that faith is faltering.

[1] 1 Thessalonians 4:18

He who opens the breach goes up before them. — Micah 2:13

Inasmuch as Jesus has gone before us, things are not as they would have been if He had never passed that way. He has *conquered every foe* that obstructed the way. Cheer up now, you faint-hearted warrior. Not only has Christ traveled the road, but He has defeated your enemies. Do you dread sin? He has nailed it to His cross. Do you fear death? He has been the death of Death. Are you afraid of hell? He has barred it against the advent of any of His children; they shall never see the gulf of perdition. Whatever foes may be before the Christian, they are all overcome. There are lions, but their teeth are broken; there are serpents, but their fangs are extracted; there are rivers, but they are bridged or fordable; there are flames, but we wear that matchless garment that renders us invulnerable to fire. The sword that has been forged against us is already blunt; the instruments of war that the enemy is preparing have already lost their point. God has taken away in the person of Christ all the power that anything can have to hurt us. Well then, the army may march safely on, and you may go joyously along your journey, for all your enemies are already conquered. What will you do but march on to take the prey? They are beaten, they are vanquished; all you have to do is share the plunder. You shall, it is true, often engage in combat; but your fight will be with a defeated foe. His head is broken; he may attempt to injure you, but his strength will not be sufficient for his malicious design. Your victory shall be easy, and your treasure shall be beyond all measure.

> *Proclaim aloud the Savior's fame,*
> *Who bears the Breaker's wond'rous name;*
> *Sweet name; and it becomes him well,*
> *Who breaks down earth, sin, death, and hell.*

❧ Evening ❧

If fire breaks out and catches in thorns so that the stacked grain or the standing grain or the field is consumed, he who started the fire shall make full restitution. — Exodus 22:6

But what restitution can be made by one who throws the firebrands of error or stirs the coals of lust and sets the souls of men ablaze with the fire of hell? The guilt is beyond estimate, and the result is irretrievable. Even if such an offender is forgiven, he will still experience grief in recognizing that he cannot undo the effects of his foolish behavior! A bad example may kindle a flame that years of amended character cannot quench. To burn the harvest is bad enough, but how much worse to destroy the eternal harvest! It may be useful for us to consider how guilty we may have been in the past, and to consider whether, even in the present, there might not be evil in us that has a tendency to cause damage to the souls of our relatives, friends, or neighbors.

The fire of conflict is a terrible evil when it breaks out in a Christian church. Where there are converts, and God is glorified, you will discover jealousy and envy doing the devil's work most effectively. Where the golden grain of blessing was being stored to reward the work of the servants, the fire of enmity comes in and leaves little else but smoke and a heap of blackness. Woe to those by whom offenses come. May they never come through us, for although we cannot make restitution, we shall certainly be the chief sufferers if we are the chief offenders. Those who feed the fire deserve fair criticism, but the one who first kindles it is most to blame. Discord usually takes hold first among the thorns; it is nurtured among the hypocrites and empty professors in the church and leaps among the righteous, blown by the winds of hell, until no one knows where it may end. O Lord, the giver of peace, make us peacemakers, and never let us aid and abet the men of strife, or even unintentionally cause the slightest division among Your people.

HIS FRUIT WAS SWEET TO MY TASTE. — SONG OF SOLOMON 2:3

Faith is described in a variety of ways in the Bible. It is *sight*: "Turn to me and be saved."[1] It is *hearing*: "Hear, that your soul shall live."[2] Faith is *smelling*: "Your robes are all fragrant with myrrh and aloes and cassia";[3] "your name is oil poured out."[4] Faith is spiritual *touch*. By this faith the woman came behind and touched the hem of Christ's garment, and by this we handle the things of the good word of life. Faith is equally the spirit's taste. "How sweet are your words to my taste, sweeter than honey to my mouth."[5] "Whoever feeds on my flesh and drinks my blood has eternal life."[6]

One of the first performances of faith is *hearing*. We hear the voice of God not only with the physical ear, but with the spiritual ear; we hear it as God's Word, and we believe it as such; that is the hearing of faith. Then our mind *looks* upon the truth as it is presented to us; that is to say, we understand it, we perceive its meaning; that is the seeing of faith. Next we discover its preciousness; we begin to admire it and find how fragrant it is; that is faith in its *smell*. Then we appropriate the mercies that are prepared for us in Christ; that is faith in its *touch*. Then follow the enjoyments, peace, delight, communion, which are faith in its taste. Any one of these acts of faith is saving. To hear Christ's voice as the sure voice of God in the soul will save us; but that which gives true enjoyment is the aspect of faith whereby we taste and see that the Lord is good. In this way we receive Christ, and He becomes, by inward and spiritual apprehension, to be the precious food for our souls. Here we learn to sit under His shadow "with great delight"[7] and find His fruit sweet to our taste.

⚘ EVENING ⚘
IF YOU BELIEVE WITH ALL YOUR HEART, YOU MAY. — ACTS 8:37

These words may address any hesitations the devout reader may have about *the ordinances*. Perhaps you say, "I am afraid to be baptized; it is such a solemn thing to declare myself to be dead with Christ and buried with Him. I do not feel at liberty to come to Communion; I am afraid of eating and drinking judgment to myself, of failing to discern the Lord's body." Come now, trembling one, Jesus has given you liberty—do not be afraid. If a stranger came to your house, he would stand at the door or wait in the hall; he would not dream of entering uninvited into your home—he is not at home. But your child enjoys complete freedom in the house; and so is it with the child of God. A stranger may not intrude where a child may venture. When the Holy Spirit has given you to feel the spirit of adoption, you may be baptized and take communion without apprehension. The same rule holds good for the *Christian's inward privileges*. Perhaps you think that you are not allowed to rejoice with joy unspeakable and full of glory; if you are permitted just to get inside Christ's door or sit at the end of His table, you will be content with that. But you will not have less privileges than the strongest saint. God makes no difference in His love to His children. A child is a child to Him; He will not make him a hired servant. The son will feast upon the fatted calf and have the music and dancing as much as if he had never wandered away. When Jesus comes into the heart, He issues a general permit to be glad in the Lord. No shackles are worn in the court of King Jesus. Our admission into full privileges may be gradual, but it is certain. Perhaps our reader is saying, "I wish I could enjoy the promises and walk at liberty in my Lord's commands." "If you believe with all your heart, you may." Loosen the chains at your neck and live in freedom, for Jesus makes you free!

[1] Isaiah 45:22   [2] Isaiah 55:3   [3] Psalm 45:8   [4] Song of Solomon 1:3   [5] Psalm 119:103   [6] John 6:54
[7] Song of Solomon 2:3

HE HAS COMMANDED HIS COVENANT FOREVER. — PSALM 111:9

The Lord's people delight in the covenant itself. It is an unfailing source of comfort to them as often as the Holy Spirit leads them into the banqueting house and waves the banner of love. They delight to contemplate *the antiquity* of that covenant, remembering that before the daystar knew its place or planets ran their course, the interests of the saints were made secure in Christ Jesus. It is peculiarly pleasing to them to remember *the certainty* of the covenant while meditating upon God's "steadfast, sure love David."[1] They delight to celebrate it as signed, sealed, and delivered! Their hearts often overflow with joy to think of its *immutability*, as a covenant that neither time nor eternity, life nor death will ever be able to break—a covenant as old as eternity and as everlasting as the Rock of Ages. They rejoice also to dine upon *the fullness* of this covenant, for in it they see all things provided for them. God is their portion, Christ their companion, the Spirit their Comforter, earth their lodge, and heaven their home. They see in it an inheritance that is reserved for every soul possessing an interest in its ancient and eternal gift. Their eyes sparkled when they saw it as a treasure-trove in the Bible; but how their souls were gladdened when they saw in the last will and testament of their Christ that it was bequeathed to them! More especially it is the pleasure of God's people to contemplate *the graciousness* of this covenant. They see that the law was made void because it was a covenant of works and depended upon merit, but they perceive this to be enduring because grace is the basis, grace the condition, grace the bulwark, grace the foundation, grace the capstone. The covenant is a treasury of wealth, a granary of food, a fountain of life, a storehouse of salvation, a charter of peace, and a haven of joy.

∾ EVENING ∾

THE CROWD, WHEN THEY SAW HIM, WERE GREATLY AMAZED AND RAN UP TO HIM AND GREETED HIM. — MARK 9:15

How great the difference between Moses and Jesus! When Moses had been forty days upon the mountain, he underwent a kind of transfiguration, so that his face shone with exceeding brightness, and he put a veil over it because the people were not able to look upon his glory. Not so our Savior. He had been transfigured with a greater glory than that of Moses, and yet we do not read that the people were blinded by the blaze of His countenance, but rather they were amazed and ran to Him and greeted Him. The glory of the law repels, but the greater glory of Jesus attracts. Though Jesus is holy and just, yet blended with His purity there is so much truth and grace that sinners run to Him amazed at His goodness, fascinated by His love; they greet Him, become His disciples, and take Him to be their Lord and Master. Reader, it may be that just now you are blinded by the dazzling brightness of the law of God. You feel its claims on your conscience, but you cannot keep it in your life. Not that you find fault with the law; on the contrary, it commands your profoundest esteem. Still you are not drawn by it to God; you are rather hardened in heart and tending toward desperation. So turn your eye from Moses with all his repelling splendor, and look to Jesus, resplendent with milder glories. Look upon His flowing wounds and thorn-crowned head! He is the Son of God and greater than Moses, but He is the Lord of love and more tender than the lawgiver. He bore the wrath of God and in His death revealed more of God's justice than Sinai displayed, but that justice is now vindicated, and it is the guardian of believers in Jesus. Look, sinner, to the bleeding Savior, and as you feel the attraction of His love, run to His arms, and you will be saved.

[1] Isaiah 55:3

Strive with all diligence to keep out the monster of unbelief. It is so dishonoring to Christ that He will withdraw His visible presence if we insult Him by tolerating it. It is true it is a weed that we can never entirely remove from the soil, but we must aim at its root with zeal and perseverance. Among hateful things it is the most to be defeated. Its hurtful nature is so poisonous that he that uses it and he upon whom it is used are both harmed by it. In your case, believer, it is most wicked, for the mercies of your Lord in the past increase your guilt in doubting Him now. When you distrust the Lord Jesus, He may well cry out, "Behold, I will press you down in your place, as a cart full of sheaves presses down." To doubt is to crown His head with thorns of the sharpest kind. It is very cruel for a well-beloved wife to mistrust a kind and faithful husband. The sin is needless, foolish, and unwarranted. Jesus has never given the slightest ground for suspicion, and it is hard to be doubted by those to whom our conduct is consistently affectionate and true. Jesus is the Son of the Highest and has unlimited wealth; it is shameful to doubt Omnipotence and distrust His sufficiency. The cattle on a thousand hills will be enough for our most hungry feeding, and the granaries of heaven are not likely to be emptied by our eating. If Christ were only a cistern, we might soon exhaust His fullness, but who can drain a fountain? Countless believers throughout the ages have drawn their supplies from Him, and not one of them has complained at the insufficiency of His resources. Dispel this lying traitor unbelief, for his only errand is to cut the bonds of communion and make us mourn an absent Savior. Bunyan tells us that unbelief has "as many lives as a cat"; if so, let us kill one life now, and continue the work until the whole nine are gone. Down with you, traitor, my heart detests you.

These words have been frequently used by the godly in their hour of departure. We may profitably consider them this evening. The object of the believer's interest in life and death is not his body or his possessions but his spirit; this is his choice treasure: If this is safe, then all is well. What is our physical condition compared with the soul? The believer commits his soul to the hand of God; it came from Him, it is His own, He has until now sustained it, He is able to keep it, and it is fitting that He should receive it. All things are safe in Jehovah's hands; what we entrust to the Lord will be secure, both now and in that day of days toward which we are hastening. It is peaceful living and glorious dying to rest in the care of heaven. At all times we should commit everything to Jesus' faithful hand; then even if life should hang on a thread, and difficulties multiply like the sands of the sea, our soul shall live in safety and delight itself in quiet resting places.

"*You have redeemed me, O LORD*, faithful God." Redemption is a solid basis for confidence. David did not know Calvary as we do, but even as redemption cheered him, so our eternal redemption will sweetly console us. Past deliverances are strong guarantees for present assistance. What the Lord has done He will do again, for He does not change. He is faithful to His promises and gracious to His saints; He will not turn away from His people.

> *Though Thou slay me I will trust,*
> *Praise Thou even from the dust,*
> *Prove, and tell it as I prove,*
> *Thine unutterable love.*

> *Thou may chasten and correct,*
> *But Thou never can neglect;*
> *Since the ransom price is paid,*
> *On Thy love my hope is stayed.*

❧ MORNING ☙
OIL FOR THE LAMPS. — EXODUS 25:6

My soul, you really need this, for your lamp will not continue to burn for long without it. Your snuff will smoke and become an offense if light is gone, and gone it will be if you run out of oil. You have no oil well springing up in your human nature, and therefore you must go to them who sell and buy for yourself, or like the foolish virgins you will have to cry, "My lamp has gone out." Even the consecrated lamps could not give light without oil; though they shone in the tabernacle, they needed to be fed; though no rough winds blew upon them, they required to be trimmed, and your need is just as great. Under the most happy circumstances you cannot give light for another hour unless fresh oil of grace is given to you.

Not every kind of oil could be used in the Lord's service; neither the petroleum that exudes so plentifully from the earth, nor the produce of fish, nor that extracted from nuts would be accepted; only one oil was selected, and that was the best olive oil. Pretended grace from natural goodness, fancied grace from priestly hands, or imaginary grace from outward ceremonies will never serve the true child of God; he knows that the Lord would not be pleased with rivers of such oil. He goes to the olive-press of Gethsemane and draws his supplies from Him who was crushed there. The oil of gospel grace is pure and free from sediment and dregs, and so the light that is fed by it is clear and bright. Our churches are the Savior's golden candelabra, and if they are to be lights in this dark world, they must have plenty of holy oil. Let us pray for ourselves, our ministers, and our churches that they may never lack oil for the light. Truth, holiness, joy, knowledge, love—these are all beams of the sacred light; but we cannot send them out into the darkness unless in private we receive oil from God the Holy Spirit.

❧ EVENING ☙
SING, O BARREN ONE. — ISAIAH 54:1

Although we may have brought forth some fruit and have a joyful hope that we are abiding in the vine, yet there are times when we feel very barren. Prayer is lifeless, love is cold, faith is weak, each grace in the garden of our heart languishes and droops. We are like flowers in the hot sun, desperately needing the refreshing shower. In such a condition what are we to do? The text is addressed to us in just such a state. "*Sing, O barren one . . . break forth into singing and cry aloud.*" But what can I sing about? I cannot talk about the present, and even the past looks full of barrenness. I can sing of Jesus Christ. I can talk of visits that the Redeemer has paid to me in the past; or if not of these, I can magnify the great love with which He loved His people when He came from the heights of heaven for their redemption. I will go to the cross again. Come, my soul, you were once heavy-laden, and you lost your burden there. Go to Calvary again. Perhaps that very cross that gave you life may give you fruitfulness. What is my barrenness? It is the platform for His fruit-creating power. What is my desolation? It is the dark setting for the sapphire of His everlasting love. I will go to Him in my poverty, I will go in my helplessness, I will go in all my shame and backsliding; I will tell Him that I am still His child, and finding confidence in His faithful heart, even I, the barren one, will sing and cry aloud.

Sing, believer, for it will cheer your own heart and the hearts of others who are desolate. Sing on, for although you are presently ashamed of being barren, you will be fruitful soon; now that God makes you *hate* to be without fruit He will soon cover you with clusters. The experience of our barrenness is painful, but the Lord's visits are delightful. A sense of our own poverty drives us to Christ, and that is where we need to be, for in Him our fruit is found.

HAVE MERCY ON ME, O GOD. — PSALM 51:1

When one of God's choice servants, William Carey, was suffering from a dangerous illness, the inquiry was made, "If this sickness should prove fatal, what passage would you select as the text for your funeral sermon?" He replied, "Oh, I feel that such a poor sinful creature is unworthy to have anything said about him; but if a funeral sermon must be preached, let it be from the words, 'Have mercy on me, O God, according to your steadfast love; according to your abundant mercy blot out my transgressions.'" In the same spirit of humility he directed in his will that the following inscription and nothing more should be cut on his gravestone:

WILLIAM CAREY, BORN AUGUST 17th, 1761:
DIED—
"A wretched, poor, and helpless worm
On Your kind arms I fall."

Only on the footing of free grace can the most experienced and most honored of the saints approach their God. The best of men are conscious above all others that they are men at best. Empty boats float high, but heavily laden vessels are low in the water; mere professors can boast, but true children of God cry for mercy upon their unprofitableness. We need the Lord to have mercy upon our good works, our prayers, our preaching, our offerings, and our living sacrifices. The blood was not only sprinkled on the doorposts of Israel's houses, but upon the sanctuary, the mercy-seat, and the altar, because as sin intrudes upon our holiest things, the blood of Jesus is needed to purify them from defilement. If mercy is needed to be exercised toward our duties, what will be said of our sins? How sweet the remembrance that inexhaustible mercy is waiting to be gracious to us, restore our backslidings, and make our broken bones rejoice!

❧ E V E N I N G ❧

ALL THE DAYS OF HIS SEPARATION HE SHALL EAT NOTHING THAT IS
PRODUCED BY THE GRAPEVINE, NOT EVEN THE SEEDS
OR THE SKINS. — NUMBERS 6:4

Nazirites had taken, among other vows, one that debarred them from the use of wine. In order that they might not violate the obligation, they were forbidden to drink the vinegar of wine or strong liquors; and to make the rule even clearer, they were not to touch the unfermented juice of grapes, nor even to eat the fruit either fresh or dried. In order to secure the integrity of the vow, they were not even allowed anything that had to do with the vine; they were, in fact, to avoid the appearance of evil. Surely this is a lesson to the Lord's separated ones, teaching them to come away from sin in every form, to avoid not merely its grosser shapes but even its spirit and likeness. Such strict walking is much despised in these days, but rest assured, dear reader, it is the safest and happiest path. He who yields a point or two to the world is in fearful peril; he who eats the grapes of Sodom will soon drink the wine of Gomorrah. A little crevice in the seawall in Holland lets in the sea, and the gap soon swells until a province is drowned. Worldly conformity, in any degree, is a snare to the soul and makes it more and more liable to presumptuous sins. The Nazirite who drank grape juice could not be completely certain whether or not it had fermented and consequently could not be clear in heart that his vow was intact. In a similar way the yielding, vacillating Christian cannot have a clear conscience but is constantly aware of his double standard. Doubtful things we need not wonder about; they are wrong for us. Tempting things we must not play with, but run from them speedily. Better to be sneered at as a Puritan than to be despised as a hypocrite. Careful walking may involve much self-denial, but it has pleasures of its own that are more than a sufficient reward.

❧ **MORNING** ☙

WAIT FOR THE LORD. — PSALM 27:14

It may seem an easy thing to wait, but it is one of the postures that a Christian soldier cannot learn without years of teaching. Marching and quick-marching are much easier for God's warriors than standing still. There are hours of perplexity when the most willing spirit, anxiously desiring to serve the Lord, does not know what role to play. Then what shall it do? Vex itself by despair? Retreat back in cowardice, turn to the right hand in fear, or rush forward in presumption? No, simply wait. *Wait in prayer*, however. Call upon God, and spread the matter before Him; tell Him your difficulty, and plead His promise of help. In dilemmas between one duty and another, it is best to be humble as a child and *wait with simplicity of soul* upon the Lord. It is sure to be well with us when we feel and know our own folly and are genuinely willing to be guided by the will of God. But *wait in faith*. Express your unstaggering confidence in Him; for unfaithful, untrusting waiting is just an insult to the Lord. Believe that if He keeps you waiting even until midnight, He will still come at the right time; the vision will come and not delay. *Wait in quiet patience*, not rebelling because things are difficult, but blessing your God for the privilege of affliction. Never grumble against the second cause, as the children of Israel did against Moses; never wish you could go back to the world again, but accept the circumstance as it is, and put it as it stands, simply and with your whole heart, without any selfish agenda, into the hand of your covenant God, saying, "Now, Lord, not my will, but Yours be done. I do not know what to do. I am at an end of myself, but I will wait until You part the floods or drive back my enemies. I will wait, even if You test me for a while, for my heart is fixed upon You alone, O God, and my spirit waits for You in the deep conviction that You will still be my joy and my salvation, my refuge and my strong tower."

❧ **EVENING** ☙

HEAL ME, O LORD, AND I SHALL BE HEALED. — JEREMIAH 17:14
I HAVE SEEN HIS WAYS, BUT I WILL HEAL HIM. — ISAIAH 57:18

It is the sole prerogative of God to remove spiritual disease. Natural disease may be instrumentally healed by men, but even then the honor is to be given to God who grants wisdom to doctors and bestows power to enable the human frame to cast off disease. As for spiritual sicknesses, these remain with the Great Physician alone; He claims it as His prerogative: "I kill and I make alive; I wound and I heal";[1] and one of the Lord's choice titles is Jehovah-Rophi, "the Lord who heals you." "I will heal your wounds" is a promise that could not come from the lips of man but only from the mouth of the eternal God. On this account the psalmist cried unto the Lord, "Heal me, O LORD, for my bones are troubled,"[2] and again, "Heal me, for I have sinned against you!"[3] For this also the godly praise the name of the Lord, saying, "[He] heals all your diseases."[4] He who made man can restore man; He who was at first the creator of our nature can re-create it. What a transcendent comfort it is that in the person of Jesus "the whole fullness of deity dwells bodily."[5] My soul, whatever your disease may be, this Great Physician can heal you. If He is God, there can be no limit to His power. Come then with the blind eye of darkened understanding; come with the limping foot of wasted energy; come with the disabled hand of weak faith, the fever of an angry temper, or the fit of shivering despondency; come just as you are, for He who is God can certainly restore you. No one can restrain the healing power that proceeds from Jesus our Lord. Legions of devils have attempted to overcome the power of the beloved Physician, and never once has He been hindered. All His patients have been cured in the past and shall be in the future, and you may be counted among them, my friend, if you will but rest yourself in Him tonight.

[1] Deuteronomy 32:39 [2] Psalm 6:2 [3] Psalm 41:4 [4] Psalm 103:3 [5] Colossians 2:9

AND FOR MY ARM THEY WAIT. — ISAIAH 51:5

In seasons of severe trial the Christian has nothing on earth that he can trust, and so he is compelled to cast himself on God alone. When his vessel is capsizing, and no human deliverance is at hand, he must simply and entirely trust himself to the providence and care of God. Happy storm that wrecks a man on such a rock as this! O blessed hurricane that drives the soul to God and God alone! Sometimes the multitude of our friends keeps us from God; but when a man is so poor, so friendless, so helpless that he has nowhere else to turn, he runs into his Father's arms, and is blessed to be there! When he is burdened with troubles so pressing and so specific that he cannot tell them to anyone but God, he may be thankful for them; for he will learn more of his Lord then than at any other time. Oh, tempest-tossed believer, it is a happy trouble that drives you to your Father! Now that you have only God to trust, make sure that you put your complete confidence in Him. Do not dishonor your Lord and Master by unworthy doubts and fears; but be strong in faith, giving glory to God. Show the world that your God is worth ten thousand worlds to you. Show rich men how rich you are in your poverty when the Lord God is your helper. Show the strong man how strong you are in your weakness when underneath you are the everlasting arms. Now is the time for feats of faith and valiant exploits. Be strong and very courageous, and the Lord your God will certainly, as surely as He built the heavens and the earth, glorify Himself in your weakness and magnify His might in the face of your distress. The grandeur of heaven's arches would be spoiled if the sky were supported by a single visible column, and your faith would lose its glory if it rested on anything discernible by the physical eye. May the Holy Spirit enable you to rest in Jesus on this closing day of the month.

❧ EVENING ❧

IF WE WALK IN THE LIGHT, AS HE IS IN THE LIGHT . . .
— 1 JOHN 1:7

As he is in the light"! Can we ever attain to this? Will we ever be able to walk as clearly in the light as He is whom we call "Our Father," of whom it is written, "God is light, and in him is no darkness at all" (verse 5)? Certainly this is the model that is set before us, for the Savior Himself said, "You therefore must be perfect, as your heavenly Father is perfect";[1] and although we may feel that we can never rival the perfection of God, yet we are to seek after it and not be satisfied until we attain to it. The youthful artist as he grasps his newly sharpened pencil can hardly hope to equal Raphael or Michelangelo; but still, if he did not have a noble *ideal* before his mind, he would only attain to something very mean and ordinary. But what is meant by the expression that the Christian is to walk in light as God is in the light? We conceive it to convey *likeness* but not *degree*. We are as truly in the light, we are as heartily in the light, we are as sincerely in the light, as honestly in the light, although we cannot be there in the same measure. I cannot dwell in the sun—it is too bright a place for my residence, but I can *walk* in the light of the sun; and so, though I cannot attain to that perfection of purity and truth that belongs to the Lord of hosts by nature as the infinitely good, yet I can set the Lord always before me and strive, by the help of the indwelling Spirit, to conform to His image. The famous old commentator John Trapp says, "We may be in the light as God is in the light for *quality*, but not for *equality*." We are to have the same light and are as truly to have it and walk in it as God does, though as for equality with God in His holiness and purity, that must be left until we cross the Jordan and enter into the perfection of the Most High. Notice how the blessings of sacred fellowship and perfect cleansing are bound up with walking in the light.

[1] Matthew 5:48

September

SEPTEMBER 1   ❧ MORNING ☙

YOU GUIDE ME WITH YOUR COUNSEL, AND
AFTERWARD YOU WILL RECEIVE ME TO GLORY. — PSALM 73:24

The psalmist felt his need of divine guidance. He had just been discovering the foolishness of his own heart, and to prevent himself from being constantly led astray by it, he resolved that God's counsel should be his guide. A sense of our own folly is a great step toward being wise, when it leads us to rely on the wisdom of the Lord. The blind man leans on his friend's arm and reaches his home in safety, and likewise we should give ourselves up implicitly to divine guidance, without doubting, assured that even though we cannot see, it is always safe to trust the All-seeing God. "*You will*" is a blessed expression of confidence. He was sure that the Lord would not neglect the necessary task. Here is a word for you, believer; rest in it. Be sure that God will be your counselor and friend; He will guide you; He will direct all your ways. In His written Word you have this assurance fulfilled in part, for Holy Scripture is His "counsel" to you. We are happy to have God's Word as our constant guide! What is the sailor without his compass? And what is the Christian without the Bible? This is the unerring chart, the map in which every shoal is described, and all the channels from the quicksands of destruction to the harbor of salvation mapped and marked by one who knows the way. O God we bless You, that we may trust You to guide us now, and even to the end! After this guidance through life, the psalmist anticipates a divine reception— "*and afterward . . . receive me to glory.*" What a thought for you, believer! God Himself will receive *you* in glory—*you*! Though you are wandering, erring, straying, still He will bring you safe at last to glory! This is your portion; live on it today, and if perplexities should surround you, go in the strength of this text straight to the throne.

❧ EVENING ☙
TRUST IN HIM AT ALL TIMES. — PSALM 62:8

Faith is the rule of both temporal as well as spiritual life; we ought to have faith in God for our earthly affairs as well as for our heavenly business. It is only as we learn to trust in God for the supply of our daily needs that we will live above the world. We are not to be idle; *that* would show we did *not* trust in God, who is always working, but in the devil, who is the father of laziness. We are not to be hasty or rash; that would be to trust chance rather than the living God, who is a God of economy and order. Acting sensibly and honestly, we must rely simply and entirely on the Lord all the time.

Let me commend to you a life of trust in God in secular things. Trusting in God, you will not be compelled to mourn as a result of using sinful means to grow rich. Serve God with integrity, and if you are unsuccessful, at least sin will not lie upon your conscience. Trusting God, you will be free from self-contradiction. The one who trusts in craftiness, sails this way today and that way tomorrow, like a sailboat tossed about by the fickle wind; but the one who trusts in the Lord is like a powerful boat cutting through the waves, defying the wind, and making one bright silvery straightforward track to her desired haven. Be courageous as you act on principle; do not bow to the varying customs of worldly wisdom. Walk on the path of integrity with confidence, and show that you are invincibly strong in the strength that confidence in God alone confers. In this way you will be delivered from anxious care, you will be untroubled by evil tidings, and your heart will be fixed, trusting in the Lord. How pleasant to float along on the stream of providence! There is no more blessed way of living than a life of dependence upon a covenant-keeping God. We do not need to worry because He cares for us; we do not need to carry burdens because He invites us to cast them upon Him.

NOW SIMON'S MOTHER-IN-LAW LAY ILL WITH A FEVER,
AND IMMEDIATELY THEY TOLD HIM ABOUT HER. — MARK 1:30

This is a very interesting little peep into the house of the apostolic fisherman. We quickly observe that household joys and cares are no hindrance to the full exercise of ministry; rather they furnish an opportunity for personally discovering the Lord's gracious work in one's own family. They may provide better instruction for the teacher than any other earthly discipline. There are those who decry marriage, but true Christianity and family life live well together. Peter's house was possibly a poor fisherman's hut, but the Lord of Glory entered it, lodged in it, and worked a miracle in it. If these words are being read this morning in some very humble cottage, let this fact encourage the inhabitants to seek the company of King Jesus. God is more often in little huts than in rich palaces. Jesus is looking around your room now and is waiting to be gracious to you. Into Simon's house illness had entered; fever in a deadly form had prostrated his mother-in-law; and as soon as Jesus came, they told Him of the sad affliction, and He hurried to the patient's bed. Do you have any illness in the house this morning? You will find Jesus the best physician by far; go to Him at once and tell Him all about the matter. Immediately lay the case before Him. It concerns one of His people, and therefore He will not regard it as trivial. Notice that immediately the Savior restored the ill woman; none can heal as He does. We dare not assume that the Lord will remove all illness from those we love, but we dare not forget that believing prayer for the sick is far more likely to be followed by restoration than anything else in the world; and where this does not happen, we must meekly bow to His will by whom life and death are determined. The tender heart of Jesus waits to hear our griefs; let us pour them into His patient ear.

❧ EVENING ☙

UNLESS YOU SEE SIGNS AND WONDERS YOU WILL NOT BELIEVE.
— JOHN 4:48

A craving for miracles was a symptom of the sickly condition of men's minds in our Lord's day; they refused solid nourishment and longed for mere wonders. The Gospel that they so greatly needed they would not have; the miracles that Jesus did not always choose to give they eagerly demanded. Even today there are many who must see signs and wonders or they will not believe. Some have said in their heart, "I must feel deep horror of soul or I never will believe in Jesus." But what if you never should feel it, as probably you never will? Will you go to hell out of spite against God because He did not treat you like someone else? One has said to himself, "If I had a dream, or if I could feel a sudden jolt of something, then I would believe." You undeserving mortals dream that my Lord is to be dictated to by you! You are beggars at His gate, asking for mercy, and you are drawing up rules and regulations as to how He will give that mercy. Do you think that He will submit to this? My Master has a generous spirit, but He also has a royal heart. He rejects all orders and maintains His sovereignty of action. Why, dear reader, if this is your case, do you crave signs and wonders? Isn't the Gospel its own sign and wonder? Isn't this the miracle of miracles, that "God so loved the world, that he gave his only Son, that whoever believes in him should not perish"? Surely that precious word, "Let the one who desires take the water of life without price"[1] and that solemn promise, "Whoever comes to me I will never cast out"[2] are better than signs and wonders! A truthful Savior ought to be believed. He is truth itself. Why will you ask the One who cannot lie for proof? The devils themselves declared Him to be the Son of God; will you mistrust Him?

[1] Revelation 22:17 [2] John 6:37

YOU WHOM MY SOUL LOVES. — SONG OF SOLOMON 1:7

It is good to be able, without any "if" or "but," to say of the Lord Jesus, "*You whom my soul loves.*" Many can only say of Jesus that they *hope* they love Him; they *trust* they love Him; but only a poor and shallow experience will be content to stay here. No one ought to give any rest to his spirit until he feels quite sure about a matter of such vital importance. We should not be satisfied with a superficial *hope* that Jesus loves us and with a bare trust that we love Him. The old saints did not generally speak with "buts" and "ifs" and "hopes" and "trusts," but they spoke positively and plainly. "I know whom I have believed,"[1] said Paul. "I know that my Redeemer lives,"[2] said Job. Get definite knowledge of your love for Jesus, and do not be satisfied until you can speak of your interest in Him as a reality—a reality that you have made sure of by receiving the witness of the Holy Spirit and His seal upon your soul by faith.

True love for Christ is in every case the Holy Spirit's work and must be accomplished in the heart by Him. He is the *efficient cause* of it; but the logical reason why we love Jesus lies in *Himself. Why* do we love Jesus? *Because He first loved us. Why* do we love Jesus? Because He *gave Himself for us.* We have life through His death; we have peace through His blood. Though He was rich, yet *for our sakes* He became poor. Why do we love Jesus? Because of the *excellency of His person.* We are filled with a sense of His beauty, an admiration of His graces, a consciousness of His infinite perfection. His greatness, goodness, and loveliness, in one resplendent ray, combine to enchant the soul till it is so delighted that it exclaims, yes, He is "altogether lovely."[3] This is a blessed love that binds the heart with chains softer than silk, and yet stronger than steel!

❧ EVENING ❧

THE LORD TESTS THE RIGHTEOUS. — PSALM 11:5

All events are under the control of providence; consequently all the trials of our outward life are ultimately traceable to God our Father. Out of the golden gate of God's ordinance the armies of trial march in rank, clad in their iron armor and armed with weapons of war. All providences are doors to testing. Even our mercies, like roses, have their thorns. Men may be drowned in prosperous seas as easily as in rivers of affliction. Our mountains are not too high, and our valleys are not too low for temptations: Trials lurk at every turn. Everywhere, above and below, we are confronted and surrounded with danger. Still no shower falls unpermitted from the threatening cloud; every drop has its order before it arrives on the earth. The trials that come from God are sent to prove and strengthen our graces and immediately illustrate the power of divine grace, to test the genuineness of our virtues and to add to their energy. Our Lord in His infinite wisdom and superabundant love sets such a high value upon His people's faith that He will not protect them from those trials by which faith is strengthened. You would never have possessed the precious faith that now supports you if the trial of your faith had not put you through the fire. You are a tree that never would have rooted as well if the wind had not rocked you to and fro and made you take a firm hold upon the precious truths of God's gracious covenant. Worldly ease is a great enemy to faith; it loosens the joints of holy zeal and snaps the sinews of sacred courage. The balloon never rises until the cords are cut; affliction provides this service for believing souls. While the wheat sleeps comfortably in the husk, it is useless to us; it must be threshed out of its resting place before its value can be known. Thus it is good that the Lord tests the righteous, for it causes them to grow rich toward God.

[1] 2 Timothy 1:12   [2] Job 19:25   [3] Song of Solomon 5:15, KJV

"I WILL; BE CLEAN." — MARK 1:41

The primeval darkness heard God say, "Let there be light," and immediately there was light. The word of the Lord Jesus is equal in majesty to that ancient word of power. Redemption, like creation, has its word of might. Jesus speaks, and it is done. Leprosy yielded to no human remedies, but it fled at once at the Lord's "I will." The disease exhibited no hopeful signs or tokens of recovery; nature contributed nothing to its own healing. But the unaided word effected the entire work on the spot and forever. The sinner is in a more miserable plight than the leper; let him imitate his example and go to Jesus, "imploring him and kneeling [say] to him . . ." Let him exercise what little faith he has, even though it should go no further than "If you will, you can make me clean." There need be no doubt as to the result of the application. Jesus heals all who come and casts out none. In reading the narrative in which our morning's text occurs, it is worthy of careful consideration that Jesus touched the leper. This unclean person had broken through the regulations of the ceremonial law and pressed into the house, but Jesus, far from chiding him, broke through the law Himself in order to meet him. He made an interchange with the leper, for while He cleansed him, He contracted by that touch a Levitical defilement. Even so Jesus Christ was made sin for us, although in Himself He knew no sin, that we might be made the righteousness of God in Him. If only poor sinners would go to Jesus, believing in the power of His blessed substitutionary work, they would soon learn the power of His gracious touch. The hand that multiplied the loaves, that saved sinking Peter, that upholds afflicted saints, that crowns believers—that same hand will touch every seeking sinner and in a moment make him clean. The love of Jesus is the source of salvation. He loves, He looks, He touches us, and *we live*.

ᔃ EVENING ᔂ

YOU SHALL HAVE JUST BALANCES, JUST WEIGHTS, A JUST EPHAH,
AND A JUST HIN. — LEVITICUS 19:36

Weights and scales and measures were all to be according to the standard of justice. Surely no Christian will need to be reminded of this in his business, for if righteousness were banished from all the world beside, it would find a shelter in believing hearts. There are, however, other balances that weigh moral and spiritual things, and these need to be examined often.

Are the balances in which we weigh our own and other men's characters quite accurate? Do we not turn our own ounces of goodness into pounds, and other people's pounds of excellence into ounces? The scales in which we measure our trials and troubles—are they properly set? Paul, who had more to suffer than we have, called his afflictions light, and yet we often consider ours to be heavy—surely something must be wrong with the weights! We must see to this matter, before we get reported to the court above for unjust dealing. Those weights with which we measure our doctrinal belief—are they quite fair? The doctrines of grace should have the same weight with us as the precepts of the Word, no more and no less; but it is to be feared that with many, one scale or the other is unfairly weighted. It is a vital matter to give honest measure in truth. Christian, be careful here. Those measures in which we estimate our obligations and responsibilities look rather small. When a rich man gives to the work of God the same amount as the poor contribute, are things properly weighted? When pastors are neglected, is that honest dealing? When the poor are despised, while ungodly rich men are held in admiration, is that a just balance? Reader, we could extend the list, but we prefer to leave it as your evening's work to identify and destroy all unrighteous balances, weights, and measures.

SEPTEMBER 5   ❧   MORNING   ☙

WOE TO ME, THAT I SOJOURN IN MESHECH,
THAT I DWELL AMONG THE TENTS OF KEDAR. — PSALM 120:5

As a Christian you have to live in the middle of an ungodly world, and it is of little use for you to cry, "Woe to me." Jesus did not pray that you should be taken out of the world, and what He did not pray for, you need not desire. It is far better to meet the difficulty in the Lord's strength and by doing so to glorify Him. The enemy is always watching for inconsistency in your conduct; therefore be very *holy*. Remember that the eyes of all are on you, and that more is expected from you than from other men. Strive to give no occasion for blame. Let your goodness be the only fault they can discover in you. Like Daniel, compel them to say of you, "We shall not find any ground for complaint against this Daniel unless we find it in connection with the law of his God."[1] Seek to be *useful* as well as consistent. Perhaps you think, "If I were in a more favorable position I could serve the Lord's cause, but I cannot do any good where I am." The worse the people are among whom you live, the more they need your exertions; if they are crooked, all the more need for you to set them straight; and if they are perverse, they need you to turn their proud hearts to the truth. Where should the doctor spend his time if not among the sick? Where is honor to be won by the soldier but in the center of the battle? And when you are weary of the strife and sin that meets you on every hand, consider that all the saints have endured the same trial. They were not carried on couches to heaven, and you should not expect to travel more easily than they. They had to risk their lives on the battlefield, and you will not be crowned until you also have endured hardship as a good soldier of Jesus Christ. Therefore, stand firm in the faith, be courageous, be strong!

❧ EVENING ☙

HAVE YOU ENTERED INTO THE SPRINGS OF THE SEA? — JOB 38:16

Some things in nature remain a mystery even to the most intelligent and enterprising investigators. Human knowledge has boundaries beyond which it cannot pass. Universal knowledge is for God alone. If this is true in the things that are seen and temporal, I can be certain that it is even more so in spiritual and eternal matters. Why, then, have I been torturing my brain with speculations about divine sovereignty and human responsibility? These deep and dark truths I am no more able to comprehend than to discover the source from which the ocean draws her watery supplies. Why am I so curious to know the reason for my Lord's providences, the motive of His actions, the design of His visitations? Will I ever be able to clasp the sun in my fist or hold the universe in my palm? Yet these are as a drop in a bucket compared with the Lord my God. Do not let me strive to understand the infinite, but spend my strength in love. What I cannot gain by intellect I can possess by affection, and that should be enough for me. I cannot penetrate the heart of the sea, but I can enjoy the healthy breezes that sweep across it, and I can sail over its blue waves with propitious winds. If I could enter the springs of the sea, the feat would serve no useful purpose either to myself or to others; it would not save the sinking ship or restore the drowned sailor to his weeping wife and children. Neither would my solving deep mysteries avail me a single whit. The simplest act of obedience to Him is better than the profoundest knowledge. My Lord, I leave the infinite to You and ask You to put far from me a love for the tree of knowledge that would keep me from the tree of life.

[1] Daniel 6:5

... IN THE MIDST OF A CROOKED AND TWISTED GENERATION,
AMONG WHOM YOU SHINE AS LIGHTS IN THE WORLD. — PHILIPPIANS 2:15

We use lights for *display*. A Christian should so shine in his life that a person could not live with him a week without knowing the Gospel. His conversation should be such that all who spend time with him would understand clearly to whom he belongs and who it is he serves and would see the image of Jesus displayed in his daily actions. Lights are intended for *guidance*. We are to help those around us who are in the dark. We are to declare to them the Word of life. We are to point sinners to the Savior and the weary to a divine resting-place. Sometimes men read their Bibles and fail to understand them; we should be ready, like Philip, to instruct the inquirer in the meaning of God's Word, the way of salvation, and the life of godliness. Lights are also used for *warning*. On our rocks and sandbanks a lighthouse is sure to be erected. Christians should know that there are many false lights everywhere in the world, and therefore the right light is needed. The wreckers of Satan are always abroad, tempting the ungodly to sin under the name of pleasure as they hoist the wrong light. It is our responsibility to set the true light upon every dangerous rock, to point out every sin and tell what it leads to, so that we may be clear of the blood of all men, shining as lights in the world. Lights also have a very *cheering* influence, and so have Christians. A Christian ought to be a comforter, with kind words on his lips and sympathy in his heart; he should carry sunshine wherever he goes and diffuse happiness around him.

> Gracious Spirit dwell with me;
> I myself would gracious be,
> And with words that help and heal
> Would Thy life in mine reveal,
> And with actions bold and meek
> Would for Christ my Savior speak.

❧ EVENING ❧

BUT IF YOU ARE LED BY THE SPIRIT, YOU ARE NOT UNDER THE LAW.
— GALATIANS 5:18

The individual who looks at his character and position from a legal point of view will not only despair when he comes to the *end* of his reckoning, but if he is a wise man he will despair at the *beginning*; for if we are to be judged on the basis of the law, none of us will be justified. How blessed to know that we live in the realm of grace and not of law! When thinking of my standing before God, the question is not, "Am I perfect in myself before the law?" but "Am I perfect in Christ Jesus?" That is a very different matter. We need not ask ourselves, "Am I without sin naturally?" but "Have I been washed in the fountain opened for sin and for uncleanness?" It is not "Am I in myself well pleasing to God?" but "Am I accepted in the Beloved?" When the Christian views his evidences from the top of Sinai, he grows alarmed about his salvation; it is far better for him to view his position in the light of Calvary. "Why," he says, "my faith has unbelief in it; it is not able to save me." Suppose he had considered *the object* of his faith instead of his faith. Then he would have said, "There is no failure in *Him*, and therefore I am safe." He sighs over his hope: "My hope is spoiled and darkened by an anxious focusing on present things; how can I be accepted?" If he had regarded *the ground* of his hope, he would have seen that the promise of God stands sure and that whatever our doubts may be, God's oath and promise never fail. Believer, it is always safer for you to be led by the Spirit into gospel freedom than to wear legal fetters. Judge yourself on what *Christ* is rather than on what *you* are. Satan will try to spoil your peace by reminding you of your sinfulness and imperfections: You can only meet his accusations by faithfully holding to the Gospel and refusing to wear the yoke of slavery.

AND WHEN THEY COULD NOT GET NEAR HIM BECAUSE OF THE CROWD,
THEY REMOVED THE ROOF ABOVE HIM, AND
WHEN THEY HAD MADE AN OPENING, THEY LET DOWN THE BED
ON WHICH THE PARALYTIC LAY. — MARK 2:4

Faith is full of creativity. The house was full, a crowd blocked the entry, but faith found a creative way of getting to the Lord and placing the paralytic before Him. If we cannot get sinners to Jesus by ordinary methods, we must use extraordinary ones. It seems, according to Luke 5:19, that roof tiles had to be removed. That would create dust and cause a measure of danger to those below; but where the case is very urgent, we must be prepared to run some risks and shock some people. Jesus was there to heal, and therefore roof or no roof, faith ventured all so that the poor paralytic might have his sins forgiven. We need more daring creative faith among us! Dear reader, let us seek it this morning for ourselves and for our fellow-workers and try today to perform some gallant act for the love of souls and the glory of the Lord.

The world is constantly creating and inventing; genius serves all the purposes of human desire: Can't faith invent too and by some creative means reach the people who are strangers to the Gospel? It was the presence of Jesus that stirred this victorious courage in the four friends of the paralytic. Is the Lord still present among us? Have we seen His face for ourselves this morning? Have we felt His healing power in our own souls? If so, then through the door or the window or the roof let us overcome every hindrance in bringing others to Jesus. When faith and love are truly set on winning souls, we will learn to be creative in our approach. If hunger for bread can break through stone walls, surely hunger for souls is not to be hindered in its efforts. O Lord, make us quick to suggest and employ methods of reaching our friends and neighbors and of introducing them to You!

THEY ARE TROUBLED LIKE THE SEA THAT CANNOT BE QUIET.
— JEREMIAH 49:23

We are unaware of what sorrow may be upon the sea at this moment. We are safe in our quiet room, but far away out to sea the hurricane may be cruelly seeking the lives of men. Imagine the bitter winds howling through the rigging, the timbers heaving as the waves beat like battering rams upon the boat! God help you, poor drenched and wearied ones! I am praying to the great Lord of sea and land, that He will make the storm calm and bring you to your desired haven! I ought not simply to pray; I should try to help those brave men who risk their lives so constantly. Have I ever done anything for them? What can I do? How often does the boisterous sea swallow up the sailor! Thousands have died where pearls lie deep. There is sorrow on the sea, which is echoed in the sad lament of widows and orphans. The salt of the sea is in the eyes of many mothers and wives. Relentless billows, you have devoured the love of women and the strength of households. What a resurrection there will be from the caverns of the deep when the sea gives up her dead! Until then there will be sorrow on the sea. As if in sympathy with the woes of earth, the sea is always fretting along a thousand shores, wailing with a sorrowful cry, booming with a hollow crash of unrest, raving with uproarious discontent, chafing with hoarse rage, or jangling with the voices of ten thousand murmuring pebbles. The roar of the sea may be glorious to a rejoicing spirit, but to the son of sorrow, the wide, wide ocean is even more forlorn than the wide, wide world. This is not our comfort, and the restless billows tell us so. There is a land where there is no more sea—our faces are firmly set toward it; we are going to the place of which the Lord has spoken. Until then we cast our sorrows on the Lord who walked upon the sea of old and who makes a way for His people through the depths.

❧ MORNING ❧

FROM ME COMES YOUR FRUIT. — HOSEA 14:8

Our fruit comes from God as a result of our union with Him. The fruit of the branch is directly traceable to the root. Sever the connection, the branch dies, and no fruit is produced. By virtue of our union with Christ we bring forth fruit. Every bunch of grapes has been first in the root; it has passed through the stem and flowed through the sap vessels and fashioned itself externally into fruit. But it was first in the stem; so also every good work is first in Christ, and then it is brought forth in us. Christian, treasure this precious union with Christ, for it must be the source of all the fruitfulness that you can ever hope to know. If you were not joined to Jesus Christ, you would be a fruitless branch indeed.

Our fruit comes from God as to *spiritual providence*. When the rain falls from heaven, when the clouds look down from on high and are about to distill their liquid treasure, when the bright sun swells the berries in the cluster, each heavenly benefit may whisper to the tree and say, "From me comes your fruit." The fruit owes much to the root—that is essential to fruitfulness—but it also owes a great deal to external influences. How much we owe to God's gracious providence, by which He provides us constantly with quickening, teaching, consolation, strength, or whatever else we need. To this we owe all of our usefulness or virtue.

Our fruit comes from God as to *skillful gardening*. The gardener's sharp-edged knife promotes the fruitfulness of the tree by thinning the clusters and by cutting off superfluous shoots. So is it, Christian, with the pruning that the Lord does to you. "My Father is the vine dresser. Every branch of mine that does not bear fruit he takes away; and every branch that does bear fruit he prunes, that it may bear more fruit."[1] Since God is the author of our spiritual graces, let us give Him all the glory for our salvation.

❧ EVENING ❧

. . . AND WHAT IS THE IMMEASURABLE GREATNESS OF HIS POWER
TOWARD US WHO BELIEVE, ACCORDING TO THE WORKING OF
HIS GREAT MIGHT THAT HE WORKED IN CHRIST WHEN HE
RAISED HIM FROM THE DEAD. — EPHESIANS 1:19-20

The resurrection of Christ, and our salvation, was brought about by nothing less than *divine power*. What will we say of those who think that conversion is accomplished by the free will of man and is due to his own kindly disposition? When we begin to see the dead rise from the grave by their own power, then may we expect to see ungodly sinners turning to Christ by their own endeavors. It is not the word preached, nor the word read in itself; all quickening power proceeds from the Holy Spirit. This power was *irresistible*. All the soldiers and the high priests could not keep the body of Christ in the tomb; death itself could not hold Jesus in its grip: Just as irresistible is the power displayed in the believer when he is raised to newness of life. No sin, no corruption, no devils in hell nor sinners on earth can resist the hand of God's grace when it intends to convert a man. If God omnipotently says, "You shall," man will not say, "I shall not." Notice that the power that raised Christ from the dead was *glorious*. It reflected honor upon God and caused dismay in the hosts of evil. So there is great glory to God in the conversion of every sinner. It was *everlasting power*. "Christ being raised from the dead will never die again; death no longer has dominion over him."[2] So we, being raised from the dead, do not go back to our dead works or to our old corruptions, but we live to God. "Because I live, you also will live."[3] "For you have died, and your life is hidden with Christ in God."[4] "Just as Christ was raised from the dead by the glory of the Father, we too might walk in newness of life."[5] Finally, in the text note *the union of the new life to Jesus*. The same power that raised the Head works life in the members. What a blessing to be quickened together with Christ!

[1] John 15:1-2 [2] Romans 6:9 [3] John 14:19 [4] Colossians 3:3 [5] Romans 6:4

SEPTEMBER 9   ❧ MORNING ❧

I WILL ANSWER YOU, AND WILL TELL YOU GREAT AND
HIDDEN THINGS THAT YOU HAVE NOT KNOWN. — JEREMIAH 33:3

There are different translations of these words. One version renders it, "I will show you great and fortified things." Another, "great and reserved things." Now, there are reserved and special things in Christian experience: Every development in the spiritual life does not take place in the same way or in the same time frame. There are the common benefits and feelings of repentance and faith and joy and hope, which are enjoyed by the entire family; but there is an upper realm of delight, communion, and conscious union with Christ, which is far from being the routine enjoyment of believers. We do not all have the high privilege of John, to lean upon Jesus' bosom; nor of Paul, to be caught up into the third heaven. There are heights in experimental [experiential] knowledge of the things of God that the eagle's eye has never seen and the philosopher's mind has never grasped. God alone can take us there; but the chariot in which He transports us, and the horses with which that chariot is pulled, are prevailing prayers. Prevailing prayer is victorious with the God of mercy, "In his manhood he strove with God. He strove with the angel and prevailed; he wept and sought his favor. He met God at Bethel, and there God spoke with us."[1] Prevailing prayer takes the Christian to the mountain and enables him to cover heaven with clouds of blessing, and earth with floods of mercy. Prevailing prayer lifts the Christian and shows him his inheritance and transfigures him into the likeness of his Lord. If you would reach to something higher than ordinary groveling experience, look to the Rock that is higher than you, and gaze with the eye of faith through the window of consistent prayer. When you open the window on your side, it will not be bolted on the other.

❧ EVENING ❧

AROUND THE THRONE WERE TWENTY-FOUR THRONES, AND
SEATED ON THE THRONES WERE TWENTY-FOUR ELDERS,
CLOTHED IN WHITE GARMENTS. — REVELATION 4:4

These representatives of the saints in heaven are said to be *around the throne.* In the passage in Solomon's Song where he sings of the King sitting at his table, some render it "a round table." From this, some expositors—I think, without straining the text—have said, "There is an equality among the saints." That idea is conveyed by the equal nearness of the twenty-four elders. The condition of glorified spirits in heaven is that of nearness to Christ, clear vision of His glory, constant access to His court, and familiar fellowship with His person. There is no difference in this respect between one saint and another, but all the people of God—apostles, martyrs, ministers, or private and obscure Christians—will all be seated *near the throne*, where they shall have a perfect view of their exalted Lord and be satisfied with His love. They will all be near Christ, all satisfied with His love, all eating and drinking at the same table with Him, all equally loved as His favorites and friends even if not all equally rewarded as His servants.

Believers on earth should imitate the saints in heaven in their nearness to Christ. We should be like the elders in heaven, sitting around the throne. Christ should be the object of our thoughts and the center of our lives. How can we endure to live at such a distance from Him? Lord Jesus, draw us nearer to Yourself. Say to us, "Abide in Me, and I in you"; and let us sing, "Holy, holy, holy is the Lord God Almighty, who was and is and is to come!"

> O lift me higher, nearer Thee,
> And as I rise more pure and fit,
> O let my soul's humility
> Make me lie lower at Thy feet;
> Less trusting self, the more I prove
> The blessed comfort of Thy love.

[1] Hosea 12:3-4

AND HE WENT UP ON THE MOUNTAIN AND CALLED TO HIM
THOSE WHOM HE DESIRED, AND THEY CAME TO HIM. — MARK 3:13

Here was sovereignty. Impatient spirits may fret and fume because they are not called to the highest places in ministry; but, reader, learn to rejoice that Jesus calls those He desires. If He leaves me as a doorkeeper in His house, I will cheerfully bless Him for His grace in allowing me to do anything in His service. The call of Christ's servants comes from above. Jesus stands on the mountain, forever above the world in holiness, zeal, love, and power. Those whom He calls must go up the mountain to Him; they must seek to rise to His level by living in constant communion with Him. They may not be able to achieve classic honors or attain scholastic eminence, but they must, like Moses, go up to the mountain of God and experience intimate communion with the unseen God if they are ever to be fit to proclaim the Gospel of peace. Jesus went away to hold high fellowship with the Father, and we must enter into the same divine companionship if we want to bless our fellowmen. No wonder that the apostles were clothed with power when they came down fresh from the mountain where Jesus was. This morning we must endeavor to ascend the mount of communion, so that we may be ordained to the lifework for which we are set apart. Let us not see the face of man today until we have met with Jesus. Time spent with Him is time well spent. We will cast out devils and work wonders if we go down into the world clothed with that divine energy that only Christ can give. It is no use going to the Lord's battle until we are armed with heavenly weapons. We *must* see Jesus; this is essential. At the mercy-seat we will linger until He makes Himself known to us and until we can truthfully say, "We were with Him on the Holy Mountain."

❧ EVENING ❦

EVENING WOLVES. — HABAKKUK 1:8

While preparing the present volume, this particular expression recurred to me so frequently that in order to be rid of its constant demand I determined to give a page to it. The evening wolf, infuriated by a day of hunger, was fiercer and more ravenous than he would have been in the morning. This furious creature may promise a picture of our doubts and fears after a day of distraction of mind, losses in business, and perhaps ungenerous tauntings from our fellowmen. How our thoughts howl in our ears: "Where is your God now?" How voracious and greedy they are, swallowing up all suggestions of comfort and remaining as hungry as ever. Great Shepherd, slay these evening wolves, and bid Your sheep lie down in green pastures, undisturbed by unbelief. The fiends of hell seen just like evening wolves, for when the flock of Christ are in a cloudy and dark day, and their sun seems to be going down, they arrive to tear and to devour. They will scarcely attack the Christian in the daylight of faith, but in the gloomy night of the soul they fall upon him. O Lord who laid down Your life for the sheep, preserve them from the fangs of the wolf.

False teachers who craftily and industriously hunt for precious life, devouring men by their falsehoods, are as dangerous and detestable as evening wolves. Darkness is their element; deceit is their character; destruction is their end. They pose the greatest threat to our safety when they wear the sheep's skin. Blessed is he who is kept from them, for thousands become the prey of grievous wolves that enter within the fold of the church.

What a wonder of grace it is when fierce persecutors are converted, for then the wolf lives with the lamb, and men of cruel, ungovernable dispositions become gentle and teachable. O Lord, convert many like this: For this we will pray tonight.

BE SEPARATE FROM THEM. — 2 CORINTHIANS 6:17

The Christian, while in the world, is not to be of the world. He should be distinguished from it in *the great object of his life*. To him, "to live" should be "Christ."[1] Whether he eats or drinks or whatever he does, he should do it all to God's glory. You may lay up treasure; but lay it up in heaven, where neither moth nor rust destroy, where thieves do not break in and steal. You may work to be rich; but make it your ambition to be "rich in faith"[2] and good works. You may pursue pleasure; but when you are happy, sing psalms and make melody in your hearts to the Lord. In your *spirit*, as well as in your aim, you should differ from the world. Waiting humbly before God, always conscious of His presence, delighting in fellowship with Him, and seeking to know His will, you will prove that you are a citizen of heaven. And you should be separate from the world in your *actions*. If a thing is right, though you lose by doing it, it must be done; if it is wrong, though you would gain from it, you must reject the sin for your Master's sake. You must have no fellowship with the unfruitful works of darkness but rather reprove them. Walk worthy of your high calling and dignity. Remember, Christian, that you are a son of the King of kings. Therefore, keep yourself unstained from the world. Do not soil the fingers that are to serve the King. Do not let your eyes become the windows of lust, eyes that will soon see the King in His beauty. Do not let your feet, which are soon to walk the golden streets, be defiled in dirty places. Do not allow your heart to be filled with pride and bitterness, but prepare it to be filled with heaven and to overflow with ecstatic joy.

> *Then rise my soul! and soar away,*
> *Above the thoughtless crowd;*
> *Above the pleasures of the day,*
> *And splendors of the proud;*
> *Up where eternal beauties bloom,*
> *And pleasures all divine;*
> *Where wealth, that never can consume,*
> *And endless glories shine.*

❧ E V E N I N G ❧

LEAD ME, O LORD, IN YOUR RIGHTEOUSNESS BECAUSE OF MY ENEMIES. — PSALM 5:8

The enmity of the world is bitter in its assault against the people of Christ. Men will forgive a thousand faults in others, but they will magnify the most trivial offense in the followers of Jesus. Instead of vainly regretting this, let us make it work for us, and since so many are watching for our collapse, let it be a special motive for walking very carefully before God. If we live carelessly, the watching world will soon see it, and multiple tongues will spread the story, exaggerated and emblazoned by the zeal of slander. They will shout triumphantly, "See! See how these Christians act! They are hypocrites to everyone." And so great damage will be done to the cause of Christ, and His name will be greatly maligned. The cross of Christ is in itself an offense to the world; let us take care that we add no offense of our own. It is "a stumbling block to Jews"[3]: Let us ensure that we put no stumbling blocks where there are enough already. "Folly to Gentiles": let us not add our folly to give apparent reason for the scorn with which the worldly deride the Gospel. How concerned we should be with ourselves! How rigid with our consciences! In the presence of adversaries who will misrepresent our best deeds and impugn our motives if they cannot censure our actions, we should be circumspect! Like pilgrims we travel under suspicion through Vanity Fair. Not only are we under surveillance, but there are more spies than we imagine, at home and at work. If we fall into the enemies' hands, we may sooner expect generosity from a wolf or mercy from a fiend than anything like patience with our infirmities from those who spice their infidelity toward God with scandals against His people. Lord, lead us always; do not allow our enemies to trip us up!

[1] Philippians 1:21 [2] James 2:5 [3] 1 Corinthians 1:23.

THE LORD IS A JEALOUS AND AVENGING GOD. — NAHUM 1:2

*B*eliever, *your Lord is very jealous of your love.* Did He choose you? He cannot bear that you should choose another. Did He buy you with His own blood? He cannot endure that you should think you are your own or that you belong to this world. He loved you with such a love that He would not remain in heaven without you; He would sooner die than have you perish, and He cannot endure that anything should stand between your heart's love and Himself. *He is very jealous of your trust.* He will not permit you to trust in yourself. He cannot stand the thought of you hewing out broken cisterns and neglecting the overflowing fountain that is always free to you. When we lean upon Him, He is glad; but when we transfer our dependence to another, when we rely upon our own wisdom or the wisdom of a friend— worst of all, when we trust in any works of our own—He is displeased and will chasten us, that He may bring us to Himself. *He is also very jealous of our company.* There should be no one with whom we converse so much as with Jesus. To remain in Him alone, this is true love; but to commune with the world, to find sufficient satisfaction in our earthly comforts, to even prefer the company of our fellow Christians to secret fellowship with Him, this grieves our jealous Lord. He longs to have us abide in Him and enjoy constant fellowship with Himself; and many of the trials that He sends us are for the purpose of weaning our hearts from created things and fixing them more closely on Him who created everything. Let this jealousy that would keep us near to Christ *also be a comfort* to us, for if He loves us so much as to care about our love, we may be sure that He will allow nothing to harm us and will protect us from all our enemies. May we have grace today to keep our hearts in holy purity for Christ alone, with sacred jealousy closing our eyes to all the fascinations of the world!

❧ EVENING ☙

I WILL SING OF STEADFAST LOVE AND JUSTICE. — PSALM 101:1

*F*aith is triumphant in trial. When reason has her feet fastened in the stocks of the inner prison, faith makes the dungeon walls ring with her happy notes as she cries, "I will sing of steadfast love and justice; to you, O LORD, I will make music." Faith pulls the dark mask from the face of trouble and discovers the angel beneath. Faith looks up at the cloud and sees that

> *It is big with mercy and will break*
> *In blessings on her head.*

There is a subject for song even in the judgments of God toward us. For, first, the trial is *not as difficult as it might have been;* next, the trouble is *not as severe as we deserved;* and our affliction is *not as crushing as the burden that others have to carry.* Faith sees that in her deepest sorrow there is no punishment. There is not a drop of God's wrath in it; it is all sent in love. Faith finds love gleaming like a jewel on the breast of an angry God. Faith wears her grief "like a badge of honor" and sings of the sweet result of her sorrows, because they work for her spiritual good. Faith says, "For this slight momentary affliction is preparing for us an eternal weight of glory beyond all comparison."[1] So faith rides out in victory, trampling down earthly wisdom and carnal knowledge, and singing songs of triumph where the battle rages.

> *All I meet I find assists me*
> *In my path to heavenly joy:*
> *Where, though trials now attend me,*
> *Trials never more annoy.*

> *Blest there with a weight of glory,*
> *Still the path I'll not forget,*
> *But, exulting, cry, it led me*
> *To my blessed Savior's seat.*

[1] 2 Corinthians 4:17

This teaches us that the *comfort* obtained by one may often prove helpful to another, just as the springs would be enjoyed by the company who came after. When we read some book that is really helpful and encouraging, we recognize that the author has gone ahead of us and discovered these refreshing springs for us as well as for himself. Many books have been like wells drilled by a pilgrim for himself but have proved quite as useful to others. We notice this especially in the Psalms—for example, 42:11: "Why are you cast down, O my soul, and why are you in turmoil within me?" Travelers have been delighted to see the footprint of man on a barren shore, and we love to see the marks of pilgrims while passing through the vale of tears.

The pilgrims dig the well, but, strangely, it fills from the top instead of the bottom. We use the means, but the blessing does not spring from the means. We dig a well, but heaven fills it with rain. The horse is prepared for the day of battle, but safety is from the Lord. The means are connected with the end, but they do not produce it themselves. Consider here how the rain covers the ground with pools, so that they become useful as reservoirs. The endeavor is not wasted, but still it does not supersede divine help.

Grace may be compared to rain for its purity, for its refreshing and energizing influence, for its coming from above, and for the sovereignty with which it is given or withheld. May our readers have showers of blessing, and may the springs be filled with water! What are the means and ordinances without the smile of heaven! They are like clouds without rain and pools without water. God of love, open the windows of heaven and pour us out a blessing!

Observe *the condescension* of this fact. Jesus, holy, harmless, undefiled, and separate from sinners, who towers above all other men—*this* Man receives sinners. This Man, who is no other than the eternal God, before whom angels veil their faces—*this* Man receives sinners. It requires an angel's tongue to describe such a mighty stoop of love. That any of *us* would be willing to reach the lost is nothing wonderful—they are, after all, our own race; but that He, the offended God, against whom the transgression has been committed, should take upon Himself the form of a servant and bear the sin of many and be willing to receive the worst of sinners—this is marvelous.

"This man receives sinners"; not in order for them to remain sinners, but He receives them in order that He may pardon their sins, justify their persons, cleanse their hearts by His purifying word, preserve their souls by the indwelling of the Holy Spirit, and enable them to serve Him, show forth His praise, and have communion with Him. Into His heart's love He receives sinners; He takes them from the refuse pile and wears them as jewels in His crown; He snatches them like branches from the fire and preserves them as costly monuments to His mercy. None are so precious in Jesus' sight as the sinners for whom He died. When Jesus receives sinners, He does not have an outdoor reception, no public square where He charitably entertains them in the way men treat passing beggars, but He opens the golden gates of His royal heart and receives the sinner right into Himself. He admits the humble penitent into personal union and makes Him a member of His body, of His flesh, and of His bones. There was never such a reception as this! This fact is certain. Even this evening, He is still receiving sinners: It is our prayer that sinners will receive Him.

AND OTHER BOATS WERE WITH HIM. — MARK 4:36

Jesus was the Lord High Admiral of the sea that night, and His presence preserved the whole convoy. It is good to sail with Jesus, even though we may be in a little boat. When we sail in Christ's company, we cannot be sure of fine weather, for great storms may toss the vessel that carries the Lord Himself, and we should not expect to find the sea less boisterous around our little boat. If we go with Jesus we must be content to face what He faces; and when the waves are rough for Him, they will be rough for us. It is through tempest and storm that we will reach land, just as He did before us. When the storm swept over Galilee's dark lake, the faces wore anxious frowns, and all hearts dreaded shipwreck.

When every attempt to ride it out proved useless, the resting Savior rose and with a word transformed the billowing tempest into the deep quiet of a calm. Then all the other boats were at rest as well as the one that carried the Lord. Jesus is the star of the sea; and though there is sorrow on the sea, when Jesus is on it, there is also joy. May our hearts make Jesus their anchor, their rudder, their lighthouse, their lifeboat, and their harbor. His Church is the Admiral's flagship; let us attend her exercises and cheer her officers with our presence. He Himself is the great attraction; let us always follow in His wake, observe His signals, steer by His chart, and never fear while He is within reach. Not one ship in the convoy shall be wrecked; the great Captain will steer every craft in safety to the desired haven. By faith we will raise our anchor for another day's cruise and sail with Jesus into a sea of tribulation. Winds and waves will not spare us, but they all obey Him; and therefore whatever squalls may occur on the outside, faith will enjoy a blessed calm within. He is always in the center of the weather-beaten company: Let us rejoice in Him. His boat has reached the harbor, and so will ours.

☙ EVENING ❧

I ACKNOWLEDGED MY SIN UNTO YOU, AND I DID NOT COVER MY INIQUITY; I SAID, "I WILL CONFESS MY TRANSGRESSIONS TO THE LORD," AND YOU FORGAVE THE INIQUITY OF MY SIN. — PSALM 32:5

David's grief for sin was bitter. Its effects were visible on his outward frame: His bones wasted away; his strength dried up like the drought of summer. He was unable to find a remedy until he made a full confession before the throne of heavenly grace. He tells us that for a time he kept silent, and his heart was filled with grief and his lips with groaning: Like a mountain stream that is blocked, his soul was swollen with torrents of sorrow. He created excuses, he tried to divert his thoughts, but it was all to no purpose; like a festering sore his anguish gathered, and, unwilling to use the scalpel of confession, his spirit was tormented and knew no peace. At last it came to this, that he must return to God in humble penitence or die outright; so he hurried to the mercy-seat and there unrolled the volume of his iniquities before the all-seeing God, acknowledging all the evil of his ways in the terms of the Fifty-first and other penitential Psalms. Having confessed, a task so simple and yet so hard for the proud, he immediately received the token of divine forgiveness; the bones that had been wasted were made to rejoice, and he emerged from his prayers to sing the joyful songs of the one whose transgression is forgiven. Do you see the value of this grace-led confession of sin? It is to be prized above everything, for in every case where there is a genuine, gracious confession, mercy is freely given—not because the repentance and confession *deserve* mercy, but for *Christ's sake*. May God be praised, there is always healing for the broken heart; the fountain is ever flowing to cleanse us from our sins. Truly, O Lord, You are a God "ready to forgive."[1] Therefore will we humbly acknowledge our iniquities.

[1] Nehemiah 9:17

SEPTEMBER 15 ❧ MORNING ❧

HE IS NOT AFRAID OF BAD NEWS. — PSALM 112:7

Christian, you ought not to be afraid of the arrival of bad news; because if you are distressed by such, *you are no different from other men.* They do not have your God to run to; they have never proved His faithfulness as you have done, and it is no wonder if they are bowed down with alarm and cowed with fear. But you profess to be of another spirit; you have been born again to a living hope, and your heart lives in heaven and not on earthly things. If you are seen to be distracted as other men, what is the value of that grace that you profess to have received? Where is the dignity of that new nature that you claim to possess?

Again, if you should be filled with alarm like others, *you would no doubt be led into the sins so common to them under trying circumstances.* The ungodly, when they are overtaken by bad news, rebel against God; they murmur and maintain that God has dealt harshly with them. Will you fall into that same sin? Will you provoke the Lord as they do?

Moreover, unconverted men often run to wrong means in order to escape from difficulties, and you will be sure to do the same if your mind yields to the present pressure. Trust in the Lord, and wait patiently for Him. Your wisest course is to do what Moses did at the Red Sea: "Stand firm, and see the salvation of the LORD."[1] For if you give way to fear when you hear bad news, you will be unable to meet the trouble with that calm composure that prepares for duty and sustains in adversity. How can you glorify God if you play the coward? Saints have often sung God's high praises in the fires, but when you act as if there were no one to help, will your doubting and despondency magnify the Most High? Then take courage and, relying in sure confidence upon the faithfulness of your covenant God, "Let not your hearts be troubled, neither let them be afraid."[2]

❧ EVENING ❧

. . . FOR THE PEOPLE OF ISRAEL WHO ARE NEAR TO HIM.
— PSALM 148:14

Distance and separation were marks of the old covenant. When God appeared even to His servant Moses, He said, "Do not come near; take your sandals off your feet";[3] and when He revealed Himself on Mount Sinai to His own chosen and separated people, one of the first commands was, "You shall set limits for the people all around."[4] In the sacred worship of the tabernacle and the temple, the thought of distance was always prominent. The majority of the people did not even enter the outer court. Into the inner court none but the priests might dare to intrude, while into the innermost place, or the holy of holies, the high priest entered but only once in the year. It was as if the Lord in those early ages was teaching man that sin was so utterly loathsome to Him that He must treat men as lepers put outside the camp; and when He came closest to them, He still made them feel the extent of the separation between a holy God and an impure sinner. When the Gospel came, we were placed on quite another footing. The word "Go" was replaced with "Come"; distance was replaced with nearness, and we who previously were far away were brought near by the blood of Jesus Christ. Incarnate Deity has no fire wall around it. "Come to me, all who labor and are heavy laden, and I will give you rest"[5] is the joyful proclamation of God as He appears in human flesh. He no longer teaches the leper his leprosy by setting him at a distance, but by Himself suffering the penalty of the leper's defilement. What a state of safety and privilege is this proximity to God through Jesus! Do you know it by experience? If you know it, are you living in the power of it? This closeness is wonderful, and yet it is to be followed by a greater nearness still, when it shall be said, "The dwelling place of God is with man. He will dwell with them, and they will be his people."[6] Lord, haste the day!

[1] Exodus 14:13 [2] John 14:27 [3] Exodus 3:5 [4] Exodus 19:12 [5] Matthew 11:28 [6] Revelation 21:3

PARTAKERS OF THE DIVINE NATURE. — 2 PETER 1:4

To be a partaker of the divine nature is not, of course, to become God. That cannot be. The essence of Deity is not to be participated in by the creature. Between the creature and the Creator there will always be a fixed gulf in terms of essence; but as the first man Adam was made in the image of God, so we, by the renewal of the Holy Spirit, are in a diviner sense made in the image of the Most High and are "partakers of the divine nature." We are, by grace, made like God. "God is love";[1] we become love—"whoever loves has been born of God."[2] God is truth; we become true, and we love what is true. God is good, and He makes us good by His grace, so that we become the pure in heart who will see God. Moreover, we become partakers of the divine nature in an even higher sense than this—in fact, in as lofty a sense as can be conceived, short of our being absolutely divine. Do we not become members of the body of the divine person of Christ? Yes, the same blood that flows in the head flows in the hand: And the same life that quickens Christ quickens His people, for "You have died, and your life is hidden with Christ in God."[3] As if this were not enough, we are married to Christ. He has betrothed us to Himself in righteousness and in faithfulness, and he who is joined to the Lord is one with Him. Marvelous mystery! We look into it, but who will understand it? One with Jesus—so much so that the branch is not more one with the vine than we are a part of the Lord, our Savior and our Redeemer! While we rejoice in this, let us remember that those who are made "partakers of the divine nature" will display this high and holy relationship in their relationships with others and will make it evident in their daily walk and conversation that they have escaped the corruption that is in the world through lust. O for more divine holiness of life!

❧ EVENING ☙

AM I THE SEA, OR A SEA MONSTER, THAT YOU SET A GUARD OVER ME?
— JOB 7:12

This was a strange question for Job to ask the Lord. He felt himself to be too insignificant to be so strictly watched and chastened, and he hoped that he was not so unruly as to need to be restrained. The inquiry was natural from one surrounded by such miseries, but after all, it is capable of a very humbling answer. It is true that man is not the sea, but he is even more troublesome and unruly. The sea obediently respects its boundary, and it does not overleap the limit, even though it is just a belt of sand. Mighty as it is, it hears the divine *"thus far,"* and when raging with tempest it still respects the word. Self-willed man, however, defies heaven and oppresses earth, and there is no end to his rebellious rage. The sea, obedient to the moon, ebbs and flows with ceaseless regularity and so renders an active as well as a passive obedience; but man, restless beyond his sphere, sleeps within the lines of duty, lazy where he should be active. He neither comes nor goes at the divine command but sullenly prefers to do what he should not and to leave undone what is required of him. Every drop in the ocean, every beaded bubble, and every yeasty foam-flake, every shell and pebble, feel the power of law and yield or move at once. If only our nature were but one thousandth as much conformed to the will of God! We call the sea fickle and false, but how constant it is! Since our fathers' days, and even before, the sea is where it was, beating on the same cliffs to the same tune. We know where to find it; it never hides, and its ceaseless pounding never fades; but where is man, fickle man? Can the wise man guess by what folly he will next be seduced from his obedience? We need more watching than the billowy sea and are far more rebellious. Lord, rule us for Your own glory. Amen.

[1] 1 John 4:8   [2] 1 John 4:7   [3] Colossians 3:3

"BRING HIM TO ME." — MARK 9:19

Despairingly the poor disappointed father turned away from the disciples to their Master. His son was in the worst possible condition, and all means had failed, but the miserable child was soon delivered from the evil one when the parent in faith obeyed the Lord Jesus' word, "Bring him to me." Children are a precious gift from God, but much anxiety comes along with them. They may be a great joy or a great bitterness to their parents; they may be filled with the Spirit of God or possessed with the spirit of evil. In all cases, the Word of God gives us one prescription for the cure of all their ills: "Bring him to me." We need to engage in agonizing prayer on their behalf while they are still babies! Sin is there; so let our prayers begin to attack it. Our cries for our offspring should precede those cries that herald their arrival into a world of sin. In the days of their youth we will see sad evidences of that dumb and deaf spirit that will neither pray properly, nor hear the voice of God in the soul, but Jesus still commands, "Bring him to me." When they are grown up, they may wallow in sin and foam with enmity against God; then when our hearts are breaking we should remember the Great Physician's words, "Bring him to me." We must never cease to pray until they cease to breathe. No case is hopeless while Jesus lives.

The Lord sometimes allows His people to be driven into a corner that they may learn how necessary He is to them. Ungodly children, when they show us our own powerlessness against the depravity of their hearts, drive us to the strong for strength, and this is a great blessing to us. Whatever our morning's need may be, may it like a strong current carry us to the ocean of divine love. Jesus can soon remove our sorrow; He delights to comfort us. Let us hurry to Him while He waits to meet us.

❧ EVENING ❧

ENCOURAGE HIM. — DEUTERONOMY 1:38

God employs His people to encourage one another. He did not say to an angel, "Gabriel, My servant Joshua is about to lead My people into Canaan—go, encourage him." God never performs unnecessary miracles. If His purposes can be accomplished by ordinary means, He will not use miraculous agencies. Gabriel would not have been half so well fitted for the work as Moses. A brother's sympathy is more precious than an angel's prestige. The swift-winged angel knew more about the Master's desires than he did about the people's needs. An angel had never experienced the difficult journey, nor faced the fiery serpents, nor had he led the stiff-necked multitude in the wilderness as Moses had done. We should be glad that God usually works for man by man. This forms a bond of brotherhood, and being mutually dependent on one another, we are united more completely into one family. Brethren, take the text as God's message to you. Work at helping others, and especially strive to *encourage* them. Talk warmly to the young and anxious inquirer; lovingly try to remove stumbling blocks out of his way. When you find a spark of grace in the heart, kneel down and blow it into a flame. Leave the young believer to discover the roughness of the road by stages, but tell him of the strength that is found in God, of the certainty of the promise, and of the benefits of communion with Christ. Aim to comfort the sorrowful and to encourage the despondent. Speak a fitting word to the weary, and lift the spirits of those who are fearful to go on their way with gladness. God encourages you by His promises; Christ encourages you as He points to the heaven He has won for you; and the Spirit encourages *you* as He works in you to will and to do of His own purpose and pleasure. Imitate divine wisdom, and encourage others according to the Word this evening.

IF WE LIVE BY THE SPIRIT, LET US ALSO WALK BY THE SPIRIT.
— GALATIANS 5:25

The two most important things in our Christian journey are the *life of faith* and the *walk of faith*. The person who grasps this is not far from being a master in experimental [experiential] theology, for they are vital points to a Christian. You will never find true faith unaccompanied by true godliness; on the other hand, you will never discover a truly holy life that does not have at its root a living faith relying upon the righteousness of Christ. Woe to those who seek the one without the other! There are some who cultivate faith and forget holiness; these may be very high in orthodoxy, but they shall be very deep in condemnation, for they hold the truth in unrighteousness! There are others who have strained after a holy life but have denied the faith, like the Pharisees of old, of whom the Master said they were "whitewashed tombs."[1] We must have faith, for this is the foundation; we must have holiness of life, for this is the superstructure. What use is the mere foundation of a building to a man on the day of tempest? Can he hide himself in it? He needs a house to cover him as well as a foundation for that house. Even so we need the superstructure of spiritual life if we want comfort in the day of doubt. But do not seek a holy life without faith, for that would be to erect a house that can provide no permanent shelter because it has no foundation on a rock. Let faith and life be put together, and like the two supports of an archway, they will make our devotion endure. Like light and heat streaming from the same sun, they are full of blessing. Like the two pillars of the temple, they are for glory and for beauty. They are two streams from the fountain of grace, two lamps lit with holy fire, two olive trees watered by heavenly care. Lord, give us today life internally, and it will reveal itself externally to Your glory.

✍ EVENING ✍

AND THEY FOLLOW ME. — JOHN 10:27

We should follow our Lord as unhesitatingly as sheep follow their shepherd, for *He has a right to lead us wherever He pleases*. We are not our own, we are bought with a price—let us recognize the rights of the redeeming blood. The soldier follows his captain, the servant obeys his master, and so we must follow our Redeemer, to whom we are a purchased possession. We are not true to our profession of being Christians if we question the summons of our Leader and Commander. Submission is our duty; quibbling is our folly. Our Lord may say to us what he said to Peter, "What is that to you? You follow Me!"[2] Wherever Jesus may lead us, *He goes before us*. If we do not know where we go, we know with whom we go. With such a companion, who will dread the dangers of the journey? The road may be long, but His everlasting arms will carry us to the end. The presence of Jesus is the assurance of eternal salvation; because He lives, we will live also. We should follow Christ in simplicity and faith, because *the paths in which He leads us all end in glory and immortality*. It is true that they may not be smooth paths—they may be covered with sharp, flinty trials; but they lead to "the city that has foundations, whose designer and maker is God."[3] All the paths of the Lord are mercy and truth to those who keep His covenant. Let us put our complete trust in our Leader, since we know that in prosperity or adversity, sickness or health, popularity or contempt, His purpose will be worked out, and that purpose will be pure, unmingled good to every heir of mercy. We will find it sweet to go up the bleak side of the hill with Christ; and when rain and snow blow into our faces, His dear love will make us far more blessed than those who sit at home and warm their hands at the world's fire. When Jesus draws us, we will run after Him. No matter where He leads us, we follow the Shepherd.

[1] Matthew 23:27   [2] John 21:22   [3] Hebrews 11:10

FOR FREEDOM CHRIST HAS SET US FREE. — GALATIANS 5:1

This "freedom" is established in heaven's charter—*the Bible*. Here is a choice passage, believer: "When you pass through the waters, I will be with you."[1] Here is another: "The mountains may depart and the hills be removed, but my steadfast love shall not depart from you."[2] These Scriptures set you free in believing. You are a welcome guest at this table of promises. Scripture is a never-failing treasury filled with boundless stores of grace. It is the bank of heaven; you may draw from it as much as you wish, without any hindrance. Come in faith; you are welcome to all the *covenant blessings*. There is not a promise in the Word that will be withheld. In the deepest tribulations let this freedom comfort you; overwhelmed by waves of distress let it cheer you; when sorrows surround you let it be your solace. This is your Father's love-token; you are free in it at all times. You are also given *free access to the throne of grace*. It is the believer's privilege to have access at all times to his heavenly Father. Whatever our desires, our difficulties, our wants, we are at liberty to spread them all before Him. It does not matter how much we may have sinned, we can ask and expect pardon. No matter how poor we are, we may plead His promise that He will provide everything we need. We have permission to approach His throne at all times—in midnight's darkest hour or in noontide's most burning heat. Exercise your right, believer, and enjoy this privilege. You are set free to all that is treasured up *in Christ*—wisdom, righteousness, sanctification, and redemption. It does not matter what your need is, for there is abundant supply in Christ, and it is there *for you*. What a "freedom" is yours! Freedom from condemnation, freedom to the promises, freedom to the throne of grace, and at last freedom to enter heaven!

❧ EVENING ☙

FOR THIS CHILD I PRAYED. — 1 SAMUEL 1:27

Devout souls delight to reflect upon those mercies that they have obtained in answer to prayer, for they can see God's special love in them. When we can name our blessings Samuel—that is, "asked of God"—they will be as dear to us as this child was to Hannah. Peninnah had many children, but they came as common blessings unsought in prayer. Hannah's one heaven-given child was far more precious, because he was the fruit of sincere pleadings. How sweet was the water that Samson found at "the spring of him who called."[3] Did we pray for the conversion of our children? How doubly sweet, when they are saved, to see in them our own petitions answered! Better to rejoice over them as the fruit of our pleadings than as the fruit of our bodies. Have we asked the Lord for some choice spiritual gift? When it comes to us, it will be wrapped up in the golden cloth of God's faithfulness and truth and will be doubly precious. Have we sought success in the Lord's work? How joyful is the prosperity that comes flying on the wings of prayer! It is always best to get blessings into our house in the legitimate way, by the door of prayer; then they are blessings indeed, and not temptations. Even when prayer is not speedy, the blessings grow all the richer on account of the delay; the child Jesus was all the more lovely in the eyes of Mary when she found Him after having searched for Him. What we gain by prayer we should dedicate to God, as Hannah dedicated Samuel. The gift came from heaven; let it go to heaven. Prayer brought it, gratitude sang over it—let devotion consecrate it. Here will be a special occasion for saying, "Of Your own I have given to You." Reader, is prayer your heartbeat or your weariness? Which?

[1] Isaiah 43:2 [2] Isaiah 54:10 [3] Judges 15:19, margin

"A SWORD FOR THE LORD AND FOR GIDEON!" — JUDGES 7:20

Gideon ordered his men to do two things: Covering up a torch in an earthen pitcher, he had them, at an appointed signal, break the pitcher and let the light shine. Then he had them blow the trumpet, crying, "A sword for the LORD and for Gideon!" This is precisely what all Christians must do. First, *you must shine*: Break the pitcher that conceals your light, throw aside the container that has been hiding your candle, and shine. Let your light shine before men; let your good works be such that when men look at you, they will know that you have been with Jesus. Then *there must be the sound*, the blowing of the trumpet. There must be active exertions for the gathering of sinners by proclaiming Christ crucified. Take the Gospel to them. Carry it to their door; put it in their path; do not allow them to escape it; blow the trumpet right against their ears. Remember that the true battle-cry of the church is Gideon's watchword, "*A sword for the LORD and for Gideon!*" God must do it; it is His own work. But we are not to be idle; He uses instruments—"A sword for the LORD *and for Gideon!*" If we only cry, "A sword for the LORD!" we will be guilty of idle presumption; and if we shout, "A sword for Gideon!" alone, we shall display an idolatrous reliance on man: We must blend the two in practical harmony: "A sword for the LORD and for Gideon!" We can do nothing in ourselves, but we can do everything by the help of our God; let us, therefore, in His name determine to go out personally and serve Him with our flaming torch of holy example and with our trumpet blasts of sincere declaration and testimony, and God will be with us, and the enemy will be put to confusion, and the Lord of hosts will reign forever and ever.

AT EVENING WITHHOLD NOT YOUR HAND. — ECCLESIASTES 11:6

In *the evening of the day* opportunities are plentiful: Men return from their work, and the zealous soul-winner finds time to share widely the love of Jesus. Do I have no evening work for Jesus? If I have not, let me no longer withhold my hand from a service that requires wholehearted endeavor. Sinners are perishing for lack of knowledge; he who loiters may find his shoes red with the blood of souls. Jesus gave both His hands to the nails. How can I keep back one of mine from His blessed work? Night and day He toiled and prayed for me. How can I give a single hour to the pampering of my body with luxurious ease? Up, lazy heart; stretch out your hand to work, or lift it up to pray. Heaven and hell are serious; so must I be, and this evening I should sow good seed for the Lord my God.

The evening of life also has its calls. Life is so short that a morning of manhood's strength and an evening of decay make up the whole of it. To some it seems long, but a dollar is a great sum of money to a poor man. Life is so brief that no man can afford to lose a day. It has been well said that if a great king were to bring us a great heap of gold and bid us take as much as we could count in a day, we would make a long day of it; we would begin early in the morning, and in the evening we would not withhold our hand. Winning souls is far nobler work; so how is it that we quit so soon? Some are spared to a long evening of green old age; if such is my case, let me use any talents I still retain and serve my blessed and faithful Lord to the final hour. By His grace I will die with my boots on and lay down my commission only when I lay down my body. Age may instruct the young, cheer the faint, and encourage the despondent. If evening has less stifling heat, it should have more calm wisdom; therefore in the evening I will not withhold my hand.

I WILL REJOICE IN DOING THEM GOOD. — JEREMIAH 32:41

How heartwarming to the believer is the delight that God takes in His saints! We cannot see any reason in ourselves why the Lord should take pleasure in us; we do not even take delight in ourselves, for we often have to groan, being burdened, conscious of our sinfulness and deploring our unfaithfulness. We are fearful that God's people cannot take much encouragement from us, for they surely can see our many imperfections and our follies, and so be caused to lament our infirmities rather than admire our graces. But we love to dwell upon this transcendent truth, this glorious mystery: As the bridegroom rejoices over the bride, so the Lord rejoices over us. We do not read anywhere that God delights in the cloud-capped mountains or the sparkling stars, but we do read that He delights in the habitable parts of the earth, and that His delights are with the sons of men. We do not even find it written that angels give His soul delight; nor does He say, concerning cherubim and seraphim, "Thou shalt be called Hephzibah . . . for the LORD delighted in thee."[1] But He does say all that to poor fallen creatures like ourselves—debased and depraved by sin, but saved, exalted, and glorified by His grace. In what strong language He expresses His delight in His people! Who could have conceived of the Eternal One bursting into a song? Yet it is written, "He will rejoice over you with gladness; he will quiet you by his love; he will exult over you with loud singing."[2] As He looked upon the world He had made, He said, "It is very good"; but when He looked on those who are the purchase of Jesus' blood, His own chosen ones, it seemed as if the great heart of the Infinite could restrain itself no longer but overflowed in divine exclamations of joy. Should we not utter our grateful response to such a marvelous declaration of His love and sing, "I will rejoice in the LORD; I will take joy in the God of my salvation?"[3]

⍺ EVENING ⍺

DO NOT SWEEP MY SOUL AWAY WITH SINNERS. — PSALM 26:9

Fear made David pray like this, for something whispered, *Perhaps, after all, you may be swept away with sinners.* That fear springs mainly from holy anxiety, arising from the recollection of past sin. Even the pardoned man will inquire, "What if at the end my sins should be remembered, and I should be left out of the company of the saved?" He thinks about his present condition—so little grace, so little love, so little holiness; and looking forward to the future, he considers his weakness and the many temptations that surround him, and he fears that he may fall and become a prey to the enemy. A sense of sin and present evil and his prevailing corruptions compel him to pray, in fear and trembling, "Do not sweep my soul away with sinners." Reader, if you have prayed this prayer, and if your character is correctly described in the Psalm from which it is taken, you need not be afraid that you will be swept away with sinners. Do you have the two virtues that David had—the outward walking in integrity and the inward trusting in the Lord? Are you resting upon Christ's sacrifice, and can you approach the altar of God with humble hope? If so, rest assured, you will never be swept away with sinners, for that calamity is impossible. At the judgment the command will be given, "Gather the weeds first and bind them in bundles to be burned, but gather the wheat into my barn."[4] If, then, you are *like* God's people, you will be *with* God's people. You cannot be swept away with sinners, for you have been purchased at too high a price. Redeemed by the blood of Christ, you are His forever, and where He is, there His people must be. You are loved too much to be swept away with reprobates. Will one who is dear to Christ perish? Impossible! Hell cannot hold you! Heaven claims you! Trust in Christ, and do not fear!

[1] Isaiah 62:4, KJV [2] Zephaniah 3:17 [3] Habakkuk 3:18 [4] Matthew 13:30

LET ISRAEL BE GLAD IN HIS MAKER. — PSALM 149:2

Rejoice, believer, but take care that your gladness has its spring *in the Lord.* You have much cause for gladness in God, for you can sing with David, "God my exceeding joy."[1] Be glad that the Lord reigns, that Jehovah is King! Rejoice that He sits on the throne and rules all things! Every attribute of God should become a fresh ray in the sunlight of our gladness. The fact that He is *wise* should make us glad, knowing as we do our own foolishness. That He is *mighty* should cause us who tremble in our weakness to rejoice. That He is *everlasting* should always be a theme of joy when we know that we wither like grass. That He is *unchanging* should provide a perpetual song, for *we* change every hour. That He is *full of grace,* that He is overflowing with it, and that this grace in covenant He has given to us, that it is ours to cleanse us, ours to keep us, ours to sanctify us, ours to perfect us, ours to bring us to glory—all this should serve to make us glad in Him. This gladness in God is like a deep river. So far we have only touched its edge; we know a little of its clear sweet, heavenly streams, but further on the depth is greater, and the current more powerful in its joy. The Christian feels that he may delight himself not only in what God is, but also in all that God *has done* in the past. The Psalms show us that God's people in olden times were keen to make much of God's actions and to have a song concerning each of them. So let God's people now rehearse the deeds of the Lord! Let them tell of His mighty acts and "sing to the LORD, for he has triumphed gloriously."[2] Let them never cease to sing, for as new mercies flow to them day by day, so their gladness in the Lord's loving acts of providence and grace should display itself in continued thanksgiving. Be glad, children of Zion, and rejoice in the Lord your God.

☙ EVENING ❧

WHEN MY HEART IS FAINT . . . LEAD ME TO THE ROCK THAT IS HIGHER THAN I. — PSALM 61:2

Most of us know what it is to be overwhelmed in heart, emptied like when a man wipes a dish and turns it upside down, submerged and thrown on our beam-ends like a boat mastered by the storm. Discoveries of inward corruption will do this, if the Lord permits the depth of our depravity to become troubled and cast up mire and dirt. Disappointments and heartbreaks will do this when billow after billow rolls over us, and we are like a broken shell thrown to and fro by the surf. Blessed be God, at such seasons we are not left without a sufficient solace: Our God is the harbor of weather-beaten sails, the hostel for forlorn pilgrims. He is higher than we are, His mercy higher than our sins, His love higher than our thoughts. It is pitiful to see men putting their trust in something lower than themselves; but our confidence is fixed on an exceeding high and glorious Lord. He is a Rock since He doesn't change, and a high Rock because the tempests that overwhelm us roll far beneath His feet; He is not disturbed by them but rules them at His will. If we get under the shelter of this lofty Rock, we may defy the hurricane; all is calm under the lee of that towering cliff. Sadly, the confusion in which the troubled mind is often cast is such that we need piloting to this divine shelter. Hence the prayer of the text. O Lord, our God, by Your Holy Spirit, teach us the way of faith; lead us into Your rest. The wind blows us out to sea—the helm does not answer to our puny hand; You alone can steer us over the bar between the sunken rocks and safe into the fair haven. We are totally dependent upon You—we need You to bring us to You. To be wisely directed and steered into safety and peace is Your gift, and Yours alone. Tonight be pleased to deal kindly with Your servants.

---

[1] Psalm 43:4   [2] Exodus 15:1

What a state of privilege! It includes our *justification* before God, but the term "blessed" in the Greek means more than that. It signifies that we are the objects of *divine satisfaction*, even of *divine delight*. How marvelous that we—worms, mortals, sinners—should be made the objects of divine love! But it is only *"in the Beloved."* Some Christians seem to be accepted in their own experience—at least that is their apprehension. When their spirit is lively and their hopes bright, they think God accepts them, for they feel so high, so heavenly-minded, so drawn above the earth! But when their souls cleave to the dust, they are the victims of the fear that they are no longer accepted. If they could only see that all their high joys do not exalt them, and all their low despondencies do not really depress them in their Father's sight, but that they stand accepted in One who never alters. This One is always the beloved of God, always perfect, always without spot or wrinkle or any such thing. How much happier they would be, and how much more they would honor the Savior if they could grasp Him! Rejoice then, believer, in this: You are blessed "in the Beloved." You look within, and you say, "There is nothing acceptable *here*!" But look at Christ, and see if everything is not acceptable *there*. Your sins trouble you; but God has cast your sins behind His back, and you are accepted and blessed in the Righteous One. You have to fight with corruption and wrestle with temptation, but you are already accepted in Him who has overcome the powers of evil. The devil tempts you, but be of good cheer—he cannot destroy you, for you are accepted in Him who has broken Satan's head. Know by full assurance your glorious standing. Even glorified souls are not more accepted than you are. They are only blessed in heaven "in the Beloved," and you are even now blessed in Christ after the same manner.

A certain man had a deeply troubled son who was afflicted with a spirit that struck him dumb. The father, having seen the futility of the attempts of the disciples to heal his child, had little or no faith in Christ. Therefore, when he was invited to bring his son to Him, he said to Jesus, "If You can do anything, have compassion on us and help us." Now there was an "if" in the question, but the poor trembling father had put the "if" in the wrong place. Jesus Christ, therefore, without commanding him to retract the "if," kindly puts it in its legitimate position. "Actually, " He seemed to say, "there should be no 'if' about My power, nor concerning My willingness; the 'if' lies somewhere else. *If you can believe*, 'all things are possible for one who believes.'" The man's trust was strengthened, he offered a humble prayer for an increase of faith, and instantly Jesus spoke the word, and the devil was cast out, with an injunction never to return. There is a lesson here that we need to learn. We, like this man, often see that there is an "if" somewhere, but we are continually blundering by putting it in the wrong place. "*If* Jesus can help me"—"*if* He can give me grace to overcome temptation"—"*if* He can grant me pardon"—"*if* He can make me successful." No; *if* you can believe, He both can and will. You have misplaced your "if." If you can confidently trust, even as all things are possible to Christ, so will all things be possible to you. Faith stands in God's power and is robed in God's majesty; it wears the royal apparel and rides on the King's horse, for it is the grace that the King delights to honor. Girding itself with the glorious might of the all-working Spirit, it becomes, in the omnipotence of God, mighty to do, to dare, and to suffer. All things, without limit, are possible to one who believes. My soul, can you believe your Lord tonight?

FOR I WAS ASHAMED TO ASK THE KING FOR A BAND OF SOLDIERS
AND HORSEMEN TO PROTECT US AGAINST THE ENEMY ON OUR WAY,
SINCE WE HAD TOLD THE KING, "THE HAND OF OUR GOD IS FOR GOOD
ON ALL WHO SEEK HIM, AND THE POWER OF HIS WRATH IS AGAINST
ALL WHO FORSAKE HIM." — EZRA 8:22

A convoy on many accounts would have been desirable for the pilgrim band, but Ezra was ashamed to ask for one. He feared that the heathen king might think his professions of faith in God were mere hypocrisy or might imagine that the God of Israel was not able to preserve His own worshipers. He could not bring his mind to depend on human instruments in a matter so evidently of the Lord, and therefore the caravan set out with no visible protection, and yet guarded by Him who is the sword and shield of His people. It is to be feared that few believers sense this holy jealousy for God; even those who in some measure walk by faith occasionally spoil the sparkle of their life by seeking help from man. It is a most blessed thing to have no props and no buttresses, but to stand upright on the Rock of Ages, upheld by the Lord alone. Would any believers seek government funds for their church if they remembered that the Lord is dishonored by their asking for Caesar's help? As if the Lord could not supply the needs of His own cause! Would we run so quickly to friends and relatives for assistance if we remembered that the Lord is glorified by our obvious reliance on His solitary arm? My soul, wait only on God. "But," says one, "are means never to be used?" Certainly they are. But our fault seldom lies in their neglect: Far more frequently it springs from foolishly believing in them instead of believing in God. Few run too far in neglecting the arm of man; but many sin greatly in making too much of it. So learn, dear reader, to glorify the Lord by leaving means untried, if by using them you would dishonor the name of the Lord.

⚕ EVENING ⚕

I SLEPT, BUT MY HEART WAS AWAKE. — SONG OF SOLOMON 5:2

Paradoxes abound in Christian experience, and here is one: The spouse was asleep, and yet she was awake. The only one who can read the believer's riddle is he who has lived through this experience. The two points in this evening's text are: a mournful sleepiness and a hopeful wakefulness. "I *slept*." Through sin that dwells in us we may become lax in holy duties, lazy in religious exercises, dull in spiritual joys, and completely indolent and careless. This is a shameful state for one in whom the quickening Spirit dwells; and it is dangerous in the highest degree. Even wise virgins sometimes slumber, but it is high time for all to shake off the chains of idleness. It is to be feared that many believers lose their strength as Samson lost his hair, while sleeping on the lap of carnal security. With a perishing world around us, to sleep is cruel; with eternity so close at hand, it is madness. Yet none of us are as awake as we should be; a few thunderclaps would do us all good, and it may be, unless we soon stir ourselves, we will have them in the form of war or disease or personal bereavements and loss. May we leave forever the couch of fleshly ease, and go out with flaming torches to meet the coming Bridegroom! "*My heart was awake*." This is a happy sign. Life is not extinct, though sadly smothered. When our renewed heart struggles against our natural heaviness, we should be grateful to sovereign grace for keeping a little vitality within this body of death. Jesus will hear our hearts, will help our hearts, will visit our hearts; for the voice of the wakeful heart is really the voice of our Beloved, saying, "Open to me." Holy zeal will surely unlock the door.

Oh lovely attitude! He stands
With melting heart and laden hands;
My soul forsakes her every sin;
And lets the heavenly stranger in.

JUST AND THE JUSTIFIER OF THE ONE WHO HAS FAITH IN JESUS.
— ROMANS 3:26

Being justified by faith, we have peace with God. Conscience no longer accuses. Judgment now decides *for* the sinner instead of against him. Memory looks back upon past sins with deep sorrow for the sin, but yet without dreading any penalty to come; for Christ has paid the debt of His people to the last jot and tittle and received the divine receipt. Unless God can be so unjust as to demand double payment for one debt, no soul for whom Jesus died as a substitute can ever be cast into hell. It seems to be one of the principles of our enlightened nature to believe that God is just; we feel that it must be so, and this terrifies us at first. But is it not marvelous that this very same belief that God is just later becomes the pillar of our confidence and peace! If God is just, I, a sinner, alone and without a substitute, must be punished. But Jesus stands in my place and is punished for me; and now, if God is just, I, a sinner, standing in Christ, can never be punished. God must change His nature before one soul for whom Jesus was a substitute can ever by any possibility suffer the punishment of the law. Therefore, Jesus having taken the place of the believer—having rendered a full equivalent to divine wrath for all that His people ought to have suffered as the result of sin—the believer can shout with glorious triumph, "Who shall bring any charge against God's elect?"[1] Not God, for He has justified; not Christ, for He has died, yes, has risen again. My hope lives not because I am not a sinner, but because I am a sinner for whom Christ died; my trust is not that I am holy, but that being unholy, *He* is my righteousness. My faith rests not upon what I am or shall be or feel or know, but in what Christ is, in what He has done, and in what He is now doing for me. Hallelujah!

✧ EVENING ✧

WHOM GOD MADE OUR WISDOM. — 1 CORINTHIANS 1:30

Man's intellect seeks for peace and by nature seeks it apart from the Lord Jesus Christ. Men of education are apt, even when converted, to look upon the simplicities of the cross of Christ with too little reverence and love. They are trapped in the old net in which the Greeks were taken and have a hankering to mix philosophy with revelation. The temptation with a man of refined thought and high education is to depart from the simple truth of Christ crucified and to invent, as the term is, a more *intellectual* doctrine. This led the early Christian churches into Gnosticism and bewitched them with all sorts of heresies. This is the root of unorthodoxy and the other high-sounding notions that in the past were so fashionable in Germany and are now so enthralling to certain classes of divines. Whoever you are, good reader, and whatever your education may be, if you are the Lord's, rest assured that you will find no peace in philosophizing divinity. You may receive the dogma of one great thinker or the dream of another profound reasoner, but what the chaff is to the wheat is what these notions are to the pure Word of God. Reason at its best can only discover the ABC's of truth, and even that lacks certainty, while in Christ Jesus there is treasured up all the fullness of wisdom and knowledge. All attempts on the part of Christians to be content with the systems that Unitarian and liberal-church thinkers approve of must fail; true heirs of heaven must come back to the grandly simple reality that makes the plowboy's eye flash with joy and rejoices the pious pauper's heart—"Christ Jesus came into the world to save sinners."[2] Jesus satisfies the most elevated intellect when He is believingly received, but apart from Him the mind of the regenerate discovers no rest. "The fear of the LORD is the beginning of knowledge."[3] "All those who practice it have a good understanding."[4]

[1]Romans 8:33 [2]1 Timothy 1:15 [3]Proverbs 1:7 [4]Psalm 111:10

HE WAS STANDING AMONG THE MYRTLE TREES IN THE GLEN.
— ZECHARIAH 1:8

The vision in this chapter describes the condition of Israel in Zechariah's day; but being interpreted in its aspect toward us, it describes the Church of God as we find it now in the world. The Church is compared to a myrtle grove flourishing in a glen. It is *hidden*, unobserved, courting no honor and attracting no attention from the careless gazer. The Church, like her Head, has a glory, but it is concealed from carnal eyes, for the time of her breaking forth in all her splendor is not yet here. The idea of *tranquil security* is also suggested to us, for the myrtle grove in the glen is still and calm, while the storm sweeps over the mountaintops. Tempests spend their force upon the craggy peaks of the Alps, but down where the stream flows that makes glad the city of our God, the myrtles flourish by still waters and are unshaken by the impetuous wind. How great is the inward tranquillity of God's Church! Even when opposed and persecuted, she has a peace that the world does not give and that, therefore, it cannot take away: The peace of God that passes all understanding keeps the hearts and minds of God's people. Doesn't the metaphor forcefully picture the peaceful, *perpetual growth* of the saints? The myrtle does not shed her leaves—she is always green; and the church in her worst time still has a blessed covering of grace about her; indeed, she has sometimes exhibited *most* vegetation when her winter has been sharpest. She has prospered most when her adversities have been most severe. Hence the text *hints at victory*. The myrtle is the emblem of peace and a significant token of *triumph*. The brows of conquerors were wreathed with myrtle and with laurel; and isn't the church always victorious? Isn't every Christian more than a conqueror through Him who loved him? Living in peace, don't the saints fall asleep in the arms of victory?

⁊ E V E N I N G ∞

WAIL, O CYPRESS, FOR THE CEDAR HAS FALLEN. — ZECHARIAH 11:2

When in the forest there is heard the crash of a falling oak, it is a sign that the woodman is around, and every tree in the whole company may tremble lest tomorrow the sharp edge of the axe should find it out. We are all like trees marked for the axe, and the fall of one should remind us that for every one, whether as great as the cedar or as humble as the cypress, the appointed hour is fast approaching. I trust we do not, by often hearing of death, become callous to it. May we never be like the birds in the steeple, which build their nests when the bells are tolling and sleep quietly when the solemn funeral peals are startling the air. May we regard death as the most serious of all events and be sobered by its approach. It ill behooves us to play while our eternal destiny hangs on a thread. The sword is out of its sheath—let us not trifle; it is ready, and the edge is sharp—let us not play with it. He who does not prepare for death is more than an ordinary fool—he is a madman. When the voice of God is heard among the trees of the garden, let fig tree and sycamore and elm and cedar all hear the sound.

Be ready, servant of Christ, for your Master comes suddenly, when an ungodly world least expects Him. See to it that you are faithful in His work, for the grave shall soon be prepared for you. Be ready, parents, see to it that your children are brought up in the fear of God, for they will soon be orphans. Be ready, businessmen, make sure that your affairs are in order and that you serve God with all your hearts, for the days of your earthly service will soon be over, and you will be called to give account for the deeds done in the body, whether they are good or bad. May we all prepare for the tribunal of the great King with a care that will be rewarded with the gracious commendation, "Well done, good and faithful servant."[1]

[1] Matthew 25:21

HAPPY ARE YOU, O ISRAEL! WHO IS LIKE YOU,
A PEOPLE SAVED BY THE LORD. — DEUTERONOMY 33:29

The person who declares that Christianity makes men miserable is himself an utter stranger to it. It would be strange indeed if it made us wretched; consider *to what a position it exalts us!* It makes us sons of God. Do you suppose that God will give all the happiness to His enemies and reserve all the mourning for His own family? Will His foes have laughter and joy, while His home-born children inherit sorrow and wretchedness? Will the sinner, who has no part in Christ, call himself rich in happiness, while we go mourning as if we were penniless beggars? No; we will rejoice in the Lord always and glory in our inheritance, for we "did not receive the spirit of slavery to fall back into fear, but you have received the Spirit of adoption as sons, by whom we cry, 'Abba! Father!'"[1] The rod of discipline must rest upon us in our measure, but it works for us the comfortable fruits of righteousness; and therefore by the help of the divine Comforter, we, a "people saved by the LORD," will rejoice in the God of our salvation. We are married to Christ; and will our great Bridegroom permit His spouse to linger in constant grief? Our hearts are knit to Him: We are His members, and though for a while we may suffer as our Head once suffered, yet even now we are blessed with heavenly blessings in Him. We have the promise of our inheritance in the comforts of the Spirit, which are neither few nor small. Inheritors of joy forever, we have foretastes of our portion. There are streaks of the light of joy to herald our eternal sunrise. Our riches are beyond the sea; our city with firm foundations lies on the other side of the river; gleams of glory from the spirit-world cheer our hearts and urge us onward. It is truly said of us, "Happy are you, O Israel! Who is like you, a people saved by the LORD."

❧ EVENING ☙

MY BELOVED PUT HIS HAND TO THE LATCH,
AND MY HEART WAS THRILLED WITHIN ME. — SONG OF SOLOMON 5:4

Knocking was not enough, for my heart was too full of sleep, too cold and ungrateful to rise and open the door; but the touch of His effectual grace has caused my soul to stir. How patient of my Beloved to wait when He found Himself shut out, and me asleep upon the bed of indolence! How great His patience to knock and knock again, and to add His voice to His knockings, beseeching me to open to Him! How could I have refused Him! My heart is base; I blush and without excuse! But the greatest kindness of all is this, that He becomes His own porter and unlocks the door Himself. Blessed is the hand that condescends to lift the latch and turn the key. Now I see that nothing but my Lord's own power can save such a naughty mass of wickedness as I am; ordinances fail, and even the Gospel has no effect upon me, until His hand is stretched out. I also see that His hand is good where everything else is unsuccessful; He can open when nothing else will. Blessed be His name, I feel His gracious presence even now. Well may my heart be thrilled within me when I think of all that He has suffered for me and of my ungenerous response. I have allowed my affections to wander. I have tolerated rivals. I have grieved Him. Sweetest and dearest of all lovers, I have treated You as an unfaithful wife treats her husband. Oh, my cruel sins, my cruel self. What can I do? Tears are a poor evidence of my repentance; my whole heart palpitates with indignation at myself. I am wretched to treat my Lord, my All in All, my exceeding great joy, as though He were a stranger. Jesus, You freely forgive, but this is not enough; prevent my unfaithfulness in the future. Kiss away these tears, and then purge my heart and bind it with seven-fold cords to Yourself, so that I may never wander from You again.

[1] Romans 8:15

❧ MORNING ❧

THE LORD LOOKS DOWN FROM HEAVEN;
HE SEES ALL THE CHILDREN OF MAN. — PSALM 33:13

Perhaps no figure of speech represents God in a more gracious light than when He is spoken of as stooping from His throne and coming down from heaven to attend to the needs and to behold the woes of mankind. We love Him who, when Sodom and Gomorrah were full of iniquity, would not destroy those cities until He had made a personal visitation to them. We cannot help pouring out our heart in affection for our Lord who turns His ear from the highest glory and puts it to the lip of the dying sinner, whose failing heart longs for reconciliation. How can we do anything but love Him when we know that He numbers the very hairs of our heads, marks our path, and orders our ways? This great truth is brought especially near to our heart when we realize how attentive He is, not merely to the passing interests of His creatures, but to their spiritual concerns. Though vast distances lie between the finite creature and the infinite Creator, yet there are links uniting both. When a tear is wept by you, do not think that God does not see it; for "As a father shows compassion to his children, so the LORD shows compassion to those who fear him."[1] Your sigh is able to move the heart of Jehovah; your whisper can incline His ear to you; your prayer can stay His hand; your faith can move His arm. Do not think that God sits on high taking no account of you. Remember that however poor and needy you are, still the Lord thinks of you. "For the eyes of the LORD run to and fro throughout the whole earth, to give strong support to those whose heart is blameless toward him."[2]

> *Oh! then repeat the truth that never tires;*
> *No God is like the God my soul desires;*
> *He at whose voice heaven trembles, even He,*
> *Great as He is, knows how to stoop to me.*

❧ EVENING ❧

AND HE SAID, "GO AGAIN," SEVEN TIMES. — 1 KINGS 18:43

Success is certain when the Lord has promised it. Although you may have pleaded month after month without evidence of response, it is not possible that the Lord should be deaf when His people are serious about a matter that concerns His glory. The prophet on the top of Carmel continued to wrestle with God and never for a moment gave way to the fear that he would not be suited for Jehovah's courts. Six times the servant returned, but on each occasion no word was spoken but "Go again." We must not dream of unbelief but hold to our faith even to seventy times seven. Faith sends expectant hope to look from Carmel's peak, and if nothing is seen, she sends again and again. So far from being crushed by repeated disappointment, faith is quickened to plead more fervently with her God. She is humbled but not crushed: Her groans are deeper, and her sighings more vehement, but she never relaxes her hold or stays her hand. It would be more agreeable to flesh and blood to have a speedy answer, but believing souls have learned to be submissive and to find it good to wait *for* as well as *upon* the Lord. Delayed answers often set the heart searching itself and so lead to contrition and spiritual reformation: Deadly blows are then struck at our corruption, and the sinful images are cleansed. The great danger is that men should faint and miss the blessing. Reader, do not fall into that sin, but continue to watch and pray. At last the little cloud was seen, the sure forerunner of torrents of rain; and even so with you, the token for good will surely be given, and you will rise as a prevailing prince to enjoy the mercy you have sought. Elijah was a man with passions just like us: His power with God did not lie in his own merits. If his believing prayer availed so much, why not yours? Plead the precious blood with unceasing persistence, and it will be with you according to your desire.

[1] Psalm 103:13 [2] 2 Chronicles 16:9

AND IF THE LEPROUS DISEASE HAS COVERED ALL HIS BODY,
HE SHALL PRONOUNCE HIM CLEAN OF THE DISEASE. — LEVITICUS 13:13

This regulation appears to be very strange, but there was wisdom in it, for the throwing out of the disease proved that the constitution was sound. This morning it may be well for us to see the typical teaching of this singular principle. We, too, are lepers and may read the law of the leper as applicable to ourselves. When a man sees himself to be completely lost and ruined, covered all over with the defilement of sin, and with no part free from pollution, when he disclaims all righteousness of his own and pleads guilty before the Lord, then is he clean through the blood of Jesus and the grace of God. Hidden, unfelt, unconfessed iniquity is the true leprosy, but when sin is seen and felt it has received its death blow, and the Lord looks with eyes of mercy upon the soul afflicted with it. Nothing is more deadly than self-righteousness or more hopeful than contrition. We must confess that we are nothing else but sin, for no confession short of this will be the whole truth. And if the Holy Spirit is at work within us, convincing us of sin, there will be no difficulty in making such an acknowledgment—it will spring spontaneously from our lips. What comfort this text provides to those under a deep sense of sin! Sin mourned and confessed, however deep and foul, will never shut a man out from the Lord Jesus. "Whoever comes to me I will never cast out."[1] Though dishonest as the thief, though immoral as the woman who was a sinner, though fierce as Saul of Tarsus, though cruel as Manasseh, though rebellious as the prodigal, the great heart of love will look upon the man who feels himself to have no health in him and will pronounce him clean when he trusts in Jesus crucified. Come to Him, then, poor heavy-laden sinner.

Come needy, come guilty, come loathsome and bare;
You can't come too filthy—come just as you are.

✥ EVENING ✥

I FOUND HIM WHOM MY SOUL LOVES. I HELD HIM, AND
WOULD NOT LET HIM GO. — SONG OF SOLOMON 3:4

Does Christ receive us when we come to Him despite all our past sinfulness? Does He never chide us for having tried all other refuges first? And is there none on earth like Him? Is He the best of all the good, the fairest of all the fair? Then let us praise Him! Daughters of Jerusalem, extol Him with tambourine and harp! Down with your idols; up with the Lord Jesus. Let the standards of pomp and pride be trampled underfoot, but let the cross of Jesus, which the world frowns and scoffs at, be lifted on high. O for a throne of ivory for our King. Let Him be set on high forever, and let my soul sit at His footstool and kiss His feet and wash them with my tears. How precious is Christ! How can it be that I have thought so little of Him? How is it I can go anywhere else for joy or comfort when He is so full, so rich, so satisfying? Fellow believer, make a covenant with your heart that you will never depart from Him, and ask the Lord to ratify it. Bid Him set you as a ring on His finger and as a bracelet on His arm. Ask Him to bind you to Him as the bride adorns herself with ornaments and as the bridegroom puts on his jewels. I would live in Christ's heart; in the hollow of that rock my soul would eternally abide. The sparrow has made a house, and the swallow a nest for herself where she may lay her young, even your altars, O Lord of hosts, my King and my God. And in the same way I would make my nest, my home, in You, and may this soul never leave again, but let me nestle close to You, Lord Jesus, my true and only rest.

When my precious Lord I find,
All my ardent passions glow;
Him with cords of love I bind,
Hold and will not let Him go.

[1] John 6:37

SING THE GLORY OF HIS NAME; GIVE TO HIM GLORIOUS PRAISE!
— PSALM 66:2

It is not left to our own option whether or not we will praise God. Praise is God's most right-eous due, and every Christian, as the recipient of His grace, is bound to praise God from day to day. It is true that we have no authoritative text for daily praise; we have no com-mandment prescribing certain hours of song and thanksgiving: But the law written upon the heart teaches us that it is right to praise God; and the unwritten mandate comes to us with as much force as if it had been recorded on the tables of stone or handed to us from the top of thundering Sinai. Yes, it is the Christian's *duty* to praise God. It is not only a pleasurable exercise, but it is the absolute obligation of his life. Those of you who are always mourning should not think that you are guiltless in this respect or imagine that you can discharge your duty to God without songs of praise. You are bound by the bonds of His love to bless His name as long as you live, and His praise should continually be in your mouth, for you are blessed in order that you may bless Him—"the people whom I formed for myself that they might declare my praise";[1] and if you do not praise God, you are not bringing forth the fruit that He has a right to expect from you. Do not let your harp hang on the willows, but take it down and strum with a grateful heart, bringing out its loudest music. Arise and declare His praise. With every morning's dawn, lift up your notes of thanksgiving, and let every set-ting sun be followed with your song. Surround the earth with your praises; circle it with an atmosphere of melody, and God Himself will listen from heaven and accept your music.

> E'en so I love Thee, and will love,
> And in Thy praise will sing,
> Because Thou art my loving God,
> And my redeeming King.

❧ EVENING ☙

A LIVING DOG IS BETTER THAN A DEAD LION. — ECCLESIASTES 9:4

Life is a precious thing, and in even its humblest form it is superior to death. This is emi-nently true in spiritual matters. It is better to be the least in the kingdom of heaven than the greatest out of it. The lowest degree of grace is superior to the noblest development of unregenerate nature. Where the Holy Spirit implants divine life in the soul, there is a precious deposit that none of the refinements of education can equal. The thief on the cross excels Caesar on his throne; Lazarus among the dogs is better than Cicero among the senators; and the most unlettered Christian is in the sight of God superior to Plato. Life is the badge of nobility in the realm of spiritual things, and men without it are only coarser or finer specimens of the same lifeless material, needing to be made alive, for they are dead in tres-passes and sins.

A living, loving gospel sermon, however unlearned in matter and lacking in style, is bet-ter than the finest discourse devoid of unction and power. A living dog keeps better watch than a dead lion and is of more service to his master; and so the poorest spiritual preacher is infinitely to be preferred to the exquisite orator who has no wisdom but that of words, no energy but that of self. The same holds true of our prayers and other religious exercises: If we are quickened in them by the Holy Spirit, they are acceptable to God through Jesus Christ, though we may think them to be worthless things, while our grand performances in which our hearts were absent, like dead lions, are mere carcasses in the sight of the living God. We need living groans, living sighs, living despondencies rather than lifeless songs and dead calms. Anything is better than death. The snarlings of the dog of hell will at least keep us awake, but dead faith and dead profession—what greater curses can a man have? Quicken us, quicken us, O Lord!

[1] Isaiah 43:21

October

CHOICE FRUITS, NEW AS WELL AS OLD, WHICH I HAVE LAID UP FOR YOU, O MY BELOVED. — SONG OF SOLOMON 7:13

The spouse desires to give to Jesus all that she produces. Our heart has all kinds of "choice fruits, new as well as old," and they are reserved for our Beloved. In this rich autumn season of fruitfulness, let us survey our supplies. We have *new* fruits. We desire to feel new life, new joy, new gratitude; we wish to make new resolves and carry them out by new endeavors; our heart blossoms with new prayers, and our soul is committing herself to new efforts. But we also have some *old* fruits. There is the choice fruit of our first love, and Jesus delights in it. There is our first faith—that simple faith by which, having nothing, we became possessors of everything. There is our joy when we first met the Lord: Let us revive it. We have our old memories of the promises. How faithful has God been! In sickness, how kindly He made our bed! In deep waters, how gently He picked us up! In the flaming furnace, how graciously He delivered us. Old fruits indeed! We have many of them, for His mercies have been more than the hairs of our head. Old sins we must regret, but then we have had repentances that He has given us, by which we have wept our way to the cross and learned the merit of His blood. We have fruits, this morning, both new and old; but here is the point— *they are all laid up for Jesus.* Without question the best and most acceptable services are those in which Jesus is the solitary aim of the soul, and His glory is the focus of all our endeavors. Let our many fruits be laid up only for Him; let us display them when He is with us, and not use them to draw attention to ourselves. Jesus, we will turn the key in our garden door, and no one will enter to rob You of one good fruit from the soil that You have watered with Your grace. All that we are and have shall be Yours, Yours alone, O Jesus, our Beloved!

Evening

THE LORD BESTOWS FAVOR AND HONOR. — PSALM 84:11

God is wonderfully generous by nature; to give is His delight. His gifts are immeasurably precious and are given as freely as the light of the sun. He gives grace to His own because He wills it, to His redeemed because of His covenant, to the called because of His promise, to believers because they seek it, to sinners because they need it. He gives grace abundantly, seasonably, constantly, readily, sovereignly; the value of the blessings is doubled by the manner in which it is given. Grace in all its forms He freely supplies to His people: Comforting, preserving, sanctifying, directing, instructing, assisting grace He generously and constantly pours into their souls, and He will always do so, whatever may happen. Sickness may come, but the Lord will give grace; poverty may descend on us, but grace will definitely be supplied; death must come, but grace will light a candle in the darkest hour. Reader, how blessed it is as years roll on, and the leaves again begin to fall, to enjoy this unfading promise, "The LORD bestows favor and honor."

The little conjunction "and" in this verse is a diamond rivet binding the present with the future: Favor and honor always go together. God has married them, and no one can separate them. The Lord will never deny a soul honor to whom He has freely granted favor; indeed, honor is nothing more than favor in its Sunday best, favor in full bloom, favor like autumn fruit, mellow and perfected. How soon we may have honor none can tell! It may be that before this month of October has run out we will see the Holy City; but if the interval is longer or shorter, we shall be honored before long. The honor of heaven, the honor of eternity, the honor of Jesus, the honor of the Father—the Lord will certainly give all this to His chosen. What a wonderful promise from a faithful God!

Two golden links of one celestial chain:
Who owns favor shall surely honor gain.

THE HOPE LAID UP FOR YOU IN HEAVEN. — COLOSSIANS 1:5

Our hope in Christ for the future is the mainspring and the mainstay of our joy down here today. Our hearts will be stirred by thinking often of heaven, for all that we can desire is promised there. Here we are tired and weary, but over there is the land of *rest* where the sweat of toil will no longer soak our shirts, and fatigue will be banished forever. To those who are weary and worn, the word *rest* is full of heaven. We are always in the field of battle; we are so tempted and so molested by foes that we have little or no peace; but in heaven we will enjoy the *victory*, when the banner shall be unfurled in triumph, and the sword will be sheathed, and we will hear our Captain say, "Well done, good and faithful servant."[1] We have suffered bereavement after bereavement, but we are going to the land of the *immortal* where graves do not exist. Here sin is a constant grief to us, but there we will be perfectly *holy*, for there will be nothing in heaven to defile it. There are no needs in the furrows of celestial fields. It is a source of deep joy to realize that the wilderness journey of our earthly pilgrimage will end and we will inherit heaven. But let us make sure that we are not just dreaming about the *future* and thus forgetting the *present*. Let all thoughts of the future serve to make us useful in the present. Through the Spirit of God the hope of heaven is the most powerful force for producing virtue; it is a fountain of joyful endeavor; it is the cornerstone of cheerful holiness. Those who have this hope in them go about their work with vigor, for the joy of the Lord is their strength. They fight hard against temptation, for the hope of the next world repels the fiery darts of the adversary. They can work without immediate reward, for they anticipate a reward in the world to come.

&. EVENING .&
. . . MAN GREATLY LOVED. — DANIEL 10:11

Child of God, do you hesitate to appropriate this title? Has your unbelief made you forget that you are also greatly loved? Surely you must have been greatly loved, to have been bought with the precious blood of Christ, as of a lamb without blemish and without spot? When God crushed His only Son for you, what was this but being greatly loved? You lived in sin and rioted in it; surely you were greatly loved for God to have been so patient with you. You were called by grace and led to a Savior and made a child of God and an heir of heaven. Doesn't this all prove a very great and superabounding love? Since that time, whether your path has been rough with troubles or smooth with mercies, it has been full of proofs that you are greatly loved. If the Lord has chastened you, it was not in anger; if He has made you poor, still in grace you have been rich. The more unworthy you feel yourself to be, the more evidence you have that nothing but unspeakable love could have led the Lord Jesus to save a soul like yours. The more disapproval you feel, the clearer is the display of God's abounding love in choosing you and calling you and making you an heir of heaven. Now, if such love exists between God and us, let us live in the influence and sweetness of it and use the privilege of our position. We should not approach our Lord as though we were strangers or as though He were unwilling to hear us—for we are greatly loved by our loving Father. "He who did not spare his own Son but gave him up for us all, how will he not also with him graciously give us all things?"[2] Come boldly, believer, for despite the whispers of Satan and the doubts of your own heart, you are greatly loved. Meditate on the exceeding greatness and faithfulness of divine love this evening, and then go to your bed in peace.

[1] Matthew 25:23 [2] Romans 8:32

OCTOBER 3   ☙   MORNING   ❧

ARE THEY NOT ALL MINISTERING SPIRITS SENT OUT TO SERVE FOR THE
SAKE OF THOSE WHO ARE TO INHERIT SALVATION? — HEBREWS 1:14

Angels are the unseen attendants of the children of God; they carry us in their hands and keep us from calamity. Loyalty to their Lord leads them to take a deep interest in the children of His love; they rejoice over the return of the prodigal to his father's house below, and they welcome the arrival of the believer to the King's palace above. In ancient times the children of God were able to actually see the angels. Today, although we do not see them, heaven is still open, and the angels of God ascend and descend upon the Son of man, so that they may visit the heirs of salvation. Seraphim still fly with live coals from the altar to touch the lips of men greatly loved. If our eyes could be opened, we would see horses and chariots of fire surrounding the servants of the Lord; for we have come to an innumerable company of angels, who are all watchers and protectors of the King's family. Spenser's line is not poetic fiction, where he sings—

How oft do they with golden pinions cleave
The flitting skies, like flying pursuivant
Against foul fiends to aid us militant!

To what dignity are the chosen elevated when the brilliant courtiers of heaven become their willing servants! Into what communion are we raised since we have communion with spotless celestials! How well are we defended since all the twenty thousand chariots of God are armed for our deliverance! To whom do we owe all this? The Lord Jesus Christ who must be forever dear to us, for through Him we are made to sit in heavenly places far above principalities and powers. It is He whose camp is around those that fear Him; He is the true Michael whose foot is upon the dragon. All hail, Jesus! Angel of Jehovah's presence, to You this family offers its morning vows.

☙ EVENING ❧

HE HIMSELF HAS SUFFERED WHEN TEMPTED. — HEBREWS 2:18

It is a common thought, and yet it tastes like honey to the weary heart—Jesus was tempted as I am. You have heard that truth many times, but have you grasped it? He was tempted by the very same sins into which we fall. Do not separate Jesus from our common humanity. If you are going through a dark room, remember Jesus went through it before you. If you are engaged in s a sore fight, remember that Jesus has stood foot to foot with the same enemy. Let us be encouraged—Christ has borne the load before us, and the blood-stained footsteps of the King of glory can be seen along the road that we travel at this hour. There is something sweeter yet—Jesus was tempted, but Jesus never sinned. My soul, it is not necessary for you to sin, for Jesus was a man, and if one man endured these temptations without sin, then in His power His followers may also flee from sin. Some new believers think that they cannot be tempted without sinning, but they are mistaken; there is no sin in *being tempted*, but there *is* sin in *yielding to temptation*. Here is comfort for those who are greatly tempted. There is still more to encourage them if they recall that the Lord Jesus, though tempted, gloriously triumphed; and as He overcame, so may His followers also, for Jesus is the representative man for His people. The Head has triumphed, and the members share in the victory. Fears are unnecessary, for Christ is with us, armed for our defense. Our place of safety is the embrace of the Savior. Perhaps we are tempted just now in order to drive us nearer to Him. Blessed be any wind that blows us into the harbor of our Savior's love! Happy wounds that make us seek the beloved Physician. Tempted ones, come to your tempted Savior, for He can sympathize with your weaknesses and will comfort every tried and tempted one.

AT EVENING TIME THERE SHALL BE LIGHT. — ZECHARIAH 14:7

We often look forward with anxiety to *the time of old age*, forgetting that at evening time it shall be light. To many saints, old age is the choicest season in their lives. A warmer breeze fans the sailor's face as he nears the shore of immortality; fewer waves ruffle his sea; quiet reigns, deep, still and solemn. From the altar of age the flashes of the fire of youth are gone, but the deepening flame of sincere feeling remains. The pilgrims have reached the promised land, the happy country, whose days are as the days of heaven upon earth. Angels visit it, celestial gales blow over it, flowers of paradise grow in it, and the air is filled with heavenly music. Some live here for years, and others arrive only a few hours before their departure, but it is an Eden on earth. We may begin to long for the time when we can recline in its shady groves and be satisfied with hope until the time of fruition comes. The setting sun seems larger than when it is high in the sky, and a splendor of glory tinges all the clouds that surround its going down. Pain does not break the calm of the sweet twilight of age, for strength is made perfect in weakness and endures it all patiently. Ripe fruits of choice experience are gathered as the rare food of life's evening, and the soul prepares itself for rest.

The Lord's people will also enjoy light in *the hour of death*. Unbelief bemoans the evening shadows, the darkening night, the end of existence. But no, cries faith, the night is almost over and the true day is at hand. Light has come, the light of immortality, the light of the Father's countenance. Gather your feet up in the bed; see the waiting throng of angels ready to bear you away. Farewell, loved one, you are gone. You wave your hand; now it is light! The pearly gates are open; the golden streets shine in the jasper light. We cover our eyes, but you behold the unseen; adieu, dear friend, you have light at evening time that we have not yet.

❧ EVENING ❧

BUT IF ANYONE DOES SIN, WE HAVE AN ADVOCATE WITH THE FATHER,
JESUS CHRIST THE RIGHTEOUS. — 1 JOHN 2:1

If anyone does sin, we *have* an advocate." Yes, though we sin, we have Him still. John does not say, "If anyone sins, they have forfeited their advocate," but "we *have* an advocate," even though we are sinners. All the sin that a believer ever did or can be allowed to commit cannot destroy his interest in the Lord Jesus Christ as his advocate. The name given here to our Lord is suggestive. "*Jesus.*" He is the kind of advocate we need, for Jesus is the name of one whose business and delight it is to save. "You shall call his name Jesus, for *he will save* his people from their sins."[1] His sweetest name implies His success. Next, it is "Jesus *Christ*"—*Christos*, the anointed. This shows *His authority* to plead. Christ has a right to plead, for He is the Father's own appointed advocate and elected priest. If He were our choice He might fail, but if God has laid help on one who is mighty, we may safely place our trouble where God has laid His help. He is Christ, and therefore authorized; He is Christ, and therefore *qualified*, for the anointing has fitted Him fully for His work. He can plead in such a way as to move the heart of God and prevail. What words of tenderness, what sentences of persuasion will the anointed use when He stands up to plead for me! One more aspect of His name remains: "Jesus Christ *the righteous*." This is not only His character but His plea. It is His character, and if the Righteous One is my advocate, then my cause is good or He would not have represented it. It is His plea, for He meets the charge of unrighteousness against me by the plea that *He* is righteous. He declares Himself my substitute and puts His obedience to my account. My soul, you have a friend perfectly fitted to be your advocate—He cannot but succeed; leave yourself entirely in His hands.

[1] Matthew 1:21

AND HE AROSE AND ATE AND DRANK, AND WENT IN THE STRENGTH OF
THAT FOOD FORTY DAYS AND FORTY NIGHTS. — 1 KINGS 19:8

All the strength supplied to us by our gracious God is meant for service, not for indulgence or pride. When the prophet Elijah found the cake baked on the coals and the jar of water placed at his head as he lay under the juniper tree, he was not being given a special treat that he could lie back and enjoy—he was being sustained so that he could fulfill his responsibilities for the next forty days and forty nights. When the Master invited the disciples to come and eat with Him, after the meal was over He said to Peter, "Feed my sheep," then added, "Follow me." It is the same for us; we eat the bread of heaven so that we can expend our strength in the Master's service. We come to the table and eat of the paschal lamb in a spirit of readiness, so that we may leave as soon as we have satisfied our hunger. Some Christians are for living *on* Christ but are not so anxious to live *for* Christ. Earth should be a preparation for heaven; and heaven is the place where saints feast most and work most. They sit down at the table of our Lord, and they serve Him day and night in His temple. They eat of heavenly food and offer perfect service. Believer, in the strength you daily gain from Christ, work for Him. Some of us have a lot to learn concerning the design of our Lord in giving us His grace. We are not to hide the precious grains of truth without giving that truth an opportunity to grow: We must sow it and water it. Why does the Lord send the rain upon the thirsty earth and give the sunshine? Is it not in order that sun and rain may help the fruits of the earth to yield food for us? Even so the Lord feeds and refreshes our souls so that we may use our renewed strength in the promotion of His glory.

❧ EVENING ❧

WHOEVER BELIEVES AND IS BAPTIZED WILL BE SAVED. — MARK 16:16

Mr. MacDonald asked the inhabitants of the island of St. Kilda how a man must be saved. An old man replied, "We will be saved if we repent and forsake our sins and turn to God." "Yes," said a middle-aged woman, "and with a true heart too." "Yes," rejoined a third, "and with prayer"; and a fourth added, "It must be the prayer of the heart." "And we must be diligent too," said a fifth, "in keeping the commandments." When each of them made their contribution, feeling that a very decent creed had been made up, they all looked and listened for the preacher's approval, but they had aroused his deepest pity. The secular mind always maps out for itself a way in which self can work and become great, but the Lord's way is quite the reverse. Believing and being baptized are not matters of merit to be gloried in—they are so simple that boasting is excluded. It may be that the reader is unsaved—what is the reason? Do you think the way of salvation as laid down in the text is dubious? How can that be when God has pledged His own word for its certainty? Do you think it too easy? Why, then, do you not obey it? Those who neglect it are without excuse. To believe is simply to trust, to depend, to rely upon Christ Jesus. To be baptized is to submit to the ordinance that our Lord fulfilled at Jordan, to which the converted ones submitted at Pentecost, to which the jailer yielded obedience on the very night of his conversion. The outward sign does not save, but it portrays our death, burial, and resurrection with Jesus and, like the Lord's Supper, is not to be neglected. Reader, do you believe in Jesus? Then, dear friend, dismiss your fears—you will be saved. Are you still an unbeliever? Then remember there is only one door, and if you will not enter by it you will perish in your sins.

BUT WHOEVER DRINKS OF THE WATER THAT I WILL GIVE HIM
WILL NEVER BE THIRSTY FOREVER. — JOHN 4:14

The person who believes in Jesus finds enough in his Lord to satisfy him now and to content him forevermore. The believer is not the man whose days are weary for lack of
comfort and whose nights are long on account of the absence of heart-cheering thought.
The believer finds in faith such a spring of joy, such a fountain of consolation that he is content and happy. Put him in a dungeon, and he will find good company; place him in a barren wilderness, and he will eat the bread of heaven; drive him away from friendship, and he
will meet the "friend who sticks closer than a brother."[1] Destroy all his shade, and he will find
shadow beneath the Rock of Ages; erode the foundation of his earthly hopes, but his heart
will still be fixed, trusting in the Lord. The heart is as insatiable as the grave until Jesus
enters it, and then it becomes a cup full to overflowing. There is such a fullness in Christ
that He alone is the believer's sufficiency. The true saint is so completely satisfied with the provision of Jesus that he no longer thirsts—except perhaps to drink more deeply at the living
fountain. In that sweet manner, believer, you will thirst; it will not be a thirst of pain, but of
loving desire; you will find it a sweet thing to be longing for a deeper enjoyment of Jesus' love.
An old saint once declared, "I have been lowering my bucket into the well so often, but
now my thirst for Jesus has become so insatiable, that I long to put the well itself to my lips
and drink right out of it." Is this the feeling of your heart now, believer? Do you feel that all
your desires are satisfied in Jesus and that you have no need now except to know more of
Him and to have closer fellowship with Him? Then come continually to the fountain, and
take the water of life freely. Jesus will never think you take too much but will always welcome
you, saying, "Drink; yes, drink abundantly, loved one."

❧ Evening ❧

HE HAD MARRIED A CUSHITE WOMAN. — NUMBERS 12:1

Moses made a strange choice, but not as surprising as the choice of Him who is a prophet
like Moses but greater than him—even our Lord Jesus! It is the wonder of angels that
the love of Jesus should be set upon poor, lost, guilty men. Each believer must, when filled
with a sense of Jesus' love, also be overwhelmed with astonishment that such love should
be lavished on an object so utterly unworthy of it. Knowing as we do our secret guiltiness,
unfaithfulness, and halfheartedness, we are dissolved in grateful admiration for the matchless freeness and sovereignty of grace. Jesus must have found the cause of His love in His own
heart; He could not have found it in us, for it is not there. Even since our conversion we
have been poor, though grace has made us rich. Holy Rutherford said of himself what we
must each subscribe to: "His relation to me is that I am sick, and He is the Physician of whom
I stand in need. Sadly how often I play fast and loose with Christ! He binds, I loose; He builds,
I tear down; I quarrel with Christ, and He agrees with me twenty times a day!" Most tender and faithful Husband of our souls, pursue Your gracious work of conforming us to
Your image, until You will present even us in our poverty to Yourself without spot or wrinkle or any such thing. Moses met with opposition because of his marriage, and both himself and his spouse were the subjects of disapproval. Can we be surprised if this empty
world opposes Jesus and His church, and particularly when notorious sinners are converted? For this is always the basis of the Pharisee's objection: "This man receives sinners."[2]
Of course He does; after all, He did not come to call the righteous but sinners to repentance.

[1] Proverbs 18:24   [2] Luke 15:1.

Our heavenly Father sends us frequent troubles *to test our faith*. If our faith is worth anything, it will stand the test. Gilt is afraid of fire, but gold is not: The *imitation* gem dreads being touched by the diamond, but the true jewel fears no test. It is a poor faith that can only trust God when friends are true, the body is healthy, and the business profitable; but it is true faith that rests in the Lord's faithfulness when friends are gone, the body is ailing, spirits are depressed, and the light of our Father's face is hidden. A faith that can say, in the deepest trouble, "Though he slay me, I will hope in him"[1] is heaven-born faith. The Lord afflicts His servants *to glorify Himself*, for He is greatly glorified in the graces of His people, who are His own handiwork. When "suffering produces endurance, endurance produces character, and character produces hope,"[2] the Lord is honored by these growing virtues. We would never know the music of the harp if the strings were left untouched, nor enjoy the juice of the grape if it were not trodden in the winepress, nor discover the sweet perfume of cinnamon if it were not pressed and beaten, nor feel the warmth of fire if the coals were not completely consumed. The wisdom and power of God are discovered by the trials through which His children are permitted to pass. Present afflictions *tend also to heighten future joy*. There must be shade in the picture to bring out the beauty of the light. Could we be so supremely blessed in heaven if we had not known the curse of sin and the sorrow of earth? Will peace not be sweeter after conflict, and rest more welcome after labor? Will the recollection of past sufferings not serve to enhance the bliss of the glorified? There are many other comfortable answers to the question with which we opened our brief meditation; let us think upon it all day long.

   EVENING
IN WHOM DO YOU NOW TRUST? — ISAIAH 36:5

Reader, this is an important question. Listen to the Christian's answer, and see if it is yours. "In whom do you now trust?" "I trust," says the Christian, "in a triune God. I trust *the Father*, believing that He has chosen me from before the foundations of the world; I trust Him to provide for me in providence, to teach me, to guide me, to correct me if need be, and to bring me home to His own house where there are many rooms. I trust *the Son*. He is very God of very God—the man Christ Jesus. I trust in Him to take away all my sins by His own sacrifice and to clothe me with His perfect righteousness. I trust Him to be my Intercessor, to present my prayers and desires before His Father's throne, and I trust Him to be my Advocate at the last great day, to plead my cause, and to justify me. I trust Him for what He is, for what He has done, and for what He has promised still to do. And I trust *the Holy Spirit*—He has begun to save me from my inbred sins; I trust Him to drive them all out; I trust Him to curb my temper, to subdue my will, to enlighten my understanding, to check my passions, to comfort my despondency, to help my weakness, to illuminate my darkness. I trust Him to dwell in me as my life, to reign in me as my King, to sanctify me completely, spirit, soul, and body, and then to take me up to dwell with the saints in light forever."

What blessed trust—to trust Him whose power will never be exhausted, whose love will never weaken, whose kindness will never change, whose faithfulness will never fail, whose wisdom will never be overruled, and whose perfect goodness can never be impaired! You are happy, reader, if this trust is yours! So trusting, you will enjoy sweet peace now and glory later, and the foundation of your trust will never be removed.

[1] Job 13:15 [2] Romans 5:3-4

PUT OUT INTO THE DEEP AND LET DOWN YOUR NETS FOR A CATCH.
— LUKE 5:4

We learn from this narrative *the necessity of human activity*. The catch of fish was miraculous, but neither the fisherman nor his boat nor his fishing tackle were ignored; they were all were used to take the fish. So in the saving of souls, God works by means; and while the present economy of grace shall stand, God will be pleased by the foolishness of preaching to save those who believe. When God works without instruments, He is glorified; but He has selected this plan of human involvement as being that by which He is most magnified in the earth. *The means themselves can accomplish nothing.* "Master, we toiled all night and took nothing!" What was the reason for this? Were they not experienced fishermen going about their business? They were not novices; they understood the work. Was the problem that they lacked skill? No. Were they lazy? No; they had worked. Did they lack perseverance? No; they had *worked all night.* Was there a lack of fish in the sea? Certainly not, for as soon as the Master came, they swam to the net in large numbers. What, then, is the reason? It is because there is no power in the means themselves apart from the presence of Jesus. Without Him we can do nothing. But with Christ we can do all things. *Christ's presence confers success.* Jesus sat in Peter's boat, and His will, by a mysterious influence, drew the fish to the net. When Jesus is lifted up in His Church, His presence is the church's power—the shout of a king is in the midst of her. "I, when I am lifted up from the earth, will draw all people to myself."[1] Let us go out this morning on our work of soul-fishing, looking up in faith, and around us at the great opportunity. Let us work until the night comes, and we will not labor in vain, for He who tells us to let down the net will fill it with fish.

❧ EVENING ❧

PRAY IN THE HOLY SPIRIT. — JUDE 20

Note the key characteristic of true prayer—"*in the Holy Spirit.*" The seed of acceptable devotion must come from heaven's storehouse. Only the prayer that comes from God can go to God. We must shoot the Lord's arrows back to Him. The desire that He writes upon our heart will move His heart and bring down a blessing, but the desires of the flesh have no power with Him.

Praying in the Holy Spirit is praying in *fervency*. Cold prayers ask the Lord not to hear them. Those who do not plead with fervency do not plead at all. We might as well talk of lukewarm fire as of lukewarm prayer—it is essential that it be red-hot. It is praying *perseveringly*. The true petitioner gathers force as he proceeds and grows more fervent when God delays to answer. The longer the gate is closed, the louder the knocking becomes; and the longer the angel lingers, the more determined he becomes to never let him go without the blessing. In God's sight tearful, agonizing, unconquerable importunity is commendable. It means praying *humbly*, for the Holy Spirit never puffs us up with pride. It is His part to convince of sin and to cause us to bow down in contrition and brokenness of spirit. We will never sing *Gloria in excelsis* except we pray to God *de profundis*: Out of the depths must we cry, or we will never behold glory in the highest. It is *loving* prayer. Prayer should be perfumed with love, saturated with love—love for our fellow believers and love for Christ. Moreover, it must be a prayer full of *faith*. A man prevails only to the extent that he believes. The Holy Spirit is the author of faith and strengthens it, so that we pray believing God's promise. Now our prayer is that this blessed combination of excellent graces, as priceless and sweet as rare spices, might be fragrant within us because the Holy Spirit is in our hearts! Blessed Comforter, exert Your mighty power within us, helping our weaknesses in prayer.

[1] John 12:32

In some ways the path to heaven is very safe, but in other respects there is *no more dangerous road*. It is surrounded with difficulties. One false step (and how easy it is to take that if grace is absent), and down we go. What a slippery path some of us have to tread! How many times do we have to exclaim with the psalmist, "My feet had almost stumbled, my steps had nearly slipped."[1] If we were strong, surefooted mountaineers, this would not matter so much; but in ourselves, *how weak we are*! On the best roads *we soon falter*; in the smoothest paths we quickly stumble. These feeble knees of ours can scarcely support our tottering weight. A feather may divert us, and a pebble can wound us. We are mere children taking our first trembling steps in the walk of faith; our heavenly Father holds us by the arms or we would soon be down. If we are kept from falling, how we should bless the patient power that watches over us day by day! Think how prone we are to sin, how apt to choose danger, how strong our tendency to stumble and fall, and these reflections will make us sing more sweetly than we have ever done, "Now to him who is able to keep you from stumbling." *We have many enemies* who try to put us down. The road is rough, and we are weak; but in addition to this, enemies hide in ambush and rush out when we least expect them and try to trip us up or throw us over the nearest cliff. Only an almighty arm can preserve us from these unseen foes who are seeking to destroy us. Such an arm is involved in our defense. He is faithful who has promised, and He is able to keep us from falling, so that with a deep sense of our utter weakness, we may cherish a firm belief in our perfect safety and say with joyful confidence

> *Against me earth and hell combine,*
> *But on my side is power divine;*
> *Jesus is all, and He is mine!*

❧ EVENING ❧
BUT HE DID NOT ANSWER HER A WORD. — MATTHEW 15:23

Genuine seekers who as yet have not obtained the blessing may find comfort in this story. The Savior did not immediately bestow the blessing, even though the woman had great faith in Him. He intended to give it, but He waited awhile. "He did not answer her a word." Were her prayers no good? Never better in the world. Was she not needy? Dreadfully needy. Did she not *feel* her need sufficiently? She felt it overwhelmingly. Was she not sincere enough? She was intensely so. Did she have no faith? She had such a high degree of it that even Jesus wondered and said, "O woman, great is your faith!" Notice then, although it is true that faith brings peace, it does not always bring it instantaneously. There may be certain reasons for faith to be tested rather than rewarded. Genuine faith may be in the soul like a hidden seed, but so far it may not have budded and blossomed into joy and peace. Silence from the Savior is the painful trial of many a seeking soul, but heavier still is the affliction of a harsh, cutting reply such as, "It is not right to take the children's bread and throw it to the dogs." Many in waiting upon the Lord find immediate delight, but this is not the case with all. Some, like the jailer, are in a moment turned from darkness to light, but others are plants of slower growth. A deeper sense of sin may be given to you instead of a sense of pardon, and in such a case you will need patience to bear the heavy blow. Poor heart, though Christ beat and bruise you, or even slay you, trust Him; even if He should give you an angry word, believe in the love of His heart. I urge you, do not give up seeking or trusting my Master because you have not yet obtained the conscious joy that you long for. Cast yourself on Him, and perseveringly depend even when you cannot rejoicingly hope.

[1] Psalm 73:2

BLAMELESS BEFORE THE PRESENCE OF HIS GLORY. — JUDE 24

Let your mind revolve around that wonderful word *"blameless"*! We are far from it now; but since our Lord never stops short of perfection in His work of love, we will reach it one day. The Savior who will keep His people to the end will also present them finally to Himself as "the church . . . in splendor, without spot or wrinkle or any such thing."[1] All the jewels in the Savior's crown are pure and without a single flaw. All the maids of honor who assist the Lamb's wife are pure virgins without spot or stain. But how will Jesus make us blameless? He will wash us from our sins in His own blood until we are as white and fair as God's purest angel; and we will be clothed in His righteousness, that righteousness that makes the saint who wears it positively blameless—yes, perfect in the sight of God. We will be unblameable and unreprovable even in His eyes. Not only will His law have no charge against us, but it will be magnified in us. Moreover, the work of the Holy Spirit within us will be altogether complete. He will make us so perfectly holy that we will have no lingering tendency to sin. Judgment, memory, will—every power and passion will be set free from the tyranny of evil. We will be holy even as God is holy, and in His presence we will dwell forever. Saints will not be out of place in heaven; their beauty will be as great as that of the place prepared for them. Oh, the intense delight of that hour when the everlasting doors will be lifted up, and we, being made fit for the inheritance, will dwell with the saints in light. Sin gone, Satan shut out, temptation past forever, and ourselves "blameless" before God—this will be heaven indeed! Let us be joyful now as we rehearse the song of eternal praise that will soon sound forth in full chorus from all the blood-washed host; let us copy David's exultings before the ark as a prelude to our ecstasies before the throne.

❧ EVENING ❧

I WILL DELIVER YOU OUT OF THE HAND OF THE WICKED, AND REDEEM YOU FROM THE GRASP OF THE RUTHLESS. — JEREMIAH 15:21

Notice the personal nature of this promise: *"I will."* The Lord Jehovah Himself intervenes to deliver and redeem His people. He pledges Himself personally to rescue them. His own arm shall do it, in order that He may have the glory. Not a word is said of any effort of our own that may be needed to assist the Lord. Neither our strength nor our weakness is taken into account, but the lone *"I,"* like the sun in the heavens, shines out resplendent in complete sufficiency. Why then do we allow ourselves to be wounded by calculating our forces and consulting with mere men? God has enough power without borrowing from our puny arm. To enjoy peace, our unbelieving thoughts must be stilled, and we must learn that the Lord reigns. There is not even a hint of help from any secondary source. The Lord says nothing of friends and helpers: He undertakes the work alone and feels no need of human arms to aid Him. All our lookings around to companions and relatives are vain; they are broken reeds if we lean upon them—often unwilling when able, and unable when they are willing. Since the promise comes from God alone, it is best for us to wait only on Him; and when we do so, our expectation never fails us. Who are the wicked, that we should fear them? The Lord will utterly consume them; they are to be pitied rather than feared. As for terrible ones, they are only terrors to those who have no God to turn to, for when the Lord is on our side, whom shall we fear? If we run into sin to please the wicked, we have cause to be alarmed; but if we maintain our integrity, the rage of tyrants will be overruled for our good. When the fish swallowed Jonah, he found him a morsel that he could not digest; and when the world devours the church, it is glad to be rid of it again. In all occasions of fiery trial, let us maintain our souls in patience.

[1] Ephesians 5:27

LET US LIFT UP OUR HEARTS AND OUR HANDS TO GOD IN HEAVEN.
— LAMENTATIONS 3:41

The act of prayer *teaches us our unworthiness*, which is a very salutary lesson for proud people like us. If God gave us favors without constraining us to pray for them, we would never know how poor we are, but a true prayer is an inventory of wants, a catalog of necessities, a revelation of hidden poverty. While prayer is an application to divine wealth, it is also a confession of human emptiness. The most healthy state of a Christian is always to be empty of self and constantly depending upon the Lord for provision; to be consistently poor in self and rich in Jesus; to be weak as water personally, but mighty through God to do great exploits. This is where prayer comes in, because while it adores God, it puts the creature where it should be—in the dust. Prayer is in itself, apart from the answer that it brings, a great benefit to the Christian. As the runner gains strength for the race by daily exercise, so for the great race of life we acquire energy by the holy exercise of prayer. Prayer thins the feathers of God's young eaglets, so that they can learn to soar above the clouds. Prayer readies God's warriors and sends them out to combat with their sinews braced and their muscles firm. The praying believer comes out of his closet, even as the sun rises from the chambers of the east, rejoicing like an athlete about to race. Prayer is the uplifted hand of Moses that defeats the Amalekites more than the sword of Joshua; it is the arrow shot from the prophet's chamber announcing defeat to the Syrians. Prayer equips human weakness with divine strength, turns human folly into heavenly wisdom, and gives the peace of God to troubled souls. We do not know what prayer cannot do! We thank You, great God, for the mercy-seat, a wonderful evidence of your marvelous loving-kindness. Help us to use it properly throughout this day!

❧ EVENING ❧

AND THOSE WHOM HE PREDESTINED HE ALSO CALLED. — ROMANS 8:30

In the second letter to Timothy, first chapter and ninth verse, we read these words: "who saved us and called us to a *holy* calling." Now here is a touchstone by which we may test our calling. It is "a holy calling, not because of our works, but because of his own purpose and grace." This calling forbids all trust in our own doings and turns us to Christ alone for salvation, but it afterwards purges us from dead works to serve the living and true God. As He who called you is holy, so must you be holy. If you are living in sin, you are not called; but if you are truly Christ's, you can say, "Nothing pains me so much as sin; I desire to be rid of it. Lord, help me to be holy." Is this the longing of your heart? Is this the substance of your life toward God and His divine will? Again, in Philippians 3:13-14 we are told of "the *upward* call of God in Christ Jesus." Is your calling an upward call? Has it refined your heart and focused it upon heavenly things? Has it elevated your hopes, your tastes, your desires? Has it raised the constant tenor of your life, so that you spend it with God and for God? We find another test in Hebrews 3:1—"you who share in a *heavenly* calling." "Heavenly calling" means a call *from* heaven. If your call comes from man alone, you are uncalled. Is your calling from God? Is it a call *to* heaven as well as *from* heaven? Unless you are a stranger here, and heaven is your home, you have not been called with a heavenly calling, for those who have been called from heaven declare that they look for a city that has foundations, whose builder and maker is God, and they find themselves strangers and pilgrims on the earth. Is your calling holy, high, heavenly? Then, beloved, you have been called of God, for such is the calling by which God calls His people.

OCTOBER 12 · MORNING ·

I WILL MEDITATE ON YOUR PRECEPTS. — PSALM 119:15

There are times when solitude is better than company, and silence is wiser than speech. We would be better Christians if we were alone more often, waiting on God and gathering through meditation on His Word spiritual strength for service in His kingdom. We ought to *ponder the things of God, because that is how we get the real nutriment out of them.* Truth is something like the cluster of the vine: In order to have wine from it, we must bruise it; we must press and squeeze it many times. The bruiser's feet must come down joyfully on the bunches or else the juice will not flow; and the grapes must be properly tread or else much of the precious liquid will be wasted. So we must, by meditation, tread the clusters of truth if we desire the wine of consolation from them. Our bodies are not supported by merely taking food into the mouth, but the process that really supplies the muscle and the nerve and the sinew and the bone is the process of digestion. It is by digestion that the outward food becomes assimilated with the inner life. Our souls are not nourished merely by listening for a while to this and then to that and then to the other part of divine truth. Hearing, reading, marking, and learning all require inward digesting to complete their usefulness, and the inward digesting of the truth lies mainly in meditating upon it. Why is it that some Christians, although they hear many sermons, make only slow advances in the Christian life? Because they neglect their closets and do not thoughtfully meditate on God's Word. They love the wheat, but they do not grind it; they want the corn, but they will not go out into the fields to gather it; the fruit hangs on the tree, but they will not pluck it; the water flows at their feet, but they will not stoop to drink it. Deliver us, O Lord, from such folly, and may this be our resolve this morning: "I will meditate on your precepts."

· EVENING ·

THE HELPER, THE HOLY SPIRIT. — JOHN 14:26

This age is peculiarly the dispensation of the Holy Spirit, in which Jesus cheers us not by His personal presence, as He will do soon enough, but by the indwelling and constant abiding of the Holy Spirit, who is forever the Comforter of the church. It is the Spirit's role to console the hearts of God's people. He convinces of sin; He illumines and instructs; but the main part of His work still lies in gladdening the hearts of the renewed, confirming the weak, and lifting up all those who are bowed down. He does this by revealing Jesus to them. The Holy Spirit consoles, but Christ *is the consolation.* If we may use the figure, the Holy Spirit is the Physician, but Jesus is the medicine. *He* heals the wound, but it is by applying the holy ointment of Christ's name and grace. He does not take of His own things, but of the things of Christ. So if we give to the Holy Spirit the Greek name of *Paraclete,* as we sometimes do, then our heart confers on our blessed Lord Jesus the title of *Paraclesis.* If one is the Comforter, the other is the Comfort. Now, with such rich provision for his need, why should the Christian be sad and despondent? The Holy Spirit has graciously committed to be your Comforter: Do you imagine, weak and trembling believer, that He will neglect this sacred trust? Do you suppose that He has undertaken what He cannot or will not perform? If it is His special work to strengthen you and to comfort you, do you suppose He has forgotten His business or that He will fail in fulfilling His loving task of sustaining you? Don't think so poorly of the tender and blessed Spirit whose name is the Comforter. He delights to give the oil of joy for mourning and the garment of praise for the spirit of heaviness. Trust in Him, and He will surely comfort you until the house of mourning is closed forever, and the marriage feast has begun.

GODLY GRIEF PRODUCES A REPENTANCE THAT LEADS
TO SALVATION. — 2 CORINTHIANS 7:10

Genuine, spiritual mourning for sin is *the work of the Spirit of God*. Repentance is too rare a flower to grow in nature's garden. Pearls grow naturally in oysters, but penitence never shows up in sinners except when divine grace produces it in them. If you have one particle of real hatred for sin, God must have given it to you, for human nature's thorns never produced a single fig. "That which is born of the flesh is flesh."[1]

True repentance *is tied directly to the Savior.* When we repent of sin, we must have one eye upon sin and the other upon the cross; or it will be even better if we fix both our eyes on Christ and see our transgressions only in the light of His love.

True sorrow for sin is *eminently practical.* No man can say he hates sin if he lives in it. Repentance makes us see the evil of sin not merely as a theory but experimentally [experientially]—as a burn victim dreads fire. We will be as afraid of it as a man who has recently been robbed is afraid of the thief on the highway; and we will shun it—shun it in everything—not only in large matters, but in small things, as men avoid little vipers as well as great snakes. True mourning for sin will make us very careful with our tongue in case it should say a wrong word; we will be very watchful over our daily actions in case in anything we offend, and each night we will end the day with painful confessions of shortcomings, and each morning awaken with earnest prayers that God would today hold us up so that we may not sin against Him.

Sincere repentance is *continual.* Believers repent until their dying day. This is not something we do only once at the beginning of our Christian lives. Nor is it an intermittent exercise. Every other sorrow passes with time, but this dear sorrow grows as we grow, and it is such sweet bitterness that we thank God He permits us to enjoy and to suffer it until we enter our eternal rest.

❧   EVENING   ☙

LOVE IS STRONG AS DEATH. — SONG OF SOLOMON 8:6

Whose love can this be that is as mighty as the conqueror of monarchs? Does it belong to the destroyer of the human race? Would it not sound like satire if it were applied to my poor, weak, and scarcely living love to Jesus my Lord? I do love Him, and perhaps by His grace I could even die for Him, but as for my love in itself, it can scarcely endure the scoffer's jest, much less a cruel death. Surely this is my Beloved's love that is spoken of here— the love of Jesus, the matchless lover of souls. His love was indeed stronger than the most terrible death, for it endured the trial of the cross triumphantly. It was a lingering death, but love survived the torment; a shameful death, but love despised the shame; a penal death, but love bore our iniquities; a forsaken, lonely death, from which the eternal Father hid His face, but love endured the curse and triumphed over all. There never was such love, never such a death. It was a desperate duel, but love bore the pain. What then, my heart? Have you no emotions stirred within you at the thought of such heavenly affection? Yes, my Lord, I long, I want to feel Your love flaming like a furnace within me. Come Yourself and excite the love of my spirit.

> *For every drop of crimson blood*
> *Thus shed to make me live,*
> *O wherefore, wherefore have not I*
> *A thousand lives to give?*

Why should I despair of loving Jesus with a love as strong as death? He deserves it: I desire it. The martyrs felt such love, and they were mere men and women, so why not I? They mourned their weakness, and yet out of weakness were made strong. Grace gave them their unflinching constancy—there is the same grace for me. Jesus, lover of my soul, shed abroad this love, even Your love, in my heart tonight.

[1] John 3:6

I COUNT EVERYTHING AS LOSS BECAUSE OF THE SURPASSING WORTH
OF KNOWING CHRIST JESUS MY LORD. — PHILIPPIANS 3:8

Spiritual knowledge of Christ will be a *personal* knowledge. I cannot know Jesus through another person's acquaintance with Him. I must know Him *myself*; I must know Him on my own account. It will be an *intelligent* knowledge—I must know *Him* not as in the visionary dreams of Him, but as the Word reveals Him. I must know His natures, divine and human. I must know His offices (Prophet, Priest and King)—His attributes—His works—His shame—His glory. I must meditate upon Him until I "comprehend with all the saints what is the breadth and length and height and depth, and to know the love of Christ that surpasses knowledge."[1] It will be an *affectionate* knowledge of Him; indeed, if I know Him at all, I must love Him. An ounce of heart knowledge is worth a ton of head learning. Our knowledge of Him will be a *satisfying* knowledge. When I know my Savior, my mind will be full to the brim—I will feel that I have that which my spirit longs for. This is the bread that satisfies all hunger. At the same time it will be an *exciting* knowledge; the more I know of my Beloved, the more I will want to know. The higher I climb, the loftier will be the summits that invite my eager footsteps. I shall want more as I get more. Like the miser's treasure, my gold will make me covet more. To conclude, this knowledge of Christ Jesus will be a most *happy* one; in fact, so elevating that sometimes it will completely lift me above all trials and doubts and sorrows; and it will, while I enjoy it, make me something more than "Man . . . born of a woman . . . few of days and full of trouble," for it will throw about me the immortality of the ever-living Savior and cover me with the golden cloak of His eternal joy. Come, my soul, sit at Jesus' feet, and learn of Him all this day.

🙟 EVENING 🙝

DO NOT BE CONFORMED TO THIS WORLD. — ROMANS 12:2

If there is any possibility of a Christian being saved while he conforms to this world, it can only be so as through fire. Such a bare salvation is almost to be dreaded as much as to be desired. Reader, would you like to leave this world in the darkness of a desponding deathbed and enter heaven like a shipwrecked sailor climbs the rocks of his native country? Then allow the world to squeeze you into its mold and refuse identity with Christ or to bear His reproach. Would you like to have a heaven below as well as a heaven above? Do you want to comprehend with all saints what are the heights and depths and to know the love of Christ that passes knowledge? Would you like to receive an abundant entry into heaven? Then do not live as a friend of the world. If you would attain the full assurance of faith, you cannot do so in communion with sinners. If you desire to be on fire for God, realize that your love will be dampened by the cold rain of a godless society. You cannot become a great Christian, you can never can be a mature believer in Christ Jesus while you give in to godless maxims and modes of life. It is incongruous for an heir of heaven to be a great friend with the heirs of hell. It has a bad look when the servant is too intimate with the king's enemies. Even small inconsistencies are dangerous. Just as small thorns make great blisters and little moths destroy fine clothes, so little frivolities and little indiscretions will rob your testimony of a thousand joys. Professing Christian on the fence, you do not know what you are losing by your conformity to the world. It cuts the tendons of your strength and makes you crawl when you ought to run. So for your own comfort's sake and for the sake of your growth in grace, if you are a Christian, be a Christian, and be a marked and distinct one.

[1] Ephesians 3:18-19

BUT WHO CAN ENDURE THE DAY OF HIS COMING . . . ?
— MALACHI 3:2

Christ's first coming was without external pomp or display of power, and yet in truth there were few who could endure its test. Herod and all Jerusalem with him were stirred at the news of the wondrous birth. Those who supposed themselves to be waiting for Him showed the fallacy of their professions by rejecting Him when He came. His life on earth was like a winnowing fan that sifted the great heap of religious profession, and only a few could survive the process. But what will His second coming be? What sinner can endure to think of it? "He shall strike the earth with the rod of his mouth, and with the breath of his lips he shall kill the wicked."[1] In Gethsemane when He said to the soldiers, "I am he," they fell backward. What will happen to His enemies when He will reveal Himself more fully as the "*I Am*"? His death shook earth and darkened heaven. What will be the dreadful splendor of that day when as the living Savior He will summon the living and the dead before Him? O that the terrors of the Lord would persuade men to forsake their sins and kiss the Son in case He is angry! Though a lamb, He is still the lion of the tribe of Judah, tearing the prey in pieces; and though He does not break the bruised reed, yet He will break His enemies with a rod of iron and dash them to pieces like a potter's vessel. None of His foes shall stand before the tempest of His wrath or hide themselves from the sweeping hail of His indignation. But His beloved blood-washed people look for His appearing with joy; in this living hope they live without fear. To them He sits as a refiner even now, and when He has tested them they shall come forth as gold. Let us examine ourselves this morning and make our calling and election sure, so that the coming of the Lord may not be the cause of fearful expectations. O for grace to discard all hypocrisy, and to be found of Him sincere and without rebuke on the day of His appearing.

EVENING

THE FIRSTBORN OF A DONKEY YOU SHALL REDEEM WITH A LAMB,
OR IF YOU WILL NOT REDEEM IT YOU SHALL BREAK ITS NECK. — EXODUS 34:20

Every firstborn creature must be the Lord's; but since the donkey was unclean, it could not be presented in sacrifice. What then? Should it be allowed to go free from the universal law? By no means. God allows for no exceptions. The donkey is His due, but He will not accept it; He will not void the claim, but yet He cannot be pleased with the victim. As a result, no way of escape remained but redemption—the creature must be saved by the substitution of a lamb in its place; or if not redeemed, it must die. My soul, here is a lesson for you. That unclean animal is you. You are justly the property of the Lord who made you and preserves you, but you are so sinful that God will not, cannot, accept you; and it has come to this—the Lamb of God must stand in your place or you must die eternally. Let all the world know of your gratitude to that spotless Lamb who has already bled for you and so redeemed you from the fatal curse of the law. Sometimes it must have been a question for the Israelite which should die—the donkey or the lamb. Surely a good man would pause to estimate and compare. Without question there was no comparison between the value of the soul of man and the life of the Lord Jesus, and yet the Lamb dies, and man the donkey is spared. My soul, adore the boundless love of God to you and others of the human race. Worms are purchased with the blood of the Son of the Highest! Dust and ashes are redeemed with a price far above silver and gold! What a doom was mine if plentiful redemption had not been found! The breaking of the neck of the donkey was but a momentary penalty, but who will measure the wrath to come to which no limit can be imagined? Inestimably dear is the glorious Lamb who has redeemed us from such a doom.

[1] Isaiah 11:4

JESUS SAID TO THEM, "COME AND HAVE BREAKFAST." — JOHN 21:12

In these words the believer is invited to enjoy a holy nearness to Jesus. "Come and eat" implies the same table, the same food, and perhaps it means to sit side by side, and even lean our head on the Savior's shoulder. It is being brought into the banqueting-house, where the banner of redeeming love waves in welcome. This invitation gives us a vision of *union with Jesus*, because Christ Himself is the only food that we can feast upon when we eat with Him. What union is this! It has a depth that reason cannot fathom. Ponder His words:; "Whoever feeds on my flesh and drinks my blood abides in me, and I in him."[1] It is also an invitation to enjoy *fellowship with the saints*. Christians may differ on a variety of points, but they all have one spiritual appetite; and if we cannot all *feel* alike, we can all *feed* alike on the Bread of Life sent down from heaven. At the table of fellowship with Jesus we are one bread and one cup. As the loving cup goes around, we commit our lives to one another. Get nearer to Jesus, and you will find yourself linked more and more in spirit to all who like yourself are supported by the same heavenly manna. If we were nearer to Jesus, we would be nearer to one another. We also see in these words the *source of strength* for every Christian. To look at Christ is to live; but for strength to serve Him, you must eat what He provides. We work too often in a sense of unnecessary weakness because we neglect this perception of the Master. None of us need to put ourselves on a low diet; on the contrary, we should fatten ourselves in the Gospel so that we may derive strength from it and extend every power to its limit in the Master's service. Then if you would realize *nearness* to Jesus, *union with Jesus*, *love* to His people, and *strength from Jesus*, "come and have breakfast" with Him by faith.

FOR WITH YOU IS THE FOUNTAIN OF LIFE. — PSALM 36:9

There are times in our spiritual experience when human counsel or sympathy or religious ordinances fail to comfort or help us. Why does our gracious God permit this? Perhaps it is because we have been living too much without Him, and so He takes away everything upon which we have been in the habit of depending, so that He may drive us to Himself. It is a great blessing to live at the fountainhead. While our water bottles are full, we are content, like Hagar and Ishmael, to go into the wilderness; but when those are empty, nothing will serve us but God Himself. We are like the prodigal; we love the pig-swill and forget our Father's house. Remember, we can fashion pigsties and husks even out of the forms of religion; they are blessed things, but if we put them in the place of God, then they are of no value. Anything becomes an idol when it keeps us away from God: Even the brazen serpent is to be despised if we worship it instead of God. The prodigal was never safer than when he was driven to his father's home, because he could be sustained nowhere else. Our Lord favors us with a famine in the land so that it may make us seek after Himself even more. The best position for a Christian is living wholly and directly on God's grace— remaining where he stood at first—"having nothing, yet possessing everything."[2] Let us never for a moment think that our standing is in our sanctification, our mortification, our graces, or our feelings. But be sure of this, that because Christ offered a full atonement, therefore we are saved; for we are complete in Him. Having nothing of our own to trust in, but resting upon the merits of Jesus, His passion and holy life provide us with the only sure ground of confidence. Beloved, when we are brought to a thirsty condition, we are sure to turn eagerly to the fountain of life.

[1] John 6:56   [2] 2 Corinthians 6:10

THEN DAVID SAID IN HIS HEART, "NOW I SHALL PERISH ONE DAY
BY THE HAND OF SAUL." — 1 SAMUEL 27:1

The thought in David's heart at this time was a *false* thought, because he certainly had no ground for thinking that God's anointing him by Samuel was intended to be left as an empty, unmeaning act. On no occasion had the Lord deserted His servant; he had often been placed in perilous positions, but not one instance had occurred in which divine intervention had not delivered him. The trials to which he had been exposed had been varied; they had not assumed one form only, but many—yet in every case He who sent the trial had also graciously ordained a way of escape. David could not put his finger on any entry in his diary and say of it, "Here is evidence that the Lord will forsake me," for the entire course of his past life proved the very reverse. He should have argued from what God *had* done for him that God would be his defender still. But is it not in the same way that *we* doubt God's help? Is it not *mistrust without a cause*? Have we ever had the shadow of a reason to doubt our Father's goodness? Hasn't His loving-kindness been marvelous? Has He ever *once* failed to justify our trust? Our God has never left us at any time. We have had dark nights, but the star of love has shone out amid the blackness; we have been in tough battles, but over our head He has held high the shield of our defense. We have gone through many trials but never to our detriment, always to our advantage; and the conclusion from our past experience is that He who has been with us in six troubles will not forsake us in the seventh. What we have known of our faithful God proves that He will keep us to the end. Let us not, then, reason contrary to the evidence. How can we ever be so ungenerous as to *doubt* our God? Lord, throw down the Jezebel of our unbelief, and let the dogs devour it.

❧ EVENING ❧

HE WILL GATHER THE LAMBS IN HIS ARMS. — ISAIAH 40:11

Our Good Shepherd has in His flock a variety of experiences. Some are strong in the Lord, and others are weak in faith; but He is impartial in His care for all His sheep, and the weakest lamb is as dear to Him as the strongest in the flock. Lambs are prone to lag behind, to wander, and are apt to grow weary; but from all the danger of these infirmities the Shepherd protects them with His arm of power. He finds newborn souls, like young lambs, ready to perish—He nourishes them until life becomes vigorous. He finds weak minds ready to faint and die—He consoles them and renews their strength. All the little ones He gathers, for it is not the will of our heavenly Father that one of them should perish. What a quick eye He must have to see them all! What a tender heart to care for them all! What a far-reaching and powerful arm, to gather them all! In His lifetime on earth He was a great gatherer of the weaker sort, and now that He dwells in heaven, His loving heart extends to the meek and contrite, the timid and feeble, the fearful and fainting here below. How gently He gathered me to Himself, to His truth, to His blood, to His love, to His Church! With what effectual grace did He compel me to come to Himself! Since my conversion, He has frequently restored me from my wanderings and once again gathered me within the circle of His everlasting arms! The best of all is that He does it all Himself. He does not delegate the task of love but condescends Himself to rescue and preserve His most unworthy servant. How will I love or serve Him enough? I long to make His name great to the ends of the earth, but what can my feebleness do for Him? Great Shepherd, add to Your mercies this humble request: Grant me a heart to love You more truly as I ought.

YOUR WAGON TRACKS OVERFLOW WITH ABUNDANCE. — PSALM 65:11

Many of the Lord's tracks overflow with abundance, but a special one is the *track of prayer*. A believer, who is often in private prayer, will not need to cry, "My leanness has risen up against me."[1] Starving souls live at a distance from the mercy-seat and become like the parched fields in times of drought. Consistent wrestling in prayer with God is sure to make the believer strong—if not happy. The nearest place to the gate of heaven is the throne of heavenly grace. Often alone, you will have plenty of assurance; seldom alone with Jesus, your faith will be shallow, polluted with many doubts and fears and not sparkling with the joy of the Lord. Since the soul-enriching path of prayer is open to the very weakest saint, since no high achievements are required, since you are not invited to come because you are an advanced saint but freely invited if you are a saint at all, see to it, dear reader, that you are often in the place of private devotion. Be regularly on your knees, for in this way Elijah drew the rain upon Israel's famished fields.

There is another special track overflowing with abundance to those who walk in it. It is the secret walk of communion that affords the delights of fellowship with Jesus! Earth has no words that can convey the holy calm of a soul leaning on Jesus. Few Christians understand it; they live in the lowlands and seldom climb to the top of the mountain; they live in the outer court and fail to enter the holy place; they do not take up the privilege of priesthood. They see the sacrifice from a distance, but they do not sit down with the priest to eat the meal and enjoy the overflowing abundance. But, reader, learn to sit under the shadow of Jesus; come up to that palm tree, and take hold of its branches. Let your Beloved be to you as the apple tree among the timber, and you shall be satisfied with goodness and abundance. Come, Lord Jesus, and visit us with Your salvation!

❧ EVENING ❧

BEHOLD, TO OBEY IS BETTER THAN SACRIFICE. — 1 SAMUEL 15:22

Saul had been commanded to completely wipe out all the Amalekites and their cattle. Instead of doing so, he preserved the king and allowed his people to take the best of the oxen and of the sheep. When called to account for this, he declared that he did it with a view to offering sacrifice to God; but Samuel met him at once with the assurance that sacrifices were no excuse for an act of direct rebellion. The sentence before us is worthy to be printed in letters of gold and to be displayed before the eyes of the present idolatrous generation, who are very fond of making a show of obedience but who utterly neglect the laws of God. Never forget that to keep strictly to the path of your Savior's command is better than any outward form of religion; and to pay attention to His precept is better than to bring animals or other precious things to lay upon His altar. If you are failing to keep the least of Christ's commands to His disciples, I urge you to be disobedient no longer. All the pretensions you make of attachment to your Master and all the devout actions that you may perform are no substitute for disobedience. "To obey," even in the slightest and smallest thing, "is better than sacrifice," however pompous. Forget the Gregorian chants, sumptuous robes, incense, and banners; the first thing that God requires of His child is obedience; and even if you gave your body to be burned and all your goods to feed the poor, if you did not listen to the Lord's commands, all your formalities would profit you nothing. It is a blessed thing to be teachable as a little child, but it is a much more blessed thing, when one has been taught the lesson, to carry it out to the letter. How many adorn their temples and decorate their priests, but refuse to obey the word of the Lord! My soul, do not share in their deceit.

[1] Job 16:8

INFANTS IN CHRIST. — 1 CORINTHIANS 3:1

Are you mourning, believer, because your spiritual life is so weak, because your faith is so small, your love so feeble? Cheer up because you have reason to be grateful. Remember *that in some things you are equal to the greatest and most mature Christian.* You are as much purchased with blood as he is. You are just as much an adopted child of God as any other believer. An infant is as truly a child of its parents as is the full-grown man. You are as completely justified, for your justification is not a matter of degree: Your little faith has made you clean every bit. You have as much right to the precious things of the covenant as the most advanced believers, for your right to covenant mercies does not lie in your growth but in the covenant itself; and your faith in Jesus is not the measure but the token of your inheritance in Him. You are as rich as the richest—if not in enjoyment, yet in real possession. The smallest star that gleams is set in heaven; the faintest ray of light has affinity with the sun. In the family register of heaven, the small and the great are written with the same pen. You are as dear to your Father's heart as the greatest in the family. Jesus is very tender toward you. You are like the faintly burning wick; a rougher spirit would say, "Put out that useless flame; it fills the room with an offensive odor!" But the feeble wick *He* will not quench. You are like a bruised reed, and any less tender hand than that of the Chief Musician would tread upon you or throw you away; but He will never break the bruised reed. So instead of being downcast by reason of what you are, you should rejoice in Christ. Am I but small and feeble in the vast company of believers? Yet in Christ I am made to sit in heavenly places. Am I poor in faith? Yet in Jesus I am heir of all things. I do not need to boast or elevate myself; even as an infant in Christ I will rejoice in the Lord and glory in the God of my salvation.

❧ EVENING ❧

GOD, MY MAKER, WHO GIVES SONGS IN THE NIGHT. — JOB 35:10

Any man can sing during the day. When the cup is full, man draws inspiration from it. When money is in plentiful supply, any man can praise the God who provides an abundant harvest or sends home a loaded ship. It is easy enough for a tuneful harp to whisper music when the winds blow; the difficulty is for music to carry when no wind is stirring. It is easy to sing when we can read the notes by daylight; but it takes a skillful singer whose song springs forth when there is not a ray of light to read by. No man can make a song in the night by himself; he may attempt it, but he will find that a song in the night must be divinely inspired. Let everything go well, I can weave songs, fashioning them from the flowers that grow upon my path; but put me in a desert, where no green thing grows, and with what shall I frame a hymn of praise to God? How shall a mortal man make a crown for the Lord without jewels? Let this voice be clear and this body full of health, and I can sing God's praise: Silence my tongue, put me on a bed of suffering, and how will I then chant God's high praises, unless He Himself provides the song? No, it is not in man's power to sing when everything is against him, unless an altar-coal shall touch his lip. It was a divine song from Habakkuk that filled the night when he sang, "Though the fig tree should not blossom, nor fruit be on the vines, the produce of the olive fail and the fields yield no food, the flock be cut off from the fold and there be no herd in the stalls, yet I will rejoice in the LORD; I will take joy in the God of my salvation."[1] So, since our Maker gives *"songs in the night,"* let us wait upon Him for the music. Chief musician, let us not remain songless because we face affliction, but tune our lips to the melody of thanksgiving.

[1] Habakkuk 3:17-18

WE ARE TO GROW UP IN EVERY WAY INTO HIM. — EPHESIANS 4:15

Many Christians remain stunted and limited in spiritual things and never seem to make progress from year to year. No surge of growth and spiritual interest is seen in them. They exist but do not *"grow up in every way into him."* Should we be content with being in the green blade when we might advance to the ear and eventually ripen into the full corn in the ear? Should we be satisfied to believe in Christ and to say, "I am safe" without wishing to know in our own experience more of the fullness that is to be found in Him? It ought not to be so; we should long as good traders in heaven's market to be enriched in the knowledge of Jesus. It is all very well to keep other men's vineyards, but we must not neglect our own spiritual growth and ripening. Why should it always be wintertime in our hearts? We must have our seedtime, it is true, but oh, for a springtime—yes, a summer season that will give promise of an early harvest. If we would ripen in grace, we must live near to Jesus—in His presence—ripened by the sunshine of His smiles. We must hold sweet communion with Him. We must leave the distant view of His face and come near, as John did, and rest our head upon His shoulder; then we will find ourselves advancing in holiness, in love, in faith, in hope—in every precious gift. As the sun rises first on mountaintops and gilds them with its light and presents one of the most charming sights to the traveler's eye, so is it one of the most delightful contemplations in the world to observe a spiritual glow on the head of some saint who has risen in stature, like Saul, above his fellows until, like a mighty snow-capped Alp, he reflects among the chosen the beams of the Sun of Righteousness and bears the glow of His radiance high for all to see, and seeing it, to glorify his Father who is in heaven.

❧ EVENING ❧

DO NOT WITHHOLD. — ISAIAH 43:6

Although this message was sent to the south and referred to the offspring of Israel, it may profitably be a summons to ourselves. We are naturally backward to all good things, and it is a lesson of grace to learn to go forward in the ways of God. Reader, are you unconverted, but do you desire to trust in the Lord Jesus? Then *do not withhold.* Love invites you; the promises assure you of success; the precious blood prepares the way. Do not let sin or fear hinder you, but come to Jesus just as you are. Do you long to pray? Would you like to pour out your heart before the Lord? *Do not withhold.* The mercy-seat is prepared for all who need mercy; a sinner's cries will prevail with God. You are invited—in fact, you are commanded—to pray; come therefore with boldness to the throne of grace.

Dear friend, are you already saved? Then *do not withhold* from union with the Lord's people. Do not neglect the ordinances of baptism and the Lord's Supper. You may be of a timid disposition, but you must fight against it, for fear that it will lead you into disobedience. There is a sweet promise made to those who confess Christ—do not miss it, in case you should come under the condemnation of those who deny Him. If you have talents, *do not withhold* from using them. Do not hoard your wealth; do not waste your time; do not let your abilities rust or your influence be unfelt. Jesus did not withhold; imitate Him by being head of the line in self-denials and self-sacrifices. *Do not withhold* from close communion with God, from boldly appropriating covenant blessings, from advancing in the divine life, from searching out the precious mysteries of the love of Christ. Do not, beloved friend, be guilty of keeping others back by your coldness, harshness, or suspicions. For Jesus' sake go forward yourself, and encourage others to do the same. Hell and the united bands of superstition and infidelity are ready for the fight. Soldiers of the cross, do not withhold!

FOR THE LOVE OF CHRIST CONTROLS US. — 2 CORINTHIANS 5:14

How much do you owe to my Lord? Has He ever done anything for you? Has He forgiven your sins? Has He covered you with a robe of righteousness? Has He set your feet upon a rock? Has He established your goings? Has He prepared heaven for you? Has He prepared you for heaven? Has He written your name in His Book of Life? Has He given you countless blessings? Has He laid up for you a store of mercies, which eye has not seen nor ear heard? Then do something for Jesus that is worthy of His love. Do not give a mere wordy offering to a dying Redeemer. How will you feel when your Master comes if you have to confess that you did nothing for Him but kept your love shut up, like a stagnant pool, neither flowing out to the poor nor to His work? Be done with that kind of love! What do men think of a love that never shows itself in action? Why, they say, "Better is open rebuke than hidden love."[1] Who will accept a love so weak that it does not stir you to a single act of self-denial, generosity, heroism, or zeal? Consider how *He* has loved you and given Himself for you! Do you know the power of that love? Then let it be like a rushing, mighty wind to your soul to sweep out the clouds of your worldliness and clear away the mists of sin. For Christ's sake let this be the tongue of fire that sits upon you: For Christ's sake let this be the divine excitement, the heavenly empowerment to bear you up from earth, the divine spirit that will make you bold as lions and swift as eagles in your Lord's service. Love should give wings to the feet of service and strength to the arms of industry. Fixed on God with a constancy that is not to be shaken, determined to honor Him with a zeal that is not to be turned aside, and pressing on with a passion that doesn't waver, let us display the constraints of love for Jesus. May the divine magnet draw us toward heaven itself.

EVENING

WHY ARE YOU TROUBLED, AND WHY DO DOUBTS ARISE IN YOUR HEARTS? — LUKE 24:38

Why do you say, O Jacob, and speak O Israel, 'My way is hidden from the LORD, and my right is disregarded by my God?'"[2] The Lord cares for everything, and the smallest creatures share in His universal providence, but His particular providence is over His saints. "The angel of the LORD encamps around those who fear him."[3] "Precious is their blood in his sight."[4] "Precious in the sight of the LORD is the death of his saints."[5] "And we know that for those who love God all things work together for good, for those who are called according to his purpose."[6] Let the fact that He is the Savior of all men but is specially the Savior of those who believe cheer and comfort you. You are His peculiar care, His royal treasure that He guards as the apple of His eye, His vineyard over which He watches day and night. "Even the hairs of your head are all numbered."[7] Let the thought of His special love *to you* be a spiritual painkiller, a soothing balm to your woe: "I will never leave *you*, nor forsake *you*."[8] God says that just as much to you as to any saint of old. "Fear not . . . I am your shield; your reward shall be very great."[9] We lose much consolation by the habit of reading His promises for the whole Church instead of taking them directly home for ourselves. Believer, grasp the divine Word with a personal, appropriating faith. Imagine that you hear Jesus say, "I have prayed for *you* that your faith may not fail."[10] Imagine you see Him walking on the water of your trouble, for He is there, and He is saying, "Do not fear—it is I." These are sweet words of Christ! May the Holy Spirit make you feel them as if they were spoken to *you*; forget others for a while—accept the voice of Jesus as addressed to you and say, "Jesus whispers consolation; I cannot refuse it; I will sit under His shadow with great delight."[11]

[1] Proverbs 27:5 [2] Isaiah 40:27 [3] Psalm 34:7 [4] Psalm 72:14 [5] Psalm 116:15 [6] Romans 8:28 [7] Matthew 10:30 [8] Hebrews 13:5 [9] Genesis 15:1 [10] Luke 22:32 [11] See Song of Solomon 2:3

This sentence is a body of divinity in miniature. Whoever grasps its meaning is a theologian, and whoever is able to dive into its fullness is a learned professor! It is a summary of the glorious message of salvation that was delivered to us in Christ Jesus our Redeemer. The sense hinges upon the word "freely." This is the glorious, the suitable, the divine way by which love streams from heaven to earth, a spontaneous love flowing out to those who neither deserved it, purchased it, nor sought after it. It is, indeed, the only way in which God can love such as we are. The text is a death-blow to all sorts of fitness: "I will love them *freely.*" Now, if there were any fitness necessary in us, then He would not love us freely; at least, this would be a hindrance and a drawback to the freeness of it. But it stands: "I will love them freely." We complain, "Lord, my heart is so hard." "I will love them *freely.*" "But I do not feel my need of Christ as I ought to." "I will not love you because you feel your need; I will love you freely." "But I do not feel that softening of spirit that I should desire." Remember, the softening of spirit is not a condition, for there are no conditions; the covenant of grace has no conditionality whatever. So we without any fitness may rest upon the promise of God that was made to us in Christ Jesus when He said, "Whoever believes in him is not condemned."[1] It is blessed to know that the grace of God is free to us at all times, without preparation, without fitness, without money, and without price! "I will love them freely." These words *invite apostates to return:* Indeed, the text was specially written for such—"I will heal their apostasy; I will love them freely." Apostate, surely the generosity of the promise will immediately break your heart, and you will return and seek your injured Father's face.

There are times when all the promises and doctrines of the Bible are of no help unless a gracious hand applies them to us. We are thirsty but too faint to crawl to the waterbrook. When a soldier is wounded in battle, it is of little use for him to know that there are those at the hospital who can bind up his wounds and medicines to ease all the pains that he now suffers: What he needs is to be carried there and to have the remedies applied. It is the same with our souls, and to meet this need there is one, even the Spirit of truth, who takes the things of Jesus and applies them to us. Do not think that Christ has placed His joys on heavenly shelves so we may climb up and retrieve them for ourselves; rather He draws near and sheds His peace abroad in our hearts. Christian, if you are tonight struggling under deep distress, your Father does not give you promises and then leave you to draw them up from the Word like buckets from a well. The promises He has written in the Word He will write afresh on your heart. He will display His love to you and by His blessed Spirit dispel your cares and troubles. Let it be known to you, if you mourn, that it is God's prerogative to wipe every tear from the eyes of His people. The good Samaritan did not say, "Here is the wine, and here is the oil for you"; he actually poured in the oil and the wine. So Jesus not only gives you the sweet wine of His promise, but He holds the golden cup to your lips and pours the lifeblood into your mouth. The poor, sick, worn-out pilgrim is not merely strengthened to walk, but he is lifted up on eagles' wings. Glorious Gospel that provides everything for the helpless, that draws near to us when we cannot reach it ourselves— it brings us grace before we seek grace! There is as much glory in the giving as in the gift. Happy people who have the Holy Spirit to bring Jesus to them!

[1] John 3:18

"DO YOU WANT TO GO AWAY AS WELL?" — JOHN 6:67

Many have forsaken Christ and have walked no more with Him; but what reason do *you* have to make a change? Has there been any reason for it in *the past*? Has Jesus not proved Himself all-sufficient? He asks you this morning, "Have I been a wilderness to you?" When your soul has simply trusted Jesus, have you ever been defeated? Have you not until now found your Lord to be a compassionate and generous friend to you, and has simple faith in Him not given you all the peace your spirit could desire? Can you even dream of a better friend than He has been to you? Then do not change the old and tried for the new and false. As for *the present*, can that compel you to leave Christ? When we are hard-pressed with this world or with the severer trials within the church, we find it a most blessed thing to rest our head upon the shoulder of our Savior. This is the joy we have today—that we are saved in Him; and if this joy is satisfying, why would we think of changing? Who trades gold for dross? We will not renounce the sun until we find a better light, nor leave our Lord until a brighter lover shall appear; and since this can never be, we will hold Him with an immortal grasp and bind His name as a seal upon our arm. As for *the future*, can you suggest anything that can arise that will render it necessary for you to mutiny or desert the old flag to serve under another captain? We think not. If life be long, He doesn't change. If we are poor, what better than to have Christ who can make us rich? When we are sick, what more do we want than Jesus to comfort and to heal? When we die, is it not written that "neither death, nor life, nor angels, nor rulers, nor things present nor things to come . . . will be able to separate us from the love of God in Christ Jesus our Lord."[1] And so we say with Peter, "Lord, to whom shall we go?"[2]

☙ EVENING ☙
WHY ARE YOU SLEEPING? RISE AND PRAY THAT YOU MAY NOT
ENTER INTO TEMPTATION. — LUKE 22:46

When is the Christian most liable to sleep? Is it not *when his temporal circumstances are prosperous*? Have you not found it so? When you had daily troubles to take to the throne of grace, were you not more awake than you are now? Easy roads make sleepy travelers. Another dangerous time is *when all goes pleasantly in spiritual matters*. Christian did not fall asleep when lions were in the way or when he was wading through the river or when fighting with Apollyon. But when he had climbed halfway up the Hill Difficulty and came to a delightful spot, he sat down and promptly fell asleep, to his great sorrow and loss. The enchanted ground is a place of balmy breezes, filled with fragrant odors and soft influences, all of which tend to lull pilgrims to sleep. Remember Bunyan's description: "Then they came to an arbor, warm, and promising much refreshing to the weary pilgrims; for it was finely wrought above head, beautified with greens, and furnished with benches and settees. It also had in it a soft couch, where the weary might lean." "The arbor was called the Slothful's Friend, and was made on purpose to attract, if it might, some of the pilgrims to take their rest there when weary." Depend upon it—it is in easy places that men shut their eyes and wander into the dreamy land of forgetfulness. Old Erskine wisely remarked, "I like a roaring devil better than a sleeping devil." There is no temptation half so danger-ous as not being tempted. The distressed soul does not sleep; it is after we enter into peace-ful confidence and full assurance that we are in danger of slumbering. The disciples fell asleep after they had seen Jesus transfigured on the mountaintop. Take heed, joyful Christian, easy days are close neighbors to temptations: Be as happy as you will—only be watchful!

[1]Romans 8:38-39 [2]John 6:68

THE TREES OF THE LORD ARE WATERED ABUNDANTLY. — PSALM 104:16

Without water the tree cannot flourish or even exist. *Vitality* is essential to a Christian. There must be *life*—a vital principle infused in us by God the Holy Spirit—or we cannot be trees of the Lord. Being a Christian merely in name is a dead thing; we must be filled with the spirit of divine life. This life is *mysterious.* We do not understand the circulation of the water, by what force it rises, and by what power it descends again. So the life within us is a sacred mystery. Regeneration is performed by the Holy Spirit entering into man and becoming man's life; and this divine life in a believer afterwards feeds upon Christ and is in this way sustained by divine food, but how it comes and where it goes who will explain to us? What a *secret* thing the water is! The roots go searching through the soil, but we cannot see them suck out the various gases or transmute the mineral into the vegetable; this work is done down in the dark. Our root is Christ Jesus, and our life is hidden in Him; this is the secret of the Lord. The source of the Christian life is as secret as the life itself. How *permanently active* is the water in the cedar! In the Christian the divine life is always full of energy—not always in fruit-bearing, but in inward operations. The believer's *graces* are not always constant motion, but his life never ceases to palpitate within. He is not always working for God, but his heart is always living in Him. As the water *reveals itself in producing the foliage and fruit of the tree*, so with a truly healthy Christian, his grace is externally displayed in his walk and conversation. If you talk with him, he cannot help speaking about Jesus. If you notice his actions, you will see that he has been with Jesus. He is so full of Christ that He must fill his conduct and conversation.

 ❧ EVENING ❦

HE . . . BEGAN TO WASH THE DISCIPLES' FEET. — JOHN 13:5

The Lord Jesus loves His people so much that every day He is still doing for them much that is analogous to washing their soiled feet. Their poorest actions He accepts; their deepest sorrow He feels; their slenderest wish He hears; and their every transgression He forgives. He is still their servant as well as their Friend and Master. He not only performs majestic deeds for them, when in all His priestly garb and function He stands up to plead for them, but He also humbly, patiently goes among His people with the basin and the towel. He does this when He puts away from us day by day our constant infirmities and sins. Last night when you bowed the knee, you mournfully confessed that much of your conduct was not worthy of your profession; and even tonight you must grieve again that you have fallen into the selfsame folly and sin from which special grace delivered you long ago. And yet Jesus displays great patience with you. He will hear your confession of sin; He will say, "I will—be clean!" He will again apply the blood of sprinkling and speak peace to your conscience and remove every spot. It is a great act of eternal love when Christ once for all absolves the sinner and places him in the family of God; but what condescending patience it is when the Savior with much long-suffering bears the repetitive follies of His wayward disciple, day by day and hour by hour washing away the multiplied transgressions of His erring but still much-loved child! To dry up a flood of rebellion is something marvelous, but to endure the constant dripping of repeated offenses, to bear with a perpetual trying of patience, this is truly divine! While we find comfort and peace in our Lord's daily cleansing, its legitimate influence upon us will be to increase our watchfulness and quicken our desire for holiness. *Is that your experience?*

BECAUSE OF THE TRUTH THAT ABIDES IN US AND WILL BE WITH US FOREVER.
— 2 JOHN 2

Once the truth of God has obtained an entrance into the human heart and subdued the whole man to itself, no power, human or infernal, can dislodge it. We entertain it not as a guest but as the master of the house. This is a *Christian necessity*, and whoever does not believe this is not a Christian. Those who feel the vital power of the Gospel and know the strength of the Holy Spirit as He opens, applies, and seals the Lord's Word would rather be torn to pieces than be torn away from the Gospel of their salvation. A thousand mercies are wrapped up in the assurance that the truth will be with us forever, will be our living support, our dying comfort, our rising song, our eternal glory. This is *Christian privilege*, and without it our faith is worth little. Some truths we outgrow and leave behind, for they are but rudiments and lessons for beginners, but this is not so with divine truth, for though it is sweet food for babies, it is in the highest sense strong meat for men. The painful truth that we are sinners is with us to humble us and make us watchful; the more blessed truth that whoever believes on the Lord Jesus will be saved remains with us as our hope and joy. Experience, far from loosening our hold on the doctrines of grace, has tied us to them more and more firmly; our grounds and motives for believing are now stronger and more numerous than ever, and we have reason to expect that it will remain this way until in death we clasp the Savior in our arms.

Wherever this abiding love of truth can be discovered, we are bound to share in fellowship and to exercise our love. No narrow circle can contain our gracious sympathies; our communion of heart must be as wide as the ocean of grace. Error may be found mingled with truth received; let us go to war with the error but still love the brother for the measure of truth that we see in him. Above all let us love and spread the truth ourselves.

❧ EVENING ❧
SO SHE SET OUT AND WENT AND GLEANED IN THE FIELD AFTER THE REAPERS,
AND SHE HAPPENED TO COME TO THE PART OF THE FIELD
BELONGING TO BOAZ, WHO WAS OF THE CLAN OF ELIMELECH. — RUTH 2:3

She happened to come. Yes, it seemed nothing but an accident, but it was divinely ruled over! Ruth had gone out with her mother-in-law's blessing, under the care of her mother-in-law's God, to humble but honorable work, and the providence of God was guiding her every step. Little did she know that among the sheaves she would find a husband, that he would make her the joint owner of all those broad acres, and that she, a poor foreigner, would become one of the ancestors of the great Messiah. God is very good to those who trust in Him and often surprises them with unexpected blessings. Little do we know what may happen to us tomorrow, but this sweet fact may cheer us—that no good thing will be withheld. Chance is banished from the faith of Christians, for they see the hand of God in everything. The trivial events of today or tomorrow may involve consequences of the highest importance. O Lord, deal as graciously with Your servants now as You did with Ruth.

How blessed would it be if, in wandering in the field of meditation tonight, we should happen to find ourselves in the place where the Lord Jesus will reveal Himself to us! O Spirit of God, guide us to Him. We would rather glean in His field than carry home the whole harvest from any other place. We would follow the footsteps of His flock, which would guide us to the green pastures where He dwells! This is a weary world when Jesus is away— we would survive easier without sun and moon than without Him—but how divinely fair all things become in the glory of His presence! Our souls know the virtue that lives in Jesus and can never be content without Him. We will wait in prayer tonight until we "happen" to come to a part of the field belonging to Jesus in which He will reveal Himself to us.

YOU LOOKED FOR MUCH, AND BEHOLD, IT CAME TO LITTLE.
AND WHEN YOU BROUGHT IT HOME, I BLEW IT AWAY.
WHY? DECLARES THE LORD OF HOSTS.
BECAUSE OF MY HOUSE THAT LIES IN RUINS, WHILE EACH OF YOU
BUSIES HIMSELF WITH HIS OWN HOUSE. — HAGGAI 1:9

Grudging souls limit their contributions to the ministry and missionary operations and call such saving good economy; little do they dream that in doing so they are impoverishing themselves. Their excuse is that they must care for their own families, and they forget that to neglect the house of God is a sure way to bring ruin upon their own houses. Our God has a method in providence by which He can cause our endeavors to succeed beyond our expectation, or He can defeat our plans to our confusion and dismay; by a turn of His hand He can steer our vessel in a profitable channel or run it aground in poverty and bankruptcy. It is the teaching of Scripture that the Lord enriches the generous and leaves the miserly to discover that withholding leads to poverty. In a very wide sphere of observation, I have noticed that the most generous Christians of my acquaintance have always been the happiest, and almost invariably the most prosperous. I have seen the generous giver rise to financial levels of which he never dreamed; and I have as often seen the mean, ungenerous soul descend to poverty by the very stinginess by which he thought to rise. Men trust good stewards with larger and larger sums, and so it frequently is with the Lord; He gives by cartloads to those who give by bushels. Where wealth is not bestowed, the Lord makes a little much by the contentment that the sanctified heart feels in his portion from which a tithe has been dedicated to the Lord. Selfishness looks first at home, but godliness seeks first the kingdom of God and His righteousness; yet in the long run selfishness is loss, and godliness is great gain. It requires faith to act toward our God with an open hand, but surely He deserves it from us; and all that we can do is a very poor acknowledgment of our amazing indebtedness to His goodness.

❧ EVENING ❧

ALL STREAMS RUN TO THE SEA, BUT THE SEA IS NOT FULL;
TO THE PLACE WHERE THE STREAMS FLOW,
THERE THEY FLOW AGAIN. — ECCLESIASTES 1:7

Everything on earth is on the move; time knows nothing of rest. The solid earth is a rolling ball, and the great sun itself is a star obediently fulfilling its course around some greater luminary. Tides move the sea; winds stir the breezy ocean; friction wears the rock: Change and death rule everywhere. The sea is not a miser's storehouse for a wealth of waters, for as by one force the waters flow into it, by another they are lifted from it. Men are born to die: Everything is hurry, worry, and vexation of spirit. Friend of the unchanging Jesus, what a joy it is to reflect upon your changeless heritage, your sea of bliss that will be forever full since God Himself shall pour eternal rivers of pleasure into it. We seek an abiding city beyond the skies, and we shall not be disappointed. The passage before us should teach us to be grateful. The ocean is a great receiver, but it is also a generous distributor. What the rivers bring, it returns to the earth in the form of clouds and rain. The man who takes everything but makes no return is out of joint with the universe. To give to others is still sowing seed for ourselves. He who is so good a steward as to be willing to use his substance for his Lord shall be entrusted with more. Friend of Jesus, are you rendering to Him in proportion to the benefit you receive? Have you been given a great deal? Where is your fruit? Have you done all you might? Can you not do more? To be selfish is to be wicked. Suppose the ocean gave up none of its watery treasure; it would bring ruin upon our race. God forbid that any of us should follow the ungenerous and destructive policy of living for ourselves. Jesus did not please Himself. All fullness dwells in Him, but from His fullness we have all received. Oh, to be like Jesus and no longer live for ourselves!

THE SAYING IS TRUSTWORTHY . . . — 2 TIMOTHY 2:11

Paul has four of these *"trustworthy" sayings.* The first occurs in 1 Timothy 1:15, "The saying is trustworthy and deserving of full acceptance, that Christ Jesus came into the world to save sinners." The next is in 1 Timothy 4:8-9, "Godliness is of value in every way, as it holds promise for the present life and also for the life to come. The saying is trustworthy and deserving of full acceptance." The third is in 2 Timothy 2:11, "The saying is trustworthy, for: If we have died with him, we will also live with him." And the fourth is in Titus 3:8, "The saying is trustworthy, and I want you to insist on these things, so that those who have believed in God may be careful to devote themselves to do good works." We may trace a connection between these faithful sayings. The first one lays the foundation of our eternal salvation in the free grace of God, as shown to us in the mission of the great Redeemer. The next affirms the double blessedness that we obtain through this salvation—the blessings of time and of eternity. The third shows the nature of the life to which the chosen people are called; we are ordained to die with Christ with the promise that "if we have died with him, we will also live with him." The last sets out the active form of Christian service, bidding us to diligently maintain good works. So we have the root of salvation in free grace, then the privileges of that salvation in the life that now is and in that which is to come; and we have also the two great branches of dying with Christ and living with Christ, loaded with the fruit of the Spirit. Treasure up these faithful sayings. Let them be the guides of your life, your comfort, and your instruction. The apostle of the Gentiles proved them to be trustworthy, and they are still trustworthy; not one word will fall to the ground. They are worthy of all acceptance; let us accept them now and prove their reliability. Let these four trustworthy sayings be written on the four corners of my house.

❧ EVENING ☙

WE HAVE ALL BECOME LIKE ONE WHO IS UNCLEAN. — ISAIAH 64:6

The believer is a new creature; he belongs to a holy generation and a peculiar people. The Spirit of God is in him, and in every respect he is far removed from the natural man. But for all that the Christian is still a sinner. He is so because of the imperfection of his nature, and he will continue as such to the end of his earthly life. The dirty fingers of sin leave marks on our cleanest clothes. Sin spoils our repentance, before the great Potter has finished it upon the wheel. Selfishness defiles our tears, and unbelief tampers with our faith. The best thing we ever did apart from the merit of Jesus only added to the number of our sins; for when we have been most pure in our own sight, still, like the heavens, we were not pure in God's sight; and as He charged His angels with folly, so He must charge us with it, even in our most angelic frames of mind. The song that seeks to emulate the angels' melodies has human discords in it. The prayer that moves the arm of God is still a bruised and battered prayer, and only moves that arm because the sinless One, the great Mediator, Jesus, has stepped in to take away the sin of our supplication. The most golden faith or the purest degree of sanctification to which a Christian ever attained on earth has still so much dross in it as to be only worthy of the flames. Every night we look in the mirror we see a sinner and need to confess, "We have become like one who is unclean, and all our righteous deeds are like a polluted garment." How precious then is the blood of Christ to hearts like ours! How priceless a gift is His perfect righteousness! And how bright is the hope of perfect holiness in heaven! Even now, though sin dwells in us, *its power is broken.* It remains, but it no longer reigns; we are in bitter conflict with it, but we are dealing with a vanquished foe. In a little while we will enter victoriously into the city where nothing defiles.

I CHOSE YOU OUT OF THE WORLD. — JOHN 15:19

Here is distinguishing grace and discriminating regard, for some are made the special objects of divine affection. Do not be afraid to dwell upon this lofty doctrine of election. When your mind is heavy and depressed, you will find it to be a spiritual tonic. Those who doubt the doctrines of grace or who throw them into the shadows miss the richest clusters of grapes; they lose the best wines, the choice food. There is no balm in Gilead comparable to it. If the honey in Jonathan's wood when simply touched illumined *the eyes*, this is honey that will illumine *your heart* as you love and learn the mysteries of the kingdom of God. You must feed on this; live upon this choice provision, and do not be afraid that it will prove too delicate a diet. Meat from the King's table will hurt none of His servants. Desire to have your mind enlarged, that you may comprehend more and more of the eternal, everlasting, discriminating love of God. When you have soared as high as election, linger on its twin peak, the covenant of grace. Covenant engagements are the mighty fortresses behind which we lie entrenched; covenant engagements with our Savior, Christ Jesus, are the quiet resting-places of trembling spirits.

> *His oath, His covenant, His blood,*
> *Support me in the raging flood;*
> *When every earthly prop gives way,*
> *This still is all my strength and stay.*

If Jesus undertook to bring me to glory, and if the Father promised that He would give me to the Son to be a part of the infinite reward of the travail of His soul, then, my soul, until God Himself shall be unfaithful, until Jesus shall cease to be the truth, you are safe. When David danced before the ark, he told Michal that election made him do so. Come, my soul, dance before the God of grace, and let your heart leap for joy!

❧ EVENING ☙

HIS HEAD IS THE FINEST GOLD; HIS LOCKS ARE WAVY, BLACK AS A RAVEN.
— SONG OF SOLOMON 5:11

Comparisons all fail to set forth the Lord Jesus, but the spouse uses the best she can find. By *the head* of Jesus we may understand His deity, "for the head of Christ is God";[1] and then the mold of purest gold is the best conceivable metaphor, but all too poor to describe one so precious, so pure, so dear, so glorious. Jesus is not a grain of gold, but a vast globe of it, a priceless mass of treasure such as earth and heaven cannot excel. The creatures are mere iron and clay—they will all perish like wood, hay, and stubble; but the ever living Head of the creation of God will shine on forever and ever. In Him is no mixture, nor smallest taint of alloy. He is forever infinitely holy and altogether divine. *The wavy locks* depict His manly vigor. There is nothing effeminate in our Lord. He is the manliest of men—bold as a lion, strong as an ox, swift as an eagle. Every conceivable and inconceivable beauty is to be found in Him, though He once was despised and rejected of men.

> *His head the finest gold;*
> *With secret sweet perfume,*
> *His curled locks hang all as black*
> *As any raven's plume.*

The glory of His head is not shorn away. He is eternally crowned with peerless majesty. *The black hair* indicates youthful freshness, for Jesus has the dew of His youth upon Him. Others grow weak with age, but He is forever a Priest like Melchizedek; others come and go, but He remains as God upon His throne, world without end. We will behold Him tonight and adore Him. Angels are gazing on Him—His redeemed must not turn their eyes away from Him. Where else is there such a Beloved? Oh, for an hour's fellowship with Him! Be gone, you intruding anxieties! Jesus draws me, and I run after Him.

[1] 1 Corinthians 11:3

This prayer begins where all true prayer must start, with the spirit of *adoption*: "Our Father." There is no acceptable prayer until we can say, "I will arise and go to my Father."[1] This childlike spirit soon perceives the grandeur of the Father "in heaven" and ascends to *devout adoration*, "hallowed be your name." The child lisping, "Abba, Father" grows into the cherub crying, "Holy, holy, holy." There is but a step from rapturous worship to the *glowing missionary spirit*, which is a sure expression of filial love and reverent adoration—"your kingdom come, your will be done, on earth as it is in heaven." Next follows the heartfelt *expression of dependence* upon God—"Give us this day our daily bread." Being further illuminated by the Spirit, the one praying discovers that he is not only dependent but sinful; so he *cries for mercy*, "Forgive us our debts, as we also have forgiven our debtors"; and being pardoned, having the righteousness of Christ imputed, and knowing his acceptance with God, he humbly *prays for holy perseverance*, "Lead us not into temptation." The man who is really forgiven is anxious not to offend again; the possession of justification leads to an anxious desire for sanctification. "Forgive us our debts"—that is justification; "Lead us not into temptation, but deliver us from evil"—that is sanctification in its negative and positive forms. As the result of all this, there follows a *triumphant ascription of praise*, "For yours is the kingdom and the power and the glory, forever. Amen." We rejoice that *our* King reigns in providence and shall reign in grace, from the river even to the ends of the earth, and of His dominion there shall be no end. So from a sense of adoption, up to fellowship with our reigning Lord, this short model of prayer conducts the soul. Lord, teach us then to pray.

◆◆ EVENING ◆◆
BUT THEIR EYES WERE KEPT FROM RECOGNIZING HIM. — LUKE 24:16

The disciples ought to have known Jesus; they had heard His voice so often and gazed upon that marred face so frequently that it is incredible they did not discover Him. Yet is it not also with you? You have not seen Jesus lately. You have been to His table, and yet you have not met Him there. You are in a dark trouble this evening, and though He plainly says, "It is I, do not be afraid," yet you cannot discern Him. Sadly, our eyes are kept from seeing Him. We know His voice, we have looked into His face, we have leaned our head upon His shoulder, and yet, though Christ is very near us, we are saying, "I wish I knew where I could find Him!" We should know Jesus, for we have the Scriptures to reflect His image, and yet how possible it is for us to open that precious book and have no glimpse of our loving Lord! Dear child of God, are you in that state? Jesus feeds among the lilies of the Word, and you walk among those lilies, and yet you do not behold Him. He is accustomed to walking through the glades of Scripture and communing with His people, as the Father did with Adam in the cool of the day, and yet you are in the garden of Scripture but cannot see Him, although He is always there. And why do we not see Him? This must be ascribed in our case, as in the disciples', to unbelief. They evidently did not expect to see Jesus, and therefore they did not know Him. To a great extent in spiritual things we get what we expect from the Lord. Only faith can bring us to see Jesus. Make it your prayer, "Lord, open my eyes, that I may see my Savior present with me." It is a blessed thing to want to see Him; but it is far better to gaze upon Him. To those who seek Him He is kind; but to those who find Him, He is dear beyond expression!

[1] Luke 15:18

I WILL GIVE THANKS TO THE LORD. — PSALM 9:1

Thanksgiving should always follow answered prayer, just as the mist of earth's gratitude rises when the sun of heaven's love warms the ground. Has the Lord been gracious to you and inclined His ear to the voice of your prayer? Then thank Him as long as you live. Let the ripe fruit fall upon the fertile soil from which it drew its life. Do not fail to sing in praise of Him who has answered your prayer and has given you the desire of your heart. To be silent about God's mercies is to incur the guilt of ingratitude; it is to act as poorly as the nine lepers who after they had been cured of their leprosy did not return to give thanks to the healing Lord. To forget to praise God is to refuse to benefit ourselves; for praise, like prayer, is one great means of promoting the growth of our spiritual lives. It helps to remove our burdens, to excite our hope, to increase our faith. It is a healthy and invigorating exercise that quickens the pulse of the believer and prepares him for new enterprises in his Master's service. To bless God for mercies received is also the way to benefit our fellowmen; "let the humble hear and be glad."[1] Others who have been in similar circumstances will take comfort if we can say, "Magnify the LORD with me, and let us exalt his name together. . . . This poor man cried, and the LORD heard him."[2] Weak hearts will be strengthened, and sagging spirits will be revived as the saints listen to our "shouts of deliverance."[3] Their doubts and fears will be rebuked as we teach and admonish one another in psalms and hymns and spiritual songs. They will also "sing of the ways of the LORD"[4] when they hear us magnify His holy name. Praise is the most heavenly of Christian duties. The angels do not pray, but they do not cease to praise both day and night; and the redeemed, clothed in white robes, with palm branches in their hands, are never tired of singing the new song, "Worthy is the Lamb."[5]

EVENING
O YOU WHO DWELL IN THE GARDENS, WITH COMPANIONS
LISTENING FOR YOUR VOICE; LET ME HEAR IT. — SONG OF SOLOMON 8:13

My sweet Lord Jesus remembers well the garden of Gethsemane, and although He has left that garden, He now dwells in the garden of His church: There He discloses Himself to those who keep His blessed company. The voice of love with which He speaks to His beloved is more musical than the harps of heaven. There is a depth of melodious love within it that leaves all human music far behind. Tens of thousands on earth, and millions above, are consumed with its harmonious accents. Some whom I know well, and whom I greatly envy, are at this moment hearkening to the beloved voice. O that I were a partaker of their joys! It is true some of these are poor, others bedridden, and some near the gates of death; but, my Lord, I would cheerfully starve with them, pine with them, or die with them if I might simply hear Your voice. Once I heard it often, but I have grieved Your Spirit. Return to me in compassion and once again say to me, "I am your salvation." No other voice can content me. I know Your voice and cannot be deceived by another; let me hear it, I pray You. I do not know what You will say, nor do I make any condition, my Beloved; simply let me hear You speak, and if it be a rebuke I will bless You for it. Perhaps the cleansing of my dull ear will require a painful surgery, but let it cost me what it will, I have only one consuming desire—to hear Your voice. Pierce my ear with Your harshest notes, but do not allow me to remain deaf to Your calls. Tonight, Lord, grant Your unworthy servant his desire, for I am Yours, and You have bought me with Your blood. You have opened my eyes to see You, and the sight has saved me. Lord, open my ear. I have read Your heart; now let me hear from Your lips.

[1] Psalm 34:2 [2] Psalm 34:3, 6 [3] Psalm 32:7 [4] Psalm 138:5 [5] Revelation 5:17

RENEW A RIGHT SPIRIT WITHIN ME. — PSALM 51:10

Abacksslider, if there is a spark of life left in him, will groan for restoration. In this renewal the same exercise of grace is required as at our conversion. We needed repentance then; we certainly need it now. We required faith that we might come to Christ at first; only the same grace can bring us to Jesus now. We needed a word from the Most High, a word from the lip of the loving One, to end our fears then; we shall soon discover, when under a sense of present sin, that we need it now. No man can be renewed without as real and true a manifestation of the Holy Spirit's energy as he felt at first, because the work is as great, and flesh and blood are as much in the way now as they ever were. Let your personal weakness, Christian, be an argument to make you pray sincerely to your God for help. Remember, David when he felt himself to be powerless did not fold his arms or close his lips, but he hurried to the mercy-seat crying, "renew a right spirit within me." Do not allow the doctrine that you, unaided, can do nothing make you sleep; but let it be a goad in your side to drive you with an awful earnestness to Israel's strong Helper. O that you may have grace to plead with God, as though you pleaded for your very life—"renew a right spirit within me." He who *sincerely* prays to God to do this will prove his honesty by using the means through which God works. Be much in prayer; live constantly on the Word of God; kill the lusts that have driven your Lord from you; be careful to watch over the future uprisings of sin. The Lord has His own appointed ways; sit by the wayside, and you will be ready when He passes by. Continue in all those blessed ordinances that will foster and nourish your dying graces; and knowing that all the power must proceed from Him, do not cease to cry, "Renew a right spirit within me."

❧   EVENING   ❧
IT WAS I WHO KNEW YOU IN THE WILDERNESS, IN THE LAND OF DROUGHT.
— HOSEA 13:5

Yes, Lord, You did indeed know me in my *fallen state*, and You did even then choose me for Yourself. When I was loathsome and self-abhorred, You received me as Your child, and You satisfied my longings. Blessed forever be Your name for this free, rich, abounding mercy. Since then, *my inward experience* has often been a wilderness; but You have kept me still as Your beloved and poured streams of love and grace into me to gladden me and make me fruitful. When my *outward circumstances* have been at the worst, and I have wandered in a land of drought, Your sweet presence has comforted me. Men have ignored me, and I have been scorned; but You have known my soul in adversities, for no affliction dims the luster of Your love. Most gracious Lord, I magnify You for all Your faithfulness to me in trying circumstances, and I deplore the fact that I have at times forgotten You and been proud of heart when I have owed everything to Your gentleness and love. Have mercy upon Your servant in this matter!

My soul, if Jesus acknowledged you in your lowly condition, be sure that you own both Himself and His cause now that you are in prosperity. Do not be puffed up by worldly successes, and do not be ashamed of the truth or of the poor church with which you have been associated. Follow Jesus into the wilderness: Bear the cross with Him when the persecution heats up. He owned you, O my soul, in your poverty and shame—never be so treacherous as to be ashamed of Him. Let me know more shame at the thought of being ashamed of my best Beloved! Jesus, my soul cleaves to You.

> *I'll turn to Thee in days of light,*
> *As well as nights of care,*
> *Thou brightest amid all that's bright!*
> *Thou fairest of the fair!*

November

THE CHURCH IN YOUR HOUSE. — PHILEMON 2

Is there a church in this house? Are parents, children, and friends all members of it, or are some still unconverted? Let us pause here and let the question go round: *Am I a member of the church in this house?* The father's heart would leap for joy, and the mother's eyes would fill with holy tears if from the eldest to the youngest all were saved! Let us pray for this great mercy until the Lord shall grant it to us. Probably it had been the dearest object of Philemon's desires to have all his household saved; but it was not at first fully granted to him. He had a wicked servant, Onesimus, who, having wronged him, ran away from his service. His master's prayers followed him, and at last, as God would have it, Onesimus was led to hear Paul preach; his heart was touched, and he returned to Philemon not only to be a faithful servant, but a beloved brother, adding another member to the church in Philemon's house. Is there an unconverted family member absent this morning? Make special supplication that they may, upon returning to their home, gladden every heart with good news of what grace has done! Is there an unconverted family member still at home? Ask God to save him also.

If there is such a church in our house, let us order it well, and let everyone conduct themselves as in the sight of God. Let us go about our daily routines with studied holiness, diligence, kindness, and integrity. More is expected of a church than of an ordinary household. Family worship must, in such a case, be more devout and hearty; internal love must be warmer and unbroken, and external conduct must be more sanctified and Christlike. We need not fear that the smallness of our number will put us out of the list of churches, for the Holy Spirit has enrolled a family-church here in the inspired book of remembrance. As a church let us now draw near to the great Head of the one Church universal, and let us beseech Him to give us grace to shine before men to the glory of His name.

∾ EVENING ∾
. . . AND THEY WERE UNAWARE UNTIL THE FLOOD CAME, AND SWEPT THEM ALL AWAY, SO WILL BE THE COMING OF THE SON OF MAN. — MATTHEW 24:39

The doom was universal. Neither rich nor poor escaped: the learned and the illiterate, the admired and the despised, the religious and the profane, the old and the young all sank in one common ruin. Some had doubtless ridiculed the preacher, but where were their merry jests now? Others had threatened Noah for his zeal, which they regarded as madness. What happened to their boastings and hard speeches? The critic who judged the old man's work drowns in the same sea that covers his sneering companions. Those who spoke patronizingly of the good man's faithfulness to his convictions, but did not share them, have sunk to rise no more, and the workers who for pay helped to build the wondrous ark are all lost also. The Flood swept them *all* away and made no single exception. Even so, outside of Christ, final destruction is sure to everyone; no rank, possession, or character will be enough to save a single soul who has not believed in the Lord Jesus. My soul, consider this widespread judgment and tremble at it.

How incredible was the general apathy! They were all eating and drinking, marrying and giving in marriage, until the awful morning dawned. There was not one wise individual upon earth outside of the ark. Folly duped the whole race, folly as to self-preservation—the most foolish of all follies. Folly in doubting the most true God—the most malignant foolishness. Is it not strange, my soul? All men are negligent of their souls until grace gives them reason; then they leave their madness and act like rational beings, but not until then.

All, blessed be God, were safe in the ark; no ruin entered there. From the huge elephant down to the tiny mouse all were safe. The timid hare was equally secure with the courageous lion, the helpless lamb as safe as the laborious ox. All are safe in Jesus. My soul, are you in Him?

FOR I THE LORD DO NOT CHANGE. — MALACHI 3:6

It is just as well for us that in all the variableness of life there is One whom change cannot affect, One whose heart can never alter, and on whose brow inconsistency can make no furrows. All other things have changed—all things are changing. The sun grows dim with age; the world is growing old; the final chapter of the worn-out vesture has begun; the heavens and earth must soon pass away; they will perish—they shall grow old like a garment. But there is One who only has immortality, of whose years there is no end, and in whose person there is no change. The delight that the sailor feels when, having been tossed about on the waves, he steps again upon the solid shore is the satisfaction of a Christian when, in all the changes of this distressing life, he rests the foot of his faith upon this truth—"*I the LORD do not change.*"

The stability that the anchor gives the ship when it has at last obtained a solid hold is like that which the Christian's hope provides him when it fixes itself upon this glorious truth. With God "there is no variation or shadow due to change."[1] Whatever His attributes were in the past, they are now; His power, His wisdom, His justice, His truth are unchanged. He has forever been the refuge of His people, their stronghold in the day of trouble, and He is still their sure Helper. He is unchanged in His love. He has loved His people with "an everlasting love";[2] He loves them now as much as ever He did, and when the creation itself is set free from its bondage to decay, His love will still endure. Precious is the assurance that He does not change! The wheel of providence revolves, but its axle is eternal love.

> *Death and change are busy ever,*
> *Man decays, and ages move;*
> *But His mercy waneth never;*
> *God is wisdom, God is love.*

❧ EVENING ❧

HOT INDIGNATION SEIZES ME BECAUSE OF THE WICKED,
WHO FORSAKE YOUR LAW. — PSALM 119:53

My soul, do you feel this holy trembling at the sins of others? For if you do not, you lack inward holiness. David's cheeks were wet with rivers of waters because of prevailing unholiness. Jeremiah desired eyes like fountains that he might lament the iniquities of Israel, and Lot was deeply troubled by the conduct of the men of Sodom. Those upon whom the mark was set in Ezekiel's vision were those who sighed and cried for the sins of Jerusalem. Gracious souls cannot help but be grieved to see what pains men take to go to hell. They know the evil of sin experimentally [experientially], and they are alarmed to see others flying like moths into its blaze. Sin makes the righteous shudder because it violates a holy law that it is in every man's highest interest to keep; it pulls down the pillars of the nation. Sin in others horrifies a believer because it makes him think of the baseness of his own heart: When he sees a transgressor he is reminded of his own frailty and vulnerability: "He fell today, and I may fall tomorrow." Sin to a believer is horrible because it crucified the Savior; he sees in every iniquity the nails and spear. How troubling it should be when the Christian learns to tolerate rather than shrink from it in disgust. Each of us must examine his heart. It is an awful thing to insult God to His face. The good God deserves better treatment; the great God claims it; the just God will have it or repay His adversary to his face. An awakened heart trembles at the audacity of sin and stands alarmed at the contemplation of its punishment. How monstrous a thing is rebellion! How dreadful a doom is prepared for the ungodly! My soul, never laugh at sin's fooleries, lest you begin to smile at sin itself. It is your enemy, and your Lord's enemy: Learn to detest it and to distance yourself from it, for only then can you give evidence of the possession of holiness, without which no one can see the Lord.

[1] James 1:17   [2] Jeremiah 31:3

BEHOLD, HE IS PRAYING. — ACTS 9:11

Prayers are instantly noticed in heaven. The moment Saul began to pray, the Lord heard him. Here is comfort for the distressed but praying soul. When our hearts are broken and we bow in prayer, we are often only able to employ the language of sighs and tears; still our groaning has made all the harps of heaven thrill with music. That tear has been caught by God and treasured in the receptacle of heaven. "Put my tears in your bottle"[1] implies that they are caught as they flow. The petitioner, whose fears prevent his words, will be well understood by the Most High. He may only look up with misty eye; but "prayer is the falling of a tear." Tears are the diamonds of heaven; sighs are a part of the music of Jehovah's court and are numbered with "the sublimest strains that reach the majesty on high." Do not think that your prayer, however weak or trembling, will be unregarded. Jacob's ladder is lofty, but our prayers shall lean upon the Angel of the covenant and so climb its starry rounds. Our God not only *hears* prayer but also *loves* to hear it. He does not forget the cry of the humble. True, He does not regard high looks and lofty words; He does not care for the pomp and pageantry of kings; He does not listen to the drums of war; He does not regard the triumph and pride of man. But wherever there is a heart enlarged with sorrow or a lip quivering with agony or a deep groan or a penitential sigh, the heart of Jehovah is open. He marks it down in the registry of His memory; He puts our prayers, like rose leaves, between the pages of His book of remembrance, and when at last the volume is opened, there will be a precious fragrance springing from it.

> Faith asks no signal from the skies,
> To show that prayers accepted rise.
> Our Priest is in His holy place,
> And answers from the throne of grace.

EVENING

THEIR PRAYER CAME TO HIS HOLY HABITATION IN HEAVEN. — 2 CHRONICLES 30:27

Prayer is the never-failing response of the Christian in any case, in every plight. When you cannot use your sword, you may take up the weapon of prayer. Your powder may be damp, your bowstring may be relaxed, but the weapon of prayer need never be out of order. Satan laughs at the javelin, but he trembles at prayer. Swords and spears need to be sharpened, but prayer never rusts; and when we think it most blunt, it cuts the best. Prayer is an open door that no one can shut. Devils may surround you on all sides, but the way upward is always open, and as long as that road is unobstructed, you will not fall into the enemy's hand. We can never be taken by siege or invasion as long as heavenly helps can come down to us and relieve us in the time of our necessities. Prayer is never out of season: In summer and in winter its merchandise is precious. Prayer gains audience with heaven in the dead of night, in the middle of business, in the heat of noonday, in the shades of evening. In every condition, whether poverty or sickness or obscurity or slander or doubt, your covenant God will welcome your prayer and answer it from His holy place. And prayer is never *futile*. True prayer is always true power. You may not always get what you ask, but you shall always have your real needs supplied. When God does not answer His children according to the letter, He does so according to the spirit. If you ask for cornmeal, will you be angry because He gives you fine flour? If you seek physical health, should you complain if instead He makes your sickness result in your spiritual health? Is it not better to have the cross sanctified than removed? This evening, my soul, do not forget to offer your petition and request, for the Lord is ready to grant your desires.

[1] Psalm 56:8

"FOR MY POWER IS MADE PERFECT IN WEAKNESS."
— 2 CORINTHIANS 12:9

A primary qualification for serving God with any amount of success, and for doing God's work well and triumphantly, is a sense of our own weakness. When God's warrior marches out to battle, strong in his own might, when he boasts, "I know that I will overcome—my own ability and my self-confidence will be enough for victory," defeat is staring him in the face. God will not enable the man who marches in his own strength. He who reckons on victory by such means has reckoned wrongly, for "not by might, nor by power, but by my Spirit, says the LORD of hosts."[1] Those who go out to fight, boasting of their ability, will return with their banners trailing in the dust and their armor stained with disgrace. Those who serve God must serve Him in His own way and in His strength, or He will never accept their service. Whatever a man does, unaided by divine strength, God can never own. The mere fruits of the earth He casts away; He will only reap corn the seed of which was sown from heaven, watered by grace, and ripened by the sun of divine love. God will empty out all that you have before He will put His own into you; He will first clean out your granaries before He will fill them with the finest of wheat. The river of God is full of water; but not one drop of it flows from earthly springs. God will have no strength used in His battles but the strength that He Himself imparts. Are you mourning over your own weakness? Take courage, for there must be a consciousness of weakness before the Lord will give you victory. Your emptiness is but the preparation for your being filled, and you are being humbled to prepare you for being lifted up.

When I am weak then am I strong,
Grace is my shield and Christ my song.

❧ EVENING ❧
IN YOUR LIGHT DO WE SEE LIGHT. — PSALM 36:9

No lips can tell the love of Christ to the heart until Jesus Himself shall speak within. Descriptions all fall flat and feeble unless the Holy Spirit fills them with life and power; until God makes Himself known to us, the soul does not see Him. If you would see the sun, would you gather together the common means of illumination and seek in that way to view its splendor? No; the wise man knows that the sun must reveal itself, and only by its own blaze can that mighty orb be seen. It is the same with Christ. "Blessed are you, Simon Bar-Jonah!" He said to Peter. "For flesh and blood has not revealed this to you."[2] Purify flesh and blood by any educational process you may select, elevate mental faculties to the highest degree of intellectual power, yet none of these can reveal Christ. The Spirit of God must come with power and overshadow the man with His wings, and then in that mystic holy of holies the Lord Jesus must display Himself to the sanctified eye, as He does not to the spiritually blind sons of men. Christ must be His own mirror. The great mass of this dim-sighted world can see nothing of the indescribable glories of Jesus. He stands before them without form or majesty, a root out of a dry ground, rejected by the vain and despised by the proud. Only where the Spirit has illumined the eye, quickened the heart with divine life, and educated the soul to a heavenly taste, only there is He understood. He is precious to the believer; He is the chief cornerstone, the Rock of your salvation, your all in all; but to others He is "a stone of stumbling, and a rock of offense."[3] Happy are those to whom our Lord reveals Himself, for His promise to such is that He will *make His home with them.* O Jesus, our Lord, our heart is open; come in, and never leave. Show Yourself to us now! Favor us with a glimpse of Your embracing loveliness.

[1] Zechariah 4:6   [2] Matthew 16:17   [3] Romans 9:33

NO WEAPON THAT IS FASHIONED AGAINST YOU SHALL SUCCEED.
— ISAIAH 54:17

The 5th of November is notable in English history for two great deliverances granted by God for us. On this day the plot of the Papists to destroy the Houses of Parliament was discovered, 1605.

> While for our princes they prepare
> In caverns deep a burning snare,
> He shot from heaven a piercing ray,
> And the dark treachery brought to day.

And secondly, today is the anniversary of the landing of King William III, at Torbay in 1688, which was crucial for the establishment of religious liberty.

This day should be celebrated not by the revelry of youth, but by the songs of saints. Our Puritan forefathers most devoutly made it a special time of thanksgiving. There is public record of the annual sermons preached by Matthew Henry on this day. Our convictions and our love of liberty should make us regard its anniversary with holy gratitude. Let our hearts and lips exclaim, "We have heard with our ears, our fathers have told us, what deeds you performed in their days, in the days of old."[1] You have made this nation the home of the Gospel; and when the enemy has risen against her, You have shielded her. Help us to offer repeated songs for repeated deliverances. Grant us more and more a hatred of sin, and hasten the day of your coming. Till then and ever, we believe the promise, "No weapon that is fashioned against you shall succeed." Should it not be laid upon the heart of every lover of the Gospel of Jesus on this day to plead for the overturning of false doctrines and the extension of divine truth? Would it not be well to search our own hearts and turn out any of the lumber of self-righteousness that may lie concealed within?

✦ EVENING ✦

GIVE THANKS TO HIM; BLESS HIS NAME! — PSALM 100:4

Our Lord would have all His people rich in high and happy thoughts concerning His blessed person. Jesus is not content that His brethren should think poorly of Him; it is His pleasure that His people should be delighted with His beauty. We are not to regard Him as a bare necessity, like bread and water, but as a luxurious delicacy, as a rare and ravishing delight. To this end He has revealed Himself as the "pearl of great price" in its peerless beauty, as the "bundle of myrrh"[2] in its refreshing fragrance, as the "rose of Sharon" in its lasting perfume, as the "lily" in its spotless purity.

As a help to high thoughts of Christ, remember the estimation that Christ has beyond the skies, where things are measured by the right standard. Think how God esteems the Only Begotten, His unspeakable gift to us. Consider what the angels think of Him, as they count it their highest honor to veil their faces at His feet. Consider what the blood-washed think of Him, as day without night they sing His well-deserved praises. High thoughts of Christ will enable us to act consistently in our relationship with Him. The more loftily we see Christ enthroned, and the more lowly we are when bowing before the foot of the throne, the more truly shall we be prepared to act our part toward Him. Our Lord Jesus desires us to think well of Him, that we may submit cheerfully to His authority. High thoughts of Him increase our love. Love and esteem go together. Therefore, believer, think much of your Master's excellencies. Study Him in His pre-incarnate glory, before He took upon Himself your nature! Think of the mighty love that drew Him from His throne to die upon the cross! Admire Him as He conquers all the powers of hell! See Him risen, crowned, glorified! Bow before Him as the Wonderful, the Counselor, the Mighty God, for only in this way will your love for Him be what it should.

[1] Psalm 44:1   [2] Song of Solomon 1:13, KJV

FOR I WILL POUR WATER ON THE THIRSTY LAND. — ISAIAH 44:3

When a believer has fallen into a low, sad state of feeling, he often tries to lift himself out of it by chastening himself with dark and gloomy fears. That is not the way to rise from the dust, but to continue in it. We may as well chain the eagle's wing to make it fly as doubt in order to increase our grace. It is not the law but the Gospel that saves the seeking soul at first; and it is not a legal bondage but gospel liberty that can restore the fainting believer afterwards. Slavish fear does not bring the backslider back to God, but the sweet wooings of love attract him to Jesus. This morning are you thirsting for the living God and unhappy because you cannot find him to the delight of your heart? Have you lost the joy of the Lord, and is your prayer, "Restore to me the joy of your salvation"?[1] Are you conscious also that you are unproductive, like the dry ground, that you are not bringing forth the fruit that God has a right to expect of you, that you are not as useful in the church or in the world as your heart desires to be? Then here is exactly the promise that you need: "For I will pour water on the thirsty land." You will receive the grace you so desperately need, and you will have it in abundance. Water refreshes the thirsty: You will be refreshed; your desires shall be satisfied. Water revives sleeping vegetable life: Your life will be restored by fresh grace. Water makes the bud develop and makes the fruit ripen; and so by God's grace you will be made fruitful in His ways. Whatever good quality there is in divine grace, you will enjoy it to the full. All the riches of divine grace you will receive in plenty; you shall be as it were drenched with it: And as sometimes the meadows become flooded by the bursting rivers, and the fields are turned into pools, so shall you be—the thirsty land shall be springs of water.

♋ EVENING ♊

THIS IS THE BLOOD OF THE COVENANT THAT GOD COMMANDED FOR YOU.
— HEBREWS 9:20

There is a strange power in the very name of blood, and the sight of it is always moving. A kind heart cannot bear to see a sparrow bleed and, unless familiarized by use, turns away with horror at the slaughter of a beast. As to the blood of men, it is a consecrated thing: It is murder to shed it in anger; it is a dreadful crime to squander it in war. Is this solemnity occasioned by the fact that the blood is the life, and the shedding of it the token of death? We think so. When we rise to contemplate the blood of the Son of God, our awe is greater yet, and we shudder as we think of the guilt of sin and the terrible penalty that the Sin-bearer endured. Blood, always precious, is priceless when it streams from Immanuel's side. The blood of Jesus seals the *covenant* of grace and makes it certain forever. Covenants of old were made by sacrifice, and the everlasting covenant was ratified in the same manner. What comfort that our salvation rests upon the sure foundation of divine commitments that cannot be dishonored! Salvation by the works of the law is a frail and broken vessel whose shipwreck is sure; but the covenant vessel fears no storms, for the blood ensures the whole. The blood of Jesus made His *covenant* valid. Wills are of no power unless the testators die. In this light the soldier's spear is a blessed aid to faith, since it proved our Lord to be really dead. There can be no doubt about that matter, and we may boldly appropriate the legacies that He has left for His people. Happy are they who see their title to heavenly blessings assured to them by a dying Savior. But does this blood not speak to us? Does it not bid us sanctify ourselves unto Him by whom we have been redeemed? Does it not call us to newness of life and incite us to entire consecration to the Lord? O that the power of the blood might be known and felt in us tonight!

[1] Psalm 51:12

BEHOLD, I HAVE ENGRAVED YOU ON THE PALMS OF MY HANDS.
— ISAIAH 49:16

No doubt part of the wonder that is concentrated in the word *"Behold"* is on account of the contrast with the unbelieving lament of the preceding sentence. Zion said, "The Lord has forsaken me; my Lord has forgotten me." How amazed the divine mind seems to be at this wicked unbelief! What can be more astounding than the unfounded doubts and fears of God's favored people? The Lord's loving word of rebuke should make us blush. He cries, "How can I have forgotten you, when I have engraved you on the palms of My hands? How dare you doubt My constant remembrance when the memorial is carved upon My own flesh?" O unbelief, what a strange marvel you are! We do not know what to wonder at most—the faithfulness of God or the unbelief of His people. He keeps His promise a thousand times, and yet the next trial makes us doubt Him. He never fails; He is never a dry well; He is never as a setting sun, a passing meteor, or a melting vapor; and yet we are as continually troubled with anxieties, molested with suspicions, and disturbed with fears as if our God were a mirage of the desert. "Behold" is *a word intended to stir our admiration*. Here, indeed, we have a theme for marveling. Heaven and earth may well be astonished that rebels should obtain such a closeness to the heart of infinite love as to be written on the palms of His hands. "I have engraved *you*." It does not say, "your name." The name is there, but that is not all: "I have engraved *you*." Consider the depth of this! "I have engraved your person, your image, your circumstances, your sins, your temptations, your weaknesses, your wants, your works; I have engraved you, everything about you, all that concerns you; I have put all of this together here." Will you ever say again that your God has forsaken you when He has engraved you on His own palms?

❧ E V E N I N G ❧
AND YOU WILL BE MY WITNESSES. — ACTS 1:8

In order to learn how to discharge your duty as a witness for Christ, look at His example. He is always witnessing—by the well of Samaria or in the temple of Jerusalem; by the sea of Galilee or on the mountainside. He is witnessing day and night; His mighty prayers are as vocal to God as His daily services. He witnesses under all circumstances. Scribes and Pharisees cannot shut His mouth; even before Pilate He witnesses a good confession. He witnesses so clearly and distinctly that there is no mistake in understanding Him. Christian, make your life a clear testimony. Be like the stream in which you can see every stone at the bottom—not like a muddy creek where you can only see the surface, but clear and transparent, so that your heart's love for God and man may be visible to all. You need not say, "I am true"; be true. Do not boast of integrity, but be upright. Then your testimony will be such that men cannot help seeing it. Never, on account of fear of feeble man, restrain your witness. Your lips have been warmed with a coal from off the altar; let them speak as heaven-touched lips should do. "In the morning sow your seed, and at evening withhold not your hand."[1] Do not watch the clouds or consult the wind; in season and out of season witness for the Savior, and if it transpires that for Christ's sake and the Gospel's you must endure suffering in any shape, do not shrink, but rejoice in the honor conferred upon you, that you are counted worthy to suffer with your Lord. And find joy also in this—that your sufferings, your losses, and persecutions shall make you a platform from which with more vigor and with greater power you will witness for Christ Jesus. Study your great example, and be filled with His Spirit. Remember that you need much teaching, much upholding, much grace, and much humility if your witnessing is to be to your Master's glory.

[1] Ecclesiastes 11:6

NOVEMBER 8   ❧ MORNING ☙

THEREFORE, AS YOU RECEIVED CHRIST JESUS THE LORD . . .
— COLOSSIANS 2:6

The life of faith is represented as *receiving—an act that implies the very opposite of any-thing like merit*. It is simply the acceptance of a gift. As the earth drinks in the rain, as the sea receives the streams, as night accepts light from the stars, so we, giving nothing, partake freely of the grace of God. The believers are not by nature wells or streams; they are just cisterns into which the living water flows; they are empty vessels into which God pours His salvation. The idea of receiving implies *a sense of realization*, making the matter a *reality*. One cannot very well receive a shadow; we receive that which is substantial: So is it in the life of faith—Christ becomes real to us. Until we come to faith, Jesus is just a name to us—a person who lived a long time ago, so long ago that His life is only a history to us now! By an act of faith Jesus becomes a real person in the consciousness of our heart. But receiving also means *grasping or getting possession of*. The thing that I receive becomes my own: I appropriate to myself that which is given. When I receive Jesus, He becomes my Savior, so much so that neither life nor death will be able to rob me of Him. All this is to receive Christ—to take Him as God's free gift, to realize Him in my heart, and to appropriate Him as mine.

Salvation may be described as the blind receiving sight, the deaf receiving hearing, the dead receiving life; but we have not only received these blessings—we have received *Christ Jesus Himself*. It is true that He gave us life from the dead. He gave us pardon from sin; He gave us imputed righteousness. These are all precious things, but we are not content with them; we have received *Christ Himself*. The Son of God has been poured into us, and we have received Him and appropriated Him. What a heart-full Jesus must be, for heaven itself cannot contain Him!

❧ EVENING ☙

THE TEACHER SAYS, WHERE IS MY GUEST ROOM, WHERE I MAY EAT
THE PASSOVER WITH MY DISCIPLES? — MARK 14:14

Jerusalem at the time of the Passover was one great inn; each householder had invited his own friends, but no one had invited the Savior, and He had no dwelling of His own. It was by His own supernatural power that He found Himself an upper room in which to keep the feast. This is still the case today—Jesus is not received among the sons of men except when by His supernatural power and grace He makes the heart anew. All doors are open enough to the prince of darkness, but Jesus must clear a way for Himself or lodge in the streets. On account of the mysterious power exerted by our Lord, the householder raised no question but at once cheerfully and joyfully opened his guest room. Who he was and what he was we do not know, but he willingly accepted the honor that the Redeemer proposed to confer upon him. In similar fashion we can still discover who are the Lord's chosen and who are not, for when the Gospel comes to some, they fight against it and will not have it; but where men receive it, welcoming it, this is a sure indication that there is a secret work going on in the soul and that God has appointed them to eternal life. Are you willing, dear reader, to receive Christ? Then there is no difficulty in the way. Christ will be your guest; His own power is working with you, making you willing. What an honor to entertain the Son of God! The heaven of heavens cannot contain Him, and yet He condescends to find a house within our hearts! We are not worthy that He should come under our roof, but what an unutterable privilege when He condescends to enter! For then He makes a feast and causes us to feast with Him upon His royal provision; we sit at a banquet where the food is immortal and provides immortality to those who feed on it. Blessed among the sons of Adam is he who entertains the angels' Lord.

SO WALK IN HIM. — COLOSSIANS 2:6

If we have received Christ Himself in our inmost hearts, our new life will display its intimate acquaintance with Him by *a walk of faith in Him*. Walking implies *action*. Our Christian life is not to be confined to our closet; our belief must be revealed in our practice. If a man walks in Christ, then he must act as Christ would act; since Christ is in him—his hope, his love, his joy, his life—he is the reflection of the image of Jesus; and men will say of that man, "He is like his Master; he lives like Jesus Christ." Walking signifies *progress*. "So walk in him." Proceed from grace to grace; run forward until you reach the ultimate degree of knowledge that a man can attain concerning Christ. Walking implies *continuance*. There must be a continual abiding in Christ. Many Christians think that in the morning and evening they ought to come into the company of Jesus, but regard the rest of the day as their own: But this is poor living; we should always be with Him, treading in His steps and doing His will. Walking also implies *habit*. When we speak of a man's walk and conversation, we mean his habits, the constant theme of his life. Now, if we sometimes enjoy Christ and then forget Him, sometimes call Him ours and then lose our hold, that is not a habit; we do not *walk* in Him. We must keep to Him, cling to Him, never let Him go, but live and have our being in Him. "Therefore, as you received Christ Jesus the Lord, so walk in him"; persevere in the same way in which you began, and, just as at the beginning Christ Jesus was the trust of your faith, the source of your life, the principle of your action, and the joy of your spirit, so let Him be the same until life's end, the same when you walk through the valley of the shadow of death and enter into the joy and the rest that remain for the people of God. O Holy Spirit, enable us to obey this heavenly precept.

❧ E V E N I N G ❧

HIS PLACE OF DEFENSE WILL BE THE FORTRESS OF ROCKS; HIS BREAD WILL BE GIVEN HIM; HIS WATER WILL BE SURE. — ISAIAH 33:16

Christian, do you doubt whether God will fulfill His promise? Will the fortresses of rock be swept away by a storm? Will the storehouses of heaven fail? Do you think that your heavenly Father, even though He knows that you need food and clothes, will forget you? When not a sparrow falls to the ground without your Father's knowledge, and the very hairs of your head are all numbered, will you mistrust and doubt Him? Perhaps your affliction will continue upon you until you dare to trust God, and then it will end. There have been many who have been tried and troubled until at last they have been driven in sheer desperation to exercise faith in God, and the moment of their faith has been the instant of their deliverance; they have seen whether God would keep His promise or not. So I urge you, doubt Him no longer! Do not please Satan, and do not trouble yourself by indulging any more those hard thoughts of God. Do not imagine that it is a small matter to doubt Jehovah. Remember, it is a *sin*; and not a little sin either, but in the highest degree criminal. The angels never doubted Him, nor the devils either: We alone, out of all the beings whom God has fashioned, dishonor Him by unbelief and tarnish His honor by mistrust. Shame on us for this! Our God does not deserve to be so poorly treated; in our past life we have proved Him to be true and faithful to His word, and with so many instances of His love and of His kindness as we have received and are daily receiving at His hands, it is base and inexcusable that we allow a doubt to lodge within our heart. From now on let us resolve to wage constant war against doubts of our God—enemies to our peace and to His honor—and with an unstaggering faith believe that what He has promised He will also perform. "I believe; help my unbelief!"[1]

[1] Mark 9:24

THE ETERNAL GOD IS YOUR DWELLING PLACE. — DEUTERONOMY 33:27

"Dwelling place" may be translated "refuge" or "abiding-place" and provides the thought that *God is our abode, our home.* There is a fullness and sweetness in the metaphor, for our home is dear to our hearts, although it may be the humblest cottage or the tiniest loft; and dearer still is our blessed God, in whom we live and move and have our being. It is at home that we *feel safe*: We shut the world out and dwell in quiet security. So when we are with our God we fear no evil. He is our shelter and retreat, our abiding refuge. At home *we take our rest*; it is there we find repose after the fatigue and toil of the day. And so our hearts find rest in God when, wearied with life's conflict, we turn to Him, and our soul dwells secure. At home also we *relax*; we are not afraid of being misunderstood, nor of our words being misconstrued. So when we are with God we can commune freely with Him, laying open all our hidden desires; for if the Lord gives favor to the humble, then they may share their secrets with Him, confident in His love. Home, too, is the place of our *truest and purest happiness*: And it is in God that our hearts find their deepest delight. We have joy in Him that far outweighs all other joy. *It is also for home that we work and labor.* The thought of it gives strength to bear the daily burden, and quickens the hands to perform the task; and in this sense we may also say that God is our home. Love for Him strengthens us. We think of Him in the person of His dear Son, and a glimpse of the suffering face of the Redeemer constrains us to work in His cause. We feel that we must work, for there are many still to be saved, and we desire to gladden our Father's heart by bringing home His wandering sons; we would fill with holy laughter the sacred family among whom we dwell. Happy then are those who have the God of Jacob for their refuge!

❧ EVENING ❧

IT IS ENOUGH FOR THE DISCIPLE TO BE LIKE HIS TEACHER.
— MATTHEW 10:25

No one will dispute this statement, for it would not be proper for the pupil to be exalted above his Teacher. When our Lord was on earth, what was the treatment He received? Were His claims acknowledged, His instructions followed, His perfections worshiped by those whom He came to bless? No. "He was despised and rejected by men."[1] His place was outside the city: Cross-bearing was His occupation. Did the world provide Him with comfort and rest? "Foxes have holes, and birds of the air have nests, but the Son of man has nowhere to lay His head."[2] This inhospitable country provided Him no shelter: It cast Him out and crucified Him. If you are a follower of Jesus and maintain a consistent, Christlike walk and behavior, you must expect to experience persecution and rejection also. Your Christian testimony will be scrutinized and criticized. People will treat it as they treated the Savior—they will despise it. Do not imagine that pagans will admire you or that the more holy and the more Christlike you are, the more peaceably people will act toward you. If they did not prize the polished gem, do you think that they will esteem the rough cut jewel? If they have referred to Jesus as Satan, how much more will they denigrate the teacher's disciples? If we were more like Christ, we would be more hated by His enemies. It is a sad dishonor to a child of God to be the world's favorite. It is a very bad omen to hear a wicked world clap its hands and shout "Well done" to the Christian man. He may begin to look to his character and wonder whether he has been doing wrong when the unrighteous give him their approval. Let us be true to our Master and have no friendship with a blind and base world that scorns and rejects Him. Far be it from us to seek a crown of honor where our Lord found only a crown of thorns.

[1] Isaiah 53:3   [2] Matthew 8:20

UNDERNEATH ARE THE EVERLASTING ARMS. — DEUTERONOMY 33:27

God—the eternal God—is Himself our support at all times, and especially when we are sinking in deep trouble. There are seasons when the Christian *sinks very low in humiliation*. Under a deep sense of his great sinfulness, he is humbled before God until he hardly knows how to pray, because he appears, in his own sight, so worthless. Well, child of God, remember that when you are at your worst and lowest, even then "underneath" you "are the everlasting arms." Sin may drag you ever so low, but Christ's great atonement is still under all. You may have descended into the depths, but you cannot have fallen so low as the uttermost; and He saves "to the uttermost."[1] Again, the Christian sometimes sinks very deeply in *sore trial from without*. Every earthly prop is cut away. What then? Still underneath him are "the everlasting arms." He cannot fall so deep in distress and affliction but what the covenant grace of an ever-faithful God will still encircle him. The Christian may be sinking under *trouble from within through fierce conflict*; but even then he cannot be brought so low as to be beyond the reach of the "everlasting arms"—they are underneath him; and, while he is sustained, all Satan's efforts to harm him achieve nothing.

This assurance of support is a comfort to any *weary but sincere worker* in the service of God. It implies a promise of strength for each day, grace for each need, and power for each duty. And, finally, *when death comes*, the promise will still hold good. When we stand in the middle of the Jordan, we will be able to say with David, "I will fear no evil, for you are with me."[2] We will descend into the grave, but we shall go no lower, for the eternal arms prevent our further fall. All through life, and at its close, we shall be upheld by the "everlasting arms"—arms that neither flag nor lose their strength, for "the everlasting God . . . does not faint or grow weary."[3]

❧   EVENING   ❧
HE CHOSE OUR HERITAGE FOR US. — PSALM 47:4

Believer, if your inheritance is meager, you should be satisfied with your earthly portion; for you may rest assured that it is best *for you*. Unerring wisdom ordained your lot and selected for you the safest and best condition. When a ship of large tonnage is to be brought up a river that has a large sandbank, if someone should ask, "Why does the captain steer through the deep part of the channel and deviate so much from a straight line?" his answer would be, "Because I could not get my ship into harbor at all if I did not keep to the deep channel." In the same way you would run aground and suffer shipwreck if your divine Captain did not steer you into the depths of affliction where waves of trouble follow each other in quick succession. Some plants die if they have too much sunshine. It may be that you are planted where you get only a little, but you are put there by the loving Farmer because only in that situation will you produce fruit unto perfection. Remember this: If any other condition had been better for you than the one in which you are, divine love would have put you there. You are placed by God in the most suitable circumstances, and if you could choose your lot, you would soon cry, "Lord, choose my heritage for me, for by my self-will I am pierced through with many sorrows." Be content with the things you have, since the Lord has ordered all things for your good. Take up your own daily cross; it is the burden best suited for your shoulder and will prove most effective to make you perfect in every good word and work to the glory of God. Busy self and proud impatience must be put down; it is not for them to choose, but for the Lord of Love!

> *Trials must and will befall—*
> *But with humble faith to see*
> *Love inscribed upon them all,*
> *This is happiness to me.*

[1] Hebrews 7:25   [2] Psalm 23:4   [3] Isaiah 40:28

THE TESTED GENUINENESS OF YOUR FAITH. — 1 PETER 1:7

Untested faith may be true faith, but it is sure to be small faith, and it is likely to remain little as long as it is without trials. Faith never prospers so well as when all things are against her: Tempests are her trainers, and bolts of lightning are her illuminators. When a calm reigns on the sea, spread the sails as you will, the ship does not move to its harbor; for on a slumbering ocean the keel sleeps too. Let the winds rush and howl, and let the waters lift themselves, though the vessel may rock and her deck may be washed with waves and her mast may creak under the pressure of the full and swelling sail, it is then that she makes headway toward her desired haven. No flowers are as lovely a blue as those that grow at the foot of the frozen glacier; no stars gleam as brightly as those that glisten in the midnight sky; no water tastes as sweet as that which springs up in the desert sand; and no faith is so precious as that which lives and triumphs in adversity. Tested faith brings experience. You could not have believed your own weakness if you had not been compelled to pass through the rivers; and you would never have known God's strength if you had not been supported in the flood. Faith increases in quality, assurance, and intensity the more it is exercised with tribulation. Faith is precious, and its trial is precious too.

Do not let this, however, discourage those who are young in faith. You will have trials enough without seeking them: The full portion will be measured out to you in due course. Meanwhile, if you cannot yet claim the result of long experience, thank God for what grace you have; praise Him for that degree of holy confidence you have now attained: Walk according to that rule, and you will still have more and more of the blessing of God, until your faith will remove mountains and conquer impossibilities.

✑ EVENING ✑

IN THESE DAYS HE WENT OUT TO THE MOUNTAIN TO PRAY, AND
ALL NIGHT HE CONTINUED IN PRAYER TO GOD. — LUKE 6:12

If ever a man might have lived without prayer, it was our spotless, perfect Lord, and yet no one ever prayed as much as He! His love for His Father was such that He loved to be in communion with Him. His love for His people was such that He desired to be regularly interceding for them. *The fact* that Jesus placed such importance on prayer is a lesson for us— He has given us an example that we may follow in His steps. *The time* He chose was admirable—it was the hour of silence when the crowd would not disturb Him, the time of inaction when everyone else had stopped work, and the season when sleep made men forget their difficulties and stop applying to Him for relief. While others found rest in sleep, He refreshed Himself with prayer. *The place* was also well selected. He was alone where none would intrude, where none could observe: And so He was free from Pharisaic ostentation and vulgar interruption. Those dark and silent hills provided a suitable prayer chapel for the Son of God. Heaven and earth in midnight stillness heard the groans and sighs of the mysterious Being in whom both worlds were blended. *The continuance* of His pleadings is remarkable: The passing hours were not too long; the cold wind did not chill His devotions; the grim darkness did not cloud His faith or loneliness prevent His persistence. We fail to watch with Him for one hour, but He never fails to watch for us night and day. *The occasion* for this prayer is notable; it was after His enemies had been enraged. Prayer was His refuge and solace; it was before He dispatched the twelve apostles. Prayer was the gate of His enterprise, the herald of His new work. Should we not learn from Jesus to resort to special prayer when we are under peculiar trial or considering new ventures for the Master's glory? Lord Jesus, teach us to pray.

THE BRANCH CANNOT BEAR FRUIT BY ITSELF. — JOHN 15:4

How did you begin to bear fruit? It was when you came to Jesus and cast yourself on His great atonement and rested on His finished righteousness. What fruit you had then! Do you remember those early days? Then the vine flourished, the tender grape appeared, the pomegranates budded, and the beds of spices produced their fragrance. Have you declined since then? If you have, we charge you to remember that time of love, and repent, and do your first works. *Commit yourself fully to the activities that you have proved to draw you closest to Christ*, because it is from Him that all your fruits proceed. Any holy activity that will bring you to Him will help you bear fruit. The sun is, no doubt, a great worker in fruit-creating among the trees of the orchard: And Jesus is even more so among the trees of His garden of grace. When have you been the most fruitless? Has it not been when you have lived farthest from the Lord Jesus Christ, when you have slackened in prayer, when you have departed from the simplicity of your faith, when your graces have engrossed your attention instead of your Lord, when you have said, "My mountain stands firm, I will never be moved" and you have forgotten where your strength lies—has not it been *then* that your fruit has ceased? Some of us have been taught that we have nothing apart from Christ by terrible humiliation of heart before the Lord; and when we have seen the utter emptiness and death of all earthly power, we have cried in anguish, "From Him all my fruit must be found, for no fruit can ever come from me." We are taught by past experience that the more simply we depend upon the grace of God in Christ and wait upon the Holy Spirit, the more we will bring forth fruit unto God. We must trust Jesus for fruit as well as for life.

AND HE TOLD THEM A PARABLE TO THE EFFECT THAT THEY
OUGHT ALWAYS TO PRAY. — LUKE 18:1

Jesus has sent His Church into the world on the same errand upon which He Himself came, and this mission includes intercession. What if I say that the Church is the world's priest? Creation is dumb, but the Church finds a mouth for it. It is the Church's high privilege to pray with acceptance. The door of grace is always open for her petitions, and they never return empty-handed. The curtain was torn *for her*; the blood was sprinkled upon the altar *for her*; God constantly invites her to bring her requests. Will she refuse the privilege that angels might envy? Is she not the bride of Christ? Can she not approach her King at any hour? Will she allow the precious privilege to be unused? The Church always needs to pray. There are always some among her who are declining or falling into open sin. There are lambs to be prayed for, that they may be carried in Christ's bosom; the strong, lest they grow presumptuous; and the weak, lest they become despairing. If we kept up prayer-meetings twenty-four hours a day all the days in the year, we might never be without a special subject for supplication. Is there ever a time when no one is sick or poor or afflicted or wavering? Is there ever a time when we do not seek the conversion of relatives, the reclaiming of backsliders, or the salvation of the lost? With congregations constantly gathering, with ministers always preaching, with millions of sinners lying dead in trespasses and sins—in a country over which the darkness of religious formalism is certainly descending—in a world full of idols, cruelties, devils—if the Church does not pray, how will she excuse her neglect of the commission of her loving Lord? Let the Church be constant in supplication; let every private believer give himself to the ministry of prayer.

AND I WILL CUT OFF FROM THIS PLACE . . . THOSE WHO BOW DOWN
AND SWEAR TO THE LORD AND YET SWEAR BY MILCOM. — ZEPHANIAH 1:4-5

These people thought they were safe because they were with both parties: they went with the followers of Jehovah and bowed at the same time to Milcom. But duplicity is abominable with God, and His soul hates hypocrisy. The idolater who distinctly gives himself to his false god has one sin less than he who brings his polluted and detestable sacrifice into the temple of the Lord, while his heart is with the world and its sins. To hold with the hare and run with the hounds is a coward's policy. In the common matters of daily life, a double-minded man is despised, but in religion he is loathsome to the last degree. The penalty pronounced in the verse before us is terrible, but it is well-deserved; for how should divine justice spare the sinner who knows the right, approves it, and professes to follow it, and all the while loves the evil and gives it dominion in his heart?

My soul, search yourself this morning and see whether you are guilty of double-dealing. You profess to be a follower of Jesus—do you truly love Him? Is your heart right with God? Are you a member of the family of old Father Honest, or are you a relative of Mr. Shady? A name for being alive is of little value if I am actually dead in trespasses and sins. To have one foot on the land of truth and another on the sea of falsehood will involve a terrible fall and a total ruin. Christ will be all or nothing. God fills the whole universe, and as a result there is no room for another god. If, then, He reigns in my heart, there will be no space for another reigning power. Do I rest alone on Jesus crucified and live alone for Him? Is it my desire to do so? Is my heart set on doing so? If yes, then blessed be the mighty grace that has led me to salvation; and if no, then, Lord, pardon my sad offense, and unite my heart to fear Your name.

✒ EVENING ✒

LABAN SAID, "IT IS NOT SO DONE IN OUR COUNTRY,
TO GIVE THE YOUNGER BEFORE THE FIRSTBORN." — GENESIS 29:26

We do not excuse Laban for his dishonesty, but we are wrong not to learn from the custom that he quoted as his excuse. There are some things that must be taken in order, and if we would win the second we must secure the first. The second may be the more lovely in our eyes, but the rule of the heavenly country must stand, and the elder must be married first. For instance, many men desire the beautiful and well-favored Rachel of joy and peace in believing, but they must first be married to the tender-eyed Leah of repentance. Everyone falls in love with happiness, and many would cheerfully work for fourteen years to enjoy it; but according to the rule of the Lord's kingdom, the Leah of real holiness must be loved in our soul before the Rachel of true happiness can be attained. Heaven stands not first but second, and only by persevering to the end can we win a portion in it. The cross must be carried before the crown can be worn. We must follow our Lord in His humiliation or we will never rest with Him in glory.

My soul, what do you say—are you so vain as to hope to be an exception to the heavenly rule? Do you hope for reward without work, or honor without endeavor? Dismiss the idle expectation, and be content with the despised things for the sake of the sweet love of Jesus, which will more than repay you. In such a spirit, working and suffering, you will find afflictions grow sweet and hard things easy. Like Jacob, your years of service will seem like only a few days on account of the love you have for Jesus; and when the dear hour of the wedding feast shall come, all your toils will be as though they never happened—an hour with Jesus will make up for years of pain and toil.

Jesus, to win Thyself so fair,
Thy cross I will with gladness bear:
Since so the rules of heaven ordain,
The first I'll wed the next to gain.

BUT THE LORD'S PORTION IS HIS PEOPLE. — DEUTERONOMY 32:9

How are they His? By His own sovereign *choice*. He chose them and set His love upon them. He did this completely apart from any goodness in them at the time or any goodness that He foresaw in them. He had mercy on whom He would have mercy and ordained a chosen company to eternal life; in this way, therefore, they are His by His unconstrained election.

They are not only His by choice, but by *purchase*. He has bought and paid for them completely, and so there can be no dispute about His title. Not with corruptible things like silver and gold, but with the precious blood of the Lord Jesus Christ, the Lord's portion has been fully redeemed. There is no mortgage on His estate; no lawsuits can be raised by opposing claimants. The price was paid in open court, and the Church is the Lord's estate forever. See the blood-mark upon all the chosen, invisible to the human eye but known to Christ, for "the Lord knows those who are his."[1] He forgets none of those whom He has redeemed from among men; He counts the sheep for whom He laid down His life and remembers carefully the Church for which He gave Himself.

They are also His by *conquest*. What a battle He had in us before we would be won! How long He laid siege to our hearts! How often He sent us terms of surrender, but we barred our gates and built our walls against Him. Do we not remember that glorious hour when He carried our hearts by storm, when He placed His cross against the wall and scaled our ramparts, planting on our strongholds the blood-red flag of His omnipotent mercy? Yes, we are indeed the conquered captives of His omnipotent love. As those chosen, who have been purchased and subdued, we know that the rights of our divine possessor are inalienable: We rejoice that we can never be our own; and we desire, day by day, to do *His* will and to declare *His* glory.

❧ EVENING ❧

SUMMON YOUR POWER, O GOD, THE POWER, O GOD,
BY WHICH YOU HAVE WORKED FOR US. — PSALM 68:28

It is wise, as well as necessary, to beseech God continually to strengthen what He has worked in us. Failure to do so finds many Christians blaming themselves for those trials and afflictions of spirit that arise from unbelief. It is true that Satan seeks to flood the fair garden of the heart and make it a scene of desolation, but it is also true that many Christians leave open the floodgates themselves and let in the dreadful deluge as a result of carelessness and lack of prayer to their strong Helper. We often forget that the Author of our faith must be the Preserver of it also. The lamp that was burning in the temple was never allowed to go out, but it had to be replenished every day with fresh oil; in the same way, our faith can only live by being sustained with the oil of grace, and we can only obtain this from God Himself. We will fail if we do not secure the needed sustenance for our lamps. He who built the world upholds it, or it would fall in one tremendous crash. He who made us Christians must maintain us by His Spirit, or our ruin will be speedy and final. So let us, then, evening by evening, go to our Lord for the grace and strength we need. We have a strong argument to plead, for it is *His own work of grace* that we ask Him to strengthen—"*the power . . . by which you have worked for us.*" Do you think He will fail to protect and provide that? Let your faith simply take hold of His strength, and all the powers of darkness, led by the master fiend of hell, cannot cast a cloud or shadow over your joy and peace. Why faint when you can be strong? Why suffer defeat when you may conquer? Take your wavering faith and faltering graces to Him who can revive and replenish them, and earnestly pray, "Summon your power, O God . . . by which you have worked for us."

[1] 2 Timothy 2:19

"THE LORD IS MY PORTION," SAYS MY SOUL. — LAMENTATIONS 3:24

It does not say, "The Lord is *partly* my portion," nor "The Lord is *in* my portion"; but He Himself makes up the sum total of my soul's inheritance. Within the circumference of that circle lies all that we possess or desire. The *Lord* is my portion. Not His grace merely, nor His love, nor His covenant, but Jehovah Himself. He has chosen us for His portion, and we have chosen Him for ours. It is true that the Lord must first choose our inheritance for us, or else we will never choose it for ourselves; but if we are really called according to the purpose of electing love, we can sing—

> *Lov'd of my God for Him again*
> *With love intense I burn;*
> *Chosen of Him ere time began,*
> *I choose Him in return.*

The Lord is our *all-sufficient* portion. God fills Himself; and if God is all-sufficient in Himself, He must be all-sufficient for us. It is not easy to satisfy man's desires. When he dreams that he is satisfied, instantly he wakes to the perception that there is still something more, and his longings remain unfulfilled. But for the believer all that we can wish for is to be found in our divine portion, so that we ask, "Whom have I in heaven but you? And there is nothing on earth that I desire besides you."[1] We can then delight ourselves in the Lord who allows us to drink of the river of His pleasures. Our faith stretches her wings and soars like an eagle into the heaven of divine love, her proper dwelling-place. "The lines have fallen for me in pleasant places; indeed, I have a beautiful inheritance."[2] Let us rejoice in the Lord always; let us show the world that we are a happy and a blessed people and cause them to exclaim, "Let us go with you, for we have heard that God is with you."

❧ EVENING ☙
YOUR EYES WILL BEHOLD THE KING IN HIS BEAUTY. — ISAIAH 33:17

The more you know about Christ, the less will you be satisfied with superficial views of Him; and the more deeply you study His transactions in the eternal covenant, His engagements on your behalf as the eternal Security, and the fullness of His grace that shines in all His offices, the more truly will you see the King in His beauty. Learn to look at Him this way. Long increasingly to see Jesus. *Meditation and contemplation* are often like windows of gold and gates of silver through which we behold the Redeemer. Meditation puts the telescope to the eye and enables us to see Jesus in a better fashion than we could have seen Him if we had lived in the days of His earthly sojourn. Our conversation ought to be more in heaven, and we should be more taken up with the person, the work, the beauty of our incarnate Lord. More meditation, and the beauty of the King would flash upon us with more splendor. Beloved, it is very probable that we will have such a sight of our glorious King as we never had before *when we come to die.* Many saints in dying have looked up from amidst the stormy waters and have seen Jesus walking on the waves of the sea and heard Him say, "It is I—do not be afraid." Yes, when the building begins to shake, and the mortar falls away, we will see Christ through the studs, and between the rafters the sunlight of heaven will come streaming in. But if we want to see the King face to face in all His beauty, *we must go to heaven* for the sight or the King must come here in person. If only He would come on the wings of the wind! He is our Husband, and we are widowed by His absence; He is our fair and faithful Brother, and we are lonely without Him. Thick veils and clouds hang between our souls and their true life: When will the day break and the shadows run away? Let the long-expected day begin!

[1] Psalm 73:25 [2] Psalm 16:6

To him be glory forever." This should be the *single* desire of the Christian. All other wishes must be subservient and serve as tributaries to this. The Christian may wish for prosperity in his business, but only inasmuch as it may help him to promote this—"To him be glory forever." He may desire to attain more gifts and more graces, but it should only be that he may declare, "To him be glory forever." You are not acting as you ought to do when you are moved by any other motive than a single focus on the Lord's glory. As a Christian, you are "from him and through him," and so you must live "to him." Do not let anything set your heart beating so fast as love for Him. Let this ambition fire your soul; may this be the foundation of every enterprise upon which you enter, and your sustaining motive whenever your zeal would grow cold. Make God your only object. Depend upon it—where self begins, sorrow begins; but if God is my supreme delight and only object,

> To me 'tis equal whether love ordain
> My life or death—appoint me ease or pain.

Let your desire for God's glory be a *growing* desire. You blessed Him in your youth; do not be content with such praises as you gave Him then. Has God prospered you in business? Give Him more as He has given you more. Has God given you experience? Praise Him by stronger faith than you exercised at the beginning. Does your knowledge grow? Then sing more sweetly. Do you enjoy happier times than you once had? Have you been restored from sickness, and has your sorrow been turned into peace and joy? Then give Him more music; put more coals and more sweet spices into the censer of your praise. Practically in your life give Him honor, offering the "Amen" of this doxology to your great and gracious Lord by your own individual service and increasing holiness.

❧ EVENING ☙

Oppressors may enforce their will on poor and needy men just as easily as they can split logs of wood, but they better be careful, for it is a dangerous business, and a splinter from a tree has often killed the woodsman. Jesus is persecuted in every injured saint, and He is strong to avenge His loved ones. Success in treading down the poor and needy is a thing to be trembled at: If the persecutors do not face immediate danger, they will face great danger in the end.

To split logs is a common everyday business, and yet it has its dangers. So then, reader, there are dangers connected with your calling and daily life that it will be good for you to be aware of. We do not refer to hazards by flood and field or by disease and sudden death, but to perils of a spiritual sort. Your occupation may be as humble as log splitting, and yet the devil can tempt you in it. You may be a domestic servant, a farm laborer, or a mechanic, and you may be greatly shielded from temptations to the bigger vices, and yet some secret sin may undo you. Those who live at home and do not mingle with the rough world may still be endangered by their very seclusion. The one who thinks himself safe is safe nowhere! Pride may enter a poor man's heart; greed may reign in a cottager's bosom; uncleanness may venture into the quietest home; and anger and envy and malice may insert themselves into the most rural dwelling. Even in speaking a few words to a doorman we may sin; a small purchase at a shop may be the first link in a chain of temptations; the mere looking out of a window may be the beginning of evil. Lord, how exposed we are! How shall we be saved! To keep ourselves is a work too hard for us: Only You Yourself are able to preserve us in such an evil world. Spread Your protection over us, and we, like little chickens, will cower down beneath You and feel ourselves safe!

A SPRING LOCKED, A FOUNTAIN SEALED. — SONG OF SOLOMON 4:12

In this metaphor, which has reference to the inner life of a believer, we have very plainly the idea of *secrecy*. It is "a spring *locked*." Just as there were springs in the East over which an edifice was built, so that no one could reach them except those who knew the secret entrance, so is the heart of a believer when it is renewed by grace: There is a mysterious life within that no human skill can touch. It is a secret that no one else knows, which the individual who is the possessor of it cannot tell his neighbor. The text includes not only secrecy but *separation*. It is not the common spring, of which every passer-by may drink; it is one kept and preserved from all others; it is a fountain bearing a particular mark—a king's royal seal, so that all can perceive that it is not a common fountain, but a fountain owned by a proprietor and placed specially by itself alone. So is it with the spiritual life. The chosen of God were separated in the eternal decree; they were separated by God in the day of redemption; and they are separated by the possession of a life that others do not have. And it is impossible for them to feel at home with the world or to delight in its pleasures. There is also the idea of *sacredness*. The locked spring is preserved for the use of some special person: And such is the Christian's heart. It is a spring kept for Jesus. Every Christian should feel that he has God's seal upon him—and he should be able to say with Paul, "From now on let no one cause me trouble, for I bear on my body the marks of Jesus."[1] Another idea is prominent—it is that of *security*. How sure and safe is the inner life of the believer! If all the powers of earth and hell could combine against it, that immortal principle must still exist, for He who gave it pledged His life for its preservation. And who or what can harm you when God is your protector?

❧ EVENING ❧
YOU ARE FROM EVERLASTING. — PSALM 93:2

Christ is *everlasting*. Of Him we may sing with David, "Your throne, O God, is forever and ever."[2] Rejoice, believer, in Jesus Christ, the same yesterday, today, and forever. Jesus always *was*. The Baby born in Bethlehem was united to the Word, which was in the beginning, by whom all things were made. The title by which Christ revealed Himself to John in Patmos was, "[Him] who is and who was and who is to come."[3] If He was not God from everlasting, we could not love Him so devoutly; we could not feel that He had any share in the eternal love that is the fountain of all covenant blessings. But since He was from all eternity with the Father, we trace the stream of divine love to Himself equally with His Father and the blessed Spirit. As our Lord always *was*, so also He *is* forevermore. Jesus is not dead; "he always lives to make intercession for them."[4] Resort to Him in all your times of need, for He is always waiting to bless you. Furthermore, Jesus our Lord ever *shall be*. If God should spare your life to fulfill your full course of threescore years and ten, you will find that His cleansing fountain is still opened, and His precious blood has not lost its power; you will find that the Priest who filled the healing fount with His own blood lives to purge you from all iniquity. When only your last battle remains to be fought, you will find that the hand of your conquering Captain has not grown feeble—the living Savior shall cheer the dying saint. When you enter heaven you shall find Him there bearing the dew of His youth; and through eternity the Lord Jesus will still remain the perennial spring of joy and life and glory to His people. You may draw living waters from this sacred well! Jesus always was, He always is, He always shall be. He is eternal in all His attributes, in all His offices, in all His might and willingness to bless, comfort, guard, and crown His chosen people.

[1] Galatians 6:17   [2] Psalm 45:6   [3] Revelation 1:8   [4] Hebrews 7:25

AVOID FOOLISH CONTROVERSIES. — TITUS 3:9

Our days are few and are far better spent in doing good than in disputing over matters that are, at best, of minor importance. The old scholars did a world of mischief by their incessant discussion of subjects of no practical importance; and our churches suffer too often from petty wars over obscure points and unimportant questions. After everything has been said that can be said, neither party is any the wiser, and therefore the discussion promotes neither knowledge nor love, and it is foolish to sow in so barren a field. Questions about issues on which Scripture is silent, on mysteries that belong to God alone, on prophecies of doubtful interpretation, and on mere modes of observing human ceremonials are all foolish, and wise men avoid them. Our business is neither to ask nor answer foolish questions, but to avoid them altogether; and if we observe the apostle's precept (Titus 3:8) to be careful to maintain good works, we will find ourselves occupied with so much profitable business that we will have no time to take much interest in unworthy, contentious, and needless strivings.

There are, however, some questions that are the reverse of foolish, which we must not avoid but fairly and honestly meet, such as these: Do I believe in the Lord Jesus Christ? Am I renewed in the spirit of my mind? Am I walking not after the flesh but after the Spirit? Am I growing in grace? Does my behavior adorn the doctrine of God my Savior? Am I looking for the coming of the Lord and watching as a servant should who expects his master? What more can I do for Jesus? Such inquiries as these demand our urgent attention; and if we have been given at all to frivolous arguments, let us now turn our critical abilities to a much more profitable service. Let us be peacemakers and endeavor to lead others both by our precept and example to "avoid foolish controversies."

◄ EVENING ►

OH, THAT I KNEW WHERE I MIGHT FIND HIM. — JOB 23:3

In Job's extremely trying circumstances, he cried for the Lord. The longing desire of an afflicted child of God is to see his Father's face once more. His first prayer is not "Oh, that I might be healed of the disease that now spreads through my body!" nor even "Oh, that I might see my children restored from the jaws of the grave, and my property returned to me from the hand of the thief!" The first and foremost cry is, "Oh, that I knew where I might find *Him*, who is my God, that I might come even to His seat!" God's children run home when the storm comes. It is the heaven-born instinct of a gracious soul to seek shelter from all ills beneath the wings of Jehovah. "He who has made God his refuge" might serve as the title of a true believer. A hypocrite, when afflicted by God, resents the infliction and, like a slave, would run from the Master who has scourged him; but not so the true heir of heaven, who kisses the hand that struck him and seeks shelter from the rod in the heart of the God who frowned upon him. Job's desire to commune with God was intensified by the failure of all other sources of consolation. The patriarch turned away from his sorry friends and looked up to the heavenly throne, just as a traveler turns from his empty water jug and makes a beeline for the well. He bids farewell to earthborn hopes and cries, "Oh, that I knew where I might find my God!" Nothing teaches us about the preciousness of the Creator as much as when we learn the emptiness of everything else. Turning away with bitter scorn from earth's hives, where we find no honey, but many sharp stings, we rejoice in Him whose faithful word is sweeter than honey or the honeycomb. In every trouble we should first seek to realize God's presence with us. Only let us enjoy His smile, and then we can bear our daily cross with a willing heart for His dear sake.

YOU HAVE TAKEN UP MY CAUSE, O LORD; YOU HAVE REDEEMED MY LIFE.
— LAMENTATIONS 3:58

Observe how *positively* the prophet speaks. He does not say, "I hope, I trust, I some-times think that God has taken up my cause"; rather he speaks of it as a matter of fact not to be disputed. "You *have* taken up my cause." Let us, by the aid of the gracious Comforter, shake off those doubts and fears that so easily mar our peace and comfort. Let this be our prayer—that we may be done with the harsh, croaking voice of conjecture and suspicion and may be able to speak with the clear, melodious voice of full assurance. Notice how *gratefully* the prophet speaks, ascribing all the glory to God alone! You will notice that there is not a word concerning himself or his own pleadings. He does not ascribe his deliverance in any measure to any man, much less to his own merit; but it is *"you"*—"You have taken up my cause, O LORD; *you* have redeemed my life." A grateful spirit should always be cultivated by the Christian; and especially after deliverances we should prepare a song for our God. Earth should be a temple filled with the songs of grateful saints, and every day should be filled with the sweet incense of thanksgiving. How *joyful* Jeremiah seems to be while he records the Lord's mercy. How triumphantly he sounds out melody! He has been in the low dungeon, and even now he is none other than the weeping prophet; and yet in the very book that is called "Lamentations," in as clear a song as Miriam's when she played her tambourine, in as piercing a note as Deborah's when she met Barak with shouts of vic-tory, we hear the voice of Jeremiah going up to heaven—"You have taken up my cause, O LORD; you have redeemed my life." O children of God, seek after a vital experience of the Lord's loving-kindness, and when you have it, speak positively of it; sing gratefully; shout tri-umphantly!

❧ Evening ❧

THE ROCK BADGERS ARE A PEOPLE NOT MIGHTY,
YET THEY MAKE THEIR HOMES IN THE CLIFFS. — PROVERBS 30:26

Conscious of their own natural defenselessness, the rock badgers resort to burrows in the rocks and are secure from their enemies. My heart, be willing to learn a lesson from these feeble folk. You are as weak and as exposed to peril as the timid badger; be as wise to seek a shelter. My best security is within the fortress of an unchanging Jehovah, where His unalterable promises stand like giant walls of rock. It will be well with you, my heart, if you can always hide yourself in the bulwarks of His glorious attributes, all of which are guar-antees of safety for those who put their trust in Him. Blessed be the name of the Lord, I have so done and have found myself like David in the cave, safe from the cruelty of my enemy. I do not have to wonder how blessed it is to trust in the Lord, for long ago, when Satan and my sins pursued me, I fled to the cleft of the rock Christ Jesus, and in His wounded side I found a delightful resting-place. My heart, run to Him afresh tonight, whatever your pres-ent grief may be. Jesus feels for you; Jesus consoles you; Jesus will help you. No king in his impregnable fortress is more secure than the rock badger in his cliff home. The master of ten thousand chariots is not one bit better protected than the little dweller in the moun-tain's cleft. In Jesus the weak are strong, and the defenseless safe; they could not be more strong if they were giants or more safe if they were in heaven. Faith gives to men on earth the protection of the God of heaven. They cannot need any more and need not wish for more. The badgers cannot build a castle, but they avail themselves of what is there already. I can-not make myself a refuge, but Jesus has provided it, His Father has given it, His Spirit has revealed it, and here again tonight I enter it and am safe from every foe.

DO NOT GRIEVE THE HOLY SPIRIT. — EPHESIANS 4:30

All that the believer has must come from Christ, but it comes solely through the channel of the Spirit of grace. Just as all blessings flow to you through the Holy Spirit, so also no good thing can come out of you in holy thought, devout worship, or gracious act apart from the sanctifying operation of the same Spirit. Even if the good seed is sown in you, it still lies dormant until He works in you to will and to do of His own good pleasure. Do you desire to speak for Jesus—how can you unless the Holy Spirit touches your lips? Do you desire to pray? Sadly, what dull work it is unless the Spirit makes intercession for you! Do you desire to subdue sin? Would you be holy? Would you imitate your Master? Do you desire to rise to superlative heights of spirituality? Are you looking to be made like the angels of God, full of zeal and love for the Master's cause? You cannot without the Spirit—"Apart from me you can do nothing."[1] O branch of the vine, you can have no fruit without the sap! O child of God, you have no life within you apart from the life that God gives you through His Spirit! So let us not grieve Him or provoke Him to anger by our sin. Let us not quench Him even in one of His faintest motions in our soul; let us foster every suggestion and be ready to obey every prompting. If the Holy Spirit is indeed so mighty, let us attempt nothing without Him; let us begin no project and carry on no enterprise and conclude no transaction without seeking His blessing. Let us give Him the due homage of feeling our entire weakness apart from Him, and then depend alone upon Him, having this for our prayer: "Open my heart and my whole being to Your fullness, and uphold me with Your Spirit when I have received that Spirit in my inward parts."

❧ EVENING ❧

LAZARUS WAS ONE OF THOSE RECLINING WITH HIM AT THE TABLE. — JOHN 12:2

He is to be envied. It was fine to be Martha and serve, but better to be Lazarus and enjoy. There are times for each purpose, and each is fitting in its season, but none of the trees of the garden yield such clusters as the vine of fellowship. To sit with Jesus, to hear His words, to mark His acts and receive His smiles was such a favor as must have made Lazarus as happy as the angels. When it has been our happy privilege to feast with our Beloved in His banqueting-hall, we would not have given half a sigh for all the kingdoms of the world, if so much breath could have bought them.

He is to be imitated. It would have been a strange thing if Lazarus had not been at the table where Jesus was, for he had been dead, and Jesus had raised him. For the risen one to be absent when the Lord who gave him life was at his house would have been dreadfully ungrateful. We too were once dead, yes, and like Lazarus bound in the grave of sin. Jesus raised us, and by His life we live. Can we be content to live at a distance from Him? Do we fail to remember Him at His table, where He deigns to feast with His brethren? This is cruel! It behooves us to repent and do as *He* has bidden us, for His least wish should be law to us. To have lived without constant fellowship with Jesus, who loved him so dearly, would have been disgraceful to Lazarus. Is it then excusable in us whom Jesus has loved with an everlasting love? To have been cold to Him who wept over his lifeless corpse would have shown a lack of feeling in Lazarus. What does it say of us over whom the Savior has not only wept but bled? Come, brethren, who read this portion; let us return to our heavenly Bridegroom and ask for His Spirit, that we may be on terms of closer intimacy with Him and never miss the opportunity to sit at the table with Him.

[1] John 15:5

ISRAEL SERVED FOR A WIFE, AND FOR A WIFE HE GUARDED SHEEP.
— HOSEA 12:12

In conversation with Laban, Jacob described what he had done: "These twenty years I have been with you. . . . What was torn by wild beasts I did not bring to you. I bore the loss of it myself. From my hand you required it, whether stolen by day or stolen by night. There I was: by day the heat consumed me, and the cold by night, and my sleep fled from my eyes."[1] Even more arduous than this was the life of our Savior here below. He watched over us until He was able to say, "Of those whom you gave me I have lost not one."[2] His hair was wet with dew, and His locks with the drops of the night. Sleep departed from His eyes, for all night He was in prayer wrestling for His people. One night Peter must be pleaded for; suddenly another claims His tearful intercession. No shepherd sitting beneath the cold skies, looking up to the stars, could ever utter such complaints because of the hardness of his toil as Jesus Christ might have brought, if He had chosen to do so, because of the sternness of His service in order to procure His bride.

> Cold mountains and the midnight air,
> Witnessed the fervor of His prayer;
> The desert His temptations knew,
> His conflict and His victory too.

It is helpful to meditate upon the spiritual parallel of Laban having required all the sheep at Jacob's hand. If they were torn by beasts, Jacob must make it good; if any of them died, he must guarantee their replacement. Was not the toil of Jesus for His Church the toil of One who was under obligation to bring every believing one safe to the hand of Him who had committed them to His charge? Look upon toiling Jacob, and you see a representation of Him of whom we read, "He will tend His flock like a shepherd."[3]

❧ EVENING ❧

THE POWER OF HIS RESURRECTION. — PHILIPPIANS 3:10

The doctrine of a risen Savior is exceedingly precious. The resurrection is the cornerstone of the entire building of Christianity. It is the keystone of the arch of our salvation. It would take a volume to set out all the streams of living water that flow from this one sacred source, the resurrection of our dear Lord and Savior, Jesus Christ. But to know that He has risen, and to have fellowship with Him as such—communing with the risen Savior by possessing a risen life—seeing Him leave the tomb by leaving the tomb of worldliness ourselves—this is even more precious still. The doctrine is the basis of the experience, but as the flower is more lovely than the root, so is the experience of fellowship with the risen Savior more lovely than the doctrine itself. I would have you believe that Christ rose from the dead so as to sing of it and derive all the consolation that it is possible for you to extract from this well-affirmed and well-witnessed fact; but I beseech you, do not rest contented even there. Though you cannot, like the disciples, see Him visibly, yet I urge you to aspire to see Christ Jesus by the eye of faith; and though, like Mary Magdalene, you may not touch Him, yet you may be privileged to converse with Him and to know that He is risen, you yourselves being risen in Him to newness of life. To know a crucified Savior as having crucified all my sins is a high degree of knowledge; but to know a risen Savior as having justified me, and to realize that He has bestowed upon me new life, having made me a new creature through His own newness of life—this is a noble style of experience. Short of it, none should rest satisfied. May you both "know him and the power of his resurrection." Why should souls who are made alive with Jesus wear the grave-clothes of worldliness and unbelief? Rise, for the Lord is risen.

[1] Genesis 31:38-40 [2] John 18:9 [3] Isaiah 40:11

FELLOWSHIP WITH HIM. — 1 JOHN 1:6

When we were united by faith to Christ, we were brought into such complete fellowship with Him that we were made one with Him, and His interests and ours became
mutual and identical. We have fellowship with Christ in His *love*. What He loves we love.
He loves the saints—so do we. He loves sinners—so do we. He loves the poor perishing
race of man and longs to see earth's deserts transformed into the garden of the Lord—so do
we. We have fellowship with Him in His *desires*. He desires the glory of God—we also
work for the same. He desires that the believers may be with Him where He is—we desire
to be with Him there too. He desires to drive out sin—behold, we fight under His banner.
He desires that His Father's name may be loved and adored by all His creatures—we pray
daily, "Your kingdom come, your will be done, on earth as it is in heaven." We have fellowship with Christ in His *sufferings*. We are not nailed to the cross, nor do we die a cruel
death, but when He is reproached, we are reproached; and it is a very sweet thing to be
blamed for His sake, to be despised for following the Master, to have the world against us.
The disciple should not be above His Lord. In our measure we fellowship with Him in His
labors, ministering to men by the word of truth and by deeds of love. Our meat and our drink,
like His, is to do the will of Him who has sent us and to finish His work. We also have fellowship with Christ in His *joys*. We are happy in His happiness; we rejoice in His exaltation. Have you ever tasted that joy, believer? There is no purer or more thrilling delight to
be known this side of heaven than that of having Christ's joy fulfilled in us, that our joy
may be full. His *glory* awaits us to complete our fellowship, for His Church will sit with
Him upon His throne as His well-beloved bride and queen.

❧ EVENING ☙

GET YOU UP TO A HIGH MOUNTAIN. — ISAIAH 40:9

Each believer should be thirsting for God, for the living God, and longing to climb the
hill of the Lord and see Him face to face. We should not rest content in the mists of the
valley when the summit of the mountain beckons us. My soul thirsts to drink deeply of the
cup that is reserved for those who reach the mountain's peak and bathe their brows in heaven.
How pure are the dews of the hills; how fresh is the mountain air; how abundant is the provision of the dwellers aloft, whose windows look into the New Jerusalem! Many saints are
content to live like men in coal mines, who do not see the sun; they eat dust like the serpent
when they might taste the food of angels; they are content to wear the miner's garb when they
might put on king's robes; tears disfigure their faces when they might anoint them with
celestial oil. I am convinced that many a believer pines in a dungeon when he might walk
on the palace roof and view the goodly land. Rouse yourself, believer, from your low condition! Discard your laziness, your lethargy, your coldness, or whatever interferes with your
sincere and pure love for Christ, your soul's Husband. Make Him the source, the center,
and the circumference of your soul's whole range of delight. What fully enchants you to
remain in a pit when you may sit on a throne? Do not live in the lowlands of bondage now
that mountain liberty is conferred upon you. Do not be satisfied any longer with your tiny
attainments, but press forward to things more sublime and heavenly. Aspire to a higher, a
nobler, a fuller life. Upward to heaven! Nearer to God!

When will Thou come unto me, Lord?
Oh come, my Lord most dear!
Come near, come nearer, nearer still,
I'm blest when Thou art near.

BUT THERE THE LORD IN MAJESTY WILL BE FOR US A PLACE
OF BROAD RIVERS AND STREAMS. — ISAIAH 33:21

Broad rivers and streams" produce fertility and abundance in the land. Places near broad rivers are remarkable for the variety of their plants and their plentiful harvests. God is all this to His Church. Having God she has *abundance*. What can she ask for that He will not give her? What need can she mention that He will not supply? "On this mountain the LORD of hosts will make for all peoples a feast of rich food."[1] Do you want the bread of life? It drops like manna from the sky. Do you want refreshing streams? The rock follows you, and that Rock is Christ. If you still have any need, it is your own fault; if you are deprived, you are not deprived in Him, but in yourself. "Broad rivers and streams" also point to *business*. Our glorious Lord is to us a place of heavenly merchandise. Through our Redeemer we have business with the past; the wealth of Calvary, the treasures of the covenant, the riches of the ancient days of election, the stores of eternity—all come to us down the broad stream of our gracious Lord. We have business, too, with the future. What ships, laden to the water's edge, come to us from heaven! What visions we have of a new heaven and a new earth! Through our glorious Lord we have business with angels—communion with the bright spirits washed in blood, who sing before the throne. Better still, we have fellowship with the Infinite One. "Broad rivers and streams" are specially intended to set forth the idea of *security*. Rivers were often a defense. Beloved, what a defense God is to His Church! The devil cannot cross this broad river of God. How he wishes he could turn the current, but do not fear, for God abides unchangeably the same. Satan may annoy, but he cannot destroy us; no galley with oars shall invade our river, neither will a majestic ship pass through.

❧ EVENING ❧

A LITTLE SLEEP, A LITTLE SLUMBER, A LITTLE FOLDING OF THE HANDS
TO REST, AND POVERTY WILL COME UPON YOU LIKE A ROBBER,
AND WANT LIKE AN ARMED MAN. — PROVERBS 24:33-34

The worst of sluggards only ask for a little slumber; they would be indignant if they were accused of complete laziness. A little folding of the hands to rest is all they desire, and they have a host of reasons to show that this indulgence is entirely legitimate. Yet by these "littles" the day runs out, and the time for work is all gone, and the field is overgrown with thorns. It is by little procrastinations that men ruin their souls. They do not intend to delay for years—a few months, they say, will bring the more convenient season—tomorrow they will attend to serious things; but the present hour is so occupied and so unsuitable that they beg to be excused. Like sands from an hourglass, time passes; life is wasted by driblets, and seasons of grace lost by little slumbers. Oh, to be wise, to catch the fleeting hour, to use the passing moments! May the Lord teach us this sacred wisdom, because otherwise a poverty of the worst kind awaits us—eternal poverty that will want even a drop of water and beg for it in vain. Like a robber steadily pursuing his victim, poverty overtakes the lazy, and ruin overthrows the undecided: Each hour brings the dreaded pursuer nearer; he doesn't pause on the way, for he is on his master's business and must not delay. As an armed man enters with authority and power, in similar fashion want will come to the idle, and death to the impenitent, and there will be no escape. O that men would become wise and would diligently seek the Lord Jesus, before the solemn day will dawn when it will be too late to plow and to sow, too late to repent and believe. In harvest, it is useless to lament that the seed-time was neglected. As of now, there is still time for faith and holy decision. May we obtain them tonight.

[1] Isaiah 25:6

... TO PROCLAIM LIBERTY TO THE CAPTIVES. — LUKE 4:18

No one but Jesus can give deliverance to captives. Real liberty comes from Him alone. It is a liberty *rightly granted*; for the Son, who is Heir of all things, has a right to make men free. The saints honor the justice of God, which now secures their salvation. It is a liberty that has been *dearly purchased*. Christ reveals it by His power, but He bought it by His blood. He makes you free, but it is by His own bonds. You go clear because He bore your burden for you: You are set at liberty because He has suffered in your place. Although the purchase price was great, *Jesus gives it freely*. He asks nothing of us as a preparation for this liberty. He finds us sitting in sackcloth and ashes and invites us to wear the fitting garment of freedom; He saves us just as we are and without any help from us. When Jesus sets us free, the liberty is *perpetually enjoyed*; no chains can bind again. Let the Master say to me, "Captive, I have delivered you," and it is done forever. Satan may plot to enslave us, but if the Lord is on our side, whom shall we fear? The world, with its temptations, may seek to ensnare us, but He who is for us is mightier than all those who are against us. The movements of our own deceitful hearts may harass and annoy us, but He who has begun the good work in us will bring it to completion in the end. The enemies of God and the antagonists of man may gather their forces together and come with concentrated fury against us, but if God acquits, who is he that condemns? The eagle that flies to its rocky perch and afterwards soars above the clouds is no more free than the soul delivered by Christ. If we are no longer under the law but free from its curse, let our liberty be *practically displayed* as we serve God with gratitude and delight. "I am your servant; the son of your maidservant. You have loosed my bonds."[1]

❧ EVENING ☙

FOR HE SAYS TO MOSES, "I WILL HAVE MERCY ON WHOM I HAVE MERCY, AND I WILL HAVE COMPASSION ON WHOM I HAVE COMPASSION." — ROMANS 9:15

In these words the Lord in the plainest manner claims the right to give or to withhold His mercy according to His own sovereign will. As the prerogative of life and death is vested in the monarch, so the Judge of all the earth has a right to spare or condemn the guilty, as may seem best in His sight. Men by their sins have forfeited all claim upon God; they deserve to perish for their sins—and if they all do so, they have no ground for complaint. If the Lord steps in to save any, He may do so if the ends of justice are not thwarted; but if He judges it best to leave the condemned to suffer the righteous sentence, none may call Him to account. All those discourses about the rights of men being placed on the same footing are foolish and impudent and ignorant; worse still are the arguments against discriminating grace, which are just the rebellions of proud human nature against God's rule. When we are brought to see our own utter ruin, and the justice of the divine verdict against sin, we no longer scoff at the truth that the Lord is not bound to save us; we do not murmur if He chooses to save others, as though He were doing us an injury, but feel that if He deigns to look upon us, it will be His own free act of undeserved goodness, for which we will forever bless His name.

How will those who are the subjects of divine election sufficiently adore the grace of God? They have no room for boasting, for sovereignty most effectually excludes it. The Lord's will alone is glorified, and the very notion of human merit is cast out to everlasting contempt. There is no more humbling doctrine in Scripture than that of election, none more deserving of gratitude, and consequently none more sanctifying. Believers should not be afraid of it but adoringly rejoice in it.

[1] Psalm 116:16

WHATEVER YOUR HAND FINDS TO DO, DO IT WITH YOUR MIGHT.
— ECCLESIASTES 9:10

Whatever your hand finds to do" refers to works that are *possible*. There are many things that our heart finds to do that we will never do. It is good for it to be in our heart; but if we would be eminently useful, we must not be content with forming schemes in our heart and talking of them; we must practically carry out *"whatever your hand finds to do."* One good deed is worth more than a thousand brilliant theories. Let us not wait for large opportunities or for a different kind of work, but just do the things we "find to do" day by day. We have no other time in which to live. The past is gone; the future has not arrived; we will never have any time but now. So do not wait until your experience has ripened into maturity before you attempt to serve God. Endeavor now to bring forth fruit. Serve God now, but be careful about the way in which you perform what you find to do—*"do it with your might."* Do it *promptly*; do not fritter away your life in thinking of what you intend to do tomorrow as if that could repay today's laziness. No one ever served God by doing things tomorrow. If we honor Christ and are blessed, it is by the things that we do *today*. Whatever you do for Christ, throw your whole soul into it. Do not give Christ a little halfhearted labor, done as a matter of course every now and then; but when you serve Him, do it with heart and soul and strength.

But where is the power of a Christian? It is not in himself, for he is perfect weakness. His power lies in the Lord of Hosts. Let us then seek His help; let us proceed with prayer and faith, and when we have done what our "hand finds to do," let us wait upon the Lord for His blessing. What we do in this way will be well done and will not fail in its effect.

❧   EVENING   ❧

FOR WHOEVER HAS DESPISED THE DAY OF SMALL THINGS SHALL REJOICE,
AND SHALL SEE THE PLUMB LINE IN THE HAND OF ZERUBBABEL.
— ZECHARIAH 4:10

Small things marked the beginning of the work in the hand of Zerubbabel, but none should despise it, for the Lord had raised up one who would persevere until the work was completed with shouts of joy. The plumb line was in good hands. Here is the comfort of every believer in the Lord Jesus. Let the work of grace be ever so small in its beginnings, *the plumb line is in good hands*. A master builder greater than Solomon has undertaken to raise the heavenly temple, and He will not fail nor be discouraged till the pinnacle shall be raised. If the plumb line were in the hand of any merely human being, we might fear for the building, but the pleasure of the Lord will prosper in Jesus' hand. The works did not proceed irregularly and without care, for *the master's hand carried a good instrument*. If the walls had been built in a hurry without proper supervision, they might have been out of line; but the plumb line was used by the chosen overseer. Jesus is always watching the construction of His spiritual temple, to ensure that it is built securely and well. We are for speed, but Jesus is for judgment. He will use the plumb line, and that which is out of line must come down, every stone of it. This explains the failure of many a flattering work, the overthrow of many a glittering profession. It is not for us to judge the Lord's Church, since Jesus has a steady hand and a true eye and can use the plumb line well. Do we not rejoice to see judgment left to Him?

The plumb line was in active use—it was in the builder's hand, a sure indication that he meant to bring the work to completion. Lord Jesus, how glad we would be to see You at Your great work. O Zion, the beautiful, your walls are still in ruins! Rise, glorious Builder, and make her desolations to rejoice at Your coming.

JOSHUA THE HIGH PRIEST STANDING BEFORE THE ANGEL OF THE LORD.
— ZECHARIAH 3:1

In Joshua *the high priest* we see a picture of each and every child of God, who has been brought near by the blood of Christ and has been taught to minister in holy things and enter into that which is within the veil. Jesus has made us priests and kings unto God, and even here upon earth we exercise the priesthood of consecrated living and hallowed service. But this high priest is said to be "*standing* before the angel of the LORD," that is, standing to minister. This should be the perpetual position of every true believer. Every place is now God's temple, and His people can serve Him just as truly at work as in His house. They should always be ministering, offering the spiritual sacrifice of prayer and praise, and presenting themselves "a living sacrifice."[1] But notice where Joshua stands to minister—it is *before the angel of Jehovah*. It is only through a mediator that we poor, defiled ones can ever become priests to God. I present what I have before the messenger, the angel of the covenant, the Lord Jesus; and through Him my prayers find acceptance wrapped up in His prayers; my praises become sweet as they are bound up with bundles of fragrant spices from Christ's own garden. If I can bring Him nothing but my tears, He will put them with His own tears in His own bottle, for He once wept; if I can bring Him nothing but my groans and sighs, He will accept these as an acceptable sacrifice, for He once was broken in heart and sighed heavily in spirit. I myself, standing in Him, am accepted in the Beloved; and all my polluted works, though in themselves only objects of divine displeasure, are so received that God smells a sweet savor. He is content, and I am blessed. Consider, then, the position of the Christian— "a priest . . . standing before the angel of the LORD."

❧ EVENING ❧

THE FORGIVENESS OF OUR TRESPASSES, ACCORDING TO THE RICHES
OF HIS GRACE. — EPHESIANS 1:7

Could there be a sweeter word in any language than that word "forgiveness" when it sounds in a guilty sinner's ear, like the joyful notes of liberation to the captive Israelite? Blessed, forever blessed, be the dear star of pardon that shines into the condemned cell and gives the perishing a gleam of hope amid the midnight of despair! Can it be possible that sin, such sin as mine, can be forgiven, forgiven altogether and forever? Hell is my portion as a sinner—there is no possibility of my escaping from it while sin remains upon me. Can the load of guilt be lifted, the crimson stain removed? Can the unbreakable stones of my prison-house ever be loosed from their mortices, or the doors be lifted from their hinges? Jesus tells me that I may still be cleared. Forever blessed be the revelation of atoning love that not only tells me that pardon is possible, but that it is secured to all who trust in Jesus. I have believed in the atoning sacrifice, even Jesus crucified, and therefore my sins are at this moment and forever forgiven by virtue of His substitutionary pains and death. What joy is this! What unimagined bliss to be a perfectly pardoned soul! My soul dedicates all her powers to Him who by His own unpurchased love became my Savior and provided for me redemption through His blood. What riches of grace does free forgiveness exhibit! To forgive at all, to forgive fully, to forgive freely, to forgive forever—here is a panorama of wonders. And when I think of how great my sins were, how dear were the precious drops that cleansed me from them, and how gracious was the method by which pardon was sealed home to me, I am in a maze of wondering, worshiping affection. I bow before the throne that absolves me, I clasp the cross that delivers me, and all my days I give to serve the Incarnate God, through whom I am this night a pardoned soul.

[1] Romans 12:1

NOVEMBER 28 ❧ MORNING ❧

FOR I REJOICED GREATLY WHEN THE BROTHERS CAME AND TESTIFIED TO
YOUR TRUTH, AS INDEED YOU ARE WALKING IN THE TRUTH. — 3 JOHN 3

The truth was in Gaius, and Gaius walked in the truth. If the first had not been the case, the second could never have occurred; and if the second could not be said of him, the first would have been a mere pretense. Truth must enter into the soul, penetrate and saturate it, or else it is of no value. Doctrines held as a matter of creed are like bread in the hand, which provides no nourishment to the body; but doctrine accepted by the heart is like food digested, which by assimilation sustains and builds up the body. In us truth must be a living force, an active energy, an indwelling reality, a part of the warp and woof of our being. If it is *in us*, we cannot then part with it. A man may lose his clothes or his limbs, but his inward parts are vital and cannot be torn away without absolute loss of life. A Christian can die, but he cannot deny the truth. Now it is a rule of nature that the inward affects the outward, as light shines from the center of the lantern through the glass: When, therefore, the truth is kindled within, its brightness soon shines in the outward life and conversation. It is said that the food of certain worms colors the cocoons of silk that they spin: And in the same way the nutriment upon which a man's inward nature lives gives a tinge to every word and deed proceeding from him. To walk in the truth conveys a life of integrity, holiness, faithfulness, and simplicity—the natural product of those principles of truth that the Gospel teaches and that the Spirit of God enables us to receive. We may judge the secrets of the soul by their appearance in the man's behavior. Today, O gracious Spirit, let it be ours to be ruled and governed by Your divine authority, so that nothing false or sinful may reign in our hearts, in case it should extend its malignant influence to our everyday lives in the community.

❧ EVENING ❧

HE SOUGHT THE WELFARE OF HIS PEOPLE. — ESTHER 10:3

Mordecai was a true patriot, and so when he was promoted to the highest position under Ahasuerus, he used his eminence to promote the prosperity of Israel. In this he was a type of Jesus who, upon His throne of glory, does not seek His own but spends His power for His people. It would be beneficial if every Christian would be a Mordecai to the Church, striving according to his ability for its prosperity. Some are placed in positions of affluence and influence; let them honor their Lord in the high places of the earth and testify for Jesus before great men. Others have what is far better, namely, close fellowship with the King of kings. Let them be sure to pray daily for the weak among the Lord's people, the doubting, the tempted, and the comfortless. It will redound to their honor if they make much intercession for those who are in darkness and dare not draw close to the mercy-seat. Instructed believers may serve their Master greatly if they offer their talents for the general good and impart their wealth of heavenly learning to others by teaching them the things of God. The very least in our churches may seek the welfare of God's people; and such a desire, if they can give no more, will be acceptable. It is at once the most Christlike and the most happy course for a believer to stop living for himself. He who blesses others cannot fail to be blessed himself. On the other hand, to seek our own personal greatness is a wicked and unhappy plan of life; its way will be grievous, and its end will be fatal.

Here is the place to ask you, my friend, whether you are to the best of your power seeking the best for the Church in your neighborhood. I trust you are not doing the Church mischief by bitterness and scandal, nor weakening it by your neglect. Friend, unite with the Lord's poor, bear their cross, do them all the good you can, and you will not miss your reward.

YOU SHALL NOT GO AROUND AS A SLANDERER AMONG YOUR PEOPLE. . . .
YOU SHALL REASON FRANKLY WITH YOUR NEIGHBOR,
LEST YOU INCUR SIN BECAUSE OF HIM. — LEVITICUS 19:16-17

Slander emits a threefold poison, for it injures the teller, the hearer, and the person who is being slandered. Whether the report is true or false, we are by this precept of God's Word forbidden to spread it. The reputations of the Lord's people should be very precious in our sight, and we should regard it as shameful to help the devil dishonor the church and the name of the Lord. Some tongues need a bridle rather than a spur. Many rejoice in putting down their brothers and sisters, as if in doing so they raised themselves. Noah's wise sons cast a covering over their father, and the one who exposed him earned a fearful curse. We may ourselves one of these dark days need leniency and silence from our family; let us offer it cheerfully to those who require it now. Let this be our family motto, and our personal bond: *Speak evil of no man.*

The Holy Spirit, however, permits us to censure sin and prescribes the way in which we are to do it. It must be done by rebuking our brother to his face, not by talking behind his back. This approach is manly, brotherly, Christlike, and under God's blessing will be useful. Do we shy away from it? Then we must lay the greater stress upon our conscience and commit ourselves to the responsibility, in case by tolerating sin in our friend we become partakers of it. Hundreds have been saved from gross sins by the timely, wise, affectionate warnings of faithful friends and family. Our Lord Jesus has set us a gracious example of how to deal with erring friends in His warning given to Peter, the prayer with which He preceded it, and the gentle way in which He endured Peter's boastful denial that he needed such a caution.

❧ EVENING ☙

SPICES FOR THE ANOINTING OIL. — EXODUS 35:8

Much use was made of this anointing oil under the law, and that which it represents is of primary importance under the Gospel. The Holy Spirit, who anoints us for all holy service, is indispensable to us if we would serve the Lord acceptably. Without His help our religious services are just an empty show, and our inward experience is a dead thing. Whenever our ministry is without unction, what miserable stuff it becomes! And the prayers, praises, meditations, and efforts of private Christians are no better. A holy anointing is the soul and life of godly devotion, its absence the most serious of all calamities. To go before the Lord without anointing would be like a common Levite thrusting himself into the priest's role—his religious services would be sins, not sacrifices. May we never embark upon holy tasks without sacred anointings. They fall upon us from our glorious Head; from His anointing we who are but the skirts of His garments receive a generous unction. Choice spices were mixed with great skill and care to form the anointing oil, to let us see how rich are all the influences of the Holy Spirit. All good things are found in the divine Comforter. Matchless consolation, infallible instruction, immortal quickening, spiritual energy, and divine sanctification are all mixed with other excellencies in the heavenly anointing oil of the Holy Spirit. It imparts a delightful fragrance to the character and person of the one upon whom it is poured. Nothing like it can be found in all the treasures of the wealthy or the secrets of the wise. It is not to be imitated. It only comes from God, and it is freely given, through Jesus Christ, to every waiting soul. Let us seek it, for we may have it, even this very evening. O Lord, anoint Your servants.

AND AMAZIAH SAID TO THE MAN OF GOD, "BUT WHAT SHALL WE DO
ABOUT THE HUNDRED TALENTS THAT I HAVE GIVEN TO THE ARMY
OF ISRAEL?" THE MAN OF GOD ANSWERED, "THE LORD IS ABLE TO GIVE
YOU MUCH MORE THAN THIS." — 2 CHRONICLES 25:9

This seemed to be a very important question for the king of Judah, and possibly it is of even more significance for the tried and tested Christian. To lose money is never pleasant, and when it involves principle, we are not always ready to make the sacrifice. "Why lose what could be put to good use? Is it not possible to pay too much for truth? Remember the children and our small income!" All these things and a thousand more would tempt the Christian to participate in dishonest gain or prevent him from carrying out his conscientious convictions when they involve serious loss. Not everyone views these matters in the light of faith; and even with the followers of Jesus, the idea that "we all have to live" carries quite a bit of weight.

"*The* LORD is able to give you much more than this" is a very satisfactory answer to the anxious question. Our Father holds the funds, and what we lose for His sake He can repay a thousandfold. Our part is to obey His will, and we may rest assured that He will provide for us. The Lord will be no man's debtor in the end. Christians know that an ounce of contentment is more valuable than a ton of gold. The person wearing a threadbare coat over a good conscience has found a spiritual treasure far more desirable than any he may have lost. God's smile and a dungeon are enough for a true heart; His frown and a palace would be hell to the trusting soul. Let the worst become worse still, let all the talents go, we have not lost our treasure, for that is above, where Christ sits at the right hand of God. In the meantime, even now the Lord makes the meek to inherit the earth, and He keeps back nothing that is good from those whose walk is blameless.

❧ EVENING ☙

. . . MICHAEL AND HIS ANGELS FIGHTING AGAINST THE DRAGON.
AND THE DRAGON AND HIS ANGELS FOUGHT BACK. — REVELATION 12:7

War always will rage between the two great sovereignties until one or the other is crushed. Peace between good and evil is an impossibility; to pretend otherwise would signal a victory for the powers of darkness. *Michael will always fight*; his holy soul is vexed with sin and will not endure it. Jesus will always be the dragon's foe, and not in any quiet sense but actively, vigorously, with full determination to exterminate evil. All His servants, whether angels in heaven or messengers on earth, will and must fight; they are born to be warriors. At the cross they enter into a covenant never to make a truce with evil; they are a warlike company, firm in defense and fierce in attack. The duty of every soldier in the army of the Lord is every day, with all his heart and soul and strength, to fight against the dragon.

The dragon and his angels will fight back; they are incessant in their onslaughts, prepared to use every kind of weaponry. We are foolish to expect to serve God without opposition: The more zealous we are, the more we can expect to be attacked by the ruffians of hell. The church may become lazy, but her great antagonist does not; his restless spirit never allows the war to pause; he hates the woman's seed and would happily devour the Church if he could. The servants of Satan share a great deal of the old dragon's energy and are usually an active crew. War rages all around, and to dream of peace is dangerous and futile.

Glory be to God, we know the end of the war. The great dragon will be cast out and forever destroyed, while Jesus and those who are with Him will receive the crown. So let us sharpen our swords tonight, and ask the Holy Spirit to make us ready for the conflict. Battle was never so important, and the crown never so glorious. Every one to their positions as warriors of the cross, and may the Lord tread Satan under your feet shortly!

December

YOU HAVE MADE SUMMER AND WINTER. — PSALM 74:17

My soul, begin this wintry month with God. The cold snows and the piercing winds all remind you that He keeps His covenant with day and night and serve to assure you that He will also keep that glorious covenant that He has made with you in the person of Christ Jesus. He who is true to His Word in the revolutions of the seasons of this poor sin-polluted world will not prove unfaithful in His dealings with His own well-beloved Son.

Winter in the soul is by no means a comfortable season, and if it is upon you just now, it will be very painful to you: But there is this comfort, namely, that *the Lord* makes it. He sends the sharp blasts of adversity to nip the buds of expectation. He scatters the frozen dew like ashes over the once fresh green meadows of our joy. He dispenses His icy morsels, freezing the streams of our delight. He does it all; He is the great Winter King and rules in the realms of frost, and therefore you cannot murmur. Losses, crosses, heaviness, sickness, poverty, and a thousand other ills are of the Lord's sending and come to us with wise design. Frosts kill harmful insects and restrain raging diseases; they break up the clods and sweeten the soul. O that such good results would always follow our winters of affliction!

How we prize the fire just now! How pleasant is its cheerful glow! Let us in the same manner prize our Lord, who is the constant source of warmth and comfort in every time of trouble. Let us draw near to Him, and in Him find joy and peace in believing. Let us wrap ourselves in the warm garments of His promises, and keep working, unlike the lazy man who refuses to plow because it is too cold; in the summer he will have nothing and will be forced to beg for bread.

❧ EVENING ❧

LET THEM THANK THE LORD FOR HIS STEADFAST LOVE, FOR HIS WONDROUS WORKS TO THE CHILDREN OF MEN! — PSALM 107:8

If we complained less and were more thankful, we would be happier, and God would be more glorified. Every day thank God for *ordinary mercies*—we refer to them as ordinary, and yet they are so priceless that without them we are ready to perish. Let us thank God for our eyes with which we see the sun, for the health and strength to walk around, for the bread we eat, for the clothes we wear. Let us thank Him that we are not among the hopeless or confined among the guilty; let us thank Him for liberty, for friends, for family associations and comforts. Let us praise Him, in fact, for everything that we receive from His generous hand, for although we deserve little, He provides an abundance. The sweetest and the loudest note in our thankful songs should be of *redeeming love*. God's redeeming acts toward His chosen are forever the favorite themes of their praise. If we know what redemption means, let us not withhold our hymns of thanksgiving. We have been redeemed from the power of our corruptions, lifted from the depth of sin in which we were naturally plunged. We have been led to the cross of Christ—our shackles of guilt have been removed. We are no longer slaves, but children of the living God, and can anticipate the time when we will be presented before the throne without spot or wrinkle or any such thing. Even now by faith we wrap ourselves in the fair linen that is to be our everlasting array and rehearse our unceasing thankfulness to the Lord our Redeemer. Child of God, can you remain silent? Stir yourselves with thoughts of your inheritance, and lead your captivity captive, crying with David, "Bless the LORD, O my soul, and all that is within me, bless his holy name."[1] Let this new month begin with new songs.

[1] Psalm 103:1

❧ **MORNING** ❧

The Lord's admiration for His Church is very wonderful, and His description of her beauty is very glowing. She is not merely *beautiful*, but "*altogether* beautiful." He views her in Himself, washed in His sin-atoning blood and clothed in His meritorious righteousness, and He considers her to be full of attraction and beauty. No wonder that this is the case, since it is simply His own perfect excellency that He admires; for the holiness, glory, and perfection of His Church are His own glorious garments worn by His well-beloved spouse. She is not simply pure or well-proportioned; she is positively lovely and fair! She has actual merit! Her deformities of sin are removed; but more, she has through her Lord obtained a meritorious righteousness by which an actual beauty is conferred upon her. Believers have a positive righteousness given to them when "he chose us in him" (Eph. 1:4). Nor is the church barely lovely—she is *superlatively* so. Her Lord styles her "most beautiful among women."[1] She has a real worth and excellence that cannot be rivaled by all the nobility and royalty of the world. If Jesus could exchange His elect bride for all the queens and empresses of earth, or even for the angels in heaven, He would not, for He puts her first and foremost! Like the moon she far outshines the stars. Nor is this an opinion that He is ashamed of, for He invites all men to hear it. He sets a "behold" before it, a special note of exclamation, inviting and arresting attention. "*Behold*, you are beautiful, my love, *behold*, you are beautiful!" (Song of Sol. 4:1). He publishes His opinion widely even now, and one day from the throne of His glory He will declare the truth of it before the assembled universe. "Come, you who are blessed by my Father" (Matt. 25:34) will be His solemn affirmation of the loveliness of His elect.

❧ **EVENING** ❧

Nothing can satisfy the entire man but the Lord's love and the Lord's own self. Some have tried to anchor in other harbors, but they have been driven out of such fatal refuges. Solomon, the wisest of men, was permitted to make experiments for us all, and to do for us what we should not attempt ourselves. Here is his testimony in his own words: "So I became great and surpassed all who were before me in Jerusalem. Also my wisdom remained with me. And whatever my eyes desired I did not keep from them. I kept my heart from no pleasure, for my heart found pleasure in all my toil, and this was my reward for all my toil. Then I considered all that my hands had done and the toil I had expended in doing it, and behold, all was vanity and a striving after wind, and there was nothing to be gained under the sun."[2] "Vanity of vanities, all is vanity."[3] What! The whole of it vanity? Is there nothing in all the wealth of kings? Nothing in that vast territory reaching from the river to the sea? Nothing in those glorious palaces? Nothing in the riches of the forests of Lebanon? In all your music and dancing and wine and luxury is there nothing? "Nothing," he says, "but sorrow, and his work is a vexation." This was his verdict when he had experimented on the paths of apparent pleasure. To embrace the Lord Jesus, to rest in His love and be fully assured of union with Him—this is all in all. Dear reader, you do not need to try these empty paths to find out whether they are better than the Christian's. If you roam the universe, you will not find another friend like Jesus; if you could have all the comforts of life but lost your Savior, you would be wretched; but if you win Christ, then you could rot in a dungeon and even there find peace. If you live in obscurity or die hungry, you will still be satisfied with favor and will be full of the goodness of the Lord.

[1] Song of Solomon 1:8 [2] Song of Solomon 2:9-11 [3] Song of Solomon 1:2

THERE IS NO FLAW IN YOU. — SONG OF SOLOMON 4:7

Having pronounced His Church positively full of beauty, our Lord confirms His praise by a precious negative: "There is no flaw in you." As if the thought occurred to the Bridegroom that the complaining world would insinuate that He had only highlighted her good parts and had purposely not mentioned those features that were deformed or defiled, in summary He declares her universally and entirely beautiful and utterly devoid of flaws. A spot can easily be removed and is the very least thing that can disfigure beauty, but even from this little blemish the believer is delivered in his Lord's sight. If He had said there is no hideous scar, no horrible deformity, no deadly ulcer, we might even then have marveled; but when He testifies that she is free from the slightest flaw, all these other forms of defilement are included, and the depth of wonder is increased. If He had simply promised to remove all flaws later on, we would still have eternal reason for joy; but when He speaks of it as already done, it fills us with a deep sense of satisfaction and delight. My soul, here is spiritual food for you; digest it properly, and be satisfied with the royal provision.

Christ Jesus has no quarrel with His spouse. She often wanders from Him and grieves His Holy Spirit, but He does not allow her faults to affect His love. He sometimes rebukes, but it is always in a tender manner, with the kindest of intentions: It is "my love" even then. There is no remembrance of our follies. He does not cherish ill thoughts of us, but He pardons and loves equally after the offense as before it. If Jesus were as mindful of injuries as we are, how could He commune with us? Too often a believer will put himself out of humor with the Lord for some slight turn in providence, but our precious Husband knows our silly hearts too well to take any offense at our ill manners.

❧ EVENING ☙

THE LORD, MIGHTY IN BATTLE! — PSALM 24:8

God is glorious in the eyes of His people, since He has worked such wonders for them, in them, and by them. *For them*, the Lord Jesus upon Calvary defeated every foe, breaking all the weapons of the enemy in pieces by His finished work of satisfactory obedience; by His triumphant resurrection and ascension He completely overturned the hopes of hell, leading captivity captive, making a show of our enemies openly, triumphing over them by His cross. Every arrow of guilt that Satan might have shot at us is broken, for who can lay anything to the charge of God's elect? Vain are the sharp swords of infernal malice and the perpetual battles of the serpent's seed, for among God's people the lame take the prey, and the feeblest warriors are crowned.

Believers will also worship the Lord Jesus for His conquests *in them*, since the arrows of their natural hatred are snapped, and the weapons of their rebellion are broken. What victories grace has won in our evil hearts! How glorious is Jesus when the will is subdued and sin dethroned! As for our remaining corruptions, they will sustain an equally sure defeat, and every temptation and doubt and fear will be completely destroyed. In the sanctuary of our peaceful hearts, the name of Jesus is great beyond compare: He has won our love, and He shall wear it. In equal measure we may look for victories *by us*. We are more than conquerors through Him who loved us. We will cast down the powers of darkness that are in the world by our faith and zeal and holiness; we will win sinners to Jesus; we will overturn false systems; we will convert nations. For God is with us, and none shall stand against us. This evening let the Christian warrior sing the war song and prepare for tomorrow's fight. Greater is He who is in us than he who is in the world.

I HAVE MANY IN THIS CITY WHO ARE MY PEOPLE. — ACTS 18:10

This should be a great encouragement in proclaiming the Gospel, since among the people in our communities—the disinterested, the rebellious, the careless—God has an elect people who must be saved. When you take the Word to them, you do so because God has ordained you to be the messenger of life to their souls, and they *must* receive it, for so the decree of predestination runs. They are as much redeemed by blood as the saints before the eternal throne. They are Christ's property, and yet perhaps they are lovers of selfish pleasures and haters of holiness; but if Jesus Christ purchased them, He will have them. God is not unfaithful to forget the price that His Son has paid. He will not suffer His substitution to be in any case an ineffectual, dead thing. Tens of thousands of redeemed ones are not regenerated yet, but regenerated they must be; and this is our comfort when we go to them with the quickening Word of God.

More than this, the ungodly are prayed for by Christ before the throne. "I do not ask for these only," says the great Intercessor, "but also for *those who will believe* in me through their word."[1] Poor, ignorant souls, they know nothing about prayer for themselves, but Jesus prays for them. Their names are on His breastplate, and before long they must bow their stubborn knee, breathing the penitential sigh before the throne of grace. The predestinated moment has not struck; but when it comes, *they will obey*, for God will have His own. *They must*, for the Spirit is not to be resisted when He comes with the fullness of power— *they must* become the willing servants of the living God. "Your people will offer themselves freely on the day of your power."[2] He will "make many to be accounted righteous."[3] "Out of the anguish of his soul he shall see and be satisfied."[4] "I will divide him a portion with the many, and he shall divide the spoil with the strong."[5]

✻ EVENING ✺
WE OURSELVES . . . GROAN INWARDLY AS WE WAIT EAGERLY FOR ADOPTION AS SONS, THE REDEMPTION OF OUR BODIES. — ROMANS 8:23

This groaning is common among God's people: To a greater or lesser extent we all feel it. It is not the groan of murmuring or complaint: It is a note of desire rather than of distress. Having received a deposit, we desire the rest of our portion; we are sighing that our entire manhood, in its trinity of spirit, soul, and body, may be set free from the last trace of the Fall; we long to discard the rags of corruption, weakness, and dishonor and to be clothed with incorruption, immortality, glory—the spiritual body that the Lord Jesus will bestow upon His people. We long for the manifestation of our adoption as the children of God. "We . . . groan," but it is "*inwardly*." It is not the hypocrite's groan, by which he would make men believe that he is a saint because he is wretched. Our sighs are sacred things, too holy and too personal for us to broadcast. We keep our longings for our Lord to ourselves. Then the apostle says we "*wait*," by which we learn that we are not to be petulant, like Jonah or Elijah when they said, "Let me die"; nor are we to whimper and sigh for the end of life because we are tired of work or wish to escape from our present sufferings till the will of the Lord is done. We are to groan for glorification, but we are to wait patiently for it, knowing that what the Lord appoints is best. Waiting implies being ready. We are to stand at the door expecting the Beloved to open it and take us away to Himself. This groaning is a test. You can learn a lot about a man by what he groans after. Some men groan after wealth—they worship money; some groan continually under the troubles of life—they are merely impatient. But the man who sighs after God, who is uneasy until he is made like Christ—that is the blessed man. May God help us to groan for the coming of the Lord and the resurrection that He will bring to us.

[1] John 17:20   [2] Psalm 110:3   [3] Isaiah 53:11   [4] Isaiah 53:11   [5] Isaiah 53:12

ASK, AND IT WILL BE GIVEN TO YOU. — MATTHEW 7:7

There was a place in England that no longer exists, where a loaf of bread was served to every passerby who chose to ask for it. Whoever the traveler was, he had only to knock at the door of St. Cross Hospital, and the loaf of bread was his to enjoy. Jesus Christ loves sinners so much that He has built a St. Cross Hospital, so that whenever a sinner is hungry, he has only to knock and have his needs supplied. He has actually done better: This Hospital of the Cross has a bath; and whenever a soul is marred and filthy, it may go to this effective fountain and be cleansed. No sinner ever went into it and found that it could not wash away his stains. Sins that were scarlet and crimson have all disappeared, and the sinner was made whiter than snow. As if this were not enough, there is attached to this Hospital of the Cross a dressing room, and a sinner making application simply as a sinner may be clothed from head to foot; and if he wishes to be a soldier, he will be provided not just with street clothes, but with armor that will cover him from the sole of his foot to the crown of his head. If he asks for a sword, that will be given to him, and a shield too. He will be denied nothing that is good for him. He will have spending money as long as he lives, and he will have an eternal heritage of glorious treasure when he enters into the joy of his Lord.

If all these things are available by simply knocking at mercy's door, then, my soul, knock hard this morning, and make large requests of your generous Lord. Do not leave the throne of grace until all your wants have been spread before the Lord and until by faith you are confident that they will all be supplied. You need not be shy about taking Jesus up on His invitation. No unbelief should hinder when Jesus promises. No coldheartedness should restrain when such blessings are to be obtained.

❧ EVENING ☙

THEN THE LORD SHOWED ME FOUR CRAFTSMEN. — ZECHARIAH 1:20

In the vision described in this chapter, the prophet saw four terrible horns. They were pushing this way and that way, dashing down the strongest and the mightiest; and the prophet asked, "What are these?" The answer was, "These are the horns that have scattered Judah." He saw before him a representation of those powers that had oppressed the Church of God. There were four horns, for the church is attacked from all quarters. The prophet had good reason to feel dismayed; but suddenly there appeared before him *"four craftsmen."* He asked, "What are these coming to do?" These were the men whom God had found to break those horns in pieces. *God will always find men for His work*, and He will find them at the right time. The prophet did not see the craftsmen at first, when there was nothing to do, but first the "horns" and then the "craftsmen." The Lord always finds *enough men*. He did not find three craftsmen, but *four*; there were four horns, and there must be four workmen. God finds *the right men*—not four men with pens to write, not four architects to draw plans, but four craftsmen to do the work. Rest assured, you who tremble for the Church of God, that when the "horns" grow troublesome, the "craftsmen" will be found. You need not worry about the weakness of the Church of God at any moment; there may be growing up in obscurity the valiant reformer who will shake the nations. Chrysostoms may come forth from our Ragged Schools, and Augustines from the thickest darkness of London's poverty. The Lord knows where to find His servants. He has in ambush a multitude of mighty men, and at His word they will take to the battle; "for the battle is the Lord's,"[1] and He will get to Himself the victory. So let us remain faithful to Christ, and He, in the right time, will raise up for us a defense, whether it be in the day of our personal need or in the season of peril to His Church.

[1] 1 Samuel 17:47

AS IS THE MAN OF HEAVEN, SO ALSO ARE THOSE WHO ARE OF HEAVEN.
— 1 CORINTHIANS 15:48

The head and members are of one nature, and not like that monstrous image that Nebuchadnezzar saw in his dream. The head was of fine gold, but the belly and thighs were of brass, the legs of iron, and the feet partly of iron and partly of clay. Christ's mystical body is no absurd combination of opposites. The members were mortal, and therefore Jesus died; the glorified head is immortal, and therefore the body is immortal too, as the record states: "Because I live, you also will live."[1] As is our loving Head, so is His body, and every member in particular. A chosen Head, therefore chosen members; an accepted Head, therefore accepted members; a living Head, therefore living members. If the head is pure gold, all the parts of the body are pure gold also. There is a double union of nature as a basis for the closest communion. Pause here, devout reader, and see if you can contemplate the infinite condescension of the Son of God in exalting your wretchedness into blessed union with His glory without being overwhelmed by the wonder of it. You are so feeble and poor that in remembering your mortality, you may say to decay, "You are my father," and to the worm, "You are my sister"; and yet in Christ you are so honored that you can say to the Almighty, "Abba, Father" and to the Incarnate God, "You are my Brother and my Husband." Surely if relationships to ancient and noble families make men think highly of themselves, we have more cause to glory than all of them. Let the poorest and most despised believer take hold upon this privilege; do not let an unthinking laziness prevent him from tracing his pedigree, and do not let him focus so much on the here and now that he fails to think profitably of this glorious, heavenly honor of union with Christ.

✍ EVENING ✍

. . . WITH A GOLDEN SASH AROUND HIS CHEST. — REVELATION 1:13

One like "a son of man" appeared to John in Patmos, and the beloved disciple noticed that He wore "a golden sash." A *sash*, for Jesus was never unprepared while on earth, but always stood ready for service; and now before the eternal throne He continues His ministry as our great High Priest. It is good for us that He has not ceased to fulfill His offices of love, since it is one of our choicest safeguards that He ever lives to make intercession for us. Jesus is never lazy; His garments are never loose as though His offices were ended; He diligently carries on the cause of His people. A *golden* sash, to declare the superiority of His service, the royalty of His person, the dignity of His state, the glory of His reward. He no longer cries out of the dust, but He pleads with authority, a King as well as a Priest. Our cause is safe enough in the hands of our enthroned Redeemer.

Our Lord presents all His people with an example. We must never unbind our sashes. This is not the time for lying down to rest; it is the season of service and warfare. We need to bind the sash of truth more and more tightly around us. It is a golden sash, and as such it will be our richest ornament. And we greatly need it, for a heart that is not well braced up with the truth as it is in Jesus and with the faithfulness that is fashioned by the Spirit will be easily entangled with the things of this life and tripped up by the snares of temptation. We possess the Scriptures in vain unless we bind them around us like a sash, surrounding our entire nature, keeping each part of our character in order, and giving compactness to our whole being. If in heaven Jesus does not remove the sash, neither should we upon earth. Stand, therefore, having fastened on the belt of truth.

[1] John 14:19

GOD CHOSE WHAT IS LOW AND DESPISED IN THE WORLD.
— 1 CORINTHIANS 1:28

Walk the streets by moonlight, if you dare, and you will see sinners then. Watch when the night is dark, and the wind is howling, and the thief is hiding in the door, and you will see sinners then. Go to the jail, and walk through the wards, and notice the men with heavy overhanging brows, men whom you would not like to meet at night, and there are sinners there. Go to the reformatories, and note those who have betrayed a rampant juvenile depravity, and you will see sinners there. Go where you will, you need not ransack the earth to find sinners, for they are common enough; you may find them in every lane and street of every city and town and village and hamlet. It is for such that Jesus died. If you will select for me the grossest specimen of humanity, if he be but born of woman, I will still have hope for him, because Jesus Christ came to seek and to save *sinners*. Electing love has selected some of the worst to be made the best. Pebbles from the brook are turned by grace into jewels for the royal crown. Worthless dross He transforms into pure gold. Redeeming love has set apart many of the worst of mankind to be the reward of the Savior's passion. Effectual grace calls deep-dyed sinners to sit at the table of mercy, and therefore none of us should despair.

Reader, by that love looking out of Jesus' tearful eyes, by that love streaming from those bleeding wounds, by that faithful love, that strong love, that pure, disinterested, and abiding love, by the heart and by the tender compassion of the Savior, we urge you not to turn away as though it was nothing to you. Rather, believe on Him and you will be saved. Trust your soul with Him, and He will bring you to His Father's right hand in everlasting glory.

EVENING
I HAVE BECOME ALL THINGS TO ALL PEOPLE, THAT BY ALL MEANS
I MIGHT SAVE SOME. — 1 CORINTHIANS 9:22

Paul's great object was not merely to instruct and to improve, but to save. Anything short of this would have disappointed him; he desired to see men renewed in heart, forgiven, sanctified, in fact saved. Have our Christian efforts been aimed at anything below this great objective? Then let us correct our ways, for what good will it be at the last great day to have taught and moralized men if they appear before God unsaved? If through life we have sought inferior objects and forgotten that men needed to be saved, then we will be held accountable. Paul knew the ruin of man's natural state and did not try to educate him, but to save him; he saw men sinking to hell and did not talk of refining them, but of saving from the wrath to come. To accomplish their salvation, he gave himself up with untiring zeal to spreading the Gospel, to warning and beseeching men to be reconciled to God. His prayers were persistent and his labors incessant. His consuming passion, his ambition, his calling was to save souls. He became a servant to all men, working for them, feeling a woe within him if he did not preach the Gospel. He laid aside his preferences to prevent prejudice; he submitted his will in things indifferent, and if men would just receive the Gospel, he raised no questions about forms or ceremonies. The Gospel was the one all-important business with him. If he might save some, he would be content. This was the crown for which he extended himself, the sole and sufficient reward of all his labors and self-denials. Dear reader, have you and I lived to win souls to this extent? Are we possessed with the same all-absorbing desire? If not, why not? Jesus died for sinners. Can we not live for them? Where is our tenderness? Where is our love for Christ, if we do not seek His honor in the salvation of men? Lord Jesus, saturate us through and through with an undying zeal for the souls of men.

YET YOU HAVE STILL A FEW NAMES IN SARDIS, PEOPLE WHO HAVE NOT
SOILED THEIR GARMENTS, AND THEY WILL WALK WITH ME IN WHITE,
FOR THEY ARE WORTHY. — REVELATION 3:4

We may understand this to refer to *justification.* "They will walk in white"; that is, they will enjoy a constant sense of their own justification by faith; they will understand that the righteousness of Christ is imputed to them, that they have all been washed and made whiter than the newly-fallen snow.

Again, it refers to *joy and gladness,* for white robes were holiday dress among the Jews. They who "have not soiled their garments" will have their faces always bright; they will understand what Solomon meant when he said, "Go, eat your bread in joy, and drink your wine with a merry heart, for God has already approved what you do. Let your garments be always white."[1] The one who is accepted by God will wear white garments of joy and gladness while they walk in sweet communion with the Lord Jesus. Why are there so many doubts, so much misery and mourning? It is because so many believers spoil their garments with sin and error, and as a result they lose the joy of their salvation and the comfortable fellowship of the Lord Jesus; they do not walk here below in white.

The promise also refers to *walking in white before the throne of God.* Those who have not soiled their garments here will most certainly walk in white in heaven, where the white-robed crowd sings perpetual hallelujahs to the Most High. They will possess joys inconceivable, happiness beyond a dream, bliss that imagination knows not, blessedness that even the stretch of desire has not reached. "Those whose way is blameless"[2] shall have all this—not of merit, nor of works, but of grace. They shall walk with Christ in white, for He has made them "worthy." In His sweet company they will drink from the fountains of living waters.

❧ EVENING ☙

IN YOUR GOODNESS, O GOD, YOU HAVE PROVIDED FOR THE NEEDY.
— PSALM 68:10

All God's gifts are prepared gifts laid away to meet wants He has foreseen. He anticipates our needs; and out of the fullness that He has treasured up in Christ Jesus, He provides from His goodness for the poor. You may trust Him for all the necessities you may face, for He has infallibly foreknown every one of them. He can say of us in all conditions, "I knew that you would be this and that." A man takes a journey across the desert, and when he has completed a day and pitched his tent, he discovers that he wants many comforts and necessities that he has not brought in his baggage. "Ah!" he says. "I did not foresee this. If I had this journey to do again, I would bring these things with me—they are necessary to my comfort." But God is already aware of all the requirements of His poor, wandering children, and when those needs occur, supplies are ready. It is goodness that He has prepared for the poor in heart, goodness and goodness only. "My grace is sufficient for you."[3] "As your days, so shall your strength be."[4]

Reader, is your heart heavy this evening? God knew it would be; the comfort that your heart requires is treasured in the sweet assurance of this text. You are poor and needy, but He has thought upon you and has the exact blessing that you require in store for you. Plead the promise; believe it and obtain its fulfillment. Do you feel that you never were so consciously sinful as you are now? Behold, the crimson fountain is open still, with all its former efficacy, to wash your sin away. You will never come into such a position that Christ cannot help you. You will never arrive at a place in your spiritual affairs in which Jesus Christ will not be equal to the emergency, for your history has all been foreknown and provided for in Jesus.

[1] Song of Solomon 9:7-8   [2] Psalm 119:1   [3] 2 Corinthians 12:9   [4] Deuteronomy 33:25

THEREFORE THE LORD WAITS TO BE GRACIOUS TO YOU.
— ISAIAH 30:18

God often *delays in answering prayer*. We have several instances of this in the Bible. Jacob did not get the blessing from the angel until near the dawn of day—he had to wrestle all night for it. The poor woman of Syrophoenicia received no answer for a long while. Paul asked the Lord *three* times for "a thorn . . . in the flesh"[1] to be taken from him, and he received no assurance that it would be removed, but instead a promise that God's grace would be sufficient for him. If you have been knocking at the gate of mercy and have received no answer, shall I tell you why the mighty Maker has not opened the door and let you in? Our Father has personal reasons for keeping us waiting. Sometimes it is to show His power and His sovereignty, so that we may learn that God has a right to give or to withhold. More often the delay is for our benefit. You are perhaps kept waiting in order that your desires may be more fervent. God knows that delay will quicken and increase desire, and that if He keeps you waiting, you will see your need more clearly and will seek more diligently, and that you will treasure the mercy all the more on account of the wait. There may also be something wrong in you that needs to be removed before the joy of the Lord is given. Perhaps your views of the gospel plan are confused, or you may be relying upon yourself instead of trusting simply and entirely in the Lord Jesus. Or God makes you wait for a while so that He may display the riches of His grace more abundantly in the end. Your prayers are all filed in heaven, and if not immediately answered they are certainly not forgotten, but in a little while they will be fulfilled to your delight and satisfaction. Do not allow despair to make you silent, but continue to present your requests to God.

∽   E V E N I N G   ∽

MY PEOPLE WILL ABIDE IN A PEACEFUL HABITATION. — ISAIAH 32:18

Peace and rest do not belong to the unregenerate; they are the peculiar possession of the Lord's people, and of them only. The God of Peace gives perfect peace to those whose hearts are fixed upon Him. Before the Fall, God gave man the Garden of Eden as his quiet resting-place; sadly, how quickly sin spoiled the fair abode of innocence. In the day of universal wrath when the Flood swept away a guilty race, the chosen family was quietly secured in the resting-place of the ark, which floated them from the old condemned world into the new earth of the rainbow and the covenant, symbolizing Jesus, the ark of our salvation. Israel rested safely beneath the blood-sprinkled dwellings of Egypt when the destroying angel smote the firstborn; and in the wilderness the shadow of the pillar of cloud and the flowing rock gave the weary pilgrims sweet repose. Today we rest in the promises of our faithful God, knowing that His words are full of truth and power; we rest in the doctrines of His Word, which are consolation itself; we rest in the covenant of His grace, which is a haven of delight. We are more highly favored than David in the cave or Jonah beneath his plant, for no one can invade or destroy our shelter. The person of Jesus is the quiet resting-place of His people, and when we draw near to Him in the breaking of the bread, the hearing of the Word, the searching of the Scriptures, prayer, or praise, we find that any form of approach to Him brings peace to our spirits.

> *I hear the words of love, I gaze upon the blood,*
> *I see the mighty sacrifice, and I have peace with God.*
> *'Tis everlasting peace, sure as Jehovah's name,*
> *'Tis stable as His steadfast throne, forevermore the same:*
> *The clouds may go and come, and storms may sweep my sky,*
> *This blood-sealed friendship changes not, the cross is ever nigh.*

[1] 2 Corinthians 12:7

• M O R N I N G •

SO WE WILL ALWAYS BE WITH THE LORD.
— 1 THESSALONIANS 4:17

Even the sweetest glimpses of Christ are short—how transitory they are! One moment our eyes see Him, and we rejoice with joy unspeakable and full of glory; but then the moment passes and we do not see Him, for our beloved withdraws Himself from us. Like a roe or a young hare He leaps over the mountains of division; He is gone to the land of spices and no longer feeds among the lilies.

If today He deigns to bless us
With a sense of pardoned sin,
He tomorrow may distress us,
Make us feel the plague within.

How sweet the prospect of the time when we will no longer see Him from a distance but rather face to face—when He will not be like a traveler staying only for a night but will enfold us in the bosom of His eternal glory. We will not see Him for a little while, but

Millions of years our wondering eyes,
Shall o'er our Savior's beauties rove;
And myriad ages we'll adore,
The wonders of His love.

In heaven we will not be interrupted by care or sins; no weeping will dim our eyes; no earthly business will distract our happy thoughts. We will have nothing to prevent us from gazing forever on the Sun of Righteousness with tireless eyes. If it is so sweet to see Him now and then, how wonderful to gaze on that blessed face forever, and without a cloud rolling between, and never have to turn one's eyes away to look on a tired and sinful world. When will this blessed day dawn? Rise, unsetting sun! If to die is to enter into uninterrupted communion with Jesus, then death is swallowed up in a sea of victory and is definitely gain.

• E V E N I N G •

THE LORD OPENED HER HEART. — ACTS 16:14

In Lydia's conversion there are many points of interest. It was brought about by *providential circumstances*. She was a seller of purple goods, from the city of Thyratira, but at just the right time for hearing Paul we find her at Philippi; providence, which is the servant of grace, led her to the right spot. Again, *grace was preparing her soul for the blessing*—grace preparing for grace. She did not know the Savior, but as a Jewess she knew many truths that were excellent stepping-stones to a knowledge of Jesus. Her conversion took place in the use of the means. On the Sabbath she went to a place of prayer, and there prayer was answered. Never neglect the means of grace. God *may* bless us when we are not in His house, but we have more reason to expect that He *will* when we are in fellowship with His people. Observe the words, "*The Lord* opened her heart." She did not open her own heart. Her prayers did not do it; Paul did not do it. The Lord Himself must open the heart to receive the things that make for our peace. He alone can put the key into the door and open it and gain entry for Himself. He is the heart's Master just as He is the heart's Maker. The first outward evidence of the opened heart was *obedience*. As soon as Lydia had believed in Jesus, she was baptized. It is a sweet sign of a humble and broken heart when the child of God is willing to obey a command that is not essential to his salvation, that is not forced upon him by a selfish fear of condemnation, but is a simple act of obedience and of communion with his Master. The next evidence was *love*, displaying itself in acts of grateful kindness to the apostles. Love for the saints has always been a mark of the true convert. Those who do nothing for Christ or His church provide no evidence of an "opened" heart. Lord, grant to us the blessing of opened hearts always!

HE WHO CALLS YOU IS FAITHFUL; HE WILL SURELY DO IT.
— 1 THESSALONIANS 5:24

Heaven is a place where we will never sin, where our battle with the evil one will be over; there will be no tempter to ensnare our feet. There the wicked cause no trouble, and the weary are at rest. Heaven is the undefiled inheritance; it is the land of perfect holiness, and therefore of complete security. But don't even the saints on earth sometimes taste the joys of blissful security? The doctrine of God's Word is that all who are in union with Christ are safe, that all the righteous shall keep to the path, that those who have committed their souls to the care of Christ will find Him to be a faithful and unchanging protector. Sustained by such a doctrine we can enjoy security even on earth—not the high and glorious security that makes us free from every slip, but that holy security that comes from the sure promise of Jesus that none who believe in Him will ever perish but will be with Him where He is. Believer, reflect often and joyfully on the doctrine of the perseverance of the saints, and honor the faithfulness of God by a holy confidence in Him.

May God bring home to you a sense of your safety in Christ Jesus! May He assure you that your name is graven on His hand and whisper in your ear the promise, "Fear not, for I am with you." Look upon Him, the great Guarantee of the covenant, as faithful and true and therefore bound and committed to present you, in your weakness, with all the chosen race, before the throne of God; and in such a sweet contemplation you will drink the cup of salvation and taste the fruits of paradise. You will have a foretaste of the enjoyments that ravish the souls of the saints in heaven if you can believe with unwavering faith that "He who calls you is faithful; he will surely do it."

YOU ARE SERVING THE LORD CHRIST. — COLOSSIANS 3:24

To what special group was this word spoken? To kings who proudly boast a divine right? No! Too often they serve themselves or Satan and forget God who patiently permits them to wear their majestic crowns for a little while. Is the apostle speaking to those so-called "right reverend fathers in God," the bishops or "the venerable archdeacons"? No; in fact, Paul knew nothing of these man-made titles. This word was not spoken even to pastors and teachers or to the wealthy and highly regarded among believers, but to servants and to slaves. Among the toiling multitudes—the journeymen, the day laborers, the domestic servants, the drudges of the kitchen—the apostle found, as we still find, some of the Lord's chosen, and he says to them, "Whatever you do, work heartily, as for the Lord and not for men, knowing that from the Lord you will receive the inheritance as your reward. You are serving the Lord Christ." This saying grants significance to the weary routine of earthly employments and sheds a halo around the most humble occupations. To wash feet may be servile, but to wash *His* feet is royal work. To untie sandals is poor employment, but to unloose the Master's shoe is a princely privilege. The shop, the barn, the kitchen, and the workbench become temples when men and women do all to the glory of God! Then divine service does not take place for a few hours and in a few places, but all life becomes holiness to the Lord, and every place and thing as consecrated as the tabernacle and its contents.

Teach me, my God and King, in all things Thee to see;
And what I do in anything to do it as to Thee.
All may of Thee partake, nothing can be so mean,
Which with this tincture, for Thy sake, will not grow bright and clean.
A servant with this clause makes drudgery divine;
Who sweeps a room, as for Thy laws, makes that and the action fine.

HIS WERE THE EVERLASTING WAYS. — HABAKKUK 3:6

What God has done on one occasion, He will do again. Man's ways are variable, but God's ways are everlasting. There are many reasons for this most comforting truth. Among them are the following: The Lord's ways are *the result of wise deliberation*; He orders everything according to the counsel of His own will. Human action is frequently the hasty result of passion or fear and is followed by regret and change; but nothing can take the Almighty by surprise or happen contrary to what He has foreseen. His ways are *the outgrowth of an unchanging character*, and in them the fixed and settled attributes of God are clearly seen. Unless the Eternal One Himself can undergo change, His ways, which are Himself in action, must remain forever the same. Is He eternally just, gracious, faithful, wise, tender? Then His ways must always be distinguished by the same excellences. Beings act according to their nature: When those natures change, their conduct also varies. But since God cannot know the shadow of turning, His ways will remain everlastingly the same. Furthermore there is no external reason that could reverse the divine ways, since they are the *embodiment of irresistible might*. The prophet tells us that the earth is split with rivers, mountains tremble, the sea lifts up its hands, and the sun and moon stand still when Jehovah marches out for the salvation of His people. Who can prevent Him or say to Him, "What are You doing?" But it is not only might that gives stability; God's ways are *the manifestation of the eternal principles of right* and therefore can never pass away. Wrong breeds decay and involves ruin, but the true and the good are marked by a vitality that time cannot diminish.

This morning let us go to our heavenly Father with confidence, remembering that Jesus Christ is the same yesterday, today, and forever, and in Him the Lord is always gracious to His people.

❧ EVENING ❧

THEY HAVE DEALT FAITHLESSLY WITH THE LORD. — HOSEA 5:7

Believer, here is a sad truth! You are the beloved of the Lord, redeemed by blood, called by grace, preserved in Christ Jesus, accepted in the Beloved, on your way to heaven, and yet you "have dealt faithlessly" with God, your best friend; faithlessly with Jesus, to whom you belong; faithlessly with the Holy Spirit, by whom you have been born again to life eternal! How faithless you have been in the matter of vows and promises. Do you remember your love in the early days, that happy time, the springtime of your spiritual life? How closely you held to your Master then, saying, "He will never charge me with indifference; my feet will never grow slow in the way of His service; I will not allow my heart to wander after other loves; in Him is blessing I could ever enjoy. I give up everything for my Lord Jesus' sake." Has it been so? Sadly if conscience speaks, it will say, "He who promised so much has performed so little. Prayer has frequently been slurred—it has been short but not sweet, brief but not fervent. Communion with Christ has been forgotten. Instead of a heavenly mind, there have been earthly preoccupations, foolish vanities, and evil thoughts. Instead of service, there has been disobedience, instead of fervency lukewarmness, instead of patience petulance, instead of faith self-reliance; and as a soldier of the cross there has been cowardice, disobedience, and desertion, to a very shameful degree." "They have dealt faithlessly." Faithless to Jesus! What words shall be used in denouncing this? Words are cheap: Let our penitent thoughts condemn the sin that is so surely in us. Faithless to Your sacrifice, O Jesus! Forgive us, and let us not sin again! How shameful to be faithless to Him who never forgets us, but who to this day stands with our names engraven on His breastplate before the eternal throne.

Salt was used in every offering made by fire to the Lord, and with its preserving and purifying properties it was the grateful emblem of divine grace in the soul. It is worthy of our careful attention that when Artaxerxes gave salt to Ezra the priest, he set no limit to the quantity, and we may be quite certain that when the King of kings distributes grace among His royal priesthood, the supply is not cut short by *Him*. In ourselves we are often in short supply, but never in the Lord. He who chooses to gather much manna will find that he may have as much as he desires. There is no famine in Jerusalem that causes the citizens to eat their bread by weight and drink their water by measure. Some things in the economy of grace are measured; for instance our vinegar and gall are given us with such exactness that we never have a single drop too much; but the salt of grace is not restricted in its provision. "Ask whatever you wish, and it will be done for you."[1] Parents need to lock up the fruit cupboard and the candy jars, but there is no need to keep the salt-box under lock and key, for few children will eat too greedily from that. A man may have too much money or too much honor, but he cannot have too much grace. When Jeshurun grew fat, he forsook God, but there is no fear of a man's becoming too full of grace: A *plethora* of grace is impossible. More wealth brings more care, but more grace brings more joy. Increased wisdom is increased sorrow, but an abundance of the Spirit is fullness of joy. Believer, go to the throne for a large supply of heavenly salt. It will season your afflictions, which are unsavory without salt; it will preserve your heart, which grows corrupt if salt is absent; and it will kill your sins even as salt kills reptiles. You need much; seek much and have much.

EVENING
GIVE ME CHILDREN, OR I SHALL DIE. — GENESIS 30:1

The cry of Rachel for physical children should be more than matched by the believer's longing for spiritual children. Our great object in living is to glorify God, and we mainly achieve this end by the winning of souls. We *must* see souls born unto God. If we do not win souls, we should mourn as the farmer who sees no harvest, as the fisherman who returns to his cottage with an empty net, or as the hunter who has roamed in vain over hill and dale. Ours should be Isaiah's language uttered with many a sigh and groan—"who has believed what they heard from us, and to whom has the arm of the Lord been revealed?"[2] As ambassadors of peace we should not cease to weep bitterly until sinners weep for their sins. If we intensely desire to see others believing in the Lord Jesus, we must act in accordance with the principle and pattern of Scripture. We must depend entirely upon the Spirit of God. Do we not fail in many of our efforts because we practically, though not doctrinally, ignore the Holy Spirit? His place as God is on the throne, and in all our enterprises He must be the beginning, the middle, and the end; we are instruments in His hand and nothing more.

We must be most of all clear upon the great soul-saving doctrine of the Atonement. "He made him to be sin who knew no sin, so that in him we might become the righteousness of God."[3] This truth that Christ died in the place of sinners gives rest to the conscience by showing how God can be just and the justifier of whoever believes. This is the great net of gospel fishermen; the fish are drawn or driven in the right direction by other truths, but this is the net itself.

We must declare the love of God in Christ Jesus. Always keep Hs abounding mercy connected to His unerring justice. Never exalt one attribute at the expense of another. Let boundless mercy be seen in calm consistency with stern justice and unlimited sovereignty.

Believer, are you longing to see spiritual offspring? Do not let the sun set on this day without imploring God to show Himself strong in this regard. Beseech Him, "Give me children, or I shall die."

Editor's note: This meditation replaces Spurgeon's original devotional, on Isaiah 54:12 and was adapted from Charles Spurgeon's Lectures to Students, page 375.

[1] John 15:7 [2] John 12:38 [3] 2 Corinthians 5:21

THEY GO FROM STRENGTH TO STRENGTH. — PSALM 84:7

They go from *strength to strength.*" There are various renderings of these words, but all of them contain the idea of progress. "They go from strength to strength." That is, they grow stronger and stronger. Usually, if we are walking we go from strength to weakness; we start fresh and in good order for our journey, but by and by the road is rough, and the sun is hot; so we sit down by the wayside and then resume our weary way. But the Christian pilgrim, having obtained fresh supplies of grace, is as vigorous after years of weary travel and struggle as when he first set out. He may not be quite so elated and buoyant, nor perhaps quite so hot and hasty in his zeal as he once was, but he is much stronger in all that constitutes real power; and if he travels more slowly, he does so more surely. Some gray-haired veterans have been as firm in their grasp of truth and as zealous in spreading it as they were in their younger days. But sadly, it must be confessed it is often otherwise, for the love of many grows cold, and iniquity flourishes; but this is their own sin and not the fault of the promise, which still holds good: "Even youths shall faint and be weary, and young men shall fall exhausted; but they who wait for the LORD shall renew their strength; they shall mount up with wings like eagles; they shall run and not be weary; they shall walk and not faint."[1] Fretful spirits sit down and trouble themselves about the future. "Unfortunately," they say, "we go from affliction to affliction." Very true, O you of little faith; but you go from strength to strength also. You will never find a bundle of affliction that does not have in it somewhere sufficient grace. God will give the strength of ripe maturity along with the burden allotted to full-grown shoulders.

❧ EVENING ❧

I HAVE BEEN CRUCIFIED WITH CHRIST. — GALATIANS 2:20

The Lord Jesus Christ acted in what He did as a great public representative person, and His dying upon the cross was the virtual dying of all His people. In Him all His people rendered justice its due and made an expiation to divine vengeance for all their sins. The apostle of the Gentiles delighted to think that as one of Christ's chosen people, he died upon the cross in Christ. He did more than believe this doctrinally—he accepted it confidently, resting his hope upon it. He believed that by virtue of Christ's death, he had satisfied divine justice and found reconciliation with God. Beloved, what a blessed thing it is when the soul can, as it were, stretch itself upon the cross of Christ and feel, "I am dead; the law has killed me, and I am therefore free from its power, because in Christ I have borne the curse, and in the person of my Substitute all that the law could do by way of condemnation has been executed upon me, for I am crucified with Christ."

But Paul meant even more than this. He not only believed in Christ's death and trusted in it, but he actually felt its power in himself causing the crucifixion of his old corrupt nature. When he saw the pleasures of sin, he said, "I cannot enjoy these: I am dead to them." Such is the experience of every true Christian. Having received Christ, he is to this world as one who is utterly dead. Yet, while conscious of death to the world, he can at the same time exclaim with the apostle, "I live." He is fully alive to God. The Christian's life is a matchless riddle. The unconverted cannot comprehend it; even the believer himself cannot understand it. Dead, yet alive! Crucified with Christ, and yet at the same time risen with Christ in newness of life! Union with the suffering, bleeding Savior and death to the world and sin are soul-cheering things. May we learn to live evermore in the enjoyment of them!

[1] Isaiah 40:30-31

ORPAH KISSED HER MOTHER-IN-LAW, BUT RUTH CLUNG TO HER.
— RUTH 1:14

Both of them had an affection for Naomi and therefore set out with her upon her return to the land of Judah. But the test came: Naomi unselfishly set before both of them the trials that awaited them and encouraged them if they cared for ease and comfort to return to their friends in Moab. At first both of them declared that they would take their stand with the Lord's people; but upon further consideration Orpah with much grief and a respectful kiss left her mother-in-law, and her people and her God, and went back to her idolatrous friends, while Ruth with all her heart gave herself up to the God of her mother-in-law. It is one thing to love the ways of the Lord when all is fair, and quite another to hold to them in the face of discouragements and difficulties. The kiss of outward profession is very cheap and easy, but the practical clinging to the Lord, which must show itself in holy devotion to truth and holiness, is no small matter. How do things stands with us? Is our heart fixed on Jesus, our body a living sacrifice? Have we counted the cost, and are we solemnly ready to suffer the loss of all things for the Master's sake? The ultimate gain will be an abundant provision, for the treasures of Egypt do not compare with the glory to be revealed. Orpah fades from view; in glorious ease and idolatrous pleasure her life melts into the gloom of death. But Ruth lives on in history and in heaven, for grace has placed her in the noble line that produced the King of kings. Blessed among women will be those who for Christ's sake renounce all; but forgotten, and worse than forgotten, will be those who in the hour of temptation violate their conscience and turn back to the world. This morning let us not be content with the form of devotion, which may be no better than Orpah's kiss, but may the Holy Spirit work in us a clinging of our whole heart to the Lord Jesus.

∾ EVENING ∾

AND LAY YOUR FOUNDATIONS WITH SAPPHIRES. — ISAIAH 54:11

Not only what is seen in the Church of God but also what is unseen is fair and precious. Foundations are out of sight, and as long as they are firm, it is not expected that they should be valuable. But in God's work everything is of the same value—nothing devalued, nothing irrelevant. The deep foundations of the work of grace are as precious as sapphires; no human mind is able to measure their glory. We build upon the *covenant of grace*, which is stronger than steel and as enduring as diamonds and upon which age makes no impact. Sapphire foundations are eternal, and the covenant remains throughout the lifetime of the Almighty. Another foundation is *the person of the Lord Jesus*, clear and spotless, as everlasting and beautiful as the sapphire, combining the deep blue of earth's ever-rolling ocean and the azure of its all-embracing sky. At one time our Lord might have been compared to the ruby as He stood covered with His own blood, but now we see Him radiant with the soft blue of love—love abounding, deep, eternal. Our eternal hopes are built upon *the justice and the faithfulness of God*, which are as clear and cloudless as the sapphire. We are not saved by a compromise, by mercy defeating justice or law suspending its operations; no, we defy the eagle's eye to detect a flaw in the groundwork of our confidence: Our foundation is of sapphire and will endure the fire.

The Lord Himself has laid the foundation of His people's hopes. It is a subject for serious inquiry whether *our* hopes are built upon such a basis. Good works and ceremonies are not a foundation of sapphires, but of wood, hay, and stubble; neither are they laid by God but by our own conceit. Foundations will all be tested before long: Woe to him whose lofty tower will come down with a crash because it was built on sand. The one who is built on sapphires may face storm or fire with confidence, for he will pass the test.

❧ MORNING ☙
COME TO ME. — MATTHEW 11:28

The call of the Christian faith is the gentle word, "Come." The Jewish law spoke harshly: "Go, pay attention to your steps as to the path in which you will walk. Break the commandments, and you will perish; keep them, and you will live." The law was a dispensation of terror that drove men before it as with a scourge; the Gospel draws with cords of love. Jesus is the Good Shepherd going before His sheep, bidding them follow Him, and leading them forward with the sweet word, "Come." The law repels; the Gospel attracts. The law shows the distance that exists between God and man; the Gospel bridges that awful chasm and brings the sinner across it.

From the first moment of your spiritual life until you are welcomed into heaven, the language of Christ to you will be, "*Come* to me." As a mother extends her hand to her tiny child and woos it to walk by saying, "*Come*," even so does Jesus. He will always be ahead of you, bidding you follow Him as the soldier follows his captain. He will always go before you to pave your way and clear your path, and you will hear His life-giving voice calling you to follow Him all through your life; in the solemn hour of death, His sweet words with which He will usher you into the heavenly world will be, "Come, you who are blessed of my Father."[1]

This is not only Christ's call to you, but if you are a believer, this is your call to Christ— "Come! Come!" You will be longing for His return; you will be saying, "Come quickly; even so come, Lord Jesus." You will desire nearer and closer fellowship with Him. As His voice to you is "Come," your response to Him will be, "Come, Lord, and stay with me. Come and occupy the throne of my heart; reign there without a rival, and consecrate me entirely to Your service."

❧ EVENING ☙
YOU HAVE NEVER HEARD, YOU HAVE NEVER KNOWN,
FROM OF OLD YOUR EAR HAS NOT BEEN OPENED. — ISAIAH 48:8

It is painful to remember that to a certain degree this accusation may be laid at the door of *believers*, who too often are in some measure *spiritually insensitive*. We may well bemoan the fact that *we* do not hear the voice of God as we should: "You have never heard." There are gentle motions of the Holy Spirit in the soul that are unheeded by us: There are whisperings of divine command and of heavenly love that are equally unobserved by our dull minds. Sadly, we have been *carelessly ignorant*—"You have never known." There are spiritual matters that we ought to have seen, corruptions that have been allowed to develop unnoticed, tender affections that are being harmed like flowers in the frost, untended by us, glimpses of the Lord that we might have perceived if we had not barricaded the windows of our soul. But we "have never known." As we think of this we are truly and deeply humbled. How we must adore the grace of God as we realize from the context that all of our folly and ignorance *was foreknown by God*, and notwithstanding that foreknowledge, He has still been pleased to deal with us in mercy! Ponder and admire the marvelous sovereign grace that could have chosen us in the sight of all this! Wonder at the price that was paid for us when Christ knew what we would be! He who hung upon the cross foresaw us as unbelieving, backsliding, cold of heart, indifferent, careless, lax in prayer, and yet He said, "I am the Lord your God, the Holy One of Israel, your Savior. Because you are precious in My eyes and honored, and I love you, I give men in return for you, peoples in exchange for your life." How wonderful and glorious is this redemption when we think how sinful we are! Holy Spirit, give us from now on a hearing ear and an understanding heart!

[1] Matthew 25:34

I REMEMBER THE DEVOTION OF YOUR YOUTH. — JEREMIAH 2:2

Let us note that Christ delights to think upon His Church and to look upon her beauty. As the bird returns often to its nest, and as the traveler hurries to his home, so the mind continually pursues the object of its choice. We cannot look too often upon the face we love; we continually desire to have what is precious to us. This is also true with our Lord Jesus. From all eternity He has been "delighting in the children of man."[1] His thoughts rolled onward to the time when His elect would be born into the world; He viewed them in the mirror of His foreknowledge. "In your book were written, every one of them, the days that were formed for me, when as yet there were none of them" (Ps. 139:16). When the world was set upon its pillars, He was there, and He set the boundaries of the people according to the number of the children of Israel. Many a time before His incarnation, He descended to this lower earth in the similitude of a man—on the plains of Mamre (Gen. 18), by the brook of Jabbok (Gen. 32:24-30), beneath the walls of Jericho (Josh. 5:13), and in the fiery furnace of Babylon (Dan. 3:19, 25). The Son of Man visited His people. Because His soul delighted in them, He could not stay away from them, for His heart longed for them. They were never absent from His heart, for He had written their names upon His hands and had graven them upon His side. As the breastplate containing the names of the tribes of Israel was the most brilliant ornament worn by the high priest, so the names of Christ's elect were His most precious jewels and glittered on His heart. We may often forget to meditate upon the perfections of our Lord, but He never ceases to remember us. Let us chide ourselves for past forgetfulness, and pray for grace that we might constantly and fondly remember Him. Lord, paint upon the eyeballs of my soul the image of Your Son.

I AM THE DOOR. IF ANYONE ENTERS BY ME, HE WILL BE SAVED AND
WILL GO IN AND OUT AND FIND PASTURE. — JOHN 10:9

Jesus, the great I AM, is the entrance into the true Church and the way of access to God Himself. He gives to the one who comes to God by Him four choice privileges.

1. *He will be saved.* The fugitive entered the gate of the city of refuge and was safe. Noah entered the door of the ark and was secure. None can be lost who take Jesus as the door of faith to their souls. Entrance through Jesus into peace is the guarantee of entrance by the same door into heaven. Jesus is the only door, an open door, a wide door, a safe door; and blessed is he who rests all his hope of admission to glory upon the crucified Redeemer.

2. *He will go in.* He will be privileged to go in among the divine family, sharing the children's food and participating in all their honors and enjoyments. He will go into the rooms of communion, to the banquets of love, to the treasures of the covenant, to the storehouses of the promises. He will go in to the King of kings in the power of the Holy Spirit, and the secret of the Lord will be with him.

3. *He will go out.* This blessing is much forgotten. We go out into the world to work and suffer, but what a mercy to go in the name and power of Jesus! We are called to bear witness to the truth, to cheer the disconsolate, to warn the careless, to win souls, and to glorify God. And as the angel said to Gideon, "Go in this might of yours,"[2] even so the Lord would have us proceed as His messengers in His name and strength.

4. *He will find pasture.* He who knows Jesus will never lack. Going in or out will be equally helpful to him: In fellowship with God he will grow, and in watering others he will be watered. Having made Jesus his all, he will find all in Jesus. His soul will be like a watered garden and like a well of water that never runs dry.

[1] Proverbs 8:31   [2] Judges 6:14

REND YOUR HEARTS AND NOT YOUR GARMENTS. — JOEL 2:13

The tearing of garments and other outward signs of religious emotion are easily displayed and are *frequently hypocritical*; but to feel true repentance is far more difficult, and consequently far less common. Men will pay attention to the most minute ceremonial regulations—for those things are *pleasing to the flesh*. But true faith is too humbling, too heart-searching, too thorough for the tastes of people of the flesh; they prefer something more ostentatious, flimsy, and worldly. Outward observances are *temporarily comfortable*; eye and ear are pleased; self-conceit is fed, and self-righteousness is puffed up: But they are *ultimately delusive*, for in the face of death, and at the day of judgment, the soul needs something more substantial than ceremonies and rituals to lean upon. Apart from vital godliness all religion is utterly vain; offered without a sincere heart, every form of worship is a solemn sham and an impudent mockery of the majesty of heaven.

Heart-rending is *divinely worked and solemnly felt*. It is a secret grief that is *personally experienced*, not in mere form, but as a deep, soul-moving work of the Holy Spirit upon the inmost heart of each believer. It is not a matter to be merely talked about and believed in, but keenly and sensitively felt in every living child of the living God. It is *powerfully humiliating* and completely sin-purging, but it is also *sweet preparation* for the gracious consolations that proud, unhumbled spirits are unable to receive; and it is *distinctly discriminating*, for it belongs to the elect of God, and to them alone.

The text commands us to rend our hearts, but they are naturally as hard as marble: How, then, can this be done? We must take them to Calvary: A dying Savior's voice rent the rocks once, and it is as powerful now. O blessed Spirit, let us hear the death-cries of Jesus, and our hearts shall be rent even as men tear their garments in the day of lamentation.

∾ EVENING ∾
KNOW WELL THE CONDITION OF YOUR FLOCKS, AND GIVE ATTENTION TO YOUR HERDS. — PROVERBS 27:23

Every wise businessman will occasionally hold a stock-taking, when he will examine his accounts, consider what he has on hand, and determine clearly whether his trade is prosperous or declining. Every man who is wise in the kingdom of heaven will cry, "Search me, O God . . . Try me";[1] and he will frequently set apart special seasons for self-examination, to discover whether things are right between God and his soul. The God whom we worship is a great heart-searcher; and in the past His servants referred to Him as "I am he who searches mind and heart, and I will give to each of you as your works deserve."[2] Let me encourage you in His name to diligently search and solemnly test your spiritual state, for fear you should come short of the promised rest. This is what every wise man does, and what God Himself does with us all. I exhort you to do the same yourself this evening. Let the oldest saint examine the basics of his piety, for gray heads may cover evil hearts: And the young professor should not despise the word of warning, for the greenness of youth may accompany the rottenness of hypocrisy. Every now and then a spiritual giant falls. The enemy still continues to sow tares among the wheat. It is not my aim to introduce doubts and fears to your mind; I rather hope that the rough wind of self-examination may help to drive them away. It is not security but fleshly security that we would kill, not confidence but carnal confidence that we would overthrow, not peace but false peace that we would destroy. By the precious blood of Christ, which was not shed to make you a hypocrite, but rather that sincere souls might declare His praise, I urge you to search and look, for fear that in the end it will be said of you, "Tekel, you have been weighed in the balances and found wanting."[3]

[1] Psalm 139:23 [2] Revelation 2:23 [3] Daniel 5:27

THE LOT IS CAST INTO THE LAP, BUT ITS EVERY DECISION
IS FROM THE LORD. — PROVERBS 16:33

If the decision about the lot is the Lord's, whose is the arrangement of our whole life? If the simple casting of a lot is guided by Him, how much more the events of our entire life—especially when we are told by our blessed Savior, "Even the hairs of your head are all numbered. Fear not, therefore; you are of more value than many sparrows."[1] It would bring a holy calm over your mind, dear friend, if you were to constantly remember this. It would relieve your mind from anxiety and enable you to walk in patience, quietness, and cheerfulness as a Christian should. When a man is anxious he cannot pray with faith; when he is troubled about the world, he cannot serve his Master, for his thoughts are serving himself. If you would "seek first the kingdom of God and his righteousness,"[2] all things would then be added to you. You are meddling with Christ's business and neglecting your own when you fret about your lot and circumstances. You have been trying to do the providing and forgetting to do the obeying. Be wise and pay attention to the obeying, and let Christ manage the providing. Come and survey your Father's storehouse, and ask whether He will allow you to starve while He has so great an abundance in store. Look at His heart of mercy; see if that can ever prove unkind! Look at His unsearchable wisdom; see if that will ever be at fault. Above all, look to Jesus Christ your Intercessor, and ask yourself, while He pleads, can your Father deal ungraciously with you? If He remembers even sparrows, will He forget one of the least of His poor children? "Cast your burden on the LORD, and he will sustain you; he will never permit the righteous to be moved."[3]

My soul, rest happy in your low estate,
Nor hope nor wish to be esteem'd or great;
To take the impress of the Will Divine,
Be that your glory, and those riches thine.

&.   EVENING   .&

THE SEA WAS NO MORE. — REVELATION 21:1

We could scarcely rejoice at the thought of losing the glorious old ocean: The new heavens and the new earth are not attractive to our imagination if in fact there is literally going to be no great and wide sea with its gleaming waves and sandy shores. Should the text not be read as a metaphor tinged with the prejudice with which the oriental mind universally regarded the sea in the olden times? A real physical world without a sea is a sad idea; it would be an iron ring without the sapphire that made it precious. There must be a spiritual meaning here. In the new dispensation there will be no *division*—the sea separates nations and divides peoples from each other. To John in Patmos the deep waters were like prison walls, shutting him out from his brethren and his work: There will be no such barriers in the world to come. Leagues of rolling billows lie between us and family members whom tonight we prayerfully remember, but in the bright world to which we go there will be unbroken fellowship for all the redeemed family. In this sense there shall be no more sea. The sea is the emblem of change; with its ebbs and flows, its glassy smoothness and its mountainous billows, its gentle murmurs and its tumultuous roarings, it is never the same for very long. It is a slave of the fickle winds and the changing moon, and its instability is proverbial. In this earthly journey we have too much of this; earth is constant only in her inconstancy. But in our heavenly state all mournful change will be unknown, and with it every fear of storms that would wreck our hopes and drown our joys. The sea of glass glows with splendor unbroken by a wave. No tempest howls along the peaceful shores of paradise. Soon we will reach that happy land where partings and changes and storms shall be ended! Jesus will guide us there. Are we in Him or not? This is the grand question.

[1] Matthew 10:30-31   [2] Matthew 6:33   [3] Psalm 55:22

I HAVE LOVED YOU WITH AN EVERLASTING LOVE. — JEREMIAH 31:3

Sometimes the Lord Jesus tells His Church His love thoughts. "He does not consider it sufficient to declare them behind her back, but in her very presence He says, 'Behold, you are beautiful, my love.'[1] It is true, this is not His ordinary method. He is a wise lover and knows when to hold back the intimation of love and when to declare it; but there are times when He will make no secret of it, times when He will put it beyond all dispute in the souls of His people" (R. Erskine's *Sermons*). The Holy Spirit is often pleased, in a most gracious manner, to witness with our spirits to the love of Jesus. He takes the things of Christ and reveals them to us. No voice is heard from the clouds, and no vision is seen in the night, but we have a testimony more certain than either of these. If an angel should fly from heaven and inform the believer personally of the Savior's love for him, the evidence would not be one bit more satisfactory than that which is born in the heart by the Holy Spirit. Ask the Lord's people who have lived the nearest to the gates of heaven, and they will tell you that they have had seasons when the love of Christ toward them has been a fact so clear and sure that they could no more doubt it than they could question their own existence. Yes, dear believer, you and I have had times of refreshing from the presence of the Lord, and then our faith has soared to the heights of assurance. We have had confidence to lean our heads upon the shoulder of our Lord, and we have not questioned our Master's affection for us. The dark question, "Lord, is it I that will betray You?" has been put far from us. He has kissed us with the kisses of His mouth and killed our doubts by the closeness of His embrace. His love has been sweeter than wine to our souls.

&. EVENING &

CALL THE LABORERS AND PAY THEM THEIR WAGES. — MATTHEW 20:8

God is a good Master; He pays His servants while they work and also when their work is done. One of His payments is this: *an easy conscience.* If you have spoken faithfully of Jesus to one person, when you go to bed at night you feel happy, thinking, "I have today discharged my conscience of that man's blood." There is a great *comfort in doing something for Jesus.* What a happiness to place jewels in His crown and allow Him to see of the travail of His soul! There is also great reward in *watching the first buddings of conviction in a soul!* To say of that girl in the class, "She has a tender heart—I do hope that the Lord is at work in her." To go home and pray over that boy who said something in the afternoon that made you think he must know more of divine truth than you had feared! Oh, the joy of hope! But as for *the joy of success*—it is unspeakable! This joy, overwhelming as it is, is a hungry thing—you pine for more of it. To be a soul-winner is the happiest thing in the world. With every soul you bring to Christ, you get a new heaven on earth. But who can conceive of the bliss that awaits us above! How sweet is the sentence, "Enter into *the joy of your master!*"[2] Do you know what the joy of Christ is over a saved sinner? This is the very joy that we are to possess in heaven. Yes, when He ascends the throne, you shall ascend with Him. When the heavens ring with "Well done, well done," you will have a part in the reward. You have worked with Him; you have suffered with Him; you will now reign with Him. You have sown with Him; you will reap with Him. Your face was covered with sweat like His, and your soul, like His, was grieved for the sins of men; now your face will be bright with heaven's splendor as is His countenance, and now your soul will be filled with heavenly joys just as His soul is.

[1] Song of Solomon 1:15 [2] Matthew 25:21, 23

FOR HE HAS MADE WITH ME AN EVERLASTING COVENANT.
— 2 SAMUEL 23:5

This covenant is *divine in its origin.* "He has made with me an everlasting covenant." Oh, that great word *"he"*! My soul, consider—God, the everlasting Father, has positively made a covenant with you; yes, the God who spoke the world into existence by a word; He, stooping from His majesty, takes hold of your hand and makes a covenant with you. Isn't this act so stupendous and such an example of condescension that it would overwhelm us forever if we could really understand it? "He has made with me an everlasting covenant." A king has not made a covenant with me—that would be something; but the Prince of the kings of the earth, Shaddai, the Lord All-sufficient, the Jehovah of ages, the everlasting Elohim— "He has made with me an everlasting covenant." But notice, it is *particular in its application.* "For he has made with *me* an everlasting covenant." Here is the sweetness of it to each believer. It is nothing for me that He made peace for the world; I want to know whether He made peace for *me*! It is a small matter that He has made a covenant; I want to know whether He has made a covenant *with me.* Blessed is the assurance that He has made a covenant with me! If God the Holy Spirit gives me assurance of this, then His salvation is mine, His heart is mine, He Himself is mine—*He is my God.*

This covenant is *everlasting in its duration.* An everlasting covenant means a covenant that had no beginning and that will never, ever end. How sweet in all the uncertainties of life to know that "God's foundation stands firm,"[1] and to have God's own promise, "I will not violate my covenant or alter the word that went forth from my lips."[2] I will sing of this through all my days and at their ending and forever.

◂ EVENING ▸

I CLOTHED YOU ALSO WITH EMBROIDERED CLOTH AND SHOD YOU WITH
FINE LEATHER. I WRAPPED YOU IN FINE LINEN AND
COVERED YOU WITH SILK. — EZEKIEL 16:10

Consider the matchless generosity with which the Lord provides for His people's apparel. They are arrayed in this way so that the divine skill is seen producing an unrivaled *"embroidered cloth,"* in which every attribute takes its part and every divine beauty is revealed. There is no art like the art displayed in our salvation, no skillful workmanship like that seen in the righteousness of the saints. Justification has engrossed learned pens in every age of the church and will be the theme of admiration in eternity. In all this splendor there is utility and durability, comparable to our being *"shod . . . with fine leather."* This skin covered the tabernacle and formed one of the finest and strongest leathers known. The righteousness that is of God by faith endures forever, and he who is shod with this divine preparation will walk through the desert in safety. The purity and dignity of our holy vestments are brought out in *"fine linen."* When the Lord sanctifies His people, they are clothed as priests in pure white; the snow itself does not excel them. They are in the eyes of men and angels fair to look upon, and even in the Lord's eyes they are without spot. Meanwhile the royal apparel is delicate and rich as *"silk."* No expense is spared, no beauty withheld, no grandeur denied.

What, then? Can we infer nothing from this? Surely there is gratitude to be felt and joy to be expressed. Come, my heart, do not refuse your evening hallelujah! Tune your pipes! Touch your chords!

> *Strangely, my soul, art thou arrayed*
> *By the Great Sacred Three!*
> *In sweetest harmony of praise*
> *Let all your powers agree.*

[1] 2 Timothy 2:19 [2] Psalm 89:34

God has a strong reserve with which to discharge this responsibility, for He is able to do everything. Believer, until you can drain the ocean dry of omnipotence, until you can break into pieces the towering mountains of almighty strength, you never need to fear. Do not think that the strength of man will ever be able to overcome the power of God. While the earth's huge pillars stand, you have enough reason to live firm in your faith. The same God who directs the earth in its orbit, who feeds the burning furnace of the sun, and trims the lamps of heaven has promised to supply you with daily strength. While He is able to uphold the universe, do not dream that He will prove unable to fulfill His own promises. Remember what He did in the past, in the former generations. Remember how He spoke and it was done, how He commanded and it stood firm. Will He who created the world grow weary? He hangs the world upon nothing; will He who does this be unable to support His children? Will He be unfaithful to His word for lack of power? Who is it that restrains the tempest? Does He not ride upon the wings of the wind and make the clouds His chariots and hold the ocean in the hollow of His hand? How can He fail you? When He has put such a faithful promise as this on record, will you for a moment indulge the thought that He has outpromised Himself or gone beyond His power to fulfill? No! You can doubt no longer.

My God, You who are my strength, I believe that this promise will be fulfilled, for the boundless reservoir of Your grace can never be exhausted, and the overflowing storehouse of Your strength can never be emptied by Your friends or plundered by Your enemies.

Now let the feeble all be strong,
And make Jehovah's arm their song.

❧ EVENING ❧

THE SHEEP FOLLOW HIM, FOR THEY KNOW HIS VOICE. — JOHN 10:4

What is it that provides the infallible evidence that you are a child of God? It is a foolish presumption to answer this by our own judgment; but God's Word reveals it to us, and we may walk confidently when we have revelation as our guide. We are told concerning our Lord, "to all who did *receive him*, who believed in his name, he gave the right to become children of God."[1] So if I have received Christ Jesus into my heart, I am a child of God. That reception is described in the same verse as *believing in the name of Jesus Christ*. If, then, I believe on Jesus Christ's name—that is, simply from my heart entrust myself to the crucified but now exalted Redeemer—I am a member of the family of the Most High. Whatever else I may not have, if I have this, I have the privilege of becoming a child of God. The Lord Jesus puts it in another way: "The sheep follow him, for they know his voice." Here is the matter in a nutshell. Christ appears as a shepherd to His own sheep, not to others. As soon as He appears, His own sheep perceive Him—they trust Him, they are prepared to follow Him. He knows them, and they know Him; there is a mutual knowledge—there is a constant connection between them. And so the evidence, the infallible mark of regeneration and adoption, is a hearty faith in the appointed Redeemer. Reader, are you in doubt, are you uncertain about whether you are one of God's children? Then do not let an hour pass until you have said, "Search me, O God, and know my heart."[2] Do not linger here, I warn you! If you must linger anywhere, let it be about some secondary matter—your health, if you wish, or the title deeds of your home. But about your soul, your never-dying soul and its eternal destiny, I urge you to be in earnest. Make certain of this eternal issue.

[1] John 1:12   [2] Psalm 139:23

FRIEND, MOVE UP HIGHER. — LUKE 14:10

When the life of grace first begins in the soul, we instinctively draw near to God, but it is with great fear and trembling. The soul, conscious of guilt and humbled by it, is over-awed with the solemnity of its position; it is prostrated by a sense of the grandeur of God, in whose presence it appears. With sincere humility it takes the lowest room. But later on, as the Christian grows in grace, although he will never forget the solemnity of his position and will never lose that holy awe that must encompass a gracious man when he is in the presence of the God who can create or destroy, yet his fear has all its terror taken out of it; it becomes a holy reverence, and no longer an overshadowing dread. He is called up higher, to greater access to God in Christ Jesus. Then the man of God, walking among the splendors of Deity and veiling his face like the glorious cherubim with those twin wings, the blood and righteousness of Jesus Christ, will, reverent and bowed in spirit, approach the throne; and seeing there a God of love, goodness, and mercy he will realize the covenant character of God rather than His absolute Deity. He will see in God His goodness rather than His greatness, and more of His love than of His majesty. Then the soul will bow just as humbly as before and enjoy a more sacred liberty of intercession; for while prostrate before the glory of the Infinite God, it will be sustained by the refreshing awareness of being in the presence of unlimited mercy and infinite love and by the realization of acceptance "in the Beloved."[1] In this way the believer is invited to come up higher and is enabled to exercise the privilege of rejoicing in God and drawing near to Him in holy confidence, crying, "Abba, Father."

So may we go from strength to strength,
And daily grow in grace,
Till in Thy image raised at length,
We see Thee face to face.

EVENING

YOURS IS THE DAY, YOURS ALSO THE NIGHT. — PSALM 74:16

Lord, You do not abdicate Your throne when the sun goes down, nor do You leave the world during all those long wintry nights to be the prey of evil. Your eyes watch us like the stars, and Your arms surround us as the band of planets belts the sky. The benefit of kindly sleep and all the influences of the moon are in Your hand, and the alarms and solemnities of night are equally with You. This is very sweet to me when walking in the midnight hours or tossing to and fro in anguish. There are precious fruits supplied by the moon as well as by the sun: May my Lord make me a favored partaker in them. The night of affliction is just as much under the arrangement and control of the Lord of Love as the bright summer days when all is bliss. Jesus is in the tempest. His love wraps the night about itself like a cloak, but to the eye of faith the sable robe is scarcely a disguise. From the first watch of the night even to the break of day the eternal Watcher observes His saints and overrules the shades and shadows of midnight for His people's highest good. We believe in no rival deities of good and evil contending for mastery, but we hear the voice of Jehovah saying, "I form light and create darkness . . . I am the LORD, who does all these things."[2] Gloomy seasons of religious indifference and social sin are not exempted from the divine purpose. When the altars of truth are defiled, and the ways of God forsaken, the Lord's servants weep with bitter sorrow, but they need not despair, for even the darkest eras are governed by the Lord and will come to an end at His command. What seems defeat to us may be victory to Him.

Though enwrapt in gloomy night,
We perceive no ray of light;
Since the Lord Himself is here,
'Tis not fitting we should fear.

[1] Ephesians 1:6 [2] Isaiah 45:7

FOR YOUR SAKE HE BECAME POOR. — 2 CORINTHIANS 8:9

The Lord Jesus Christ was eternally *rich*, glorious, and exalted; but "though *he was rich*, yet for your sake he became poor." As the wealthy believer cannot be true in his fellowship with his poor brethren unless from his wealth he ministers to their needs, so (the same rule holding with the head as between the members) it is impossible that our Divine Lord could have had fellowship with us unless He had given to us from His own abounding wealth and had become poor so as to make us rich. If He had remained upon His throne of glory, and we had continued in the ruins of the Fall without receiving His salvation, fellowship would have been impossible on both sides. Our position by the Fall, apart from the covenant of grace, made it as impossible for fallen man to communicate with God as it is for Satan to be in communion with Christ. In order, therefore, that communion might be enjoyed, it was necessary for the rich relative to bestow his estate upon his poor relatives, for the righteous Savior to give to His sinning brethren from His own perfection, and for we, the poor and guilty, to receive of His fullness grace for grace, so that in giving and receiving, the One might descend from the heights, and the other ascend from the depths, and in this way be able to embrace each other in true and hearty fellowship. Poverty must be enriched by Him in whom are infinite treasures before it can begin to commune; and guilt must lose itself in imputed and imparted righteousness before the soul can walk in fellowship with purity. Jesus must clothe His people in His own garments or He cannot admit them into His palace of glory; and He must wash them in His own blood or else they will be too defiled for the embrace of His fellowship.

Believer, herein is love! For *your sake* the Lord Jesus "became poor" that He might lift you up into communion with Himself.

🙢 EVENING 🙠

AND THE GLORY OF THE LORD SHALL BE REVEALED, AND
ALL FLESH SHALL SEE IT TOGETHER. — ISAIAH 40:5

We anticipate the happy day when every knee will bow before Christ; when the gods of the heathen shall be cast to the moles and the bats; when empty religion will be exploded, and the crescent of Mohammed will topple, never again to cast its harmful rays upon the nations; when kings shall worship before the Prince of Peace, and all nations shall call the Redeemer blessed. Some despair of this. They look on the world as a ship breaking up and going to pieces, never to float again. We know that the world and all that is in it will one day be burned up, and afterwards we look for new heavens and for a new earth; but we cannot read our Bibles without the conviction that—

Jesus shall reign where'er the sun
Doth his successive journeys run.

We are not discouraged by the length of His delays; we are not disheartened by the long period that He assigns to the church in which to struggle with little success and much defeat. We believe that God will never tolerate this world, which has once seen Christ's blood shed upon it, remaining as the devil's stronghold. Christ came here to deliver this world from the detested sway of the powers of darkness. What a shout that will be when men and angels unite to cry "Hallelujah! For the Lord our God Almighty reigns"[1] What a satisfaction it will be in that day to have had a part in the fight, to have helped to break the arrows of the bow, and to have shared in winning the victory for our Lord! Happy are those who entrust themselves to this conquering Lord, and who fight side by side with Him doing their part in His name and by His strength! How unhappy are those on the side of evil! It is a losing side, and it is a matter in which to lose is to lose and to be lost forever. On whose side are you?

[1] Revelation 19:6

Let us today go down to Bethlehem, and in company with wondering shepherds and adoring Magi let us see Him who was born King of the Jews, for we by faith can claim an interest in Him and can sing, "*For to us* a child is born, *to us* a son is given."[1] Jesus is God incarnate, our Lord and our Savior, and yet our brother and friend; let us adore and admire Him. Let us notice at the very first glance *His miraculous conception*. It was a thing unheard of before, and unparalleled since, that a virgin should conceive and bear a son. The first promise concerned *the seed of the woman*, not the offspring of the man. Since venturesome woman led the way in the sin that resulted in paradise lost, she, and she alone, ushers in the Regainer of Paradise. Our Savior, although truly man, was as to His human nature the Holy One of God. Let us reverently bow before the holy Child whose innocence restores to manhood its ancient glory; and let us pray that He may be formed in us, the hope of glory. Do not fail to note *His humble parentage*. His mother has been described simply as "the virgin," not a princess or prophetess, nor a woman of influence. True, the blood of kings ran in her veins; and her mind was not weak or untaught, for she could sweetly sing a song of praise. Yet how humble her position, how poor the man to whom she was engaged, and how miserable the accommodation provided for the newborn King!

Immanuel—God with us in our nature, in our sorrow, in our daily work, in our punishment, in our death, and now with us, or rather we with Him, in resurrection, ascension, triumph, and Second Advent splendor.

❧ EVENING ☙

AND WHEN THE DAYS OF THE FEAST HAD RUN THEIR COURSE,
JOB WOULD SEND AND CONSECRATE THEM, AND HE WOULD RISE
EARLY IN THE MORNING AND OFFER BURNT OFFERINGS ACCORDING TO
THE NUMBER OF THEM ALL. FOR JOB SAID, "IT MAY BE THAT
MY CHILDREN HAVE SINNED, AND CURSED GOD IN THEIR HEARTS."
THUS JOB DID CONTINUALLY. — JOB 1:5

What Job did early in the morning, after the family festivities, it will be good for the believer to do for himself before he rests tonight. Amid the cheerfulness of household gatherings it is easy to slide into sinful frivolity and to forget our declared character as Christians. It ought not to be so, but sadly it is, that our days of feasting are very seldom days of sanctified enjoyment but too frequently degenerate into unholy amusement. It is possible to experience joy as pure and sanctifying as a dip in the rivers of Eden: Holy gratitude should be just as purifying an element as grief. Sadly for our poor hearts, facts prove that the house of mourning is better than the house of feasting. Come, believer, how have you sinned today? Have you been forgetful of your high calling? Have you been like others in using empty words and unguarded speech? Then confess the sin, and flee to the sacrifice. The sacrifice sanctifies. The precious blood of the Lamb removes the guilt and purges the defilement of our sins of ignorance and carelessness. This is the best ending of a Christmas day—to wash anew in the cleansing fountain. Believer, come to this sacrifice continually; if it is good tonight, it is good every night. To live at the altar is the privilege of the royal priesthood; to them sin, bad as it is, is nevertheless no cause for despair, since they draw near once more to the sin-atoning victim, and their conscience is purged from dead works.

> *Gladly I close this festive day,*
> *Grasping the altar's hallow'd horn;*
> *My slips and faults are washed away,*
> *The Lamb has all my trespass borne.*

[1] Isaiah 9:6

THE LAST ADAM. — 1 CORINTHIANS 15:45

Jesus is the representative head of His people. In Adam every heir of flesh and blood has a personal interest, because he is the covenant head and representative of the race when considered under the law of works; so under the law of grace, every redeemed soul is one with the Lord from heaven, since He is the Second Adam, the Sponsor and Substitute of the elect in the new covenant of love. The apostle Paul declares that Levi was in the loins of Abraham when Melchizedek met him: It is a certain truth that the believer was in the loins of Jesus Christ, the Mediator, when in eternity the covenant settlements of grace were decreed, ratified, and made sure forever. Whatever Christ has done, He has accomplished for the whole body of His Church. We were crucified in Him and buried with Him (read Col. 2:10-13), and to make it still more wonderful, we are risen with Him and even ascended with Him to the seats on high (Eph. 2:6). It is in this way that the Church has fulfilled the law and is "blessed *in the Beloved.*"[1] She is regarded with satisfaction by the just Jehovah, for He views her in Jesus, and does not look upon her as separate from her covenant head. As the Anointed Redeemer of Israel, Christ Jesus has nothing distinct from His Church, but all that He has He holds for her. Adam's righteousness was ours so long as he maintained it, and his sin was ours the moment that he committed it; and in the same way, all that the Second Adam is or does is ours as well as His because He is our representative. Here is the foundation of the covenant of grace. This gracious system of representation and substitution, which moved Justin Martyr to cry out, "O blessed change, O sweet permutation!" is the very groundwork of the Gospel of our salvation and is to be received with strong faith and rapturous joy.

EVENING

I AM WITH YOU ALWAYS. — MATTHEW 28:20

The Lord Jesus is among His people; He walks between the golden candlesticks; His promise is, "I am with you always." He is as surely with us now as He was with the disciples at the lake when they saw coals of fire and fish being prepared for breakfast. Not physically, but still in reality, Jesus is with us. And an important truth this is, for where Jesus is, *love becomes passionate.* Of all the things in the world that can set the heart burning, there is nothing like the presence of Jesus! A glimpse of Him is so overwhelming that we are ready to say, "Turn away Your eyes from me, for they have overcome me." Even the fragrance of the aloes and the myrrh and the cinnamon, which linger on His perfumed garments, causes the sick and the faint to grow strong. A moment's leaning of the head upon that gracious chest, welcoming His divine love into our poor cold hearts, and suddenly we are no longer cold but shine like seraphs, equal to every task and capable of bearing every suffering. If we know that Jesus is with us, *every power will be heightened*, and every grace will be strengthened, and we will cast ourselves into the Lord's service with heart and soul and strength; therefore the presence of Christ is to be desired above all things. *His presence will be realized most by those who are most like Him.* If you desire to see Christ, you must grow in conformity to Him. Bring yourself, by the power of the Spirit, into union with Christ's desires and motives and plans of action, and you are likely to be favored with His company. Remember, *His presence may be enjoyed.* His promise is as true as ever. He delights to be with us. If He does not come, it is because we hinder Him by our indifference. He will reveal Himself to our sincere prayers and graciously allow Himself to be detained by our cries and by our tears, for these are the golden chains that bind Jesus to His people.

[1] Ephesians 1:6

CAN REEDS FLOURISH WHERE THERE IS NO WATER? — JOB 8:11

The reed is spongy and hollow, and so is a hypocrite; there is no substance or stability in him. It is shaken back and forth in every wind, just as the outwardly religious yield to every influence; for this reason the reed is not broken by the storm, neither are hypocrites called to face persecution. I would not willingly be a deceiver or be deceived; perhaps the text for today may help me to test myself to see whether I am a hypocrite or not. The reed by nature lives in water and owes its very existence to the mire and moisture in which it has taken root; let the water drain away, and the reed withers very quickly. Its greenness is absolutely dependent upon circumstances; a continuous supply of water makes it flourish, and a drought destroys it at once. Is this my case? Do I only serve God when I am in good company or when faith is profitable and respectable? Do I love the Lord only when I am enjoying comforts from His hands? If so I am just a hypocrite, and like the withering reed, I will perish when death deprives me of outward joys. But can I honestly maintain that when there have been few bodily comforts, and my surroundings have been adverse to grace rather than at all helpful to it, I have still maintained my integrity? Then I have hope that there is genuine vital godliness in me. The reed cannot grow without water, but the Lord's plants can and do flourish even when there is a drought. A godly man often grows best when his worldly circumstances are daunting. He who follows Christ for money is a Judas; those who follow for loaves and fishes are children of the devil; but those who stay close out of love to Himself are His own beloved ones. Lord, let me find my life in *You*, and not in the shifting sands of this world's favor or gain.

❧ EVENING ❧

AND THE LORD WILL GUIDE YOU CONTINUALLY. — ISAIAH 58:11

The LORD will guide you." Not an angel, but the Lord will guide you. He said He would not go through the wilderness before His people, but an angel would go before them to lead them in the way; but Moses said, "If *your* presence will not go with me, do not bring us up from here."[1] Christian, God has not left you in your earthly pilgrimage to be guided by an angel: He Himself leads the procession. You may not see the cloudy, fiery pillar, but the Lord will never forsake you. Notice the word *will*—"The LORD *will* guide you." This makes it certain! We may be sure that God will not forsake us! His precious shalls and wills are better than men's promises. "I will never leave you nor forsake you."[2] Then observe the adverb *"continually."* We are not merely being led sometimes, but we have a perpetual guide; not occasionally left to our own understanding, and so to wander, but continually hearing the guiding voice of the Great Shepherd; and if we keep close to His heels, we will not drift but will be led by a right way to our eternal dwelling. If you have to change your position in life, if you have to emigrate to another country, if it should happen that you are poverty-stricken or suddenly promoted to a more responsible position than the one you now occupy, if you are thrown among strangers or cast among foes, don't tremble, for "the LORD will guide you continually." There are no dilemmas out of which you will not be delivered if you live near to God and your heart is kept warm with holy love. You will not go astray in the company of God. Like Enoch, walk with God, and you cannot miss your road. You have infallible wisdom to direct you, unchangeable love to comfort you, and eternal power to defend you. "The LORD"—mark the word—"the LORD will guide you continually."

[1] Exodus 33:15   [2] Hebrews 13:5

AND THE LIFE I NOW LIVE IN THE FLESH I LIVE BY FAITH IN THE SON OF GOD. — GALATIANS 2:20

When the Lord in mercy drew near and saw us in our deadness, He first of all said, "Live"; and He did this, *first*, because life is absolutely essential in spiritual matters, and until it is given we are incapable of seeing or entering the kingdom. Now the life that grace confers upon believers at the moment of their conversion is none other than the life of Christ, which, like the sap from the stem, runs into us, the branches, and establishes a living connection between our souls and Jesus. Faith is the grace that perceives this union, having proceeded from it as its firstfruit. It is the neck that joins the body of the Church to its all-glorious Head.

> *A faith that shines more bright and clear,*
> *When tempests rage without,*
> *That when in danger knows no fear,*
> *In darkness feels no doubt.*

Faith lays hold upon the Lord Jesus with a firm and determined grasp. It knows His excellence and worth, and no temptation can induce faith to place its trust elsewhere. And Christ Jesus is so delighted with this heavenly grace that He never ceases to strengthen and sustain that faith by the loving embrace and all-sufficient support of His eternal arms. This establishes a living, sensible, and delightful union that produces streams of love, confidence, sympathy, contentment, and joy, from which both the bride and Bridegroom love to drink. When the soul can clearly see this oneness between itself and Christ, the pulse may be felt as beating for both, and the one blood as flowing through the veins of each. Then the heart is as near heaven as it can be on earth and is prepared for the enjoyment of the most sublime and spiritual kind of fellowship.

> *Lord, give me such a faith as this,*
> *And then, whate'er may come,*
> *I taste e'en now the hallowed bliss,*
> *Of an eternal home.*

❦ EVENING ❧
I HAVE NOT COME TO BRING PEACE, BUT A SWORD. — MATTHEW 10:34

The Christian will be sure to make enemies. It will be one of his objects to make none; but if doing what is right and believing what is true should cause him to lose every earthly friend, he will regard it as a small loss, since his great Friend in heaven will be even more friendly and will reveal Himself to him more graciously than ever. You who have taken up His cross, don't you know what your Master said? "I have come to set a man against his father, and a daughter against her mother . . . And a person's enemies will be those of his own household." Christ is the great Peacemaker; but before peace, He brings war. Where the light comes, the darkness must vanish. Where truth is, the lie must flee; or if it remains, there must be a stern conflict, for the truth cannot and will not lower its standard, and the lie must be trampled underfoot. If you follow Christ, you will have all the dogs of the world yelping at your heels. If you live in such a manner as to stand the test of the last judgment, you can depend upon it that the world will not speak well of you. He who has the friendship of the world is an enemy to God; but if you are true and faithful to the Most High, men will resent your uncompromising commitment, since it is a testimony against their iniquities. You must do the right and not fear the consequences. You will need the courage of a lion to pursue a course that turns your best friend into your fiercest foe; but for the love of Jesus you must take your stand. To risk reputation and affection for the truth's sake is so demanding that to do it constantly you will need a degree of moral principle that only the Spirit of God can work in you. Do not turn your back like a coward, but play the man. Follow boldly in your Master's steps, for He has made this rough journey before you. Better a brief warfare and eternal rest than false peace and everlasting torment.

TILL NOW THE LORD HAS HELPED US. — 1 SAMUEL 7:12

The phrase "till now" is like a hand pointing in the direction of the *past*. Twenty years or seventy, and still "till now the LORD has helped us." Through poverty, through wealth, through sickness, through health, at home, abroad, on the land, on the sea, in honor, in dishonor, in perplexity, in joy, in trial, in triumph, in prayer, in temptation, "till now the LORD has helped us." We delight to look down a long avenue of trees. It is delightful to gaze from end to end of the long vista, a sort of verdant temple, with its branching pillars and its arches of leaves. In the same way look down the long aisles of your years at the green branches of mercy overhead and the strong pillars of loving-kindness and faithfulness that support your joys. Are there no birds singing in those branches? Surely there must be many, and they all sing of mercy received "till now."

But the word also points *forward*. For when a man reaches a certain point and writes "till now," he is not yet at the end; he still has a distance to go. More trials, more joys; more temptations, more triumphs; more prayers, more answers; more toils, more strength; more fights, more victories; and then he faces sickness, old age, disease, death. Is it over then? No! Then there is wakening in Jesus' likeness, thrones, harps, songs, psalms, white raiment, the face of Jesus, the company of saints, the glory of God, the fullness of eternity, the infinity of bliss. Be of good courage, believer, and with grateful confidence raise your banner, for—

> *He who hath helped thee hitherto*
> *Will help thee all thy journey through.*

When read in light of heaven, how glorious and marvelous a prospect will the "till now" provide for your grateful eye!

❧ EVENING ☙
WHAT DO YOU THINK ABOUT THE CHRIST? — MATTHEW 22:42

The great test of your soul's health is, *What do you think about Christ?* Is He the best of friends—"distinguished among ten thousand"[1]—your all in all? When Christ is held in such esteem, all the faculties of the spiritual man are energized. I can gauge your piety by this standard: Does Christ take a high or low position with you? If you have thought little of Christ, if you have been content to live without His presence, if you have cared only slightly for His honor, if you have neglected His laws, then I know that your soul is sick—God grant that it may not be a sickness leading to death! But if the first thought of your spirit has been, *How can I honor Jesus?*—if the daily desire of your soul has been, "O that I knew where I might find him!"[2] I tell you that you may face a thousand infirmities, and even hardly know whether you are a child of God at all, and yet I am persuaded beyond a doubt that you are safe, since Jesus is great in your esteem. I'm not concerned about your rags—what do you think of *His* royal apparel? I'm not concerned about your wounds, though they bleed profusely—what do you think of *His* wounds? Are they like glittering rubies in your esteem? I think none the less of you, though you lie like Lazarus on the refuse pile, and the dogs lick you—I do not judge you by your poverty: What do you think of the King in His beauty? Does He sit enthroned in your heart? Would you set Him higher if you could? Would you be willing to die if you could add another trumpet to the melody that proclaims His praise? Then it is well with you. Whatever you may think of yourself, if Christ is great to you, you will be with Him in the end.

> *Though all the world my choice deride,*
> *Yet Jesus shall my portion be;*
> *For I am pleased with none beside,*
> *The fairest of the fair is He.*

[1] Song of Solomon 5:10   [2] Job 23:3

BETTER IS THE END OF A THING THAN ITS BEGINNING.
— ECCLESIASTES 7:8

Look at David's Lord and Master; consider His beginning. He was despised and rejected by men, a man of sorrows and acquainted with grief. Then look at the end! He sits at His Father's right hand, waiting until His enemies are made his footstool. "As he is so we are also in this world."[1] You must bear the cross or you will never wear the crown; you must wade through the water or you will never walk the golden pavement. Cheer up, then, poor Christian. "Better is the end of a thing than its beginning." View the creeping worm— how contemptible its appearance! It is the beginning of a thing. Mark that insect with gorgeous wings, playing in the sunbeams, sipping at the flowers, full of happiness and life—that is the worm's end. You are that caterpillar, wrapped up in the chrysalis of death; but when Christ appears, you will be like Him, for you will see Him as He is. Be content to be like Him, a worm and no man, so that like Him you may be satisfied when you wake up in His likeness. The rough-looking diamond is put upon the wheel of the gem-smith. He cuts it on all sides. It loses much—much that seemed costly to itself. The king is crowned; the diadem is put upon the monarch's head accompanied by the trumpet's joyful sound. A glittering ray flashes from that coronet, and it beams from that same diamond that was so recently fashioned at the wheel. You may venture to compare yourself to such a diamond, for you are one of God's people; and this is the time of the cutting process. Let faith and patience have their perfect work, for in the day when the crown is set upon the head of the King, eternal, immortal, invisible, one ray of glory shall stream from you. "They shall be mine, says the LORD of Hosts, in the day when I make up my treasured possession."[2] "Better is the end of a thing than its beginning."

∾ EVENING ∾

DO YOU NOT KNOW THAT THE END WILL BE BITTER?
— 2 SAMUEL 2:26

Reader, if you are merely a professor and not a possessor of the faith that is in Christ Jesus, the following lines are a true sketch of your end.

You are a respectable attender at a place of worship; you go because others go, not because your heart is right with God. This is your beginning. I will suppose that for the next twenty or thirty years you will be spared to continue in this way, professing religion by an outward attendance upon the means of grace, but having no heart in the matter. Tread softly, for I must show you the deathbed of someone just like you. Let us gaze upon him gently. A clammy sweat is on his brow, and he wakes up crying, "O God, it is hard to die. Did you send for my pastor?" "Yes, he is coming." The pastor comes. "Sir, I fear that I am dying!" "Have you any hope?" "I cannot say that I have. I fear to stand before my God. Oh, pray for me." The prayer is offered for him with sincere earnestness, and the way of salvation is for the ten-thousandth time put before him, but before he has grasped the rope, I see him sink. I may put my finger upon those cold eyelids, for they will never see anything here again. But where is the man, and where are the man's true eyes? It is written, "In Hades, being in torment, he lifted up his eyes."[3] Why did he not lift up his eyes before? Because he was so accustomed to hearing the Gospel that his soul slept under it. If you should lift up your eyes in hell, how bitter will be your wailings. Let the Savior's own words reveal the woe: "Father Abraham, have mercy on me, and send Lazarus to dip the end of his finger in water, and cool my tongue, for I am in anguish in this flame."[4] There is a frightful meaning in those words. May you never have to spell it out by the red light of God's wrath!

[1] 1 John 4:17 [2] Malachi 3:17 [3] Luke 16:23 [4] Luke 16:24

ON THE LAST DAY OF THE FEAST, THE GREAT DAY,
JESUS STOOD UP AND CRIED OUT,
"IF ANYONE THIRSTS, LET HIM COME TO ME AND DRINK." — JOHN 7:37

Patience had her perfect work in the Lord Jesus, and until the last day of the feast He pleaded with the Jews, even as on this last day of the year He pleads with us and waits to be gracious to us. The long-suffering of the Savior is truly admirable as He bears with some of us year after year despite our insults, rebellions, and resistance to His Holy Spirit. Wonder of wonders that we are still in the land of mercy!

Mercy expressed herself most plainly, for Jesus "*cried,*" which implies not only the loudness of His voice, but the tenderness of His tones. He entreats us to be reconciled. "God making his appeal through us," says the apostle, "we implore you on behalf of Christ . . ." What earnest, pathetic terms are these! How deep the Father's love that causes Him to weep over sinners and, like a mother, to tenderly call His children to Himself! Surely at the sound of such a cry our willing hearts will come.

Provision is made most generously: Everything that man needs to quench his soul's thirst is available. To his conscience the Atonement brings peace; to his understanding the Gospel brings the richest instruction; to his heart the person of Jesus is the noblest object of affection; to the whole man the truth as it is in Jesus supplies the purest nourishment. Thirst is terrible, but Jesus can remove it. Even if the soul were utterly famished, Jesus can restore it.

Proclamation is made most freely, that every thirsty one is welcome. No other distinction is made but that of thirst. Whether it be the thirst of greed, ambition, pleasure, knowledge, or rest, he who suffers from it is invited. The thirst may be bad in itself, and not be a sign of grace, but a mark of inordinate sin that longs to satisfy itself with deeper lust; but it is not goodness in the creature that brings him the invitation—the Lord Jesus sends it freely and without respect of persons.

Personality is declared most fully. The sinner must come to Jesus—not to works, ordinances, or doctrines but to a personal Redeemer who Himself bore our sins in His own body on the tree. The bleeding, dying, rising Savior is the only ray of hope to a sinner. Oh, for grace to come now and drink, before the sun sets upon the year's last day!

No waiting or preparation is even hinted at. Drinking represents a reception that has no special requirements. A fool, a thief, a harlot can drink; our sinfulness is no barrier to the invitation to believe in Jesus. We need no golden cup, no fine china, in which to convey the water to the thirsty; the mouth of poverty is welcome to stoop down and drink of the life-giving stream. Blistered, leprous, filthy lips may touch the stream of divine love; they cannot pollute it but will themselves be purified. Jesus is the fount of hope. Dear reader, listen to the dear Redeemer's loving voice as He cries to each of us, "If anyone thirsts, let him come to me and drink."

THE HARVEST IS PAST, THE SUMMER IS ENDED, AND
WE ARE NOT SAVED. — JEREMIAH 8:20

Not saved! Dear reader, is this your sorry condition? Warned of the judgment to come, invited to escape for your life, and yet at this moment *not saved*! You know the way of salvation, you read it in the Bible, you hear it from the pulpit, it is explained to you by friends, and still you neglect it, and therefore you are *not saved*. You will be without excuse when the Lord shall execute judgment. The Holy Spirit has blessed the Word that has been preached in your hearing, and times of refreshing have come from the divine presence, and yet you are still without Christ. All these hopeful seasons have come and gone—your summer and your harvest have past—and still you are *not saved*. Years have followed one another into eternity, and your last year will soon be here: Youth has gone, manhood is going, and still you are *not saved*. Let me ask you—*will you ever be saved*? Is there any likelihood of it? Already the most favorable seasons have left you unsaved. Will other occasions alter your condition? Every means has failed with you—the best of means, used perseveringly and with the utmost affection. What more can be done for you? Affliction and prosperity have equally failed to impress you; tears and prayers and sermons have been wasted on your barren heart. Are not the probabilities dead against your ever being saved? Is it not more than likely that you will stay as you are till death forever bars the door of hope? Do you recoil from this idea? Yet it is a most reasonable one: He who is not washed in so many waters will in all probability go filthy to his end. The convenient time never has come—why should it ever come? It is logical to fear that it will never arrive and that like Felix you will find no convenient occasion until you are in hell. Think carefully about hell and of the dreadful probability that you will soon be there!

Reader, suppose you should die unsaved—no words can picture your doom. Write out your dreadful predicament in tears and blood; talk of it with groans and gnashing of teeth: You will be punished with everlasting destruction and banished from the glory of the Lord and from the glory of His power. Allow my words to startle you into serious thought. Be wise, be wise in time, and before another year begins believe in Jesus, who is able to save you completely. Consecrate these last hours to lonely thought, and if you are brought to deep repentance, it will be well; and if it leads to a humble faith in Jesus, it will be best of all. See to it that this year does not pass away with you still unforgiven. Do not let the new year's midnight bells sound upon a joyless spirit! Now, *now*, NOW believe and live.

ESCAPE FOR THY LIFE;
LOOK NOT BEHIND THEE,
NEITHER STAY THOU
IN THE PLAIN;
ESCAPE TO THE MOUNTAIN,
LEST THOU BE CONSUMED.

SCRIPTURE INDEX